ENCYCLOPEDIA
OF MORMONISM

EDITORIAL BOARD

ENCYCLOPEDIA OF MORMONISM

Edited by
Daniel H. Ludlow

Volume 3

*The History, Scripture, Doctrine, and Procedure
of The Church of Jesus Christ of Latter-day Saints*

Macmillan Publishing Company
New York

Maxwell Macmillan Canada
Toronto

Maxwell Macmillan International
New York   Oxford   Singapore   Sydney

Macmillan Publishing Company
866 Third Avenue, New York, NY 10022

Maxwell Macmillan Canada, Inc.
1200 Eglinton Avenue East, Suite 200, Don Mills, Ontario M3C 3N1

Library of Congress Catalog Card No.:91–34255

Printed in the United States of America

printing number
4 5 6 7 8 9 10

Macmillan Inc. is part of the Maxwell Communication
Group of Companies.

Library of Congress Cataloging-in-Publication Data

Encyclopedia of Mormonism/edited by Daniel H. Ludlow.
    p. cm.
   Includes bibliographical references and index.
   ISBN 0-02-879605-5 (4 vol. set).—ISBN 0-02-904040-X (5 vol.
set).—ISBN 0-02-879600-4 (v. 1)
   1. Church of Jesus Christ of Latter-Day Saints—Encyclopedias.
2. Mormon Church—Encyclopedias.   3. Mormons—Encyclopedias.
I. Ludlow, Daniel H.
BX8605.5.E62 1992
289.3'03—dc20   91–34255
                                         CIP

N

NAME OF THE CHURCH

The name The Church of Jesus Christ of Latter-day Saints was given by the Lord in revelation to Joseph SMITH on April 26, 1838 (D&C 115:4). The Church had been known as The Church of Christ from 1830 to 1834 (D&C 20:1); The Church of the Latter Day Saints in 1834; and The Church of Christ of Latter Day Saints from 1836 to 1838. The Church is commonly, but unofficially, referred to today as the Mormon Church and its members as Mormons because of their belief in the Book of Mormon. But the use of the term "Mormon" to refer to the Church is unsatisfactory from the point of view of Church members because it does not convey the conviction that Jesus Christ is the head of the Church and that members strive to live Christian lives. In the Book of Mormon, Christ's disciples asked him, "Tell us the name whereby we shall call this church" (3 Ne. 27:3). He answered, "How be it my church save it be called in my name? For if a church be called in Moses' name then it be Moses' church, or if it be called in the name of a man then it be the church of a man; but if it be called in my name then it is my church, if it so be that they are built upon my gospel" (3 Ne. 27:8). By implication, calling the Church by the name Mormon would make it Mormon's Church. While most Church members are not offended by the title Mormon, they prefer the name that prop-erly underscores their relationship to Christ.

Members of the Church are often referred to as SAINTS, meaning men and women who are committed to live in accordance with the gospel. The New Testament similarly refers to followers of Christ as saints. The term "Latter-day" comes from the belief that the world is passing through the last days prior to the second coming of Christ.

BIBLIOGRAPHY

Anderson, Richard Lloyd. "I Have a Question." *Ensign* 9 (Jan. 1979):13–14.

Nelson, Russel M. "'Thus Shall My Church Be Called.'" *Ensign* 20 (May 1990):16–18.

SUSAN EASTON BLACK

NAME EXTRACTION PROGRAM

Name extraction programs sponsored by the LDS Church are based upon the doctrine of SALVATION OF THE DEAD. Names, dates, and places are the key elements in precisely identifying individual ancestors. Name extraction consists of systematically transcribing this information from original vital records. Church members perform TEMPLE ORDINANCES for those whose names have been thus identified.

The FAMILY HISTORY DEPARTMENT of the Church (formerly the Genealogy Department) initiated the first name extraction program, called Records Tabulation, in 1961. Department employees extracted data primarily from filmed copies of English parish registers. In 1978 the Church deployed name extraction to stake centers, the new program being called Stake Record Extraction. Since that date, name extraction is done by local Church members. Besides records of England, those of Mexico, Germany, Scotland, Finland, Sweden, Norway, and Denmark have been heavily extracted. From 1961 to 1989, over 100 million names were thus copied.

The department begins the extraction process by sending a microfilm to a stake. Extractors transcribe the desired information onto cards. Data entry workers at regional centers input information onto computer diskettes. To ensure accuracy, two transcriptions of each entry are made and compared to find and resolve discrepancies.

Names derived from the name extraction program are listed in the Church's INTERNATIONAL GENEALOGICAL INDEX. The sources from which the names have been extracted are listed by locality in the Parish and Vital Records Listing. Alphabetized printouts of the names extracted from each source are also prepared and made available for research through the Church's main FAMILY HISTORY LIBRARY in Salt Lake City and branch family history centers around the world.

The department increased its name extraction efforts in 1986 with the introduction of the Family Record Extraction Program. This differs from the older program in that a paper photocopy of the original record is given to extractors and they transcribe the information in their homes at their convenience. The extracted information is "data entered" at the stake center by means of a personal computer and submitted on diskettes to a central data base in Salt Lake City.

KAHLILE MEHR

NAME OF GOD

Latter-day Saints invoke the name of God in prayers, in ordinances such as baptism, in testimony bearing, and in sermons. In certain ceremonies, they take upon themselves God's sacred name in covenantal pledges to keep his commandments. They also employ the various names of God to distinguish between members of the Godhead. Consequently, the names of God are considered very sacred and are not to be taken in a vain way or spoken in profanity.

The word from the Hebrew Bible most commonly translated "God" or "gods" is 'elohim, the plural of 'eloah or 'el which means "lofty one" or "exalted one." The plural ending –im may indicate royal loftiness as well as plurality (see ELOHIM).

The formal name of God in the Old Testament is "Jehovah" or "YHWH" (Hebrew yhwh), which comes from a root suggesting "I was, am, and will be forever." Some consider yhwh to be a name too sacred to be spoken; consequently, in many Bible versions, yhwh is translated "LORD" (see JEHOVAH, JESUS CHRIST).

Joseph Smith's FIRST VISION and later revelations confirmed the separate identity of the Father and the Son. To distinguish them individually in some scriptures, however, is very difficult. For instance, Jesus Christ has spoken the words of the Father by divine investiture as if he were the person of the Father (cf. MFP 5:26–34; John 14:24). Jesus continually emphasized the "oneness" or unity of mind and purpose of the Godhead and set it forth as an example to disciples. The term "God," therefore, may apply equally to the Father and the Son. The prayer of Jesus to his Father after the Last Supper was that followers might be "one, even as we are" (John 17:1–26; cf. 3 Ne. 11:27, 32–36; D&C 132:12).

The principal name of the Eternal Father is not clearly stated in scripture although several names and titles appear (see GOD THE FATHER: NAMES AND TITLES OF GOD). Where identification is appropriate, Latter-day Saints have designated the Father by the exalted name-title Elohim (MFP 5:26).

The use of sacred names plays an important part in LDS WORSHIP. For example, Latter-day Saints have been instructed to address God in prayer with the title "Our Father" and to offer prayers in the name of Jesus Christ (Matt. 6:9; 3 Ne. 13:9; see PRAYER). In baptismal prayers and sacrament prayers, faithful members covenant to take upon themselves the name of Christ. The participants commit themselves to remember Christ, which means to be an example of him to the world, to love him, to have faith in him, and to walk in his way (cf. 2 Ne. 31:19–20; Mosiah 5:7–12).

Jesus Christ has specifically commanded that his Church should bear his name. He said, further, that his people will be called by that name at the last day (3 Ne. 27:1–12; Mosiah 5:7–14; D&C 115:4).

The Lord has also revealed that ordinances and blessings performed in his name by his authorized servants are binding in heaven as well as on earth (D&C 132:45–46; 128:9). Ordinances, such as baptism, marriage, and vicarious work in temples, are performed in the "name of the Father, and of the Son, and of the Holy Ghost."

In modern times, as in the past, the Lord has cautioned men and women not to utter his name in vain speech (Ex. 20:7; D&C 63:60–64) nor to defile it through improper conduct (*see* BLASPHEMY; PROFANITY). He has directed his people to keep pledges and "keep yourselves from evil to take the name of the Lord in vain, for I am the Lord your God, even the God of your fathers" (D&C 136:21).

[*See also* Jesus Christ, Names and Titles of.]

BIBLIOGRAPHY

Madsen, Truman G. "'Putting on the Names': A Jewish–Christian Legacy." In *By Study and Also by Faith*, ed. J. Lundquist and S. Ricks, Vol. 1, pp. 458–81. Salt Lake City, 1990.

Talmage, James E. *AF*. Salt Lake City, 1915.

GLADE L. BURGON

NATIVE AMERICANS

LDS BELIEFS. The Book of Mormon, published in 1830, addresses a major message to Native Americans. Its title page states that one reason it was written was so that Native Americans today might know "what great things the Lord hath done for their fathers."

The Book of Mormon tells that a small band of Israelites under LEHI migrated from Jerusalem to the Western Hemisphere about 600 B.C. Upon Lehi's death his family divided into two opposing factions, one under Lehi's oldest son, LAMAN (*see* LAMANITES), and the other under a younger son, NEPHI₁ (*see* NEPHITES).

During the thousand-year history narrated in the Book of Mormon, Lehi's descendants went through several phases of splitting, warring, accommodating, merging, and splitting again. At first, just as God had prohibited the Israelites from intermarrying with the Canaanites in the ancient promised land (Ex. 34:16; Deut. 7:3), the Nephites

were forbidden to marry the Lamanites with their dark skin (2 Ne. 5:23; Alma 3:8–9). But as large Lamanite populations accepted the gospel of Jesus Christ and were numbered among the Nephites in the first century B.C., skin color ceased to be a distinguishing characteristic. After the visitations of the resurrected Christ, there were no distinctions among any kind of "ites" for some two hundred years. But then unbelievers arose and called themselves Lamanites to distinguish themselves from the Nephites or believers (4 Ne. 1:20).

The concluding chapters of the Book of Mormon describe a calamitous war. About A.D. 231, old enmities reemerged and two hostile populations formed (4 Ne. 1:35–39), eventually resulting in the annihilation of the Nephites. The Lamanites, from whom many present-day Native Americans descend, remained to inhabit the American continent. Peoples of other extractions also migrated there.

The Book of Mormon contains many promises and prophecies about the future directed to these survivors. For example, Lehi's grandson Enos prayed earnestly to God on behalf of his kinsmen, the Lamanites. He was promised by the Lord that Nephite records would be kept so that they could be "brought forth at some future day unto the Lamanites, that, perhaps, they might be brought unto salvation" (Enos 1:13).

The role of Native Americans in the events of the last days is noted by several Book of Mormon prophets. Nephi₁ prophesied that in the last days the Lamanites would accept the gospel and become a "pure and delightsome people" (2 Ne. 30:6). Likewise, it was revealed to the Prophet Joseph SMITH that the Lamanites will at some future time "blossom as the rose" (D&C 49:24).

After Jesus' resurrection in Jerusalem, he appeared to the more righteous Lamanites and Nephites left after massive destruction and prophesied that their seed eventually "shall dwindle in unbelief because of iniquity" (3 Ne. 21:5). He also stated that if any people "will repent and hearken unto my words, and harden not their hearts, I will establish my church among them, and they shall come in unto the covenant and be numbered among this the remnant of Jacob [the descendants of the Book of Mormon peoples], unto whom I have given this land for their inheritance"; together with others of the house of Israel, they will build the NEW JERUSALEM (3 Ne. 21:22–23). The Book of Mormon teaches that the descendants of

Chief Washakie and his Shoshone braves. Washakie was friendly to the white settlers in Wyoming and many of his people were baptized by LDS missionaries who preached among them.

Lehi are heirs to the blessings of Abraham (*see* ABRAHAMIC COVENANT) and will receive the blessings promised to the house of Israel.

THE LAMANITE MISSION (1830–1831). Doctrine and a commandment from the Lord motivated the Latter-day Saints to introduce the Book of Mormon to the Native Americans and teach them of their heritage and the gospel of Jesus Christ. Just a few months after the organization of the Church, four elders were called to preach to Native Americans living on the frontier west of the Missouri River (*see* LAMANITE MISSION).

The missionaries visited the Cattaraugus in New York, the Wyandots in Ohio, and the Shawnees and Delawares in the unorganized territories (now Kansas). Members of these tribes were receptive to the story of the Restoration. Unfortunately, federal Indian agents worrying about Indian unrest feared that the missionaries were inciting the tribes to resist the government and ordered the missionaries to leave, alleging that they were "disturbers of the peace" (Arrington and Bitton, p. 146). LDS pro-Native American beliefs continued to be a factor in the tensions between Latter-day Saints and their neighbors in Ohio, Missouri, and Illinois, which eventually led to persecution and expulsion of the Latter-day Saints from Missouri in 1838–1839 and from Illinois in 1846 (*see* MISSOURI CONFLICT).

RELATIONS IN THE GREAT BASIN. When the Latter-day Saints arrived in the Great Salt Lake Valley in 1847, they found several Native American tribal groups there and in adjacent valleys. The Church members soon had to weigh their need to put the limited arable land into production for the establishment of Zion against their obligation to accommodate their Native American neighbors and bring them the unique message in the Book of Mormon.

Brigham YOUNG taught that kindness and fairness were the best means to coexist with Native Americans and, like many other white Americans at the time, he hoped eventually to assimilate the Indians entirely into the mainstream culture. He admonished settlers to extend friendship, trade fairly, teach white man's ways, and generously share what they had. Individuals and Church groups gave, where possible, from their limited supplies of food, clothing, and livestock. But the rapid expansion of LDS settlers along the Wasatch Range, their preoccupation with building Zion, and the spread of European diseases unfortunately contravened many of these conciliatory efforts.

A dominating factor leading to resentment and hostility was the extremely limited availability of life-sustaining resources in the Great Basin, which in the main was marginal desert and mountain terrain dotted with small valley oases of green. Although Native Americans had learned to survive, it was an extremely delicate balance that was destroyed by the arrival of the Latter-day Saints in 1847. The tribal chiefs who initially welcomed the Mormons soon found themselves and their people being dispossessed by what appeared to them to be a never-ending horde, and in time they responded by raiding LDS-owned stock and fields, which resources were all that remained in the oases which once supported plants and wildlife that were the staples of the Native American diet. The Latter-day Saints, like others invading the western frontier, concerned with survival in the wilderness, responded at times with force.

An important factor in the conflict was the vast cultural gap between the two peoples. Native Americans in the Great Basin concentrated on scratching for survival in a barren land. Their uncanny survival skills could have been used by the Mormons in 1848, when drought and pestilence nearly destroyed the pioneers' first crops and famine seriously threatened their survival.

The Utes, Shoshones, and other tribal groups in the basin had little interest in being farmers or cowherders, or living in stuffy sod or log houses. They preferred their hunter-gatherer way of life under the open sky and often resisted, sometimes even scoffed at, the acculturation proffered them. Nor did they have a concept of land ownership or the accumulation of property. They shared both the land and its bounty—a phenomenon that European Americans have never fully understood. The culture gap all but precluded any significant acculturation or accommodation.

Within a few years, LDS settlers inhabited most of the arable land in Utah. Native Americans, therefore, had few options: They could leave, they could give up their own culture and assimilate with the Mormons, they could beg, they could take what bounty they could get and pay the consequences, or they could fight. Conflict was inevitable. Conflict mixed with accommodation prevailed in Utah for many years. Violent clashes occurred between Mormons and Native Americans in 1849, 1850 (Chief Sowiette), 1853 (Chief Walkara), 1860, and 1865–1868 (Chief Black Hawk)—all for the same primary reasons and along similar lines. Conflict subsided, and finally disappeared, only when most of the surviving Native Americans were forced onto reservations by the United States government.

Still, the LDS hand of fellowship was continually extended. Leonard Arrington accurately comments that "the most prominent theme in Brigham's Indian policy in the 1850s was patience and forbearance. . . . He continued to emphasize always being ready, using all possible means to conciliate the Indians, and acting only on the defensive" (Arrington, p. 217). Farms for the Native Americans were established as early as 1851, both to raise crops for their use and to teach them how to farm; but most of the "Indian farms" failed owing to a lack of commitment on both sides as well as to insufficient funding. LDS emissaries (such as Jacob Hamblin, Dudley Leavitt, and Dimmick Huntington) continued, however, to serve Native American needs, and missionaries continued to approach them in Utah and in bordering states. Small numbers of Utes, Shoshones, Paiutes, Gosiutes, and Navajos assimilated into the mainstream culture, and some of that number became Latter-day Saints. But overall, reciprocal contact and accommodation were minimal. By the turn of the century, contact was almost nil because most Native Americans lived on reservations far removed from LDS communities. Their contact with whites was mainly limited to government sol-

Native American members of the Church participate in a ward sacrament meeting (1985). Photographer: Marty Mayo.

diers and agency officials and to non-Mormon Christian missionaries.

RELATIONS IN RECENT TIMES. Beginning in the 1940s, the Church reemphasized reaching out to Native Americans. The Navajo-Zuni Mission, later named the Southwest Indian Mission, was created in 1943. It was followed by the Northern Indian Mission, headquartered in South Dakota. Eventually, missionaries were placed on many Indian reservations. The missionaries not only proselytize, but also assist Native Americans with their farming, ranching, and community development. Other Lamanite missions, including several in Central and South America and in Polynesia, have also been opened. Large numbers of North American Indians have migrated off reservations, and today over half of all Indians live in cities. In response, some formerly all-Indian missions have merged with those serving members of all racial and ethnic groups living in a given geographical area.

An Indian seminary program was initiated to teach the gospel to Native American children on reservations, in their own languages if necessary

A Native American meets with President George Albert Smith. Courtesy Special Collections Department, University of Utah Libraries.

(see SEMINARY). Initially, Native American children of all ages were taught the principles of the gospel in schools adjacent to federal public schools on reservations and in remote Indian communities. The Indian seminary program has now been integrated within the regular seminary system, and Indian children in the ninth through twelfth grades attend seminary, just as non-Indian children do.

The INDIAN STUDENT PLACEMENT SERVICES (ISPS) seeks to improve the educational attainment of Native American children by placing member Indian children with LDS families during the school year. Foster families, selected because of their emotional, financial, and spiritual stability, pay all expenses of the Indian child, who lives with a foster family during the nine-month school year and spends the summer on the reservation with his or her natural family. Generally, the children enter the program at a fairly young age and return year after year to the same foster family until they graduate from high school.

From a small beginning in 1954, the program peaked in 1970 with an enrollment of nearly 5,000 students. The development of more adequate schools on reservations has since then reduced the need for the program and the number of participants has declined. In 1990, about 500 students participated. More than 70,000 Native American youngsters have participated in ISPS, and evaluations have shown that participation significantly increased their educational attainment.

In the 1950s, Elder Spencer W. KIMBALL, then an apostle, encouraged BRIGHAM YOUNG UNIVERSITY to take an active interest in Native American education and to help solve economic and social problems. Scholarships were established, and a program to help Indian students adjust to university life was inaugurated. During the 1970s more than 500 Indian students, representing seventy-one tribes, were enrolled each year. But enrollment has declined, so a new program for Indian students is being developed that will increase the recruiting of Native American students to BYU and raise the percentage who receive a college degree. The Native American Educational Outreach Program at BYU presents educational seminars to tribal leaders and Indian youth across North America. It also offers scholarships. American Indian Services, another outreach program originally affiliated with BYU, provides adult education and technical and financial assistance to In-

President Spencer W. Kimball escorts Milli Cody [Garrett], "Miss Indian BYU" for 1974–1975 to a campus reception. Courtesy Doug Martin.

dian communities. In 1989, American Indian Services was transferred from BYU to the Lehi Foundation, which continues this activity.

In 1975, George P. Lee, a full-blooded Navajo and an early ISPS participant, was appointed as a General Authority. He was the first Indian to achieve this status and served faithfully for more than ten years. Elder Lee became convinced that the Church was neglecting its mission to the Lamanites, and when he voiced strong disapproval of Church leaders, he was excommunicated in 1989.

The Church has always had a strong commitment to preaching the gospel to Native Americans and assisting individuals, families, communities, and tribes to improve their education, health, and religious well-being. Programs vary from time to time as conditions and needs change, but the underlying beliefs and goodwill of Latter-day Saints toward these people remain firm and vibrant.

BIBLIOGRAPHY

Arrington, Leonard J. *Brigham Young: American Moses.* New York, 1985.

———, and Davis Bitton. *The Mormon Experience: A History of the Latter-day Saints.* New York, 1979.

Chadwick, Bruce A., Stan L. Albrecht, and Howard M. Bahr. "Evaluation of an Indian Student Placement Program." *Social Casework* 67, no. 9 (1986):515–24.

Walker, Ronald W. "Toward a Reconstruction of Mormon and Indian Relations, 1847–1877." *BYU Studies* 29 (Fall 1989):23–42.

BRUCE A. CHADWICK
THOMAS GARROW

NATURAL MAN

The phrase "natural man" is understood by Latter-day Saints to be an unrepentant person; it does not imply that mortals are by nature depraved or evil, but only that they are in a fallen condition. Natural man describes persons who are "without God in the world, and they have gone contrary to the nature of God" (Alma 41:11). The Lord declared to Joseph SMITH: "Every spirit of man was innocent in the beginning; and God having redeemed man from the fall, men became again, in their infant state, innocent before God" (D&C 93:38).

The ATONEMENT of Christ does not automatically free mankind from a fallen condition, although it does guarantee all a physical resurrection. Rather, it makes possible for men and women to escape the condition of natural man by accepting the Atonement and nurturing the LIGHT OF CHRIST within them. King BENJAMIN was told by an angel that "the natural man is an enemy to God, and has been from the fall of Adam." But a person can "put off the natural man" by yielding to "the enticings of the Holy Spirit," and can become "a saint through the atonement of Christ the Lord, . . . [by becoming] as a child, submissive, meek, humble, patient, full of love" (Mosiah 3:19). The phrase natural man, therefore, does not describe a condition that causes sin but a consequence of sin, of going against the commandments of God. As the prophet ABINADI taught, "he that persists in his own carnal nature, and goes on in the ways of sin and rebellion against God, remaineth in his fallen state" (Mosiah 16:5). In such rebellion, one is left without excuse. As explained by SAMUEL THE LAMANITE:

> Whosoever doeth iniquity, doeth it unto himself; for behold, ye are free; ye are permitted to act for yourselves; for behold, God hath given unto you a knowledge and he hath made you free. He hath given unto you that ye might know good from evil, and he hath given unto you that ye might choose life or death [Hel. 14:30–31; see also AGENCY].

The apostle PAUL speaks of the natural man as being in a state incapable of understanding spiritual truth. "But the natural man receiveth not the things of the Spirit of God: for they are foolishness unto him: neither can he know them, because they are spiritually discerned" (1 Cor. 2:14). Moreover, the natural man "walk[s] according to the course of this world, fulfilling the desires of the flesh and of the mind" (Eph. 2:2–3).

Because the natural man is unrepentant and indulgent, one must overcome this condition through repentance and submission to the Spirit of God. President Brigham YOUNG stated that God "has placed us on the earth to prove ourselves, to govern, control, educate and sanctify ourselves, body and spirit" (JD 10:2, in Discourses of Brigham Young, ed. J. Widtsoe, p. 57, Salt Lake City, 1971). Parley P. Pratt, an apostle, explains how the Holy Ghost aids in the process:

> [It] increases, enlarges, expands and purifies all the natural passions and affections; and adapts them, by the gift of wisdom, to their lawful use. It inspires, develops, cultivates and matures all the fine-toned sympathies, joys, tastes, kindred feelings and affections of our nature [Key to the Science of Theology, 10th ed., p. 101, Salt Lake City, 1973].

Repentance is manifested as "[yielding] to the enticings of the Holy Spirit, . . . [being] willing to submit to all things which the Lord seeth fit to inflict upon him, even as a child doth submit to his father" (Mosiah 3:19). Neal A. Maxwell of the Quorum of the Twelve Apostles has pointed out that humility and selflessness develop a capacity for discipline and a control of natural appetites. This is a difficult process, which requires that "men and women of Christ magnify their callings without magnifying themselves" (p. 16).

BIBLIOGRAPHY

Maxwell, Neal A. "Put Off the Natural Man, and Come Off Conqueror." Ensign 20 (Nov. 1990):14–16.

Millet, Robert L. Life in Christ, pp. 23–35. Salt Lake City, 1990.

R. J. SNOW

NATURE, LAW OF

Rational inquiry into nature (physis) was for Greek philosophers the way to know reality. The natural was originally radically distinguished from law (nomos), which identified merely human conventions. Thus, for example, it is natural for humans to speak, but it is not natural to speak Greek. Hence, law was not initially thought of by such philosophers as natural, though it was natural for humans to be governed by such conventions. Later the terms "nature" and "law" began to be linked to describe a prepolitical golden age without rules, contracts, property, or marriage. Understood in this way, "natural law," after the decline from the golden age, did not provide the model for civil law, but instead identified a realm accessible to reason that transcends the world. Roman Catholic theologians eventually borrowed the expression "natural law" from pagan philosophy to ground a structured social ethic. Thomas Aquinas, in his Aristotelian restructuring of Christianity, distinguished four levels of law: eternal, divine, natural, and human. Eternal law, the mind of God and structure of reality, he held, is known both through revelation as divine law and through reason as natural law, and human law should strive to reflect the natural law.

Though Latter-day Saints sometimes speculate about the reasons for the positive law given through divine REVELATION and also about the moral sense of mankind (see ETHICS), a moral natural law is not clearly delineated in the LDS canon. Some suggest that rough equivalents for a moral natural law might be elicited from scripture. But theology, grounded in philosophical speculation, is typically seen as a competitor to divine revelation. Such speculation remains tentative and problematic. Hence, there is little talk of a moral natural law among Latter-day Saints.

LDS scriptures, rather than relying upon notions of a moral natural law, speak of God's commandments, statutes, and ordinances, of God's will and plans and purposes, of the ordering of the world (including its metes and bounds) of law given by God, and so forth. The laws mentioned in the scriptures seem, instead, to be instances of divine positive law, though they are not arbitrary, since as moral prescriptions they form the terms of the COVENANT entered into in the hope that blessings will flow from obedience to God. It is assumed that God's commandments rest on reasons not fully accessible to human inquiry or explication.

There is, however, another strand of thought among Latter-day Saints, one that affirms what might be called the "laws of nature," where that term identifies the regularities found by the sciences. These laws are seen as descriptive, not prescriptive or normative. They are thought either to be set in place by God or to exist independently of God's will and hence function as conditions that must be managed as plans are worked out by man in cooperation with God. Such views are entertained by many Latter-day Saints, especially those trained in the natural sciences, but they have not been systematically set forth or integrated with the teachings in the scriptures.

It is the prophetic gift that makes available the terms of the covenant with God, and such covenants are accompanied by blessings and cursings. Latter-day Saints thus emphasize obedience to what amounts to divine positive law and not to the dictates of nature as known by human reason.

BIBLIOGRAPHY

d'Entreves, A. P. *Natural Law.* London, 1951.

Madsen, Truman G. "Joseph Smith and the Problems of Ethics." In *Perspectives in Mormon Ethics,* ed. Donald E. Hill, pp. 29–48. Salt Lake City, 1983.

LOUIS C. MIDGLEY

NAUVOO

Nauvoo, Illinois, headquarters of the Church and home for many of its members from 1839 to 1846, began and ended as a community in exile. In 1838–1839 Latter-day Saints fled from Missouri seeking religious refuge from mob persecution. They found shelter in eastern Iowa and western Illinois, where they established new communities. Joseph Smith named the principal city Nauvoo, meaning, he said, "a beautiful location, a place of rest." When the Saints left Nauvoo for the Rocky Mountains seven years later, they were again religious exiles in search of a home.

The community at Nauvoo grew rapidly on land purchased from settlers and speculators willing to sell on contract. Joseph Smith, acting as agent for the Church, bought the Illinois farms of Hugh and William White and investment tracts from Isaac Galland and Horace Hotchkiss—in all, 660 acres. He resold one-acre Nauvoo lots surveyed on the flats along the river, in competition with other LDS developers who platted land on nearby bluffs. A survey established streets three rods wide within city boundaries overlaying existing "paper" towns of Commerce and Commerce City. In December 1840, Nauvoo became a legal entity under the NAUVOO CHARTER, issued by the Illinois legislature and providing the Saints better legal protection than they had ever known. Nauvoo was now home.

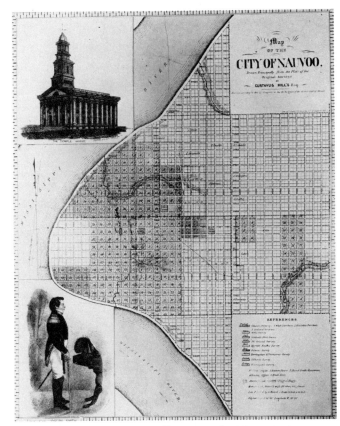

Map of the City of Nauvoo, Illinois, on the Mississippi River, c. 1842.

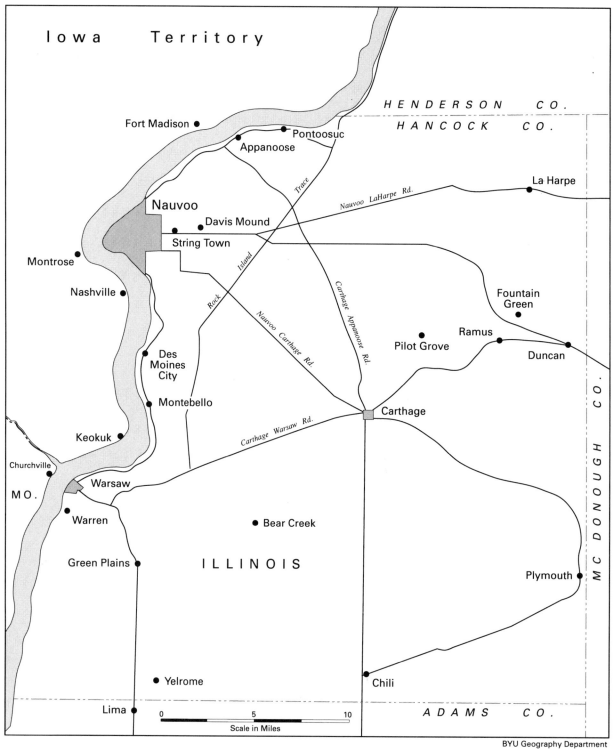

BYU Geography Department

Church history sites near Nauvoo, Illinois, 1839–1846.

Nauvoo, Illinois. Streets and buildings, 1846. ⟶

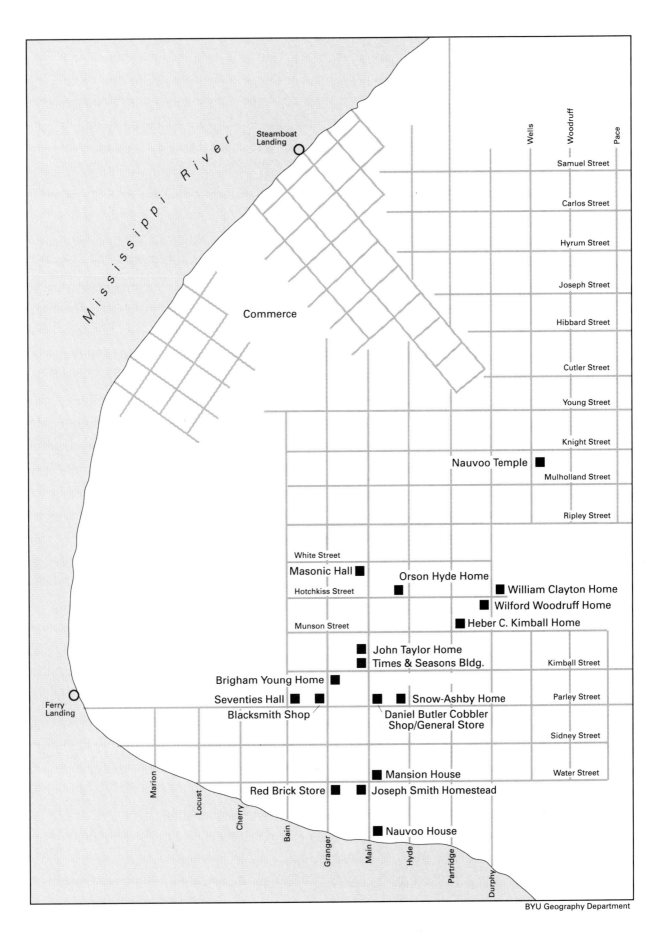

As exiled Latter-day Saints from Missouri and Ohio gathered to their new stake of ZION, missionaries in the United States and Great Britain baptized many new converts (*see* MISSIONS OF THE TWELVE TO THE BRITISH ISLES). Encouraged by Joseph Smith, American and Canadian converts moved westward to Nauvoo. Some used canal boats and lake steamers, others covered wagons and horseback, and a few simply walked. Beginning in 1840, thousands sailed the Atlantic from Liverpool, England, and took steamboats up the Mississippi from New Orleans. This was a religious migration, an individual and family response to religious beliefs, aided by Church emigration agents in Liverpool, who organized companies and appointed shepherds for those fleeing to Zion (*see* IMMIGRATION AND EMIGRATION).

Newcomers were welcomed in Nauvoo by friends, relatives, missionaries, and the Prophet Joseph Smith himself. Renting a room or finding other temporary quarters became increasingly difficult during the boom years 1841–1843. As quickly as possible, new settlers hired scarce contractors and craftsmen to build houses. Lumber, harvested from nearby virgin forests or shipped in, and, later, bricks made in Nauvoo, went into hundreds of comfortable but small, new homes. Nauvoo became a boom town.

Gardens on the city lots furnished vegetables, herbs, fruits, and berries. Meat and potatoes, when available, and corn—ground into meal for boiling, baking, and frying—were staples in everyone's diet. On nearby prairies, farmers plowed, cooperatively enclosed, and then planted hundreds of acres in corn, wheat, and potatoes. LDS tradesmen found ready work in Nauvoo, as did merchants eager to import manufactured goods from St. Louis, Cincinnati, and the East Coast.

Nauvoo boosters and their political opponents in neighboring towns exaggerated their estimates of Nauvoo's population for differing purposes. Illinois census takers in 1845 counted 11,057 residents. Adding growth through late 1845 and including the city's environs boosted the estimate to 15,000 at Nauvoo's peak, almost equal to a faster-growing Chicago.

To meet public needs, civic groups built a music hall and cultural hall, and PRIESTHOOD QUORUMS planned their own meeting halls. Church-sponsored construction of the NAUVOO HOUSE, a grand hotel, and the Nauvoo temple gave Nauvoo's growth religious meaning.

Though all members contributed as means and faith allowed toward erection of the temple, they did not all live in Nauvoo. Some remained in their hometowns because of economic or family pressures. Others joined the march to Nauvoo but found homesites and land away from headquarters. On a 13,000-acre, Church-purchased site in Lee County, Iowa, just across the river from Nauvoo, the Saints founded a town called Zarahemla and nine other smaller settlements. Joseph Smith organized an Iowa stake and approved settlement there and in several new towns in western Illinois. Besides Nauvoo, Church members in Hancock County lived at Ramus (now Webster); in Adams County at Lima, Quincy, Mount Hope (now Columbus), and Freedom (near Payson); in Morgan County at Geneva; in Sangamon County at Springfield; and in Pike County at Pleasant Vale (now Canton). Additionally, presiding elders organized Church branches wherever clusters of members lived in North America and the British Isles.

Wherever they lived, Latter-day Saints looked to the Prophet Joseph Smith for religious leadership. His revelations and sermons published in Nauvoo achieved Churchwide distribution. For residents, the Prophet offered firsthand preaching,

Joseph Smith and his family moved into the Mansion House in August 1843. Later a wing was added to the east side of the main structure for a total of twenty-two rooms. Beginning in January 1844, Ebenezer Robinson managed the Mansion House as a hotel, and the Prophet maintained six rooms for himself and his family. Emma Smith lived here until 1871, when she moved into the Nauvoo House, where she died in 1879.

teaching, and counseling. Besides these, his influence in Nauvoo was enlarged through his roles as land agent, mayor, militia leader, magistrate, and merchant. No wonder that after his death and the repeal of its charter, the city was renamed the City of Joseph.

During his last years at Nauvoo, the Prophet unfolded additional aspects of the restored gospel. He responded to questions about basic LDS beliefs with thirteen ARTICLES OF FAITH, which described fundamental doctrines. He published another revealed scriptural record, the BOOK OF ABRAHAM. He taught new insights into the common origins of all mankind and their eternal destiny, particularly in a eulogy for a member, King Follett (*see* KING FOLLETT DISCOURSE). Many of the new teachings pointed toward the temple, and looked toward a collective effort to perform ordinances for the salvation of deceased ancestors and the exaltation of faithful Saints. The first BAPTISMS FOR THE DEAD were done in the Mississippi River, but by late November 1841, proxy baptisms commenced in the temple font. Meanwhile, with the temple not yet complete, several men, including two of the Twelve, received the first temple ENDOWMENTS on May 4, 1842, in an upstairs room at the President's office-store. The following year their wives and other men and women received the same ordinances, providing a corps of initiates to administer temple ordinances to thousands of others in the Nauvoo Temple beginning in December 1845.

The temple was a central focus of Nauvoo religious life. The Saints supported its construction with tithes of time and means, and they longed to receive anticipated temple blessings. For those privileged to live in Nauvoo, the temple and its associated theology gave new and eternal meaning to birth, marriage, life, and death.

Though Joseph Smith's personal leadership dominated Nauvoo's religious life, an institutional structure supported his efforts and carried on after his death in 1844 (*see* MARTYRDOM OF JOSEPH AND HYRUM SMITH). During the Nauvoo years, the Quorum of the Twelve accepted an increased role. First organized in 1835, members gained experience first as mission leaders in England and then as administrators in Nauvoo. With the FIRST PRESIDENCY and other authorities, they shared opportunities to preach scriptural commentaries on Sunday from the stand in the grove near the temple, and to address the Saints at general con-

Seventies Hall, Nauvoo, was a meeting place for various priesthood quorums. Built in 1844, it housed a training school for missionaries, a small library, and a museum of artifacts from around the world. It was reconstructed on its original foundation in 1971–1972.

ferences. Among the most significant meetings in Nauvoo, these April and October conferences brought together thousands of the Saints for business and instruction. Similar gatherings convened elsewhere for scattered branches. Minutes published in the British *Millennial Star* and Nauvoo *Times and Seasons* helped keep members elsewhere informed of Church business, membership growth, and preachings. Church periodicals issued the first installments of Joseph Smith's HISTORY OF THE CHURCH, a project he pursued diligently with his clerks from 1838 until his death in 1844.

The women's RELIEF SOCIETY, organized in 1842, administered to the needs of the poor and taught principles of sexual purity. In this, they assisted the bishops of Nauvoo's fledgling WARDS— new administrative units for tending to temporal needs and monitoring religious worthiness. After Brigham YOUNG and the Twelve succeeded the Prophet as leaders, the SEVENTY and other Melchizedek Priesthood quorums grew rapidly in numbers and importance. The Seventy built a hall, sponsored a library, and prepared themselves for missions and for temple blessings.

While Latter-day Saints in Nauvoo gave primary allegiance to their religious affiliation, their lives reflected experiences typical of others in Jacksonian America. Non-Mormons living in and

Brigham Young's residence in Nauvoo, as it appeared around 1900.

around Nauvoo joined with them in the celebration of Independence Day. Military processions, band music, patriotic speeches, and other festivities attracted citizens who arrived on horseback and in carriages and riverboats. Christmas observances were highlights for family and friends, with progressive dinners, singing, and dancing. Membership in Mormon Freemasonry lodges, organized in 1841–1842, affirmed group loyalty within the Church and encouraged fraternal ties with others. Contrary to expectations, however, the rapid growth of the lodges created controversy that strained relationships with other masons (*see* FREEMASONRY IN NAUVOO).

Mormon-American society in Nauvoo, leavened increasingly by a British and Scandinavian immigrant influence, included typical nineteenth-century entertainment and recreational opportunities. Brass bands played at dances and patriotic gatherings, accompanied Church choirs, and performed for temple capstone ceremonies. Adult and youth choirs, instrumentalists, and vocalists entertained and edified at social and religious gatherings. The music performed came out of the host society, though some hymns were newly written for LDS services. Mormon poets regularly memorialized events and people and set significant religious messages to rhyme for biweekly periodicals. Thespians in Nauvoo presented popular theatricals or sponsored traveling performing troupes in the Nauvoo cultural hall. Other occasional attractions included art exhibits, the circus, and riverboat excursions (*see* SOCIAL AND CULTURAL HISTORY).

Children had few toys, mostly homemade wagons, tops, and dolls. They enjoyed games such as fox and geese or leapfrog. Youths engaged in pastimes such as playing with marbles, wrestling, foot racing, hunting, fishing, stick-pulling, bowling, and baseball. Adults joined in many of these recreational activities and sometimes passed the time with card games, carriage rides, or parlor socials. When not providing necessities, Nauvooans also pursued education and learning. To get basic training in reading, writing, and arithmetic for their families, parents hired tutors or enrolled children in one of dozens of classes offered by Nauvoo's part-time teachers. Tuition was paid through providing teachers board and room and scarce cash. The University of Nauvoo existed only in a few scattered classes. Male adults and younger men organized lyceums and debating societies to develop rhetorical skills. They argued religious as well as political topics to prepare participants for missionary and civic service. Books were scarce in private homes, but a membership lending library offered two hundred donated volumes on science, world religion, history, and literature. Nauvoo's religious and secular newspapers, the *Times and Seasons* and *Nauvoo Neighbor* (originally *The Wasp*), edited by prominent LDS citizens, circulated to Latter-day Saints on two continents. In an "Age of the Common Man," Nauvoo's social and educational life was one of broad enjoyment and participation.

As elsewhere in American society, the family was the focus of everyday life. Women met domestic needs through a combination of their own labor and income from their husbands' work. The family produced and prepared food, though Nauvoo merchants imported or traded many foodstuffs. Women often made everyday clothing, bed coverings, rugs, and such things as towels and curtains from purchased cloth. Furniture, kitchen utensils, and tools for trades were imported or brought along by immigrants. Home remedies, supplemented by priesthood blessings, were administered in faith for healing. Infant mortality was high, and death for all a constant possibility from malarialike diseases, untreatable illnesses, and accidents.

For Latter-day Saints in Nauvoo, the family took on new religious meaning. Conversion unfortunately often divided families, though letters from Nauvoo nurtured bonds and encouraged reunion. Proxy temple ordinances offered opportunity for uniting families across generations and beyond the grave. Select associates accepted the Prophet's private challenge to make covenants of marriage with plural wives (*see* PLURAL MARRIAGE), though the doctrine was not preached publicly until 1852 in Utah. In preparation for the temple, teaching of the doctrine of eternal families added a unique touch to LDS family life. SEALING ordinances for husbands and wives gave marriage and the family in Nauvoo an eternal perspective.

Just when life appeared to be back to normal after the martyrdom, the loss of Nauvoo's charter and mob harassment in 1845 threatened the peace of Joseph Smith's City Beautiful. Political and schismatic opponents predicted "the end of 'Mormonism.'" Disaffected Latter-day Saints threatened religious unity and offered guardianship and new prophetic leadership in opposition to the Twelve. The Church survived, but Nauvoo's position as the Church center ended. The governing Quorum of the Twelve announced plans at the October 1845 conference to evacuate by the following spring.

Throughout the winter, residents organized for the exodus even as they rushed to complete their temple and receive its ordinances (*see* WESTERN MIGRATION: PLANNING AND PROPHECY). They purchased oxen, made wagons, sold properties, and outfitted themselves for the long trek into the western wilderness as they also prepared temple clothing and did finishing work inside the temple on the hill. Brigham Young and the Twelve appointed agents to dispose of unsold property and organized emigration companies as they oversaw construction details on the temple. By December, just before departure began, thousands of the Nauvoo faithful began to receive their long-awaited temple endowments. Before winter's end more than 6,000 received temple ordinances and thus were willing to leave. After seven eventful years, the Latter-day Saints moved on again, transplanting their covenant society to a new promised land.

Looking northeast toward the Nauvoo Temple, 1846, at the time of the Latter-day Saint exodus (daguerreotype). Nauvoo grew rapidly between 1839 and 1846. Dugouts and simple log structures were soon replaced by traditional frame or brick homes. Charles W. Carter collection.

Hill, Marvin S. "Mormon Religion in Nauvoo: Some Reflections." *Utah Historical Quarterly* 44 (1976):170–80.

Kimball, Stanley B. "Nauvoo West: The Mormons of the Iowa Shore." *BYU Studies* 18 (1978):132–42.

Miller, David E., and Della S. Miller. *Nauvoo: The City of Joseph.* Salt Lake City, 1974.

GLEN M. LEONARD

BIBLIOGRAPHY

Flanders, Robert B. "To Transform History: Early Mormon Culture and the Concept of Time and Space." *Church History* 40 (1971):108–17.

Godfrey, Kenneth W. "Some Thoughts Regarding an Unwritten History of Nauvoo." *BYU Studies* 15 (1975):417–24.

——. "The Nauvoo Neighborhood: A Little Philadelphia or a Unique City Set Upon a Hill?" *Journal of Mormon History* 11 (1984):78–97.

NAUVOO CHARTER

By legislation signed into law on December 16, 1840, the Illinois General Assembly granted corporate city status to Nauvoo. Among literally hundreds of Illinois settlements, only Alton, Chicago, Galena, Quincy, and Springfield shared such distinctive legal status. Expectations of what would result ran high for both Latter-day Saints and their neighbors.

Many Illinoisans, shocked at the harsh treatment given the Latter-day Saints by the Missourians (*see* MISSOURI CONFLICT), sought to succor the beleaguered followers of Joseph SMITH by helping them politically and providing legal safeguards. Moreover, the economic fabric of the state suffered from the deepening effects of the panics of 1837 and 1839, and many legislators saw an economic boon in the future immigration of several thousand new settlers. Encouraged by state political leaders, the Saints believed that a city charter would guarantee them a kind of security they had never yet enjoyed. Even State Supreme Court Justice Stephen A. Douglas, despite prior judicial decisions to the contrary, opined that a corporate charter was irrevocable and perpetual.

The Nauvoo document, neither the longest nor the shortest city charter, was much like the charters of other Illinois cities. More than half the sections were modeled on the Springfield charter. City status allowed governance by a council chosen by an electorate; unlike other city councils in Illinois, the Nauvoo Council contained aldermen, councillors, and a mayor. The Nauvoo instrument also differed from others in being not one but three charters, granting corporate status the city, a university, and a city militia. Previous practice was to establish schools and also militia units by separate acts. The University of the City of Nauvoo, governed by the city council, was the only city-operated university in the state.

One important provision stated that the Nauvoo Council could pass any ordinances not repugnant to the constitutions of the United States or that of Illinois. This, in effect, empowered the Nauvoo body to stand in a federated position with the Illinois General Assembly. Ordinances passed by the Nauvoo Council could be in direct violation or disregard of state law and still be valid in Nauvoo, provided they did not conflict with specific powers granted by the federal and state constitutions. Leaders of the city militia, known as the NAUVOO LEGION, and the university trustees could also pass laws, limited only by state and federal constitutions.

Almost at once this power became a focal point of misunderstanding and controversy, though the same delegation of authority was also in three of the other five city charters. Since this provision was not unique, adverse reaction to it clearly had a good deal to do with how others viewed Latter-day Saints and the implementation of the provision by Nauvoo and its leaders. The Nauvoo Municipal Court, the third such court provided for by the Illinois General Assembly, also became a point of contention. While the city courts of Chicago and Alton convened under one judge, the principal Nauvoo judge was the mayor of the city, sitting as chief justice, with the aldermen as associate justices. Adversaries argued that the way Joseph Smith, as mayor of Nauvoo, used the legislative and judicial powers granted by law resulted in "anti-republican" abuses.

In granting the charter, some legislators may have hoped to protect Latter-day Saints from PERSECUTION, but it proved to be a two-edged sword. When the Illinois majority turned against Nauvoo but lacked legal tools to curb the city's power and influence, it turned to extralegal means. Later, after violence, it also succeeded in getting Nauvoo's charter repealed. Although based solidly on precedents not termed "anti-republican" until Latter-day Saints obtained and used them, the Nauvoo Charter nevertheless ultimately fell short of providing the Saints the peace and protection they desired.

BIBLIOGRAPHY

Kimball, James L., Jr. "The Nauvoo Charter: A Reinterpretation." *Journal of the Illinois State Historical Society* 54 (Spring 1971):66–78.

JAMES L. KIMBALL, JR.

NAUVOO ECONOMY

Nauvoo, for seven years the headquarters of the Church, was a river city with an agricultural hinterland set amid a preestablished, second-generation frontier society of non-Mormons. Founded in 1839 by LDS refugees from the MISSOURI CONFLICT, it existed as an LDS community only until 1846. Additions to its fast-growing population came mostly through new converts, many from England, who almost always brought skills and sometimes wealth. Though commerce in goods and services was brisk, Nauvoo's primary import was converts (*see* IMMIGRATION AND EMIGRATION), and its primary export, MISSIONARIES.

Nauvoo was neither communal nor communitarian. Still, the influences of the corporation of the

Nauvoo, Illinois, 1859, by Johannes Schroeder (1859, oil on metal, 10″ × 13″). Nauvoo was a Mississippi boom town, competing with several other communities for business. Through industry and organization, the Mormons and others in Nauvoo established successful businesses as printers, gunsmiths, coopers, farmers, and merchants.

Church pervaded society and economy. In Nauvoo, Joseph SMITH voiced a prophetic, hurrying urgency to build the city and its TEMPLE, an urgency that loomed over all. Nauvoo was the first full-scale model of the kingdom of God on earth as envisioned by Joseph Smith. The Nauvoo Saints thus directed great energy toward "building up the Kingdom," which, in economic terms, meant building the city and establishing its economic infrastructure.

Like other communities of its day, Nauvoo had blacksmiths, coopers, potters, gunsmiths, and tinsmiths, but most in demand were the sawyers, brick makers, and carpenters. Construction was the principal industry. The hamlet of Commerce, Illinois, whose site Nauvoo overran, had few buildings, so the demand for housing was great. The Saints did not envision group housing in the fashion of Moravians, Shakers, and other communitarian societies, but they wanted detached single-family dwellings of Anglo-American rural tradition. The same was true for commercial and industrial buildings. With numerous small buildings reared upon large lots in more or less orderly rows, orga-

nized in a grid of wide streets with open land between for outbuildings, gardens, orchards, and grazing plots, Nauvoo became the prototypical Mormon city (*see* CITY PLANNING).

Public works made up a major part of Nauvoo construction. Work never started on an ambitious plan to dam the Mississippi to facilitate industrial development, but work did begin on a canal across the town peninsula. The plan was to bypass the Des Moines Rapids of the Mississippi, an obstacle that made the site a river portage much of the year; but the project was abandoned when the workers encountered limestone bedrock. The stone was subsequently quarried for the NAUVOO TEMPLE.

The Nauvoo Temple, a focal point of Nauvoo religious and economic life, was essential for Nauvoo to be a literal manifestation of the kingdom. Temple building tested the religious zeal and the economic resources of all the Saints, both in Nauvoo and elsewhere. Residents were expected to "tithe for the temple" in time, goods, or money. Saints not yet gathered to Nauvoo were urged to do so quickly so that they could be part of the enterprise. Those who could not do so were to support temple construction with cash. The Twelve Apostles wrote the English Saints in 1841, "The first great object before us, and the Saints generally, is to [complete] the Temple . . . to secure the salvation of the Church" (*HC* 4:449). For Joseph Smith, completion of the temple was the first priority. The 1841 revelation authorizing the temple also threatened rejection of the Church unless the building was completed in "a sufficient time" (D&C 124:30–32). Even so, when Joseph Smith was killed in 1844, the walls were only half built.

Though building the temple was a labor of love, its economic cost put a severe drain on the city's resources. Capital was diverted from enterprises needed to provide goods and employment. Even Joseph Smith, though enthusiastic about the temple, recognized the problem. "I prophesy," he said in 1843, that "as soon as we get the Temple built, so that we shall not be obliged to exhaust our means thereon, we will have means to gather the Saints by thousands and tens of thousands" (*HC* 5:255).

Nauvoo's economy developed during the national depression of 1839–1843. The refugee founders were virtually destitute, but few Americans of any station had sound money during that period. The banks had failed, and specie had fled. The Saints fashioned an ingenious but shaky exchange system based on barter, letters of credit, informal IOUs, and "bonds-for-deed"—bonds given in land sales in lieu of deeds, a necessity because the whole Nauvoo tract was purchased on a long-term contract without deed until full payment. The system worked because the economy was generally expanding and the Saints trusted each other and were bound by common purpose.

The land purchase, the temple, the NAUVOO HOUSE (a large hotel), and the whole kingdom-building project upon which the Saints believed their salvation depended were headed by Joseph Smith and his ecclesiastical organization. Because Nauvoo represented an intermingling of the sacred and the secular under a prophet-leader, when he was killed in 1844, the survival of the project depended upon how and by whom he was succeeded (*see* SUCCESSION IN THE PRESIDENCY). Those who accepted the leadership of Brigham YOUNG and the Quorum of the Twelve transplanted the system of political economy fashioned in Nauvoo to the West (*see* PIONEER ECONOMY; WESTWARD MIGRATION, PLANNING AND PROPHECY). Some who did not and who chose to move away from the model of Nauvoo

later joined the REORGANIZED CHURCH OF JESUS CHRIST OF LATTER DAY SAINTS.

BIBLIOGRAPHY

Flanders, Robert. *Nauvoo: Kingdom on the Mississippi.* Urbana, Ill., 1965.

Miller, David, and Della Miller. *Nauvoo: The City of Joseph.* Santa Barbara and Salt Lake City, 1974.

Rowley, Dennis. "Nauvoo: A River Town." *BYU Studies* 18 (Winter 1978):255–72.

ROBERT B. FLANDERS

NAUVOO EXPOSITOR

The *Nauvoo Expositor* was the newspaper voice of APOSTATES determined to destroy the Prophet Joseph SMITH and The Church of Jesus Christ of Latter-day Saints in the spring of 1844. During the last few months of Joseph Smith's life, an opposition party of disgruntled members, apostates, and excommunicants coalesced into a dissenting church. The principals claimed to believe in the Book of Mormon and the RESTORATION OF THE GOSPEL, but rejected what they termed Nauvoo innovations, notably PLURAL MARRIAGE. Claiming that Joseph was a fallen PROPHET, the dissenters set out, through the *Expositor*, to expose the Prophet's supposed false teachings and abominations. They held secret meetings, made plans, and took oaths to topple the Church and kill Joseph Smith. The publication of the newspaper was crucial to their stratagem.

When the press for the *Expositor* arrived in Nauvoo on May 7, 1844, it stirred great excitement among Mormons and non-Mormons alike, but there was no immediate interference. Within three days the owners, all leaders of the opposition movement, issued a broadside prospectus for their newspaper. One month later, on June 7, the first and only issue of the *Nauvoo Expositor* appeared and caused an immediate furor in the community. Nauvoo residents were incensed at what they saw as its sensational, yellow-journalistic claims about Nauvoo religion, politics, and morality. They were also struck with sharp foreboding. Francis Higbee, one of the proprietors of the newspaper, set an ominous tone when he described Joseph Smith as "the biggest villain that goes unhung."

The literary quality of the paper was inferior. A contemporary non-Mormon critic described it as "dull or laughable," with "lame grammar and turgid rhetoric" (Oaks, p. 868). But the *Expositor*'s polemics against the Church and Joseph Smith were threatening and polarizing. The anti-Mormons were exultant about the *Expositor*, but Church members demanded that something be done.

As mayor of Nauvoo, Joseph Smith summoned the city council. Following fourteen hours of deliberation in three different sessions, the council resolved on Monday, June 10, about 6:30 P.M., that the newspaper and its printing office were "a public nuisance" and instructed the mayor "to remove it . . . without delay." Joseph Smith promptly ordered the city marshal to destroy the press and burn all copies of the paper. At 8:00 P.M. the marshal carried out the mayor's orders (HC 6:432–49). That action, justified or not, played into the hands of the opposition. It riled anti-Mormon sentiment throughout Hancock County and provided substance for the charges used by the opposition to hold Joseph Smith in CARTHAGE JAIL, where he was murdered on June 27, 1844 (*see* MARTYRDOM OF JOSEPH AND HYRUM SMITH).

BIBLIOGRAPHY

Godfrey, Kenneth W. "Causes of Mormon/Non-Mormon Conflict in Hancock County, Illinois, 1839–1846." Ph.D. diss., Brigham Young University, 1967.

Oaks, Dallin H. "The Suppression of the Nauvoo Expositor." *Utah Law Review* 9 (Winter 1965):862–903.

Oaks, Dallin H., and Marvin S. Hill. *Carthage Conspiracy: The Trial of the Accused Assassins of Joseph Smith*. Urbana, Ill., 1979.

REED C. DURHAM, JR.

NAUVOO HOUSE

A revelation to Joseph Smith in January 1841 commanded the Saints to build both the NAUVOO TEMPLE and the Nauvoo House, a hotel that would be "a delightful habitation for man, and a resting place for the weary traveler" (D&C 124:60). The Saints were not to isolate themselves from the world, but to provide attractive accommodations for strangers and tourists while they "contemplate the word of the Lord; and the corner-stone I have appointed for Zion" (D&C 124:23).

Joseph Smith donated the land for the Nauvoo House, and many Latter-day Saints purchased

One of the first projects of the Church in Nauvoo was to build a hotel called the Nauvoo House. This uniface stock certificate was issued by the Nauvoo House Association, an Illinois corporation. In D&C 124, many Church members were called upon by name to invest capital in this project. Courtesy Rare Books and Manuscripts, Brigham Young University.

stock. The design of architects Lucien Woodworth and William Weeks called for an L-shaped brick building forty feet deep and three stories high. Construction began in the spring of 1841 and progressed (with interruptions) into 1845. Eventually, the work was discontinued in an effort to complete the Nauvoo Temple.

When the Saints left Nauvoo in 1846, the Nauvoo House walls were up above the windows of the second story. The large unfinished building on the south end of Main Street facing the Mississippi River became the property of Joseph Smith's widow, Emma SMITH. Subsequently, Emma's second husband, Lewis C. Bidamon, tore down the extremities of the L-shaped structure and used their bricks to complete the central portion as a smaller hotel, variously known as the Bidamon House and the Riverside Mansion. He and Emma lived there from 1871 until they died. After Bidamon's death, the REORGANIZED CHURCH OF JESUS CHRIST OF LATTER DAY SAINTS purchased the Nauvoo House and still owns it.

BIBLIOGRAPHY

Flanders, Robert Bruce. *Nauvoo: Kingdom on the Mississippi*, pp. 179–90. Urbana, Ill., 1965.

Holzapfel, Richard N., and T. Jeffery Cottle. *Old Mormon Nauvoo, 1839–1846*. Provo, Utah, 1990.

HELENE HOLT

NAUVOO LEGION

The Illinois legislative act of December 1840 that incorporated the city of Nauvoo also authorized creation of a military body or militia that came to be known as the Nauvoo Legion. Perhaps influenced by genuine disgust with the way the Latter-day Saints had been treated in Missouri, the Illinois legislature acted liberally. Under the NAUVOO CHARTER, Latter-day Saints could manage their own affairs, provided they did not violate the state or federal constitutions.

The organization of a militia unit was customary in settlements with sufficient population, a practice as old as the Republic. Nauvoo residents were particularly anxious to have their own military protection after having been victims of mob violence and having suffered expulsion from Missouri (*see* HAUN'S MILL MASSACRE; MISSOURI

Lieut. Gen. Joseph Smith, by Sutcliffe Maudsley (1842, egg tempera on paper, 9″ × 5″). On June 25, 1842, Joseph Smith sat for this portrait in uniform as leader of the citizen-militia Nauvoo Legion. Militia units like this were common in the area and were helpful in protecting citizens' rights and property. This artist is the only known painter who created portraits of Joseph Smith from life (discussed in detail, *Ensign* 11 [Mar. 1981]:62–73). Courtesy Buddy Youngreen.

CONFLICT). By 1840, they realized that they could not always rely on federal or state authorities for protection from such violence.

The Nauvoo Court Martial, consisting of the legion's commissioned officers, was given extensive authority. Among other things, it could "make, ordain, establish, and execute all such laws and ordinances as may be considered necessary for the benefit, government, and regulation of said Legion; provided [that] said Court Martial shall pass no law or act, repugnant to, or inconsistent with, the Constitution of the United States, or of this State [Illinois]" (*HC* 4:244).

As part of the state militia, the Nauvoo Legion was at the disposal of the governor of Illinois "for the public defense, and the execution of the laws of the State or of the United States." Significantly, it was also at the disposal of the mayor of Nauvoo for "executing the laws and ordinances of the city corporation" (*HC* 4:244).

The city council ordinance that created the Nauvoo Legion authorized the rank of lieutenant general for its commanding officer, an extraordinary authorization, since no other militia officer in the United States held rank above that of major general. The court martial elected Joseph Smith, commander of the legion.

The parades and other activities of the legion—which included mock battles—attracted visitors from near and far. Indeed, the legion became so popular that many non-Mormons joined the ranks. At its peak, it is said to have numbered 5,000 men, the largest such body in Illinois. But there were problems. According to historian B. H. Roberts:

> [The Nauvoo Legion] excited the jealousy and envy of the rest of the militia in surrounding counties, and all the laudable efforts of the legion to become an efficient body with a view of assisting in the execution of the state and national laws, if occasion should require, were construed by their enemies to mean a preparation for rebellion. . . . Hence that which was to be a bulwark to the city, and a protection to the saints, was transformed by their enemies into an occasion of offense, and an excuse for distrusting them [*CHC* 2:59–60].

Joseph SMITH mobilized the Nauvoo Legion to defend the city and declared martial law in June 1844 as tensions mounted between the Latter-day Saints, dissenters, and hostile neighbors. Joseph Smith and his brother Hyrum were among those arrested by another Illinois militia and placed in CARTHAGE JAIL, where they were killed by members of yet another militia (*see* MARTYRDOM OF JOSEPH AND HYRUM SMITH). Six months later, the Illinois legislature revoked the Nauvoo Charter. At that point, the Nauvoo Legion ceased to exist as a state militia, although as an unofficial body it continued to provide some protection to the beleaguered Latter-day Saints.

During the exodus westward later, some former members of the Nauvoo Legion served in the MORMON BATTALION. This 500-man body, authorized by the U.S. government in 1846 as part of the campaign against Mexico, marched from Council Bluffs to San Diego.

The name Nauvoo Legion was revived in Utah and applied to the organized militia of the state of DESERET and later of UTAH TERRITORY. This legion was called upon in 1849 to subdue marauding Indians, and its members served in the so-called Walker War of 1853–1854, named after Wakara, a Ute chieftain. With the approach of the UTAH EXPEDITION in 1857–1858, the Utah militia harassed and burned U.S. Army supply trains and prepared, if necessary, to prevent the entry of U.S. troops into Salt Lake City. In 1862, during the American Civil War, two units of the Nauvoo Legion protected overland mail and telegraph lines. Later, with a force of some 2,500 men, it fought against Indians in Utah's Black Hawk War (1865–1868).

Always more responsive to Mormon leadership than to the federal appointees who succeeded Brigham Young as governor of Utah, the legion was rendered inactive by an 1870 proclamation of Acting Governor J. Wilson Shaffer, who forbade gatherings of the militia except on his express orders. The Nauvoo Legion was finally disbanded as a result of the Edmunds-Tucker Act of 1887. In 1894 the National Guard of Utah was organized as Utah's militia.

BIBLIOGRAPHY

Gardner, Hamilton. "The Nauvoo Legion, 1840–1845—A Unique Military Organization." *Journal of the Illinois State Historical Society* 54 (Summer 1961):181–97.

PHILIP M. FLAMMER

NAUVOO NEIGHBOR

The *Nauvoo Neighbor* was a weekly newspaper published and edited by John TAYLOR in NAUVOO, Illinois, from May 3, 1843, through October 29, 1845. It replaced *The Wasp* (begun April 16, 1842, with William Smith as editor). Funded by subscriptions and advertising, the *Neighbor* regularly featured literature, science, religion, agriculture, manufacturing, commerce, and local, national, and international news. It reported actions of the state legislature, the Nauvoo City Council, and local courts.

As an advocate of truth, the *Neighbor* detailed conflicts involving the members of the Church, their neighbors, their enemies, and state and federal governments. It also carried correspondence between the Prophet Joseph SMITH and Henry Clay (both U.S. presidential candidates) as well as the letters between Emma SMITH and Governor Thomas Carlin concerning Joseph Smith's harassment by Missouri officials. It detailed the *Nauvoo Expositor* case and the events of the assassinations of Joseph and Hyrum SMITH in CARTHAGE JAIL, including other newspaper accounts and correspondence. The *Nauvoo Neighbor* is a valuable record of the events and attitudes in and around Nauvoo from 1843 to 1845.

BIBLIOGRAPHY

Nauvoo Neighbor. Microfilm, Lee Library, Brigham Young University.

DARWIN L. HAYES

NAUVOO POLITICS

Political power played an important role both in the development of the LDS community in Illinois and in its demise. The political situation was complex, inviting rivalry and controversy.

On the eve of the arrival of the Latter-day Saints, Commerce (NAUVOO), in Hancock County, Illinois, was situated in a pro-Whig enclave in a state where Democrats dominated all political offices except the supreme court. In Hancock County, however, the two parties were so evenly matched that a few hundred votes could be decisive. But in the state legislature, even voting as a unit, a community the size of that of the Latter-day Saints could have only moderate influence. County offices were more vulnerable; the number of votes needed for election to such offices as sheriff, county commissioner, and probate judge was under one thousand. A liberal provision in the Illinois constitution enfranchised all adult immigrants after only six months' residence—a contentious issue in a state where party lines were sharply drawn, especially with the regular arrival of new British immigrants in Nauvoo (*see* IMMIGRATION AND EMIGRATION).

Joseph Smith's decision to use LDS voting strength sprang from a desire for security from PERSECUTION and for self-government. Conscious of the divine imperative to gather the Saints and build the physical KINGDOM OF GOD on earth, he came to see politics as one means of enlarging and protecting his community. At first, the Saints were politically neutral. But in 1840–1841 they voted solidly Whig in Illinois, though they had voted Democrat in Missouri. This alienated some Democrats, but most politicians courted the LDS bloc vote in Illinois, just as others courted the Roman Catholic vote in New York.

The first example of possible "vote trading" by Latter-day Saints was the legislative vote in favor of the NAUVOO CHARTER in December 1840, promoted by Democrats but also voted for by the Whig Abraham Lincoln. The resulting Nauvoo Municipal Court, NAUVOO LEGION, and Agricultural and Manufacturing Association formed the backbone of a self-governing theocracy, which was anathema to frontier Illinoisans.

The prevalence of lawyer-politicians and the frequency of Missouri arrest warrants enmeshed Joseph Smith in vote trading. One clear example was LDS support for the Whig John T. Stuart in the congressional election of 1841, a direct result of assistance rendered to Joseph Smith by the Whigs Orville H. Browning and Cyrus Walker when Smith was arrested following a Missouri extradition order. Joseph Smith was technically a fugitive, having fled Missouri after six months in LIBERTY JAIL awaiting trial (*see* SMITH, JOSEPH: TRIALS OF JOSEPH SMITH). However, not all lawyers were Whigs. The judge in the 1841 case was Stephen A. Douglas, an ambitious Democrat determined to win the LDS vote. His efforts were successful in December 1841 when Joseph Smith declared for the Democrats; Hancock County subsequently lost its Whig identity.

Seeing Nauvoo as a political threat, non-Mormons in Hancock County organized politically on an anti-Mormon platform. Successful in the county elections in 1841 (they were unopposed in many contests), they were singularly unsuccessful in 1842 with nominations for the state legislature. Existing partisan affiliations were too strong for the emergence of a third party, and the Whigs had usurped the anti-Mormon cause in the 1842 gubernatorial elections. The Democratic candidate for governor, Thomas Ford, an opponent of the Nauvoo Charter, won the election.

Governor Ford advised Joseph Smith to stay out of politics. Smith seemed inclined to do that until Ford, in June 1843, issued another writ for the Prophet's arrest on a Missouri requisition. After the Whig Cyrus Walker, a prominent criminal lawyer, using the controversial habeas corpus provisions of the Nauvoo Charter, effected Joseph Smith's release from custody, the Prophet pledged his vote to Walker. But his brother Hyrum SMITH, a Democrat, announced that he believed the Saints should vote for Walker's opponent, Joseph P. Hoge. The Latter-day Saints in Nauvoo, part of the Sixth Congressional District, voted for Hoge, but those in the Fifth Congressional District voted for the Whig O. H. Browning, running against Douglas.

This marked the beginning of disillusionment with the LDS vote by both parties. In particular the Whigs, who had retreated from anti-Mormonism in 1842–1843 in the hope of finding favor, now openly opposed LDS political and judicial power. In 1843, even within Nauvoo, Joseph Smith found politics problematic. There was internal dissent over city elections in February, and in August, Mayor Smith complained of being roughly treated by pro-Democrats in city elections. Also, the prominent Church leader William Law publicly challenged Hyrum's "Hoge testimony."

In January 1844, after canvassing U.S. presidential hopefuls for support in obtaining redress for Missouri depredations and finding none, Joseph Smith announced his own candidacy. Some saw this as a bid for political power, consistent with the goal of furthering the political kingdom of God; others felt that because Joseph Smith was not likely to win national election, he simply wanted a platform for presenting his message. The leading anti-Mormon newspaper in Illinois, the *Warsaw Signal*, greeted the move with customary derision but nonetheless viewed it as an audacious and threatening development.

All Joseph Smith's attempts to gain political influence were objectionable to the apostate group that launched the NAUVOO EXPOSITOR newspaper, the destruction of which set in motion the events leading to Smith's death in June 1844 (*see* MARTYRDOM OF JOSEPH AND HYRUM SMITH). In this volatile atmosphere, anti-Mormons gained strength by accusing Governor Ford of pursuing pro-Mormon policies in order to secure Democratic votes. The Latter-day Saints gradually lost support until, in January 1845, their charter was repealed, disincorporating Nauvoo. Unauthorized municipal elections continued in Nauvoo, however, and Latter-day Saints voted in county and state elections, still favoring the Democrats. From then until the Saints left in 1846 (see WESTWARD MIGRATION, PLANNING AND PROPHECY), this persistent involvement of Mormons in politics continued to inflame non-Mormons and rally them to press for Mormon expulsion.

Politics and political power were indispensable to the rise and strength of Nauvoo and to the protection of the Prophet Joseph Smith. But mismanagement of political power may also have contributed to the city's downfall.

[See also Politics: Political History.]

BIBLIOGRAPHY

Flanders, Robert B. *Nauvoo: Kingdom on the Mississippi.* Urbana, Ill., 1965.

Gayler, George R. "The Mormons and Politics in Illinois: 1839–1844." *Journal of the Illinois State Historical Society* 49 (1956):48–66.

Hampshire, Annette P. *Mormonism in Conflict: The Nauvoo Years.* New York, 1985.

ANNETTE P. HAMPSHIRE

NAUVOO TEMPLE

The Nauvoo Temple, its tower and spire visible from a distance of twenty miles, was the principal structure in the city of NAUVOO. Facing west, it stood on the summit of a gently sloping bluff overlooking the lower part of the city and the Mississippi River.

Built from a high-quality grayish-white to tan limestone, its imposing walls were erected and finished with great skill. The walls were three feet thick at ground level, with some individual stones weighing as much as 4,000 pounds. The building measured 128 feet long and 88 feet wide. The top of the tower stood 158 feet above ground level and was graced by a golden statue of an angel flying in a horizontal position (doubtless inspired by the prophecy in Rev. 14:6–7).

Prominent features of the stone walls were thirty tall, heavily ornamented pilasters, nine on each side and six on each end. Each pilaster was embellished by a large moonstone at the base and a sunstone at the top. The moon- and sunstones were bas-relief features, hand-chiseled in solid stone. A stone star also graced each pilaster. These cosmic symbols typified the three DEGREES OF GLORY in the life to come (1 Cor. 15:41; D&C 76).

Construction of the building began in the fall of 1840. Cornerstones were set with impressive ceremonies during a general CONFERENCE on April 6, 1841. Financial setbacks and persecution continually interfered with the construction, even up to the days of its completion and dedication.

William Weeks became the official architect and supervised most of the construction. The building was a complexity of architectural styles, yet much of it was also original, inspired by what the Prophet Joseph SMITH had seen in VISION. He closely guided Weeks in the design of the temple as he had seen it, requiring, for example, that it have round windows on the second level (*HC* 6:196–97).

The call to build so large a structure taxed the resources of a destitute people. The final cost exceeded $1,000,000. Funds came largely from tithes and offerings of Church members, some donating their life savings. Many gave months of physical labor with little or no remuneration, working from early morning until sundown, even during harsh weather.

Stone for the building was quarried near the city. Wood was brought in from Wisconsin in the form of huge rafts of sawed lumber, which were floated down the Mississippi to Nauvoo. Some British converts contributed a large bell weighing over 1,500 pounds. As the Saints left Nauvoo, the bell was removed and taken west as part of the migration, where it was later mounted on a tower on Temple Square, Salt Lake City.

The main feature at the basement level was a large white limestone laver resting on the backs and shoulders of twelve life-sized stone oxen. This was the baptismal font to be used particularly for the ORDINANCE of BAPTISM FOR THE DEAD. The basement floor was paved with brick. The first story contained a large room in the center, which served as an auditorium. At each end of this large hall were elaborate pulpits, each graded into four tiers of seats to accommodate the AARONIC PRIESTHOOD and MELCHIZEDEK PRIESTHOOD

This model of the Nauvoo Temple (constructed 1841–1846) shows the sunstones and starstones at the tops of the columns and the moonstones at their bases. For Latter-day Saints, a holy temple is a meeting place where heaven and earth come into close contact. Baptisms for the dead were performed in the Nauvoo Temple beginning in 1841, endowments in 1845–1846.

leaders. The main floor was fitted with seats, the backs of which could be reversed, allowing congregations to face either direction. The second story was an exact duplicate of the first. The attic story contained two main sections. A half-story on the west end was divided by cloth partitions and used for the ENDOWMENT ordinances. The main attic section, under the pitched roof, was used for SEALING ordinances and celestial or eternal MARRIAGES. The entire attic was plastered and painted, and the floors were covered with carpets.

Occasional ceremonial use took place during construction, especially baptisms for the dead. Even though not fully completed, the temple was filled to capacity by members coming for ordinances during the months just prior to the exodus— ordinances on behalf both of the living and the dead. In addition to its sacral uses, the temple served as a multipurpose meeting place. Regular

Sunday services and even some general conferences were held in the building. The structure also provided some facilities as a Church office building. The planning and organization of the western migration took place in the temple.

As most of the Saints left Nauvoo under threat of mob violence in early February 1846, a special crew stayed behind and completed the temple. Three months later the building was considered complete and was publicly dedicated on May 1, 1846. Dedication services were repeated over a three-day period and witnessed by thousands. Visitors paid a one-dollar admission fee, and the funds were used to help workmen move their families and join the main body of the Church on the plains to the west.

When most of the remaining Church members were driven from the city in September of 1846, the temple was temporarily abandoned.

One of the few surviving sunstones from the Nauvoo Temple, at the Nauvoo State Park. Another sunstone is in the Smithsonian Museum, Washington, D.C.

Mob forces desecrated and defiled the sacred structure. Some physical damage, though not extensive, was sustained. Attempts were later made to sell the temple, but these proved unsuccessful. The building was consumed by fire in October 1848, by the deliberate act of arson. Only the bare walls were left standing. A French Icarian community purchased the site and was preparing to reclaim the structure when it was struck by a tornado, which knocked down some of the walls and damaged others so severely that they had to be razed. Much of the structural stone was later reused in other Nauvoo buildings.

Today the temple site has been repurchased by the Church. A Nauvoo Temple exhibit is a key part of the Nauvoo Visitors Center. A small model built to scale is on the exact location of the original temple. The well that supplied water for the baptismal font is preserved. Some sunstones and moonstones that once adorned the building remain here and in museums as a reminder of the beauty of this once majestic temple.

BIBLIOGRAPHY

Colvin, Don F. "A Historical Study of the Mormon Temple at Nauvoo, Illinois." Master's thesis, Brigham Young University, 1962.

Harrington, Virginia S. *Rediscovery of the Nauvoo Temple.* Salt Lake City, 1971.

DON F. COLVIN

NEHOR, NEHORISM

See: Antichrists; Secret Combinations

NEPHI₁

The first of several leaders named Nephi in the Book of Mormon, Nephi₁ was an influential prophet and the founder of the NEPHITE people. He was apparently well-educated, faithful and obedient to God, courageous, and bold. An inspired prophet, he had visions of Jesus Christ and of the world's future; he also interpreted the prophecies of others, such as his father, LEHI, and Isaiah. He authored the first two books in the Book of Mormon, which provide virtually all known information about him. He was a skilled craftsman and leader, and succeeded Lehi as leader of the family (ahead of his three older brothers). Above all, he trusted in God: "My voice shall forever ascend up unto thee, my rock and mine everlasting God" (2 Ne. 4:35).

HISTORY. Nephi was born c. 615 B.C. His father, the prophet Lehi, led his family group out of Jerusalem just after 600 B.C., through the Arabian desert, and across the ocean to the Western Hemisphere. While in the wilderness, Nephi saw a vision that was to shape many of his basic views; it is partially reported in 1 Nephi 11–14. In the promised land, he was designated by his father to succeed him as leader of the family (2 Ne. 1:28–29), but his older brothers LAMAN and Lemuel rebelled and half the group associated with them. Nephi was inspired to flee with all who believed in the warnings and revelations of God (2 Ne. 5:6) and set up a new city, the city of Nephi.

Nephi established his people on sound political, legal, economic, and religious bases. They acclaimed him king, although he resisted this action initially. He taught them to be industrious and to provide for their needs, and he prepared them with training and weapons for defense against their enemies. He followed the law of Moses, built a temple like the temple of Solomon (though without "so many precious things"), and anointed his younger brothers Jacob and Joseph as priests and teachers to instruct the people and lead them in spiritual matters (2 Ne. 5:10, 16, 26). Before he died, he appointed a new king (called the "second Nephi"; Jacob 1:11) and appointed his brother Jacob as the caretaker of religious records (Jacob 1:1–4, 18).

VISIONS. Because of the great visions and revelations he received, Nephi shared a role with his father as a founding prophet. At a young age he was inspired by the Holy Spirit and believed his father's words. He heard the voice of the Lord telling him that he would become a ruler and teacher over his brothers (1 Ne. 2:22). He witnessed the vision of the TREE OF LIFE shown earlier to his father (1 Ne. 8), which showed him the future birth, baptism, and ministry of Jesus Christ, as well as the future rise and demise of his own people. He was shown also the future establishment of the Gentiles in the Western Hemisphere and the restoration of the gospel in their midst (1 Ne. 11–14). Because of these revelations, Nephi was able to teach his people the gospel or "doctrine of Christ"—the means by which they could come unto Christ and be saved (2 Ne. 30:5; 31:2–32:6). His carefully formulated teaching of this doctrine provided a model that other Nephite prophets invoked repeatedly (see GOSPEL).

Because the Nephites had received the fulness of the gospel of Jesus Christ, their strict observance of the LAW OF MOSES was oriented toward its ultimate fulfillment in Jesus, and Nephi explained to his people that they should observe the law of Moses as a means of keeping Christ's future atonement always in their minds (2 Ne. 25:29–30). The law itself had become "dead" to those who were "made alive in Christ" and who knew that Jesus was the one to whom they could look directly "for a remission of their sins" (2 Ne. 25:25–27).

RECORD KEEPING AND LITERACY. Nephi founded the extensive Nephite tradition of record keeping (see BOOK OF MORMON PLATES AND RECORDS). He was inspired to keep two separate accounts, both of which were continued for hundreds of years. The official record kept by the kings, known as the large plates of Nephi, began

with the book of Lehi and contained the historical chronicles of the Nephites for one thousand years. The GOLD PLATES given to Joseph Smith contained Mormon's abridged version of Nephi's large plates and provided most of the text for the Book of Mormon (from the book of Mosiah to the book of Mormon). However, thirty years after leaving Jerusalem, Nephi was instructed by God to compose a second record focusing on spiritual matters. Known as the small plates of Nephi, this record contains Nephi's retrospective account of the founding events and subsequent prophecies of a line of prophets and priests that descended from Jacob down to about 200 B.C. The opening books in today's printed Book of Mormon, 1 Nephi through Omni, come from this record. Nephi's revelations and inspired teachings shaped the religious understanding of his followers, the Nephites.

When Nephi began writing his small plates, he was a mature prophet-king. The record reveals his concern with helping his people and their descendants to understand the future atonement of Jesus Christ and the legitimacy of his own calling as their ruler and teacher. In composing this record, Nephi used his father's record and his own earlier and more comprehensive record, both unavailable today.

The exceptional literacy of the later Nephite leaders may have been due to the fact that Nephi was a man of letters. The text suggests that he was probably fluent in both Hebrew and Egyptian and states that he had been "taught somewhat in all the learning" of the Jews and of his father (1 Ne. 1:1–3).

Nephi displayed literary learning in the way he organized his writings and in the variety of literary forms and devices he employed, including those of narrative, rhetoric, and poetry, including a psalm. The techniques, stories, prophecies, and teachings of Nephi provided models and substance for his successors (see BOOK OF MORMON LITERATURE). He loved the writings of Isaiah and quoted them extensively (e.g., 1 Ne. 20–21; 2 Ne. 12–24), often providing interpretations.

THE MAN AND HIS MESSAGES. Nephi constructed the book of 1 Nephi on a tightly balanced and interrelated set of founding stories and revelations, all designed to show "that the tender mercies of the Lord are over all those whom he hath chosen, because of their faith, to make them mighty even unto the power of deliverance" (1 Ne.

1:20). Nephi supports this thesis in 1 Nephi with stories of how God has intervened in human affairs to deliver his faithful followers, and Nephi in particular, from their enemies. But these are only types and shadows. Nephi's true proof is set forth in 2 Nephi, where he says that the atonement of Jesus Christ makes available to all who have faith in Christ a liberation from sin and spiritual redemption from hell and the devil, their greatest enemy. All men and women who follow the example of Christ and enter into his way through repentance and baptism will be blessed with a baptism of fire and the Holy Ghost—which brings a remission of sin and individual guidance—so that they might endure to the end in faith and receive eternal life (2 Ne. 31).

Into a more spiritual account on his small plates, Nephi also wove a vivid defense of his own political primacy by using allusions to MOSES and JOSEPH OF EGYPT (Reynolds, 1987). In defending his ruling position as a younger son, Nephi tells how the two oldest sons rejected their father and the Lord and how he (Nephi) was selected and blessed by the Lord and his father. He relates how, with the help of the Lord, he acquired the brass plates (1 Ne. 3–4), persuaded Ishmael and his family to join Lehi's group (1 Ne. 7), prevented starvation in the wilderness (1 Ne. 16), and constructed a ship and sailed it successfully across the ocean (1 Ne. 17–18). In these exploits, Nephi was consistently opposed and threatened, even with death, by Laman and Lemuel; but in each crisis, he was miraculously delivered by the power of the Lord and blessed to complete his task.

Though unable to bridge the gulf between himself and his brothers, Nephi's writings reveal that he was a man with an impressive range of human sensitivities, and he yearned for their welfare. He developed his enormous faith in his father and in the Lord at a young age and never faltered. Consequently, he obeyed without murmuring. He pondered his father's prophecies and repeatedly asked the Lord for personal understanding and direction. He had a deep love and sense of responsibility for his people: "I pray continually for them by day, and mine eyes water my pillow by night, because of them" (2 Ne. 33:3). He also had charity for all other people. Nephi gloried in plainness and in truth, and he knew that his words were harsh against unrepentant sinners (2 Ne. 33:5–9). He anguished deeply because of temptations and his own sins, and particularly because of his feelings of anger against his enemies (2 Ne. 4:26–29). His spiritual strength and depth were grounded in the knowledge that Jesus Christ had heard his pleas and had redeemed his soul from hell (2 Ne. 33:6).

BIBLIOGRAPHY

Bergin, Allen E. "Nephi, A Universal Man." *Ensign* 6 (Sept. 1976):65–70.

Cannon, George Q. *The Life of Nephi*. Salt Lake City, 1883; repr. 1957.

Reynolds, Noel B. "Nephi's Outline." *BYU Studies* 20 (Winter 1980):131–49.

———. "The Political Dimension in Nephi's Small Plates." *BYU Studies* 27 (Fall 1987):15–37.

Sondrup, Steven P. "The Psalm of Nephi: A Lyric Reading." *BYU Studies* 21 (Summer 1981):357–72.

Turner, Rodney. "The Prophet Nephi." In *The Book of Mormon: First Nephi, the Doctrinal Foundation*, ed. M. Nyman and C. Tate, pp. 79–97. Provo, Utah, 1988.

NOEL B. REYNOLDS

NEPHI₂

Nephi₂ succeeded his father HELAMAN₃ in 39 B.C. as the Nephite chief judge, evidently at a young age. Because of wickedness among the Nephites, he resigned the judgment seat in 30 B.C. and went with his younger brother Lehi to preach the gospel of Jesus Christ among the Lamanites. Although imprisoned and threatened with death, they were preserved by the power of God and converted thousands of Lamanites (Hel. 5).

Nephi returned thereafter to Zarahemla, boldly condemned the corrupt Nephite leaders, miraculously revealed the identity of a murderer, and exercised the power of God to invoke a famine on the Nephites. Although the Nephites repented occasionally, their conversion and the peace that followed did not last. When time was about to expire on the prophecy of SAMUEL THE LAMANITE regarding the birth of Christ, Nephi passed the records to his son Nephi₃ and left, never to be heard of again (3 Ne. 1:3; 2:9).

BIBLIOGRAPHY

Welch, John W. "Longevity of Book of Mormon People and the Age of Man." *Journal of the Collegium Aesculapium* 3 (1985):34–42.

MELVIN J. THORNE

NEPHI₃

Nephi₃ was the eldest son of Nephi₂. He was given responsibility for all the Nephite records in 1 B.C. (3 Ne. 1:2). Because of his great faith and his concern for his people, he was told by the voice of Jesus the day before Jesus' birth that the Savior would be born "on the morrow." Later, he consolidated, led, and defended the righteous, moving them to the land Bountiful. He survived the destructions occurring in the Western Hemisphere at the Savior's death (3 Ne. 8–9) and was the first to whom the resurrected Christ gave the power to baptize (3 Ne. 11:18–12). He served as the leading disciple in the Church spoken of in this part of the Book of Mormon and saw his people enjoy years of peace and righteousness.

BIBLIOGRAPHY

Arnold, Marilyn. "The Nephi We Tend to Forget." *Ensign* 8 (Jan. 1978):68–71.

MELVIN J. THORNE

NEPHI₄

Nephi₄ was the son of NEPHI₃. Nephi₄ kept the Nephite records during the extraordinarily blessed era that followed the appearance of Jesus Christ to the Nephites. He saw his people live in love, unity (having all things in common), righteousness, and obedience because the love of God abounded in their hearts. A type of UNITED ORDER or LAW OF CONSECRATION was practiced by them during this time. His people experienced the rebuilding of cities, prosperity, miracles, peace, and happiness. Little else is known about his life. He died sometime after A.D. 110 (see 4 Ne. 1:1–19).

MELVIN J. THORNE

NEPHITES

[*The Nephites are the primary group who kept the record known as the Book of Mormon. This complex population was initially descended from* Lehi *through four of his sons (Sam, Nephi₁, Jacob, and Joseph) and their friend Zoram, although the descendants of other people also joined themselves to the Nephites from time to time (see* Book of Mormon Peoples). *The Nephites were dis-* tinguished by their belief in the gospel of Jesus Christ, as taught by Lehi and Nephi, as opposed to the lack of faith of the* Lamanites, *often their enemies but also descendants of Lehi.*

For an account of Nephite life, see Book of Mormon Economy and Technology. *Political and legal practices among the Nephites are described in* Book of Mormon, Government and Legal History in. *The traditions of record keeping among the Nephites are summarized in* Book of Mormon Plates and Records. *Nephite religious belief and culture are detailed in* Book of Mormon Religious Teachings and Practices. *Nephite women and their contributions are reported in* Book of Mormon, Women in.]

NEUM

Neum was an ancient Israelite PROPHET whose words were contained on the PLATES of brass, a record carried to the Western Hemisphere from JERUSALEM about 600 B.C. by the Book of Mormon prophet LEHI and his colony. Neum's work is not preserved in the Hebrew Bible or other known sources. Concerning the time of his writing, it is only definite that he predated Lehi's departure.

Neum is mentioned only once in the Book of Mormon. In writing to his future readers, NEPHI₁ cited him along with other prophets who foretold aspects of the mortal mission of JESUS CHRIST. According to Neum's words, the God of ABRAHAM, Isaac, and Jacob (Jesus Christ) would be crucified (1 Ne. 19:10). This confirmed what Nephi himself had seen previously in a vision (1 Ne. 11:32–33).

KENT P. JACKSON

NEVADA, PIONEER SETTLEMENTS IN

Latter-day Saints constructed Nevada's first log cabins and founded what became the state's first permanent white settlement when, in 1849, would-be gold miners established a trading post at present-day Genoa (Carson Valley, near Reno) to supply those en route to the goldfields in northern California.

The present state of Nevada lay within the original boundaries of Utah Territory as established by Congress in 1850, and in 1855 territorial governor Brigham YOUNG appointed Orson HYDE, an apostle, as probate judge and sent him to Carson Valley to organize a county government. Hyde called for more LDS settlers to establish political control of the area and to proselytize and "civilize" the Indians of that region. The following year about 250 Latter-day Saints arrived. Problems promptly developed between them and non-Mormons who resented LDS political control. Reports that they were to be recalled to Utah kept the LDS settlers off balance, and some of the leading members soon departed. As the U.S. Army approached Utah from the east in 1857 (see UTAH EXPEDITION), the remaining colonists were recalled to Salt Lake City.

The Las Vegas Mission was founded in 1855 to proselytize local Indians and teach them agriculture and peaceful ways. Latter-day Saints there labored among the Paiutes, converting many of them and establishing a farm for them. In 1856 the colony, reinforced by men sent from Salt Lake City, established a lead-mining mission. Lead mining was largely unsuccessful, partly due to silver in the ore and the difficulty of separating them. In 1857, after the lead miners returned to Utah, the remainder of the missionaries received permission to return as well. Most departed later that year, after word reached them of the army's approach to Utah.

In 1865 Brigham Young sent colonists to settle on the Muddy River, in present-day Moapa Valley, to grow cotton and other semitropical crops and to assist with possible LDS overland immigration from a projected port on the Colorado River. In 1867 the boundaries of Nevada Territory, which was created from the western part of Utah Territory in 1861, were extended southward, annexing part of Arizona Territory, including the Muddy settlements. Most Latter-day Saints abandoned these towns in 1871 when they were ordered to pay back taxes to Nevada; farming marginal lands, the settlers lacked the cash to meet additional assessments. The LDS resettlement of Moapa Valley was resumed in 1877 with the founding of Bunkerville, a UNITED ORDER community.

LDS families founded several small communities north of the Muddy River beginning in 1864. Some of these settlers remained despite the problems with taxation, particularly in Panaca, which has remained largely LDS.

In 1898 the LDS settlements of Lund, Preston, and Georgetown were established in White Pine County on land ceded to the Church in lieu of property confiscated under the provisions of the Edmunds-Tucker Act of 1887 (see ANTIPOLYGAMY LEGISLATION).

BIBLIOGRAPHY

Arrington, Leonard J. *The Mormons in Nevada*. Las Vegas, 1979.

Hunter, Milton R. *Brigham Young the Colonizer*. Santa Barbara, Calif., 1973.

TED J. WARNER

NEW ERA

The *New Era* is the official English language publication of The Church of Jesus Christ of Latter-day Saints for YOUTH (ages 12–18), their parents, and their Church leaders and teachers. Established in 1971 during a period of consolidation of all Church MAGAZINES, the *New Era* is published monthly. In its earliest days, it was addressed to readers twelve to twenty-six years old (to include single college students), but after four years its scope was reduced to twelve- to eighteen-year-olds to coincide with the age levels of the AARONIC PRIESTHOOD and YOUNG WOMEN programs. Its features include inspirational messages from GENERAL AUTHORITIES; stories about young Latter-day Saints throughout the world; first-person accounts of FAMILY LIFE, MISSIONARY experiences, CONVERSION stories, and spiritual insights; personality profiles; a question-and-answer section; a news and information section; Church history; poetry; photography; and humor. Another special feature is *Mormonads*, which appear as one-page "advertisements" of GOSPEL ideals. Some of these ads are made into posters and sold through Church DISTRIBUTION CENTERS and LDS book outlets.

Special issues of the *New Era* have covered such topics as Christlike service, courtship and marriage, sharing the gospel, the Aaronic Priesthood, the Young Women program, career preparation, leadership, its own tenth anniversary, and a guide to "surviving and thriving in the 1990s." Special insertions have included a recording of speeches by PRESIDENTS OF THE CHURCH, a leadership game, and an advent calendar based on the life of Christ.

The *New Era* is a significant source of LDS fiction and music. It sponsors an annual creative talent contest for the youth of the Church with categories in writing, art, photography, and music. The winning entries are published in subsequent issues of the magazine. Consequently, the *New Era* is known for its policy of encouraging promis-

The *New Era* is a magazine published for youth, ages 12–18. This boy in Poland (1990) was converted to the gospel through a friend who sent him a copy of the *New Era.* Courtesy Peggy Jellinghausen.

ing young LDS authors, artists, and composers, which includes an internship program in writing and editing for LDS college students who show promise.

The *New Era* has a reputation for being positive and idealistic, and it does not hesitate to combat problems like drug abuse, depression, alcoholism, immorality, suicide, exploitation of "nannies," and eating disorders. It has also won awards for design and typographical excellence.

The magazine's charter statement reflects its editorial philosophy: "As an official line of communication to the youth of the Church, the *New Era* is to provide a positive, uplifting voice for young people to hear. Therefore, each issue must be an example of editorial, photographic, and artistic excellence. The *New Era* shows every twelve- through eighteen-year-old Latter-day Saint what blessings can come from living the restored gospel. Readers learn from the examples and testimonies of others that being spiritually committed, wholesome, and LDS is the most desirable way to be, that righteous living is the only source of peace and happiness in life." Its managing editors have been Brian K. Kelly (1972–1989) and Richard M. Romney since 1989.

BIBLIOGRAPHY

Gostick, Adrian. "So You Want to Write for the *New Era*?" *New Era* 21 (Aug. 1991).

Todd, Jay M. "The New Era." *New Era* 1 (1971):3.

Wilkins, Richard G. "How to Write for the *New Era* Without Developing Ulcers." *New Era* 7 (Feb. 1977):16–19.

RICHARD M. ROMNEY

NEW AND EVERLASTING COVENANT

The new and everlasting covenant is the gospel of Jesus Christ. The sum of all gospel COVENANTS that God makes with mankind is called "*the* new and everlasting covenant" and consists of several individual covenants, each of which is called "*a* new and *an* everlasting covenant." It is "new" when given to a person or a people for the first time, and "everlasting" because the gospel of Jesus Christ and PLAN OF SALVATION existed before the world was formed and will exist forever (*MD*, pp. 479–80).

Baptism, marriage, and all other covenants from God necessary for salvation are new and everlasting (D&C 22:1; 45:9; 66:2; 132:4–7). Holy covenants have been introduced anew in each of the DISPENSATIONS OF THE GOSPEL from Adam to Joseph SMITH, and have been available whenever the gospel of Jesus Christ has been upon the earth. Therefore, these covenants are spoken of as everlasting. Covenants of salvation and exaltation are everlasting in the sense also that once entered into they are forever binding and valid only if they are not broken by transgression.

All covenants between God and mankind are part of the new and everlasting covenant (D&C 22; 132:6–7). Thus, celestial marriage is *a* new and *an* everlasting covenant (D&C 132:4) or the new and everlasting covenant of *marriage*. Some covenants, such as baptism, have force in all dispensations. Other covenants are made for special purposes in particular dispensations; CIRCUMCISION as a sign of a covenant is of this type (*MD*, p. 479). The same eternal covenant conditions may be established through other ritual signs at other times.

Covenants and promises instituted by God are governed by certain stipulations and conditions that he has set and that his children must comply with to make the covenant or promise valid (*DS* 1:152–160). The Lord's house is a house of order, and all things are done according to law (D&C 130:20–21; 132:8–11):

> For all who will have a blessing at my hands shall abide the law which was appointed for that blessing, and the conditions thereof, as were instituted from before the foundation of the world.

> And as pertaining to the new and everlasting covenant, it was instituted for the fulness of my glory. . . .

> And verily I say unto you, that the conditions of this law are these: All covenants, contracts, bonds,

obligations, oaths, vows, performances, connections, associations, or expectations, that are not made and entered into and sealed by the Holy Spirit of promise, of him who is anointed, both as well for time and for all eternity, . . . by revelation and commandment through the medium of mine anointed, . . . are of no efficacy, virtue, or force in and after the resurrection from the dead; for all contracts that are not made unto this end have an end when men are dead [D&C 132:5–7].

The Lord has said, "I, the Lord, am bound when ye do what I say; but when ye do not what I say, ye have no promise" (D&C 82:10).

BIBLIOGRAPHY

Smith, Hyrum M., and Janne M. Sjodahl. *Doctrine and Covenants Commentary*, pp. xiv, 822. Salt Lake City, 1972.

D. CECIL CLARK

NEW HEAVEN AND NEW EARTH

This phrase depicts the EARTH's destiny of renewal, one cosmic aspect of the RESTORATION OF ALL THINGS. In LDS theology, "the earth will be renewed and receive its paradisiacal glory" (A of F 10). That renewal will include restoration of its former components—for example, the return of the city of ENOCH—and also its former purity and Edenic state.

Ancient biblical prophets taught that the beginnings of this fulfillment are to be associated with the coming of the MESSIAH and his millennial reign. The phrase reflects the vision of Isaiah (65:17; 66:22) and the revelation of JOHN (Rev. 2:17; 3:12; 5:9; 14:3; 21:1). Book of Mormon prophets likewise speak of a new heaven and a new earth (Ether 13:9) and of "all things" becoming new (3 Ne. 15:2). The Doctrine and Covenants contains prophecies that every corruptible "element shall melt with fervent heat; and all things shall become new, that [God's] knowledge and glory may dwell upon all the earth" (D&C 101:23; cf. 29:23–24; 42:35, 62, 67; 45:66; 84:2–4; 133:56).

The Hebrew root for "new" (*chadash*) points to a time of refreshing rather than replacement. Consistent with this understanding, Mormons expect that the earth will not be destroyed but glorified, not transcended but transformed, and that ultimately the polarization of earth and heaven will be overcome. Faithful Saints are promised the

"fulness of the earth" (D&C 59:16) and "an inheritance upon the earth when the day of transfiguration shall come, when the earth shall be transfigured" (D&C 63:20–21).

The earth fills the "measure [the purpose] of its creation" (D&C 88:19, 25) and its biography follows typologically that of mankind. It has fallen from paradise, it has been baptized in water, and it will be baptized by fire. It will die (Isa. 51:6; D&C 45:22; 88:26) and be "quickened again," and will not only regain its pristine condition but a higher state still (D&C 88:25–26). "This earth will be Christ's" (D&C 130:9). It will have a one-thousand-year sabbatical and then become a veritable URIM AND THUMMIM in fulfillment of John's vision of its appearance as a "sea of glass" (D&C 130:7–9; Rev. 2:17), a habitation worthy of God. "It will be rolled back into the presence of God," and "crowned with celestial glory" (*TPJS*, p. 181; cf. *WJS*, p. 60). Then those who have been "quickened by a portion of the celestial glory shall then receive of the same, even a fulness" (D&C 88:29). God, "in whose bosom it is decreed that the poor and the meek of the earth shall inherit it" (D&C 88:17), will fulfill his promise "that bodies who are of the celestial kingdom may possess it forever and ever; for for this intent was it made and created, and for this intent are they sanctified" (D&C 88:20).

BIBLIOGRAPHY

Turner, Rodney. *Footstool of God: Earth in Scripture and Prophecy*. Orem, Utah, 1983.

THOMAS J. RISKAS, JR.

NEW JERUSALEM

For Latter-day Saints, the gathering of ISRAEL in the last days, and the building of the city of ZION and of the New Jerusalem, are closely related concepts.

The tenth ARTICLE OF FAITH, written by the Prophet Joseph SMITH in 1842, declares that the New Jerusalem will be built upon the American continent. He learned this as he translated the Book of Mormon (3 Ne. 20:22; Ether 13:2–6). Additional revelation on this subject came in September 1830 and was further clarified in the subsequent months (D&C 28:9; 42:33–36, 62, 67; 57:3). In July 1831, Joseph Smith traveled to Jackson

County, Missouri, at the command of the Lord, where it was announced that the long-awaited gathering of Israel would commence. The city of Zion (also called the New Jerusalem) and its temple would be built in Independence, Missouri (D&C 57:1–3).

Even as the ancient tribes of Israel were scattered north of the Holy Land and their identity was lost, their prophets foretold a gathering of Israel in the last days in a consecrated land (Jer. 31:1–12). Zion would be reestablished. This prophecy includes the promise that the "pure in heart" will receive the higher principles and truths of the full GOSPEL OF JESUS CHRIST (D&C 97:21; 100:16; 101:18). Both where and how they live will come about under divine influence. Since favorable spiritual conditions may exist anywhere in the world, cities of Zion and of Zion people, the "pure in heart," could be located anywhere in the world (D&C 97:21). However, there is to be a "center place," or capital city, of Zion. It is referred to both as "the city of Zion" and as "the city of New Jerusalem" (D&C 57:2; 84:2; cf. 45:66–67).

The writings of Ether, written prior to 125 B.C., abridged by MORONI₂ in the Book of Mormon, prophesy of the preparations for the coming of the MESSIAH and of a New Jerusalem in the Western Hemisphere. It is to be built by the remnant of the seed of JOSEPH OF EGYPT (Ether 13:3–10). Ether also speaks of the destruction of Jerusalem of old, adding that it will be rebuilt with a temple and become a holy city (Ether 13:11).

Also, the book of Revelation speaks of "the holy city, new Jerusalem, coming down from God out of heaven" (Rev. 21:2, 10). This may relate to the return of the city of Enoch, the Zion that in Enoch's day was caught up into heaven (Moses 7:12–21, 59–64).

The future rebuilding of the Holy Land for the house of Judah and the building of the New Jerusalem in the Western Hemisphere for the house of Joseph are associated with the return of the Messiah to the earth. Of this era, the 1845 Proclamation of the Twelve (MFP 1:252–66) says:

> He will assemble the Natives, the remnants of Joseph in America; and make them a great, and strong, and powerful nation: and he will civilize and enlighten them, and will establish a holy city, and temple and seat of government among them, which shall be called Zion.
>
> And there shall be his tabernacle, his sanctuary, his throne, and seat of government for the whole continent of North and South America for ever. In short, it will be to the western hemisphere what Jerusalem will be to the eastern. . . .
>
> The city of Zion, with its sanctuary and priesthood, and the glorious fulness of the gospel, will constitute a standard which will put an end to jarring creeds and political wranglings, by uniting the republics, states, provinces, territories, nations, tribes, kindred, tongues, people and sects of North and South America in one great and common bond of brotherhood. Truth and knowledge shall make them free, and love cement their union. The Lord also shall be their king and their lawgiver; while wars shall cease and peace prevail for a thousand years [pp. 259–60].

The prophet Isaiah declared that in a future time "out of Zion shall go forth the law, and the word of the Lord from Jerusalem" (Isa. 2:2–3; cf. Micah 4:1–2). Latter-day Saints believe this refers to the two Zion headquarters in the two hemispheres from which the Messiah, the returned Son of God, will reign triumphantly over the whole earth.

GRAHAM W. DOXEY

NEW MEXICO, PIONEER SETTLEMENTS IN

Although the MORMON BATTALION traversed New Mexico from its northeast to its southwest corner in 1846, the next significant LDS contact in that territory did not occur until nearly three decades later. In 1876 two members of a group of LDS missionaries otherwise assigned to Mexico found notable success in proselytizing among the Zuni in western New Mexico. Subsequent labors among the Zuni were less successful, but a number of Navajos were converted. In 1876, missionaries founded the settlement of Savoia, about twenty miles east of the Zuni village, and were joined by LDS converts from the southern states. The southerners soon moved to LDS settlements on the Little Colorado River in Arizona, and in 1882 the remaining settlers, reinforced by expatriates from the Little Colorado, relocated a few miles south. Eventually named Ramah, the village continues as a predominantly LDS community. Ramah was a major focus in a landmark interdisciplinary study of five cultures by Harvard University scholars in the mid-twentieth century.

Meanwhile, Latter-day Saints settled along the San Juan River at Fruitland, in northwestern New Mexico, in 1878. Kirtland and Waterflow, additional LDS villages along the San Juan, were initiated in the early 1880s, and Bluewater, a short distance to the north, was founded in 1894. In 1912, Fruitland became headquarters for the Young Stake, which also included wards and branches in nearby southwestern Colorado.

Farther south but also near New Mexico's western border, a group of Latter-day Saints settled in the Luna Valley, beginning in 1883. The Luna Ward was closely associated with LDS congregations across the border in Arizona.

Additional LDS congregations were established in western New Mexico at Pleasanton, Socorro County (1882–1889); and at Virden, Hidalgo County (from 1915). The latter was settled by refugees from the Mormon colonies in Mexico dislodged by the Mexican Revolution.

Most LDS wards and branches established in the twentieth century served minorities in communities east of these predominantly Mormon villages. In the first third of the century, congregations were organized at Albuquerque, Gallup, Taos, Silver City, Clovis, Tres Piedras, Pagosa Springs, and Thoreau. By 1990, as a result of widespread proselytizing and of in-migration, there were 49,000 Latter-day Saints in New Mexico.

BIBLIOGRAPHY

Divett, Robert T. "New Mexico and the Mormons." *Greater Llano Estacado Southwest Heritage* 6 (Spring 1976):14–19.

Telling, Irving. "Ramah, New Mexico, 1876–1900: An Historical Episode with Some Value Analysis." *Utah Historical Quarterly* 21 (Apr. 1953):117–36.

Vogt, Evon Z., and Ethel M. Albert, eds. *People of Rimrock: A Study of Values in Five Cultures.* Cambridge, Mass., 1966.

RICHARD L. JENSEN

NEWSPAPERS, LDS

The Latter-day Saints have seldom been without a Church-sponsored or -oriented newspaper from the days of *The Evening and the Morning Star* (Independence, Missouri, 1832–1833, and Kirtland, Ohio, 1833–1834) to the current *Deseret News* (Salt Lake City, 1850–) and *Church News* (1931–). Even during their exodus to the West, the Saints could read their *Frontier Guardian* (Kanesville,

Iowa, 1849–1852). For a time they supported both a religious Church paper and a single-sheet local newspaper. Such paired papers were *The Upper Missouri Advertiser* (Independence, 1832–1833) and *The Evening and the Morning Star*; the *Northern Times* (Kirtland, c. 1835–1836) and the *Latter Day Saints' Messenger and Advocate* (1834–1837); and the *Wasp* (Nauvoo, 1842–1843) replaced by the *Nauvoo Neighbor* (1843–1845) and the *Times and Seasons* (1839–1846).

When Latter-day Saints settle in an area, they often start an unofficial Church-oriented paper to share local news and to keep posted on the international Church. Some of the best-known unofficial twentieth-century local LDS newspapers are *California Intermountain News* (Los Angeles, 1935–1985, which became *Latter-day Sentinel* 1985–1989), the *Latter-day Sentinel* (Phoenix, Arizona 1979–1989), and the *Hawaii Record Bulletin* (Honolulu, 1977–), currently *Hawaii LDS News*.

[*See* the chart of Church periodicals in the Appendix.]

BIBLIOGRAPHY

McLaws, Monte Burr. *Spokesman for the Kingdom: Early Mormon Journalism and the Deseret News, 1830–1898.* Provo, Utah, 1977.

JACK A. NELSON

NEW TESTAMENT

During the early centuries of the Christian era, the New Testament gospels were the principal written witness of Jesus as the Christ. No other collection of writings carried the insight, the power of teaching, and, consequently, the spiritual appeal to Christians. The New Testament also stands as the foundation of the RESTORATION of the gospel in the latter days. It was while reading in the Epistle of JAMES (1:5) that the youthful Joseph SMITH was inspired to pray to the Lord about his confusion over religious matters, leading to his FIRST VISION (JS—H 1:7–20). The New Testament is one of the STANDARD WORKS or canonized scriptures accepted by Latter-day Saints, who seek spiritual strength and enlightenment from its pages. Further, they accept the New Testament sketches as accurate portrayals of the life and ministry of Jesus Christ as well as the ministry of his apostles and their associates, that reveal much of the order and organization of the earliest New Testament Church. Moreover, the New Testament includes many of God's covenants and commandments given personally by Jesus and, after his ascension, through his apostles. Latter-day Saints also value the New Testament prophecies about the latter days.

The writings of the New Testament were likely all produced within the first Christian century of the Christian era. Even so, its collection of texts went through three centuries of changes, and acceptance or rejection, before it acquired its recognized and current form, first listed in the Easter letter of Athanasius in Egypt in A.D. 367. The third synod of Carthage (A.D. 397) canonized the books of the New Testament as represented in the letter of Athanasius because each writing had three qualifications: apostolic authority, support of a major Christian community, and an absence of false teachings.

The rise of so-called heresies in the second century demonstrated the loss of prophetic revelation and thus marked the need for Christians to turn back to the apostles for authoritative writings. One of the heretics, Marcion (c. A.D. 130), limited his early collection of scripture to one gospel, Luke, and to the letters of Paul, which he freely edited.

THE GOSPELS.   For at least two reasons Latter-day Saints view the New Testament gospels as essentially accurate accounts of the life and ministry of Jesus Christ. First, many pre-Christian prophecies, especially in the Book of Mormon, detailed specific events in Jesus' life, including his mother's name, circumstances of his birth, his baptism, his selection of twelve apostles, the miracles he performed, his rejection and suffering, and his death and resurrection (e.g., 1 Ne. 11:13–36; Mosiah 3:5–11; see JESUS CHRIST: MINISTRY OF JESUS CHRIST). Second, Joseph Smith's inspired work in the JOSEPH SMITH TRANSLATION OF THE BIBLE (JST) led him to add clarifying details to the setting and content of certain stories about Jesus and to view many of Jesus' PARABLES and teachings as applicable to the latter days.

The Gospel of Matthew is characterized by two distinct features: frequent use of Old Testament references and six of Jesus' discourses (see MATTHEW, GOSPEL OF). It is assumed that Matthew's frequent use of Old Testament references

indicates both a Jewish audience and the view that Christianity was the fulfillment of prophetic Judaism.

Significantly for Latter-day Saints, portions of this gospel receive attention in extrabiblical scriptures. For instance, the Book of Mormon records that when the resurrected Jesus visited disciples in the Western Hemisphere (c. A.D. 34), he delivered a sermon almost identical to the SERMON ON THE MOUNT, underscoring the validity and universality of the sermon (3 Ne. 12–14; Matt. 5–7; see also BEATITUDES). Additionally, Joseph Smith's work on the JST led him to make inspired revisions, the most frequently noted being those in the Sermon on the Mount and in Jesus' discourse about the fate of Jerusalem and his second coming (Matt. 24; see JOSEPH SMITH—MATTHEW).

While only modest attention has been given to Mark's gospel in LDS scholarly writings, Church members have traditionally found great value in studying its pages. Its portrayal of Jesus may be the most dynamic, and may ultimately go back to the eyewitness recollections of PETER, the chief apostle.

The Gospel of Luke, called by some scholars "the most beautiful book" in the world, holds special interest for Latter-day Saints for several reasons, including its narrative of the Christmas story, its seventeen parables not recorded elsewhere, its strong emphases on remission of sin and Jesus' sympathy for all people, its account of the call and mission of the SEVENTY disciples, and the distinct prominence it gives to women.

The Gospel of JOHN was written that "ye might believe that Jesus is the Christ" (John 20:31). Besides presenting a series of Jesus' discourses not contained in the other gospels, John uses a series of "Messianic metaphors" to disclose Jesus' divine nature and his mission: Word; Lamb; Living Water; I am; Bread of Life; Living Bread; Light of the World; Good Shepherd; Resurrection; the Way, Truth and Life; and the True Vine. Many of these metaphors also appear in the Doctrine and Covenants, a latter-day scripture, where such language is expanded and applied to the restored Church. Further, Jesus' discussion of "other sheep," recorded only in John 10:14–16, was specifically referred to by the risen Jesus during his visit to disciples in the Western Hemisphere when he wanted to make a point about those to whom he was sent to minister (3 Ne. 15:12–24). During that same post-Resurrection visit, Jesus used several phrases and descriptions—particularly of himself and his work—that are characteristic of John's gospel (e.g., 3 Ne. 11:10–11, 14, 27, 32–36).

THE ACTS OF THE APOSTLES. From the narrative of the ascension of Jesus through the account of the ministry of Paul, the book of Acts relates the spiritual ministry of apostolic witnesses during the early years of Christianity. Latter-day Saints are interested that, in replacing Judas, one apostle was chosen to complete the twelve and that Peter set the qualifications of apostles: They must know the ministry of Jesus, they must be ordained, and they must be witnesses of his resurrection (Acts 1:21–22). Latter-day apostles in the Church are also "special witnesses of the name of Christ in all the world" (D&C 107:23; cf. 27:12; 84:108). In addition, the book of Acts indicates the rich outpouring of the Holy Ghost in the early Church, both in the form of guiding revelation and in manifestations of the GIFTS OF THE SPIRIT, characteristics that Latter-day Saints experience and value. Further, certain prophetic statements have particular meaning. For example, Latter-day Saints understand Paul's prophecy to the elders of Ephesus concerning mutinous problems within the early Church to be an inspired declaration about the impending APOSTASY (Acts 20:29–30). Moreover, they view Peter's prediction of Jesus' return from heaven at "the times of restitution of all things" as commencing with the latter-day restoration of the gospel (3:19–21). Further, the book of Acts has a good deal to say about the organization, doctrines, and character of the preaching of the early Christian church.

THE EPISTLES. Letters in the new testament are traditionally divided into two groups, the writings of Paul and the general epistles.

The style of Paul's writings varies from the almost formal exposition in Romans to the charming persuasion in Philemon. In addition to teachings valued by other Christians, Latter-day Saints exhibit particular interest in certain doctrines, ecclesiastical offices, and practices noted in Paul's works. For instance, the place of the Gentiles in the history of salvation (Rom. 9–11) is also addressed in the Book of Mormon (e.g., 1 Ne. 13:20–14:7; 22:6–11; 2 Ne. 10:8–18; see GENTILES, FULNESS OF); joint-heirship with Christ (Rom. 8:16–17) is taught in modern revelation (D&C 84:35–38; see HEIRS); adoption into the covenant

people of God (Rom. 8:14–15) is taught in the Book of Mormon (e.g., 2 Ne. 30:2; see LAW OF ADOPTION); the value of spiritual gifts (1 Cor. 12; cf. 1 Thes. 5:19–20) is emphasized in modern scripture (D&C 46); the importance of CHARITY or LOVE (1 Cor. 13) is underscored particularly by words of the prophet Mormon (Moro. 7:40–48); Paul's list of virtues to be sought (Philip. 4:8) is the base of Joseph Smith's thirteenth ARTICLE OF FAITH; the encroaching apostasy (Gal. 1:6–9) and disunity in the early church (1 Cor. 1:10–13), as well as Paul's prophecy about the inevitability of the apostasy (2 Thes. 2:1–4; cf. 1 Tim. 4:1–3), formed an important focus of the risen Jesus' words to Joseph Smith in the First Vision (JS—H 1:18–19); the fulfillment of the LAW OF MOSES in Christ (e.g., Gal. 3) is emphatically affirmed by the risen Jesus in the Book of Mormon (3 Ne. 15:3–10; cf. 9:19–20); and his literal physical resurrection, attended by many proofs (1 Cor. 15), is underlined and augmented by the appearances of the risen Jesus to disciples in the Western Hemisphere (c. A.D. 34; 3 Ne. 11–28) and in statements to Joseph Smith (cf. D&C 130:22). In matters of Church organization, Latter-day Saints find Paul's discussions of apostolic leadership (Gal. 1:18–19; 2:9–10) and his mention of priesthood offices such as apostles, prophets, EVANGELISTS (Eph. 2:19–21; 4:11–13), and BISHOPS and DEACONS (1 Tim. 3) to be significant for Church administration. In terms of practices or ordinances, Latter-day Saints value Paul's statements on the SACRAMENT (1 Cor. 10:14–21; 11:23–30; cf. 3 Ne. 18:28–29; Moro. 4–5), his mention of BAPTISM FOR THE DEAD (1 Cor. 15:29), and his instructions on the LAYING ON OF HANDS (1 Tim. 4:14; 5:22). These things exist in the LDS Church as a result of latter-day revelation, and the New Testament epistles attest to their presence in the early Church.

Concerning the general epistles, that of James stands out in the LDS view because of its influence on the young Joseph Smith. In addition to the passage that led him to pray for divine guidance (James 1:5), Latter-day Saints value both the teaching that the quality of one's faith in Christ is mirrored in one's daily actions (James 2:14–26; see FAITH; GRACE) and the practice of blessing the sick (James 5:14–15). From the writings of Peter, perhaps the most frequently cited are those that speak of Jesus' mission among departed spirits while his body lay in the tomb (1 Pet. 3:18–20; 4:6), an important subject in latter-day revelation (D&C 138;

see SALVATION OF THE DEAD). In addition, passages that discuss the TRANSFIGURATION (2 Pet. 1:17–18) and the inspired means whereby prophecy is to be interpreted (2 Pet. 1:19–21) hold interest for Latter-day Saints. Because they are led by apostles and believe that an apostasy occurred from the early Christian church, Latter-day Saints have been drawn to the components of the apostolic witness in John's letters (1 Jn. 1:1) and to indications that a serious apostasy was already under way in the early Church (1 Jn. 4:1–3; 3 Jn. 1:9–10).

BOOK OF REVELATION. Besides naming the apostle John as the author of this work (1 Ne. 14:18–28), latter-day scripture has focused both on issues mentioned in the book of Revelation (D&C 77) and on additional material written by John (D&C 7; see JOHN, REVELATIONS OF). Latter-day Saint interest has focused on matters that have to do with the latter days (cf. *TPJS*, pp. 287–94), including the discussions of the eventual demise of evil and the millennial reign of Christ and his righteous followers (Rev. 19–20), the anticipation of the NEW JERUSALEM (Rev. 21), and the vision of "another angel [flying] in the midst of heaven, having the everlasting gospel to preach unto them that dwell on the earth" (Rev. 14:6). This latter passage has usually been interpreted as referring to the angel MORONI, who visited Joseph Smith in 1823 and revealed to him the burial place of the GOLD PLATES. Moreover, Latter-day Saints understand the warning against adding to or taking away from the book (Rev. 22:18–19) as applying specifically to the book of Revelation rather than to an expanding canon of scripture that they value (cf. Deut. 4:2; 12:32; 2 Ne. 29:3–14).

BIBLIOGRAPHY

Anderson, Richard L. *Understanding Paul*. Salt Lake City, 1983.

Bruce, Frederick Fyvie. *New Testament History*. Garden City, N.Y., 1972.

Conybeare, W. J., and John S. Howson. *The Life and Epistles of St. Paul*. Grand Rapids, Mich., 1968 (reprint).

Edersheim, Alfred. *The Life and Times of Jesus the Messiah*, 2 vols. Grand Rapids, Mich., 1950 (reprint).

Jackson, Kent P., and Robert L. Millet, eds. *Studies in Scripture*, Vol. 5. Salt Lake City, 1986.

McConkie, Bruce R. *Doctrinal New Testament Commentary*, 3 vols. Salt Lake City, 1965–1973.

———. *The Promised Messiah: The First Coming of Christ*. Salt Lake City, 1978.

———. *The Mortal Messiah: From Bethlehem to Calvary*, 4 vols. Salt Lake City, 1979–1981.

Millet, Robert L., ed. *Studies in Scripture*, Vol. 6. Salt Lake City, 1987.

Sperry, Sidney B. *Paul's Life and Letters*. Salt Lake City, 1955.

Talmage, James E. *JC*. Salt Lake City, 1915.

ROBERT C. PATCH

NEW YORK, EARLY LDS SITES IN

[*Many events in early Latter-day Saint history occurred in the Finger Lakes region of western New York and nearby northern Pennsylvania from 1820 to 1831. Western New York became known as the Burnt-over District because of the intense religious revivals that swept the area from the 1790s to the 1840s, affecting the families of many early LDS converts. See, generally,* Historical Sites *and* History of the Church: c. 1820–1831.

The Palmyra-Manchester neighborhood was the home of the Joseph Smith family and the location of Joseph's First Vision; see Sacred Grove. *In this area he obtained the* Gold Plates; *see* Cumorah *and* Moroni, Visitations of. *In 1830 the Book of Mormon was published in Palmyra with the financial assistance of a local resident, Martin* Harris.

Joseph Smith was employed near Harmony, Pennsylvania, in 1825. There he met his future wife, Emma Hale Smith; *they were married at nearby South Bainbridge (Afton), New York, in 1827. Joseph and Emma lived until 1830 in Harmony, where Joseph translated most of the Book of Mormon. The restoration of the* Aaronic Priesthood *occurred in this vicinity in May 1829, and the* Melchizedek Priesthood *was restored between Harmony and* Colesville. *Some of the earliest converts to the Church belonged to its Colesville branch.*

In Fayette, New York, Joseph Smith completed the Book of Mormon translation in June 1829, at the home of Peter Whitmer, Sr., where the Organization of the Church *also took place, April 6, 1830.*]

NEW ZEALAND, THE CHURCH IN

The Church of Jesus Christ of Latter-day Saints first reached New Zealand on October 27, 1854, when President Augustus Farnham, of the Australian MISSION, Elder William Cooke, and Thomas Holder, a PRIEST in the AARONIC PRIESTHOOD, arrived from AUSTRALIA. The missionaries worked first among European immigrants and then among the native Maoris, and the Church grew slowly at first, then steadily, so that by 1990 New Zealand had about 70,000 Latter-day Saints, two MISSIONS, and sixteen STAKES.

The first two people baptized into the LDS Church in New Zealand were Martha Holder and her daughter Louisa. The first Church branch was established in April 1855 among the European immigrants in Karori, a suburb of Wellington. The April 15, 1881, assignment of Elder William J. McDonnel to go to the Maori people coincided with prophecies of at least five separate Maori *tohungas* (tribal priests) that the true church of God would soon come to New Zealand. The best-known of these prophecies was the one given by Paora Potangaroa in 1881. Collectively they helped the Maoris to readily identify with the Church when its missionaries came among them (Britsch, pp. 274–76). In 1883–1884, Elders Alma Greenwood and Ira Hinckley, Jr., were especially successful among the Maoris, baptizing several hundred converts and organizing thirteen branches.

SCRIPTURES IN THE MAORI LANGUAGE. Before the LDS missionaries arrived, the Bible had already been published in Maori by earlier Christian missionaries, but expanding Maori membership created an urgent need to have the Book of Mormon translated. Ezra F. Richards and Sondra Sanders, assisted by Henare Potae, Te Pirihi Tutokohi, and James Jury, local Maori members, published the first translation in 1889. During World War I, President Joseph F. SMITH approved a second translation of the Book of Mormon, and Elder Matthew Cowley, a young missionary with unusual skill in the Maori language, was assigned to the work. He made changes in approximately 2,500 verses in the original translation, and the second edition appeared in 1917. Elder Cowley was then assigned to translate the Doctrine and Covenants and the Pearl of Great Price, assisted by Wiremu Duncan and Stuart Meha. These translations appeared in 1919.

RELIEF SOCIETY, PRIMARY, AND THE MUTUAL IMPROVEMENT ASSOCIATION. The first branch RELIEF SOCIETY in New Zealand was organized in 1878, with Ann Jones as president. The first Maori Relief Society was organized in 1901, with Sister Mangu Reweti as president. In 1904, Sister Emma E. Wright, the wife of a missionary, was called as the first president of the Mission Relief Society, which coordinated the local units. Thereafter until 1931, the wife of the mission president presided over the mission Relief Society, PRIMARY, and

One of the five buildings of the Latter-day Saints' Maori Agricultural College, near Hastings, Hawke's Bay District, New Zealand, in 1919. The Church operated this school for Maori boys from 1912 to 1931, when its buildings were destroyed by an earthquake. Courtesy Edith W. Morgan.

Young Women Mutual Improvement Association (YWMIA, now YOUNG WOMEN). Then in 1931, Hepera Takare Duncan became the first local sister to preside over the Mission Relief Society.

The first MIA was organized in the Auckland branch in 1907, and the first units among the Maoris came in 1918. Sister Una Thompson is remembered for her leadership of the MIA in those early years. The first Primaries were organized in 1913, with Sisters Ere Hapati Mete and Bessie Greening as presidents. Between 1928 and 1931, Sister Arta Romney Ballif, wife of the principal of the Maori Agricultural College, was instrumental in building the Primary association throughout the mission.

CHURCH SCHOOLS. Because many Maori converts lived in outlying areas with no schools for their children, the Church established schools in local branch meetinghouses as early as 1886. In 1907 the FIRST PRESIDENCY of the Church authorized creation of a secondary school to train boys in farming, technology, and leadership skills, and to teach them religion. Accordingly, Maori Agricultural College was dedicated on April 6, 1913, in Korongata, Hastings, Hawkes Bay. A February 1931 earthquake rendered the buildings unsafe, and the Church closed the college.

Because many of the alumni of the college had become prominent Church leaders by the 1940s, Mission President Matthew Cowley recommended that a coeducational secondary school be established in New Zealand, with capacity increased from eighty to more than five hundred students.

The First Presidency approved building the present Church College of New Zealand (CCNZ) at Temple View, near Hamilton. Since its inception in 1955, CCNZ has played a significant role in the educational and spiritual development of thousands of LDS high school students.

NEW ZEALAND TEMPLE.   Prior to 1958, Latter-day Saints in New Zealand had to travel to the Hawaii Temple to receive the significant ORDINANCES available only in temples. The decision to build a temple in New Zealand was announced by President David O. MCKAY in February 1955 and brought great joy among the local SAINTS. The temple and college buildings were to be built simultaneously under the newly conceived Church Building Missionary Program, which provided for supervisory craftsmen to be called from the United States to construct the buildings with a local voluntary missionary labor force of hundreds of members, mainly Maoris, who would learn construction skills on the job. In less than two and a half years, both the temple and the college were completed at minimal expense, and hundreds of previously unskilled and unemployed Maori members had learned building skills and were qualified for gainful employment. E. Albert and Vernice Gold Rosenvall were called as the first president and matron. President McKay dedicated the temple on April 20, 1958, and the college on April 26.

The New Zealand Temple, Hamilton, New Zealand. Dedicated in 1958, its spire rises 157 feet.

The Building Missionary Program was so successful that it was used for several years to construct Church buildings in other parts of the world. For years the New Zealand Temple served Church members living throughout the South Pacific, but since September 1984, temples have been in service in Australia, Samoa, Tonga, and Tahiti.

MATTHEW COWLEY.   With the coming of World War II, all American missionaries were called home, but President Matthew and Sister Elva Taylor Cowley chose to remain in New Zealand with their family to supervise the work during the war. It was September 1945 before the Cowleys were released after seven and a half years of service. At the October 1945 GENERAL CONFERENCE, Matthew Cowley was called to be a member of the QUORUM OF THE TWELVE APOSTLES and was affectionately called their "Polynesian Apostle" by the Saints of the South Pacific. Six other men with New Zealand connections have been called as GENERAL AUTHORITIES, all in the QUORUMS OF THE SEVENTY: Douglas J. Martin, a native New Zealander, and former New Zealand mission presidents Rufus K. Hardy, John J. Lasater, Glenn L. Rudd, Robert L. Simpson, Philip T. Sonntag, and Rulon G. Craven.

The year 1958 was pivotal for the Church in New Zealand. In that year the temple and the college were completed, the first stake was organized in Auckland, and the mission was divided into two missions. Since then, the Church has shown increasing growth in New Zealand.

BIBLIOGRAPHY

Britsch, R. Lanier. "New Zealand." In *Unto the Islands of the Sea: A History of the Latter-day Saints in the Pacific*, pp. 215–345. Salt Lake City, 1986.

Clement, Russell T., comp. *Mormons in the Pacific: A Bibliography*. Laie, Hawaii, 1981.

ROBERT L. SIMPSON

NOAH

Noah is one of God's most notable prophets, patriarchs, and ministering messengers. He became a second father—with ADAM—of all mankind following the Flood and later returned to earth as the angel Gabriel to announce the births of JOHN THE BAPTIST and Jesus Christ (*HC* 3:386; *TPJS*, p. 157).

LDS REVELATION has amplified what is known about Noah in the Bible.

Lamech, son of Methuselah and grandson of ENOCH, begat Noah, fulfilling COVENANTS that the Lord made with Enoch that a remnant of his posterity would always be found among all nations (Moses 7:52) and that Noah would be born of his lineage through Methuselah (Moses 8:2). Lamech chose the name Noah because of the "comfort" the child would bring to his family in their toil (8:9). Though Noah had brothers and sisters, nothing about them is known (8:10).

A promised child of noble ancestry, including Adam and other "preachers of righteousness" (Moses 6:22–23), Noah was ordained to the PRIESTHOOD at age ten by Methuselah (D&C 107:52), an unusually young age when compared with the ages at which other antediluvian patriarchs were ordained (D&C 107:42–51).

Though Noah lived in times of wickedness (Moses 8:20–22, 28–30), Noah successfully raised three sons who "hearkened unto the Lord . . . and they were called the sons of God" (8:13). Unfortunately, his "fair" granddaughters "sold themselves" by marrying wicked husbands, losing the benefits of living in a righteous environment (8:14–15). He taught the gospel of the anticipated Savior Anointed (Jesus Christ), as Enoch had, including FAITH, REPENTANCE, BAPTISM in the name of the Savior and reception of the HOLY GHOST (Moses 8:16, 19, 23–24). He warned that failure to heed his message would bring the floods upon his hearers (D&C 138:41; Moses 8:24).

Noah was "perfect in his generation; and he walked with God" (Moses 8:27). Like Adam, he received dominion over the EARTH and all living things (HC 3:386). Thus, Methuselah's PROPHECY "that from his [own] loins should spring all the kingdoms of the earth (through Noah)" was dramatically fulfilled (Moses 8:3).

Noah stands "next in authority to Adam in the Priesthood" (HC 3:386), and "in third position from the Lord" (Petersen, p. 2), and conferred the power of the priesthood on his righteous posterity (D&C 84:14–15).

Eighteen centuries after announcing Christ's birth, Noah—again as Gabriel—visited the Prophet Joseph SMITH to restore priesthood KEYS (D&C 128:21). Noah is to return to earth after Christ's second coming to attend the MARRIAGE SUPPER OF THE LAMB (D&C 27:5–7).

BIBLIOGRAPHY

Parrish, Alan K. "The Days of Noah." In Studies in Scripture, ed. R. Millet and K. Jackson, Vol. 2, pp. 145–59. Salt Lake City, 1985.

Petersen, Mark E. Noah and the Flood. Salt Lake City, 1982.

ANDREW C. SKINNER

NON-MORMONS, SOCIAL RELATIONS WITH

The social milieu of the Church in modern times may be compared to that of the New Testament Church. In each situation, a PECULIAR PEOPLE amid multiple religious traditions and structures engendered hostility.

In and around Palmyra, New York, prior to the organization of the Church, the Smith family was welcomed in the community. But the announcements of new revelation, new scripture, and direct communication with God engendered a negative social reaction. Within a year, the family and all other members of the Church moved from that area. None returned for nearly eighty-five years. Similar hostilities developed in other areas (see ANTI-MORMONISM; PERSECUTION). The missionary outreach of the fledgling Church extended into England, Scandinavia, and western Europe, where churches were mostly state-controlled, and alternative faiths were oppressed. To listen to, sympathize with, or join the Latter-day Saints often meant that one would be disowned by parents and relatives, socially ostracized, fined, jailed, or even in some instances threatened with death. The resulting stream of LDS emigrants to Church settlements in Ohio, Missouri, and Illinois was so extensive that even in the melting-pot atmosphere of America, they were often confronted immediately with suspicion and opposition.

Following its withdrawal from New York, the Church established its headquarters in Kirtland, Ohio. There the vigorous missionary thrust continued to bring into the Church many people with commitment and dedication, leaving little time in their lives for social relationships with those outside the Church, who often shunned friendly overtures when they were made. The reaction of many churches was strongly negative to the LDS influence, and the typical responses of Latter-day Saints was to draw closer to each other for mutual protection and support. Communication was sporadic and fleeting at best. Misunderstandings grew.

Under divine command, the Church relocated in northern Missouri, where rapid growth multiplied tensions and frictions. The specter of growing LDS economic and political power in five counties amplified the social stress. There was also the complication of "apostates," or dissidents, who often joined anti-Mormon coalitions. The "old settlers" and the new LDS ones were polarized. The Church's social and political difficulties in Missouri culminated in Governor Lilburn Boggs' infamous EXTERMINATION ORDER and resulted in some 1,500 LDS families being forced to abandon their farms, homes, and other possessions and flee for their lives into Illinois. There, a new LDS gathering place called NAUVOO was founded.

For a time Nauvoo was a community almost unto itself. Its singular status, the inclusive character of its life patterns, and the extension of the religious vision into all aspects of culture were stabilized by a strong self-sufficient charter and even a militia, the NAUVOO LEGION. Many visitors came to view the new city, and efforts to promote cultural and intellectual exchange increased. Joseph Smith and about 1,500 other Church members joined the Masonic lodges in Nauvoo and nearby Keokuk and Montrose to promote fraternal relations (see FREEMASONRY IN NAUVOO). However, once again the old settlers outside the Church clashed with the LDS settlers, and hostilities grew.

Driven westward, the Saints settled in the Great Basin, where comparative freedom and peace enabled them to pursue their social, intellectual, and spiritual goals. For several decades social exchange and the development of intercultural relations with those outside the group were limited. The Church was the leading influence—social, political, economical, and educational. Relative calm and cooperation prevailed until tensions mounted, primarily over the practice of plural marriage. A half century passed before this issue was resolved, and in 1896, Utah Territory in the Great Basin became a state (see UTAH STATEHOOD).

In the twentieth century, congenial relations have developed between the Church and other groups and institutions throughout the United States and the world. Church membership has become increasingly diverse and widespread, and new motivations for communication, goodwill, and cooperation have arisen. The needs of modern society have cried out for improved relations among faiths and people worldwide. The critical need for efforts and participation that unite churches and social organizations has become more apparent. Problems relating to the hungry and homeless, the illiterate and underprivileged, the drug-addicted and abused, and the victims of disintegrating family life have increased on a worldwide scale. The relative stability of LDS society is attractive to many who seek leadership and example. Latter-day Saints and their neighbors have increasingly recognized common ground and common causes. They participate extensively in such groups as Boy Scouts, chambers of commerce, service clubs, the YMCA, the United Fund, local school systems, and a variety of professional and benevolent civic organizations (see CIVIC DUTIES).

Although social relations of Church members with others are generally much more congenial in the late twentieth century than earlier, some sources of friction persist. Some negative responses continue to arise in other church communities because of LDS missionary efforts, with Latter-day Saints sometimes accused of being aggressive in both religious and nonreligious contexts.

[See also Interfaith Relations; Social and Cultural History.]

DARL ANDERSON
DAVID K. UDALL
ELEANOR PARK JONES

O

OATH AND COVENANT OF THE PRIESTHOOD

Among the most important covenants is the oath and covenant of the priesthood, a set of mutual promises between God and those who receive the Melchizedek Priesthood. Doctrine and Covenants 84:33–42 states the obligations involved, affirming the rewards that will be given to those who faithfully discharge their oath, and confirming the consequences of breaking this covenant.

The priesthood holder's first responsibility is to receive in good faith and with honest intent both the Aaronic and the Melchizedek priesthoods. The covenant then obligates that priesthood holder to magnify his callings by fulfilling all the responsibilities associated with the office, teaching the word of God, and laboring with all his might to advance the purposes of the Lord (*see* MAGNIFYING ONE'S CALLING; cf. Jacob 1:19). The priesthood holder is required to "obtain a knowledge of the gospel . . . [and] to render service—service in carrying the restored gospel, with all the blessings of the priesthood, to the peoples of the earth; and service in comforting, strengthening, and perfecting the lives of one another and all the Saints of God" (Romney, p. 43).

God then promises that those who fulfill their part of the agreement will be "sanctified by the Spirit unto the renewing of their bodies," will become "the sons of Moses and of Aaron and the seed of Abraham" and members of "the church and kingdom, and the elect of God," and will receive the Father's kingdom, and, thus, "all" that the "Father hath shall be given unto" them (D&C 84:33–38). Latter-day Saints see in the first of these promises a change that purifies not only the minds of worthy priesthood holders, but also their bodies, until they are enlivened and strengthened to minister among the nations of the earth. Those who keep this covenant are then counted among those in the celestial kingdom, "into whose hand the Father has given all things—they are they who are priests and kings, who have received of his fulness, and of his glory; . . . they are gods, even the sons of God" (D&C 76:55–58).

This oath and covenant of the priesthood also carries a severe warning. The Lord has stated that anyone who breaks this covenant and "altogether turneth therefrom, shall not have forgiveness of sins in this world nor in the world to come" (D&C 84:41).

Ancient prophets received the priesthood by oath and covenant. Latter-day Saints understand several Old and New Testament covenantal texts to refer to the oath and covenant by which the priesthood has been received through all generations (e.g., Num. 25:13; 1 Chr. 16:15–17; Ps. 110:4; Heb. 7:20–21, 28). Enoch, Melchizedek, Abraham, and all others who received the fulness of the gospel of Jesus Christ have obtained the priesthood after the order of the Son of God in a covenant-based relationship with the Lord (e.g., JST Gen. 13:13; 14:27–30). In this way, the priesthood has been transmitted to man since the beginning of time with an eternal obligation and unfailing promise, both of which the Lord communicates through the sacred medium of an oath and a covenant.

BIBLIOGRAPHY

Asay, Carlos E. "The Oath and Covenant of the Priesthood." *Ensign* 15 (Nov. 1985):43–45.

Brown, Hugh B. "Participation: The Way to Salvation." *IE* 66 (June 1963):506–507.

Kimball, Spencer W. "Becoming Pure in Heart." *Ensign* 15 (Mar. 1985):2–5.

Monson, Thomas S. *First British Area General Conference Report*, pp. 142–46. Salt Lake City, 1972.

Romney, Marion G. "The Oath and Covenant Which Belongeth to the Priesthood." *Ensign* 2 (July 1972):43–45.

MICHAEL K. YOUNG

OATHS

Oaths are solemn declarations used to affirm a statement or strengthen a promise. Anciently, oath-swearing formed an important part of social, political, economic, and religious interaction. God himself uses an oath and promise in his covenants with man (cf. Jer. 22:5; Amos 6:8; D&C 97:20). In covenant-making, ritual oaths attest the fidelity of those entering into the COVENANT. Sometimes an oath is sworn that anticipates punishment in case of failure to perform a specified act, and in some cases the covenant process symbolically depicts specific punishments (Jer. 34:18–19).

Oath-swearing was common among the Book of Mormon peoples. NEPHI₁ swore an oath to Zoram assuring him full status in Lehi's family (1 Ne. 4:32–34), and Zoram swore to accompany Nephi and his brothers into the wilderness, after which their "fears did cease concerning him" (1 Ne. 4:37). Oaths of office were administered to judges (Alma 50:39). In a manner reminiscent of biblical and other Near Eastern peoples, the NEPHITES swore to support MORONI₁ in defensive war, and used their rent garments to represent the punishment they wished upon themselves should they fail (Alma 46:21–22).

Oaths were also used with evil intent. For sinister purposes, the Gadianton robbers and the JAREDITES swore secret oaths that had once been sworn by Cain (Hel. 6:21–26; Ether 8:15; Moses 5:29).

Oaths continue to play a role in Latter-day Saint religion and ritual. The higher PRIESTHOOD is received through an "oath and covenant" (D&C 84:39–40; cf. Heb. 7:11–22) of faithfulness. Following a pattern similar to ancient covenant-making, Latter-day Saints make holy covenants in TEMPLES. In their worship and prayer they use the word AMEN, which in Hebrew means "verily," "truly," or "let it be affirmed," and is considered a form of an oath comparable to expressions used in ancient Israel (Deut. 27:14–26; cf. D&C 88:135). The raising of the right hand of the congregation in periodic CONFERENCES in approval for those called to Church positions is viewed as a silent oath signifying one's determination to sustain those persons in their CALLINGS.

Frequent and superficial use of oaths can become an abuse and may diminish their sincere and sacred functions and oaths made "in vain" are profane and blasphemous. Christ admonished his followers to avoid oaths sworn without real intent and told them to make their commitments simply by saying "yes" or "no" (Matt. 5:33–37; 23:16–22).

BIBLIOGRAPHY

Johnson, Roy. "The Use of Oaths in the Old Testament and the Book of Mormon." *F.A.R.M.S.*, Provo, Utah, 1982.

Szink, Terrence. "An Oath of Allegiance in the Book of Mormon." In *Warfare in the Book of Mormon*, ed. S. Ricks and W. Hamblin. Salt Lake City, 1990.

TERRENCE L. SZINK

OBEDIENCE

Obedience in the context of the gospel of Jesus Christ means to comply with God's will, to live in accordance with his teachings and the promptings of his Spirit, and to keep his COMMANDMENTS. Disobedience means to do anything less, whether it be to follow Satan and his will, to live in accordance with one's own selfish wants and desires, or to be a "slothful" person who must be "compelled in all things" (D&C 58:26).

Part of God's purpose in designing mortal life for his children was to "prove them herewith, to see if they will do all things whatsoever the Lord their God shall command them" (Abr. 3:25; cf. D&C 98:14). Passing such a test is necessary for one to progress to become like God because he, himself, lives in accordance with law and principles of justice (Alma 42:22–26; see GODHOOD). Thus, obedience to DIVINE LAW is essential to ETERNAL PROGRESSION, and those who live obediently in this life will "have glory added upon their heads for ever and ever" (Abr. 3:26).

The importance of obedience is further emphasized by the fact that God permits sorrows and suffering on this earth in part to help teach obedience. Thus Jesus Christ, the exemplar, learned "obedience by the things which he suffered" (Heb. 5:8; cf. Alma 7:12), and the Lord's people "must needs be chastened until they learn obedience, if it must needs be, by the things which they suffer" (D&C 105:6). On the other hand, God has also promised that he will provide a way for his children to obey him (cf. 1 Ne. 3:7).

In the LDS view, although it can sometimes be difficult to be obedient because it requires making difficult choices among alternatives, it does bring BLESSINGS in this life and in eternity. In fact, all blessings depend upon obedience: "When we obtain any blessing from God, it is by obedience to that law upon which it is predicated" (D&C 130:21). Disobedience may result in the loss of blessings in this world and may bring curses or punishments in the next life as well. Therefore, when God gives a commandment, he frequently specifies both the blessings that come from obedience and the curses or punishments that come from disobedience. Accordingly, the commandment to "honour thy father and thy mother" specifies the potential blessing "that thy days may be long upon the land which the Lord thy God giveth thee" (Ex. 20:12); and the commandment to Book of Mormon peoples to serve God on the American continent came with the promise of being "free from bondage" or, in the case of noncompliance, the curse of being "swept off" (Ether 2:8–12; see AGENCY).

God also recognizes the need to obey the laws of governments. Thus he states: "Let no man break the laws of the land, for he that keepeth the laws of God hath no need to break the laws of the land. Wherefore, be subject to the powers that be, until he reigns whose right it is to reign" (D&C 58:21–22). Joseph SMITH reiterated this principle: "We believe in . . . obeying, honoring, and sustaining the law" (A of F 12).

The purest and best motivation for obedience to godly law is LOVE: "If ye love me, keep my commandments" (John 14:15). However, because God wants his children to grow spiritually, he neither requires nor desires unwilling or begrudged compliance, nor "blind obedience." Every person has the right, and even the responsibility, to learn whether a commandment, prompting, or teaching comes from God. However, because God also requires faithful response—"the heart and a willing mind" (D&C 64:34)—from his children, he does sometimes require obedience of the type wherein one complies humbly with his teachings, promptings, or commandments even before totally understanding the reasons for them. ADAM gave such obedience when commanded by the Lord to offer the firstlings of his flocks. "After many days," when an angel asked him why he was offering such sacrifice, Adam replied: "I know not, save the Lord commanded me." The angel then taught Adam the reason for the offering: It represented the atoning SACRIFICE that Jesus Christ would eventually make on behalf of all human beings (Moses 5:5–8).

God does not hold people responsible or punish them for disobedience to laws and commandments that they have not had opportunity to learn and understand. King BENJAMIN taught that Christ's "blood atoneth for the sins of those who have fallen by the transgression of Adam, who have died not knowing the will of God concerning them, or who have ignorantly sinned" (Mosiah 3:11).

As with Adam, men and women who willingly obey the commandments of God because they love him will receive greater KNOWLEDGE and understanding of God and his purposes. Disobedience brings no such growth in knowledge or understanding, and may result in loss of previously gained knowledge and ability or opportunity to make further choices (D&C 1:33). In other words, it can result in both spiritual and temporal captivity for the disobedient. Thus, Jacob taught the Nephites that they were free to choose "liberty and eternal life" or to choose "captivity and death" (2 Ne. 2:27).

BIBLIOGRAPHY

Packer, Boyd K. "Obedience." *BYU Speeches of the Year.* Provo, Utah, 1971.

CHERYL BROWN

OCCUPATIONAL STATUS

Occupational and employment data collected in the United States, Canada, Britain, Japan, and Mexico from 1980 to 1983 indicate that members of the Church differ in some respects from the general populations in which they live, but are generally similar.

In the United States, LDS men tend to be about 7 percent more likely than the rest of the population to be in the labor force. LDS women have labor-force participation rates almost identical to U.S. women generally, but LDS women are about 4 percent more likely to work part-time rather than full-time. In single-parent families, LDS women are some 16 percent more likely to be employed than other single mothers. LDS mothers with children under six years of age are 9 percent less likely to be in the labor force than other U.S. mothers of preschoolers.

Among LDS men and women who are employed, occupational distributions are very similar to the United States generally. LDS men are slightly more likely to be professionals and a little less likely to be machine or equipment operators, but in all other occupational categories the percentages tend to be virtually the same.

In Canada the occupational and employment figures tend to be very similar to the United States. Canadian LDS men are 7 percent more likely to have employment than the general population, and about half of the LDS women are employed and 9 percent more likely than others to work part-time. The occupational breakdowns in Canada for LDS men and women tend to follow the national patterns within a few percentage points.

Church survey data from Britain, Mexico, and Japan for the years 1981–1983 show that British LDS men had 87 percent participation in the labor force, the highest of the countries examined. The employment rate for LDS men in Mexico was 67 percent; in Japan, 77 percent; and in the United States, 85 percent. Japanese LDS women active in the Church were generally in the labor force at a slightly higher rate (5 percent higher) than other women in Japan.

When Church populations are compared, greater concentrations of white-collar workers are usually found in areas where members are mainly urban. Their proportion in specific white-collar categories varies somewhat in each country. In 1981–1983, LDS men were found more in managerial, administrative, and production positions in the five countries that were examined. Men and women were in professions in about the same proportion in all countries except Mexico, where greater numbers of women are in the professions (especially teaching), while LDS women were overrepresented in clerical, sales, and service occupations.

WILLIAM G. DYER

OCEANIA, THE CHURCH IN

The Church of Jesus Christ of Latter-day Saints has been established in Oceania (the islands of the central and southern Pacific) since 1844, when its missionaries first arrived in French Polynesia and organized a branch there. The Church moved into Hawaii in 1850, New Zealand in 1854, Samoa in 1888, Tonga in 1891, and other islands after World War II. By 1990 the Church in Oceania had grown to over 100,000 members living in several MISSIONS and hundreds of STAKES, WARDS, and branches, and it had TEMPLES in Samoa, Tahiti, and Tonga (*see also* HAWAII and NEW ZEALAND).

FRENCH POLYNESIA. The Prophet Joseph SMITH sent four missionaries, Addison Pratt, Benjamin Franklin Grouard, Noah Rogers, and Knowlton F. Hanks (who died at sea), to the islands of the Pacific in May 1843. Arriving at Tubuai Island, 350 miles south of Tahiti, on April 30, 1844, they established the first branch of the Church in Oceania in July 1844, with eleven members. When friction with the French territorial government ended the first period of missionary work in 1852, the Church had nearly 2,000 converts scattered on at least twenty islands.

The mission was refounded in 1892, when William A. Seegmiller and Joseph W. Damron, Jr., were sent to Tahiti from the Samoan mission. Growth was negligible until 1950, when the Church placed leadership in the hands of local members and moved the proselytizing missionaries from the Tuamotu Islands to Tahiti. This move accelerated Church growth. Three other factors also contributed to more rapid growth after 1953: increased use of the French language, use of organized proselytizing plans, and the building of modern MEETINGHOUSES.

Mormon missionaries in 1887. Photographer: Edward Cliff.

The first stake organized in French Polynesia was the Papeete Tahiti Stake, on May 14, 1972, with Raituia Tehina Tapu as stake president. Church President Spencer W. KIMBALL broke ground for the Papeete Tahiti Temple on February 13, 1981, and Gordon B. Hinckley, first counselor in the FIRST PRESIDENCY, dedicated the completed structure on October 27–29, 1983. LDS scriptures are available in Tahitian and French.

SAMOA. LDS missionary work in Samoa officially began on June 18, 1888, when Joseph Harry Dean and Florence Ridges Dean arrived on Tutuila. There had been an unofficial start in January 1863, when Walter Murray Gibson sent two Hawaiian elders, Kimo Pelio and Samuela Manoa, to Samoa to teach the restored gospel; they baptized about fifty people. Pelio died in 1876, and Manoa married and settled on the little island of Aunuu, from which he wrote letters to Hawaii and Church headquarters asking for assistance. One of those letters prompted the Deans to go to Samoa from Hawaii.

Growth of the Church in Samoa was steady from 1888 on. During their first four months the Deans baptized forty people and formed a branch. By 1899 the Church had 1,139 Samoan Latter-day Saints scattered across the major islands. Local leaders led most branches, and Samoan priesthood holders and their wives served missions. Church schools were operated in a number of villages, and three "central" residential schools were created on the islands of Tutuila, Upolu, and Savai'i. The Church has continued to operate many schools, the most important being the Church College of Western Samoa, a high school in Apia, Western Samoa. Gathering places for Church families to establish homes were founded at Mapusaga on Tutuila, American Samoa, in 1903 and at Sauniatu, Upolu, in Western Samoa, in 1904.

In 1902, Church headquarters were established at Pesega, near Apia, on land donated by Ah Mu, a Chinese member. The Apia Samoa Temple, the Church College of Western Samoa, a stake center, the mission headquarters, and the missionary training center are all built on that land. The Book of Mormon was translated and published in Samoan in 1903, and the Doctrine and Covenants and the Pearl of Great Price, in 1963.

On March 18, 1962, the Apia Stake was organized with Percy John Rivers, a descendant of Ah Mu, as stake president. On February 19, 1981, President Spencer W. Kimball broke ground for

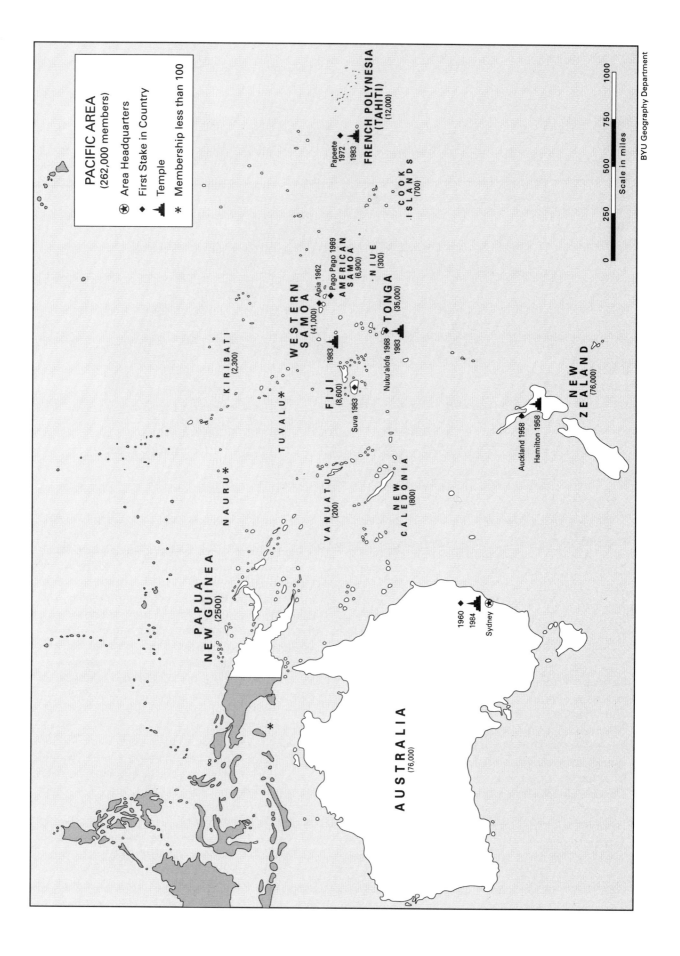

PACIFIC AREA
(262,000 members)

⊛ Area Headquarters

◆ First Stake in Country

⚒ Temple

∗ Membership less than 100

FRENCH POLYNESIA
(TAHITI)
(12,000)

Papeete
1972
1983

COOK
ISLANDS
(700)

WESTERN
SAMOA
(41,000)

Apia 1962

Pago Pago 1969
AMERICAN
SAMOA
(6,900)

1983

NIUE
(300)

TONGA
(35,000)

Nuku'alofa 1968
1983

KIRIBATI
(2,300)

TUVALU ∗

FIJI
(8,600)

Suva 1983

NAURU ∗

VANUATU
(200)

NEW
CALEDONIA
(800)

NEW
ZEALAND
(76,000)

Auckland 1958
Hamilton 1958

PAPUA
NEW GUINEA
(2500)

∗

AUSTRALIA
(76,000)

1960
1984
Sydney

0   250   500   750   1000
Scale in miles

BYU Geography Department

the Samoa Temple at Pesega, and the completed structure was dedicated on August 5–7, 1983.

TONGA. LDS missionaries first visited the "Friendly Islands" on July 15, 1891, when Brigham Smoot and Alva J. Butler arrived at Nuku'alofa, Tongatapu Island, from Samoa. However, this first phase of the Tongan mission was short-lived because of political and religious circumstances. In June 1907, William O. Facer and Heber J. McKay reopened missionary work in Tonga, this time at Vava'u, the northern island group. Until 1916, when Willard L. Smith arrived as the first mission president, Tonga was part of the Samoan mission. Until the early 1950s, Church growth in Tonga was slow, being retarded by misunderstandings with the government. When those difficulties were resolved, the Church showed significant growth in Tonga, reflecting the maturity in leadership, understanding of Church organization, and depth of spirituality of the Tongan Saints. The Nuku'alofa Stake was organized on September 5, 1968, with Orson Hyde White as stake president. As growth continued, Church President Spencer W. Kimball broke ground for a temple near Nuku'alofa on February 18, 1981. It was dedicated August 9, 1983, by his counselor, President Gordon B. Hinckley.

Education has played an important role in the Church in Tonga. Of the many schools established, the most important are Liahona High School (1952) on Tongatapu and Saineha High School (1978) on Vava'u. The Book of Mormon was published in Tongan in 1946 and the Doctrine and Covenants and the Pearl of Great Price, in 1959.

FIJI. Although Tongan and other Latter-day Saints had lived and held Church meetings in Fiji for many years, not until May 1954 were missionaries sent to Suva from the Samoan mission to officially commence LDS proselytizing. Boyd L. Harris and Sheldon L. Abbott organized the Suva Branch on September 5, 1954. An initial boost in Church growth occurred when Church President David O. McKay visited Suva in January 1955 and decided that a large chapel should be built, which he dedicated three years later on May 4, 1958. That building was part of President McKay's vision

Temple Square and Eagle Gate, by Relief Society members, Vavau District, Tonga (c. 1935, tapa cloth— pigment on bark). Created by LDS women who loved a temple that most of them would never see, this detail shows the six-spired Salt Lake Temple and the domed Tabernacle on Temple Square in Salt Lake City. Nearly fifty years later, on August 9, 1983, an LDS temple was dedicated in Nuku'alofa, Tonga. Church Museum of History and Art.

for Fiji and manifested to the government and people alike that the LDS Church was in Fiji to stay.

Fiji was assigned to the Samoan and Tongan missions until July 1971, when it was made an independent mission. Since then, the Fiji Suva Mission has had many South Pacific areas assigned to it for a time, such as New Caledonia, Niue, the Cook Islands, Kiribati, Vanuatu, and Rotuma. Church growth and development in Fiji have been steady. In 1969 the Suva chapel also housed a Church-sponsored elementary school. Seminary classes began in 1973, and two years later, the LDS Fiji Technical College (equivalent to a U.S. vocational high school) opened on a new campus in Suva. By 1984, 372 students, mostly LDS, were enrolled.

Overall Church membership also continued to grow in Fiji, and in February 1976, one thousand Fijian Latter-day Saints attended an area conference held by President Spencer W. Kimball. On June 5, 1983, Howard W. Hunter organized

The Church of Jesus Christ of Latter-day Saints in Australia, New Zealand, and the South Pacific Islands as of January 1, 1991.

the Suva Fiji Stake, with Inosi Naga as stake president. The Book of Mormon was published in Fijian in 1980.

NEW CALEDONIA.   Some LDS Tahitian laborers migrated to New Caledonia during the 1950s and established small units of the Church there. Under the direction of the French Polynesia (Tahiti) mission president, the Noumea Branch was organized in October 1961. Years of negotiations between mission leaders and the New Caledonian government led to permission for LDS missionaries to proselytize. On May 2, 1968, Elder Thomas S. Monson, of the Quorum of the Twelve Apostles, dedicated New Caledonia for the preaching of the gospel. Two months later, the first missionary couple arrived. In 1990 the full program of the Church had been established, and New Caledonia was under the Fiji Suva Mission.

GUAM AND MICRONESIA.   Latter-day Saints have lived on many of the Micronesian islands since World War II. But only Guam has had LDS servicemen's groups and branches consistently. President Joseph Fielding SMITH dedicated Guam to the preaching of the gospel on August 25, 1955, and the first full-time missionaries were sent there in January 1957. However, until the mid-1970s, missionary work was confined primarily to U.S. military personnel and their families. Since that time, expansion into the many islands of Micronesia has been rapid. In the spring of 1980, the Church created the Micronesia Guam Mission, with Ferron C. Losee as president. Book of Mormon selections were published in Marshallese and Pohnpeian in 1984 and 1987, respectively.

KIRIBATI.   LDS missionary efforts in the Republic of Kiribati (formerly the Gilbert Islands) have proven quite fruitful. On October 19, 1975, six Gilbertese students who had studied at Liahona High School in Tonga returned to the island of Tarawa and commenced missionary work. They had been ordained elders and were serving in the Fiji Suva Mission. At about the same time, the Church took over a small middle school in 1977 and renamed it Moroni Community School. It has served as the physical focus of the Church in Kiribati. Relative to the small population, Church growth has been rapid. In 1990 the Church was also established in Belau, the Cook Islands, Marshall, Niue, Nauru, Northern Marietta, Tuvalu, and Vanuata.

BIBLIOGRAPHY

Britsch, R. Lanier. *Unto the Islands of the Sea: A History of the Latter-day Saints in the Pacific.* Salt Lake City, 1986.

Clement, Russell T., comp. *Mormons in the Pacific: A Bibliography.* Laie, Hawaii, 1981.

R. LANIER BRITSCH

Papeete Tahiti Temple in 1986 in Pirae, Tahiti (dedicated 1983). The design shows influences of local French and Polynesian culture. Courtesy Floyd Holdman.

OHIO, LDS COMMUNITIES IN

[*The Church became established in Ohio after Sidney* Rigdon *and his Reformed Baptist congregations at Mentor and Kirtland converted in October–November 1830. Others around the vicinity of* Kirtland *joined the Church. A December 1830 revelation initiated a* Gathering *of Church members to Ohio (D&C 37:1–2), where they were to be "endowed with power from on high" (D&C 38:32). See* History of the Church: 1831–1844.

Joseph Smith *and Sidney Rigdon lived at Hiram, Ohio, from September 1831 to September 1832, where both were tarred and feathered. There Joseph Smith received sixteen revelations later published in the* Doctrine and Covenants.

Between 1831 and 1838, Kirtland served as Church headquarters. See such entries as Kirtland: LDS Community; Schools of the Prophets; *and* Whitney Store. *Here many more revelations were received, and in the Kirtland Temple, in 1836, Latter-day Saints experienced an increased outpouring of spiritual manifestations and visitations.*

By 1838, the Church had organized more than two dozen branches in communities mostly in northeastern Ohio.

Some early Ohio converts had formed a communal society prior to their conversion. This communitarian impulse was redirected by a revelation, Doctrine and Covenants: Section 42; see Consecration in Ohio. *Management of temporal affairs was seen as an integral part of building the* Kingdom of God *on the earth. Joseph Smith's role in the development of the* Kirtland Economy *became a focal point of dissent in the wake of the failure of an unchartered Kirtland bank during the Panic of 1837.*

In early 1838, threatened by malcontents, Joseph Smith and other Church leaders fled Kirtland, moving Church headquarters to Missouri. Most Latter-day Saints soon left Ohio, although a Church organization was maintained at Kirtland for several years.]

OIL, CONSECRATED

Olive oil is used by members of The Church of Jesus Christ of Latter-day Saints in blessing the sick and in performing initiatory ORDINANCES in the TEMPLE. Before oil is used, it is consecrated in a short ceremony. An officiating MELCHIZEDEK PRIESTHOOD bearer, holding an open vessel containing pure olive oil, consecrates it by the authority of the priesthood and in the name of Jesus Christ for its intended purposes. The oil is then stored and used upon occasion as required.

The use of oil in religious rites can be seen in the record of Old Testament times, when it was used to anoint objects (Gen. 28:18–19; Lev. 8:10–12), as an offering (Ex. 25:1–6), and to anoint priests (Ex. 29:7; Lev. 21:10–12) and kings (1 Sam. 10:1; 16:3). In the New Testament, oil was used to anoint the sick (Mark 6:13; James 5:14).

Two New Testament PARABLES illustrate possible symbolisms of oil both as a therapeutic ointment and as a source of light. The good Samaritan, finding the injured traveler, "bound up his wounds, pouring in oil and wine" (Luke 10:34). In another parable wise virgins "took oil in their vessels with their lamps" and thus were in possession

of material to provide light, to celebrate the coming of the bridegroom, Christ (Matt. 25:1–13).

The reason for using olive oil rather than any other kind of oil is never clearly stated in the scriptures. To say that olive oil is preferred because it is the oil indigenous to the Holy Land would be simplistic. A more likely explanation results from examining the wide range of meanings symbolized by the olive tree and the oil derived from the olive fruit, the only major culinary oil that is derived from a fruit. The olive branch has long been a token of peace. The olive tree is used in scripture as a symbol for the house of Israel (Hosea 14:6; Rom. 11:17; Jacob 5; D&C 101:43–62).

PAUL Y. HOSKISSON

OLD TESTAMENT

The Old Testament is one of the STANDARD WORKS, or SCRIPTURES, accepted by The Church of Jesus Christ of Latter-day Saints, which values it for its prophetic, historical, doctrinal, and moral teachings. The Old Testament recounts an epochal series of ancient DISPENSATIONS during which people received periodic guidance through divine COVENANTS and COMMANDMENTS, many of which remain basic and timeless. In relation to the Old Testament, it is significant for Latter-day Saints that in September 1823 the angel Moroni quoted a series of Old Testament PROPHECIES when he revealed the location of an ancient record written on GOLD PLATES to the Prophet Joseph SMITH, whose translation yielded the Book of Mormon (JS—H 1:36–41). Moreover, Joseph Smith's extensive labors on the Old Testament and the accompanying revelations to him (June 1830–July 1833), which led to the JOSEPH SMITH TRANSLATION OF THE BIBLE (JST) and certain informative sections of the Doctrine and Covenants, underscore the importance of these scriptural texts. In addition, from the Book of Mormon it is clear that before 600 B.C. the prophet LEHI and his colony carried to the Western Hemisphere from Jerusalem a record on the PLATES of brass that included many Old Testament texts (1 Ne. 5:10–15), leading Lehi and his descendants to look forward to a redeemer (1 Ne. 19:22–23) and giving them a guide for their moral and spiritual development (Mosiah 1:3, 5).

The Old Testament, even by the name Old Covenant, is thus not outmoded in the LDS view.

It contains narrative, wisdom, and prophetic literature from ancient epochs; and even though some "plain and precious" parts have been lost, many of these have been restored in LDS scripture (1 Ne. 13:40). It frames a series of ancient covenants with Jehovah (Jesus Christ) as distinguished from the higher covenants in the New Testament (e.g., Matt. 26:28; Luke 22:20; 1 Cor. 11:25; 2 Cor. 3:6; Heb. 7:22). Latter-day Saints view them all as elements in the same divine PLAN OF SALVATION.

ETERNAL COVENANTS AND COMMANDMENTS. Latter-day Saints feel a need to learn and practice the principles prescribed in all the divine covenants and commandments, which are eternally valid. To know and understand God's eternal purposes requires a study of the past eras documented in the Old Testament, together with those available in other ancient and modern scriptures. For example, Latter-day revelations help Latter-day Saints read the Old Testament with fuller appreciation for the continuity of the eternally significant concepts taught by the prophets in the scriptures.

From the beginning, the divine covenants associated with salvation have been taught through prophetic words, and some have been typified by sacrificial ordinances. A revelation to Moses, restored through Joseph Smith, states that animal sacrifice was required from the days of Adam and Eve (Moses 5:5) and that such sacrifices were "a similitude of the sacrifice of the Only Begotten of the Father" (Moses 5:7).

Another Old Testament covenant verified in modern revelation is the ABRAHAMIC COVENANT. It pertains not alone to literal descendants of Abraham but also to those adopted into Abraham's family because of their faith in the true God and their baptism into the gospel of Christ (Gen. 12:1; Gal. 3:26–29). These "descendants" of Abraham are charged with bringing the blessings of this covenant to all nations, through teaching about the true and living God and making known his plan of salvation (Abr. 2:9–11). Responsibility for knowing and acting in accordance with the covenant of Abraham has been transmitted to latter-day heirs by revelation (D&C 110:12). Moreover, a promise by the resurrected Jesus is recorded in the Book of Mormon that descendants of his ancient covenant people Israel, who have been scattered abroad, shall "be gathered in from the east and from the west, and from the south and from the north; and they shall be brought to the knowledge of the Lord their

God, who hath redeemed them" (3 Ne. 20:13). They are to be established in their lands of inheritance and will accomplish their ancient and culminating responsibility of building the kingdom of the Lord (3 Ne. 20:21–46; cf. Isa. 52:1–15). For Latter-day Saints the RESTORATION "of all things" (Acts 3:21) includes many Old Testament principles, doctrines, and ideals.

TEMPORARY AND ETERNAL LAWS. Latter-day Saints do not believe that when Jesus fulfilled the LAW OF MOSES he thereby abrogated the law, the prophets, and the writings of the Old Testament (3 Ne. 15:5–8). Indeed, he fulfilled the law of sacrifice by allowing his own blood to be shed (Alma 34:13) and by replacing certain ancient worship performances (3 Ne. 12:18–20; 15:2–10). Thus, the feast of Passover became the commemorative sacrament of the Last Supper (Luke 22:1–20): The paschal lamb culminated in the Lamb of God (Ex. 12:5, 21; 1 Cor. 5:7; 1 Pet. 1:19; Rev. 5:6). Sacrifice of animals culminated in Jesus' ultimate sacrifice, of which they were mere types, but the sacrifice of "a broken heart and contrite spirit" continues (3 Ne. 9:19–20; cf. Rom. 12:1).

Jesus reiterated many moral and spiritual laws taught by Moses and the prophets. These include laws regarding REVERENCE for God, respect for parents, CHASTITY in moral conduct, avoiding violence and MURDER, and practicing honesty with fellow beings (e.g., Matt. 5:17–48; cf. 3 Ne. 12:17–48; Luke 16:19–31; 24:13–47). The Book of Mormon prophet ABINADI reiterated the Ten Commandments and was adamant about the necessity of teaching and living according to their standards (Mosiah 12:33–37; 13:12–26). And latter-day revelation confirms the same necessity for any who would please the Lord (e.g., D&C 20:17–19; 42:18–29; 52:39).

For Latter-day Saints, all principles of morality and righteousness taught by Old Testament prophets remain valid. Micah, for instance, asks, "What doth the Lord require of thee, but to do justly, and to love mercy, and to walk humbly with thy God?" (Micah 6:8). The Lord taught through Habakkuk that divinely inspired visions will surely come to fulfillment, even if far off; therefore, "the just shall live by his faith" (Hab. 2:3–4). Moses urged the Israelites to live according to God's laws as good examples to others: "Keep therefore and do them [the laws and ordinances], for this is your wisdom and your understanding in the sight of the nations, which shall hear all these statutes, and say, Surely this great nation is a wise and understanding people" (Deut. 4:6). Jesus appealed to Deuteronomy and Leviticus concerning the first and second commandments, to love God and one's fellow beings (Deut. 6:4–5; Lev. 19:18, 33–34; Mark 12:28–34).

This, however, is not to say that all worship practices admonished in "the law and the prophets" were to be perpetuated eternally. About 150 B.C., the Book of Mormon prophet Abinadi explained, "I say unto you that it is expedient that ye should keep the law of Moses as yet; but I say unto you, that the time shall come when it shall no more be expedient to keep the law of Moses. And moreover, I say unto you, that salvation doth not come by the law alone; and were it not for the atonement, which God himself shall make for the sins and iniquities of his people, that they must unavoidably perish, notwithstanding the law of Moses" (Mosiah 13:27). The risen Jesus rehearsed teachings which he had fulfilled from the law and the prophets, the Psalms and "all the scriptures," to the disciples on the road to Emmaus and to the eleven apostles gathered in Jerusalem (Luke 24:13, 27, 33, 44). Only certain things had an end in him (3 Ne. 15:8; Gal. 3:24).

Latter-day Saints therefore value those Old Testament laws and doctrines that are eternal, believing that they were "given by inspiration of God" and are "profitable for doctrine, for reproof, for correction, for instruction in righteousness" (2 Tim. 3:16).

PROPHETIC ANTICIPATION OF THE MESSIAH. More than five centuries before the time of Christ, JACOB, a Book of Mormon prophet, stated that his people knew of Christ through the teachings of Moses and the prophets, and thus had hope of his coming (Jacob 4:4–5). And NEPHI₁ added, "For this end hath the law of Moses been given; and all things which have been given of God from the beginning of the world, unto man, are the typifying of [Christ]" (2 Ne. 11:4). On another occasion, Jacob said that "all the holy prophets . . . believed in Christ," and that his people faithfully kept the law of Moses, "it pointing our souls to [Christ]." Indeed, they saw in Abraham's offering of Isaac "a similitude of God and his Only Begotten Son" (Jacob 4:4–5). Amulek, a later Book of Mormon teacher (c. 75 B.C.), when speaking of the "great and last sacrifice" of the Son of God, declared that

"this is the whole meaning of the law, every whit pointing to that great and last sacrifice . . . [of] the Son of God" (Alma 34:13–14).

The relevance of prophetic teachings and ordinances for bringing people to Christ is shown by Jesus' own references to such rites and teachings. While coming down from the MOUNT OF TRANSFIGURATION, he spoke to Peter, James, and John about things "written of the Son of man, that he must suffer many things, and be set at nought" (Mark 9:12; cf. Isa. 53:3–7). In his hometown of Nazareth, he announced his fulfillment of Isaiah's prophecy of the Messiah's actions of healing and making people free (Luke 4:21; Isa. 61:1–2). After healing a man on the Sabbath, Jesus told those who would condemn him that the time was nigh that even the dead would hear his voice alluding, no doubt, to prophecies of that event (John 5:25; cf. Isa. 24:22). His parting words to that same audience were, "Had ye believed Moses, you would have believed me: for he wrote of me" (John 5:46; cf. Deut. 18:15–19 and Acts 3:22–23; 1 Ne. 22:21; 3 Ne. 20:23). Even in his last mortal hour, as he suffered and fulfilled the promises of redemption, Jesus quoted the first line of Psalm 22—"My God, my God, why hast thou forsaken me?"—as if to point to the imminent fulfillment of the remaining lines of the Psalm (Matt. 27:46; cf. Ps. 22:7–8, 12–19).

Early Christian missionaries converted many to Christ among those who "searched the scriptures daily" (Acts 17:10–12). Those scriptures included what is now known as the Old Testament. Christian teachers succeeded in showing "by the scriptures that Jesus was Christ" (Acts 18:24–28). PAUL declared that scriptures "written aforetime were written for our learning, that we through patience and comfort of the scriptures might have hope" of salvation (Rom. 15:4).

Concerning Christ's future advent, more than a score of "royal" and "messianic" psalms anticipate the Lord's reign in the final age. Psalms 72 and 100 are typical (see PSALMS, MESSIANIC PROPHECIES IN). Moreover, in the prophetic books of the Old Testament more chapters look forward to his triumphant final reign than point toward his first advent and sacrifice (e.g., Isa. 40, 43, 45, 52, 60, 63, 65; Ezek. 37–48; Dan. 12; Zech. 12–14).

PROPHECIES FOR PRESENT AND FUTURE. For Latter-day Saints, the present era of the gospel of Jesus Christ began not only with Joseph Smith's

FIRST VISION but also with the visits of other divine messengers, who quoted Old Testament prophecies with the promise that they were about to be fulfilled. The angel Moroni quoted to Joseph Smith some of the eschatological prophecies of Malachi, Isaiah, Joel, and—according to Wilford WOODRUFF—Daniel, and promised their fulfillment (JS—H 1:29, 33, 36–41; JD 24:241).

Latter-day Saints use both ancient and modern prophecies to bring the gospel light to the GENTILES so that all can be mutually blessed (Isa. 49:5–22; D&C 86:11; 110:12; 124:9). In the LAST DAYS the God of heaven will set up his kingdom to embrace all people, rolling forth until it fills the earth (Dan. 2:31–45; D&C 65). The Lord "shall bring again Zion" and, in doing so, will publish peace and salvation, proclaiming, "Thy God reigneth!" Then all nations will see the salvation of God (Isa. 52:7–10). All can be a part of ZION, "the pure in heart" (D&C 97:19–21). "Saviours shall come up on mount Zion," as Obadiah said, "and the kingdom shall be the LORD's" (Obad. 1:21; D&C 103:7–10).

BIBLIOGRAPHY

Ludlow, Daniel H. A Companion to Your Study of the Old Testament. Salt Lake City, 1981.

Ludlow, Victor L. Unlocking the Old Testament. Salt Lake City, 1981.

Matthews, Robert J. "A Plainer Translation": Joseph Smith's Translation of the Bible. Provo, Utah, 1975.

McConkie, Bruce R. The Promised Messiah. Salt Lake City, 1978.

Nyman, Monte S., ed. Isaiah and the Prophets. Provo, Utah, 1984.

Reynolds, Noel B. "The Brass Plates Version of Genesis." In By Study and Also by Faith, ed. J. Lundquist and S. Ricks, Vol. 2, pp. 136–73. Salt Lake City, 1990.

Sperry, Sidney B. The Voice of Israel's Prophets. Salt Lake City, 1965.

———. The Spirit of the Old Testament. Salt Lake City, 1970.

ELLIS T. RASMUSSEN

OMNIPOTENT GOD; OMNIPRESENCE OF GOD; OMNISCIENCE OF GOD

The Church of Jesus Christ of Latter-day Saints uses the familiar terms "omnipotent," "omnipresent," and "omniscient" to describe members of the GODHEAD.

OMNIPOTENCE. The Church affirms the biblical view of divine omnipotence (often rendered as "almighty"), that GOD is supreme, having power over all things. No one or no force or happening can frustrate or prevent him from accomplishing his designs (D&C 3:1–3). His power is sufficient to fulfill all his purposes and promises, including his promise of ETERNAL LIFE for all who obey him.

However, the Church does not understand this term in the traditional sense of absoluteness, and, on the authority of modern REVELATION, rejects the classical doctrine of CREATION out of nothing. It affirms, rather, that there are actualities that are coeternal with the persons of the Godhead, including elements, intelligence, and law (D&C 93:29, 33, 35: 88:34–40). Omnipotence, therefore, cannot coherently be understood as absolutely unlimited power. That view is internally self-contradictory and, given the fact that evil and suffering are real, not reconcilable with God's omnibenevolence or loving kindness (see THEODICY).

OMNIPRESENCE. Since Latter-day Saints believe that God the Father and God the Son are gloriously embodied persons, they do not believe them to be bodily omnipresent. They do affirm, rather, that their power is immanent "in all and through all things" and is the power "by which all things are governed" (D&C 88:6, 7, 13, 40–41). By their knowledge and power, and through the influence of the Holy Ghost, they are omnipresent.

OMNISCIENCE. Latter-day Saints differ among themselves in their understanding of the nature of God's knowledge. Some have thought that God increases endlessly in knowledge as well as in glory and dominion. Others hold to the more traditional view that God's knowledge, including the FOREKNOWLEDGE of future free contingencies, is complete. Despite these differing views, there is accord on two fundamental issues: (1) God's foreknowledge does not causally determine human choices, and (2) this knowledge, like God's power, is maximally efficacious. No event occurs that he has not anticipated or has not taken into account in his planning.

BIBLIOGRAPHY

Roberts, B. H. "The Doctrine of Deity." Seventy's Course in Theology, third year. Salt Lake City, 1910.

DAVID L. PAULSEN

ONLY BEGOTTEN SON OF GOD

See: Jesus Christ: Only Begotten in the Flesh

OPPOSITION

Opposition and AGENCY are eternal and interrelated principles in the theology of The Church of Jesus Christ of Latter-day Saints. Agency is man's innate power to choose between alternative commitments and finally between whole ways of life. Opposition is the framework within which these choices and their consequences are possible.

In his account of the FALL OF ADAM, LEHI teaches that the philosophy of opposites is at the heart of the plan of redemption. Had ADAM and EVE continued in a state of premortal innocence, they would have experienced "no joy, for they knew no misery; doing no good, for they knew no sin" (2 Ne. 2:23). Hence, Lehi concludes, "it must needs be, that there is an opposition in all things . . . [otherwise] righteousness could not be brought to pass, neither wickedness, neither holiness nor misery, neither good nor bad" (2 Ne. 2:11).

Latter-day Saints understand that contrast and opposition were manifest in PREMORTAL LIFE as well as on EARTH (Abr. 3:23–28; Moses 6:56) and that the distinction between good and evil is eternal. Prior to earth life the spirits of all men had opportunities to choose God and demonstrate love for him by obeying his LAW (Matt. 22:37) or to yield to satanic proposals for rebellion and coercion (2 Ne. 2:11–15; cf. Luke 16:13; 2 Ne. 10:16). Different, indeed opposite, consequences followed these choices (Abr. 3:26).

Scripture relates the principle of opposition to crucial states of human experience. Among them are life and death, knowledge and ignorance, light and darkness, growth and atrophy.

LIFE AND DEATH. As a consequence of Adam and Eve's partaking of the fruit of the tree of knowledge of good and evil, they and all their posterity became subject to physical death and to the afflictions and degeneration of the mortal body (2 Ne. 9:6–7). They also became subject to spiritual death, which means spiritual separation from God because of SIN. However, through Christ, provision had already been made for their redemption (2 Ne. 2:26), the overcoming of both deaths, and

the return to the presence of God. In the span of eternity, the worst form of death is subjection to Satan and thereby exclusion from the presence of God (2 Ne. 2:29). Christ came to bring life, abundant life, everlasting life with God (John 10:28; 17:3; D&C 132:23–24).

KNOWLEDGE AND IGNORANCE. Opposition was, and is, a prerequisite of authentic KNOWLEDGE, "for if they never should have bitter they could not know the sweet" (D&C 29:39; cf. 2 Ne. 2:15). Such knowledge is participative. Because "it is impossible for a man to be saved in ignorance" (D&C 131:6), the Prophet Joseph SMITH taught, "A man is saved no faster than he gets [such] knowledge" (TPJS, p. 217; cf. 357). One may aspire to all truth (D&C 93:28), but not without confronting the heights and depths of mortal experience, either vicariously or actually.

LIGHT AND DARKNESS. Latter-day Saints find a parallel between light and darkness, the concept of the "two ways," and the idea of the warring "sons of darkness" and "sons of light" apparent in the DEAD SEA SCROLLS. Jesus teaches that "if therefore the light that is in thee be darkness, how great is that darkness!" (Matt. 6:23) and that "he who sins against the greater light shall receive the greater condemnation" (D&C 82:3). Finally, the sons and daughters of God are to reach the point where "there shall be no darkness in [them]" (D&C 88:67).

GROWTH AND ATROPHY. The principle of opposition also implies that people cannot be tested and strengthened unless there are genuine alternatives (Abr. 3:23–25) and resistances. Life is a predicament in which there are real risks, real gains, real losses. From such tests emerge responsibility, judgment, and soul growth. Latter-day Saints believe that this encounter with choice and conditions for progression will continue forever. It follows that in the gospel framework, once one is committed, there is no such thing as neutrality or standing still. Joseph Smith taught, "If we are not drawing towards God in principle, we are going from Him" (TPJS, p. 216).

One may err in religion by attempting to reconcile the irreconcilable; so one may assume opposition when there is none. In some forms of Judaism and Christianity, for example, the view prevails that the flesh and the spirit are opposed and antithetical. PAUL is often cited in this connection. But a close reading of Paul and other writers shows that "flesh" most often applies to man bound by SIN, and "spirit" to one regenerated through Christ. Thus, it is not the flesh, but the vices of the flesh that are to be avoided. And it is not the earth, but worldliness (wickedness) that is to be transcended (JST Rom. 7:5–27). Similarly, Latter-day Saints do not finally pit faith against reason, or the spirit against the senses, or the life of contemplation against the life of activity and service. Only when these are distorted are they opposed, for when the self is united under Christ, they are reconciled.

In the plan of redemption, opposition is not obliterated but overcome: evil by good, death by life, ignorance by knowledge, darkness by light, weakness by strength.

BIBLIOGRAPHY

Roberts, B. H. *The Gospel.* Liverpool, 1888.

———. *Comprehensive History of the Church.* Vol. 2, pp. 403–406. Salt Lake City, 1930.

KAY P. EDWARDS

ORDINANCES

[*This entry consists of two articles:* An Overview, *a general discussion of the nature of ordinances in the broadest sense, and* Administration of Ordinances, *the actual ecclesiastical procedures involved in the authorization and performance of ordinances in the Church.*]

OVERVIEW

The word "ordinance" is derived from the Latin *ordinare,* which means to put in order or sequence; or to act by authorization or command. Members of The Church of Jesus Christ of Latter-day Saints regard religious ordinances not as arbitrarily established but as purposefully instituted by GOD and eternal in scope.

The power to perform ordinances whose validity is recognized by God is inseparably connected with the divine AUTHORITY conferred on mortal man, that is, the PRIESTHOOD of God: "Which priesthood continueth in the church of God in all generations. . . . Therefore, in the ordinances thereof, the power of godliness is manifest. And without the ordinances thereof, and the authority of the priesthood, the power of godliness is

not manifest unto men in the flesh" (D&C 84:17, 20–21).

Ordinances in the Church contain instructions and rich SYMBOLISM. Anointing with consecrated OIL (e.g., as in the TEMPLE) is reminiscent of the use of sacred oil in the coronation of kings and the calling of PROPHETS in ancient days. Laying hands on the head of the sick symbolically suggests the invocation and transmission of power from on high. The "waters of baptism" richly symbolize the actuality of new birth.

Latter-day scriptures give ample evidence that God has established unchangeable, eternal ordinances as essential elements of the PLAN OF SALVATION and redemption (Isa. 24:5; Mal. 3:7; Alma 13:16; D&C 124:38). The Prophet Joseph SMITH taught that "the ordinances of the Gospel . . . were laid out before the foundations of the world" and "are not to be altered or changed. All must be saved on the same principles" (*TPJS,* pp. 367, 308).

A biblical example of the necessity of ordinances can be found in the Lord's statement to Nicodemus that one must "be born again" (John 3:3). The Prophet Joseph Smith taught that "being born again comes by the spirit of God through ordinances" (*TPJS,* p. 162). The process of salvation is experienced as a "mighty change in your hearts" (Alma 5:14) under the guidance and assistance of the Spirit of God through keeping the divine ordinances. The test of obedience is reiterated in modern times, a pattern that is said to apply "in all cases under the whole heavens." One is fully accepted of God and is "of God" if, and only if, she or "he obey mine ordinances" (D&C 52:14–19). Some ordinances are universal in nature (cf. Lev. 18:4; Rom. 13:2; Alma 30:3; D&C 136:4), while others are rites and ceremonies decreed for special purposes within the Lord's work (e.g., Num. 18:8; Heb. 9:10; Alma 13:8; D&C 128:12).

Ordinances, in the sense of rituals and ceremonies, embrace the entire mortal life of God's sons and daughters and are performed by the Lord's authorized representatives, the bearers of his priesthood. Indeed, ordinances are the visible aspect of priesthood efficacy, the operation of proper divine authority conferred upon mortal man.

Some ordinances are prerequisite for entering celestial glory (BAPTISM, GIFT OF THE HOLY GHOST) and for EXALTATION (priesthood ordination, temple endowment, celestial marriage). Each human who lives, who has ever lived, or who will yet live upon the earth has need of these ordinances. Therefore, ordinances are to be performed vicariously in behalf of those who had no opportunity to receive them during their mortal lives.

Other ordinances enhance the physical, emotional, and spiritual welfare of their recipients though they may not be prerequisites for celestial glory or entering into the actual presence of God the Father. Such additional ordinances include the naming of children, confirmation, consecration of oil, dedication of buildings, and dedication of graves. Administering to the sick contributes to health and well-being and to emotional relief and comfort. Spiritual guidance is provided by the bestowal on children of patriarchal and paternal blessings. Vital COVENANT renewal occurs in partaking of the SACRAMENT, when one makes a solemn commitment to conduct one's self appropriately as a bearer of the name of Christ, to always remember him, and to keep the commandments that he has given. Such obedience increases susceptibility to the guidance and sanctification of the Spirit.

Ordinances reflect the truth that the Lord's Church is a house of order. They also remind members of their standing in God's kingdom on earth.

Not only should the one performing an ordinance qualify to do so, but those receiving the ordinance should prepare themselves for the occasion. The fourth ARTICLE OF FAITH says, "We believe that the first principles and ordinances of the Gospel are: first, Faith in the Lord Jesus Christ; second, Repentance; third, Baptism by immersion for the remission of sins; fourth, Laying on of hands for the gift of the Holy Ghost." These initiatory steps are in precise and divinely appointed sequence, and by following them one moves "from grace to grace" as did the Son of God himself (D&C 93:13; cf. Luke 2:52). Indeed, modern revelation teaches, "If a man gets the fulness of the priesthood of God, he has to get it in the same way that Jesus Christ obtained it, and that was by keeping all the commandments and obeying all the ordinances of the House of the Lord" (TPJS, p. 308).

When ordinances are performed with authority and power, they are followed by divine blessings. They have "efficacy, virtue, [and] force"

(D&C 132:7). They are enlightening to the mind and enlivening to the whole soul (JS—H 1:74). The first man, after he entered the process of baptism, was "quickened in the inner man" (Moses 6:65). Ordinances unify man with God, and man with man: "Behold, thou art one in me, a son of God; and thus may all become my sons" (Moses 6:68).

BIBLIOGRAPHY
Smith, Joseph F. GD.

IMMO LUSCHIN

ADMINISTRATION OF ORDINANCES

Ordinances performed in The Church of Jesus Christ of Latter-day Saints are to "be done in order" (D&C 20:68) by one who is ordained. The common linguistic root of the words "ordinance," "order," and "ordain" implies fixed succession, privilege, right, and solemn responsibility.

The administration of all ordinances presupposes worthiness of the administrator and the recipient. Most are performed by the LAYING ON OF HANDS of one properly ordained. It must be "known to the church that he [the officiator] has authority" (D&C 42:11), which can be traced in a documented line to the source of all AUTHORITY, Jesus Christ. All ordinances are performed in the name of the Son, Jesus Christ, and in the authority of the AARONIC PRIESTHOOD or MELCHIZEDEK PRIESTHOOD. For some ordinances, such as BAPTISM and administration of the SACRAMENT, the scriptures prescribe exact words. For others, such as administration to the sick, the pronouncement of the recipient's name and a statement of the authority of the officiator are followed by a spontaneous blessing as inspiration directs.

Ordinances that are essential to SALVATION must be performed under the direction of those who hold the KEYS to assign the administration (see Heb. 5:4; cf. D&C 132:7). The validity of ordinances performed, and their divine ratification or SEALING, require this approval.

In harmony with biblical precedent and latter-day commandment, all saving and exalting ordinances, from baptism to temple MARRIAGE, are performed in the presence of WITNESSES, and a proper and faithful record is made and kept in the archives of the Church (2 Cor. 13:1; cf. D&C 128:2–5). Thus, ordinances become "a law on earth and in heaven" and, unless the COVENANTS are violated, they cannot be annulled, "according to the decrees of the great Jehovah" (D&C 128:6–10).

BIBLIOGRAPHY
Melchizedek Priesthood Handbook. Salt Lake City, 1989.

IMMO LUSCHIN

ORDINATION TO THE PRIESTHOOD

Ordination to the priesthood is required in The Church of Jesus Christ of Latter-day Saints of all who administer the ORDINANCES of the gospel of Jesus Christ.

The pattern of ordaining men to PRIESTHOOD OFFICES and CALLINGS is found in the Bible as well as in sacred history. Joshua was ordained by MOSES (Num. 27:18–23), and Christ chose and ordained his APOSTLES (John 15:16). Latter-day Saints believe these ordinations involved the LAYING ON OF HANDS. The sequence of ordaining ancient prophets and thereby transmitting author-

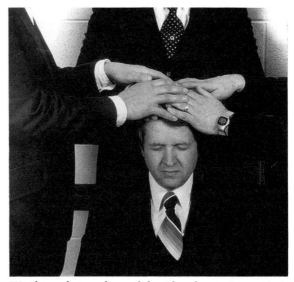

Worthy male members of the Church are given priesthood authority and ordained to offices within the priesthood by the laying on of hands by those in authority (A of F 5). Photograph, 1982; courtesy Floyd Holdman.

Christ Ordains the Apostles (detail), by Harry Anderson (1964, oil on canvas, 5' × 12'). Christ called and ordained twelve apostles early in his Galilean ministry (Matt. 10:1–4). "Ye have not chosen me, but I have chosen you, and ordained you, that ye should go and bring forth fruit, and that your fruit should remain" (John 15:16). Church Museum of History and Art.

ity from Adam to Noah is outlined in modern REVELATION (D&C 84:6–16; 107:40–52).

LDS officers trace their "line of authority" in steps back to the Lord Jesus Christ. Modern conferrals of priesthood authority are based on the specific historical claim of ordinations under the hands of ancient worthies (see AARONIC PRIESTHOOD: RESTORATION OF; MELCHIZEDEK PRIESTHOOD: RESTORATION OF). Priesthood authority and power from on high can be transmitted by the laying on of hands to all men who qualify for it in a spirit of humility. They who are ordained by an authorized agent of God look upon their ordinations as coming from the Lord himself (cf. Alma 13:1). An 1830 revelation declared in the voice of the Lord, "I will lay my hand upon you by the hand of my servant" (D&C 36:2).

Efficacy of ordination depends not simply upon the formula or words, but upon worthiness and the sanction of the Spirit. One may forfeit his priesthood authority by abusing it. The priesthood is not a domineering power. "No power or influence can or ought to be maintained by virtue of the priesthood, only by persuasion, by long-suffering, by gentleness and meekness, and by love unfeigned" (D&C 121:41).

In LDS understanding, those who are ordained to the priesthood are not an elite or professional priestly class distinct from laymen. They are all laymen. It is taught that "a man must be called of God by prophecy and the laying on of hands" by those who are in authority (A of F 5; cf. 1 Tim. 4:14). "By prophecy" means the right to receive and the power to interpret manifestations of the divine will.

At the age of twelve, all worthy LDS men may receive the Aaronic Priesthood and be ordained to the office of DEACON. At later ages they may be ordained TEACHERS and PRIESTS. Adult male converts are generally ordained priests shortly after BAPTISM. An ordained BISHOP is SET APART to preside over the Aaronic Priesthood and to serve as the PRESIDING HIGH PRIEST of his WARD. He authorizes all ordinations in the Aaronic Priesthood in his ward, which are performed either by a priest or a member of the Melchizedek Priesthood, often the father. Other priesthood holders usually join in the ordination standing in a circle around the seated person and laying their hands on his head. The one serving as voice invokes the authority of the priesthood and the name of Jesus Christ and pronounces the specific ordination, with accompanying words of counsel and promise.

Worthy men eighteen years of age and older may receive the Melchizedek Priesthood and be ordained ELDERS. Men called to presiding positions in the Church such as BISHOPRICS, HIGH COUNCILS, and STAKE PRESIDENCIES, as well as PATRIARCHS and APOSTLES, are ordained high priests.

At the present time only those called to serve as GENERAL AUTHORITIES in a quorum of SEVENTY are ordained to the office of seventy. Members of the QUORUM OF THE TWELVE APOSTLES are ordained apostles. Counselors in the First Presidency generally, but not always, also hold the office of apostle. The PROPHET of the Church is the Senior Apostle. When he becomes the presiding officer, he is ordained and set apart as the PRESIDENT OF THE CHURCH by the Quorum of the Twelve Apostles.

HOYT W. BREWSTER, JR.

ORGANIC EVOLUTION

See: Creation; Creation Accounts; Evolution

ORGANIZATION

[*This entry is divided into two parts:*

Organizational and Administrative History
Contemporary Organization

The first article summarizes 160 years of Church organization and programs, and Contemporary Organization *examines the organization of the Church in 1990. There are separate entries for most major officers and units. See* Auxiliary Organizations *for an overview of subsidiary units that support the work of* Priesthood. *For details of local organization, consult* District, Ward, *and* Stake *entries; see also those associated with* Mission. Correlation of the Church, Administration *reviews more recent efforts to streamline and coordinate all Church curricula and administration.*]

ORGANIZATIONAL AND ADMINISTRATIVE HISTORY

Church organization and administration since 1830 have been the result of the restoration of ancient PRIESTHOOD authority and offices, of decisions made by living PROPHETS receptive to divine revelation, and of practical responses to changing world and Church circumstances. From its inception the Church has been hierarchical, with authority flowing from the PRESIDENT OF THE CHURCH. Most positions are filled by lay members called to serve without remuneration, and members are entitled to sustain or not sustain decisions and officers proposed by their leaders (*see* COMMON CONSENT; LAY PARTICIPATION AND LEADERSHIP).

THE FOUNDATION. Joseph SMITH and Oliver COWDERY received priesthood ordination and baptism under the direction of heavenly messengers in 1829. They then baptized others. This cluster of believers gathered on April 6, 1830, for the formal ORGANIZATION OF THE CHURCH, with Joseph Smith as First Elder and Oliver as Second Elder. Two months later the Church held its first conference and soon established a tradition of semiannual general conferences. From the beginning, Church officers were sustained by conference vote, and members and officials received certificates of membership or ordination from conferences.

During the first two years of the Church, DEACONS, TEACHERS, PRIESTS, and ELDERS constituted the local ministry. "The Articles and Covenants" served as a handbook explaining the duties of these officers (*see* DOCTRINE AND COVENANTS: SECTION 20).

First Presidency and Quorum of the Twelve Apostles (engraving, 1853). Top row: Heber C. Kimball, President Brigham Young, Willard Richards. Apostles (second row) Orson Hyde, Parley P. Pratt, Orson Pratt, Wilford Woodruff, (third row) John Taylor, George A. Smith, Amasa Lyman, Ezra T. Benson, (fourth row) Charles C. Rich, Lorenzo Snow, Erastus Snow, Franklin D. Richards.

A revelation in 1831 instituted the office of BISHOP, initially one for Missouri and another for Ohio. Temporal affairs were their primary stewardship at first; they received consecrations of property in the 1830s, tithes afterward, and cared for the poor. Soon bishops also received responsibility for disciplinary procedures and for the AARONIC PRIESTHOOD. Not until 1839, in Nauvoo, Illinois, did the Church have bishops assigned to local geographical subdivisions called WARDS, under the jurisdiction of the bishop responsible for the larger region.

The office of HIGH PRIEST was instituted in 1831, with Joseph Smith as the PRESIDING HIGH PRIEST over the Church. In 1832 he chose counselors to assist him, initiating what became the FIRST PRESIDENCY. Revelation in March 1833 (D&C 90) gave the presidency supreme authority over all affairs of the Church; their roles at the head of the hierarchy remain essentially unchanged. Late in 1833 a second general officer, the PATRIARCH TO THE CHURCH, was called and ordained.

In 1834 two STAKES—geographic entities—were formed (one in Ohio and the second in Missouri) to direct the operation of BRANCHES (congregations) and local officers. Stakes were led by a three-man STAKE PRESIDENCY and a twelve-member HIGH COUNCIL (D&C 102). High councils arbitrated disputes, investigated and tried charges of misconduct, and generally oversaw local ecclesiastical operations. Outside stake boundaries, members clustered into isolated branches led by elders or priests.

In 1835 the QUORUM OF THE TWELVE APOSTLES and the QUORUM OF THE SEVENTY were organized. The Twelve, subordinate to the First Presidency, were assigned by revelation to preside outside organized stakes as a traveling high council. This included ordaining and supervising other officers of the Church outside stakes, including patriarchs. They were also to direct proselytizing in all lands, assisted by the SEVENTY. The Seventy's presidency of seven, called the FIRST COUNCIL OF THE SEVENTY, were sustained with other GENERAL AUTHORITIES in August 1835.

By 1835 revelations defined two orders of priesthood: the higher, or MELCHIZEDEK PRIESTHOOD, including the offices of high priest, seventy, and elder; and the lesser, or Aaronic Priesthood, comprising priests, teachers, and deacons. PRIESTHOOD QUORUMS in the stakes consisted of up to ninety-six elders, forty-eight priests, twenty-four teachers, and twelve deacons, each with its own presidency except the priests, whose president is a bishop.

In the fall of 1835 the Church published the first edition of the Doctrine and Covenants. The three revelations placed first (now sections 20, 107, and 84) described priesthood and its organization.

Visitations by Moses, Elias, and Elijah in 1836 restored the KEYS OF THE PRIESTHOOD and responsibility to gather scattered Israel and the SEALING powers by which families could be linked for eternity in TEMPLES (see DOCTRINE AND COVENANTS: SECTIONS 109–110). These keys are still the basis for LDS missionary, family history/genealogy, and temple work.

After a mission to Great Britain, in 1839–1841, the Twelve received broadened responsibility, under the First Presidency, for Church government within the stakes as well as outside them, a responsibility they have carried since. In Nauvoo they received temple ordinances and the keys necessary to govern the Church if there were no First Presidency.

To complete Church organization and prepare the women, along with the men, for the temple, in 1842 Joseph Smith organized the women's RELIEF SOCIETY IN NAUVOO. A counterpart of priesthood organization for men, the RELIEF SOCIETY was seen as a more integral part of Church organization than were later AUXILIARY ORGANIZATIONS.

In 1841 Joseph Smith established the office of Trustee-in-Trust to manage Church properties at the general level. The role of bishops in temporal affairs thus became subordinate to that of the Trustee-in-Trust, generally the PRESIDENT OF THE CHURCH. In Nauvoo, and for the next decade after, a Council of Fifty assisted as political and temporal administrators.

The last body in the governing hierarchy to emerge was the PRESIDING BISHOPRIC. Until 1847 the Church had two general bishops, but that year Bishop Newel K. Whitney became Presiding Bishop. When his successor (1851), Bishop Edward Hunter, received two regular counselors in 1856, the three constituted the first full Presiding Bishopric. Initially, the Presiding Bishopric's primary responsibility was the overall management of temporal affairs, including the supervision of ward bishops in their temporal duties. Beginning in the 1850s, the Presiding Bishopric also oversaw Aaronic Priesthood matters.

The First Presidency, Twelve, Seventy, and Presiding Bishopric—all dating from this first generation—continue to be the main administrative officers of the Church. These General Authority offices are generally life-tenured callings except in cases of calls to a higher position or removal for cause or health problems, though emeritus status has recently been introduced. The Second Quorum of the Seventy is comprised of men called to serve a five-year period. Between 1941 and 1976 additional General Authorities known as ASSISTANTS TO THE TWELVE also served. The office of Patriarch to the Church, which earlier had

The Council House, Salt Lake City, completed in 1850, was one of the early public and church buildings in Utah. The territorial legislature met here; a public library was here; endowments were given here; and for several years the University of Deseret occupied the building. It was destroyed by fire in 1883.

administrative functions, was eventually limited to giving PATRIARCHAL BLESSINGS to Church members outside stakes, and in 1979 was discontinued.

After Joseph Smith's death in 1844, the Twelve Apostles led the Church under the direction of senior apostle and quorum president Brigham YOUNG. In 1847 he was sustained as President in a new First Presidency. SUCCESSION IN THE PRESIDENCY continues to adhere to that basic pattern.

THE PIONEER ORGANIZATION. After migration to the West in the late 1840s, Church organization adapted to facilitate COLONIZATION of the undeveloped Great Basin. Church officers directed the establishment of hundreds of colonies and helped provide settlements with economic, political, judicial, social, and spiritual programs. Often, one of the Twelve presided in larger settlements. Mormon villages combined private enterprise and economic cooperation, with bishops or stake presidents supervising the dispensing of land, building of roads, digging of ditches and canals, and conducting of business ventures (*see* CITY PLANNING; PIONEER ECONOMY). Although civil government gradually assumed an increasing role, the Church remained a significant influence in local and regional affairs throughout the pioneer period.

In a largely cashless economy with little investment capital, Church leaders promoted colonization and industrial enterprises by calling individuals on special missions and by using Church resources to foster community enterprises. A Church public works program, directed by the First Presidency and managed by the Presiding Bishopric, provided employment and helped build the SALT LAKE TEMPLE and TABERNACLE and create other community improvements. In the 1870s Brigham Young directed the organization of UNITED ORDERS, economic endeavors managed by stake presidents and bishops. Since TITHING donations were usually in "kind" rather than cash, local bishops and the Presiding Bishopric directed a gigantic barter and transfer system that paid for needed services, fed public works employees, and assisted the needy.

Much Church effort went toward assisting with immigration to the Great Basin (*see* IMMIGRATION AND EMIGRATION). The PERPETUAL EMIGRATING FUND, a revolving loan fund, helped poorer immigrants, including HANDCART immigrants, make the trek. In the 1860s Church wagon trains were sent from Utah to convey immigrants from the railroad terminus. After they arrived in Utah, the First Presidency and Presiding Bishopric directed immigrants to settlements where they were needed.

In the 1850s and thereafter, the ward became the primary Church organization in the lives of the Saints. In the pioneer era, bishops selected by the First Presidency and priesthood "block teachers" called by bishops were the main ward officers. General Authorities maintained contact through semiannual general conferences in Salt Lake City, visits to the settlements, DESERET NEWS articles, and epistles.

Missionary work, most of it outside the Great Basin, also had to be organized. In 1850 several of the Twelve opened new missions in Europe. Usually an apostle residing in Britain supervised all European missionary work. Missions were divided into conferences, districts, and branches, each with a president selected by the line officer above him.

During the 1860s and 1870s auxiliary organizations started locally and then became general Church organizations under the supervision or presidency of General Authorities. These included SUNDAY SCHOOLS; the RETRENCHMENT ASSOCIATION, predecessor to the Young Ladies' Mutual Improvement Association (YLMIA; *see* YOUNG WOMEN); the Young Men's Mutual Improvement Association (YMMIA; *see* YOUNG MEN); and the PRIMARY for children. Relief Society for women was revived in Utah and established throughout the Church beginning in 1867.

In 1877 President Brigham Young implemented a massive reordering of wards, stakes, and priesthood quorums. This reform removed the Twelve from local leadership assignments, created new quorums for elders and Aaronic Priesthood, expanded the role of bishops as ward leaders, gave stakes increased responsibility, and, for the first time, involved most young men in Aaronic Priesthood offices. These and other changes at that time, such as quarterly stake conferences and reporting procedures, remained standard for nearly a century.

During the changes of 1877, Elder Orson PRATT explained the Church's organizational flexibility in terms that also foreshadowed future developments:

> To say that there will be a stated time, in the history of this church, during its imperfections and weaknesses, when the organization will be perfect, and that there will be no further extension or addition to the organization, would be a mistake. Organization is to go on, step after step, . . . just as the people increase and grow in the knowledge of the principles and laws of the kingdom of God [*Deseret News Weekly*, July 18, 1877].

Led by PROPHETS, SEERS, AND REVELATORS, the Church has exhibited its flexibility in adapting to changing needs and circumstances.

ELABORATION AND CONTINUITY. The Church faced the 1880s with a well-developed and well-functioning organization; in addition, it was beginning to create auxiliary organizations for children and youth. Over decades these would mature and be fine-tuned to function more effectively in an increasingly complex world.

Church pioneering institutions also remained. During the 1880s and 1890s, the Church continued to direct colonization and economic development (*see* ECONOMIC HISTORY OF THE CHURCH). Building on the cooperative movement of the 1860s and the united orders of the 1870s, by the 1880s the First Presidency was coordinating development and regulated economic competition through a central Board of Trade and similar stake boards. During this period as well, revelations to President John TAYLOR initiated a revitalization of quorums of Seventy and moved these quorums toward becoming stake rather than general Church entities.

Federal prosecutions of polygamists during the 1880s disrupted Church administration as General Authorities, stake presidents, and bishops went into hiding or left Utah (*see* ANTIPOLYGAMY LEGISLATION). Franklin D. Richards, an apostle whose plural wife had died, carried on many of the public functions of general Church leadership under the direction of the First Presidency, who were in hiding. With general Church ownership of property severely restricted, stakes, wards, and individuals formed nonprofit associations to hold Church property, including temples, meetinghouses, tithing houses, and livestock. After the MANIFESTO OF 1890 and the granting of amnesty,

Church leaders resumed their full administrative duties.

During the 1880s stake boards or committees were created for YMMIA, YLMIA, Relief Society, Primary, and Sunday School to promote and supervise auxiliary work locally. In 1889 the Relief Society began holding conferences in connection with the Church's general conferences, as did the Primary. By 1902 each of the auxiliaries was publishing its own magazine.

Though an extensive bureaucracy was not necessary until rapid international growth began in the 1960s, between 1900 and 1930 the Church modernized management and constructed important new facilities. The Church acquired HISTORICAL SITES, supported HOSPITALS, established recreation centers in local meetinghouses, and erected new offices in Salt Lake City, including a Bishop's Building (1910) for the Presiding Bishopric and auxiliary organizations, and the Administration Building (1917), in which the First Presidency and Quorum of the Twelve still have their offices. Zions Securities Corporation was created to manage taxable Church properties, and the Corporation of the President was established to oversee ecclesiastical properties.

Church leaders also attended to programs for youth. Early CORRELATION efforts saw the autonomy of Church auxiliaries decline as the Church assumed greater control over auxiliary magazines; the YMMIA's IMPROVEMENT ERA became a magazine for priesthood and Church readership. In 1911 the Church adopted the Boy Scout program as part of the YMMIA (*see* SCOUTING). In response to the secularization of Utah schools during the late nineteenth century, the Church had created stake ACADEMIES and conducted religion classes after school for elementary-school children. By 1910 a General Board of Education supervised thirty-four stake academies; Brigham Young College in Logan, Utah; Latter-day Saint University in Salt Lake City; and BRIGHAM YOUNG UNIVERSITY in Provo, Utah. By the 1920s the Church had closed most of its academies or transferred them to the state. Starting in 1912 released-time SEMINARIES provided religious instruction for high school students. In 1926 the first INSTITUTE OF RELIGION for college students opened adjacent to the University of Idaho (*see* CHURCH EDUCATIONAL SYSTEM).

Correlation efforts also extended to the work of priesthood, including missionary work, and to auxiliaries. A Priesthood Committee on Outlines

Construction on the Gardo house began under the direction of Brigham Young and was completed during John Taylor's administration. The Gardo house was the official Salt Lake residence of President John Taylor, and it was used by President Wilford Woodruff as a Church office. Begun under direction of Brigham Young for one of his wives, it was eventually purchased from the Church by the Federal Reserve Bank of San Francisco. It was razed in 1921. Photographer: Albert Wilkes. Courtesy Utah State Historical Society.

began publishing lesson materials for each priesthood quorum during a priesthood revitalization movement (1908–1922). Church leaders also grouped deacons, teachers, and priests by age and defined their duties more fully; instituted weekly ward priesthood meetings, conducted by the bishops; and improved ward (formerly "block") teaching. After 1923 members of the Quorum of the Twelve directly supervised Melchizedek Priesthood work while the Presiding Bishopric supervised the Aaronic Priesthood, and in 1928 the Church published its first Melchizedek Priesthood handbook. A Priesthood-Auxiliary Movement, in 1928–1937, made Sunday School the instructional arm and YMMIA the activity arm of priesthood. This plan defined auxiliaries as aids to the priesthood and made the adult Gospel Doctrine class in Sunday School an integral part of adults' Sunday activity. Junior Sunday School for children became part of the Sunday School program Churchwide in 1934.

The Presiding Bishopric began providing aggressive leadership to Aaronic Priesthood work and to the YMMIA in 1938, and shortly thereafter they were given supervision of the young women. They provided counsel to bishops and stake presidents on Aaronic Priesthood, buildings, records and reports, and ward teaching through a weekly bulletin, *Progress of the Church.*

Beginning in 1925 a mission home in Salt Lake City provided training for new full-time missionaries. During the 1920s radio and motion pictures first helped missionaries convey the LDS message. Stake missionary work (part-time proselytizing by local members), started locally by 1915, was supervised by the First Council of Seventy after 1936. In 1937 the first missionary handbook was published, and in 1952 missionaries began using *A Systematic Program for Teaching the Gospel,* the Church's first official proselytizing outline. In 1954 a Missionary Committee, under General Authorities, began overseeing missionary appointments, the mission home in Salt Lake City, and publicity and literature. A Language Training Mission for full-time missionaries called to foreign lands opened in 1961 at Provo, Utah, and in 1978 it was expanded to become a MISSIONARY TRAINING CENTER for most new missionaries. Eventually Mission Training Centers were established in other countries; collectively these provide intensive training in dozens of languages.

In 1936, to ease hardships caused by the Great Depression, the First Presidency introduced the Church Security Program. Renamed the Welfare Program in 1938, it established through existing priesthood channels a network of farms, canneries, and factories that sent food, clothing, furniture, and household goods to BISHOP'S STOREHOUSES to assist the needy and, later, disaster victims. Soon after World War I, the Relief Society developed a SOCIAL SERVICES department to help families. This was gradually expanded to provide professional assistance, available through priesthood leaders, in such matters as counseling, therapy, and adoptive services. Eventually Social Services joined health services, employment bu-

reaus, and other guidance programs as part of WELFARE SERVICES.

To meet the needs of LDS servicemen far from home wards and stakes, the Church responded with servicemen's groups on military bases, LDS chaplains, servicemen's coordinators, a Military Relations Committee, servicemen's conferences, seminars to prepare young men for the service, and an English-speaking servicemen's stake in West Germany (*see* MILITARY AND THE CHURCH). NATIVE AMERICANS also received renewed administrative attention. An Indian mission was formed in 1936 in the American Southwest, a general-level Indian Committee in the late 1940s, and the INDIAN STUDENT PLACEMENT SERVICES beginning in 1947.

CHALLENGES OF GROWTH AND INTERNATIONALIZATION. Between 1960 and 1990, Church membership more than quadrupled, with especially rapid growth outside the United States. Many organizational developments during these decades were designed to streamline operations, enhance communication and leadership training, and focus resources on the needs of Church members far from headquarters.

First Presidency (1901–1910). Left to right: President Joseph F. Smith, second counselor Anthon H. Lund, first counselor John R. Winder. Courtesy Rare Books and Manuscripts, Brigham Young University.

The Church Administration Building, at 47 East South Temple Street, Salt Lake City, completed in 1917, serves as the main office building for the Church President, his counselors, the Quorum of the Twelve Apostles, and other General Authorities.

By the 1960s three kinds of organizations were operating within the Church: (1) an ecclesiastical system under a priesthood chain of command; (2) auxiliaries, each with its own general officers, manuals, conferences, and publication; and (3) professional services and departments for education, social work, legal affairs, building, communications, accounting, etc. Early in the 1960s, efforts began to correlate these organizations. A Correlation Committee consolidated and simplified Church curriculum, publications, meetings, and activities. Further elements of the correlation program, implemented in 1964, grouped priesthood responsibilities into four categories: missionary, genealogy, welfare, and home teaching. Ward teaching became HOME TEACHING, giving the priesthood quorums new responsibility for carrying Church programs to LDS families. Wards developed PRIESTHOOD EXECUTIVE COMMITTEES and WARD COUNCILS to coordinate functions and reach out to individuals. In 1965 FAMILY HOME EVENING was established Churchwide and, in 1970, Monday nights were set aside for families; special manuals provided suggestions for gospel-oriented family activities.

Beginning in 1965 all messages from general Church agencies to wards and stakes were funneled into the PRIESTHOOD BULLETIN. Regional publications merged in 1967 into a unified INTERNATIONAL MAGAZINE, published in several languages. In 1971 Church magazines in the United States and Great Britain were restructured with the publication of the ENSIGN for adults, the NEW ERA for teens, and the FRIEND for children. By 1970 the Church had implemented a worldwide translation and distribution organization with publishing and DISTRIBUTION CENTERS in European countries, the Americas, and the Pacific Rim.

Members of the First Council of the Seventy were ordained high priests in 1961 in order to better assist the Twelve in overseeing the growing number of wards and stakes. REGIONAL REPRESENTATIVES and Mission Representatives of the Twelve were called in 1967 and 1972, respectively (and merged in 1974). These officers played a key role in training and advising local leaders, an increasing number of whom were relatively recent converts with little administrative experience.

Spencer W. KIMBALL's presidency (1973–1985) saw important administrative changes, often in the direction of regionalizing responsibilities. Several functions previously reserved for General Authorities were delegated to stake presidents. In 1975 the First Quorum of the Seventy was reinstated as a body of General Authorities; a decade later the office of Seventy became exclusively a General Authority position. Regional Representatives received limited line authority to supervise stake work (1976). In 1978 the Twelve became more directly involved in such ecclesiastical matters as curriculum, activity programs, and Scouting; the Presiding Bishopric retained responsibility for temporal programs but no longer for the youth. To enhance general Church supervision of local operations throughout the world and at the same time facilitate regionalization, in 1984 an AREA PRESIDENCY (a president and two counselors, all of the Seventy) was organized for each of several major geographic areas. As the Church expands, boundaries are redrawn, and the number and importance of area presidencies increase.

Church programs have also been redesigned to meet the needs of an increasingly international membership. During the 1960s a labor missionary program (modeled after one that earlier constructed a college and a temple in New Zealand, and numerous chapels, especially in the South Pacific) helped the Church build meetinghouses in all parts of the world (see BUILDING PROGRAM). In the mid-1970s the Church divested itself of hospitals that benefited primarily residents of the intermountain West and focused increased attention on the construction of chapels and temples world-

The Quorum of the Twelve Apostles (1953): Front (left to right): Joseph Fielding Smith, Harold B. Lee, Spencer W. Kimball, Ezra Taft Benson, Mark E. Petersen, Matthew Cowley. Back (left to right): Henry D. Moyle, Delbert L. Stapley, Marion G. Romney, LeGrand Richards, Adam S. Bennion, Richard L. Evans. The first four became Presidents of the Church in succession (1970–).

wide—this time not by labor missionaries but by professional builders. A consolidated Sunday three-hour meeting schedule for priesthood, SACRAMENT MEETING, and auxiliary meetings was introduced in the United States and Canada in 1980 and later worldwide. By the 1980s a SATELLITE COMMUNICATIONS NETWORK linked headquarters with many local stakes; that, and the widespread use of videotapes, made general conferences and communications from Church headquarters much more accessible. By 1990 much of the training of local leaders had been assumed by area presidencies and regional representatives.

In the 1980s Church financing became increasingly centralized, relieving local units of a major burden. Beginning in 1982 ward and stake buildings were funded fully from general Church funds (from tithes). In 1990 general funds also became the source for financing all local operations in the United States and Canada (*see* FINANCES OF THE CHURCH).

Though the basic administrative officers date from the founding generation, the challenges faced and the way the Church organizes itself to meet those challenges have changed dramatically. Such changes will continue. As President John Taylor said in 1886, the priesthood must not be fettered by "cast iron rules," for it is "a living, intelligent principle, and must necessarily have freedom to act" as circumstances require (First Council of the Seventy, Minutes, Dec. 15, 1886, Church Archives).

BIBLIOGRAPHY

Allen, James B., and Glen M. Leonard. *The Story of the Latter-day Saints*. Salt Lake City, 1976.

Cowan, Richard O. *The Church in the Twentieth Century*. Salt Lake City, 1985.

Hartley, William G. "The Priesthood Reform Movement, 1908–1922." *BYU Studies* 13 (Winter 1973):137–56.

———. "The Priesthood Reorganization of 1877: Brigham Young's Last Achievement." *BYU Studies* 20 (Fall 1979):3–36.

Quinn, D. Michael. "The Evolution of the Presiding Quorums of the LDS Church." *Journal of Mormon History* 1 (1974):21–38.

Widtsoe, John A. *Priesthood and Church Government.* Salt Lake City, 1954.

WILLIAM G. HARTLEY

CONTEMPORARY ORGANIZATION

Members of The Church of Jesus Christ of Latter-day Saints believe that certain organizational principles, laws, and arrangements are divinely inspired. As evidence of this they point to callings and offices in the contemporary organization of the Church (e.g., prophet, apostle, the seventy, and evangelist or patriarch) that were also present in the early Christian church. Several early revelations, including the original articles of Church organization and government (D&C 20) and the revelation on PRIESTHOOD (D&C 107), are seen by members of the Church as sources of a divinely inspired organizational pattern. All offices and callings are filled by lay leaders, as the Church has no professional clergy. Even full-time missionaries and GENERAL AUTHORITIES are drawn from the laity (*see* LAY PARTICIPATION AND LEADERSHIP).

PRINCIPLES OF ORGANIZATION. Six basic principles that can be inferred from the revelations have shaped the historical and contemporary organization of the Church.

First is the guiding principle that the Church functions in the context of God's eternal plan. Latter-day Saints believe that God's work and glory is to "bring to pass the immortality and eternal life" of mankind (Moses 1:39). To further this plan, the Church pursues a complex mission that can be described as threefold: (1) proclaiming the gospel of Jesus Christ to every nation, kindred, tongue, and people; (2) perfecting the Saints by preparing them to receive the ordinances of the gospel and, by instruction and discipline, to gain exaltation; and, (3) redeeming the dead by performing vicarious ordinances in the temple for those who have lived on the earth (Kimball, p. 5). The structures, programs, and processes of the contemporary organization of the Church are designed to fulfill one or more dimensions of the Church mission.

The second principle establishes the priesthood of God as the organizing authority of the Church. Structurally, the Church follows a strict hierarchical form, and authority is exercised through priesthood KEYS, which determine who presides over the Church and who directs its affairs at each organizational level. The PRESIDENT OF THE CHURCH is the only person on earth authorized to exercise all priesthood keys. But through his authority different keys are delegated to individuals when they are called and "set apart" to specific positions of priesthood leadership and responsibility.

Third is the principle of presidencies and councils (*see* PRESIDENCY, CONCEPT OF; PRIEST-

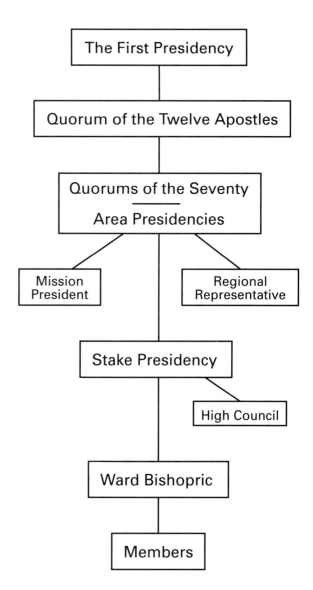

HOOD COUNCILS). Presidents, because they hold priesthood keys and are entitled to the powers of presidency, possess the ultimate decision-making authority for their assigned stewardships. Nevertheless, all presidents are instructed to meet in presidencies and councils to hear various points of view. For example, it is the responsibility of counselors to presidents to give counsel; in Church disciplinary councils, council members may even be assigned to represent competing points of view. The same patterns are observed in the presidencies of the AUXILIARY ORGANIZATIONS, even though no priesthood keys may be involved.

Fourth is the law of COMMON CONSENT. Church leaders are selected through revelation by those in authority. Before new leaders may serve, they must receive a formal sustaining vote from the members whom they will serve or over whom they will preside. When members of the Church sustain leaders, they commit themselves to support these leaders in fulfilling their various stewardships.

Fifth is the principle of orderly administration. The organization of the Church follows prescribed policies and procedures that in the contemporary Church are defined in the GENERAL HANDBOOK OF INSTRUCTIONS, the *Melchizedek Priesthood Handbook*, and other handbooks and manuals for specific programs. An order or pattern is indicated for such procedures as ordinations, ordinances, and blessings; conducting meetings; extending callings and releases to members in various callings in the Church; keeping records and reports; controlling finances; and exercising Church discipline (*see* DISCIPLINARY PROCEDURES).

Sixth, the contemporary organization of the Church continues to change in response to the demands of rapid international growth. New auxiliary organizations and new levels of geographic representation (e.g., REGION and AREA) have been added since the original revelations were received. Nevertheless, the influence of the first five organizing principles can still be seen at every organizational level, in both the ecclesiastical order and the administrative support system of the Church. In this respect, the contemporary organization of the Church is a product of both constancy and change.

Most people experience the organization of the LDS Church principally at the local level, where congregations are organized into WARDS. Although the local ward organization meets most of

First Presidency (1963–1965). Left to right: First counselor Hugh B. Brown, President David O. McKay, and second counselor N. Eldon Tanner.

the religious needs of the members within its boundaries, many specialized services are provided at a higher level. In addition, ward officers are in continuing contact with a hierarchy of priesthood leaders linking them directly to the central authorities in Salt Lake City. Wards are organized into STAKES, stakes into regions, and regions into areas, which constitute the major international divisions of the Church organization. The present article will describe the organization beginning with the most general level and ending with the local wards.

A body of priesthood leaders called the General Authorities heads the organization of the Church. They are full-time ecclesiastical leaders drawn from the laity, and they receive modest living allowances from returns on investments made by the Church, not from the tithes and offerings paid by members of the Church. The General Authorities consist of the FIRST PRESIDENCY of the Church, the QUORUM OF THE TWELVE APOSTLES or Council of the Twelve, the quorums of the SEVENTY, and the PRESIDING BISHOPRIC.

These General Authorities preside over the entire ecclesiastical organization of the Church, from the central headquarters in Salt Lake City, and its area offices in major cities in different parts of the world. They also manage the departments of the central office, which are composed largely of full-time employees who serve the administrative needs of the Church from offices in Salt Lake City and other locations as needed. This administrative support system functions in cooperation with the normal ecclesiastical channels, maintaining clear and direct lines of authority and responsibility between local and general officers of the Church.

THE FIRST PRESIDENCY. The First Presidency is the highest council of the Church, and is composed of the President of the Church and usually two counselors. The First Presidency performs the central and authoritative role of receiving revelation and establishing policies and procedures for the Church. When the President dies, the senior apostle (i.e., the member of the Quorum of the Twelve Apostles with the longest tenure) becomes President of the Church, and he chooses his counselors usually from among the other apostles, without regard to seniority. A new apostle is then chosen to fill the complement of twelve.

Since the First Presidency is a policymaking body, relatively few organizations and departments of the Church administrative support system report directly to it. For example, the various units of the CHURCH EDUCATIONAL SYSTEM (CES), including INSTITUTES and SEMINARIES, report through a Board of Education. Brigham Young University, BYU–Hawaii, Ricks College, the LDS Business College, and several small colleges and schools located outside the United States also report through their boards of trustees.

The Church Auditing Department, the Budget Office, and the Personnel Department report directly to the First Presidency or its committees, as do the advisers to the MORMON TABERNACLE CHOIR and the MORMON YOUTH SYMPHONY AND CHORUS. Although not a part of the Church administrative system, TEMPLE PRESIDENTS likewise report directly to the First Presidency.

THE COUNCIL OF THE TWELVE. The Council, or Quorum, of the Twelve Apostles is a quorum "equal in authority and power" to the First Presidency, meaning that when the First Presidency is dissolved (which occurs upon the death of the President of the Church) the Council of the Twelve exercises all of the power and authority previously reserved to the First Presidency until a new First Presidency is organized (D&C 107:23–24). The Council of the Twelve is presently organized into four executive groups—the Correlation Executive Committee composed of the Council of the Twelve's three most senior apostles; the Missionary Executive Council; the Priesthood Executive Council; and the Temple and Family History Executive Council.

The Correlation Executive Council reviews the work of the three other councils. It also directs the Correlation Department, which evaluates manuals and other materials disseminated to the membership of the Church and conducts research for the General Authorities (see CORRELATION). The Evaluation Division of the Correlation Department includes lay-member committees responsible for reviewing all Church materials, research, and the translation of materials.

The Missionary Executive Council directs the work of the Missionary Department of the Church, which provides support to a worldwide proselytizing effort. It is made up of several major sections, including the Proselyting Resource Division; several MISSIONARY TRAINING CENTERS; the Missionary Operations Division, for handling day-to-day missionary activities; and the Media Division.

The Priesthood Executive Council directs the Priesthood Department and the Curriculum Department of the Church (see CURRICULUM). The Priesthood Department supervises the activities of the MELCHIZEDEK PRIESTHOOD and the auxiliaries of the Church. Among these auxiliary organizations are the PRIMARY (for young children), the YOUNG MEN and YOUNG WOMEN (for youth ages twelve to eighteen), the RELIEF SOCIETY (for adult women), and the SUNDAY SCHOOL. The members of the general presidencies of the Relief Society, Young Women, and Primary are women who are called to serve on a part-time basis, while members of the general presidencies of the Young Men and Sunday School are members of the quorums of the Seventy. The principal role of the general presidencies of the auxiliaries is to train and serve the leaders and members of their respective organizations in the stakes and wards of the Church. The Curriculum Department is responsible for planning, developing, and producing printed, audio, and audiovisual materials for the Church. It includes the Curriculum Planning and Development Division, the Audiovisual Planning and Development Division, the Publications Coordination Division, the Scriptures Coordination Division, and the Church Magazines Division.

The Temple and Family History Executive Council directs the Temple Department, the Family History Department, and the Historical Department of the Church. The Temple Department supervises the operation of the Church's temples throughout the world. The major divisions of the Temple Department are the Recording and Ordinance Procedures Division, the Ordinance Recording Systems Division, and the Audiovisual Services Division. The Family History Department manages the genealogical research done by members of the Church all over the world and assists members in researching their ancestors (see FAMILY HISTORY, GENEALOGY; GENEALOGY). It engages in the acquisition and storage of genealogical records, manages the worldwide system of genealogical libraries, and supervises the preparation of individual names for temple ordinance work. The Historical Department acquires, organizes, preserves, and oversees the use of materials of enduring value to the Church. The department includes the Archives Division, the Library Division (for historical research), and the Museum Division.

Members of the Missionary, Priesthood, and Temple and Family History executive councils also have "first contact" assignments in various areas of the Church. This means that these members of the Council of the Twelve work with specific area presidencies and are ultimately responsible for all the work of the Church in their assigned areas.

THE QUORUMS OF THE SEVENTY. Members of the First Quorum of the Seventy are called to serve usually until they reach seventy years of age, while members of the Second Quorum of the Seventy are normally called to serve for five years. Members of the quorums of the Seventy serve under the direction of the Presidency of the Seventy. The seven presidents of the Seventy presently serve as Executive Directors of, respectively, the Correlation, Missionary, Priesthood (two Executive Directors assigned), Curriculum, Temple, and Family History departments of the Church. Members of the quorums of the Seventy are assigned to serve in area presidencies throughout the world. Area presidencies oversee both the local units and the missions of the Church. Each mission is presided over by a MISSION PRESIDENT, who oversees the proselytizing activities of approximately two hundred missionaries.

Those members of the quorums of the Seventy assigned to the areas of North America work at the general headquarters of the Church in Salt Lake City. They also receive assignments as assistant executive directors over the departments of the Church or as members of general presidencies of the Young Men and Sunday School organizations of the Church.

THE PRESIDING BISHOPRIC. The Presiding Bishopric is made up of three General Authorities— the Presiding Bishop and two counselors— responsible for many of the temporal affairs of the Church. They report directly to the First Presidency of the Church and oversee the WELFARE SERVICES, Physical Facilities, Materials Management, Information Systems, Finance and Records, Investments, LDS FOUNDATION, and Security departments of the Church. The members of the Presiding Bishopric also support directors for temporal affairs assigned to each of the areas of the Church, who oversee all the temporal affairs of the Church in their assigned areas.

The Welfare Services Department is charged with helping members of the Church to care for themselves and for the poor and needy. The department consists of the Employment Services Division, DESERET INDUSTRIES (organized for the employment and rehabilitation of disadvantaged members of the Church), and the Production/ Distribution Division (responsible for the production, processing, and distribution of sustenance to temporarily disadvantaged Church members).

The Physical Facilities Department provides, maintains, and manages Church buildings and sites in the United States and Canada, and provides functional support for Church-owned physical facilities throughout the world. The department is divided into the Architecture and Engineering Division, the Headquarters Facilities Division, the Real Estate Division, and the Temple and Special Projects Division.

The Materials Management Department provides Church members and the local units of the Church with equipment, functional services, supplies, sacred clothing, and published materials.

The divisions of this department include Printing Services, Beehive Clothing (a production facility for articles of sacred clothing), the Purchasing Division, the Translation Division, the Vehicle Fleet Division, and the Food Services Division.

The Information Systems Department provides information services to the administrative departments and the areas, regions, stakes, and wards of the Church. The department is composed of the Client Services Division, the Operations Services Division (Data Center), and the Applications Services Division.

The Finance and Records Department protects the assets and vital administrative records of the Church. It is organized into the Treasury Services, Controller, Tax Administration, Risk Management, and Membership and Statistical Records divisions.

The Investments Department is responsible to the Presiding Bishopric for investment securities and investment properties of the Church and is organized into separate divisions to perform these responsibilities (*see* BUSINESS: CHURCH PARTICIPATION IN).

The purpose of the LDS Foundation is to encourage and facilitate charitable giving to the Church and its programs. The LDS Foundation consists of the Donor Services, Donor Services Support, and Administrative Services divisions.

Finally, the Security Department is charged with providing security for properties at Church headquarters and other locations and personal protection as determined by the First Presidency. The department is organized into divisions responsible for each activity.

THE LOCAL UNITS OF THE CHURCH. The General Authorities oversee the geographical areas of the Church and normally become involved in local Church affairs through regional representatives. Regional representatives, like stake and ward leaders, serve on a part-time basis. All are lay members, and receive no financial compensation from the Church for their services. Regional representatives perform an advisory and training role. Their principal responsibility is to train local Church leaders in their assigned regions, as directed by the Council of the Twelve through the area presidencies.

The local units of the Church are stakes and wards. Stakes are centers of Church activity. The size of a stake may range from 2,000 to 7,000 members, and each stake provides its members with the full range of programs and services of the Church. Each stake is presided over by a STAKE PRESIDENT and two counselors, assisted by a HIGH COUNCIL of twelve or more men. The stake presidency and high council form the Stake Priesthood Executive Committee, which directs all stake activities. The Stake Priesthood Executive Committee is usually divided into the Stake Melchizedek Priesthood Committee and the Stake Aaronic Priesthood Committee. The Stake Melchizedek Priesthood Committee, under the direction of the stake president (chairman) and a counselor in the stake presidency (vice-chairman), supervises Melchizedek Priesthood quorums and trains quorum and group leaders. The Stake Aaronic Priesthood Committee, chaired by the other counselor in the stake presidency, meets to correlate and supervise stake and multiward Aaronic Priesthood programs. Finally, the Stake Council, formed of the members of the Stake Priesthood Executive Committee and the presidents of the stake auxiliaries, meets regularly to coordinate the planning of stake programs and activities.

Wards are the basic ecclesiastical unit of the Church. They normally have between 200 and 800 members and are presided over by a BISHOP and two counselors. The operation of substantially all the programs of the Church takes place in wards. Moreover, all Aaronic Priesthood quorums are ward quorums, in contrast to Melchizedek Priesthood quorums, which are primarily supervised by stakes. The organization of wards resembles the organization of stakes, with the BISHOPRIC serving as the presidency of the ward and the Ward Priesthood Executive Committee and the WARD COUNCIL serving as the major councils. Ward members meet together frequently for spiritual and social purposes: According to President Harold B. Lee, "Perhaps the most important of all the work done in the Church is done in the wards." In areas where there is a smaller Church membership, members are organized into local BRANCHES and DISTRICTS under the direction of missions, until there is sufficient membership strength to organize them as self-operating wards and stakes.

The contemporary organization of the Church is unique in its complexity and its use of lay members, though experience indicates that many details of that organization are necessarily subject to change. It is the intent of the Church to provide multiple opportunities for its members to serve in formal organizational roles and to perform Christian service, such as visiting the sick, caring for the poor, and serving as missionaries. Accordingly, a ward of 400 members may involve as many as 250 of those members in a variety of ward and stake positions. Members view their positions in the Church as "callings." Those who are in positions of Church authority seek inspiration from God in determining which member should receive a particular calling and then extend the call accordingly. Soon thereafter, the member is sustained by the body of membership that he or she serves, and is then set apart to the position by the presiding authority. Members of the Church expect to serve in a variety of positions throughout their lives. Although some positions are seen to carry greater status—roughly correlated with the ecclesiastical hierarchy—there is no prescribed sequence of Church positions. For example, a man might serve as a stake president and, upon his release, be called as a Sunday School teacher. Members accept such changes as inspired and as new opportunities to serve.

BIBLIOGRAPHY

The Church of Jesus Christ of Latter-day Saints. "Instructions to Bishops." Salt Lake City, Dec. 13, 1967.

Coleman, Neil K. "A Study of the Church of Jesus Christ of Latter-day Saints as an Administrative System, Its Structure and Maintenance." Ph.D. diss., New York University, 1967.

Kimball, Spencer W. "A Report of My Stewardship." *Ensign* 11 (May 1981):5–7.

LEE TOM PERRY
PAUL M. BONS
ALAN L. WILKINS

ORGANIZATION OF THE CHURCH, 1830

On Tuesday, April 6, 1830, under the direction of the Prophet Joseph SMITH, a group of friends assembled in Peter Whitmer, Sr.'s log farmhouse to organize the Church, later named The Church of Jesus Christ of Latter-day Saints (*see* NAME OF THE CHURCH). Whitmer, a German immigrant from Pennsylvania, had come to Fayette, New York, in the Seneca Lake region in 1809. Joseph and Emma SMITH and Oliver COWDERY had lived and worked in the Whitmer farmhouse in 1829 while they completed the translation of the Book of Mormon.

The Organization of the Church—April 6, 1830, by Robert E. Barrett (1989, 36″ × 44″). As instructed by the Lord, Joseph Smith presided over the organization of the Church on April 6, 1830. Six men participated in the organization. About fifty believers and friends were present. Courtesy Robert E. Barrett.

Prior to this date, Joseph Smith and his small but growing group of believers had held meetings regularly in Fayette, Manchester, and Colesville, New York, but April 6 was the day given them by revelation to organize formally as a church, in compliance with laws regulating the creation of new churches in New York State. It appears that the legal requirements were checked and steps taken to comply with New York law prior to the organization. The law required notice on two successive sabbaths, nomination and election of three to nine trustees, and nomination of two members to preside at the election (Carmack, p. 16). These steps assured formal status to the fledgling Church, validating property and ecclesiastical actions in the eyes of the state. Joseph Smith's official history reports his conclusion that the organizers held the meeting agreeable to the laws of the country (*see* JOSEPH SMITH—HISTORY). There is no record of any challenge to the action, and thereafter the Church conducted both religious rites and business transactions on a regular basis.

The organizational meeting commenced with prayer. The small congregation, made up of about fifty men and women, unanimously voted approval to organize a new church and elected Joseph Smith, Oliver Cowdery, Hyrum SMITH, Peter Whitmer, Jr., Samuel H. Smith, and David WHITMER as trustees. They also unanimously elected Joseph Smith and Oliver Cowdery as teachers and first and second elders of the newly organized Church of Christ. Smith ordained Cowdery as an elder of the Church, and in turn Cowdery ordained Smith, even though they had previously ordained each other to the priesthood office of ELDER (*see* MELCHIZEDEK PRIESTHOOD: RESTORATION). The second ordination signified that the two elders were empowered to act in the new Church. They blessed and shared the bread and wine of the Lord's Supper with those present in honor of the special occasion, bestowed the GIFT OF THE HOLY GHOST on each individual member present by the LAYING ON OF HANDS, and confirmed each of those previously baptized as members. Smith and Cowdery called and ordained men to different offices of the PRIESTHOOD. Those present at the meeting enjoyed an unusual outpouring of the Spirit of the Lord. After the spiritual feast, they dismissed the formal meeting. Having authority bestowed upon them, the newly appointed Church officers baptized several persons, including Joseph SMITH, Sr., Martin HARRIS, and Orrin Porter Rockwell. On this day the Prophet Joseph Smith also received revelations to guide the Church (cf. D&C 21).

Important events such as the restoration of priesthood AUTHORITY and the translation and publishing of the Book of Mormon preceded this date, and subsequent revelations and administrative changes defined and expanded Church organization, but Latter-day Saints consider April 6, 1830, as the birthday of the Church.

BIBLIOGRAPHY

Anderson, Richard L. "The House Where the Church Was Organized." *IE* 73 (Apr. 1970):16–19, 21–25.

Carmack, John K. "Fayette, the Place the Church Was Organized." *Ensign* 19 (Feb. 1989):15–19.

Porter, Larry C. "A Study of the Origins of The Church of Jesus Christ of Latter-day Saints in the States of New York and Pennsylvania, 1816–1831." Ph.D. diss., Brigham Young University, 1971.

JOHN K. CARMACK

ORGANIZATION OF THE CHURCH IN NEW TESTAMENT TIMES

Latter-day Saints "believe in the same organization that existed in the Primitive Church, namely, apostles, prophets, pastors, teachers, evangelists, and so forth" (A of F 6). They believe that Jesus Christ bestowed his PRIESTHOOD on those he called and appointed to positions of responsibility in the church he organized. They believe that in the "Primitive Church" a person had to be "called of God, by prophecy, and by the laying on of hands, by those who [were] in authority, to preach the Gospel and administer in the ordinances thereof" (A of F 5, cf. John 15:16; 20:22–23; Acts 6:6; 13:1–3). The Church established by Christ provided for a general leadership composed of apostles and prophets, with each local congregation under the direction of an "overseer," a bishop. The apostles were charged to bear the good news of the GOSPEL OF JESUS CHRIST to all the world and to organize converts into churches or mutually supportive communities of saints.

The latter-day restoration of this administrative structure is distinctive, but shares some features retained also by Protestant and Catholic traditions. It resembles Protestantism in its attempt to return to the basic doctrines and procedures of the early Church. However, it shares a more Catholic conviction of the need for authoritative church leadership and a centralized organization. The Church of Jesus Christ of Latter-day Saints is particularly distinctive in its belief in the leadership of living PROPHETS who guide it through REVELATION.

The LDS position is in agreement with the several allusions to Church structure in the NEW TESTAMENT. In 1 Corinthians 12:28, Paul describes the organization of the Church as "first apostles [*apostoloi*, "sent ones," i.e., representatives, agents], secondarily prophets." In Ephesians 2:20, the Church at Ephesus is said to be "built upon the foundation of the apostles and prophets, Jesus Christ himself being the chief corner stone." Three of the apostles—PETER, JAMES, and JOHN—are clearly a leading group (like a FIRST PRESIDENCY), and Peter seems to lead this group in initiating authoritative action and receiving revelation (Matt. 16:18; Acts 1–5; 8–10). Latter-day Saints regard Peter as the prophet or president of the Church in New Testament times.

The early church also had BISHOPS (*epískopoi*, "overseers, supervisors," 1 Tim. 3:1), ELDERS (*presbúteroi*, Acts 15:22; 16:4; 20:17, where a council of elders is grouped with the apostles), TEACHERS (*didáskaloi*, 1 Cor. 12:28, here mentioned just after the apostles and prophets; Eph. 4:11), DEACONS (*diákonoi,* "servants, helpers," Philip 1:1), and a group of SEVENTY (Luke 10:1) who gave missionary service. All of these offices have LDS equivalents.

However, Latter-day Saints do not claim an exact, one-to-one correspondence between the primitive Church and the restored Church. Continuing revelation provides for continual adaptations of the basic ecclesiastical pattern. For instance, in the early New Testament Church the three leading apostles were part of the council of the twelve, while in the latter-day Church they generally are a separate quorum. In the early Church, elders appear to have been older members of a congregation, while in the LDS Church they are often, or usually, younger men. Deacons and teachers were adults in the primitive Church (1 Tim. 3:12) and in the early LDS Church. In the twentieth-century Church, however, young men ordinarily receive these priesthood offices at the ages of twelve and fourteen. The LDS Church has no officer entitled EVANGELIST (*euaggelistēs,* "good-message announcer") or pastor (*poimēn,* "shepherd," Eph. 4:11–14); but Joseph Smith taught that the evangelist was a PATRIARCH, an official who gives revelatory "fatherly" blessings (*see TPJS,* p. 151); and a pastor, although not an ordained officer in the priesthood, could well be any leader who serves as a "shepherd of the flock" (*MD,* p. 557).

[*See also* Apostasy.]

BIBLIOGRAPHY

Dahl, Larry E., and Charles D. Tate, Jr., eds. *The Lectures on Faith in Historical Perspective.* Provo, Utah, 1990.

See Bruce R. McConkie, *Mormon Doctrine* (Salt Lake City, 1966), for articles on separate offices in The Church of Jesus Christ of Latter-day Saints; Thomas F. O'Dea, *The Mormons,* pp. 174–86 (Chicago, 1957); James Talmage, *The Articles of Faith,* chap. 11, pp. 198–216 (Salt Lake City, 1971); and D. Michael Quinn, "From Sacred Grove to Sacral Power Structure," *Dialogue* 17.2 (1984):9–34.

See *The Interpreter's Dictionary of the Bible* (Nashville, Tenn., 1962), for articles on separate offices from a non-Mormon perspective; F. Agnew, "The Origin of the New Testament Apostle Concept: A Review of Research," *Journal of Biblical Literature* 105 (1986):75–96; and A. Lemaire, "The Ministries in the New Testament: Recent Research," *Biblical Theology Bulletin* 3 (1973):133–66.

TODD COMPTON

ORGAN TRANSPLANTS AND DONATIONS

Because the transplanting of body parts raises some concerns regarding ethics and moral issues, the Church has issued the following statement: "Whether an individual chooses to will his own bodily organs or authorizes the transplant of organs from a deceased family member is a decision for the individual or the deceased member's family. The decision to receive a donated organ should be made with competent medical counsel and confirmation through prayer" (*General Handbook of Instructions,* 11–6).

The transplanting of certain organs is now being done with increasing success. For example, transplantation of the cornea has been done for many years, and now a better than 90 percent chance of vision restoration is expected in cases of blindness due to corneal disease. As successful replacements increasingly occur, more people become aware of the various diseases and disorders that can be treated and cured by transplantation, and more people want to become recipients. According to the American Council on Transplantation, more than 50,000 people benefited from organ transplants in 1989. And according to the Intermountain Transplant Program, "more than 100,000 could benefit if enough organs and tissue were available."

Organs and tissue that can now be transplanted include the cornea, kidney, pancreas, heart, liver, skin, bone, veins, tendons, lung, bone marrow, and blood. Heart and liver donations are immediate matters of life and death. Donated kidneys replace thrice-weekly dialysis treatments. A donated pancreas may "cure" someone's diabetes. Donated eyes provide not only corneas for sight-restoring corneal transplants but also vital eye tissue for other surgical procedures and for research into blinding eye disorders.

According to organizations handling organs for transplantation, only those who meet strict criteria are considered for donors. These criteria include careful testing for infectious diseases, including AIDS. Because of these procedures and advances in transplant techniques, donors and recipients do not face the risks faced a few years ago.

In some instances, as where a kidney is needed, a close relative can serve as a donor. (A healthy person can continue a normal life with one kidney.) In the case of some organs, such as the cornea of the eye, the donated organ usually comes from one who signs a statement indicating a desire to donate organs upon death. In the event of an accident or untimely death, the donor's eyes may then be used with the consent of the family.

BIBLIOGRAPHY

General Handbook of Instructions, 11-6. Salt Lake City, 1989.

WAYNE A. MINEER

ORIGINAL SIN

While The Church of Jesus Christ of Latter-day Saints teaches that the transgression of ADAM and EVE brought death into the world and made all mortals subject to temptation, suffering, and weakness, it denies that any culpability is automatically transmitted to Adam and Eve's offspring. All mortals commit sin, but they will be punished "for their own sins, and not for Adam's transgression" (A of F 2).

IN OTHER FAITHS. The doctrine of original sin as taught traditionally states that, due to the FALL OF ADAM, infants are born tainted with actual SIN, resulting in the "privation of sanctifying grace"; this dogma "does not attribute to the children of Adam any properly so-called responsibility for the act of their father," nor is it a voluntary sin "in the strict sense of the word," yet it is a "real sin" (S. Harent, "Original Sin," in *Catholic Encyclopedia*, 1911 ed., Vol. 11, p. 315). All people, according to this doctrine, except the Virgin Mary and Jesus Christ, inherit an actual, existing personal guilt (*see* IMMACULATE CONCEPTION). A corollary of this belief is the doctrine of INFANT BAPTISM, holding that infants are to be baptized to remove this sin because those who die without baptism remain unsanctified and forever excluded from heaven and the presence of God.

The doctrine of original sin derives from an interpretation given to the writings of Paul, particularly Romans 5:12–21, by some theologians of the second and third centuries. More than any other, Augustine in the fifth century transformed Paul's teachings on the Fall into the doctrine of original sin. His views were adopted as doctrine and formally canonized by the decrees of the Council of Trent in the sixteenth century. According to this view, Adam's sin is considered "original" because it arose with the "origin" of man.

Protestantism largely accepts this doctrine. John Calvin stated: "We believe that all the posterity of Adam is in bondage to original sin, which is a hereditary evil" (R. Reed, *The Gospel as Taught by Calvin* [Grand Rapids, Mich., 1979], p. 33). Protestant views emphasize the inherited nature of the sin, reflecting the German word for "original sin," *Erbsunde* (literally "inherited sin"). Rabbinic Judaism teaches of two inclinations, one evil and one good; and some Jews consider "circumcision as a means of escaping damnation" (Samuel Cohon, *Essays in Jewish Theology* [Cincinnati, Ohio, 1987], p. 265).

IN LDS DOCTRINE. Latter-day Saints believe that infants inherit certain effects of the Fall, but not the responsibility for any sin as a result of Adam's or Eve's transgression. From the foundation of the world, the atonement of Jesus Christ makes amends "for the sins of those who have fallen by the transgression of Adam" (Mosiah 3:11). Therefore, baptism is not needed until children reach a state of accountability, generally at the age of eight years, for little children cannot sin and are innocent (*see* CHILDREN: SALVATION OF CHILDREN). They are redeemed from the beginning by the grace of Jesus Christ (D&C 29:46–47), whose atonement cleanses them of the effects of the Fall (D&C 137:10). The Prophet Mormon wrote the following words of Christ: "Little children are whole, for they are not capable of committing sin; wherefore the curse of Adam is taken from them in me, that it hath no power over them" (Moro. 8:8).

In one account in the Pearl of Great Price, Adam learned that he had been forgiven for his transgression in the Garden of Eden, and that "the Son of God hath atoned for original guilt, wherein the sins of the parents cannot be answered upon the heads of the children" (Moses 6:54). However, as a consequence of the Fall, evil is present in the world and all "children are conceived in sin, [and] so when they begin to grow up, sin conceiveth in their hearts, and they taste the bitter, that they may know to prize the good" (Moses 6:55). Begetting children in marriage is not a sin (cf. Heb. 13:4), but the propensity for sin is inherited.

No mortal person bears the burden of repenting for Adam's transgression. Nevertheless, all inherit the effects of the Fall: All leave the presence of God at birth, all are subject to physical death, and all will sin in some measure. From the moment of conception, the body inherits the seed of mortality that will eventually result in death, but only as a person becomes accountable and chooses evil over good do personal sins result in further separation from God. Thus Adam was counseled: "Wherefore teach it unto your children, that all men, everywhere, must repent, or they can in nowise inherit the kingdom of God, for no unclean thing can dwell there" (Moses 5:57).

BIBLIOGRAPHY

Haag, Herbert. *Is Original Sin in Scripture?* New York, 1969.

McConkie, Bruce R. *A New Witness for the Articles of Faith*, pp. 81–104. Salt Lake City, 1985.

BYRON R. MERRILL

ORIGIN OF MAN

The view of the "origin of man" in The Church of Jesus Christ of Latter-day Saints differs significantly from that in most other modern traditions. Its prime concern is to affirm that humans were created as SPIRITS by and in the image of God, which determined their form and nature long before they became earthly organisms. Questions about what biological or cultural mechanisms might have produced *Homo sapiens* and over what period of time that often dominate secular discussions are of limited interest for Latter-day Saints.

The clearest presentation of the Church position may be a 1909 statement by the FIRST PRESIDENCY entitled "The Origin of Man," where four essential points are made: (1) God created humans (Gen. 1:27–28); (2) God created ADAM, "the origin of the human family" and "the first man"; (3) CREATION was sequential: first spiritual, later physical; and (4) each human body displays the characteristics of the individual premortal SPIRIT that inhabits it. Other ideas included in the statement are that humanity was not "a development from the lower orders of creation" but a "fall" from a higher state of existence; that an understanding of all the details about the origin of man is not vital to one's salvation, although the matter is related to several important truths; that the subject cannot be fully clarified by human learning alone; and that only certain relevant facts are now known, to which the Church adheres.

Subsequent official statements indicate that the details of how Adam became "the first man" are considered not to have been revealed clearly enough to settle questions of process. Emphasized instead is an eternal perspective wherein the individual as an "undeveloped offspring of celestial parentage is capable, by experience through ages and aeons, of evolving into a God" (*IE* 28:1091).

Since the rise of Darwinism in 1860, individual Latter-day Saints, both leaders and members, have occasionally participated in public discussion about EVOLUTION, since the official position of the Church on man's origin is not definitive in all respects. Mormons have expressed a wide range of views that are reminiscent of the well-known debates among Christians. Since a large number of Latter-day Saints entered careers in science early in this century, some have attempted to reconcile scientific facts and ideas with statements from the scriptures and prophetic leaders that are emphasized in the LDS tradition. Others have argued that in this area science merely offers "theories of men" and should therefore be discounted.

Many sympathetic to science interpret certain statements in LDS scripture to mean that God used a version of evolution to prepare BODIES and environmental surroundings suitable for the premortal spirits. For example, one scriptural description of creation says, "the Gods *organized the earth to bring forth* . . . every thing that creepeth upon the earth after its kind" (Abr. 4:25 [emphasis added]). Certain statements of various GENERAL AUTHORITIES are also used by proponents of this idea to justify their opinions.

Other Latter-day Saints accept a more literal reading of scriptural passages that suggest to them an abrupt creation. Proponents of this view also support their positions with statements from scripture and General Authorities (*see* EARTH).

While the current state of revealed truth on the LDS doctrine of man's origin may permit some differences of opinion concerning the relationship of science and religion, it clearly affirms that God created man, that the FALL OF ADAM was foreknown of God and was real and significant, and that the ATONEMENT of Christ was foreordained and necessary to reverse the effects of the Fall. Perhaps because these claims embrace the main doctrinal issues relevant to the condition of man, the description of the actual creation process does not receive much attention from the general membership of the Church or from the authorities.

BIBLIOGRAPHY

Jeffrey, Duane E. "Seers, Savants and Evolution: The Uncomfortable Interface." *Dialogue* 8, Nos. 3/4 (1973):41–75.

"Mormon View of Evolution." *IE* 28 (Sept. 1925):1090–91; reprinted in *MFP* 5:244.

"The Origin of Man." *IE* 13 (Nov. 1909):75–81; reprinted in *MFP* 4:199–206.

Packer, Boyd K. "The Law and the Light." In *The Book of Mormon: Jacob Through Words of Mormon, To Learn with Joy*, ed. M. Nyman and C. Tate, pp. 1–31. Salt Lake City, 1990.

JOHN L. SORENSON

ORTHODOXY, HETERODOXY, HERESY

Concepts of orthodoxy, heterodoxy, and heresy are found in virtually all religious traditions. This is also the case among Latter-day Saints, but with important distinctions that arise from the emphasis placed on individual agency, accountability, behavior, and growth.

The traditional terms "orthodoxy," "heterodoxy," and "heresy" are used rarely by Latter-day Saints. Moreover, in words like "orthodoxy" and "heresy" the stress is on religious belief rather than on religious practice. In the determination of an individual's standing within the LDS tradition, emphasis is placed more on what a member says or does than on what he or she believes. Thus, the terms "orthodoxy," "heterodoxy," and "heresy," in a traditional sense, are less significant to Latter-day Saints.

In general, the word "orthodoxy," which derives from the Greek *orthos*, "straight" or "right," and *doxa*, "opinion" or "belief," means adhering to what is commonly accepted, customary, or traditional. The term "heterodoxy" means not being in agreement with accepted teachings or holding beliefs that go contrary to established norms. The word "heresy," from the Greek *hairesis*, initially was a value-free term based on the word meaning "to choose" or "to act with purposive effort." This term came to mean any school, movement, or religious system of belief that was freely chosen. By the second century A.D., however, "heresy" was used in a strictly negative sense, referring to the doctrine of those who publicly dissented from or denied any of the established teachings of the tradition to which they belonged. The dissenter was thus a "heretic."

The traditional Christian concept of "church" (*ekklēsia*) excluded the concept of private "choice" (*hairesis*). Religious groups characteristically identify certain beliefs and practices that they view as being primary or foundational. On that basis they establish criteria for determining what is deemed acceptable belief and behavior for their adherents, often appealing to an established canon of scripture, to recognized sources of authority, and to the requirements of an organized ecclesiastical structure. How these criteria are interpreted and implemented determines the extent to which deviant belief or practice is allowed or tolerated.

Instead, the Church admonishes its members to use their agency to do all they can to accept and live all the teachings and principles of the gospel of Jesus Christ (Moro. 10:32–33), knowing that they will eventually be held accountable for their choices and, for those who have lived worthily, lay claim to the promises made to them when they entered into covenants with God. Each member, at any given time, may be at any stage in this process. Each is encouraged to grow closer to the Heavenly Father and to emulate the Savior in thought and action. Members are urged to expand their knowledge of truth, grace upon grace, line upon line, and precept upon precept. Provided one continues in this effort, relying on the means of repentance that lead from baptism to eternal life, no rigid conceptual checkpoints or belief requirements are imposed to challenge a person's membership in the Church.

Distinctions arise, however, when worthiness to teach, to preach, to hold office, or to participate in temple worship comes into question. The more a person may influence others by virtue of his or her Church assignments or activities, the greater is the concern about worthiness to serve. In these instances, members are asked if they follow certain basic Church tenets (*see* INTERVIEWS; TEMPLE RECOMMEND). These include, among others, having faith in God the Father and in his Son Jesus Christ, believing in the fundamental concepts set forth in the ARTICLES OF FAITH, acknowledging Joseph SMITH as a prophet of God, and sustaining the current President of the Church, the GENERAL AUTHORITIES, and local Church leaders. They also are asked if they abide by certain prescribed patterns of conduct (*see* PRAYER; RIGHTEOUSNESS; CHASTITY; WORD OF WISDOM; TITHING; FAMILY; CALLINGS; ACTIVITY IN THE CHURCH). The goal is that each Latter-day Saint will obtain a personal

TESTIMONY of all gospel truths and will increasingly understand and live in accordance with those truths.

All members who live the gospel are promised the companionship of the Holy Ghost and personal revelation to help them grow in their knowledge of the Lord and to bring their lives into greater conformity with his will while they work out their "own salvation with fear and trembling" (Philip. 2:12). Thus, there will always be individual diversity within the overall unity of the Church, as each member grows in his or her chosen way in harmony with fundamental principles. Such choice and individuality are looked upon as sources of strength within the tradition so long as individuals remain within the confines of the doctrine of Jesus Christ (3 Ne. 11:31–35), the consistent teachings of the scriptures, and the clear words of the living prophets on what is required of each member to gain his or her salvation and exaltation.

Those who break their covenants or whose conduct brings discredit upon the Church may be dealt with in a DISCIPLINARY PROCEDURE. Occasionally such action may arise when a member publicly disavows certain basic tenets of the faith, actively teaches against Church doctrines, or tries to subvert the work of the Church. However, most disciplinary action is taken because a member's dealings with others are deemed to be morally improper. Virtually every disciplinary action has as its ultimate purpose to assist a member in the difficult process of repentance, which can in time result in his or her being restored to full fellowship in the Church.

BIBLIOGRAPHY

Barlow, Philip L., ed. *A Thoughtful Faith*. Centerville, Utah, 1986.

Bradford, M. Gerald. "On Doing Theology." *BYU Studies* 14 (Spring 1974):345–58.

Widtsoe, John A. "What Is Orthodoxy." In *Evidences and Reconciliations*, pp. 276–78. Salt Lake City, 1960.

M. GERALD BRADFORD

P

PAGEANTS

In the Church, pageants are outdoor theatrical productions that celebrate a place, person, or event in religious history. Some pageants depict the earthly mission of the Savior and his dealings with covenant peoples in Jerusalem and the New World, both before and after his resurrection. Other pageants dramatize some historical aspect of how the Church in this dispensation fulfills its mission of taking the gospel of Jesus Christ to every nation, kindred, tongue, and people (cf. Rev. 14:6).

Most pageants are initiated and sponsored by local Church leaders and carried out by Church members who reside in the area where the pageant is performed. They are usually presented out-of-doors on temporary stages on the site of the event or on or near the grounds of LDS temples. Typically they present a sequence of short but elaborate scenes that unseen speakers narrate over an audio system. The pageants often feature original music prerecorded by a professional orchestra and delivered through an audio system powerful enough to be heard for several hundred meters. Pageant casts consist of businessmen, homemakers, teenagers, children, college students, grandparents, craftsmen, and professional actors whose involvement is voluntary and without remuneration. Each pageant is typically presented for about seven performances to as many as 20,000 people at a single performance. No admission fee is charged.

LDS pageants often feature appropriately costumed casts of as many as 600 performers, and may include live orchestras, choirs, and dancers. Each pageant is different in form as well as content. The "City of Joseph" pageant in Nauvoo, Illinois, is a conventional musical play. The Calgary (Canada) Nativity Pageant in December portrays how the Savior's birth is a blessing to all peoples. "The Man Who Knew," in Clarkston, Utah, is a narrative drama about the life of Martin HARRIS.

The CUMORAH PAGEANT, near Rochester, New York, has been presented at the hill CUMORAH since 1937. It depicts how Joseph SMITH learned about and acquired the plates of gold from which the Book of Mormon was translated and it presents a dramatized sampling of some of the epic events and prophecies described in them. Cast members include young adults called from other areas of the Church to participate in the July–August productions. Other pageants, such as at the Manti, Utah, or Oakland, California, temples, depict the restoration of the gospel. The Mesa, Arizona, pageant presents the story of the Savior's life. Other pageants are performed in Independence, Missouri; Castle Valley, Utah; and Auckland, New Zealand.

LAEL J. WOODBURY

PALMYRA/MANCHESTER, NEW YORK

The Palmyra/Manchester area of New York is significant to the LDS Church because the Joseph SMITH, Sr., family settled there in 1816, and the hill CUMORAH, from which came the gold plates of the Book of Mormon, is nearby. Many events in early Church history occurred in the vicinity, including Joseph Smith's FIRST VISION, and also the visits of the ANGEL MORONI leading to the translation and publication of the Book of Mormon in Palmyra. A number of persons, including Martin HARRIS, Oliver COWDERY, and E. B. Grandin, prominent in the early scenes of the Church, also lived in the vicinity. Four revelations now published in the Doctrine and Covenants were received in the area (see D&C 2, 19, 22, 23).

The Joseph Smith, Sr., family arrived in the village of Palmyra, New York, in 1816 from their home in Norwich, Vermont. By the fall of 1817 they made a down payment on a 100-acre farm two miles south of the village in the adjoining township of Farmington (which became Manchester in 1822). During the winter of 1817–1818, they began the construction of a log house, which was completed by the fall of 1818 (Enders, p. 16). A 1982 archaeological dig revealed the exact location of the log cabin on the southern edge of Palmyra township (Berge, pp. 24–26).

In the early spring of 1820, Joseph Smith, Jr., sought the Lord in prayer and experienced the First Vision, in a grove of trees near the home, and three years later, on the evening of September 21–22, 1823, the angel Moroni visited him in the log cabin and gave him instructions about the coming forth of the Book of Mormon. The hill Cumorah where Joseph first viewed the gold plates and received annual visits from Moroni is about three miles to the southeast, on the Canandaigua Road.

From 1822 to 1826 the Smiths built a frame house in Manchester; and in January 1827 Joseph and his new bride, Emma Hale Smith, came to that home to work on the farm. Attempts to steal the gold plates required their being concealed both under the hearthstone of the house and in the cooper's shop.

The Book of Mormon was printed by Egbert B. Grandin in his Palmyra Bookstore, with Martin Harris's mortgaged farm guaranteeing that the printing costs would be met. With the organization of the Church on April 6, 1830, at Fayette, the Manchester/Palmyra area was identified as one of three branches.

The Church still has interest in the area, maintaining VISITORS CENTERS in the Grandin printing shop and bookstore; at the Smith farm and SACRED GROVE; and also at the hill Cumorah, where an appropriate monument and building have been erected, and where an annual pageant is held. A portion of the Martin Harris farm is also owned by the Church. Members of the Smith family and others prominent in the early history of the Church are buried in the cemeteries of the area.

[See also History of the Church, c. 1820–1831; New York: Early LDS Sites in.]

BIBLIOGRAPHY

Berge, Dale L. "Archaeological Work at the Smith Log House." Ensign 15 (Aug. 1985):24–26.

Enders, Donald L. "A Snug Log House": A Historical Look at the Joseph Smith, Sr., Family Home in Palmyra, New York." Ensign 15 (Aug. 1985):14–23.

Porter, Larry C. "A Study of the Origins of The Church of Jesus Christ of Latter-day Saints in the States of New York and Pennsylvania, 1816–1831." Ph.D. diss., Brigham Young University, 1971.

LARRY C. PORTER

PAPYRI, JOSEPH SMITH

The term "Joseph Smith papyri" refers narrowly to twelve extant pieces of the Egyptian papyrus that the Prophet Joseph Smith acquired from Michael H. Chandler in July 1835. Located in the Church Archives, these fragments range in size from 7.5 in. x 12.5 in. to 6.5 in. x 4.5 in. Facsimile No. 1 in the BOOK OF ABRAHAM came from one of these fragments. Broadly, the term also refers to Facsimiles Nos. 2 and 3 in the same book and to papers and all the Egyptian materials of the KIRTLAND period of Church history containing small sections of copied papyrus text. The discovery and transmission of the mummies and papyri are discussed in BOOK OF ABRAHAM: ORIGIN.

The origin of the ancient writings is fascinating to trace. In 1798 Napoleon's Egyptian conquest reawakened Europe to Egypt's treasures. One Italian collector, Antonio Lebolo, excavated in Egypt between 1817 and 1821. In 1820 he worked at

Thebes, near El Gourna; Chandler said that Lebolo's mummies came from there (Todd, pp. 45, 130). About 1822 Lebolo returned to Italy, where he died on February 19, 1830. In 1831 his son Pietro investigated why shipping merchant Albano Oblasser had not reimbursed him for eleven mummies. In 1833 Pietro authorized Francesco Bertola, in Philadelphia, to sell eleven mummies that Oblasser had sent to a partnership in New York (Peterson, pp. 145–47).

How Chandler obtained his possessions is not known. It is known that Lebolo mummies and papyri were exhibited in Philadelphia (April–May 1833) and Baltimore. By September 1833, six had been shown in Harrisburg and one had been publicly dissected in Philadelphia. In June of 1835, four mummies and papyri were exhibited at Cleveland, twenty miles southwest of Kirtland (Todd, pp. 108–143).

In early July 1835, Chandler visited Kirtland, where he met Joseph Smith and inquired "if he had a power by which he could translate the ancient Egyptian. Mr. Smith replied that he had" (P. Pratt, *Millennial Star*, July 1842). Chandler presented some hieroglyphics, which others suppos-

edly had interpreted. Joseph Smith left and returned with a written English translation corresponding to the interpretation Chandler had already received. The Prophet displayed interest in the papyri, but Chandler would not break up his exhibit. Shortly thereafter, Church members purchased for $2,400 "four human figures . . . with two or more rolls of papyrus" (*HC* 2:235). Oliver COWDERY remembered that it was "two rolls . . . [with] two or three other small pieces," the text written "with black, and a small part, red ink or paint" (*Messenger and Advocate*, Dec. 31, 1835). Within three days, Joseph Smith translated some "hieroglyphics, and much to our joy found that one of the rolls contained the writings of ABRAHAM, another, writings of JOSEPH OF EGYPT." Joseph Smith spent from July 17 to 31 "continually . . . translating an alphabet . . . and arranging a grammar" of Egyptian (*HC* 2:236–38). On October 1, while he worked on the alphabet, the "principles of astronomy as understood by Father Abraham . . . unfolded" (*HC* 2:286). On November 17 he "exhibited the alphabet" (*HC* 2:316). He recorded "translating the Egyptian records" on October 7, November 19–20 (20th: "made rapid progress"),

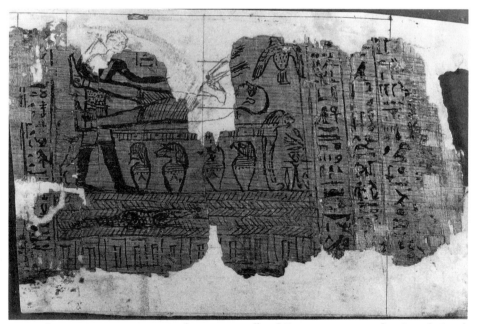

Facsimile No. 1, an extant piece from some rolls of Egyptian papyrus that Joseph Smith acquired in 1835, illustrates some of the text in the book of Abraham, translated by Joseph Smith. The Prophet said the upper right bird figure represents the angel of the Lord, the prone man represents Abraham, and the upper left figure represents the idolatrous priest who attempted to sacrifice Abraham.

and November 24–26 (*HC* 2:289, 318, 320). LDS Church Archives contain Book of Abraham texts (Abr. 1:1–2:18) from this period.

In 1837 a visitor wrote: "These records were torn, . . . some parts entirely lost, but Smith is to translate the whole by divine inspiration and that which is lost, like Nebuchadnezzar's dream, can be interpreted as well as that which is preserved." Joseph Smith let the mummies and papyri be moved to nearby towns, and in 1836 they were in the KIRTLAND TEMPLE. Despite care, the papyri had been damaged. Consequently, they were cut into pieces, and some were pasted on paper for preservation. By January 4, 1838, there were at least "two undivided thirds." During 1838–1839, the papyri and mummies spent the winter in Quincy, Illinois, where they were exhibited, a practice that continued until 1856 (Todd, pp. 197–203).

In 1842 Joseph Smith worked to prepare the facsimiles for publication and, likely, wrote his "Explanations," which are printed with them; on February 23, he instructed the printer on making the plate for Facsimile No. 1, which with its "Explanation" was printed in the March 1 issue of the *Times and Seasons*, with Abraham 1:1–2:18. On March 4 he instructed the printer on Facsimiles Nos. 2 and 3; on March 8–9 he did "translating" and "revising" (*HC* 4:518, 543–48). The final installment of the Book of Abraham (2:19–5:21) and Facsimile No. 2 with its "Explanation" were printed in the March 15 issue; Facsimile No. 3 and its "Explanation" were printed May 16.

Although the papyrus rolls had been shortened, a visitor in February 1843 saw "a long roll of manuscript, [being told] it was the 'writing of Abraham'" and was shown "another roll" (Todd, p. 245). After Joseph Smith's death, the Egyptian artifacts were held principally by his mother, and then by Emma SMITH after Lucy's death on May 14, 1856. On May 25, 1856, Emma sold "four Egyptian mummies with the records with them" to Mr. Abel Combs (*IE*, Jan. 1968, pp. 12–16). (Pioneers brought one fragment west.) Combs then sold two mummies with some papyri, which were sent to the St. Louis Museum (1856); they ended up in the Chicago Museum (1863), where they apparently burned in 1871. The fate of Combs's two other mummies and papyri is unknown, but some papyri remained, for in 1918 Mrs. Alice Heusser of Brooklyn, a daughter of Combs's housekeeper, approached the New York Metropol-

itan Museum of Art (MMA) with papyri once owned by Joseph Smith. In 1947 MMA acquired papyri from her widower. In May 1966 Aziz S. Atiya of the University of Utah saw eleven Heusser fragments at MMA. He informed Church leaders, and on November 27, 1967, the Church acquired the fragments; one of them is Facsimile No. 1.

Egyptologists who have studied the fragments in recent years generally identify them as religious texts, some from the Book of the Dead dating from 500–300 B.C., and some from the Book of Breathings dating from about A.D. 100. Since the rediscovery of the fragments, researchers have sought to learn if any of them, other than Facsimile No. 1, is related to the Book of Abraham.

[*See also* Book of Abraham: Facsimiles.]

BIBLIOGRAPHY

Nibley, Hugh. *The Message of the Joseph Smith Papyri.* Salt Lake City, 1975.

Peterson, H. Donl. "Sacred Writings from the Tombs of Egypt." In *The Pearl of Great Price: Revelations from God,* ed. D. Peterson and C. Tate. Provo, Utah, 1989.

Todd, Jay M. *Saga of the Book of Abraham.* Salt Lake City, 1969.

JAY M. TODD

PARABLES

Parables are short didactic narratives that make use of characters, situations, and customs familiar to their audience. They are meant to convey a spiritual message, but the reader usually must infer the message from the story, which generally is a presentation of some aspect of daily life. Because they are stories, parables are sometimes more memorable and more interesting than direct exhortation. Parables are seen to have several layers of meaning and may be understood differently, depending on the sensitivity and spiritual preparation of the hearer. For Latter-day Saints, it is significant that through the Prophet Joseph SMITH the Lord offered some additional parables and used those given during Jesus' ministry to enrich that part of the message of the RESTORATION of the gospel that points to events of the latter days.

In the JOSEPH SMITH TRANSLATION OF THE BIBLE (JST), Joseph Smith reworked some of the parables of Christ recorded in the synoptic gospels. In addition, he often referred to Christ's parables in discourses and articles. In revelations from the Lord, he received at least three original parables not in the New Testament (D&C 38:26–27; 88:51–61; 101:43–62). For those in the New Testament that he reworked, because he recognized that the meaning of a parable is in its relevance to the original audience, he used as a key for interpretation the situation that drew the parable from Christ (*TPJS*, pp. 276–77). Then under inspiration he interpreted virtually all the parables of Matthew 13 to apply to the latter days or to the mission of the restored Church of helping to prepare people for the SECOND COMING of Christ (cf. D&C 45:56; 63:53–54; *TPJS*, pp. 94–99).

Joseph Smith showed many of Christ's parables to be relevant to the mission of the latter-day Church. For example, Doctrine and Covenants section 86 interprets the parable of the wheat and the tares (cf. Matt. 13:24–30, 36–43) as portraying the APOSTASY and the restoration of Christ's true gospel: "The apostles were the sowers of the seed," but "after they have fallen asleep . . . the tares choke the wheat and drive the church into the wilderness" (D&C 86:2–3). However, the wheat, or Christ's true church, resprouts: "In the last days, . . . the Lord is beginning to bring forth the word, and the blade is springing up and is yet tender" (D&C 86:4). The JST applies this parable to the latter days: "In that day, before the Son of Man shall come, he shall send forth his angels and messengers of heaven" (JST, Matt. 13:42). These angels and messengers are called to strengthen the wheat in the LAST DAYS before the wicked will be destroyed. The focus of this parable thus becomes the time just before the end of the world (cf. D&C 101:65–66).

Other references further link Christ's parables to the latter-day Church. The JST version of the parable of the ten virgins (Matt. 25:1–13) begins, "At that day, before the Son of man comes, the kingdom of heaven shall be likened unto ten virgins" (JST, Matt. 25:1). The Doctrine and Covenants also refers to this parable: At "the coming of the Son of Man . . . there will be foolish virgins among the wise; and at that hour cometh an entire separation of the righteous and the wicked" (D&C 63:53–54; cf. 45:56–57). Of the parable of the mustard seed (Matt. 13:31–32), "the least of all seeds: but when it is grown, it is the greatest among herbs" (Matt. 13:32), Joseph Smith wrote, "Now we can discover plainly that this figure is given to represent the Church as it shall come forth in the

last days" (*TPJS*, p. 98). He also saw a comparison with the Book of Mormon:

> Let us take the Book of Mormon, which a man took and hid in his field . . . to spring up in the last days, or in due time; let us behold it coming forth out of the ground, . . . even towering, with lofty branches, and God-like majesty, until it, like the mustard seed, becomes the greatest of all herbs. And it is truth, and it has sprouted and come forth out of the earth, and righteousness begins to look down from heaven, and God is sending down His powers, gifts and angels, to lodge in the branches thereof [*TPJS*, p. 98].

In discussing other parables, Joseph Smith compared the three measures of meal in which a woman hid leaven (Matt. 13:33) to the three witnesses to the Book of Mormon (*TPJS*, p. 100). The treasure hidden in a field for which a man "selleth all that he hath, and buyeth that field" (Matt. 13:44) is likened to the Saints' "selling all that they have, and gathering themselves together unto a place that they may purchase for an inheritance" (*TPJS*, p. 101). To the "householder, which bringeth forth out of his treasure things that are new and old" (Matt. 13:52), the Prophet Joseph Smith compared "the Book of Mormon coming forth out of the treasure of the heart, . . . the covenants given to the Latter-day Saints, [and] the translation of the Bible—thus bringing forth out of the heart things new and old" (*TPJS*, p. 102).

Other parables were used in the Doctrine and Covenants to offer counsel for particular incidents. In 1833, Latter-day Saints in Jackson County, Missouri, were driven from their homes by armed mobs. In a revelation received by Joseph Smith on December 16, 1833, two parables suggested appropriate action. The first parable (D&C 101:43–62) is original, although it echoes Christ's parable of the wicked husbandmen (cf. Matt. 21:33–44). A nobleman sends servants to his vineyard to plant twelve olive trees and then to protect the vineyard by raising a hedge, setting watchmen, and erecting a tower. His servants at first obey but then become slothful. An enemy comes at night, breaks down the hedge and the olive trees, and takes over the vineyard. The nobleman calls the servants to task and then asks all the men of his house to go "straightway unto the land of [his] vineyard, and redeem [his] vineyard" (D&C 101:56). This parable, interpreted two months later in a subsequent revelation (D&C 103), served as the basis of ZION'S CAMP, a militia of LDS men called to march from

Ohio to Missouri for the purpose of recovering the land of their fellow Saints.

The other parable cited in the December 1833 revelation (D&C 101:81–91) is that of the woman and the unjust judge (Luke 18:1–8). The judge grants the woman's suit because her continual pleading annoys him. Likewise the displaced Saints of the time were urged to "importune at the feet of the judge," then the governor, then the president of the United States, until they obtained redress (D&C 101:85–89).

These parables, as well as others he employed (cf. D&C 35:16; 38:24–27; 45:36–38; 88:51–61), add a richness to Joseph Smith's teachings.

BIBLIOGRAPHY

Brooks, Melvin R. *Parables of the Kingdom.* Salt Lake City, 1965.

Burton, Alma P., ed. *Discourses of the Prophet Joseph Smith,* pp. 196–204. Salt Lake City, 1965.

Jeremias, Joachim. *The Parables of Jesus.* London, 1954.

SUSAN HOWE

PARADISE

Paradise is a Persian word (*para-daeza*, meaning "enclosure") that came into Greek and meant a pleasant place, such as a park or garden. Later it came to refer generally in scripture to that place where righteous spirits go after death. The word "paradise" is not found in the Old Testament, but occurs three times in the New Testament: Luke 23:43, where the Savior on the cross says to the thief, "Today shalt thou be with me in paradise"; 2 Corinthians 12:2–4, where Paul alludes to his vision of the third heaven and also to paradise; and Revelation 2:7, which describes the righteous who partake of the TREE OF LIFE in the midst of God's paradise (cf. D&C 77:2, 5). The latter two uses of paradise seem to refer to the highest degree of heaven (the CELESTIAL KINGDOM) rather than to the SPIRIT WORLD. Another sense of paradise pertains to the condition of the GARDEN OF EDEN, which was paradisiacal in nature. Article of Faith 10 declares that "the earth will be renewed and receive its paradisiacal glory," which is to say that it will eventually return to the edenic state that existed before the FALL OF ADAM (*see* NEW HEAVEN AND NEW EARTH).

The Savior's reference to paradise in Luke 23:43 pertains neither to heaven, nor to a specific place of righteous spirits, but to the spirit world in general, since the thief was not prepared to enter into the abode of the righteous. It is a misconception that this passage justifies "deathbed REPENTANCE," that is, the idea that one can delay repentance until death and still enter a heavenly condition. The gospel of Jesus Christ requires that persons use the gift of mortal life to learn to control appetites, thus preparing themselves to meet God and to acquire the divine nature (Rom. 8:29; Alma 34:32–35). The Prophet Joseph SMITH taught that the thief on the cross was to be with Jesus Christ "in the world of spirits" (he did not say paradise or heaven). "Hades, Sheol, paradise, spirits in prison, are all one: it is a world of spirits. The righteous and the wicked all go to the same world of spirits" (*TPJS*, pp. 309–310).

It is apparent from the scriptures, however, that even though the spirit world is one world, there exists a division between righteous and disobedient spirits. Luke 16:22–26 indicates a division and also a gulf fixed between the place of the righteous (Abraham's bosom) and the place of the wicked (cf. 1 Ne. 15:28–29). Between his death and his RESURRECTION, the Savior visited the spirit world (1 Pet. 3:18–20; 4:6; D&C 138) and bridged the gulf by giving righteous spirits authority to cross the gulf and carry the gospel to the spirits dwelling in darkness. This darkness is sometimes referred to as SPIRIT PRISON, HELL, or even "outer darkness" (Alma 40:13–14).

The Book of Mormon and the Doctrine and Covenants teach that paradise is the part of the spirit world where the righteous, those who in mortality obeyed God's commandments and were faithful to their COVENANTS, await the resurrection. ALMA teaches that the spirits of the righteous "are received into a state of happiness, which is called paradise, a state of rest, a state of peace, where they shall rest from all their troubles and from all care, and sorrow" (Alma 40:12). It was in paradise that righteous spirits like ADAM, EVE, and ABRAHAM greeted the Savior on his appearance in the spirit world after his crucifixion (D&C 138:38–49). Paradise is a temporary condition. At the resurrection it "must deliver up the spirits of the righteous" (2 Ne. 9:13). Even though the righteous spirits attain to a greater state of rest and happiness (Alma 40:12) than is possible in this life, they look "upon the long absence of their spirits from their bodies as a bondage" (D&C 138:50). When the Savior visited the spirit world, he taught these righteous spirits in paradise and "gave them power to come forth, after his resurrection from the dead, to enter into his Father's kingdom, there to be crowned with IMMORTALITY AND ETERNAL LIFE, and continue thenceforth their labor as had been promised by the Lord, and be partakers of all blessings which were held in reserve for them that love him" (D&C 138:51–52). As teaching and missionary work proceed in the spirit prison and ORDINANCES for the dead are performed in temples on the earth, the once uninformed and the disobedient but now repentant and purified spirits may enter into paradise and enjoy association with the righteous and the blessings of the gospel. The Prophet Joseph Smith taught, "There is never a time when the spirit [of man] is too old to approach God. All are within the reach of pardoning mercy, who have not committed the unpardonable sin, which hath no forgiveness, neither in this world, nor in the world to come. There is a way to release the spirits of the dead; that is by the power and authority of the Priesthood—by binding and loosing on earth" (*TPJS*, pp. 191–92).

[*See also* Spirit World.]

BIBLIOGRAPHY

Young, Brigham. *Discourses of Brigham Young*, comp. John A. Widtsoe, pp. 376–81. Salt Lake City, 1946.

M. CATHERINE THOMAS

PARMLEY, LAVERN WATTS

Martha LaVern Watts Parmley (1900–1980) served as general president of the PRIMARY of The Church of Jesus Christ of Latter-day Saints from 1951 to 1974, a period when the Church was adapting its programs to serve the needs of a rapidly growing, worldwide membership. She was born January 1, 1900, in Murray, Utah, to LDS parents. LaVern served as a Primary teacher at age fourteen. She married Thomas Jennison Parmley on June 28, 1923. After her husband completed a doctorate at Cornell University in New York, the Parmleys returned to Utah. They were the parents of three children.

When she returned from New York, LaVern Parmley became a member of a STAKE Primary board. After serving on that board for three years, she was called as a member of the Primary General Board in 1942. Six months later, she was appointed second counselor to Primary President May Green Hinckley. She became first counselor to a new president, Adele Cannon Howells, a year later, a position she held until her call as Primary general president in 1951.

As president, LaVern Parmley was instrumental in adapting the Primary programs to meet a new set of challenges. When the Boy Scouts of America lowered its admission age to eleven, Church and Primary leaders discussed whether the Primary or the YOUNG MEN's organization should direct the activities of the eleven-year-old boys. Although the National Scout Committee initially opposed having women leaders direct a scouting program, the Primary obtained permission for women to administer SCOUTING activities for boys until they turned twelve. The Primary also adopted Cub Scouting, thereby assuming responsibility for four years of scouting. LDS women

LaVern W. Parmley (1900–1980), fifth general president of the Primary Association, served from 1951 to 1974.

helped open the Boy Scouts program to women leaders nationwide. They served not only in local troops but eventually on local and national boards. In 1967 Parmley became the first woman member of a national scouting committee and later served on several scouting boards. She received the highest honors awarded by the Boy Scouts of America, including the Silver Buffalo award.

President Parmley also supervised the adaptation of the Primary organization to serve the needs of a growing, widely distributed world membership. When Primary membership doubled during her first decade as president, she doubled the members on the Primary General Board. She set up committees to establish new activities, including an annual sacrament meeting presentation by the children, special Primaries for handicapped children, and a reverence program. As editor of the CHILDREN'S FRIEND, she restructured its format to make it a magazine for children (see FRIEND). Under her direction, teacher training, which began with Primary, developed into a well-ordered general Church program.

As the Church grew, stake Primary conventions and general Primary conferences were discontinued. The Church began to centralize the publication of educational materials, and Primary publications were reduced. President Parmley responded to these challenges by standardizing lesson materials and by preparing audiovisual and printed materials for presentation to Primary leaders in regional meetings.

A major challenge during her administration was the need to accommodate the Primary program to the CORRELATION process implemented in 1961 to place all Church programs under the authority and direction of the priesthood. As part of the process, responsibility for Primary lessons was transferred to the Church Correlation Committee. In a spirit of cooperation, President Parmley helped merge the goals and programs of the Primary into a larger Church-sponsored program for children.

President Parmley helped promote the construction of a new Primary Children's Hospital (later Primary Children's Medical Center), completed in 1952, and encouraged donations from Primary children. As Primary president, she served as chairman of the board for the hospital until 1970. When the Health Service Corporation was organized later that year to oversee all LDS hospitals, she was appointed a board member. In 1975, after she was released as Primary president, the Primary Children's Hospital was transferred to Intermountain Health Care, a private nonprofit corporation (see HOSPITALS).

LaVern Parmley presided over the Primary Association at a time when its programs became more complex and wide-ranging than at any earlier time in its history. As its president during a period of rapid Church growth and expansion, she traveled more than any Primary president before her, providing firsthand supervision and unity in an organization otherwise subject to much local variation. Her contributions are reflected in the organization and direction of Primary today.

BIBLIOGRAPHY

Madsen, Carol Cornwall, and Susan Staker Oman. *Sisters and Little Saints.* Salt Lake City, 1979.

Parmley, Martha LaVern Watts. Oral history interview with Jill Mulvay Derr, 1974–1976. Church Archives, Historical Dept., Salt Lake City.

JESSIE L. EMBRY

PASSOVER

See: Law of Moses

PATRIARCH

[*This entry consists of two articles*: Stake Patriarch *and* Patriarch to the Church. *A patriarch is a Church priesthood calling. Each stake has one or more patriarchs and their duties are given in the first article. The second article gives the history of the Church office Patriarch to the Church.*]

STAKE PATRIARCH

Each STAKE in the Church has at least one patriarch ordained, as the Prophet Joseph SMITH wrote, "for the benefit of the posterity of the Saints as it was with Jacob in giving his patriarchal blessing unto his sons" (*WJS*, p. 6). Age is not a factor, and the call, which is for voluntary service in giving patriarchal blessings to stake members, may come to any worthy, spiritually mature high priest.

The fathers from Adam to Jacob are seen as patriarchs of this order. The word "patriarch" is often used in the Bible as a title of honor for the early leaders of the Israelites. It is perhaps in this sense that Peter spoke of "the patriarch David"

(Acts 2:29). Stephen spoke of the sons of Jacob as "the twelve patriarchs" (Acts 7:8–9). These men may have been natural patriarchs, being fathers, and some of them may also have been ordained to the patriarchal priesthood. By right of this priesthood and under inspiration, they could confer upon their sons and daughters promises, privileges, and duties like unto those of the family of Abraham.

The Doctrine and Covenants speaks of "evangelical ministers," which is understood to refer to patriarchs. The Council of the Twelve Apostles has the responsibility of calling and ordaining stake patriarchs "as they shall be designated unto them by revelation" (D&C 107:39). This responsibility is now generally delegated to stake presidents. A stake patriarch may also give patriarchal blessings outside his stake to members of his own family. If he moves to another stake, his jurisdiction there requires approval through the Council of the Twelve.

The training and preparation of patriarchs includes spiritual enhancement through prayer and righteous living, constant study of the scriptural and historical heritage of the calling, and occasional meetings where they are instructed by their leaders.

Members of the Church receive a blessing from a stake patriarch only on a bishop's recommendation following an interview. Approval is based on a desire and readiness to receive the blessing, and on personal worthiness as shown by faithfulness in the gospel and Church service. The blessing is given in a quiet setting, usually a room in the stake center or the home of the patriarch. Parents, a spouse, or other immediate family members may be invited to witness the blessing. The recipient is seated. The patriarch lays his hands on the head of the person and invokes the inspiration of the Holy Ghost. In the spirit of fasting and prayer all present are united in faith to seek inspired insight into the birthright blessings and destinies of the recipient. The patriarch also seeks inspiration to specify the dominant family line that leads back to Abraham. Then, as manifested by the Spirit, the patriarch gives admonitions, promises, and assurances.

The stake patriarch always records and transcribes the blessings he gives. The original copy is sent to the patriarchal division of the Church Historical Department. A copy given to the individual becomes a permanent record that is held sacred. It is usually available only to the recipient, or later to his family and descendants.

The appointment of stake patriarchs does not preempt the calling and right of every father in the Church who holds the MELCHIZEDEK PRIESTHOOD also to give each of his children father's blessings. Both ordained patriarchs and priesthood-bearing fathers have the power, through spiritual inspiration, to give a priesthood blessing that will look down the corridor of time and expand the vision, strengthen the faith, and clarify the life mission of the one receiving the blessing.

BIBLIOGRAPHY

Widtsoe, John A. *Evidences and Reconciliations*, chap. 16, pp. 321–25. Salt Lake City, 1967.

ARIEL S. BALLIF

PATRIARCH TO THE CHURCH

Before 1979, Patriarch to the Church was a Church officer whose chief duty was to confer patriarchal blessings on Church members who generally did not have the service of stake patriarchs readily available to them. The Prophet Joseph SMITH explained that an "evangelist" (as in Ephesians 4:11) is a "patriarch" (*TPJS*, p. 151); that is, he confers the blessings of a patriarch upon members of the Church. Patriarchs are currently ordained in individual stakes of the Church, but for many years there was a patriarch to the entire Church. He was considered one of the GENERAL AUTHORITIES.

On December 18, 1833, in KIRTLAND, OHIO, Joseph SMITH, Sr., was ordained the first Patriarch to the Church (D&C 107:39–56), with jurisdiction throughout the Church. Upon his death, he was succeeded by his oldest living son, Hyrum SMITH, who served until he was martyred on June 27, 1844. William Smith, a younger brother, was ordained Patriarch to the Church on May 24, 1845, by the Quorum of the Twelve Apostles, but William was rejected by the Church on October 6, 1845, for misconduct. The office was vacant until January 1, 1849, when John Smith, brother of Joseph Smith, Sr., was called. He served until his death on May 23, 1854.

A second John Smith, son of Hyrum Smith, was Patriarch to the Church from February 18, 1855, until November 6, 1911. Hyrum Gibbs Smith, grandson of the second John Smith, then served from May 9, 1912, until February 4, 1932.

For ten years Acting Patriarchs were called who were not in the direct hereditary line. They included Nicholas G. Smith (October 1932 to October 1934), Frank B. Woodbury (June 1935 to October 1937), and George F. Richards (October 1937 to October 1942).

The call returned to the hereditary line on October 3, 1942, with the call of Elder Joseph Fielding SMITH (1899–1964), a great-grandson of Hyrum Smith. He was released at his own request on October 7, 1946, because of poor health. Eldred G. Smith, eldest son of Hyrum Gibbs Smith, was called in April 1947.

In 1979 the office of Patriarch to the Church was retired "because of the large increase in the number of stake patriarchs and the availability of patriarchal service throughout the world." Eldred G. Smith was designated "a Patriarch Emeritus, which means that he is honorably relieved of all duties and responsibilities pertaining to the office of Patriarch to the Church" (*CR* [Oct. 1979]:25).

BIBLIOGRAPHY

Smith, Joseph Fielding. In *Doctrines of Salvation*, comp. Bruce R. McConkie, Vol. 3, pp. 104–108, 162–72. Salt Lake City, 1956.

CALVIN R. STEPHENS

PATRIARCHAL BLESSINGS

The practice of a father blessing his sons and daughters can be traced from earliest times. ADAM, as the first patriarch and father of the human race, blessed his son SETH, promising that "his posterity should be the chosen of the Lord, and that they should be preserved unto the end of the earth" (D&C 107:42). Abraham, Isaac, and Jacob blessed their children, opening up a vision of their inheritance and their destinies (e.g., Gen. 28:4; 49:3–27).

Each family in the Church, and the larger family that is the Church, perpetuates this heritage. Members have the right to go to the stake patriarch for a Church blessing. Stake patriarchs are ordained wherever the Church is organized that all may have this privilege.

Patriarchal blessings are given by the authority of the MELCHIZEDEK PRIESTHOOD which "is to hold the keys of all the spiritual blessings of the Church" (D&C 107:18).

When God covenanted with Abraham that through his posterity all the families of the earth would be blessed, he promised "the blessings of the Gospel, which are the blessings of salvation, even of life eternal" (Abr. 2:11). The scope of these promises, both here and hereafter, is outlined in modern day scripture:

> Abraham received promises concerning his seed, and of the fruit of his loins . . . which were to continue so long as they were in the world; and as touching Abraham and his seed, out of the world they should continue. . . . This promise is yours also, because ye are of Abraham, and the promise was made unto Abraham [D&C 132:30–31].

An essential part of a patriarchal blessing is a declaration of lineage. The patriarch seeks inspiration to specify the dominant family line that leads back to Abraham. The majority of modern blessings have designated EPHRAIM or MANASSEH as the main link in this tracing, but others of every tribe of Israel have also been named. Whether this is a pronouncement of blood inheritance or of adoption does not matter (see Abr. 2:10). It is seen as the line and legacy through which one's blessings are transmitted. Thus the blessings "of Abraham, Isaac and Jacob" are conferred.

In addition, as the patriarch seeks the SPIRIT he may be moved to give admonitions, promises, and assurances. Individual traits of personality and strengths and weaknesses may be mentioned. Against the backdrop of the prophetic anticipation of world events, individual roles and CALLINGS may be named. One's spiritual gifts, talents, skills, and potentials may be specified with their associated obligations of gratitude and dedication. Karl G. Maeser described these blessings as "paragraphs from the book of one's possibilities" (Alma P. Burton, *Karl G. Maeser: Mormon Educator*, p. 82 [Salt Lake City, 1953]).

It is continually taught in the Church that the fulfillment of patriarchal blessings, as of all divine promises, is conditioned on the faith and works of the individual. Typically, blessings close with such a statement as, "I pronounce these blessings upon your head according to your faith and your diligence in keeping the commandments of the Lord."

The practice of giving patriarchal blessings is a constant reminder of the honor and glory of family: that one is not alone and that every person stands on the shoulders of those who have gone before. They prompt those who receive blessings to "look unto Abraham, your father," (2 Ne. 8:2) to "do the works of Abraham" (D&C 132:32; cf. John 8:39), to be willing to be "chastened and tried even as Abraham" (D&C 101:4), and to recognize that Abraham's willingness in offering up his son was "a similitude of God and his Only Begotten Son" (Jacob 4:5). In short, the command to honor one's father and mother does not end with death, nor with the unfolding growth of the human family.

All patriarchal blessings are recorded and transcribed; copies are preserved in official Church archives and by the recipient. They are held sacred by those receiving them.

In the history of ISRAEL, as of the Latter-day Saints, the moving appeal of these blessings is incalculable. They open many doors to self-awareness. They have inspired men and women of renown, as well as those in the most obscure and remote places, to lose themselves in a realization of mission; to serve and give in the spirit of CONSECRATION. They have been a strength amidst the tests and temptations of life, a comfort in the darkness of bereavement and loss, and an anchor in stormy days, a "daily help in all the affairs of life" (Widtsoe, p. 74).

BIBLIOGRAPHY

Widtsoe, John A. *Evidences and Reconciliations.* Salt Lake City, pp. 72–77.

WILLIAM JAMES MORTIMER

PATRIARCHAL ORDER OF THE PRIESTHOOD

To Latter-day Saints, the patriarchal order of the priesthood is the organizing power and principle of celestial family life. It is the ultimate and ideal form of government. It answers the query of Elder Parley P. Pratt: "Who can endure to be forever banished and separated from father, mother, wife, children and every kindred affection and from every family tie?" (Pratt, *Utah Genealogical and Historical Magazine* 23 [Apr. 1932]:59).

In The Church of Jesus Christ of Latter-day Saints there are two priesthood divisions: the Aaronic and the Melchizedek. The highest order of the MELCHIZEDEK PRIESTHOOD is patriarchal authority. The order was divinely established with father ADAM and mother EVE. They are the fount and progenitors of all living, and they will appear at the culmination of earth's history at the head of the whole sealed family of the redeemed. The promises given to ABRAHAM and SARAH pertain to this same order.

Three principles underlie the patriarchal order. First, the primal parents of the race were in their paradisiacal state in Eden united in eternal bonds before death entered their lives. Second, the fall of man and the continual source of degeneration in this world have resulted in the estrangement of parents from God, from each other, and from their children. Third, the healing of this broken harmony is the essence of ETERNAL LIFE, as is the perpetuation of powers of creation and procreation—eternal increase.

The patriarchal order is, in the words of Elder James E. Talmage, a condition where "woman shares with man the blessings of the Priesthood," where husband and wife minister, "seeing and understanding alike, and cooperating to the full in the government of their family kingdom" (*Young Woman's Journal* 25 [Oct. 1914]:602–603). A man cannot hold this priesthood without a wife, and a woman cannot share the blessings of this priesthood without a husband, sealed in the TEMPLE.

Concerning patriarchal authority, the Prophet Joseph SMITH admonished the Saints: "Go to and finish the [Nauvoo] temple, and God will fill it with power, and you will then receive more knowledge concerning this priesthood" (*TPJS*, p. 323, cf. D&C 107:18, 20). This priesthood and its associated powers were introduced in NAUVOO, Illinois, in 1843. It was first conferred upon the FIRST PRESIDENCY, the APOSTLES, and their wives (*WJS*, pp. 244–45).

Today dedicated husbands and wives enter this order in the temple in a COVENANT with God. The blessings of this priesthood is given only to husbands and wives together. Their covenants extend beyond this life (D&C 76:59, 60), beyond death (D&C 132:20–24), and into the resurrection, to eternal lives, the eternal giving and receiving of life.

Thus united, they work in love, faith, and harmony for the glorification of their family. If they are not united in obedient love, if they are not one, they are not of the Lord. Eventually, through this order, families will be linked in indissoluble bonds all the way back to the first parents, and all the way forward to the last child born into this world. This priesthood order will be both the means and the end of reconciliation, redemption, peace, joy, and eternal life.

LYNN A. MCKINLAY

PATTEN, DAVID W.

David Wyman Patten (1799–1838), son of Benenio (Benoni) Patten and Abigale (Edith) Cole, was born in Theresa, Jefferson County, New York, on November 14, 1799. He left his home at an early age and settled near Dundee, Monroe County, Michigan. In 1828 he married Phoebe Ann Babcock. They had no children.

Patten first became acquainted with the Book of Mormon around 1830. In May 1832 he received a letter from his brother John, who was living in Green County, Indiana, noting that he had joined The Church of Jesus Christ of Latter-day Saints. Patten journeyed to Indiana and was baptized by his brother on June 15, 1832. Two days later he was ordained an elder by Elisha H. Groves. On September 2, 1832, he was ordained a high priest by Hyrum Smith.

Until his death in 1838, Patten served almost continuously as a missionary for the Church. He established numerous branches of the Church on each of his proselytizing journeys and was renowned for his spiritual gift of healing.

On February 14, 1835, Patten was chosen as one of the Twelve Apostles and was ordained the following day by Oliver Cowdery. On May 2, 1835, the Prophet Joseph SMITH directed that the seniority of the Twelve be determined according to the members' ages. Patten was uncertain of his exact birth date, and Thomas B. Marsh (born 1800) was mistakenly adjudged to be the older of the two, and thus was made the President of the Quorum.

During the latter part of 1836, Elder Patten settled in Far West, Missouri. Following Church action taken against the presidency of the stake in Missouri (David Whitmer, William W. Phelps, and John Whitmer) in early February 1838, Thomas B. Marsh and Patten were appointed as Presidents pro tem of the Church in Missouri. On April 6, 1838, Patten and Brigham Young were sustained as assistant presidents of the Church in Missouri, with Thomas B. Marsh as President pro tem.

In April 1838, Joseph Smith received a revelation instructing Patten to prepare for a mission with the Twelve the following spring (D&C 114); however, Patten did not live to fulfill the assignment. He died on October 25, 1838, from a wound suffered in a battle at Crooked River when a contingent of Caldwell County militia (all Mormons), under his leadership, attempted to rescue three Latter-day Saints who had been taken prisoners by a company of Missourians from Ray County. He was buried in Far West, Missouri, two days later. In January 1841 a revelation was given to Joseph Smith in which the Lord indicated that David W. Patten "is with me at this time" (D&C 124:19, 130).

BIBLIOGRAPHY

Jenson, Andrew. *Latter-day Saint Biographical Encyclopedia*, Vol. 1, pp. 76–80. Salt Lake City, 1901.

Wilson, Lycurgus A. *Life of David W. Patten, the First Apostolic Martyr*. Salt Lake City, 1900.

ALEXANDER L. BAUGH

PAUL

The Church recognizes Paul as a true APOSTLE of Jesus Christ. No other early Apostle has had the impact on subsequent believers through both his personal example and his written words that Paul has. The early Christian apostle to the Gentiles, in his New Testament letters, produced a rich source of Christian doctrine and the single most important doctrinal influence upon many of the denominations of modern Christendom. Without Paul, the doctrine of justification by faith in Christ would be largely missing from the Bible, and considerably less would be known about grace, the Lord's Supper, church structure, the Apostasy, or the role of gifts of the spirit in the Church.

BIOGRAPHICAL SKETCH.   Details of Paul's life are found in his letters and in the book of Acts. Born in Tarsus of Cilicia (modern southeastern Turkey), Paul was multicultural. As a Jew, he was known by the name of Saul and was educated in Jerusalem as a Pharisee under the famous rabbi Gamaliel. He was also a Roman citizen by birth, a rare privilege for a Jew at that time. Finally, he was familiar with Greek language and culture through his early environment in the Hellenistic city of Tarsus. Thus, he was able to deal with Jews, Romans, and Greeks on their own cultural terms—a great advantage for his later missionary work.

As a Pharisee working for the Jewish high priest, Saul was an early and zealous persecutor of Christians and personally assented to the execution of Stephen (Acts 7:58–8:3). However, as Saul traveled toward Damascus to arrest Christians there, the resurrected Christ appeared to him in a vision. As a result of this experience, Saul embraced the cause of Christ and spent the rest of his life in his service.

After baptism, Saul "went into Arabia, and returned again unto Damascus" (Gal. 1:17). He was so effective in preaching Christ that he provoked much Jewish opposition and was eventually compelled to flee for his life. Returning to Jerusalem after three years, he met briefly with Peter and James, the Lord's brother, and then went to Cilicia and Syria, where he spent approximately the next decade preaching the gospel.

Barnabas brought Saul to Antioch, whence they left on their first missionary journey. On this journey, Saul began using his Roman name, Paul, and established his basic strategy for missionary work. Whenever he entered a city, Paul went first to the Jews, preaching Christ in their synagogues. Usually they would reject his message, but Gentiles associated with the synagogues would frequently be converted; Paul would then turn his attention to teaching the Gentiles of that city and would establish a branch of the Church made up of Gentiles and perhaps a few Jewish converts.

Two more missionary journeys of over three years each are described in Acts, and Paul was successful in teaching the gospel and establishing churches throughout much of present-day Turkey and Greece. Returning to Jerusalem after his third missionary journey, Paul met with such intense Jewish opposition to his presence in the temple that he was put into custody by the Romans and held in prison in Caesarea for two years before being sent to Rome for trial. Though shipwrecked on the way, he was eventually imprisoned in Rome and was executed around A.D. 64, during the reign of the emperor Nero.

The Prophet Joseph SMITH gave a description of Paul: about five feet tall, dark hair, penetrating eyes, and a powerful orator (*TPJS*, p. 180; *WJS*, p. 59). He also indicated that Paul was acquainted with ENOCH (*TPJS*, p. 170) and that Abel "was sent down from heaven unto Paul to minister consoling words, and to commit unto him a knowledge of the mysteries of godliness" (*TPJS*, p. 169).

PAUL'S TEACHINGS. One of Paul's greatest contributions to the New Testament is his forceful statement of justification (that is, being absolved of guilt) by faith in Christ (cf. Gal. 2–3; Rom. 2–5). Early on, Paul had taught his gentile converts that they did not need to live the LAW OF MOSES in order to be justified before God. It was sufficient to make and keep the gospel COVENANT, the covenant of faith, to do this, while outward observance of the law of Moses was not (Gal. 2:16). In particular, after Christ's atonement, there was no longer any necessity of observing the earlier law and covenant of Moses, which were rendered obsolete by the law and covenant of the gospel (cf. Heb. 8:6–13; 3 Ne. 9:17–20). Thus, Paul's Gentile converts did not need to become Jews in order to become Christians (cf. Acts 15:5–29), for human beings are "justified by faith without the deeds of the law" (Rom. 3:28). A complete commitment to the gospel of Jesus Christ, the covenant of faith, automatically fulfills all previous obligations before God, including the obligations of the law of Moses.

Paul also taught the related doctrine of salvation by grace. Latter-day Saints recognize at least four ways in which Paul spoke of salvation as an operation of the grace of God. First, through the atonement of Christ, a free gift, Adam's posterity is not accountable for the transgression of Adam (Rom. 5:18–21). Second, it naturally follows that death—a consequence of Adam's transgression—will be done away by the gift of resurrection that will be graciously given to all human beings (1 Cor. 15:21–22). Third, the fact that God has offered a new covenant of faith in place of the old rules of performances and ordinances, which mankind then was not able to live perfectly, is in itself an act of grace. And fourth, that the Savior volunteered to suffer and die for the sake of others is the greatest expression of the grace of God. Thus, salvation is accessible to mankind only through the gracious acts and gifts of God. As Paul said, "We have access by faith into this grace wherein we stand, and rejoice in hope of the glory of God" (Rom. 5:2). However, in Paul's theology, the doctrines of salvation by grace and justification by faith do not eliminate but require the absolute necessity for high personal standards of conduct (1 Cor. 6:9–11; Gal. 5:19–21).

Paul also taught that God's knowledge is unlimited and that God's plan has anticipated all future events and cannot be thwarted. God knows the end from the beginning and has already prepared the inheritance of those who choose to keep his will (Eph. 1:4–14). Though the King James Version of the Bible uses the problematic word "predestinated" (Greek, *proorizō*), Latter-day Saints do not understand it to mean that some are saved and some are damned according to a prior decision by God. Latter-day Saints prefer the term FOREORDINATION to "predestination" and insist that the FOREKNOWLEDGE OF GOD does not impinge upon the free agency of human beings.

Not all, or possibly not even most, of Paul's letters have been preserved. Latter-day Saints believe that if a more complete collection of Paul's letters had survived, it would reflect a theology much like that of the restored gospel of latter days. They see support for this in the number of references in Paul to doctrines that are now peculiar to the Latter-day Saints, such as BAPTISM FOR THE DEAD (1 Cor. 15:29), the three DEGREES OF GLORY (1 Cor. 15:39-41; 2 Cor. 12:2), the PREMORTAL LIFE (Eph. 1:4), and the necessity of an ecclesiastical organization that includes apostles and prophets (Eph. 2:19-20; 4:11-13). Latter-day Saints assume that Paul did not expand on these topics in his extant writings because they were written to people who already knew about them.

Paul is a major source of predictions of the apostasy of the early Christian church. He is quoted in Acts 20:29-30 as warning the elders from Ephesus and Miletus that grievous wolves would descend after his departure, "not sparing the flock," and that disaffected members would tear up the Church from within. He warned the Thessalonians not to expect the coming of Christ before the Apostasy had taken place (2 Thes. 2:2-3). Significantly, he reminded both groups that this warning had been part of his preaching from the first (2 Thes. 2:5; Acts 20:31).

Latter-day Saints do not see in Paul an opposition to women, sex, or marriage. Rather, Paul's general statement of principle on marriage is "Let every man have his own wife, and let every woman have her own husband" (1 Cor. 7:2; cf. Heb. 13:4). Paul goes on to address special circumstances (1 Cor. 7:8-16) and admonishes all people to care first for the things of God (verses 25-38), but his advice regarding particular situations should not be confused with his general policy. Husbands are to love their wives, and vice versa (Eph. 5:28), for "neither is the man without the woman, neither the woman without the man, in the Lord" (1 Cor. 11:11). It is clear that women were valued associates and held positions of responsibility in Paul's congregations (cf. Rom. 16:1-4).

Paul's influence upon Joseph Smith and the Latter-day Saints is seen at many points. Joseph Smith referred to "the admonition of Paul" (cf. Philip. 4:8) in describing the highest moral aspira-

tions of the Latter-day Saints (A of F 13). The language of Paul is discernible in most of the Articles of Faith (e.g., in A of F 4 on the first principles of the gospel [cf. Heb. 6:1-2]; in A of F 5 on ordination to the priesthood [cf. 1 Tim. 4:14]; in A of F 6 on the officers of the Primitive Church [cf. Eph. 4:11]; and in A of F 7 on the gifts of the spirit [cf. 1 Cor. 12:8-12]), and part of the sublime hymn to charity (1 Cor. 13:4-8) is also found in the Book of Mormon (Moro. 7:45-46). These are taken as indications that Jesus was the ultimate source of all of these teachings.

Of Paul's life, the Prophet Joseph Smith observed:

> Follow the labors of this Apostle from the time of his conversion to the time of his death, and you will have a fair sample of industry and patience in promulgating the Gospel of Christ. Derided, whipped, and stoned, the moment he escaped the hands of his persecutors he as zealously as ever proclaimed the doctrine of the Savior. . . . Paul rested his hope in Christ, because he had kept the faith, and loved His appearing and from His hand he had a promise of receiving a crown of righteousness [*TPJS*, pp. 63-64].

[*See also* Joseph Smith Translation of the Bible (JST); New Testament.]

BIBLIOGRAPHY

Anderson, Richard Lloyd. *Understanding Paul*. Salt Lake City, 1983.

McConkie, Bruce R. *Doctrinal New Testament Commentary*, Vols. 2-3. Salt Lake City, 1970-1973.

Sperry, Sidney B. *Paul's Life and Letters*. Salt Lake City, 1955.

J. PHILIP SCHAELLING

PEACE

See: War and Peace

PEARL OF GREAT PRICE

[*The Pearl of Great Price consists of a diverse collection of sacred works that are accepted as scripture by Latter-day Saints. The article* Contents and Publication *offers an overview of the individual texts in the collection as well as details about the history of how the documents were brought together and were then received as scripture by Church members. The article titled* Literature *briefly treats the variety of literary features that characterize the Pearl of Great Price.*

CONTENTS AND PUBLICATION

One of the four STANDARD WORKS accepted as scripture by The Church of Jesus Christ of Latter-day Saints, the Pearl of Great Price includes various documents known as "Selections from the Book of Moses," "The Book of Abraham," "Joseph Smith—Matthew," "Joseph Smith—History," and "The Articles of Faith."

It was first published at Liverpool, England, in 1851 by Franklin D. Richards, then president of the British Mission and a member of the QUORUM OF THE TWELVE APOSTLES, in response to requests from converts for further information about

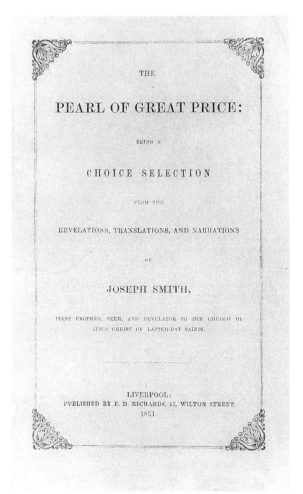

Cover of the first edition of the Pearl of Great Price, published by Elder Franklin D. Richards at Liverpool in 1851 as a "choice selection" of revelations, translations, and narrations of Joseph Smith. The Pearl of Great Price was accepted as a standard work by the body of the Church in 1880. Courtesy Rare Books and Manuscripts, Brigham Young University.

their new church. In addition to selected revelations from Genesis in the JOSEPH SMITH TRANSLATION OF THE BIBLE (JST) and the BOOK OF ABRAHAM, the 1851 edition contained Matthew 24 as revealed to the Prophet Joseph SMITH in 1831 (currently titled JOSEPH SMITH—MATTHEW); "A Key to the Revelations of St. John" (now D&C 77), a revelation received by Joseph Smith on December 25, 1832 (now D&C 87); and Joseph Smith's 1838 account of his early VISIONS and translation of the Book of Mormon (now JOSEPH SMITH—HISTORY). It also incorporated certain extracts from the Doctrine and Covenants (sections 20, 107, and 27), thirteen untitled statements previously published in the *Times and Seasons* in March 1842 and now known as the ARTICLES OF FAITH, and a poem titled "Truth" that later became the LDS hymn "Oh Say, What Is Truth?"

The book of Moses originally consisted of several revelations given to Joseph Smith as he was revising the Bible under inspiration, beginning in June 1830. In the 1851 edition of the Pearl of Great Price, these excerpts were untitled. The 1878 edition added the titles "Visions of Moses" (chap. 1) and "Writings of Moses" (chaps. 2–8). These revelations were first printed in Church newspapers between 1832 and 1851 (Clark, pp. 9–17).

The book of Abraham is linked to Joseph Smith's work on rolls of papyri that the Church obtained in 1835. Soon after he began studying the rolls, he produced a record of the life of the patriarch Abraham and a description of the creation of the world similar to that in Genesis and the book of Moses. In 1842 the Nauvoo *Times and Seasons* and the *Millennial Star* in England printed the available text and facsimiles. It is certain that the materials incorporated into the books of Moses and Abraham were extracts and that more information was available than has ever been included in the printed editions of the Pearl of Great Price.

The second edition of the Pearl of Great Price, the first American edition, was published at Salt Lake City in 1878 and added "A Revelation on the Eternity of the Marriage Covenant, Including Plurality of Wives," which is now known as Doctrine and Covenants section 132. On October 10, 1880, in general conference at Salt Lake City, the membership of the Church accepted the Pearl of Great Price as a standard work. When additional changes were made—including page size and format—another vote in 1890 reaffirmed the acceptance of the Pearl of Great Price as scripture.

James E. Talmage, later a member of the Quorum of the Twelve Apostles, under assignment of the FIRST PRESIDENCY, divided the work into chapters and verses, added some titles (such as "The Book of Moses"), and eliminated some portions, such as the materials also published in the Doctrine and Covenants. These changes were formally approved by Church membership at the October conference of 1902.

At general conference on April 3, 1976, Joseph Smith's vision of the CELESTIAL KINGDOM received in the Kirtland Temple on January 21, 1836, and President Joseph F. SMITH's vision of the redemption of the dead (October 3, 1918) were added to the Pearl of Great Price. In 1979 these two revelations were transferred to the Doctrine and Covenants as sections 137 and 138.

BIBLIOGRAPHY

Clark, James R. *The Story of the Pearl of Great Price*. Salt Lake City, 1955.

Millet, Robert L., and Kent P. Jackson, eds. *Studies in Scripture*, Vol. 2. Salt Lake City, 1985.

Peterson, H. Donl, and Charles D. Tate, Jr., eds. *The Pearl of Great Price: Revelations from God*. Provo, Utah, 1989.

KENNETH W. BALDRIDGE

LITERATURE

Drawing the effective metaphor of its title from the literary treasures of the Savior's parables (Matt. 13:45), this book of scripture—despite its diversity of sections—consistently sustains a grandeur of language enriched throughout with vivid word pictures and the subtle touches of diverse literary techniques.

For example, Enoch hears and describes the personified soul of the earth alliteratively as the "*m*other of *m*en" agonizing from the bowels of the earth that she is "*w*eary" of "*w*ickedness." The tension of the drama resolves itself as the voice uses assonance in pleading for "r*i*ghteousness" to "ab*i*de" for a season (Moses 7:48).

Also remarkable is the artistic control of tone throughout the narrative of JOSEPH SMITH—HISTORY. Despite his having been the victim of severe persecution, Joseph objectively selects connotative words that allow the readers to discover for themselves the abuse he had suffered. In describing the deep schisms among the sects in his village, he skillfully calls into question the "great love" and "great zeal" of the clergy in their efforts to have everybody "converted," as they were "pleased to call it." The irony of tone remains dignified but becomes incrementally more poignant as he next refers to their "seemingly good feelings" being "more pretended than real"; he finalizes his deep disappointment by leaving no doubt regarding the irony: "So that all their good feelings one for another, if they ever had any, were entirely lost in a strife of words and a contest about opinions" (JS—H 1:6).

The final verse in the Pearl of Great Price addresses the value of artistry not only in writing but also in all aspects of life. Referring to the literarily beautiful writings of Paul, it affirms Joseph Smith's conviction that the Latter-day Saints must search the handiwork of God for all that is "virtuous, lovely, or of good report" (A of F 13).

O. GLADE HUNSAKER

PEARL OF GREAT PRICE, JESUS CHRIST IN

See: Jesus Christ in the Scriptures: Pearl of Great Price

"PECULIAR" PEOPLE

Latter-day Saints consider themselves a peculiar people in the biblical sense of being a covenant people with the Lord. Their lifestyle, stemming from the doctrines and practices of the Church, also makes them a different or peculiar people. In any dispensation, followers of Jesus Christ produce a distinct culture:

> Is there a gospel culture? . . . Is there a gospel community or society? . . . Zion has always been described as a city, an organized society, set apart from the world. If the community preserves its integrity for any length of time, it is bound to emerge as a separate culture. The earliest reference to the culture I have in mind is Israel as the "peculiar people." Moses and Aaron disengaged the children of Israel from the culture of Egypt, the most distinctive culture of its time. The Lord tells them: "Ye have seen what I did unto the Egyptians, and how I bare you on eagles' wings, and brought you unto myself. Now therefore, if ye will obey my voice indeed, and keep my covenant, then ye shall be a peculiar treasure unto me above all people" [Ex. 19:4–5; Nibley, pp. 22–23].

But to the extent that a covenant people do not honor their allegiance to God, they become more like the cultures they are raised in and are indistinguishable from those who know not God (see Smith, W., 1959). Nevertheless, when a people honor their commitment to God, there are evidences that distinguish them and make them peculiar to the population at large. "By their fruits ye shall know them" (Matt. 7:20; see also 1 Jn. 3:10–18; Moro. 7:5–17).

Large comparisons of LDS behavior patterns with those of the general population are not extensive in the research literature, but because Latter-day Saints comprise 70 percent of the population of Utah, comparisons of Utah data with regional and national samples give a reliable estimate of how Latter-day Saints differ from the general population. And demographers who have compared Utah Latter-day Saints with those living elsewhere in the United States find more similarities than differences, and conclude that "Utah Mormons are not distinctive compared to Mormons elsewhere" (Heaton, "Demography," p. 193).

Latter-day Saints are taught to live by a health code requiring abstention from alcohol, tobacco, tea, and coffee (see WORD OF WISDOM). Utah ranks lowest of the fifty states in the consumption of all types of alcoholic beverages. Utah's mortality rate from diseases related to alcohol and tobacco use (heart disease/stroke and cancer) is very low (Smith, James E., p. 69).

Latter-day Saints value education highly, and the percentage of the Utah population completing up to three years of high school ranks first in the nation (93 percent), and Utah is seventh in the nation in both graduation rates from high school (80 percent) and from four-year colleges (20 percent) (Van Mondfrans, Smith, and Moss, pp. 198–99). Moreover, the relationship between education and religiosity among Latter-day Saints is the opposite of the national trend, with the most educated Mormons being the most actively involved in the Church (Albrecht).

For Latter-day Saints married in a temple, family commitments are not only for mortality but for eternity, and divorce rates among temple-married Latter-day Saints have traditionally been much lower than for those who marry by civil authority or marry non-Latter-day Saints (Thomas, p. 49). Also, premarital sexual involvement is a sin in LDS doctrine, and Utah unmarried teenagers report substantially lower rates of sexual intercourse than either the regional or national averages. Moreover, higher rates of sexual abstinence among unmarried adolescents in Utah are positively correlated with religious affiliation and attendance (especially LDS membership) and with the following characteristics, which reflect LDS counsel: living with both biological parents, educational aspirations, the avoidance of early and steady dating, abstention from drug and alcohol use, and personal belief in premarital abstinence (Governor's Task Force on Teenage Pregnancy Prevention, "Preventing Teenage Pregnancy in Utah," Oct. 3, 1988, p. 39; see LIFESTYLE; see also Miller, McCoy, and Olson).

Many of the "peculiar" features of LDS lives reflect faith in the counsel of modern prophets who offer revelation about how followers of Jesus Christ should operate in the world without becoming of the world. This counsel has included among many other things encouraging the observance of FAMILY HOME EVENING, keeping JOURNALS, planting gardens, avoiding debt, not dating until the age of sixteen, and preparing food and resources to meet emergencies.

BIBLIOGRAPHY

Albrecht, Stan L. "The Consequential Dimension of Mormon Religiosity." BYU Studies 29 (Spring 1989):57–108.

Chadwick, Bruce A. "Teenage Pregnancy and Out-of-Wedlock Births." In Utah in Demographic Perspective. ed. T. Martin, T. Heaton, and S. Bahr, pp. 23–36. Salt Lake City, 1986.

Heaton, Tim B. "The Demography of Utah Mormons." In Utah in Demographic Perspective, ed. T. Martin, T. Heaton, and S. Bahr, pp. 181–93. Salt Lake City, 1986.

———. "Four C's of the Mormon Family: Chastity, Conjugality, Children, and Chauvinism." In The Religion and Family Connection: Social Science Perspectives, ed. Darwin L. Thomas, pp. 107–24. Provo, Utah, 1988.

Miller, Brent C.; J. Kelly McCoy; and Terrance D. Olson. "Dating Age and Stage as Correlates of Adolescent Sexual Attitudes and Behavior." Journal of Adolescent Research 1 No. 3 (1986):361–71.

Nibley, Hugh W. "Comments, Hugh [W.] Nibley." In Mormonism: A Faith for All Cultures, ed. F. LaMond Tullis, pp. 22–28. Provo, Utah, 1978.

Smith, James E. "Mortality." In Utah in Demographic Perspective, ed. T. Martin, T. Heaton, and S. Bahr, pp. 59–69. Salt Lake City, 1986.

Smith, Wilford E. "The Urban Threat to Mormon Norms." Rural Sociology 24 (1959):355–61.

———. "Mormon Sex Standards on College Campuses, or Deal Us Out of the Sexual Revolution!" Dialogue 10 (1976):76-81.

Thomas, Darwin L. "Do Early Marriages Tend to End in Disaster?" New Era 3 (Mar. 1973):48–50.

Van Mondfrans, Adrian; Ralph B. Smith; and Vanessa Moss. "Education." In *Utah in Demographic Perspective*, ed. T. Martin, T. Heaton, and S. Bahr, pp. 195–215. Salt Lake City, 1986.

WILFORD E. SMITH

PERDITION, SONS OF

See: Sons of Perdition

PERFECTION

Through all generations, God has commanded his children to be perfect. His mandates to Abraham, "Walk before me, and be thou perfect" (Gen. 17:1), and to the Israelites, "Thou shalt be perfect with the Lord thy God" (Deut. 18:13), were one with his charge, "Be ye therefore perfect, even as your Father which is in heaven is perfect" (Matt. 5:48; cf. 3 Ne. 12:48).

Although the Savior's injunction is an unequivocal call to perfection, Latter-day Saints recognize that only he was totally without blemish or stain and was perfect in an infinite and absolute sense. "And being made perfect, he became the author of eternal salvation unto all them that obey him" (Heb. 5:9).

Human beings are required to seek perfection in certain respects that are attainable in mortality only through Christ. The New Testament refers to "them that are perfect" (1 Cor. 2:6; cf. Matt. 19:21; James 3:2; Heb. 12:23), and the Greek word *teleios*, meaning "perfect," also means "complete, whole, fully initiated, mature." Such maturity and completeness consist of receiving the fulness of the gospel, walking by faith in the Lord Jesus Christ, repenting of one's sins, receiving necessary ordinances, being faithful to covenants with the Lord, obeying the Lord and submitting to his will, seeking first the kingdom of God and his righteousness, and having charity, "the bond of perfectness and peace" (D&C 88:125).

Latter-day prophets have taught that men and women can become perfect "in the spheres in which [they] are called to act . . . [and that] we may become as perfect in our sphere as God is perfect in his higher and more exalted sphere" (Smith, p. 252; cf. *JD* 6:99; 2:129; 10:223). Mortal beings have the comforting assurance that God "giveth no commandments unto the children of men, save he

shall prepare a way for them that they may accomplish the thing which he commandeth them" (1 Ne. 3:7).

Mormons believe that Jesus Christ provides the means for all humans to become perfect. He is "the way, the truth, and the life: no man cometh unto the Father but by [him]" (John 14:6). Through his atoning sacrifice all men and women can repent and become perfected by having their sins and errors and the desire for sin removed. Ultimately, eternal life and godly perfection are gifts of God (D&C 14:7), rooted in the grace of God, redemption, individual righteousness, and being born of God. Human effort falls short; God's gift of grace compensates for this shortcoming, "for we know that it is by grace that we are saved, after all we can do" (2 Ne. 25:23).

The process by which faithful Saints advance toward perfection is gradual, made step by step. Just as the Savior "continued from grace to grace, until he received a fulness" (D&C 93:13), so God gives his children milk before meat (1 Cor. 3:2; Heb. 5:12; D&C 19:22). "It is not requisite that a man should run faster than he has strength" (Mosiah 4:27). This process is variously described as a "ladder" (*TPJS*, p. 348), a "road" (*DS* 2:18–19), and a "process to be pursued throughout one's lifetime" (Kimball, p. 6). In 1831 the Lord admonished the Saints to "continue in patience until ye are perfected" (D&C 67:13).

Although to many the goal of perfection seems overwhelming, Christ promised, "My yoke is easy, and my burden is light" (Matt. 11:30). While obedience to the commandments is essential, the spirit of perfection is contrary to ever-lengthening checklists of outward acts visible to others. Rather, prophets invite all to "come unto Christ, and be perfected in him, and deny yourselves of all ungodliness; . . . and love God with all your might, mind and strength, then is his grace sufficient for you" (Moro. 10:32). Therein lies the power to overcome sin and discouragement.

The man or woman who seeks the perfection of the Redeemer participates in the Father's work of saving and exalting mankind: "He proceeds to help his frail fellow men in their attempts to progress; thus becoming a partner with God in working out the plan of salvation" (Widtsoe, p. 180). Latter-day Saints believe that they must become perfected and one in spirit, as individuals and as a body (Eph. 4:12), in order to inherit the kingdom of God.

[*See also* HOLINESS; SANCTIFICATION.]

BIBLIOGRAPHY

"Becoming Justified and Sanctified." In *Relief Society Personal Study Guide*, pp. 63–69. Salt Lake City, 1989.

Kimball, Spencer W. "Hold Fast to the Iron Rod." *Ensign* 8 (Nov. 1978):4–6.

Lund, Gerald N. "Are We Expected to Achieve Perfection in this Life?" *Ensign* 16 (Aug. 1986):39–41.

Smith, Joseph F. *Gospel Doctrine*, p. 252. Salt Lake City, 1939.

Widtsoe, John A. *Evidences and Reconciliations*, p. 180. Salt Lake City, 1960.

CAROL LEE HAWKINS

PERPETUAL EMIGRATING FUND (PEF)

To assist Latter-day Saints in the eastern United States and Europe to gather to Church headquarters in the West (*see* GATHERING), the Church inaugurated the Perpetual Emigrating Fund Company in 1849. It is probable that before its demise in 1887, the Emigrating Company assisted more than 30,000 individuals to travel to Utah.

The PEF used Church assets and private contributions to assist individuals commensurate with their inability to pay. With limited funds, fewer individuals could be assisted than wished to participate. Those receiving priority included individuals with skills urgently needed in the West, those whose relatives or friends had contributed to the PEF, and those with longest membership in the Church. Cost-cutting measures, including group contracting, doubling up families in wagons, and organizing HANDCART COMPANIES, were also adopted to make the available funds stretch as far as possible.

PEF assistance was always extended as a loan rather than as a gift. Sponsored emigrants signed a note obligating themselves to repay the PEF as they were able. Though it sometimes required years, and some never fully retired their debt, many repaid their loan in cash, commodities, or labor. In 1880, on the fiftieth anniversary of the organization of the Church, President John TAYLOR, in the tradition of the Israelite jubilee year, forgave half of the outstanding debt owed by the poor to the fund, while those who were able to pay were still expected to do so. In late 1887, under provisions of the Edmunds-Tucker Act (*see* ANTIPOLYGAMY LEGISLATION), the U.S. government dissolved both the Corporation of The Church of Jesus Christ of Latter-day Saints and the Perpetual Emigrating Fund Company.

[*See also* Immigration and Emigration.]

Monarch of the Sea, the largest sailing vessel to transport LDS immigrants from Europe to America, carried the two largest companies of 955 and 974 people, in 1861 and 1864 respectively. Immigration to Utah was made possible for many more by borrowing from the Perpetual Emigrating Fund. Courtesy Peabody Museum, Salem, Massachusetts.

BIBLIOGRAPHY

Arrington, Leonard J. *Great Basin Kingdom*. Cambridge, Mass, 1958.

Jensen, Richard J. "The British Gathering to Zion." In *Truth Will Prevail: The Rise of The Church of Jesus Christ of Latter-day Saints in the British Isles, 1837–1987*, pp. 165–98. Cambridge, England, 1987.

DAVID F. BOONE

PERSECUTION

Jesus told his followers that they would be persecuted, but promised them a great reward in heaven (Matt. 5:11–12). Latter-day Saints believe that righteously enduring persecution can bring blessings in both this life and the next. Although suffering is as unwelcome to Latter-day Saints as to any other people, they strive to respond with patience and faith and to avoid bitterness or revenge (Matt. 5:43–47; D&C 101:35; cf. 98:23–27).

Although Latter-day Saints claim no greater suffering than many others who have also been persecuted for their religious beliefs through the ages, many Latter-day Saints have been persecuted, beginning with Joseph SMITH (see JS—H 1:33). As the Church grew, persecutions increased; the Latter-day Saints faced threats, murder, rape, mayhem, property damage, and revilement in Kirtland, Ohio (1831–1838), in Missouri (1831–1839), and in the area of Nauvoo, Illinois (1839–1846), culminating in the assassinations of Joseph and Hyrum Smith at Carthage, Illinois, in 1844 (Hull, pp. 643–52).

The isolation and safety of the Great Basin in the American West, to which the main body of the Church fled beginning in 1846–1847, lasted only a few years before persecutions were renewed. The Great Basin area became part of the United States in 1848 after the Mexican-American War, and soon federal laws against the practice of plural marriage forced many Latter-day Saints into hiding or to settlements in Mexico and Canada. More than one thousand Latter-day Saints, mostly polygamous husbands, were fined and imprisoned. Ultimately, ANTIPOLYGAMY LEGISLATION disenfranchised the Saints and disincorporated the Church, allowing confiscation of Church property. After the 1890 MANIFESTO enjoining plural marriage, anti-Mormon persecution declined substantially, but other hostilities persisted.

Anti-Mormon literature has often incited and precipitated persecution, from early attempts to discredit Joseph Smith and the Book of Mormon, to recent films misrepresenting LDS doctrine. LDS missionaries have sometimes especially been persecuted. Some missionaries sent to England and Scandinavia in the 1830s and 1850s were confronted by mobs, threats, imprisonment, and physical harm. Several missionaries and potential converts were murdered in the United States at the height of antipolygamy agitation during the 1870s. As recently as 1990, two LDS missionaries were killed in Huancayo, Peru, by anti-American terrorists, and Church property was vandalized or destroyed in several South American countries.

Scriptural examples provide comfort and perspective to Latter-day Saints by showing that in God's eternal plan persecutions are sometimes allowed, with blessings then coming to the persecuted (Ivins, pp. 408–413). The biblical stories of Joseph (Gen. 37–46) and Esther (Esth. 2–9) demonstrate that faith can overcome persecution and bring honor to the persecuted. In the Book of Mormon, the Ammonites provide a poignant example of a people who became dedicated to righteousness, willing to suffer persecution and death rather than break their covenants (Alma 24). Many have also been comforted by the Lord's words to Joseph Smith when he was falsely accused and wrongfully imprisoned. Despite his many trials, the Lord reminded Joseph that the Savior had endured even more, and promised him, "All these things shall give thee experience, and shall be for thy good" (D&C 122:7). He expanded the Prophet's perspective to eternity with the statement "Fear not what man can do, for God shall be with you forever and ever" (D&C 122:9).

The LDS response to persecution is to temper sorrow and anger in accordance with scriptural counsel. The Savior's admonition to turn the other cheek (Matt. 5:39–42) is expanded in the Doctrine and Covenants: Great rewards are promised to those who do not seek retribution and retaliate, but the persecuted may seek for justice after they have suffered repeated offenses and given their adversaries adequate prior warnings (D&C 98:23–31). Patience and tolerance are admonished in the Book of Mormon (Alma 1:21) and in Articles of Faith 11 and 13. A true Latter-day Saint hopes to be reconciled to, and perhaps even to convert, an enemy.

BIBLIOGRAPHY

Allen, James B. "Why Did People Act That Way? Some Observations on Religious Intolerance and Persecution in the American Past." *Ensign* 8 (Dec. 1978):21–24.

Arrington, Leonard J., and Davis Bitton. *The Mormon Experience*, chaps. 3–5, 9. New York, 1979.

The Church of Jesus Christ of Latter-day Saints, ed. *My Kingdom Shall Roll Forth*, chap. 8. Salt Lake City, 1979.

Hull, T. "Persecution: The Heritage of the Saints." *IE* 4 (July 1901):643–52.

Ivins, A. "Is Persecution a Result of Transgression or Righteousness." *IE* 27 (Mar. 1924):408–413.

LISA BOLIN HAWKINS

PERSONAL ANCESTRAL FILE®

Personal Ancestral File® is a genealogical software package produced by the Church for IBM-compatible, Macintosh, and Apple personal computers that enables users to organize, store, and search genealogical information; contribute genealogies to ANCESTRAL FILE™; and match and merge information from other genealogical data bases with their own files.

The package consists of three major programs: Family Records, Research Data Filer, and Genealogical Information Exchange. The Family Records program enables users to assemble pedigrees; group families together, showing relationships between family members for each generation; search pedigree lines; add, modify, and delete information about individuals; and display information on the screen and print it on genealogical forms. Research Data Filer helps users manage original research, including searching, sorting, and printing information by event, place, date, name of person, or relationship to others. Genealogical Information Exchange enables users to send Family Records data to another Personal Ancestral File user, prepare diskette submissions of names for LDS temple ordinance processing or contribution to Ancestral File, and copy data from one diskette to another.

BIBLIOGRAPHY

Long, Jack. "Personal Ancestral File 2.1." *MacWorld* (Sept. 1989):242–44.

Trivette, Donald B. "Personal Ancestral File Helps Organize Facts of Family History." *PC Magazine* (June 13, 1989):452.

DAVID M. MAYFIELD

PETER

Simon bar-Jona, later known as Cephas or Peter, became the senior and chief apostle of Jesus Christ. He was evidently the presiding officer over the ancient Church after Christ's death. In the present dispensation, as a resurrected being, he restored apostolic authority to the Prophet Joseph SMITH and Oliver COWDERY.

The New Testament contains more information about Peter than about any of the other apostles. This provides some indication of his ministry, his character, and his relationship to the Savior. In contrast to the sometimes impetuous younger Peter portrayed in the Gospels, the apostle's later ministry and epistles bespeak a mature leader of patient faith whose sincere concern is for the spiritual well-being of the flock that Jesus entrusted to him (John 21:15–17). Differences persist, however, in the portraits of Peter derived from the various biblical accounts, and these are extrapolated in scholarly analyses of the role and theology of Peter. Recourse to later Christian writings from the second and third centuries reveals other views about Peter's position in the pristine Church. It cannot be presumed, therefore, that all that is written about him is clearly factual.

Originally from Bethsaida, a small fishing port somewhere on the north shore of the Sea of Galilee, Peter resided in the town of Capernaum with his wife and mother-in-law at the time of his apostolic call. Peter's given name was Simon and his patronymic, bar-Jona, identifies him as the son of Jonah (Matt. 16:17). The name Simon *(Simōn)* and that of his brother Andrew *(Andreas)* are derived from the Greek renditions of their names. Living in a region where, in addition to the native Aramaic, Greek was widely used as a language of business and trade, Peter may have been conversant with the tongue in which his scriptural writings were later penned. Although Peter was a fisherman by occupation, and despite the description of Peter and John by the elders of the Sanhedrin as being "without learning" (Acts 4:13), the Galilean apostles were literate men, probably without normal rabbinical training but with broad general understanding and capability.

Peter was among the first of Jesus' disciples. To him, then called Simon, was extended a special call, marked by the reception of a new name, which in Jewish tradition "denoted the conferring of a special divine mission" (Winter, p. 5). John describes Christ's bestowal upon Simon bar-Jona of the title "Cephas, which is by interpretation, A stone" (John 1:42). The Aramaic *kepha* and its Greek equivalent, *petros*, are common nouns and prior to that time were unused as proper names. A dispute of long duration continues among Catholic and Protestant scholars (Winter, pp. 6–25; Horsley, pp. 29–41) concerning the definition of *petros*, "a rock or stone," and *petra*, "a large mass of rock," as these words pertain to Peter's name and its connection to Christ's wordplay "Thou art Peter, and upon this rock I will build my church" (Matt. 16:18). LDS doctrine holds that revelation was the rock denoted by Jesus and that Peter's call to become the prophet to lead the early Church is here foretold. Relevant to this passage, Joseph Smith applied the term "seer" to define *cephas* (JST John 1:42), and Bruce R. McConkie (pp. 133, 380–83) relates this to the seership, or power of continuing revelation, which he further connects to the KEYS of the kingdom (Matt. 16:19) bestowed on Peter, the chief apostle, upon the MOUNT OF TRANSFIGURATION, an account of which immediately follows in Matt. 17:1–13.

Peter's primacy in the ancient Church derived from apostolic authority. His first place among the twelve apostles is clear in a number of contexts: all New Testament lists of the apostles mention Peter first; the phrase "Peter and they that are with him" describes the apostles (e.g., Luke 8:45); and Peter acts as their spokesman in posing questions to Jesus (e.g., Luke 12:41). Miracles, teaching incidents, and special events (e.g., Matt. 14:25–31; Mark 14:26–42; Luke 5:1–10) center around Peter alone or on him as the key apostle involved (Muren, p. 150). After the trial of Jesus before Caiaphas, Peter stayed nearby in the dark and the cold. Although during Jesus' trial he denied certain allegations about association or affiliations with the disciples, and acquaintance with Jesus, Peter was the first apostle to whom the resurrected Christ appeared (Luke 24:33–35; 1 Cor. 15:5).

Peter's leading position is perceived by Latter-day Saints as one of presidency. Two LDS Church Presidents have likened Peter's office to that of the President of the QUORUM OF THE TWELVE APOSTLES (McKay, p. 20; Kimball).

The apostles JAMES and JOHN occupied a position second to that of Peter. Together these three were privileged to attend Jesus on three most sacred occasions: at Jesus' raising of Jairus' daughter from the dead (Mark 5:35–43), at his glorification

on the Mount of Transfiguration (Matt. 17:1–13; Mark 9:2–9), and at his suffering in the garden of Gethsemane (Mark 14:26–42). Latter-day Saints attribute the presence of Peter, James, and John on these occasions to the priesthood office that they held among the apostles. Joseph Smith taught that the Savior, Moses, and Elias, when transfigured before them, gave the keys of the MELCHIZEDEK PRIESTHOOD to Peter, James, and John (*TPJS*, p. 158; *see* MOUNT OF TRANSFIGURATION).

Through this authority, Peter, James, and John directed the Church in the name of Jesus Christ after his death. Peter presided over the selection of a new apostle to replace Judas (Acts 1:15–26) and over the ministry on the Day of Pentecost (Acts 2). Peter confronted the Sanhedrin, performed miracles, and preached the gospel of Christ (Acts 3–4). In many of these activities John was Peter's companion, but Peter took the lead. Through important revelations pertaining to the extension of the gospel to the Gentiles (Acts 10), Peter's calling as prophet, seer, and revelator is evident (Muren, pp. 150–52). Although modern revelation provides much clarification of information in this regard, Peter's role of presiding over Church councils and directing the general apostolic effort is patently demonstrable through examination of the New Testament and other early Christian sources (Brown, pp. 9–16, 1973).

Because of his ancient office, it was Peter who, with the assistance of James and John, was commissioned to restore apostolic authority to a new gospel dispensation and to endow Joseph Smith with the same priesthood keys that Christ had given to Peter, thereby reauthorizing the performance of the ordinances of salvation by the authority of the priesthood (*see* MELCHIZEDEK PRIESTHOOD: RESTORATION OF).

Peter's two epistles in the New Testament contain an abundance of inspired and inspiring teachings and exhortations. Throughout 1 and 2 Peter, concern is expressed for the salvation and sanctification of the flock, reminding the faithful that this can be obtained only through knowledge of Jesus Christ and performance of the ordinances of the priesthood (cf. *TPJS*, pp. 297, 303–305; Muren, pp. 153–56). Peter also provides information about the salvation of the dead (1 Pet. 3:18–22; 4:6), and he exhorts all members of the Church to be holy, to feed the flock, to be humble, and to secure salvation through making their calling and election sure (1 Pet. 4–5; 2 Pet. 1). A final concern is expressed for the spiritual welfare of the Church, which Peter warns will soon experience the teaching of false doctrines that will threaten individual salvation (2 Pet. 2–3). Of these epistles Joseph Smith remarked, "Peter penned the most sublime language of any of the apostles" (*TPJS*, p. 301).

BIBLIOGRAPHY

Brown, Raymond E.; Karl Donfried; and John Reumann, eds. *Peter in the New Testament*. Minneapolis, Minn., 1973.

Brown, S. Kent. "James the Just and the Question of Peter's Leadership in the Light of New Sources." In *Sperry Lecture Series*, pp. 9–16. Provo, Utah, 1973.

Horsley, A. Burt. *Peter and the Popes*. Salt Lake City, 1989.

Kimball, Spencer W. "Peter, My Brother." In *BYU Speeches of the Year*. Provo, Utah, 1971.

McConkie, Bruce R. *Doctrinal New Testament Commentary*, Vol. 1. Salt Lake City, 1978.

McKay, David O. *Ancient Apostles*. Salt Lake City, 1964.

Muren, Joseph C. "Peter." In *A Symposium on the New Testament*. Salt Lake City, 1980.

Winter, Michael M. *Saint Peter and the Popes*. Westport, Conn., 1960.

JOHN FRANKLIN HALL

PHILOSOPHY

Philosophy (the "love of wisdom") originated in the Western world in ancient Greece. The attempt to find wisdom by ancient thinkers such as Socrates, Plato, and Aristotle led them also to investigate the world (nature), the unseen world (METAPHYSICS), and how we know (EPISTEMOLOGY). Wonder about nature through progressively refined epistemological procedures led through the centuries to modern scientific methods. As philosophers developed standards for accurate description and generalization, new sciences were born and detached themselves from philosophy: the first was physics, and the latest is linguistics. But the basic problems of epistemology, metaphysics, and ethics (including aesthetics and the philosophy of religion) dominate present philosophy as much as they did in ancient times. Although the solutions are more varied now, the basic issues remain the same.

Latter-day scriptures do not present a philosophical system, but they do contain answers to many classic philosophical issues. These scriptures preclude ex nihilo creation, idealism (immaterialism), a chance theory of causation, and absolute determinism. They affirm the eternality and agency of the individual person, the necessary existence of evil apart from God, a nonrelativistic good (righteousness), and the doctrine that all mortals are the offspring and heirs of God. God is affirmed as a perfected physical being who governs all things in pure love and who continues to communicate with his children on earth by personal revelation.

Observers of the LDS position have ascribed philosophical labels and tendencies to it, but that position usually will not fit neatly into the stock answers. It is empirical, yet rational; pragmatic, yet idealistic; oriented toward eternity, yet emphasizing the importance of the here and now. Affinities are found with the Cartesian certainty of personal existence, the positivist insistence on sensory evidence, the Enlightenment emphasis on elimination of paradox, and the postmodern respect for the "other." The ultimate standard for all being, truth, and good is Christ himself.

Contemporary analytic and existential movements in philosophy have had little impact on LDS thought, not because it is not aware of them, but because it has different answers to the questions they pose. The knowledge of God is established through careful experimentation with God's promises, which results in tangible consequences, culminating in the possibility of seeing God face to face. Existential angst is recognized and met by personal guidance from God to establish a path to righteousness and fulfillment, the general features of which each person must follow, but with individual parameters. The relativism of situational ethics is answered in spiritual assurance and power to do those things that are eternally worthwhile. Mind-body dualism is answered by the material nature of spirit (more refined matter) (D&C 131:7).

Answers to the questions How may I know? What is the seen world? What is the unseen world? and How shall I be wise? are all answered personally for every fully participating Latter-day Saint. The equivalent of epistemology in an LDS frame is the ORDINANCES, focusing on the ordinance of PRAYER. Through the ordinances and in connection with other epistemologies come all of the light and knowledge sufficient to live a spiritually successful life. Questions about the natural world are answered by one's culture as corrected by personal revelation. One must have some guidance on questions of metaphysics, and such is found in holy scripture and confirmed to each individual through personal REVELATION. The ultimate question as to how to be wise is answered both in general and in particular. The general answer is that to be wise is to love God with all of one's heart, might, mind, and strength, and to love our neighbor as God loves us (D&C 59:5). The particular answer is to repent of sinning and to live by the whisperings of the Holy Spirit and the counsels of the living prophet (Isa. 50:10–11).

While LDS culture does not encourage philosophizing directly, every LDS person is encouraged to become a profound theologian. Becoming such necessitates a heavy commitment to active study "in theory, in principle, in doctrine" to search out the weighty matters of time and eternity (D&C 97:14), which include the basic questions of the philosophers. The imperative "study it out in your mind" (D&C 9:7–8) is a standard for all LDS persons, not just for academics. "Time, and experience and careful and ponderous and solemn thought" (TPJS, p. 37) are not inimical to but are the preface to and foundation for personal revelation.

BIBLIOGRAPHY

Madsen, Truman G. "Joseph Smith and the Ways of Knowing," pp. 25–63. BYU Extension Publications, Seminar on the Prophet Joseph Smith, 1962.

Oaks, Dallin H. "Ethics, Morality, and Professional Responsibility." In *Perspectives in Mormon Ethics*, ed. Donald G. Hill, Jr., pp. 193–200. Salt Lake City, 1983.

Yarn, David H., Jr. "Some Metaphysical Reflections on the Gospel of John." *BYU Studies* 3 (Autumn 1960):3–10.

CHAUNCEY C. RIDDLE

PHYSICAL BODY

Latter-day Saints believe that the physical human body was created by God in his express image, and that one of the most important purposes of earth life is for the spirit children of God to obtain a physical body and grow through the experience of MORTALITY.

The physical body, with all its structures and physiological systems, appetites and passions, strengths and frailties, serves as the mortal housing of the spirit. Before BIRTH, the spirit leaves God's presence and comes to this world to take up a physical body. In mortality, the body is imperfect and will eventually die. In due time, the physical body of every human will be resurrected in its "proper and perfect frame" (Alma 40:23) and the spirit will be restored to it in a state of immortality.

Together, the physical body and the spirit constitute the SOUL (D&C 88:15). The salvation of the soul requires PERFECTION of both body and spirit. GOD THE FATHER and JESUS CHRIST, both perfected and glorified beings, possess tangible resurrected bodies of flesh and bone (D&C 130:22). The Prophet Joseph SMITH stated, "No person can have this salvation except through a tabernacle" (TPJS, p. 297; see also D&C 93:35). To become like God, his children, too, must obtain physical bodies. "We came to this earth that we might have a body and present it pure before God in the celestial kingdom. The great principle of happiness consists in having a body" (TPJS, p. 181).

These beliefs are crucial to LDS understanding of the importance of the physical body. Many religions view the human corporeal nature as a state of constant conflict between the righteous enticings of the spirit and the vices of the flesh, ending only when death frees the spirit from the body. In contrast, Latter-day Saints strive for righteous harmony between the two, seeking perfection and discipline of the spirit along with training and health of the body. Health includes both physical and moral hygiene. The WORD OF WISDOM and other scriptural admonitions concerning health are intended to be followed to ensure a clean and clear mind and vigorous longevity "unto the renewing of their bodies" (D&C 84:33). CHASTITY, in both deed and thought, and physical and moral health are conditions essential for spiritual sensitivity, receiving a TESTIMONY, and personal REVELATION.

Latter-day Saints view the possession of a body as an eternal privilege and a blessing. The righteous decision to accept the plan of God the Father and come into this world was rewarded with the gift of a human body. Humans are free to choose their actions while in the flesh, and they are privileged to experience the pleasures and pains of being alive. This is a blessing not enjoyed by those who followed Satan's lead and were cast out of God's presence, never to have a mortal body. During Christ's ministry, he found several occasions to cast out DEVILS. In the most notable incident, the spirits requested that Christ not cast them out entirely, but that he allow them to enter the bodies of nearby swine (Mark 5:6–13). For Latter-day Saints this suggests how much the followers of Satan desire a physical body. RESURRECTION, the ultimate and perfect unification of body and spirit, gives spirits the power to overcome SPIRITUAL DEATH: "For behold, if the flesh should rise no more our spirits must become subject to that angel who fell from before the presence of the Eternal God, and became the devil, to rise no more" (2 Ne. 9:8).

For Latter-day Saints the physical body, in all its developmental, anatomical, and physiological complexities and functions, is evidence of God's creative hand. It is, in itself, miraculous. Furthermore, the day-to-day vitality of the body can be attributed to divine regulation; as expressed by King BENJAMIN, it is God who "has created you from the beginning, and is preserving you from day to day, by lending you breath, that ye may live and move and do according to your own will, and even supporting you from one moment to another" (Mosiah 2:21).

The upkeep and maintenance of the body are important in LDS belief. Disease is a natural condition that disturbs the normal function of the body's physical processes. When ill or injured, Latter-day Saints exercise faith toward recovery. Worthy priesthood holders, by administering a BLESSING of health, may call upon the power of God to aid in the healing process. At the same time, Latter-day Saints are encouraged to take full advantage of modern medicine and technology in the prevention and cure of sickness and do not find this inconsistent with accepting the blessings of the priesthood, for they see an ultimate unity between SPIRIT and MATTER.

BIBLIOGRAPHY

Lockhart, Barbara. "The Body: A Burden or a Blessing." *Ensign* 15 (Feb. 1985):56–60.

Madsen, Truman G. *Eternal Man*, pp. 43–51. Salt Lake City, 1966.

Nelson, Russell M. "Self Mastery." *Ensign* 15 (Nov. 1985):30–32.

KENT M. VAN DE GRAAFF

PHYSICAL FITNESS AND RECREATION

The Church has always endorsed recreation and fitness as desirable and worthy of promotion. Recreational activities can strengthen social connections and a sense of community. Proper physical activities are any that are "clean, beneficial to health, conducive to true happiness and in harmony with the highest moral standards" ("Wholesome Recreation," p. 430). A latter-day apostle stated, "Recreation—good Latter-day Saint recreation—is one of the devices by which we may help the young people of this Church to learn and love the gospel of the Lord, Jesus Christ, and thereby learn to live righteously" (Petersen, p. 554).

During the nineteenth century, when most religions were condemning play as sinful (T.D., p. 178), Joseph SMITH and Brigham YOUNG advocated recreation as part of their religious teaching. Both men participated in recreational activities and sanctioned wholesome amusements. Moreover, it was noted of Brigham Young that "he not only enjoyed recreational pursuits himself, but some of his august religious speeches were on this subject" (Skidmore, p. 25). In the early days of the Church, recreation also provided respite from work, drudgery, hardship, and persecution. It is likely that the large number of converts from many nationalities and cultures, although they were drawn together by a testimony of Christ and the restoration of the gospel, were more easily assimilated into the new community of Saints when recreational activities were a common denominator (Skidmore, p. 9). According to one researcher on recreation, the Church was the first religious organization to construct halls adjacent to, or adjoining, chapels for the formal promotion of such activities as games and sports, music, drama, speech, and dance (Brinley, pp. 43, 104–105).

The PHYSICAL BODY is viewed as a temple of God that the individual has stewardship from God to care for properly: "I speak of the religious doctrine which teaches that the human body is sacred, the veritable tabernacle of the divine spirit which inhabits it, and that it is a solemn duty of mankind to protect and preserve it from pollutions and unnecessary wastage and weakness" (Richards, p. 208). Isaiah recorded a promise to those who are willing to "wait upon the Lord" that they would "run and not be weary; and . . . walk, and not faint" (40:31). This promise is affirmed in the revelation to Joseph Smith known as the WORD OF WISDOM (D&C 89:20). Physical and spiritual health is promised as a consequence of obedience to spiritual law and observance of specific dietary and health habits.

BIBLIOGRAPHY

Brinley, Eldon D. "The Recreational Life of the Mormon People." Ph.D. diss., New York University, 1943.

Evans, Richard L. "Great Miracle: Housing for Body and Mind." *Church News* (Aug. 26, 1967):16.

McKay, David O. "The Whole Man." *IE* 55 (Apr. 1952):221–22.

Petersen, Mark E. "Building Spirituality Through Recreation." *IE* 51 (Sept. 1948):554–55, 598.

Richards, Stephen L. *Where Is Wisdom.* Salt Lake City, 1955.

Skidmore, Rex A. *Mormon Recreation In Theory and Practice: A Study of Social Change.* Philadelphia, 1941.

T.D. "Repose." *Nation* 2 (Feb. 1866):178.

"Wholesome Recreation: Ward Teacher's Message for August, 1939." *IE* 42 (July 1939):430.

CLARK T. THORSTENSON

PIONEER DAY

July 24, Pioneer Day, is celebrated yearly in "Mormon Country" and increasingly on an international scale among Latter-day Saints. On this date in 1847, the first Mormon pioneers (143 men, 3 women, 2 children) led by Brigham YOUNG, entered the uninhabited Salt Lake Valley. They began the pioneer settlement of more than 400 communities in the intermountain West, Canada, and Mexico. Before the completion of the transcontinental railroad in 1869, 80,000 Mormon refugees and converts went west in perpetual immigration. Six thousand lost their lives and were buried along the way.

"In the annals of the American Frontier," wrote historian Purnell H. Benson, there is "no more thrilling story" (p. 423). On July 24 this story is commemorated annually by a huge parade in Salt Lake City and is also celebrated frequently in drama (e.g., the *Promised Valley* musical), poetry, and song. The holiday is typically marked by sunrise services and, throughout LDS communities,

A Pioneer Day parade in Eureka, Utah. Traditionally, Latter-day Saints dress in pioneer costume and reenact the entry of the Mormon pioneers into the Salt Lake Valley in 1847. Pancake breakfasts, picnics, and pageantry mark Pioneer Day, even outside the Intermountain West. Courtesy Utah State Historical Society.

by Old West reenactments. In Church programs, commemorative addresses are given and family journals and reminiscences are revived. The close conjunction of the festivities of July 4 and 24 tends to focus on the Mormon exodus as a quest for religious freedom. But like the Puritan movement and the Jewish *aliyah*, it was at root a quest for the sacred. It grew out of the vision of a consecrated community, the KINGDOM OF GOD on earth. The festivities of July 24 attempt to regain and extend that vision.

[*See also* Celebrations.]

BIBLIOGRAPHY

Benson, Purnell H. *Religion in Contemporary Culture*, pp. 420–27. New York, 1960.

Shipps, Jan. *Mormonism: The Story of a New Religious Tradition*, pp. 64, 129. Urbana, Ill., 1985.

D. JAMES CANNON

PIONEER ECONOMY

The Church of Jesus Christ of Latter-day Saints was the major force contributing to the economic development of the Great Basin region in the nineteenth century. This was true until the completion of the transcontinental railroad in 1869, and to a large extent even through the remainder of the century. Though the railroad ended the isolation of the Great Basin and brought both economic benefits and new challenges to HOME INDUSTRIES, the Church's economic role did not decline significantly until the end of the pioneer period (*see* ECONOMIC HISTORY OF THE CHURCH).

Church involvement in the economy was rooted in theology. According to LDS belief, building up the KINGDOM OF GOD on earth—developing it and beautifying it for the return of the Savior—is a prime task of God's people. LDS pioneers believed that the Church was the agent of God and his people in building the kingdom. The responsibility to promote its progress and perfection rested upon Church officials. It thus became a religious duty to produce, to build, and to prepare for the MILLENNIUM. Digging canals, tending herds, cultivating crops, and constructing telegraph lines, railroads, and factories were all viewed as acts of religious devotion similar to prayer, worship, and other strictly religious activities.

Partly because economic activity had religious significance, it was clearly understood that all such was to be conducted in harmony with gospel principles. Precious-metal mining and other economic activities that did not contribute to basic production and stable communities were not endorsed. Individualism, profiteering, and speculation were eschewed. Instead, the individual member was enjoined to be "one with his brethren." Not only were they to work together in harmony, but Latter-day Saints were also expected to maintain relative equality in the possession and enjoyment of this world's goods.

President Brigham Young recognized early on the economic importance of women in making a harsh land productive. Not only were women partners with men in agriculture and home production—the more so with many men called away on missions—but they were also specifically encouraged by President Young to be involved as telegraph operators and shopkeepers, and he enlisted them throughout the territory to work in SILK CULTURE.

Building the pioneer kingdom required the erection of a "two-decker" economy—a foundation of agricultural and handicraft production to satisfy the most pressing wants of the settlers and the steady increment of immigrants, along with a superstructure of investment to provide for future growth. In general, programs were concerned with three types of activities. First, leaders sought to increase the agents of production by a widespread missionary program and by promotion and organization of emigration (*see* IMMIGRATION AND EMIGRATION; PERPETUAL EMIGRATING FUND). Between 1847 and 1880 more than 70,000 converts immigrated to the Great Basin to work on farms, in factories, and to participate in COLONIZATION projects.

Second, Church leaders sought to aid capital formation. This they did by sending out exploration parties to discover new resources, by developing these resources under Church sponsorship, by mobilizing the savings of its members in the Great Basin and in Europe, and by diverting resources from the production of consumables to the production of reproducible wealth. Sizable groups were sent to southern Utah to mine and manufacture iron, to southern Nevada to mine silver and lead, to northern and central Utah to mine coal, to southern California to establish an entrepôt, to southern Utah to raise cotton and other semitropical products, to various places in northern Utah and southern Idaho to utilize grazing lands, and to hundreds of irrigable areas throughout the Great Basin to establish colonies, construct irrigation systems, and engage in farming (*see also* AGRICULTURE; CITY PLANNING).

In mobilizing savings to support these developmental projects, the basic organizational device was the office of the trustee-in-trust. Usually the PRESIDENT OF THE CHURCH, as trustee-in-trust, held, bought, and sold property; collected donations and expended them; and in general used the common fund of the community in constructing the infrastructure of communications, transportation, merchandising, and education. This was sometimes done by chartered companies such as the Deseret Iron Company, the Deseret Sugar Manufacturing Company, and the Deseret Telegraph Company. The President of the Church could also direct regionwide economic initiatives such as the 1850s CONSECRATION movement, the 1860s cooperative movement, and the 1870s UNITED ORDERS.

A second organizational device was the network of tithing houses, that received contributions in kind of butter, eggs, calves, chickens, hay, wheat, and other produce that were then used to support workers on school buildings, tanneries, woolen factories, gristmills, roads, and other projects. In the largely cashless pioneer economy, the tithing house system also made it possible to spend credit earned for labor or goods in one community in another. Tithing Office script and credits, ultimately controlled and reconciled through the books of the trustee-in-trust, thus helped to grease the wheels of commerce in the Great Basin.

Third, pioneer Church leaders also sought to overcome an adverse balance of trade for the region. They solicited investments by members wherever they were located and promoted sales outside the region of livestock, grain, salt, cotton, dried fruits, wool products, and other exportables. In this connection, the Church was able to turn to advantage the discovery of gold in California in 1848. The Church acquired about $150,000 in gold dust during the 1850s from returning miners, from contributions of its members in California, and from men assigned to California expressly for the purpose of obtaining specie to help boost the Utah economy.

The balance of payments problem was one reason the Church discouraged the importation of unnecessary consumables. Leaders urged Latter-day Saints to refrain from using imported tea, coffee, tobacco, liquor, or "fashionable" clothing from the East (homemade was considered more saintly). In order to prevent "outside" merchants from becoming wealthy in this trade, Church leaders bought out most of them, imposed a boycott on trading with others, and channeled the bulk of the territory's imports through the Church-controlled Zion's Cooperative Mercantile Institution (ZCMI).

The Church assumed much of the burden of promoting economic activity that, under different circumstances, might have been assumed by eastern capitalists or the federal government. By influencing the movement of population and new investment, and by controlling community pricing through the tithing houses, the Church regulated the allocation of resources to maximize the gross product. By continuously funneling new families into the various settlements and valleys, the Church also prevented the creation of a class system and contributed to a greater equality of income. In so doing, LDS leaders expressed greater confidence in the efficacy of their own administered economy than in the ability of an impersonal price system to optimally allocate resources and induce rapid and diversified economic development.

BIBLIOGRAPHY

Arrington, Leonard J. *Great Basin Kingdom: An Economic History of the Latter-day Saints, 1830–1900.* Cambridge, Mass., 1958.

———. "Religion and Planning in the Great Basin, 1847–1900." *Proceedings of the Thirty-second Annual Conference of the Western Economic Association*, pp. 37–41. Salt Lake City, 1957.

LEONARD J. ARRINGTON

PIONEER LIFE AND WORSHIP

The first members of The Church of Jesus Christ of Latter-day Saints worshiped like the converts of many new religions: their devotions were democratic, fervent, local, and spontaneous. "High Church" priestly gowns, sacerdotal objects, or complicated liturgy were not used—then or later. Equally remote were the formal creeds and confessions of the frontier sects. Only as Church growth brought the need for orderly administration, toward the last third of the nineteenth century, did the Latter-day Saints gain a measure of formal devotion.

The early Saints were not left without direction. As early as June 1829, ten months prior to the formal ORGANIZATION OF THE CHURCH, Joseph SMITH and Oliver COWDERY sought guidance about Church performances. "The church shall meet together oft for prayer & supplication," read an early copy of the manuscript that resulted. "Each member shall speak & tell the church of their progress in the way of Eternal life" (Oliver Cowdery, "Articles of the Church of Christ," 1829, LDS Library Archives). The document, which drew on previous revelations and Book of Mormon injunctions, later became the Church's "Articles and Covenants." The first revelation to be canonized, it became, arguably, the Church's single most important statement on religious WORSHIP and procedure (see DOCTRINE AND COVENANTS: SECTIONS 20–21).

It defined a simple structure. There were three sacramental ORDINANCES: BAPTISM by immersion, confirmation of the spirit, and the bread and the cup of the Lord's Supper (see SACRAMENTS). Routines were equally modest, prescribing prayer, frequent MEETINGS, home visits by teachers, local PRIESTHOOD governance, and quarterly CONFERENCES to regulate Churchwide business. Traveling elders took this blueprint to the early, scattered congregations.

KIRTLAND, OHIO, one of the Church's early centers, typified the resulting system. There were many meetings. Leaders might hold frequent "councils" and "schools" at the Newel K. Whitney store. They joined members in private homes on Sundays and on weekdays for prayer and worship meetings, often with millennial singing and testifying accompanied by the display of pentecostal gifts. Fast and testimony meetings might be held on Thursdays, with attention given to the needs of the poor (see FASTING). Abstinence from food brought piety to worshipers, and what was saved assisted the needy. Kirtland members also attempted wider, congregational assemblies. With no other gathering place at first available, they met in the open air or in Kirtland's sixteen-by-twenty-four-foot schoolhouse. After the completion of the KIRTLAND TEMPLE in 1836, meetings were held there with as many as several hundred people in attendance.

These routines set the pattern for Latter-day Saint worship as the Church moved from Ohio to Missouri, Illinois, and Nebraska. While leaders might organize and direct meetings, individual Saints could also do so. Prayer meetings, often the redoubt of women, proceeded at times without ecclesiastical direction. General Church meetings were often as democratic. Members simply summoned others by ringing the community bell. Content was also unstructured. "We shall devote this day to preaching—exhortation—singing—praying and blessing children," promised a Church leader prior to the start of the Church's April general conference in 1845 (T&S, 6:953–57). With congregational sessions still held in open air, some might chat on the perimeters while the more centrally situated struggled to hear.

NAUVOO brought the innovation of ward worship. At first a political division as in other American cities, wards in Nauvoo became religious units. Church-appointed BISHOPS presided over the jurisdictions, levying quotas for Church building projects, conducting neighborhood (block) or ward teaching (see HOME TEACHING), and overseeing the needs of the poor and, increasingly, the holding of meetings. Here began, for the first time, Church-directed neighborhood worship. The system was regularized at WINTER QUARTERS, Nebraska, during the exodus west. Brigham YOUNG instructed bishops to "organize and watch over their wards, have weekly meetings therein; also see that those under their charge have work and that none suffer through want, also [they should] instruct their wards to establish schools" (Manuscript History of Brigham Young, 1846, p. 474, Church Archives).

The Saints' propensity for "going to meeting," as they called congregational worship, increased after they settled in the Great Basin. Community meetings were first held in the Salt Lake City fort, with a haystack affording shade and a small cannon serving as a podium. Later a "bowery" was built within the fort by erecting posts, interlacing them with beams, and covering the affair with boughs and leaves. Boweries became a staple of Salt Lake and outlying community worship—in some communities they were not replaced by tabernacles for several decades. After the abandonment of the fort bowery, Salt Lake City settlers erected another on TEMPLE SQUARE, eventually giving it adobe walls and a ceiling of debris and soil. Still bigger boweries followed, largely to attend to the needs of the Church's general conferences when no community building could seat the flood of the people who attended.

During the pioneer period the most prominent building on Temple Square was the Tabernacle (later called the "Old Tabernacle" to differentiate it from the present-day TABERNACLE built in the 1860s). Unlike the stopgap adobe and soil bowery, it boasted stone walls and had no interior posts. "The Tabernacle on the inside is built quite in the form of a Theatre," wrote a traveler, "benches rising one behind another until the outer row is a great way from the pulpit. The building is executed on the inside so that it is one story under ground and in entering its steps descend" (Reminiscence of Addison Moses Crane, Huntington Library, San Marino, California). While lacking architectural distinction, it answered practical purposes. Finished in 1852, its 60-by-120-foot expanse provided 2,500 unobstructed seats and fairly good acoustical quality.

At first Temple Square community worship services were most important. The entire settlement was expected to gather each Sunday, usually at ten in the morning and two in the afternoon. A brass band might begin the preliminaries, followed by the "crying out" of the recently arrived post, notices of lost and found articles, or the announcement of upcoming political, social, and religious events. These newsy routines generally ended with the establishment of the DESERET NEWS in 1850.

During opening exercises, leaders might enter the hall to assume positions on the "stand," while followers drifted to their unassigned benches (increasingly members were asked not to occupy the rostrum without invitation). The lack of prepared sermons sometimes brought problems. Without a seasoned speaker present, authorities might summon a Church officer from other activity. The afternoon meeting was occupied by the administration of the Lord's Supper and a continuation of impromptu sermonizing, often by members of the congregation. Each meeting usually lasted for two hours or more.

There was variety and sometimes even theater. Leaders might invite LDS preachers, Indian chiefs, or, more frequently, returning missionaries to speak. Church leaders often preached gospel "discourses" that mixed spiritual and temporal themes—and sometimes the serious and the humorous. Elder Joseph Young, President of the

First Quorum of Seventy, "got up lively & spirited & caused much merriment," recorded the minutes on one occasion. "Pres[iden]t [Brigham] Young followed—on Charity—amusingly" (September 9, 1855, Minutes of Meetings, Church Archives). Speakers might preach, dialogue with the congregation, issue reproof and correction, and on occasion disfellowship or excommunicate wayward members.

With Temple Square meetings disadvantaged by a growing lack of intimacy due to increased membership and uncomfortable conditions during inclement weather, emphasis slowly shifted to local and ward activity. There, "blessing meetings" were held to confirm the baptized or rebaptized, and to bless. One ward boasted a "singing school." Thursday fast and testimony meetings continued in most neighborhoods, and bishops also held youth meetings. While the male priesthood quorums generally met on a multiward basis, special men's meetings were held in wards to aid immigration, levy taxes, or oversee road, canal, school, and chapel construction. Women continued their prayer meetings, RELIEF SOCIETY meetings in the 1850s for Indian relief, and restructured Relief Society gatherings in the 1870s for instruction, testimony, and relief for the unfortunate.

The most important ward gathering was the Sunday evening worship service, held usually an hour or two after the Temple Square afternoon service. "Meeting at E. M. Saunder's house," read the minutes of one. "Filled to overflowing. Pres John Young opened the meeting by singing and prayer. [He] made some remarks, ex[h]orted the brothern to use their privelages in occupying the time. Was followed by the Brotheren in quick succession. Brotheron and sisters delivered their testimony concerning the work of the Lord. [Many] spake in toungs, and prophesied" (Jan. 18, 1852, Nineteenth Ward Book A, Church Archives). The meeting began at 6 P.M. and ended three and one-half hours later.

MUSIC played an important part in any LDS service. "My soul delighteth in the song of the heart," read an early revelation; "yea, the song of the righteous is a prayer unto me" (D&C 25:12). Emma SMITH, Joseph's wife, collected and published in 1835 the first hymnal, which was actually a diminutive volume of poetry (music was borrowed from popular or favorite melodies). The settlers continued their musical tradition in the intermountain West. Only two weeks after their arrival, the nucleus of what would become the TABERNACLE CHOIR formed around a group of English and Welsh singers. As pioneering progressed, President Young insisted that each colonizing party have a music leader, called "musical missionaries," to sing, lead choirs, and play instruments in outlying settlements. He personally subsidized the Nauvoo Brass Band, which became a prototype. By the 1860s there were at least forty bands in the territory; by 1875 there were twice that number. Travelers Jules Remy and Julius Benchley were impressed. "Mormons have a feeling for sacred music," they concluded. "Their women [particularly] sing with soul" (A Journey to Great-Salt-Lake City, 1861, 2:56, 374–75).

Latter-day Saints also expressed their devotions in sacramental ordinances. COMMUNION, or "the sacrament," as Latter-day Saints call it, was a primary means. Occasionally suspended due to the unworthiness or insouciance of partakers, the SACRAMENT generally was a weekly ritual on Temple Square and at least a monthly one in local wards. Forms varied. Sometimes speakers stopped in mid-discourse to bless the emblems, which priesthood teachers then passed to the congregation's men, women, children, and even non-Mormon visitors as the preaching resumed. On other occasions bishops or young men consecrated the bread and water, which increasingly was substituted for wine. For Latter-day Saints the ordinance was a symbolic remembrance of Christ's flesh and blood and a renewal of the covenant of discipleship. Simple and unadorned, avoiding complex formulations such as transubstantiation, it was the central LDS public act of worship.

There were others. During a pioneer's lifetime, baptism might be administered several times as a token of special covenant. In addition to the original baptismal vow, accepting Christ and establishing Church membership, Saints were baptized on such special occasions as the dedication of the Nauvoo Temple, the exodus west, arrival in the SALT LAKE VALLEY, and during the Churchwide reformations of 1856–1857 (see REBAPTISM; REFORMATION OF 1856–1857) and 1875–1876, when "reconfirmations" were also administered. Moreover, members used rebaptism in the process of personal repentance and faith healing, and they also performed proxy baptisms in behalf of deceased ancestry. At a time when the acceptance of the restored gospel often severed a convert's ties to family, neighborhood, and vocation, the outward

sign of baptism provided powerful emotional and psychological reconfirmation. With weekly meeting attendance figures starkly low, it was the means by which many Latter-day Saints expressed their continuing religious commitment.

The temple ENDOWMENT was another way of uniting pioneer life with the sacred. With no temple completed during the pioneer period, members received their endowments on hills or mountaintops or in an upper room, but more frequently, after its dedication in 1855, in the Salt Lake ENDOWMENT HOUSE. Here they were instructed on mankind's spiritual journey through the eternities and performed ordinances pertaining to ETERNAL LIFE. Without the opportunity for doing frequent proxy endowments, a ritual that became common in the twentieth century, these ceremonies entered everyday pioneer life in two ways. Members wore temple garments or marked shirts as a sign of their temple commitments, and many joined a PRAYER CIRCLE. Salt Lake City had more than seven of these groups, at least one scheduled for each night of the week, and outlying settlements had at least one. At these gatherings, members bore testimony, discussed doctrine, consecrated oil for anointing the sick, reviewed personal and group needs, and united in temple ritual and prayer.

There were broader, community devotions as well. In the early years, quorums of SEVENTY held jubilees, which united dance, exhortation, music, socializing, and general celebration. Starting in 1849 annual, communitywide Pioneer Day fetes used similar activities to mark the coming of the first pioneers. Reminiscent of the community worship and socializing of the biblical feast days, general conferences twice each year gathered thousands to Salt Lake City for worship and mingling. Finally, the Saints often united for "reform." While most often a local phenomenon, at times the "spirit of reformation" spread through the territory or was officially initiated and sanctioned. During these periods, Latter-day Saints subjected themselves to preaching, religious catechizing, confession, and the cleansing of sin, followed by a renewal of the sacramental ordinances.

There was a final expression of LDS worship. Beyond their traditional expressions and devotions, nineteenth-century Saints acted on their religious feeling by seeking to establish the temporal KINGDOM OF GOD. They "gathered to Zion" (see GATHERING; ZION), settled, had children, built homes and communities, and refined themselves. Leaders might complain of their wayward meeting attendance or inattention to detail. Yet their community building, at least in a broad sense, was a sacral experience that revealed their formidable religious energy and devotion.

BIBLIOGRAPHY

Though no comprehensive survey of nineteenth-century Latter-day Saint worship exists, several narrower studies are especially helpful. Consult Leonard J. Arrington and Davis Bitton, "The Nineteenth Century Ward," in *The Mormon Experience*, pp. 206–219, New York, 1979; Joseph Heinerman, "The Mormon Meetinghouse: Reflections of Pioneer Religious and Social Life in Salt Lake City," *Utah Historical Quarterly* 50 (Fall 1982):340–53; and Ronald W. Walker, "'Going to Meeting' in Salt Lake City's Thirteenth Ward, 1849–1881: A Microanalysis," in *New Views of Mormon History*, ed. Davis Bitton and Maureen Ursenbach Beecher, pp. 138–61, Salt Lake City, 1987. For an example of Temple Square preaching rhetoric, see Ronald W. Walker, "Raining Pitchforks: Brigham Young as Preacher," *Sunstone* 8 (May–June 1983):4–9.

RONALD W. WALKER

PLAN OF SALVATION, PLAN OF REDEMPTION

Latter-day Saints believe that eons ago, GOD, in his infinite wisdom and never-ending mercy, formulated a plan whereby his children could experience a physical existence, including mortality, and then return to live in his presence in eternal felicity and glory. This plan, alternately called "the plan of salvation" (Jarom 1:2; Alma 42:5; Moses 6:62), "the plan of redemption" (Jacob 6:8; Alma 12:25; 42:11), and the "great plan of happiness" (Alma 42:8), provided both the way and the means for everyone to receive SALVATION and gain ETERNAL LIFE. Eternal life is God's greatest gift to his children (D&C 6:13), and the plan of salvation is his way of making it available to them. Although the term "plan of salvation" is used repeatedly in latter-day scripture, it does not occur in the Bible, though the doctrines pertaining to it are discoverable in its pages.

The Father is the author of the plan of salvation; JESUS CHRIST is its chief advocate; the HOLY SPIRIT helps carry it out, communicating God's will to men and helping them live properly.

THE PREMORTAL EXISTENCE. Latter-day Saints believe that all humans are spirit children of heavenly parents (see GOD THE FATHER; MOTHER IN HEAVEN), and they dwelt with them prior to BIRTH on this earth (Heb. 12:9; cf. Jer. 1:5; Eph. 1:4). In that PREMORTAL LIFE, or FIRST ESTATE, those spirit children could not progress fully. They needed a PHYSICAL BODY in order to have a fulness of joy (D&C 93:33–34), and the spirits also needed to be placed in an environment where, by the exercise of AGENCY, they could prove their willingness to keep God's commandments (Abr. 3:25). On the other hand, if they succumbed to TEMPTATION, they would be shut out from God's presence, for "no unclean thing can dwell with God" (1 Ne. 10:21; Eph. 5:5). To bring those who yielded to temptation back into God's presence, a plan of redemption had to be set in place, and this required a redeemer.

A COUNCIL IN HEAVEN was held of all the spirits, and two individuals volunteered to serve as the redeemer. One was Lucifer, a son of the morning (Isa. 14:12; D&C 76:26), who said he would "redeem all mankind, that one soul shall not be lost," but they would have no choice in the matter. Their agency would be destroyed (Moses 4:1–3). Such a proposal was out of harmony with the plan of the Father, for the agency of mankind is an absolute prerequisite to progress. JEHOVAH, the premortal Jesus Christ, had first stepped forward and volunteered to give his life as payment for all SINS. He set no plan or conditions of his own, but said, "Father, thy will be done, and the glory be thine forever" (Moses 4:2). He was selected by the Father.

When Lucifer would not accept the Father's choice, a WAR IN HEAVEN ensued, and he was cast out for rebellion (Moses 4:3; D&C 76:25), along with those who followed him, numbering about a third of the spirits (Rev. 12:4, 7–9; D&C 29:36–38). After Satan's expulsion, the Father's plan was carried forward. Three events ordained and instituted by God before the creation of the Earth constitute the foundation stones upon which the plan of salvation rests. These are the CREATION, the FALL OF ADAM, and the ATONEMENT OF JESUS CHRIST. "These three divine events—the three pillars of eternity—are inseparably woven together into one grand tapestry known as the eternal plan of salvation" (McConkie, p. 81).

THE CREATION. One of the purposes for creating this earth was for God's spirit children to obtain physical bodies and learn to walk by FAITH. Earth life is the SECOND ESTATE. The scriptures teach that by the power of his Only Begotten Son, the Father has created "worlds without number" (Moses 1:33; cf. John 1:3; Heb. 1:2), but the Lord has revealed to us detailed information only about this world (Moses 1:40).

Ecclesiastes states that "whatsoever God doeth, it shall be forever" (Eccl. 3:14). God does not work for temporal ends (D&C 29:34–35). The scriptures specify that when God created the earth, it was in a paradisiacal and deathless state. If ADAM and EVE had not transgressed and fallen, "all things which were created must have remained in the same state in which they were after they were created; and they must have remained for ever, and had no end" (2 Ne. 2:22; cf. Moses 3:9; *DS*, pp. 75–77).

THE FALL.   An earth in a deathless and paradisiacal state did not fulfill conditions needed for the progression of God's children (*see* PURPOSE OF EARTH LIFE). The Book of Mormon gives some reasons why the Fall was part of the foreordained plan of God. Agency is of paramount importance in the proving process. Critical to agency are choices or alternatives. LEHI taught that "there must needs be an opposition in all things" (2 Ne. 2:11). But in the state in which Adam and Eve found themselves, there was no such opposition. They had physical bodies, but were in a state of innocence. There was no death, sin, sorrow, or pain. Furthermore, in that state they would have had no children (2 Ne. 2:22–23). It appears that a major reason Lucifer and his followers had access to those on earth is the necessity that everyone be enticed by both good and evil (2 Ne. 2:16).

Eve was beguiled by Satan to partake of the forbidden fruit, exercised her agency and did so. Adam also chose to partake, realizing that if he did not, Eve and he would be separated and the command to multiply and replenish the earth would be thwarted. Therefore, "Adam fell that men might be" (2 Ne. 2:25). "With the eating of the 'forbidden fruit,' Adam and Eve became mortal, sin entered, blood formed in their bodies, and death became a part of life. . . . After Adam fell, the whole creation fell and became mortal. Adam's fall brought both physical and spiritual death into the world upon all mankind" (Bible Dictionary, p. 670; *DS* 1:77; Hel. 14:16–17; *see also* SPIRITUAL DEATH). Later, both Adam and Eve rejoiced in the opportunities

that had come to them because of the fall (Moses 5:10–11).

The Fall was part of God's plan for mankind and came as no surprise. "All things have been done in the wisdom of him who knoweth all things" (2 Ne. 2:24). Latter-day Saints affirm that Adam and Eve were actual beings, the first parents, and that the Fall was a literal event both in time and place. Elder Joseph Fielding SMITH explained, "If Adam did not fall, there was no Christ, because the atonement of Jesus Christ is based on the fall of Adam" (*DS* 1:120). Elder James E. Talmage wrote, "It has become a common practice with mankind to heap reproaches on the progenitors of the family, and to picture the supposedly blessed state in which we would be living but for the fall; whereas our first parents are entitled to our deepest gratitude for their legacy to posterity" (*AF*, p. 70).

THE ATONEMENT.   The Atonement is the crowning phase of the plan of salvation, without which all else would have been without purpose and all would have been lost. Atonement literally means "at-one-ment" and carries the idea of reconciliation, or the reuniting, of the human family with Heavenly Father. Understanding reconciliation necessitates an examination of the operation of the laws of JUSTICE AND MERCY.

God's perfect love, patience, long-suffering, and care for humanity's eternal welfare are the manifestations of his mercy. God is also just and so cannot look upon sin with the "least degree of allowance" (Alma 45:16). Perfect justice requires that every violation of God's law be punished and every act of obedience to the law be rewarded or blessed (D&C 130:20–21). Mercy and justice are basic to God's nature, and neither can be ignored. If the demands of justice were the only consideration and mercy ignored, no one could come back into God's presence, for "all have sinned and come short of the glory of God" (Rom. 3:23). If God were to excuse sin, then mercy would rob justice. Such cannot be. "What, do ye suppose that mercy can rob justice? I say unto you, Nay; not one whit. If so, God would cease to be God" (Alma 42:25).

In the atonement of Jesus Christ, justice and mercy are combined to bring about the plan of redemption. As the Only Begotten Son of a divine Father and a mortal mother (see MARY, MOTHER OF JESUS), Jesus was subject to the effects of the fall of Adam (mortality, temptation, pain, etc.), but had the power to live a perfect, sinless life (Heb.

3:15; D&C 45:4) and to lay down his life and take it up again (John 5:26; 10:17). In LDS doctrine, the miraculous conception and VIRGIN BIRTH of Jesus Christ are accepted as literally true and absolutely essential to the working of the plan of salvation. Because of his sinless life, justice had no claim on him. Because of his infinite, divine power, he could pay the price of sin for all of God's children and satisfy justice in their behalf (D&C 45:3–5). His was not a human sacrifice, but an infinite, eternal sacrifice (Alma 34:40). He atoned not only for the fall of Adam but also for the individual sins of every person. He extends forgiveness to everyone upon the condition of repentance.

In Gethsemane, Christ took upon himself the burden of the sins of the world and suffered for them in a way that is incomprehensible to mortals. "He suffereth the pains of all men, yea, the pains of every living creature, both men, women, and children, who belong to the family of Adam" (2 Ne. 9:21). This incomprehensible agony was so intense that it caused Jesus, "even God, the greatest of all, to tremble because of pain, and to bleed at every pore, and to suffer both body and spirit" (D&C 19:18; Mosiah 3:7; cf. Luke 22:42). Because he had power over death, Jesus endured (*JC*, p. 613). The shame, suffering, trials, scourging, and crucifixion were such that a mortal, finite being cannot fathom the price required before the Redeemer could say, "It is finished!" (John 19:30). God's great plan of redemption was implemented, and justice was not robbed by mercy, but rather was *paid* in full by the atoning blood of Jesus Christ. This payment for everyone's sins is called the grace of Jesus Christ. Without it, all stand condemned to eternal damnation. Hence, NEPHI₁ declared, "It is by grace that we are saved, after all we can do" (2 Ne. 25:23). Paul also taught the doctrine of salvation by grace (Eph. 2:8–9)—that is, without Christ's atonement, nothing any mortal could do would suffice.

Some aspects of Christ's atonement are unconditional. All mortal beings will be resurrected and brought back into the presence of God for the judgment regardless of the kind of lives they have lived (1 Cor. 15:22; 2 Ne. 9:12–15; Hel. 14:16–17), thus redeeming all humankind from both the mortal and spiritual deaths occasioned by the fall of Adam. Another unconditional aspect of Christ's mercy applies to young children who are not capable of understanding the difference between good and evil and therefore are not accountable. They cannot sin or be tempted of Satan (D&C 29:47;

Moro. 8:8). "They are all alive in [Christ] because of his mercy" (Moro. 8:19; cf. D&C 29:46). LDS doctrine states that all children who die before the age of ACCOUNTABILITY (age eight) are saved in the CELESTIAL KINGDOM (D&C 137:10). Mercy extends also to those who through mental handicaps do not reach the mental age of eight, the level of accountability (D&C 29:50).

However, for those who are mentally accountable, part of their estrangement from God is the direct result of their own sins, in addition to Adam's transgression. Unless something is done in their behalf, they will not be allowed to return to the presence of God after their judgment, for no unclean thing can enter there (1 Ne. 10:21). The Lord has set in place certain principles and ORDINANCES called the gospel, which must be followed to have Christ's full atoning power applied to one's own sins: (1) FAITH IN JESUS CHRIST, (2) REPENTANCE, (3) BAPTISM by immersion for the remission of sins by one having AUTHORITY, and (4) the GIFT OF THE HOLY GHOST by the LAYING ON of hands (*see* ARTICLES OF FAITH). Paul and others emphasized that humans are saved by GRACE and not by their own WORKS (Eph. 2:8). This is true because no mortals can work perfectly enough to save themselves. No mortals have, or can have, the power to overcome the effects of the fall of Adam, or even their own sins. Everyone must depend on the atoning blood of the Savior for salvation. With equal clarity and firmness, the Savior and his servants have taught that how people live is a condition for bringing the power of the Atonement to bear in their own lives. "Not every one that saith unto me, Lord, Lord, shall enter into the kingdom of heaven; but he that doeth the will of the Father" (Matt. 5:21). "The hearers of the law are [not] just before God, but the doers of the law shall be justified" (Rom. 1:18; 2:13). "They which do [the works of the flesh] shall not inherit the kingdom of God" (Gal. 5:21). "Behold, [Christ] offereth himself a sacrifice for sin, to answer the ends of the law, unto all those who have a broken heart and contrite spirit; and unto none else can the ends of the law be answered" (2 Ne. 2:7).

THE SPIRIT WORLD AND THE THREE DEGREES OF GLORY. When mortals complete their sojourn on earth and pass through the portal called death, they enter the postmortal SPIRIT WORLD. As part of the plan of salvation, the Lord set a time between death and the RESURRECTION when men and women can continue their progression and further learn principles of perfection before they are brought to the final judgment (Alma 40:6–21). Jesus Christ went to the postmortal spirit world while his body lay in the tomb to preach the gospel to them (1 Pet. 3:19–20; 4:6; D&C 138:11–37) so that those spirits in the postmortal spirit world could hear and accept or reject the gospel. Since baptism, the gift of the Holy Ghost, temple endowment, and SEALING are earthly ordinances, Latter-day Saints perform the ordinances vicariously for the dead in their temples (see SALVATION FOR THE DEAD). Because individuals differ so widely in their obedience to God's commandments, LDS theology rejects the traditional Christian concepts of the single option of heaven or hell in explaining the final destiny of souls (see SOUL). Through a vision given to the Prophet Joseph Smith (D&C 76), the Lord has shown, as he also revealed to Paul, that there are several DEGREES OF GLORY in mankind's eternal reward (D&C 76; cf. 1 Cor. 15:42).

The plan of salvation was created by the Father, brought into reality by the atoning sacrifice of his Beloved Son, and facilitated by the gifts of the Holy Ghost. It embraces the Creation, the Fall, and the Atonement, including the Resurrection, and sweeps across all time from the premortal existence to the final state of IMMORTALITY and eternal life.

BIBLIOGRAPHY

McConkie, Bruce R. *A New Witness for the Articles of Faith*, pp. 81–104, 144–59. Salt Lake City, 1985.

Packer, Boyd K. *Our Father's Plan*. Salt Lake City, 1984.

Taylor, John. *The Mediation and Atonement of Our Lord and Savior Jesus Christ*. Salt Lake City, 1882.

GERALD N. LUND

PLATES, METAL

[*The Book of Mormon mentions several records, most of which were inscribed on metal plates. The text of the Book of Mormon was inscribed on metal plates; see* Book of Mormon Plates and Records; Book of Mormon: The Words of Mormon; *and* Gold Plates. *In addition, the scriptural record possessed by the Book of Mormon colony that fled Jerusalem and came to the Americas under the leadership of the prophet Lehi was engraved on plates of brass; see* Book of Mormon: An Overview. *This colony continued to prepare metal plates, which were then used to inscribe records both sacred and secular; see* Book of Mormon Economy and Technology. *It is also known that a prophet named Ether inscribed on metal leaves the record of his people, the earliest Book of Mormon group to migrate to the Western Hemisphere; see* Book of Mormon: Book of Ether *and* Jaredites. *The final set of plates abridged by Mormon were seen by the* Book of Mormon Witnesses. *For information about the major writers or abridgers of these plates, see* Mormon; Moroni$_2$; Mosiah$_2$; *and* Nephi$_1$.]

PLURAL MARRIAGE

Plural marriage was the nineteenth-century LDS practice of a man marrying more than one wife. Popularly known as polygamy, it was actually polygyny. Although polygamy had been practiced for much of history in many parts of the world, to do so in "enlightened" America in the nineteenth century was viewed by most as incomprehensible and unacceptable, making it the Church's most controversial and least understood practice. Though the principle was lived for a relatively brief period, it had profound impact on LDS self-definition, helping to establish the Latter-day Saints as a "people apart." The practice also caused many nonmembers to distance themselves from the Church and see Latter-day Saints more negatively than would otherwise have been the case.

Rumors of plural marriage among the members of the Church in the 1830s and 1840s led to persecution, and the public announcement of the practice after August 29, 1852, in Utah gave enemies a potent weapon to fan public hostility against the Church. Although Latter-day Saints believed that their religiously-based practice of plural marriage was protected by the U.S. Constitution, opponents used it to delay Utah statehood until 1896. Ever harsher ANTIPOLYGAMY LEGISLATION stripped Latter-day Saints of their rights as citizens, disincorporated the Church, and permitted the seizure of Church property before the MANIFESTO OF 1890 announced the discontinuance of the practice.

Plural marriage challenged those within the Church, too. Spiritual descendants of the Puritans and sexually conservative, early participants in plural marriage first wrestled with the prospect and then embraced the principle only after receiving personal spiritual confirmation that they should do so.

The family of Alvin F. Heaton and his two wives Sarah Jane Carroll (married in 1880) and Lucy Spencer (married in 1882), in Moccasin Springs, Arizona (1907). In 1890 the Manifesto announced that no new plural marriages were to be authorized.

In 1843, one year before his death, the Prophet Joseph Smith dictated a lengthy revelation on the doctrine of marriage for eternity (D&C 132; see MARRIAGE: ETERNAL MARRIAGE). This revelation also taught that under certain conditions a man might be authorized to have more than one wife. Though the revelation was first committed to writing on July 12, 1843, considerable evidence suggests that the principle of plural marriage was revealed to Joseph Smith more than a decade before in connection with his study of the Bible (see JOSEPH SMITH TRANSLATION OF THE BIBLE), probably in early 1831. Passages indicating that revered patriarchs and prophets of old were polygamists raised questions that prompted the Prophet to inquire of the Lord about marriage in general and about plurality of wives in particular. He then

learned that when the Lord commanded it, as he had with the patriarchs anciently, a man could have more than one living wife at a time and not be condemned for adultery. He also understood that the Church would one day be required to live the law (D&C 132:1-4, 28-40).

Evidence for the practice of plural marriage during the 1830s is scant. Only a few knew about the still unwritten revelation, and perhaps the only known plural marriage was that between Joseph Smith and Fanny Alger. Nonetheless there were rumors, harbingers of challenges to come.

In April 1839, Joseph Smith emerged from six months' imprisonment in LIBERTY JAIL with a sense of urgency about completing his mission (see HISTORY OF THE CHURCH: C. 1831–1844). Since receiving the SEALING key from ELIJAH in the

KIRTLAND TEMPLE (D&C 110:13–16) in April 1836, the Prophet had labored to prepare the Saints for additional teachings and ordinances, including plural marriage.

Joseph Smith realized that the introduction of plural marriage would inevitably invite severe criticism. After the Kirtland experience, he knew the tension it would create in his own family; even though Emma, with faith in his prophetic calling, accepted the revelation as being from God and not of his own doing, she could not reconcile herself to the practice. Beyond that, it had the potential to divide the Church and increase hostilities from outside. Still, he felt obligated to move ahead. "The object with me is to obey & teach others to obey God in just what he tells us to do," he taught several months before his death. "It mattereth not whether the principle is popular or unpopular. I will always maintain a true principle even if I Stand alone in it" (TPJS, p. 332).

Although certain that God would require it of him and of the Church, Joseph Smith would not have introduced it when he did except for the conviction that God required it then. Several close confidants later said that he proceeded with plural marriage in Nauvoo only after both internal struggle and divine warning. Lorenzo Snow later remembered vividly a conversation in 1843 in which the Prophet described the battle he waged "in overcoming the repugnance of his feelings" regarding plural marriage.

> He knew the voice of God—he knew the commandment of the Almighty to him was to go forward—to set the example, and establish Celestial plural marriage. He knew that he had not only his own prejudices and pre-possessions to combat and to overcome, but those of the whole Christian world . . . ; but God . . . had given the commandment [The Biography and Family Record of Lorenzo Snow, pp. 69-70 (Salt Lake City, 1884)].

Even so, Snow and other confidants agreed that Joseph Smith proceeded in Nauvoo only after an angel declared that he must or his calling would be given to another (Bachman, pp. 74–75). After this, Joseph Smith told Brigham Young that he was determined to press ahead though it would cost him his life, for "it is the work of God, and He has revealed this principle, and it is not my business to control or dictate it" (Brigham Young Discourse, Oct. 8, 1866, Church Archives).

Nor did others enter into plural marriage blindly or simply because Joseph Smith had spoken, despite biblical precedents. Personal accounts document that most who entered plural marriage in Nauvoo faced a crisis of faith that was resolved only by personal spiritual witness. Those who participated generally did so only after they had obtained reassurance and saw it as religious duty.

Even those closest to Joseph Smith were challenged by the revelation. After first learning of plural marriage, Brigham Young said he felt to envy the corpse in a funeral cortege and "could hardly get over it for a long time" (JD 3:266). The Prophet's brother Hyrum Smith stubbornly resisted the very possibility until circumstances forced him to go to the Lord for understanding. Both later taught the principle to others. Emma Smith vacillated, one day railing in opposition against it and the next giving her consent for Joseph to be sealed to another wife (see comments by Orson Pratt, JD 13:194).

Teaching new marriage and family arrangements where the principles could not be openly discussed compounded the problems. Those authorized to teach the doctrine stressed the strict covenants, obligations and responsibilities associated with it—the antithesis of license. But those who heard only rumors, or who chose to distort and abuse the teaching, often envisioned and sometimes practiced something quite different. One such was John C. Bennett, mayor of Nauvoo and adviser to Joseph Smith, who twisted the teaching to his own advantage. Capitalizing on rumors and lack of understanding among general Church membership, he taught a doctrine of "spiritual wifery." He and associates sought to have illicit sexual relationships with women by telling them that they were married "spiritually," even if they had never been married formally, and that the Prophet approved the arrangement. The Bennett scandal resulted in his excommunication and the disaffection of several others. Bennett then toured the country speaking against the Latter-day Saints and published a bitter anti-Mormon exposé charging the Saints with licentiousness.

The Bennett scandal elicited several public statements aimed at arming the Saints against the abuses. Two years later enemies and dissenters, some of whom had been associated with Bennett, published the NAUVOO EXPOSITOR, to expose, among other things, plural marriage, thus setting in motion events leading to Joseph Smith's death (see MARTYRDOM OF JOSEPH AND HYRUM SMITH).

Far from involving license, however, plural marriage was a carefully regulated and ordered system. Order, mutual agreements, regulation, and covenants were central to the practice. As Elder Parley P. Pratt wrote in 1845,

> These holy and sacred ordinances have nothing to do with whoredoms, unlawful connections, confusion or crime; but the very reverse. They have laws, limits, and bounds of the strictest kind, and none but the pure in heart, the strictly virtuous, or those who repent and become such, are worthy to partake of them. And . . . [a] dreadful weight of condemnation await those who pervert, or abuse them [*The Prophet*, May 24, 1845; cf. D&C 132:7].

The Book of Mormon makes clear that, though the Lord will command men through his prophets to live the law of plural marriage at special times for his purposes, monogamy is the general standard (Jacob 2:28-30); unauthorized polygamy was and is viewed as adultery. Another safeguard was that authorized plural marriages could be performed only through the sealing power controlled by the presiding authority of the Church (D&C 132:19).

Once the Saints left Nauvoo, plural marriage was openly practiced. In WINTER QUARTERS, for example, discussion of the principle was an "open secret" and plural families were acknowledged. As early as 1847, visitors to Utah commented on the practice. Still, few new plural marriages were authorized in Utah before the completion of the ENDOWMENT HOUSE in Salt Lake City in 1855.

With the Saints firmly established in the Great Basin, Brigham Young announced the practice publicly and published the revelation on eternal marriage. Under his direction, on Sunday, August 29, 1852, Elder Orson Pratt publicly discussed and defended the practice of plural marriage in the Church. After examining the biblical precedents (Abraham, Jacob, David, and others), Elder Pratt argued that the Church, as heir of the keys required anciently for plural marriages to be sanctioned by God, was required to perform such marriages as part of the RESTORATION. He offered reasons for the practice and discussed several possible benefits (see *JD* 1:53–66), a precedent followed later by others. But such discussions were after the fact and not the justification. Latter-day Saints practiced plural marriage because they believed God commanded them to do so.

Generally plural marriage involved only two wives and seldom more than three; larger families like those of Brigham Young or Heber C. KIMBALL

were exceptions. Sometimes the wives simply shared homes, each with her own bedroom, or lived in a "duplex" arrangement, each with a mirror-image half of the house. In other cases, husbands established separate homes for their wives, sometimes in separate towns. Although circumstances and the mechanics of family life varied, in general the living style was simply an adaptation of the nineteenth century American family. Polygamous marriages were similar to national norms in fertility and divorce rates as well. Wives of one husband often developed strong bonds of sisterly love; however, strong antipathies could also arise between wives.

Faced with a national antipolygamy campaign, LDS women startled their eastern sisters, who equated polygamy with oppression of women, by publicly demonstrating in favor of their right to live plural marriage as a religious principle. Judging from the preaching, women were at least as willing to enter plural marriage as men. Instead of public admonitions urging women to enter plural marriage, one finds many urging worthy men to "do their duty" and undertake to care for a plural wife and additional children. Though some were reluctant to accept such responsibility, many responded and sought another wife. It was not unheard of for a wife to take the lead and insist that her husband take another wife; yet, in other cases, a first marriage dissolved over the husband's insistence on marrying again.

As with families generally, some plural families worked better than others. Anecdotal evidence and the healthy children that emerged from many plural households witness that some worked very well. But some plural wives disliked the arrangement. The most common complaint of second and third wives resulted from a husband's displaying too little sensitivity to the needs of plural families or not treating them equally. Not infrequently, wives complained that husbands spent too little time with them. But where husbands provided conscientiously even time and wives developed deep love and respect for each other, children grew up as members of large, well-adjusted extended families.

Plural marriage helped mold the Church's attitude toward DIVORCE in pioneer Utah. Though Brigham Young disliked divorce and discouraged it, when women sought divorce he generally granted it. He felt that a woman trapped in an unworkable relationship with no alternatives deserved a chance to improve her life. But when a husband sought relief from his familial responsibilities, President Young consistently counseled him to do his duty and not seek divorce from any wife willing to put up with him.

Contrary to the caricatures of a hostile world press, plural marriage did not result in offspring of diminished capacity. Normal men and women came from plural households, and their descendants are prominent throughout the Intermountain West. Some observers feel that the added responsibility that fell early upon some children in such households contributed to their exceptional record of achievement. Plural marriage also aided many wives. The flexibility of plural households contributed to the large number of accomplished LDS women who were pioneers in medicine, politics and other public careers. In fact, plural marriage made it possible for wives to have professional careers that would not otherwise have been available to them.

The exact percentage of Latter-day Saints who participated in the practice is not known, but studies suggest a maximum of from 20% to 25% of LDS adults were members of polygamous households. At its height, plural marriage probably involved only a third of the women reaching marriageable age—though among Church leadership plural marriage was the norm for a time. Public opposition to polygamy led to the first law against the practice in 1862, and, by the 1880s, laws were increasingly punitive. The Church contested the constitutionality of those laws, but the Supreme Court sustained the legislation (see REYNOLDS V. UNITED STATES), leading to a harsh and effective federal antipolygamy campaign known by the Latter-day Saints as "the Raid." Wives and husbands went on the "underground" and hundreds were arrested and sentenced to jail terms in Utah and several federal prisons. This campaign severely affected the families involved, and the related attack on Church organization and properties greatly inhibited its ability to function (see HISTORY OF THE CHURCH: C. 1877–1898). Following a vision showing him that continuing plural marriage endangered the temples and the mission of the Church, not just statehood, President Wilford WOODRUFF issued the Manifesto in October 1890, announcing an official end to new plural marriages and facilitating an eventual peaceful resolution of the conflict.

Earlier polygamous families continued to exist well into the twentieth century, causing further political problems for the Church, and new plural marriages did not entirely cease in 1890. After having lived the principle at some sacrifice for half a century, many devout Latter-day Saints found ending plural marriage a challenge almost as complex as was its beginning in the 1840s. Some new plural marriages were contracted in the 1890s in LDS settlements in Canada and northern Mexico, and a few elsewhere. With national attention again focused on the practice in the early 1900s during the House hearings on Representative-elect B. H. Roberts and Senate hearings on Senator-elect Reed Smoot (see SMOOT HEARINGS), President Joseph F. SMITH issued his "Second Manifesto" in 1904. Since that time, it has been uniform Church policy to excommunicate any member either practicing or openly advocating the practice of polygamy. Those who do so today, principally members of FUNDAMENTALIST groups, do so outside the Church.

BIBLIOGRAPHY

Bachman, Danel W. "A Study of the Mormon Practice of Plural Marriage before the Death of Joseph Smith." M.A. thesis, Purdue University, 1975.

Bashore, Melvin L. "Life Behind Bars: Mormon Cohabs of the 1880s." *Utah Historical Quarterly* 47 (Winter 1979): 22-41.

Bennion, Lowell ("Ben"). "The Incidence of Mormon Polygamy in 1880: 'Dixie' versus Davis Stake." *Journal of Mormon History* 11 (1984): 27–42.

Bitton, Davis. "Mormon Polygamy: A Review Article." *Journal of Mormon History* 4 (1977): 101–118.

Embry, Jessie L. *Mormon Polygamous Families: Life in the Principle*. Salt Lake City, 1987.

Foster, Lawrence. *Religion and Sexuality: The Shakers, The Mormons, and the Oneida Community*. Oxford, 1981.

James, Kimberly Jensen. "'Between Two Fires': Women on the 'Underground' of Mormon Polygamy." *Journal of Mormon History* 8 (1981): 49-61.

Van Wagoner, Richard S. *Mormon Polygamy: A History*. Salt Lake City, 1986.

Whittaker, David J. "Early Mormon Polygamy Defenses." *Journal of Mormon History* 11 (1984): 43-63.

DANEL W. BACHMAN
RONALD K. ESPLIN

POLICIES, PRACTICES, AND PROCEDURES

The FIRST PRESIDENCY and the QUORUM OF THE TWELVE APOSTLES have developed policies, practices, and procedures to give order and continuity throughout the units of the Church and to provide guidelines for its leaders. These guidelines, policies, and procedures have been formalized in the GENERAL HANDBOOK OF INSTRUCTIONS, which is distributed to priesthood leaders of the Church. The handbook is revised and brought up to date from time to time to keep instructions current. The following statements have been selected as samples from the latest edition of that handbook (1989), and references are to section and page numbers in that edition.

MORAL ISSUES

Abortion. "Abortion is one of the most revolting and sinful practices of this day. Members must not submit to, be a party to, or perform an abortion. The only exceptions are when—

1. Pregnancy has resulted from incest or rape;
2. The life or health of the woman is in jeopardy, in the opinion of competent medical authority;
3. The fetus is known, by competent medical authority, to have severe defects that will not allow the baby to survive beyond birth" (11-4).

As far as has been revealed, a person may repent and be forgiven for the sin of abortion (*see* ABORTION).

Abuse and Cruelty. "Members who abuse or are cruel to their spouses, children, or other family members violate the laws of God and man" (11-4; *see* ABUSE, SPOUSE AND CHILD).

Artificial Insemination. "Artificial insemination with semen from anyone but the husband is discouraged. . . . Artificial insemination of single sisters is not approved" (11-4; *see* ARTIFICIAL INSEMINATION).

Chastity and Fidelity. "God's standard for sexual morality has always been clear: 'Thou shalt not commit adultery' (Ex. 20:14). In modern and . . . ancient times God has commanded all of his children to lead strictly [chaste] lives before and after marriage—intimate relations being permissible only between a man and a woman legally and lawfully married. Accordingly, intimate relations outside of marriage are out of harmony with God's eternal plan for his children. To be morally clean, a person must refrain from adultery and fornication, from homosexual or lesbian relations, and from every other unholy, unnatural, or impure practice" (11-4; *see* CHASTITY, LAW OF; MARRIAGE).

Donation of Sperm. "The donation of sperm is discouraged" (11-4).

In Vitro Fertilization. "In vitro fertilization using semen other than that of the husband or an egg [from anyone] other than the wife is discour-

aged. However, this is a personal matter that ultimately must be left to the judgment of the husband and wife" (11-4).

Rape or Sexual Abuse Victims. "Victims of the evil acts of others are not guilty of sin." Church officers should help victims of rape and other sexual abuse "regain their sense of innocence and overcome any feelings of guilt" (11-5).

Sex Education. "Parents have primary responsibility for the sex education of their children. Teaching this subject honestly and plainly in the home greatly improves the chance that young people will avoid serious problems. . . . Where schools have undertaken sex education, it is appropriate for parents to seek to ensure that the instructions given their children are consistent with sound moral and ethical values" (11-5; *see* MARRIAGE; SEX EDUCATION; SEXUALITY).

Suicide. People who take their own lives "may not be responsible for [their] acts. Only God can judge such a matter" (11-5; *see* SUICIDE).

Surgical Sterilization (Including Vasectomy). "Surgical sterilization should only be considered (1) where medical conditions seriously jeopardize life or health, or (2) where birth defects or serious trauma have rendered a person mentally incompetent and not responsible for his or her actions. Such conditions must be determined by competent medical judgment and in accordance with law. Even then, the person or persons responsible for this decision should consult with each other and with their bishop (or branch president) and receive divine confirmation through prayer" (11-5).

Surrogate Motherhood. The Church discourages surrogate motherhood (11-5).

MEDICAL AND HEALTH ISSUES

Acquired Immune Deficiency Syndrome (AIDS). "Local leaders should encourage members with AIDS to consult competent medical authority. Leaders and members should treat a member who has AIDS with dignity and compassion. Though AIDS can afflict innocent victims, the principal guides to safety are chastity before marriage, total fidelity in marriage, abstinence from any homosexual relations, avoidance of illegal drugs, and reverence and care for the body" (11-5; *see* AIDS).

Euthanasia. "A person who participates in euthanasia—deliberately putting to death a person suffering from incurable conditions or diseases—violates the commandments of God" (11-5; *see* PROLONGING LIFE).

Organ Transplants. The decision of whether to will one's personal body organs or authorize "the transplant of organs from a deceased family member [rests with] the individual or the deceased person's family. The decision to receive a donated organ should be made with competent medical counsel and confirmation through prayer" (11-6; *see* ORGAN TRANSPLANTS AND DONATIONS).

Prolonging Life. "When severe illness strikes, Church members should exercise faith in the Lord and seek competent medical assistance. However, when dying becomes inevitable, it should be looked upon as a blessing and a purposeful part of eternal existence. Members should not feel obligated to extend mortal life by means that are unreasonable" (11-6; *see* PROLONGING LIFE; PURPOSE OF EARTH LIFE, LDS PERSPECTIVE).

Stillborn Children. "Although temple ordinances are not performed for stillborn children, no loss of eternal blessings or family unity is implied. The family may record the name of a stillborn child on the family group record followed by the word *stillborn* in parentheses. Memorial or graveside services may or may not be held as determined by the parents" (11-6; *see* STILLBORN CHILDREN).

Word of Wisdom. In addition to avoiding the use of tea, coffee, and alcoholic beverages, members should not misuse legal drugs and "should not use any substance that contains illegal drugs or other harmful or habit-forming ingredients" (11-6; *see* ALCOHOLIC BEVERAGES; COFFEE; DRUG ABUSE; TEA; WORD OF WISDOM).

ADMINISTRATIVE ISSUES

Church Discipline. "The purposes of Church discipline are to (1) save the souls of transgressors; (2) protect the innocent; and (3) safeguard the purity, integrity, and good name of the Church. [It] includes giving cautions in private interviews, imposing restrictions in probations, and withdrawing fellowship or membership" (10-1). Church discipline is administered by leaders of local congregations; it can affect only a person's standing in the Church. "A person who is disfellowshipped is still a member of the Church, but is no longer in good standing. . . . A person who is excommunicated is no longer a member of the Church and cannot enjoy any membership privileges" (10-5). "All persons who are excommunicated, disfellowshipped, or placed on formal probation by a disciplinary council have a right to appeal the decision" (10-8).

The bishop, or another appropriate priesthood leader, should continue to help a disciplined person return to full fellowship in the Church (*see* DISCIPLINARY PROCEDURES).

Funerals. "When a funeral service is held in a Church building or conducted by a Church officer, it is a Church meeting. A member of the bishopric conducts the service. . . . Bishops may offer the use of Church meetinghouses for the funeral services of nonmembers. Such services may be held in the manner prescribed by the deceased person's church and, if the family desires, may be conducted by a clergyman of that church, provided the service is dignified and appropriate" (2-7; *see* BURIAL; CREMATION; DEATH AND DYING).

Income Taxes. Church members in any nation are to obey applicable tax laws. "If a member disapproves of tax laws, he may attempt to have them changed by legislation or constitutional amendment, or, if he has a well-founded legal objection, he may attempt to challenge them in the courts. A member who refuses to file a tax return, to pay required income taxes, or to comply with a final judgment in a tax case is in direct conflict with the law and with the teachings of the Church" (11-2; *see* CIVIC DUTIES; CIVIC RIGHTS; CONSTITUTIONAL LAW; LAW).

Political Action. "The Church does not endorse political parties or candidates. Branch, ward, or stake meetinghouses and other Church facilities, and Church directories or mailing lists must not be used in any way for political purposes." (11-2; *see* CHURCH AND STATE; CIVIC DUTIES; CIVIC RIGHTS; CONSTITUTIONAL LAW).

Prayers. "Both men and women may offer prayers in Church meetings" (11-3; *see* MEETINGS, MAJOR CHURCH; PRAYER).

BIBLIOGRAPHY

General Handbook of Instructions. Salt Lake City, 1989.

FRANK O. MAY, JR.

POLITICS

[*Included in this entry are four articles:*

Political History
Political Teachings
Political Culture
Contemporary American Politics

The first article traces the history of the political issues in which The Church of Jesus Christ of Latter-day Saints has been involved since the restoration of the gospel. The second article examines the official teachings of LDS scriptures and prophets on political questions. The third article examines the perception of a political subculture in the membership of the Church. The last article examines the participation of the Church and its members in contemporary politics throughout the world.

The Church has on occasion been involved in political issues. Specific political controversies can be found organized by time periods in the series of articles entitled History of the Church *and organized geographically in articles on particular communities, such as* Kirtland, Ohio.

Several articles take up specific political issues. Missouri Conflict *and* Nauvoo Politics *detail two major political experiences of the young LDS community that ended in forcible expulsion and loss of life and property. To see the unfolding political connection of the Mormons to the United States after the 1848 move west, read the following articles in this order:* Utah Territory; Utah Expedition; Antipolygamy Legislation; Reynolds v. United States; Manifesto of 1890; Utah Statehood; *and the* Smoot Hearings.

The extent to which the Constitution of the United States of America *will protect distinctive religious practices is a question brought in many forms to American courts. The experience of the Church and its members in the courts is summarized in* Legal and Judicial History. *The efforts of the Church to gain recognition and religious freedoms through direct negotiations with governments throughout the world are described in* Diplomatic Relations. *The attitudes and teachings of the Church derived from its scriptures and these experiences in law and politics are described in articles on* Church and State; Civil Rights; Constitutional Law; Politics: Political Teachings; *and* War and Peace.]

POLITICAL HISTORY

LDS involvement in American politics began with the conflicts between Mormons and non-Mormons in the 1830s and 1840s that led to the founding of a religious and political community in the Great Basin, organized by the U.S. Congress as UTAH TERRITORY. Mormonism emerged as a national political issue in the presidential election of 1856 with the Republican platform's condemnation of the "twin relics of barbarism"—southern slavery and Mormon polygamy. Political involvement continued in the social and political order of the state of Utah where, because of the high number of Latter-day Saints, there is identification between the political community and the dominant religion.

From its inception in western New York in 1830, the LDS Church was politically controversial. The deepest cause of conflict directly or indi-rectly affecting political relationships between Latter-day Saints and others was the belief in continuing REVELATION. Non-Mormons viewed the claim of continuing revelation and the social and political forms built on that claim as threats to democratic self-government. While the Book of Mormon was being printed, a mass meeting of Palmyra residents pledged to boycott it. The Prophet Joseph SMITH was arrested several times on charges brought, according to his accusers, "to open the eyes and understanding of those who blindly follow" him. When the Church was hardly large enough to "man a farm, or meet a woman with a milk-pail," recalled Sidney RIGDON, non-Mormons were already accusing them of wanting "to upset the Government" (*HC* 6:289).

The turmoil of the New York period was only a harbinger of intense conflicts to follow. As the practical implications of belief in new revelation and obedience to a new prophet became clear, anti-Mormon opposition intensified. For the Prophet and his followers, divine calling made possible—indeed, morally incumbent—the effort to create a just society, which the revelations called ZION. For non-Mormon neighbors, these efforts constituted challenges that they determined to resist.

Belief in continuing revelation had profound implications for the organization of political society among the Latter-day Saints. The establishment of Zion required the unity of the LDS community in RIGHTEOUSNESS. The effort brought social, economic, and political innovations, including the GATHERING of the Saints, CONSECRATION and stewardship, the UNITED ORDER, and PLURAL MARRIAGE. In all matters relevant to building Zion, the LDS community looked to the Prophet for guidance, concentrating power, even against his own inclinations, in his hands.

Efforts to establish Zion excited fear and animosity. Made uneasy by ever-increasing numbers of Latter-day Saints and shocked or bemused by their economic and social experiments, many non-Mormons viewed the Saints as alien and hostile, even as a threat to their freedoms as Americans. Because the Church seemed to erase the distinction between CHURCH AND STATE—in American liberal political thought an important pillar of liberty—some felt that it portended the rise of religious despotism. The result was recurring political conflict, which time and again threatened the LDS community.

The efforts to build a NEW JERUSALEM in America began in 1831 with the gathering to Ohio and the designation of Zion in Jackson County, Missouri. As Church members built these new communities, differences with neighbors, and resulting tensions, were immediately evident. In Ohio, Joseph Smith and Sidney Rigdon were tarred and feathered by a mob. Random acts of violence threatened the young LDS community (see KIRTLAND, OHIO; OHIO, LDS COMMUNITIES IN).

Matters were still worse in Missouri, where, in 1833, citizens of Jackson County banded together to remove the Latter-day Saints from the county, "peaceably if we can, forcibly if we must" (HC 1:374). They were justified, they claimed, because Mormonism was an evil for which the laws made no provision. Missourians saw these newcomers as "deluded fanatics" or "designing knaves" who claimed "to hold personal communication and converse face to face with the Most High God" and who threatened to take political control of the county (HC 1:375; see also HISTORY OF THE CHURCH: C. 1831–1844; MISSOURI: LDS COMMUNITIES IN JACKSON AND CLAY COUNTIES).

By late fall of 1833, the Latter-day Saints had been driven from Jackson County. Most found temporary refuge in Clay County, where they were at first kindly received. Eventually, however, antagonisms developed there as well when it became apparent that Saints would not be going back to their homes and lands in Jackson County. Before violence erupted, Church members abandoned Clay County in 1836 for the newly organized Caldwell County, created by the legislature specifically as a home for Mormons (see MISSOURI: LDS COMMUNITIES IN CALDWELL AND DAVIESS COUNTIES).

By the summer of 1838, trouble had erupted again. In Kirtland, economic failure associated with the Panic of 1837 contributed to dissent. Some criticized Joseph Smith's exercise of authority and charged him with "Popery," or the combining of spiritual authority and temporal power. As tensions escalated, Joseph Smith and most of the faithful left Ohio for Missouri. In Caldwell County, critics within the Church also soon took up the cry, creating such profound consternation that the community forced them out. Dissenters then stirred up non-Mormons who were already fearful of growing LDS strength. In this situation of rising tensions, Sidney Rigdon defiantly declared independence from mob depredations and vowed that the Saints would meet future force with force. All that was required for a violent conflagration was a tiny spark.

Not surprisingly, political rivalry provided the spark. On August 6, 1838, non-Mormons in Daviess County, into which the rapidly increasing LDS population had spilled, attempted to prevent Latter-day Saints from voting at Gallatin, Missouri. A brawl resulted, and exaggerated accounts of the incident soon mobilized armed bands on both sides. After several skirmishes, a pitched battle occurred, with both sides suffering casualties. Following exaggerated reports of this battle, Governor Lilburn Boggs ordered the state militia to treat the Mormons as enemies to be exterminated or driven from the state (see EXTERMINATION ORDER; MISSOURI CONFLICT). After Joseph Smith and other leaders were imprisoned, the Latter-day Saints were disarmed and then were forced from Missouri. After months of imprisonment, jailed Church leaders eventually escaped or were released.

Moving to Illinois, the Latter-day Saints built a new city, NAUVOO, along the banks of the Mississippi River. Apparently convinced that there would be no peace as long as Church members were politically at the mercy of non-Mormons, Joseph Smith sought and obtained political power for the new city. In the NAUVOO CHARTER, the Illinois legislature empowered the city to make any ordinances not prohibited by the CONSTITUTION OF THE UNITED STATES or that of Illinois and to organize a militia with power to execute said laws.

While Nauvoo flourished under the protection of the new city government and its own militia, the NAUVOO LEGION, trouble soon developed. Non-Mormons resented Nauvoo's political power, which was based on increasing LDS numbers and on their willingness to vote as a bloc to reward political friends and punish political enemies (see NAUVOO POLITICS). Bloc voting was both a reflection of the social unity of the LDS community and a defensive reaction to the abuses suffered in Missouri. Yet critics condemned the Saints for "yielding implicit obedience" to a "pretended prophet of the Lord" who, they charged, was a dangerous character entertaining "the most absolute contempt for the laws of man" (HC 6:4–5).

Even within the Church there was again restiveness, for the private introduction of plural marriage and Joseph Smith's increasing political power contributed to dissent. Dissidents established a newspaper, the NAUVOO EXPOSITOR, and attacked Joseph Smith for supposed moral imperfections and poor leadership. Declaring the *Expositor* a public nuisance, the Nauvoo City Council authorized Mayor Joseph Smith to order city police to destroy its press. In the resulting furor, the anti-Mormon *Warsaw Signal* called on the citizens of Illinois to take direct military action against the Prophet. Others spoke of extermination. With violence clearly a possibility, Joseph Smith allowed himself to be arrested on charges stemming from the *Expositor* incident and was imprisoned in Carthage, the county seat, where on June 27, 1844, he was murdered by a mob (*see* CARTHAGE JAIL; MARTYRDOM OF JOSEPH AND HYRUM SMITH).

The Prophet's death brought a lull in hostilities, which provided time to complete the NAUVOO TEMPLE and to make preparations to move to a new home in the West. When conflict broke out again in September 1845, Church leaders announced their intention to leave Illinois in the spring. By the summer of 1846, most Latter-day Saints had departed. Those remaining were forced out by an anti-Mormon attack on the city in September 1846.

The Missouri and Illinois cataclysms convinced Brigham YOUNG and other Church leaders that the Latter-day Saints needed not just political power but political autonomy. According to the prevailing constitutional interpretation of states' rights, the federal government was largely prohibited from interfering with a state's domestic institutions (slavery, for example). To obtain such autonomy, Latter-day Saints did not necessarily have to remove themselves from the boundaries of the United States but only from existing states and territories. As the first settlers in a new area, they could possibly obtain the political autonomy necessary for protection within the federal Union.

As the Latter-day Saints embarked on their westward migration, some dreamed of an independent LDS nation, while others envisioned the establishment of a territory or state within the United States. When Church leaders selected the Great Basin as their probable destination, it was legally a remote part of Mexico. The MORMON BATTALION contributed, at least marginally, to the effort by which the United States obtained title to the Southwest, including the Great Basin.

The first LDS pioneers entered the valley of the Great Salt Lake in July 1847. Until late 1848,

when the Quorum of the Twelve Apostles established themselves in the valley, the settlement was governed by the Salt Lake Stake presidency and HIGH COUNCIL. President Brigham Young charged these local officials to "observe those principles which have been instituted in the Stakes of Zion for the government of the Church, and to pass such laws and ordinances as shall be necessary for the peace and prosperity of the city for the time being" (Morgan, p. 69). In December 1848, Church leaders petitioned Congress for a territorial organization. Later, they drafted a constitution for a proposed STATE OF DESERET, with a bill of rights containing a strongly worded guarantee of religious liberty, and applied for admission to the Union. Brigham Young was elected governor of the would-be state.

In Congress, this hoped-for admission became enmeshed in the political maelstrom over slavery in U.S. territories raised by the Treaty of Guadalupe Hidalgo. In the Compromise of 1850, Congress organized the Latter-day Saints as the Territory of Utah. The compromise, adopting the principle of popular sovereignty, allowed settlers in the newly acquired territories to decide whether they would have slavery. Utah, attempting to remain aloof from the dispute over slavery, offended both anti- and proslavery congressmen by ignoring the matter in its constitution.

From the beginning of Utah's territorial period, relations between the LDS community and the federal government were tense. The first non-Mormon territorial officials became embroiled in controversy within days of their arrival and soon returned to the East, spreading inflammatory reports that deeply influenced congressional and public opinion. Later federal appointees were also critical. And the Church deeply agitated public opinion when it officially avowed plural marriage in 1852.

In the presidential election of 1856, the Republican party used public antipolygamy feeling to attack the Democratic party for its stand on slavery in the territories. Democrats in Congress had passed the 1854 Kansas-Nebraska Act, which, by repealing the Missouri Compromise, removed the last legal restraints on the spread of slavery to U.S. territories and established popular sovereignty as the political principle governing slavery in the territories. The Republican party, intent on restoring the Missouri Compromise by repudiating popular sovereignty, inserted the "twin relics" plank in the

1856 Republican platform in an effort to tar the Democratic party with Mormon polygamy. The point was that if the Democrats truly believed that the citizens of the territories alone had the power to legislate on slavery, logically they must also accept that the citizens of the territories should have the sole power to legislate on matrimony. Polygamy and slavery, according to the author of the "twin relics" plank, "rested precisely on the same Constitutional basis," and so "to make war upon polygamy, and at the same time strengthen the case against slavery as much as possible," he linked them together (Poll, p. 127).

The Republican strategy succeeded. Democratic party leaders concluded that to protect popular sovereignty as it related to slavery, they had to take a firm stand against polygamy. Senator Stephen Douglas, popular sovereignty's chief patron, attacked the Mormons as subversive aliens who recognized the authority of Brigham Young "and the government of which he is the head" above that of the United States. He accused Latter-day Saints of prosecuting "a system of robbery and murders upon American citizens" (*see* DANITES) and called for the application of "the knife" to "this pestiferous, disgusting cancer" of Mormonism, "which is gnawing at the very vitals of the body politic" (*CHC* 4:221–22). It is possible that embarrassment over the linkage of polygamy and popular sovereignty contributed to U.S. President James Buchanan's decision, on the basis of vague and unsubstantiated reports, to take the extraordinary step of sending an army to Utah in 1857 to enforce federal law (*see* UTAH EXPEDITION). The ostensible purpose of the army was to ensure that the territory accepted the replacement of Brigham Young as governor, but it had also been suggested to Buchanan that he might be able to upstage the commotion over slavery in the territories with the excitement of an anti-Mormon crusade.

A Republican-controlled Congress passed the first ANTIPOLYGAMY LEGISLATION in 1862. The Morrill Act outlawed polygamy and overturned certain acts of the Utah legislature, including one incorporating the Church, which shielded the practice of polygamy. The Civil War delayed enforcement, and when the federal government returned to the Utah situation after the war, it found that the act was unenforceable because territorial courts were in LDS hands. To remedy this situation, Congress passed the Poland Act of 1874, transferring control over criminal proceedings—

including cases involving polygamy—from local courts to federally appointed officials. This act marked the transformation of the confrontation over plural marriage into a struggle over political power in Utah. The 1882 Edmunds Act prohibited polygamists (including virtually all Church leaders) from voting or holding office. It also established a federally appointed commission to control territorial elections, including voter registration. Utah women were among the first in the nation to vote, and WOMAN SUFFRAGE was now also under attack. The most sweeping legislation, the 1887 Edmunds-Tucker Act, required an antipolygamy test oath for voting and holding office, disfranchised women, disbanded the territorial militia, took control of public schools, abolished the Church's PERPETUAL EMIGRATING FUND, dissolved the Church as a legal entity, and seized much of its property. In the late 1880s, demands were made in Congress for even more stringent measures.

Latter-day Saints vigorously protested that this legislation violated their constitutionally protected right of the free exercise of religion, and in a series of cases, they challenged the antipolygamy legislation in the courts. REYNOLDS V. UNITED STATES was decided by the U.S. Supreme Court in 1879. The appeal attacked the Morrill Act for failing to acknowledge the religious motivation behind plural marriage. A unanimous Court held, however, that to allow Latter-day Saints' religious beliefs to excuse them from obeying the law would be to "make the professed doctrines of religious belief superior to the law of the land, and in effect to permit every citizen to become a law unto himself" (98 U.S. [1879]). The *Reynolds* decision distinguished between religious opinions and religious practices, leaving the former free while allowing for government regulation of the latter (*see* CIVIL RIGHTS; LEGAL AND JUDICIAL HISTORY OF THE CHURCH).

Decisions in later polygamy cases undermined that distinction, allowing for the direct or indirect regulation of religious opinion. The Court upheld the disfranchisement provisions of the Edmunds Act in *Murphy v. Ramsey*. Congress, according to the Court, was responsible for preparing the territories for statehood and self-government. In Utah this required curbing the political power of polygamists because nothing was more important in the founding of a self-governing commonwealth than "the idea of family, as consisting in and springing from the union for life of one man and one woman in the holy estate of matrimony" (114 U.S. 15 [1885]). The Court in *Davis v. Beason* upheld an Idaho test oath that disfranchised any member of any organization that taught its members "to commit the crime" of polygamy. According to the Court, the free exercise clause of the First Amendment did not protect individuals in advocating "any form of worship" and "any tenets, however destructive of society," merely by asserting them to be a part of their religious beliefs (133 U.S. 333 [1890]). In *The Late Corporation of the Church of Jesus Christ of Latter-day Saints v. United States*, the Supreme Court sustained the disincorporation and escheat provisions of the Edmunds-Tucker Act. The opinion described the Church corporation as a contumacious organization that, in defiance of the authority of the government, continued to encourage polygamy, "a crime against the laws, and abhorrent to the sentiments and feelings of the civilized world" (136 U.S. 1 [1890]). With plenary authority over the political affairs of territories, Congress had the power to abolish the Church corporation and the government could dispose of its property.

The Poland, Edmunds, and Edmunds-Tucker laws curtailed LDS political power. An all-out attack on plural marriage came in the late 1880s, in what Latter-day Saints called "the Raid." The thrust against the Church struck deeper than the practice of polygamy, however: it struck at the heart of the LDS community and threatened its survival in a world that, since the 1830s, had shown itself hostile. The deeper threat was reflected in the massive economic, social, and political dislocations occasioned by the Raid. Finally, facing even the loss of its TEMPLES, in 1890 Church President Wilford WOODRUFF concluded that "for the temporal salvation of the church" it was necessary to end the practice of plural marriage. In his MANIFESTO OF 1890, he announced his intention to submit to the antipolygamy laws and to use his influence to induce Church members to do the same.

The Manifesto was only the beginning of the changes introduced by Church leaders in the 1890s to accommodate the Latter-day Saint community to the social, economic, and political forms of the larger society. They dissolved the local People's party, which had dominated electoral politics in Utah from its organization in the early 1870s, and encouraged members to affiliate with the Republican and Democratic national parties. They sup-

ported the development of a public school system. Finally, leaders reduced direct Church involvement in the economic life of the territory by selling off most business interests (*see* ECONOMIC HISTORY OF THE CHURCH; PIONEER ECONOMY). The reward for their willingness to accommodate themselves to the forms of American liberalism came in 1896 with UTAH STATEHOOD. Latter-day Saints relinquished important elements of the social, economic, and political order that they had established in the Great Basin in exchange for a measure of the political power and autonomy that decades of confrontation and conflict had demonstrated were necessary for their survival as a community.

The modus vivendi that Church leaders worked out with the American political community as the prerequisite for statehood reduced, but by no means ended, direct Church involvement in politics. In the first years after statehood, Church leaders quietly supported and participated in a system of power sharing between Mormons and non-Mormons, Democrats and Republicans. For example, the state's two seats in the U.S. Senate were divided between Latter-day Saints and non-Mormons until the election of 1916, when the Seventeenth Amendment (ratified 1913), providing for direct popular election of senators, removed the matter from the control of party or Church leaders.

Church leaders signaled their intention to curb their own political activity in the so-called Political Manifesto of 1896, which emphasized the importance of the religious duties of Church officers and required them to obtain approval of ecclesiastical superiors before seeking public office. This rule was applied more stringently for Democratic- than Republican-inclined Church officials. Church authorities in the 1890s encouraged the development of the Republican party among Church members, many of whom had avoided the party because of its harsh opposition to plural marriage.

Church leaders since 1896, with only a few exceptions, have avoided taking stands that by either identifying the Church with, or casting the Church in opposition to, either major political party would encourage a religious polarization of the parties. But they have been willing to take an official stand on such issues as public welfare and the repeal of PROHIBITION in the 1930s, Sunday closing laws in the 1950s, right-to-work laws and liquor by the drink in the 1960s, the Equal Rights Amendment (ERA) in the 1970s, and ABORTION in the 1970s, 1980s, and 1990s. While the Church by no means inevitably has its way in Utah politics, it is a pervasive influence in the state. Latter-day Saints help shape the political agenda of Utah, in large part determining the issues that are or are not live, and dictating the terms in which issues accepted as live are debated. Generally, the overwhelming majority of all officeholders, both Republican and Democratic, are LDS.

What the Latter-day Saints relinquished in order to secure statehood for Utah indicates what was really at stake in the nineteenth-century political conflicts. Both sides were well aware that the struggle was over more than a "peculiar institution." For Latter-day Saints, plural marriage symbolized obedience to the will of God revealed through latter-day prophets. For anti-Mormons, polygamy symbolized the potential for theocratic control, rooted in the religion's belief in continuing revelation. Territorial governor Caleb West told the Mormons in 1888 that the cause of their woes was their belief that "God governs them immediately, not alone in faith and morals, but in all affairs and relations of life, and that the counsel of the priesthood is the Supreme Voice of God and must be obeyed" (governor to Territorial Assembly, Jan. 9, 1888). The tenet of continuing revelation, an issue since the beginning, largely accounted for the struggles between the Latter-day Saints and the federal government over political power in early Utah. It generated continuing tensions in the politics of Utah, and containing them required the exercise of prudent statesmanship by leaders of both church and state. At the same time, the vitality of Utah as a democratic political community in the early twentieth century was the foundation for the relative peace that Latter-day Saints have enjoyed since then. That such peace remained somewhat precarious was evident when well-organized LDS lobbying efforts in several states against the ERA in the 1970s threatened to reawaken major apprehensions of priesthood influence on LDS voters.

Outside the United States, LDS efforts for legal recognition and freedom of operation under restrictive regimes were remarkably successful by 1990, precisely because Church leaders convinced government leaders that priesthood directives would not promote political activity that confronted constituted authority—would not, in fact, promote political activity in any particular direction. The fact that LDS political behavior both in

Utah and in U.S. government service was observably stable and responsible was thus significant for the functioning and expansion of the Church in an international setting.

BIBLIOGRAPHY

Alexander, Thomas G. *Mormonism in Transition: A History of the Latter-day Saints, 1890–1930.* Urbana and Chicago, 1986.

Firmage, Edwin Brown, and Richard Collin Mangrum. *Zion in the Courts: A Legal History of the Church of Jesus Christ of Latter-day Saints, 1830–1900.* Urbana and Chicago, 1988.

Hill, Marvin S. *Quest for Refuge: The Mormon Flight from American Pluralism.* Salt Lake City, 1989.

Lyman, Edward Leo. *Political Deliverance: The Mormon Quest for Utah Statehood.* Urbana and Chicago, 1986.

Morgan, Dale L. "The State of Deseret." *Utah Historical Quarterly* 8 (Apr., July, Oct. 1940):65–239.

Poll, Richard D. "The Mormon Question Enters National Politics, 1850–1856." *Utah Historical Quarterly* 25 (1957):117–31.

ROGER M. BARRUS

POLITICAL TEACHINGS

Concerning the general duties of government and citizen, latter-day scriptures and the prophets of The Church of Jesus Christ of Latter-day Saints teach that governments should protect freedoms and provide for the public interest and that citizens should honor and uphold laws and governments. LDS theology endorses aspects of both individualism and communitarianism, and harmonizes these conflicting ideas by teaching that community members can share and promote ideals and principles but should never use force to achieve such conditions. Church leaders encourage members to be participants in public affairs even as they emphasize the separation of the management of CHURCH AND STATE. The Church rarely gives official counsel to its members regarding political issues. As with other religions, various opinions exist among Latter-day Saints as to how political teachings and principles should be applied.

Section 134 of the Doctrine and Covenants is a useful starting point for examining the major beliefs of members of the LDS Church concerning politics and government. In an 1835 meeting to discuss plans for publishing the Doctrine and Covenants, Church leaders prepared a declaration to the world concerning "earthly governments and law." Some members of the Church had been accused of being opposed to law and order, and were subsequently victimized by mobbings and violence. The declaration provided guidelines for the Saints in rebutting the charges of their enemies. Penned by Oliver Cowdery, with the possible participation of W. W. Phelps, this is one of the few sections of the Doctrine and Covenants not given by revelation to Joseph Smith.

Two central themes run throughout this section and related passages. First, the duty of government is to provide for the public interest in general and to protect freedom of conscience and religious belief in particular. Governments "were instituted of God for the benefit of man." Laws are to be enacted "for the good and safety of society" and to "secure to each individual the free exercise of conscience, the right and control of property, and the protection of life." Government officials are to make laws that are "best calculated to secure the public interest; at the same time, however, holding sacred the freedom of conscience" (D&C 134:1–2, 5). The separation of church and state is imperative: it is not "just to mingle religious influence with civil government, whereby one religious society is fostered and another proscribed in its spiritual privileges" (D&C 134:9). Governments do not have the right "to interfere in prescribing rules of worship, to bind the consciences of men, nor dictate forms for public or private devotion." They "should restrain crime, but never control conscience; should punish guilt, but never suppress the freedom of the soul." Governments have an affirmative duty to protect citizens "in the free exercise of their religious belief," but they do not have the right to "deprive citizens of this privilege, or proscribe them in their opinions," as long as such citizens do not promote sedition (D&C 134:4–7).

Second, the duty of citizens is to honor and sustain laws and governments. All people are "bound to sustain and uphold the respective governments in which they reside, while protected in their inherent and inalienable rights." Governments are responsible "for the protection of the innocent and the punishment of the guilty"; citizens are to "step forward and use their ability in bringing offenders against good laws to punishment" (D&C 134:5–6, 8).

Other passages in LDS scripture reflect these themes of governmental and citizenship duties. Members of the Church are to befriend the "constitutional law of the land" that supports the "principle of freedom in maintaining rights and privileges" (D&C 98:5–6). Church leaders have regularly indicated their belief that the CONSTITUTION OF THE UNITED STATES OF AMERICA is an inspired document. Citizens are to seek and uphold honest, wise, and good government leaders (D&C 98:10). Book of Mormon writers emphasize that every person is to enjoy "rights and privileges alike" and that political decisions are to be made "by the voice of the people" (Mosiah 29:25–27, 32).

New Testament admonitions to "render therefore unto Caesar the things which are Caesar's" (Matt. 22:21), to "be subject to principalities and powers, to obey magistrates" (Titus 3:1), and to "submit yourselves to every ordinance of man" (1 Pet. 2:13) also provide guidance to members of the Church concerning their obligations as citizens. In all nations, Latter-day Saints are encouraged to support their lawful governments; to participate actively in politics, civic affairs, and public service; and to support and promote just and righteous causes.

Because of its emphasis on free AGENCY, individual ACCOUNTABILITY, and freedom of belief and conscience, LDS theology is quite compatible with Western traditions of liberal democracy that champion individual and minority rights, personal freedom, and religious pluralism. Laws are to ensure "the rights and protection of all" so that every person "may act in doctrine and principle pertaining to futurity, according to the moral agency which [God has] given unto him, that every man may be accountable for his own sins in the day of judgment" (D&C 101:77–78).

From a broader view of politics, however, Latter-day Saints have much greater expectations for collective action. Their theology includes a strong commitment to achieve a unified, cooperative society, characterized by spiritual convictions, strong social bonds, collective responsibilities, and material EQUALITY. Joseph Smith taught that "the greatest temporal and spiritual blessings which always come from faithfulness and concerted effort, never attended individual exertion or enterprise" (*TPJS*, p. 183). UNITY and cooperation in temporal affairs are preconditions for spiritual progress: "If ye are not one ye are not mine" (D&C 38:27); "If ye are not equal in earthly things ye cannot be equal in obtaining heavenly things" (D&C 78:6; *see also* ZION).

Respect for individual rights and a strong commitment to collective action come together in the belief that communities can be built on shared principles and ideals, but force can never be employed to achieve those ends. Unity and cooperation cannot be attained by coercion, but only through love: power is to be exercised by "persuasion, by long-suffering, by gentleness and meekness, and by love unfeigned" (D&C 121:41). The goals of individual RIGHTEOUSNESS and COMMUNITY are well captured in this description of the city of Enoch from the Pearl of Great Price: "And the Lord called his people ZION, because they were of one heart and one mind, and dwelt in righteousness; and there was no poor among them" (Moses 7:18).

While Latter-day Saints aspire to such a community of the faithful, they have been encouraged throughout their history to participate in public affairs even under other conditions. "It is our duty," said Joseph Smith, "to concentrate all our influence to make popular that which is sound and good, and unpopular that which is unsound. 'Tis right, politically, for a man who has influence to use it" (HC 5:286). Brigham Young charged members of the Church, "Let every man and woman be industrious, prudent, and economical in their acts and feelings, and while gathering to themselves, let each one strive to identify his or her interests with the interests of this community, with those of their neighbor and neighborhood, let them seek their happiness and welfare in that of all" (JD 3:330).

In 1903 the First Presidency of the Church issued a statement emphasizing the separation of religious and political activity:

> The Church . . . instructs in things temporal as well as things spiritual. . . . But it does not infringe upon . . . the domain of the state. . . . Every member of the organization in every place is absolutely free as a citizen. . . . In proclaiming "the kingdom of heaven's at hand," we have the most intense and fervent conviction of our mission and calling. . . . But we do not and will not attempt to force them upon others, or to control or dominate any of their affairs, individual or national [MFP 4:79, 82].

In 1968, the First Presidency issued a statement concerning the obligations of citizenship:

> We urge our members to do their civic duty and to assume their responsibilities as individual citizens in seeking solutions to the problems which beset our cities and communities.
>
> With our wide ranging mission, so far as mankind is concerned, Church members cannot ignore the many practical problems that require solution if our families are to live in an environment conducive to spirituality. . . .
>
> Individual Church members cannot, of course, represent or commit the Church, but should, nevertheless, be "anxiously engaged" in good causes, using the principles of the Gospel of Jesus Christ as their constant guide [see Appendix, "Doctrinal Expositions of the First Presidency"].

There are differing views among Church members concerning how to put these principles into practice. From one view, government intervention ought to be minimal in order to encourage VOLUNTEERISM, freedom of choice, and individual responsibility. Others believe governments should pursue a wide range of collective purposes and promote shared values. There are also differences concerning the role of religious ideas in political discourse. Some believe, much like those in other churches who have not hesitated to mix politics and religion in issues such as CIVIL RIGHTS, abortion, and environmental pollution (see EARTH), that religious principles having corresponding secular purposes should be part of public debate and be enacted into law if they can gain sufficient support in the political system. Others favor a more distinct separation between religious belief and public discourse, where public debate is limited to issues and values that can be defended on "rational" grounds, so that religious beliefs do not influence the making of laws (see POLITICS: POLITICAL CULTURE).

Brigham Young stated clearly the LDS commitment to a broad conception of collective effort in working toward a vision of a celestial community, while expressing ambivalence about earthly politics: "As for politics, we care nothing about them one way or the other, although we are a political people. . . . It is the Kingdom of God or nothing with us" (Millennial Star 31 [1869]:573).

BIBLIOGRAPHY

Cannon, Donald Q. "Church and State." In Insights into the Doctrine and Covenants: The Capstone of our Religion, ed. R. Millet and L. Dahl, pp. 183–96. Salt Lake City, 1989.

Firmage, Edwin Brown. "Eternal Principles of Government: A Theological Approach." Ensign 6 (June 1976):11–16.

Nibley, Hugh. "Beyond Politics." In Nibley on the Timely and the Timeless: Classic Essays of Hugh W. Nibley, ed. T. Madsen, pp. 279–305. Provo, Utah, 1978.

GARY C. BRYNER

POLITICAL CULTURE

Contrary to some popular characterizations, Latter-day Saints do not all think or vote alike on political matters and do not share a distinctive political subculture. American Latter-day Saints tend to be slightly more pragmatic, less cynical, more optimistic, and less alienated than the average American citizen, but only in minor variations from the broad national political culture. The earliest Latter-day Saints were Americans before they became Latter-day Saints. If Latter-day Saints as a group were markedly less or more optimistic or less or more cynical than the average U.S. citizen, that might indicate the presence of a distinctive political subculture, but there is no evidence for this.

A political culture is generally understood to be a patterned set of ways of thinking about how politics and governing ought to be carried out, and a subculture is a somewhat differing view peculiar to a smaller area or group. During the nineteenth century, when Latter-day Saints "gathered" together in well-structured communities throughout the intermountain West, there was a distinctive Mormon political subculture. It was based on a model of consensus politics and a deference to ecclesiastical AUTHORITY, which set it apart from the dominant American political culture of the time. This subculture slowly dissipated as the intermountain LDS commonwealth was integrated into the larger political and economic patterns of the United States, despite the continued majority status of Latter-day Saints in many communities.

In a strict sense, there is no such thing today as "a Mormon political culture." The mark of such a subculture is the frequency and likelihood of certain political behaviors observable over time and in well-defined situations, not the source of the ideas that it expresses. While various tenets of their faith may predispose many Latter-day Saints to one side of some political disputes in the United States, such a predisposition is not sufficient to indicate the presence of a unique political subculture.

In the late twentieth century, Latter-day Saints are found in many different countries, living under many different political systems. That which ties them together is a set of religious beliefs, not an identifiable set of habits of thinking or acting about politics. Were a cross-polity survey to be taken, the empirical beliefs, likes and dislikes, values, and priorities of Latter-day Saints in political matters would be polity-specific. German Latter-day Saints, for example, would resemble other Germans more than they would Mexican, French, or Samoan Latter-day Saints.

Some maintain, nonetheless, that there is an identifiable LDS political subculture in America, or at least in Utah. This perspective may confuse a regional pattern of attitudes and behaviors with a religious one. It also reflects the ubiquitous disagreements between minorities and the majority in any population. Latter-day Saints in Utah (the only state where they constitute a majority of the population) are no more sensitive to the feelings of alienation and oppression perceived by members of other denominations than are other religious or cultural majorities in other parts of the world.

Since statehood in 1896, Utah has been in the mainstream of American politics. In the twenty-two presidential elections between 1904 and 1988, Utah gave its electoral (and majority) votes to the national winner all but three times. The partisan preferences of Utah voters are essentially the same as those of other intermountain and western voters in presidential and congressional elections. Divisions between voters are essentially partisan, not ecclesiastical, even in strongly LDS areas.

Belief in the LDS worldview does not produce predictable or demonstrable similarities in political habits of thought and expectations, regardless of geographical, economic, or social differences. The often fervent divisions among LDS voters over political issues and candidates cast serious doubt on the existence of any unifying, religiously determined political behaviors.

Latter-day Saints' attitudinal orientations are generally intensifications of typically American attitudes. For example, the idea of political efficacy—the feeling citizens have that they can influence what the government does and the belief that government listens to what ordinary citizens say—is a key indicator of the type of political culture a country has. In all cross-polity surveys, U.S. citizens demonstrate significantly higher levels of political efficacy than citizens of any other country. Perhaps because of the stress in LDS theology on the value of individual effort and the right of individual agency, Latter-day Saints demonstrate higher levels of efficacy than most other groups in American political life. How directly related to religious beliefs such attitudes may be is difficult to establish empirically. However, there may be some overlap or holdover from earlier times.

Latter-day Saints also ascribe a higher level of legitimacy to political leaders, possibly a holdover from the mingling of ecclesiastical and political authority in nineteenth-century Utah. Finally, voting participation statistics indicate that the growing political alienation in America has made few inroads in strongly LDS areas.

A crucial determinant of a community's or a nation's political stability and governmental effectiveness is the extent to which its citizens give their primary political loyalties to it rather than to a particular region, tribe, or religion. Although Latter-day Saints are deeply attached to their religion, for this attachment to affect their political behavior has been the exception rather than the rule. For example, during the 1930s and 1940s the President of the Church and at least one of his counselors were implacably opposed to the policies of President Franklin D. Roosevelt and expressed their views publicly and privately. Nevertheless, Utah voters joined decisively with national majorities voting for the Democratic candidates from 1932 through 1948. In the ten presidential elections since 1952, only in 1964 did Utah vote Democratic, again joining an overwhelming national majority. This Republican hegemony is found not only in LDS areas but also nearly all the western states.

There is no detectable pattern or set of political behaviors common to Latter-day Saints. Appearances of a unique LDS political homogeneity disappear when regional and national trends are taken into account. No institutional or doctrinal mechanism exists for passing on a political culture, especially in light of the high percentage of converts. The growing international character of the Church and its membership will no doubt produce even greater political heterogeneity among Latter-day Saints in the future.

BIBLIOGRAPHY

Poll, Richard D., et al. *Utah's History*, pp. 97–112, 153–73, 243–74, 387–404, 409–428, 481–96, 515–30, 669–80. Provo, Utah, 1978.

WM. CLAYTON KIMBALL

CONTEMPORARY AMERICAN POLITICS

Latter-day Saints are an integral part of the politics of the intermountain West of the United States. They play important roles in U.S. politics and government, and members have held high positions in all three branches of the federal government and in many state and local governments. The Church encourages its members throughout the world to be involved in government and civic affairs (*see* CIVIC DUTIES). Official Church statements on such matters as the Equal Rights Amendment (ERA) and the MX missile have been important in the politics of these issues.

On most issues and in most elections, the Church has remained neutral, admonishing its members to study the issues and vote according to their conscience. A member of the First Presidency said in 1951:

> The Church, while reserving the right to advocate principles of good government underlying equity, justice, and liberty, the political integrity of officials, and the active participation of its members, and the fulfillment of their obligations in civic affairs, exercises no constraint on the freedom of individuals to make their own choices and affiliations. . . . Any man who makes representation to the contrary does so without authority and justification in fact [Richards, p. 878].

The Church encourages individual choice in elections, although through the 1960 election Church leaders often publicly endorsed or indicated their personal preference for U.S. presidential candidates (Jonas, p. 335). Despite any corporate interest it may have in Utah (*see* BUSINESS: CHURCH PARTICIPATION IN), the Church has not become directly involved in elections in those jurisdictions for many years.

While many non-LDS candidates have been elected to public office in Utah, Church membership and affiliation do appear to be important to political success in Utah, as well as in some surrounding areas of the intermountain West with large LDS populations. Candidates for office sometimes advertise their Church affiliation, Church leadership positions, and family size as part of their political campaigns. Local Church officials sometimes become involved in politics either as candidates or as supporters of candidates. Some voters incorrectly infer an implicit Church endorsement of candidates or issues in these situations.

While the Church rarely takes an official stand on candidates or issues, it does possess substantial political power. Its membership constitutes an overwhelming majority (70 percent) in the state of Utah and significant portions of the population in Idaho, Arizona, and Nevada. It also exercises political influence through its corporate and business interests. The Church's business interests and its print and broadcast media (BONNEVILLE INTERNATIONAL) give it a means to participate in politics. Editorials from these media are often considered to reflect the views of the Church.

Church members in the late twentieth century are generally Republicans, often strong Republicans, though in earlier generations Democratic influence prevailed. Data on Utah indicate that 69 percent of the Latter-day Saints are Republicans, a figure higher than the 57 percent of Utahans who are Republicans and the 47 percent of western Americans who are Republicans. Increased Church activity is even more strongly correlated to Republican partisan identification. This relationship between Church activity and attachment to the Republican party is also related to age; younger, very active Latter-day Saints are most likely to classify themselves Republicans. Party identification among members of the Church has the same behavioral consequences as it does among non-Mormons nationwide. Most members of the Church are politically conservative, both by self-classification and in attitudes toward economic, social, and lifestyle issues. The conservatism of many Church members reinforces their partisan preferences, especially with regard to the national political parties. Little is known about the partisan or ideological predispositions of LDS members outside the United States.

Recent nationally prominent LDS political figures also tend to be disproportionately Republican, although for all of U.S. history, LDS congressmen and senators have been only about 50 percent Republican. LDS congressmen tend to come from Utah and surrounding states, but include several California members of the U.S. House of Representatives. Utah, Idaho, Michigan, and Arizona have all had LDS governors. LDS-elected gubernatorial officials and national legislators represent an even partisan balance.

Several Latter-day Saints have played key roles in recent Republican administrations. President Eisenhower's cabinet included apostle and later President of the Church Ezra Taft Benson as secretary of agriculture. President Nixon's cabinet included David M. Kennedy as secretary of the treasury, and George Romney as secretary of housing and urban development. The Ford, Reagan, and Bush administrations also had several members of the Church as key staff. Church members played a generally less visible role in the Democratic administrations of Kennedy, Johnson, and Carter.

Church members have been important participants in the judicial branch as well. While no member of the Church has been appointed to the U.S. Supreme Court, several Latter-day Saints have served as court of appeals, district court, and state supreme court judges.

The Church has been most visible politically in discussion of moral issues. In 1976, after years of silence on political issues, the Church issued a statement opposing the ERA: "We recognize men and women as equally important before the Lord, but with differences biologically, emotionally, and in other ways. ERA, we believe, does not recognize these differences. There are better means for giving women, and men, the rights they deserve" ("First Presidency Issues Statement Opposing Equal Rights Amendment," *Ensign* 6 [Dec. 1976]:79). This formal institutional opposition sparked significant local organizing by private Church members acting on their own accord against the amendment in Florida, Illinois, Maryland, Nevada, and Virginia. Not all Church members opposed the amendment. Some had spoken publicly in support of the amendment before the Church position was announced.

During the early 1980s the Church took a position on the MX missile controversy. Many Church leaders had long been critical of war and armaments. But others were in favor of preparations for defense. Thus, elected officials could find Church authorities either favoring or opposing defense spending, new weapons systems, and foreign military activities. Utah representatives in Washington tend to promote defense spending, and Utah has a large defense industry.

In 1981, Church President Spencer W. Kimball and his counselors issued a strongly worded letter opposing the deployment of the MX missile in the desert of western Utah and neighboring eastern Nevada. The statement criticized not only the MX missile but also the form of warfare it exemplified: "With the most serious concern over the pressing moral question of possible nuclear conflict, we plead with our national leaders to marshal the genius of the nation to find viable alternatives which will secure at an earlier date and with fewer hazards the protection from possible enemy aggression, which is our common concern" ("First

Presidency Statement on Basing of MX Missile," *Ensign* 11 [June 1981]:76).

The Church has also opposed legalized GAMBLING, including state-run lotteries ("Church Opposes Government-Sponsored Gambling," *Ensign* 16 [Nov. 1986]:104–105), and has made moral arguments against liberalizing access to alcoholic beverages.

BIBLIOGRAPHY

Arrington, Leonard J., and Davis Bitton. *The Mormon Experience: A History of the Latter-day Saints*, pp. 243–307. New York, 1979.

Jonas, Frank. "Utah: The Different State." In *Politics in the American West*, ed. F. Jonas. Salt Lake City, 1969.

Richards, Stephen L. "Awake, Ye Defenders of Zion." *IE* 54 (Dec. 1951):877–80.

DAVID B. MAGLEBY

POLYGAMY

[*The main article on this subject is* Plural Marriage. *Under the direction of the Prophet Joseph Smith, some members of The Church of Jesus Christ of Latter-day Saints began to practice plural marriage, also referred to as "celestial marriage." This was viewed as a divine commandment to "raise up seed unto" God* (Jacob 2:30). *The revelation of God concerning eternal marriage is D&C 132. See* Doctrine and Covenants: Sections 131–32. *The latter also contains strong warnings against marital infidelity. See* Adultery; Chastity; Marriage: Eternal; *and* Sexuality.

On the federal and public opposition to Mormon polygamy, see Antipolygamy Legislation; Legal and Judicial History of the Church; Mormons, Image of; *and* Reynolds v. United States. *On attitudes of Mormon women toward polygamy, see* Retrenchment Association *and* Woman's Exponent.

The Church of Jesus Christ of Latter-day Saints officially discontinued the practice of plural marriage in 1890. See Manifesto of 1890.

Some schismatic groups have not accepted the revelation of God to Wilford Woodruff, fourth President of the Church, ending Church-sanctioned plural marriage and therefore continue the practice today. See Fundamentalists.

See generally History of the Church: c. 1844–1877 *and* c. 1878–1898; Smith, Emma; Smith, Joseph: Teachings of; Snow, Eliza R.; Woodruff, Wilford; *and* Young, Brigham.]

POLYNESIAN CULTURAL CENTER

The Polynesian Cultural Center is located in Laie, Hawaii, on the north shore of the island of Oahu. It is a 42-acre visitor attraction owned and operated by The Church of Jesus Christ of Latter-day Saints for the purpose of preserving and sharing the heritage of Pacific island cultures while providing employment, scholarships, and grants to students at the adjacent BRIGHAM YOUNG UNIVERSITY—HAWAII.

In seven authentically recreated villages, representative dwellings, furniture, and artifacts from Fiji, old Hawaii, Samoa, Tonga, Tahiti, Maori New Zealand, and the Marquesas Islands are featured in a landscape of island foliage and lagoons. Visitors may observe or participate in demonstrations of arts, crafts, dances, music, games, and food preparation presented by villagers and performers, many of whom come from the cultures they portray. Various kinds of island cuisine are available in restaurants and snack bars. Daytime and evening shows and concerts are held on the grounds and in the 2,773-seat amphitheater. An IMAX theater with an ultra-large screen shows cultural and educational films shot on locations in the South Pacific.

Precursors to the present production consisted mainly of a *hukilau*—a fishing festival with luau and entertainment. That production was begun by Church members in the 1940s and continued for several years in Laie. In 1959 students and faculty at the Church College of Hawaii (now Brigham Young University—Hawaii) organized "Polynesian Panorama," a production of songs and dances that played regularly to audiences in Waikiki.

In 1962 Church President David O. MCKAY authorized construction of the present center. Special "labor missionaries" donated their skills, using building materials from Hawaii and the other islands represented. The original 12-acre center opened on October 12, 1963. Hugh B. Brown, a counselor to President McKay in the Church's FIRST PRESIDENCY, presided at the opening ceremonies. In 1975–1976 the center was redesigned and greatly enlarged.

The labor missionaries helped realize the dream of Matthew Cowley, an apostle who worked for years with the Latter-day Saints in New Zealand, when he said, "I hope to see the day when my Maori people will have a little village at Laie with a beautiful carved house. . . . The Tongans will have a little village out there, and the Tahitians and Samoans—all those islanders of the sea!" (O'Brien, p. 73).

The center is a nonprofit organization that attracts almost a million visitors a year. It is administered locally by a president and governed by a board of directors chaired by a member of the Church's QUORUM OF THE TWELVE APOSTLES.

BIBLIOGRAPHY

O'Brien, Robert. *Hands Across the Water: The Story of the Polynesian Cultural Center.* Laie, Hawaii, 1983.

CHARLES JAY FOX

POLYNESIANS

Polynesia is most frequently identified as those Pacific islands lying within an enormous triangle extending from New Zealand in the south to Hawaii in the north and the Easter Islands in the extreme east. The major Polynesian ethnic groups include Hawaiians, New Zealand Maoris, Samoans, Tongans, and Tahitians.

A basic view held in the Church is that Polynesians have ancestral connections with the Book of Mormon people who were descendants of Abraham and that among them are heirs to the blessings promised Abraham's descendants (*see* ABRAHAMIC COVENANT). Since 1843, the Church has undertaken extensive missionary efforts in the Pacific islands, and large numbers of Polynesians have joined the Church (*see* NEW ZEALAND; OCEANIA).

The belief that Polynesian ancestry includes Book of Mormon people can be traced back at least to 1851, when George Q. Cannon taught it as a missionary in Hawaii (he was later a counselor in the First Presidency). President Brigham YOUNG detailed the belief in a letter to King Kamehameha V in 1865. Other Church leaders have since affirmed the belief, some indicating that among Polynesian ancestors were the people of Hagoth, who set sail from Nephite lands in approximately 54

Primary officers, teachers, and children of the French Polynesia Mission (now the Tahiti Papeete Mission) in the early 1970s. LDS missionaries arrived in the Society Islands in 1844. Local members customarily fill leadership positions as soon as possible. Many Pacific Islands have a high percentage of Latter-day Saints in their total populations.

This Maori "rangatira" (chief) and family were members of the Church in New Zealand (c. 1917). Courtesy Edith W. Morgan.

B.C. (cf. Alma 63:5–8). In a statement to the Maoris of New Zealand, for instance, President Joseph F. SMITH said, "I would like to say to you brethren and sisters . . . you *are* some of Hagoth's people, and there is NO PERHAPS about it!" (Cole and Jensen, p. 388.) In the prayer offered at the dedication of the Hawaii Temple, President Heber J. GRANT referred to the "descendants of Lehi" in Hawaii (*IE* 23 [Feb. 1920]:283).

Among scholars, the exact ancestry of the Polynesian peoples is a matter of debate. While some non-LDS scientists have insisted on their Western Hemisphere origins, the prevailing scientific opinion from anthropological, archaeological, and linguistic evidence argues a west-to-east migratory movement from Southeast Asia that began as early as 1200 B.C.

What seems clear from the long-standing debate is that considerable interaction was maintained over the centuries from many directions. The island peoples had both the vessels and the skill to sail with or against ocean currents. It would be as difficult to say that no group could have migrated from east to west as to argue the opposite in absolute terms. Church leaders, who have attested

to Polynesian roots in the Nephite peoples, have not elaborated on the likelihood of other migrating groups in the Pacific or of social mixing and intermarriage.

Throughout the Church's history in the islands, Polynesian members have demonstrated spiritual receptivity, maturity, and leadership. In 1990, more than 100,000 Polynesians, including approximately 30 percent of the Tongans and 20 percent of the Samoans, were members of the Church. In all areas of Polynesia, local leaders preside over organized stakes and wards. Missionary work continues, much of it under the direction of local mission presidents and missionaries. In Tonga and Samoa, for example, almost the entire force of missionaries is made up of local youth, and hundreds of others have been called to serve missions elsewhere in the world.

Some Polynesian Latter-day Saints have left their homelands and established communities abroad. Honolulu, Auckland, and Los Angeles have extensive LDS Polynesian populations. Thousands of LDS Polynesians have also migrated to Utah's Wasatch Front area and to Missouri, California, and Texas.

BIBLIOGRAPHY

Britsch, R. Lanier. *Moramona*. Laie, Hawaii, 1989.

————. *Unto the Islands of the Sea.* Salt Lake City, 1989.

Clement, Russell T. "Polynesian Origins: More Word on the Mormon Perspective." *Dialogue* 13 (Winter 1980):88–89.

Cole, W. A., and E. W. Jensen. *Israel in the Pacific.* Salt Lake City, 1961.

Loveland, Jerry. "Hagoth and the Polynesian Tradition." *BYU Studies* 17 (Autumn 1976):59–73.

ERIC B. SHUMWAY

PORNOGRAPHY

Pornography refers to explicit depictions of sexual activity in written or pictorial form in an exploitive style. The purpose of these presentations is erotic arousal for commercial gain. Most of it presents highly inaccurate, unscientific, and distorted information about human SEXUALITY. It is, in a sense, sex miseducation marketed for financial gain in a variety of formats, including books, magazines, motion pictures, television, videotapes, and even telephone. The Church of Jesus Christ of Latter-day Saints condemns all forms of pornography.

The Church views sexuality positively—as a sacred gift from God with the primary purposes of reproducing life upon the earth and bonding the husband and wife together in an eternal, affectionate, committed relationship. High standards of personal morality and sexual conduct, including CHASTITY before marriage and fidelity in marriage, are taught as norms for Church members. These standards are perceived as reflecting God's will and counsel for his earthly children.

Pornography is seen as degrading sex and creating an unhealthy extramarital sexual interest in individuals, thereby contributing to a weakening of the marital relationship. Much of this filmed, photographed, or written "prostitution" is actually antisexual because it gives a great deal of false information about human sexuality. Also, since much pornography depicts violence and aggression against females, it raises risks of conditioning viewers to sanction these as acceptable behavior. The best evidence suggests that all sexual deviations are learned, and pornography appears to be a major facilitator in the acquisition of these deviations.

Introducing immoral or inappropriate sexual stimuli into the mind of those who view it can create fantasies that may never be erased. It has the potential for corrupting the values of, and degrading, those who indulge. It suggests behaviors that could negatively affect or even destroy one's marriage and family. Pornography, in a sense, is an attack on the family and the marriage covenant as well as on the bonds of affection or trust that hold a marriage and family together.

Additionally, involvement in pornography promotes a voyeuristic interest in sex, one form of sexual illness. This is a regressive fantasy approach to sexuality with major health risks. These various hazards have been documented at length by the U.S. Pornography Commission, convened under the sponsorship of the U.S. Department of Justice.

The experience of many men and adolescent males who repeatedly experiment with, or voluntarily expose themselves to, pornography suggests four possible consequences. First, there is a risk of addiction. Once involved with it, many get "hooked," as with a highly addictive drug, and keep coming back in a compulsive fashion for more. Second, they desire increasingly deviant material. In time, they need rougher and more explicit material to get the same kicks, arousal, and excitement as initially. Third, they become desensitized to the inappropriateness or abnormality of the behavior portrayed, eventually accepting and embracing what at first had shocked and offended them. Fourth, with appetite whetted and conscience anesthetized, they tend to act out sexually what they have witnessed. This almost always disturbs the most intimate aspects of marital and family relationships and attacks the participants' spiritual nature. As an individual acts out his desires and appetites, there is a significant risk of venereal infections, some of which are incurable and life-threatening. When this occurs, the health and life of the marital partner is also jeopardized.

The Church strongly counsels its members to avoid involvement with pornography for the many reasons cited above. An important additional reason is that involvement with it is also perceived as leading to a loss of contact with, and consciousness of, God and the Holy Spirit. It can lead to a psychological, sexual, and spiritual regression. Becoming addicted to pornography can lead to a loss of control and eventually to the loss of moral agency.

The Church counsels its members to be responsible citizens in the communities where they live, to join organizations that attempt to improve community values, to let their voices be heard, and to work for, in legal ways, limits being placed on the dissemination, broadcast, sale, and rental of illegal pornographic materials.

BIBLIOGRAPHY

"Church Leaders Suggest Ways to Fight Pornography." *Ensign* 14 (Apr. 1984):37–39.

Cline, Victor B. "Obscenity: How It Affects Us, How We Can Deal with It." *Ensign* 14 (Apr. 1984):32–37.

———, ed. *Where Do You Draw the Line?* Provo, Utah, 1974.

Monson, Thomas S. "Pornography—The Deadly Carrier." *Ensign* 9 (Nov. 1979):66–67.

Shapiro, Gary R. "Leave the Obscene Unseen." *Ensign* 19 (Aug. 1989):27–29.

VICTOR B. CLINE

POSTEARTH LIFE

See: Afterlife

POVERTY, ATTITUDES TOWARD

For Latter-day Saints, as for all Christians, attending to the needs of the poor is service to God (Matt. 25:31–40; Mosiah 2:17; D&C 42:38) and an expression of the greatest spiritual gift, the attitude of charity (1 Cor. 13:13). King BENJAMIN explained in the Book of Mormon that, as a result of true repentance, people are filled with the love of God and the desire to administer to those in need (Mosiah 4:16). It is no excuse that "the man has brought upon himself his misery," for all are beggars dependent upon God, who gives generously (Mosiah 4:17–23). Benjamin required that the poor also carry this attitude and covet not—those who cannot give are to say in their hearts, "I give not because I have not, but if I had I would give" (Mosiah 4:24–25). Giving to the poor is essential to retaining a remission of one's sins and walking guiltless before God (Mosiah 4:26). Anyone who cries unto God sends up a petition in vain without giving "to those who stand in need" (Alma 34:28).

In 1935 the Church established an extensive welfare services program to assist those in need. In addition, all members of the Church are encouraged to give their time and resources wherever possible. Efforts to help the poor are designed to relieve suffering by supplying immediate needs

(cf. Luke 10:29–42; 16:19–39), to build self-sufficiency through employment, and to teach people to give willingly (D. McKay, *CR* [Oct. 1941]:54; *see* WELFARE SERVICES). Widows or orphans are to be provided for (James 1:27; D&C 83:6), especially those destitute because of persecution (D&C 42:30, 39; 52:40; 104:14–18). Indolence on the part of those who are able to work is condemned (Prov. 20:4; 1 Tim. 5:8, 13; D&C 42:42); the poor are to contribute their own labor, whenever possible (Deut. 15:7–11; 24:19; 2 Thes. 3:10). Through the efforts of all living the gospel law in an ideal society worthy of the presence of the Lord, there are "no poor among them" (Moses 7:18; Acts 4:32–35; 4 Ne. 1:2–3; D&C 42:30–33; *see* ZION).

Those who willingly give to the poor are promised many blessings, including eternal life (Luke 18:18–23; Matt. 25:31–40), deliverance (Ps. 41:1), forgiveness (Alma 4:13–14), happiness (Prov. 14:21), material rewards (Prov. 19:17; 28:27; Jacob 2:17–19; Deut. 24:19), and answers to prayers (Alma 34:28). Strong condemnations are repeated against those who refuse to share with the poor (2 Ne. 9:30; D&C 56:16). Caring for the poor is a significant moral challenge and obligation (Deut. 15:11; *CWHN* 9:193).

Under the LAW OF MOSES, the poor were to be treated generously (Epsztein, pp. 108–134). The corners of fields were left for them to reap (Lev. 19:9–10; Deut. 24:19–21); the produce of the land every seventh year was given first to the poor and the stranger (Ex. 23:10–11; Lev. 25:3–7); loans to the poor were interest free (Lev. 25:35–37; Ex. 22:25–27); Hebrews sold into bondage to other Hebrews were emancipated and generously supplied after six years of service (Ex. 21:2–6; Deut. 15:12–15); and the tithes not used by the Levites were given to the poor (Deut. 14:28–29; 26:12–13). Still, this did not absolve the responsibility to do more if another remained in need (Deut. 15:11).

The law of CONSECRATION, revealed to Joseph Smith in 1831 (D&C 42), invited the members to give all they possessed to the Church, receive back what they needed (their stewardships), use what they received to provide for themselves, and give their surplus to the Church. These surpluses and the residues of their inheritances were held in the BISHOP'S STOREHOUSE and used first to help the poor (Cook, 1985). Latter-day scriptures speak warnings equally to the rich and to the poor: "Wo unto you rich men, that will not give your substance to the poor, for your riches will canker your souls. . . . Wo unto you poor men, whose hearts are not broken, whose spirits are not contrite, and whose bellies are not satisfied, and whose hands are not stayed from laying hold upon other men's goods, whose eyes are full of greediness, and who will not labor with your own hands!" (D&C 56:16–17).

Most fundamental, however, is the generosity of individuals. As a minimum, most Latter-day Saints believe they should fast for two meals (twenty-four hours) each month and give the equivalent of these two meals, or more, as a FAST OFFERING. In addition, many believe they are expected to do more, to contribute to organized charities and to give personal assistance in the form of money, training, and encouragement (*see* ECONOMIC AID; HUMANITARIAN SERVICE).

[*See also* Wealth, Attitudes Toward.]

BIBLIOGRAPHY

Cook, L. W. *Joseph Smith and the Law of Consecration.* Provo, Utah, 1985.

Epsztein, Leon. *Social Justice in the Ancient Near East and the People of the Bible.* London, 1986.

Nibley, Hugh W. *Approaching Zion.* Salt Lake City, 1990.

DAVID J. CHERRINGTON

PRATT, ORSON

As a member of the first QUORUM OF THE TWELVE APOSTLES of the modern dispensation, Orson Pratt participated in almost every phase of the Church's history from 1830 until his death in 1881. As a missionary, editor, pioneer, and pamphleteer, he was one of the most influential leaders of the Church in the nineteenth century.

Pratt was born September 19, 1811, at Hartford, Washington County, New York. At the age of eighteen he began seeking a RELIGIOUS EXPERIENCE, and within a year he had been taught the gospel by his brother Parley P. PRATT, who had himself recently joined the Church. On his nineteenth birthday, Orson was baptized into the Church by his brother.

Orson Pratt spent his first years in the Church on a variety of short-term missions in the eastern United States and Canada. He also attended the SCHOOL OF THE PROPHETS in Kirtland, Ohio, marched to Missouri with ZION'S CAMP in 1834,

was ordained one of the Standing High Council in Missouri (July 1834), and in February 1835 was chosen as a member of the newly organized Quorum of the Twelve Apostles.

From 1839 to 1841 he participated in the very successful MISSION OF THE TWELVE TO THE BRITISH ISLES, spending much of his time in Scotland. At Edinburgh in September 1840, he published his first missionary tract, *A[n] Interesting Account of Several Remarkable Visions.* An important pamphlet, it contained the first *public* recording of Joseph SMITH'S FIRST VISION and also summarized basic LDS beliefs, a list that bears some resemblance to the 1842 ARTICLES OF FAITH in the WENTWORTH LETTER of Joseph Smith.

Orson Pratt's return to America in 1841 thrust him into a maelstrom of rumors and gossip in Nauvoo: that the Prophet Joseph Smith was teaching PLURAL MARRIAGE. His reactions to the situation led to his excommunication in August 1842. However, after several months of seeking the truth regarding both Joseph Smith's revelations and the newly introduced practice of plural marriage, Pratt accepted both with such assurance that he spent the rest of his life in their defense. He was rein-

Orson Pratt (1811–1881), apostle, pioneer, author, scientist (pictured here c. 1865). Photographer: G. Wunsch.

stated in the Quorum of the Twelve Apostles in January 1843.

Following Joseph Smith's death in 1844, Pratt supported the right and responsibility of the Quorum of the Twelve Apostles to preside over the Church. In 1847 he was a member of the Pioneer Company traveling to the Great Basin. On July 21 of that year he and Erastus Snow were the first of that company to enter the Salt Lake Valley. Several days later he preached the first sermon there. His journals are an important source for pioneer history.

From 1848 to 1851 Pratt presided over the Church in Europe. In addition to his many responsibilities regarding proselytizing, immigration, and editing the LDS MILLENNIAL STAR, he wrote and published sixteen pamphlets in defense of LDS doctrines. These include his treatises *Divine Authority, or the Question, Was Joseph Smith Sent of God?* (1848); *The Kingdom of God* (1848–1849); and *Divine Authenticity of the Book of Mormon* (1850–1851).

When he returned to Salt Lake City, Elder Pratt was assigned by President Brigham YOUNG to publicly preach a sermon announcing the doctrine of plural marriage at a special missionary conference in August 1852. Following the meetings he was assigned by Brigham Young to publish in Washington, D.C., a periodical in defense of plural marriage. The twelve-month run of *The Seer* in 1853 provides the most detailed defense of the doctrine in LDS literature.

In 1856, again presiding over the European Mission, Elder Pratt produced additional pamphlets on specific gospel principles. Eight tracts were issued separately, then bound together in 1857 under the title *Tracts by Orson Pratt.* . . . After Brigham Young's death in 1877, Pratt was assigned by John TAYLOR to help prepare new editions of the modern LDS scriptures. He had provided much of the critical work for the 1876 edition of the Doctrine and Covenants, and he did the same for the 1879 edition of the Book of Mormon (dividing it into chapters and verses and adding references), and for the 1879 American edition of the Pearl of Great Price.

Throughout his life Orson Pratt pursued his strong interest in mathematics and astronomy. In 1866 he published his major mathematical work, *New and Easy Method of Solution of the Cubic and Biquadratic Equations*, and in 1879 issued *Key to the Universe*. In these works and in various lectures to many early LDS audiences, he was a positive force in the scientific education of the American pioneers. By the time his last scientific work was published, he was suffering from diabetes. He preached his last public discourse on September 18, 1881, and died on October 3 in Salt Lake City. He had married seven wives and fathered forty-five children.

Elder Pratt's greatest impact upon the Church came through his precisely written theological studies. Within each work he moved carefully from one axiom to the next, developing his position with the same exactness he used in presenting a mathematical proof. His concern for definitiveness and his ability to simplify, to reduce things to their lowest common denominator, made his written works valuable to missionaries defending the faith in mission fields throughout the world.

Orson Pratt's religious pamphlets grew out of a missionary context. Their importance lies partly in the extended arguments and "proofs" for the central tenets of LDS theology. In most of his writing, however, he was an elaborator, a systematizer, and a popularizer of LDS thought, rather than an innovator or an originator. In almost every area he learned the substance either directly from the Prophet Joseph Smith or indirectly from his dynamic and visionary older brother Parley, also an LDS apostle and author. Orson Pratt was at his best in developing the ideas of others and expanding them into fully elaborated statements.

BIBLIOGRAPHY

England, Breck. *The Life and Thought of Orson Pratt.* Salt Lake City, 1985.

Hogan, Edward R. "Orson Pratt as a Mathematician." *Utah Historical Quarterly* 41 (Winter 1973):59–68.

Lyon, T. Edgar. "Orson Pratt—Early Mormon Leader." Master's thesis, University of Chicago, 1932.

———. "Orson Pratt, Pioneer and Proselyter." *Utah Historical Quarterly* 24 (July 1956):261–73.

Skabelund, Donald. "Cosmology on the American Frontier: Orson Pratt's Key to the Universe." *Centaurus: International Magazine of the History of Mathematics, Science, and Technology* 11 (1965):190–204.

Whittaker, David J. "Orson Pratt: Prolific Pamphleteer." *Dialogue* 15 (Autumn 1982):27–41.

———. "The Bone in the Throat: Orson Pratt and the Public Announcement of Plural Marriage." *Western Historical Quarterly* 18 (July 1987):293–314.

DAVID J. WHITTAKER

PRATT, PARLEY PARKER

One of the most significant LDS missionaries, writers, poets, and thinkers to emerge during the early years of the LDS Restoration was Parley Parker Pratt (1807–1857). He was a central figure in expounding the doctrines of the gospel, and his publications set a standard for future pamphleteers. He was a member of the original Quorum of the Twelve Apostles in this dispensation and a leader in the migration to the Great Basin.

Pratt was born April 12, 1807, in Burlington, Otsego County, New York, the third son of Jared and Charity Pratt. He married Thankful Halsey on September 9, 1827, at Canaan, New York, and they made their home in Amherst township, Lorain County, Ohio. In Ohio, Parley became a member of the Reformed Baptist Society (Campbellite) through the preaching of Sidney RIGDON.

Parley P. Pratt (1807–1857), converted through the Book of Mormon in 1830, became one of the Church's leading writers and early apostles. His writings are spirited and open-ended, holding continuous revelation to be the key in the science of theology. He was killed in Arkansas in 1857. Daguerreotype, c. 1853, attributed to Marsena Cannon.

While traveling on the Erie Canal in western New York, Parley came in contact with a Baptist deacon named Hamblin, who introduced him to a copy of the Book of Mormon. He then investigated the LDS Church and was baptized in Seneca Lake by Oliver COWDERY on September 1, 1830. In turn, he converted his younger brother, Orson PRATT, and baptized him on September 19, 1830.

From 1830 to 1857, Parley P. Pratt was constantly engaged in a variety of missionary assignments. Of special note was a 1,500-mile journey from Fayette, New York, to the western boundaries of Missouri with Oliver Cowdery, Peter Whitmer, Jr., and Ziba Peterson (D&C 32:1–2) on a mission to the Lamanites, beginning in October 1830 (see LAMANITE MISSION). En route, these missionaries converted some 130 persons in the Kirtland–Mentor area, including Sidney Rigdon and Frederick G. Williams, future members of the First Presidency. Upon reaching Missouri, Pratt was among the first members of the Church to stand upon the land later designated for the City of Zion, Independence, Jackson County (cf. D&C 57:2–3).

Parley Pratt was ordained an apostle on February 21, 1835, and sustained as a member of the Quorum of the Twelve. The first LDS hymnal (1835) included three hymns he had written. During a mission to the eastern states with the Twelve in the summer of 1835, Parley published eleven more hymns in conjunction with a long narrative poem in six chapters entitled *The Millennium, A Poem.* This volume became the first book of LDS poetry.

Pratt proselytized extensively in Upper Canada, leading to the conversion of John TAYLOR and his wife Leonora, Joseph Fielding, and Joseph's sisters, Mary and Mercy Fielding (see SMITH, MARY FIELDING). In 1838, he suffered persecution with the Saints in Missouri and spent nine months imprisoned in Richmond and Columbia before escaping to Illinois in July 1839.

Parley and Orson Pratt left Nauvoo, Illinois, on August 19, 1839, on an apostolic mission to the British Isles (see MISSIONS OF THE TWELVE TO THE BRITISH ISLES). At a conference in Preston, England, Parley was named editor of the newly created *Latter-day Saints' Millennial Star* (see MILLENNIAL STAR), which became the Church's longest continuous periodical—1840 to 1970.

Upon his return to Nauvoo, Parley was called to preside over the branches of the Church in New

VOICE OF WARNING

AND

INSTRUCTION TO ALL PEOPLE,

CONTAINING

A DECLARATION OF THE FAITH AND
DOCTRINE OF THE CHURCH OF
THE LATTER DAY SAINTS,

COMMONLY CALLED MORMONS.

BY P. P. PRATT, MINISTER OF THE GOSPEL.

Behold the former things are come to pass, and new things
do I declare : before they spring forth, I tell you of them.—
Isa. xlii. 9.

Produce your cause, saith the Lord ; bring forth your strong
reasons, saith the King of Jacob.—Isa. xli. 21

New=York:
PRINTED BY W. SANDFORD, 29 ANN-ST.

MDCCCXXXVII.

1837

Parley P. Pratt's *A Voice of Warning and Instruction to All People* (1837) was the first Latter-day Saint book, other than the Book of Mormon, the Book of Commandments, the Doctrine and Covenants, and the 1835 hymnal. Widely used by missionaries in proclaiming the message of the gospel, it was very popular throughout the nineteenth century. Courtesy Rare Books and Manuscripts, Brigham Young University.

England and the Mid-Atlantic states with headquarters in New York City. Here he published a periodical entitled *The Prophet.*

February 1846 found Parley and his family crossing the territory of Iowa on a forced move from Illinois. During the summer and autumn of 1847, he traveled with his household to the Salt Lake Valley.

In 1851 the First Presidency called Elder Pratt to preside over a "General Mission to the Pacific" with headquarters in San Francisco. Sensing a duty to the peoples of Latin America, he, with his wife Phebe Soper, and Elder Rufus Allen,

sailed to Valparaiso, Chile, in September 1851. Frustrated by language difficulties, poverty, the death of an infant son, and the ecclesiastical and political conditions in Chile, the missionaries returned to San Francisco in March 1852.

His publication *A Voice of Warning* (1837) became a model for other writers. The format, which employed descriptions of basic LDS doctrines and biblical references, arguments, and examples, was used by most Church writers for the next century. It was the first use of a book, other than the standard works, to spread the gospel message (Crawley, 1982, p. 15). His contributions to the dissemination of doctrine were extensive, and among his most significant works are *Late Persecutions of the Church of Jesus Christ of Latter-day Saints . . . With a Sketch of Their Rise, Progress and Doctrine* (1840); *Key to the Science of Theology* (1855); *The Millennium and Other Poems: To Which is Annexed, a Treatise on the Regeneration of Matter* (1840); and the *Autobiography of Parley Parker Pratt* (1874). (For additional publications, see Crawley, 1990; Robison, 1952.)

In 1856 Elder Pratt was called to another mission to the Eastern states. While returning to the West on May 13, 1857, he was killed by a man who had been seeking to murder him. This occurred about twelve miles northeast of Van Buren, Arkansas (S. Pratt, 1975). A monument now marks the site of his burial. Through the enduring legacy of his doctrinal writings, hymns, and poems, Parley Parker Pratt continues to instruct and inspire each new generation.

BIBLIOGRAPHY

Crawley, Peter L. "Parley P. Pratt: Father of Mormon Pamphleteering." *Dialogue* 15 (Autumn 1982):13–26.

———. *The Essential Parley P. Pratt.* Salt Lake City, 1990.

Pratt, Parley P. *Autobiography of Parley P. Pratt*, ed. Parley P. Pratt, Jr. Salt Lake City, 1874 and 1938.

Pratt, Steven. "Eleanor McLean and the Murder of Parley P. Pratt." *BYU Studies* 15 (Winter 1975):225–56.

Robison, Parley Parker. *The Writings of Parley Parker Pratt.* Salt Lake City, 1952.

LARRY C. PORTER

PRAYER

Prayer marked the beginning of The Church of Jesus Christ of Latter-day Saints when God the Father and his son Jesus Christ appeared in answer to the Prophet Joseph SMITH's plea to know which of the neighboring churches he should join. Young Joseph Smith had followed JAMES's invitation: "If any of you lack wisdom, let him ask of God, that giveth to all men liberally. . . . But let him ask in faith, nothing wavering" (James 1:5–6). God answered the boy's sincere and earnest plea (JS—H 1:5–20). And this FIRST VISION shows prayer as the way to commune with God and receive REVELATION from him. Faith, sincerity, obedience, and seeking are attributes that lift the soul to God; this is the essential character of prayer for the Latter-day Saint.

Adam and Eve began praying to God after they were cast out of the Garden of Eden. "And Adam and Eve, his wife, called upon the name of the Lord, and they heard the voice of the Lord from the way toward the Garden of Eden, speaking unto them, and they saw him not" (Moses 5:4). Though they were separated from God, communication with him was possible and important, for the Lord commanded, "Thou shalt repent and call upon God in the name of the Son forevermore" (Moses 5:8).

Among Latter-day Saints, this commandment to pray still applies. The Lord instructs, "Ask, and ye shall receive; knock, and it shall be opened unto you" (D&C 4:7; cf. Matt. 7:7). Home teachers, for instance, are to "visit the house of each member,

Mother and three children praying. This picture was sent to their father who was away serving a mission. Courtesy Rare Books and Manuscripts, Brigham Young University.

and exhort them to pray vocally and in secret" (D&C 20:47). Other scriptures emphasize these important commandments: "Pray always lest that wicked one have power in you, and remove you out of your place" (D&C 93:49). "Pray always, lest you enter into temptation and lose your reward" (D&C 31:12). "For if ye would hearken unto the Spirit which teacheth a man to pray ye would know that ye must pray; for the evil spirit teacheth not a man to pray, but teacheth him that he must not pray. But behold . . . ye must pray always, and not faint; . . . ye must not perform any thing unto the Lord save in the first place ye shall pray unto the Father in the name of Christ, that he will consecrate thy performance unto thee, that thy performance may be for the welfare of thy soul" (2 Ne. 32:8–9). Thus, the scriptures make clear that prayer is a commandment as well as an opportunity to communicate with God and to receive blessings and direction from him.

The Church uses set prayers only in temple ORDINANCES, in the two SACRAMENT prayers, and in the BAPTISMAL PRAYER. "By revelation the Lord has given the Church . . . set prayers for use in our sacred ordinances. . . . [These] relate to the atonement of the Lord Jesus Christ, his crucifixion, and his burial and resurrection. All of the ordinances in which we use these prayers place us under solemn covenants of obedience to God" (Kimball et al., p. 56). In all other instances, Latter-day Saints express themselves in their own words.

Although few set prayers occur in their worship, Latter-day Saints follow a pattern when praying. Prayers are addressed to the Father in Heaven, following the example set by Christ when instructing his disciples how to pray (Matt. 6:9; 3 Ne. 13:9). His prayer serves as a pattern: Disciples are to praise and thank God, ask for daily physical needs, and plead for the spiritual power to forgive, be forgiven, and resist temptation. Jesus used simple, expressive language in his prayers, avoiding vain repetition and flowery phrases (Matt. 6:5–13; 3 Ne. 13:5–13; 19:20–23, 28–29; cf. 3 Ne. 17:14–17; 19:31–34). More important than the words is the feeling that accompanies prayer. Christ reiterated a clear, prophetic warning: "This people draweth nigh unto me with their mouth, and honoureth me with their lips; but their heart is far from me" (Matt. 15:8; cf. Isa. 29:13). In praising God, in offering thanks, in asking for needs—remembering to pray that God's will be done—language is to be reverent, humble, and sincere.

President Spencer W. KIMBALL commented, "In all our prayers, it is well to use the pronouns *thee*, *thou*, *thy*, and *thine* instead of *you*, *your*, and *yours* inasmuch as they have come to indicate respect" (p. 201). Unnecessary repetition of God's name is avoided, as are idle clichés. Prayers close by stating that the prayer is offered in the name of Jesus Christ, concluding with amen. When someone prays in behalf of a group, the members customarily repeat the final "amen" aloud, expressing acceptance of what has been said. In private, the individual or family members kneel with bowed heads and closed eyes. In public, the one praying usually stands, but also observes behavior appropriate to prayer. A prayer's length is determined somewhat by the occasion, but generally prayers are reasonably concise, expressing thanks and petitioning God for what the group needs, avoiding a sermon or display of verbal skills. For both invocations and benedictions the Church teaches that the one praying should express worship rather than make a display or preach a sermon.

Prayer is both an individual and a family form of worship. Usually, the day begins and ends with prayer. At least once daily, LDS families should pray together (*see* FAMILY PRAYER). The father, or the mother in his absence, calls on one member to pray for the family. As days pass, each family member has the opportunity to lead family prayer. A blessing on the food that offers thanks to God also precedes each meal, the younger children often offering this simple prayer, at first with the help of a parent. In addition, one is encouraged to pray whenever the desire or need occurs: to give thanks for a special blessing, to ask for help in difficult circumstances, or to speak with God on any matter of concern. Prayers begin and end all formal Church meetings and often begin other occasions for which Latter-day Saints have responsibility, such as Church-sponsored athletic contests, concerts, and plays.

Another practice associated with prayer is the fast observed on the first Sunday of the month. Latter-day Saints abstain from two consecutive meals, ending their FASTING with a FAST AND TESTIMONY MEETING, bearing public testimony of God and Christ and giving thanks for God's goodness and blessings. In addition, whenever circumstances dictate, special pleas to God are combined with fasting, occasionally observed by a whole congregation to petition for special blessings outside the ordinary course of events (see D&C 27:18).

The comprehensive scope of prayer has been outlined by the Book of Mormon prophet ALMA₂: "I would that ye should be humble, . . . asking for whatsoever things ye stand in need, both spiritual and temporal; always returning thanks unto God for whatsoever things ye do receive" (Alma 7:23). Amulek, a noted Book of Mormon teacher, followed these essential qualities of prayer when he counseled men and women to pray about physical needs: "Cry unto [God] when ye are in your fields, yea, over all your flocks. Cry unto him in your houses, yea, over all your household, both morning, mid-day, and evening . . . Cry unto him over the crops of your fields, that ye may prosper in them. Cry over the flocks of your fields, that they may increase" (Alma 34:20–21, 24–25). Thus, a student may pray about studies, a merchant about business, a mother and father about the welfare of their children. Although prayer may be for physical needs, spiritual results may also occur, and vice versa. A student who prays about studies is not likely to cheat on examinations; a merchant who prays about business is not likely to be dishonest.

Alma₂ sought still other spiritual blessings:

O Lord, my heart is exceedingly sorrowful; wilt thou comfort my soul in Christ. O Lord, wilt thou grant unto me that I may have strength, that I may suffer with patience these afflictions which shall come upon me, because of the iniquity of this people. . . . O Lord, wilt thou grant unto us [Alma and fellow missionaries] that we may have success in bringing [our brethren] again unto thee in Christ. Behold, O Lord, their souls are precious, . . . therefore, give unto us, O Lord, power and wisdom that we may bring these, our brethren, again unto thee [Alma 31:31–35].

The intent of Alma's prayer underlies the missionary program of the Church. Alma's disciple Amulek also told his people to "cry unto [God] against the devil, who is an enemy to all righteousness" (Alma 34:23). The spiritual blessings one might pray for include comfort when sorrowing, strength to resist temptation, wisdom to discern good and evil, compassion to forgive others, and understanding of God's will for one's life. An important purpose of prayer is to thank God for life itself and for all that makes life valuable. Ingratitude is an offense against God because it is a failure to recognize his power and love (D&C 59:14–21). Giving thanks is a way of praising God by acknowledging his ever-present hand.

Latter-day Saints are taught that preparation is necessary if one is to communicate effectively with God. A tranquil time and place allow quiet contemplation on the specific requests one may make. Joseph Smith went to a nearby grove to pray for an answer to his question, and received his glorious vision. Job was told, "Prepare thine heart, and stretch out thine hands toward him" (Job 11:13). Alma₂ listed the qualities of a heart prepared for prayer: "I would that ye should be humble, and be submissive and gentle; easy to be entreated; full of patience and long-suffering . . . being diligent in keeping the commandments of God. . . . And see that ye have faith, hope, and charity, and then ye will always abound in good works" (Alma 7:23–24). MORONI₂ stressed the need for "a sincere heart, . . . real intent, . . . [and] faith in Christ" (Moro. 10:4).

Latter-day Saints believe that relationships with others must also harmonize with Christ's teachings. Christ taught that God's forgiveness could not be obtained unless the sinner were willing to forgive those who had sinned against him (Matt. 6:14–15; Mark 11:25–26). A prepared heart is also a giving heart. Amulek spoke of this quality: "I say unto you, do not suppose that [praying] is all; for . . . if ye turn away the needy, and the naked, and visit not the sick and afflicted, and impart of your substance, if ye have, to those who stand in need—I say unto you, if ye do not any of these things, behold, your prayer is vain, and availeth you nothing" (Alma 34:28).

When one's heart is prepared, God promises answers. The elders of the early Church were promised that "if ye are purified and cleansed from all sin, ye shall ask whatsoever you will in the name of Jesus and it shall be done" (D&C 50:29). In even stronger terms this assurance is repeated to all who pray: "I, the Lord, am bound when ye do what I say; but when ye do not what I say, ye have no promise" (D&C 82:10). However, it is wise to pray that God's will be done, even if it means denial of a request. God warns that asking for what "is not expedient" will turn to one's "condemnation" (D&C 88:64–65).

One answer to a faithful prayer is illustrated through the experience of Oliver COWDERY, an early elder of the Church, when he attempted to help with translating the Book of Mormon. He was told to "study it out in [his] mind" and, if his translation were right, it would be confirmed with a burning in his bosom; if wrong, a "stupor of thought" would come (D&C 9:8–9). When prayers are answered, one experiences peace of mind and assurance that God has heard, even though the answer may be no. The Savior's submissiveness as he prayed in GETHSEMANE shows the way: "Nevertheless not my will, but thine, be done" (Luke 22:42).

BIBLIOGRAPHY

Kimball, Spencer W. *Faith Precedes the Miracle*, pp. 21–58. Salt Lake City, 1972.

———. *The Teachings of Spencer W. Kimball*, ed. Edward L. Kimball, pp. 115–27. Salt Lake City, 1982.

Kimball, Spencer W., *Prayer*. Salt Lake City, 1977.

McConkie, Bruce R. *Doctrinal New Testament Commentary*, Vol. 1, pp. 233–37. Salt Lake City, 1975.

MAE BLANCH

PRAYER CIRCLE

The prayer circle is a part of Latter-day Saint TEMPLE WORSHIP, usually associated with the ENDOWMENT ceremony. Participants, an equal number of men and women dressed in temple clothing, surround an altar in a circle formation to participate unitedly in prayer.

The circle is an ancient and universal symbol of perfection. In a public discourse, Joseph SMITH once used a ring as an image of eternity, "one eternal round," without beginning or end (*TPJS*, p. 354). The formation of the prayer circle suggests wholeness and eternity, and the participants, having affirmed that they bear no negative feelings toward other members of the circle (cf. Matt. 5:23–24), evoke communal harmony in collective prayer—a harmony underscored by the linked formation, uniformity of dress, and the unison repetition of the words of the leader. The prayer has no set text, but is, among other things, an occasion for seeking the Lord's blessing upon those with particular needs whose names have been submitted for collective entreaty.

Prayer in circle formation can be traced to many early Christian sources. In the apocryphal Acts of John, for example, participants are bidden to "make as it were a ring, holding one another's hands, and [Jesus] standing in the midst" led the prayer (James, p. 253). Other texts require the participants to prepare by washing or reconciling themselves, or to receive secret words and signs, or to dress in special clothing; some suggest a ritual ring dance.

"Prayer rings" were also common in nineteenth-century Protestant revivals, and Freemasons of the period arranged themselves in circular formation around an altar, repeating in unison the received Masonic signs (see FREEMASONRY AND THE TEMPLE).

Despite these analogues, the LDS prayer circle is a distinctive ceremony, integrally connected with temple worship. The ceremony may have been introduced in May 1842, when Joseph Smith taught the endowment to several of his closest associates; and a prayer circle group was formed on May 26, 1843, with Joseph Smith as its leader. This prayer circle, referred to in many early records as the "Quorum of the Anointed," to which others (including women) were gradually initiated, met and prayed together regularly during the last year of Joseph Smith's life and continued after his martyrdom in June 1844 until endowments began to be performed in the Nauvoo Temple in December 1845.

Although deriving in all instances from temple worship, some prayer circles were formally organized apart from the endowment ceremony. Membership in these special prayer circles, which began in 1851 and continued until 1929, did not depend upon Church position. Other prayer circles were formed for priesthood groups: stake presidencies and high councils, priesthood quorums, ward bishoprics—all of them formed under the authority of the First Presidency and generally in response to specific requests. On May 3, 1978, the First Presidency announced that all prayer circles outside the temple were to be discontinued. Apart from the endowment ceremony, the only prayer circles still held are part of the weekly meeting of the First Presidency and Quorum of the Twelve and the monthly meeting of all General Authorities in the Salt Lake Temple.

BIBLIOGRAPHY

James, M. R. *Apocryphal New Testament*. Oxford, 1924.

Nibley, Hugh. "The Early Christian Prayer Circle." *BYU Studies* 19 (Fall 1978):41–78; reprinted in *CWHN* 4:45–99.

Quinn, D. Michael. "Latter-day Saint Prayer Circles." *BYU Studies* 19 (Fall 1978):79–105.

GEORGE S. TATE

PREACHING THE GOSPEL

Prior to his ascension, the resurrected Savior charged his apostles to "teach all nations, baptizing them in the name of the Father, and of the Son, and of the Holy Ghost: teaching them to observe all things whatsoever I have commanded you" (Matt. 28:19–20). This charge reiterates the call of Abraham (Abr. 2:6, 9–11) and has been unequivocally renewed in the latter days (D&C 110:12): "And the voice of warning shall be unto all people" (D&C 1:4). "This calling and commandment give I unto you concerning all men . . . [they] shall be ordained and sent forth to preach the everlasting gospel among the nations" (D&C 36:4–5). "For, verily, the sound must go forth from this place unto all the world, and unto the uttermost parts of the earth—the gospel must be preached unto every creature, with signs following them that believe" (D&C 58:64). The Church of Jesus Christ of Latter-day Saints responds to this charge by sending missionaries to people of all persuasions throughout the world (see MISSIONS).

The calling to preach the gospel has a distinctive meaning among Latter-day Saints. All who are in the Church are directly or indirectly indebted to missionaries for their introduction to the gospel. Historically, missionary labor has been carried out by members of the Church who have gone "two by two" (D&C 42:6; 52:10; cf. Luke 10:1; John 8:17) into every land and clime of the free world (see MISSIONARY, MISSIONARY LIFE). LDS missionary labor is not a profession or vocation. It is voluntary and unpaid. The majority of those who presently serve for an average of two years are young men and women, but many older couples of various professions or walks of life also serve. MISSION PRESIDENTS are themselves laymen called to serve usually for three years. At this writing (1991), some 40,000 LDS full-time missionaries are serving.

In addition, there are other modes of preaching the gospel. Members may be called to fulfill stake missions that are coordinated in time spent with their regular occupations or professions. They devote about ten hours per week (usually evenings) to missionary work in their own stake area. The "Every member a missionary" program emphasized by President David O. MCKAY involves members inviting friends or interested persons into their homes for discussions of gospel principles. A General Missionary Fund is maintained by member contributions, which help some persons in undeveloped countries to supplement their savings and serve full-time missions. Whether laboring at home or abroad, Latter-day Saints are constantly admonished that the witness and testimony of the gospel are only effective if they reflect genuine and continual discipleship of Jesus Christ. The gospel is to be taught in mildness and in meekness, in demonstration of the Spirit, and in love unfeigned (D&C 38:41; 99:2; 121:41).

The command of the Lord to preach the gospel to all nations has a twofold purpose: to bring people to an understanding of the gospel of Jesus Christ, and also to sound the warning voice to leave mankind without excuse (*see* VOICE OF WARNING).

BIBLIOGRAPHY

Smith, Joseph Fielding. *DS* 1:307–324.

MAX L. PINEGAR

PREDESTINATION

The Church of Jesus Christ of Latter-day Saints rejects the belief in predestination—that God predetermines the salvation or the damnation of every individual. The gospel teaches that genuine human freedom and genuine responsibility—individual AGENCY in both thought and action—are crucial in both the development and the outcome of a person's life. Church doctrine rejects the strict dual option providing only heaven or hell as an outcome, since people vary widely in their levels of spiritual attainment. At the same time, Latter-day Saints recognize both the indispensable need for the grace of God manifested through Jesus Christ and the effective spiritual guidance that comes through divine FOREORDINATION.

The LDS position is based in part on the teachings of Paul that God "will render to every man according to his deeds" and that "there is no

California Mission meeting by the Cliff House, near San Francisco, May 1897, Mission President Ephraim H. Nye speaking. Latter-day Saints strive to preach the gospel in every land, in every place, and to every person.

respect of persons with God" (Rom. 2:6, 11). These two principles provide a basis for understanding Paul's use of the term "predestination." The term apparently connoted "to be ordained beforehand for godly labor." In the sense that one's potential or calling has been recognized and declared, this interpretation conforms with the Greek term Paul used, *proorizō*, and does not denote an irreversible or irresistible predetermination.

Latter-day Saints are to "look unto God in every thought" (D&C 6:36), because no person can save himself. But neither can God redeem anyone without that person's effort and collaboration. All are free to accept or reject God's help and powers of redemption. It is clearly taught in scripture that with his help both justification and sanctification will be "just and true" (D&C 20:30). "But there is a possibility that man may fall from grace and depart from the living God; therefore let the church take heed, and pray always, lest they fall into temptation; yea, and even let those who are sanctified take heed also" (D&C 20:32, 33).

RICHARD D. DRAPER

PRE-EXISTENCE (PRE-EARTHLY EXISTENCE)

[The term "pre-existence," or more accurately, "premortal existence," refers to a period of individual conscious and accountable life before birth into mortality on this earth. It is Latter-day Saint doctrine that living things existed as individual spirit beings and possessed varying degrees of intelligence in an active, conscious spirit state before mortal birth and that the spirit continues to live and function in the mortal body. The revelations teach that premortal spirit bodies have general resemblance to their physical counterparts.

Articles pertaining to the premortal existence are Animals; Birth; Council in Heaven; Devils; First Estate; Foreordination; God the Father; Intelligences; Jehovah; Jesus Christ: Firstborn in the Spirit; Mother in Heaven; Premortal Life; Soul; Spirit; Spirit Body; War in Heaven.]

PREMARITAL SEX

Throughout the centuries, the Lord has declared very clearly that sexual relations outside of marriage are sin (cf. Ex. 20:14; Deut. 5:18; 22:13–30; 2 Sam. 13:12; Matt. 5:27–30; 19:18; Acts 15:20; 21:25; 1 Cor. 5:1; 6:18–20; Alma 39:3–6; D&C

42:22–26). In like manner, The Church of Jesus Christ of Latter-day Saints teaches that premarital sex is sin and counsels its members to abstain from it. Recognizing that the "new morality," which advocates that consenting partners may do whatever their appetites urge them to do, is nothing more than the "old immorality," the Church rejects the popular view that sex before marriage is not sinful and is justifiable as "normal and natural." Rather, the Church teaches that sex should be a sacred expression of love between a husband and wife and that both men and women should abstain from sexual activity until their marriage. It teaches that sex before marriage is an expression of lust, not love, and admonishes its members not to participate in it or in any other kinds of activities that excite sexual desires. The Church teaches that those who have participated in premarital sex may repent of their sin, reminding them that true repentance requires that they abstain from sexual relations except with their legal spouse.

[*See also* Chastity; Marriage; Repentance.]

BIBLIOGRAPHY

Kimball, Spencer W. *The Miracle of Forgiveness*, pp. 213–32. Salt Lake City, 1969.

H. REESE HANSEN

PREMORTAL LIFE

Prior to mortal BIRTH individuals existed as men and women in a spirit state and thus coexisted with both the Father and the Son. That period of life is also referred to as the FIRST ESTATE or PRE-EXISTENCE.

The Bible presents the concept that mankind had a preparation period prior to mortal birth. The Lord said to Jeremiah: "Before I formed thee in the belly I knew thee; and before thou camest forth out of the womb I sanctified thee, and I ordained thee a prophet unto the nations" (Jer. 1:5), and the "Preacher" asserted "The spirit shall return unto God who gave it" (Eccl. 12:7). In other scriptures, such as Alma 13:3, it is written that priests were "called and prepared from the foundation of the world according to the foreknowledge of God, on account of their exceeding faith and good works."

There is indeed indication that the INTELLIGENCE dwelling in each person is coeternal with God. It always existed and never was created or made (D&C 93:29). In due time that intelligence was given a SPIRIT BODY, becoming the spirit child of God the Eternal Father and his beloved companion, the MOTHER IN HEAVEN. This spirit, inhabited by the eternal intelligence, took the form of its creators and is in their image (Ballard, p. 140).

To the Prophet Joseph SMITH it was revealed that we are all literal spirit sons and daughters of heavenly parents. He received a revelation of information once made known to Moses: "I [God] made the world, and men before they were in the flesh" (Moses 6:51). This likewise reflects the implication in Numbers 16:22 that God is the Father of all, and hence he is "the God of the spirits of all flesh."

Intelligences were organized before the world was, and among these were many great and noble ones, such as Abraham and Moses. God stood in their midst, saw that they were good, and chose them for responsibilities on earth and throughout eternity (Abr. 3:21–23). Jesus, the firstborn spirit, was preeminent among them. "Jesus . . . existed with the Father prior to birth in the flesh; and . . . in the pre-existent state He was chosen and ordained to be the one and only Savior and Redeemer of the human race" (JC, p. 6).

Revelation indicates that all things, even the earth itself, had a spirit existence before the physical creation. Elder Joseph Fielding SMITH wrote, "Not only has man a spirit, and is thereby a living soul, but likewise the beasts of the field, the fowl of the air, and the fish of the sea have spirits, and hence are living souls. . . . The fish, the fowl, the beasts of the field lived before they were placed naturally in this earth, and so did the plants that are upon the face of the earth. The spirits that possess the bodies of the animals are in the similitude of their bodies" (DS 1:63–64). The biblical passage that says the Lord God made "every plant of the field before it was in this earth, and every herb of the field before it grew" (Gen. 2:5) is clarified in a parallel scripture with the words: "For I, the Lord God, created all things, of which I have spoken, spiritually before they were naturally upon the face of the earth . . . and I, the Lord God, had created all the children of men and not yet a man to till the ground; for in heaven created I them" (Moses 3:5).

The Prophet Joseph Smith taught that "God himself, finding he was in the midst of spirits and glory, because he was more intelligent, saw proper to institute laws whereby the rest [of the intelligences] could have a privilege to advance like himself" (TPJS, p. 354). His plan included sending his sons and daughters to earth (the SECOND ESTATE), to obtain a body of flesh and bones and learn by experience through earthly vicissitudes, with no memory of the first estate and with the agency to fail or succeed.

In a council in heaven to preview earth life, the Lord called before him his spirit children and presented the PLAN OF SALVATION by which they would come to this earth, partake of mortal life with physical bodies, pass through a probation in mortality, and progress to a higher exaltation. The matter was discussed as to how, and upon what principle, the salvation, exaltation, and eternal glory of God's sons and daughters would be brought about (cf. DS 1:58). The Firstborn of God volunteered to implement the plan of salvation (Abr. 3:27). Lucifer, who was also a son of the Father, came forward with a counterproposal: "Behold, send me, I will be thy Son, and I will redeem all mankind, that not one soul shall be lost and surely I will do it; wherefore, give me thine honor" (Moses 4:1). Already of exalted status, Lucifer sought to aggrandize himself without regard to the rights and agency of others, seeking to destroy the agency of man (JC, p. 7–8). The Father said, "I will send the first" (Abr. 3:27).

This decision led the hosts of heaven to take sides, and a third part rose in rebellion and, with Lucifer, were cast out of heaven. "They were denied the privilege of being born into this world and receiving mortal bodies. . . . The Lord cast them out into the earth, where they became the tempters of mankind" (DS 1:65; cf. Jude 1:6).

Elder James E. Talmage wrote, "The offer of the firstborn Son to establish through His own ministry among men the gospel of salvation, and to sacrifice himself, through labor, humiliation and suffering even unto death, was accepted and made the foreordained plan of man's redemption from death, of his eventual salvation from the effects of sin, and of his possible exaltation through righteous achievement" (JC, p. 18). Elder Joseph Fielding Smith explained, "God gave his children their free agency even in the spirit world, by which the individual spirits had the privilege, just as men have here, of choosing the good and rejecting the evil, or partaking of the evil to suffer the consequences of their sins" (p. 318–19).

The Book of Mormon prophet ALMA₂ further explains the opportunities presented to the spirit children of God in the premortal existence: "In the *first place* being left to choose good or evil; therefore they having chosen good and exercising exceedingly great faith, are called with a holy calling . . . on account of their faith, while others would reject the Spirit of God on account of the hardness of their hearts and blindness of their minds, while, if it had not been for this they might have had as great privilege as their brethren. Or in fine, in the *first place* they were on the same standing with their brethren; thus this holy calling being prepared from the foundation of the world for such as would not harden their hearts, being in and through the atonement of the Only Begotten Son" (Alma 13:3–5; *emphasis added*). The "first place" here refers to one's first estate or premortal existence.

The doctrine of FOREORDINATION suggested in the above passage is understood to mean that many may come to earth with preassigned callings and responsibilities. The Prophet Joseph Smith taught, "Every man who has a calling to minister to the inhabitants of the world was ordained to that very purpose in the Grand Council of heaven before this world was" (*TPJS*, p. 365). Abraham was shown the noble and great premortal spirits, and the Lord said to him, "Thou art one of them; thou wast chosen before thou wast born" (Abr. 3:22–23). The apocryphal book of Tobit also suggests the concept that in a premortal life there were assignments that could affect mortality (6:17). However, even though some may be foreordained to special missions on earth, Elder Joseph Fielding Smith stated that "no person was foreordained or appointed to sin or to perform a mission of evil" (*DS* 1:61). Foreordinations and appointments do not proscribe one's agency or free will.

The character of one's life in the SPIRIT WORLD probably influences disposition and desires in mortal life. From among those who were the noble and great ones in that former world, the Lord selected those to be his prophets and rulers on earth in the second estate, for he knew them before they were born, and he knows who will be likely to serve him in mortality. Characteristics of the spirit, which were developed during experiences of the former existence, may play an important part in man's progression through mortal life (cf. *DS* 1:60). "Even before they [the prophets] were born, they, with many others, received their first lessons in the world of spirits and were prepared to come forth in the due time of the Lord to

labor in his vineyard for the salvation of souls of men" (D&C 138:56).

This concept that God's spirit children developed some characteristic capabilities, but yet come to earth in forgetfulness, is similar to that expressed in Wordsworth's "Ode, Intimations of Immortality from Recollections of Early Childhood": "Our birth is but a sleep and a forgetting: . . . Trailing clouds of glory do we come from God, who is our home" (verses 58, 64–65). Elder Orson Hyde, an apostle, declared that lack of memory does not mean that mankind did not have a premortal life. He explained that many people leave their homeland to live in another country, yet after a number of years memory of that earlier country can be almost obliterated as though it never existed. "We have forgotten! . . . But our forgetfulness cannot alter the facts" (*JD* 7:315).

Thus, to Latter-day Saints premortal life is characterized by individuality, agency, intelligence, and opportunity for ETERNAL PROGRESSION. It is a central doctrine of the theology of the Church and provides understanding to the age-old question "Whence cometh man?"

BIBLIOGRAPHY

Ballard, Melvin J. *Sermons and Missionary Services of Melvin J. Ballard*, comp. Bryant S. Hinckley, p. 140. Salt Lake City, 1949.

Smith, Joseph Fielding. "Is Man Immortal?" *IE* 19 (Feb. 1916):318–19.

GAYLE OBLAD BROWN

PRESIDENCY, CONCEPT OF

The administrative/leadership CALLING of presidency is part of the presiding structure at all levels in virtually every unit of The Church of Jesus Christ of Latter-day Saints. A presidency generally consists of the president (or BISHOP) and two counselors, with assistance from secretaries and/or CLERKS. Presidencies are responsible for all members and programs within their organizational jurisdiction and range from the FIRST PRESIDENCY of the Church to a presidency of a small priesthood quorum or class.

Presidents are usually called by the next higher level in the ORGANIZATION, and their calling is "sustained" by COMMON CONSENT of the group over which they will preside. Counselors are then nominated by the president, but are likewise approved and called by the higher level. They are designated first and second counselors to establish relative AUTHORITY and areas of responsibility. The president makes specific assignments to counselors, but in general they assist and support the president in gathering information, analyzing problems, making decisions, and implementing programs.

Decision making in a presidency is not a democratic voting process. The counselors sit in council with the president and give counsel, but the president is responsible to make decisions and to work for unanimity if it has not already been reached. Counselors are similar to a vice-president or assistant administrator except that they do not have independent decision-making power for organizational subunits. The two most common presidencies in the Church, the STAKE PRESIDENCY and the ward BISHOPRIC, call or release all individuals in positions under their jurisdiction, usually in consultation with the appropriate PRIESTHOOD QUORUM or AUXILIARY presidency. When a president is released, the counselors are automatically also released.

A statement representative of the responsibilities of a president contained in the DOCTRINE AND COVENANTS includes sitting in council with members, teaching them, edifying them, and presiding over the organization (D&C 107:79–95). The LDS presidency model ensures that no one administrator is responsible alone but always has others who share the burden and perspective of the office and in most matters can act in the president's absence. The authority of the president is clear, but the shared responsibility adds strength and assistance and provides an opportunity for individual development, which is helpful for future leadership.

J. BONNER RITCHIE

PRESIDENT OF THE CHURCH

The President of the Church is the PROPHET, SEER, AND REVELATOR who is authorized to direct the affairs of the Church throughout the earth. He speaks and acts under divine guidance from Jesus Christ, who is the HEAD OF THE CHURCH. Presidents of the Church to 1991 have been Joseph SMITH, Brigham YOUNG, John TAYLOR, Wilford WOODRUFF, Lorenzo SNOW, Joseph F. SMITH,

Heber J. GRANT, George Albert SMITH, David O. MCKAY, Joseph Fielding SMITH, Harold B. LEE, Spencer W. KIMBALL, and Ezra Taft BENSON.

In principle and in practice, no other office or calling elicits the same love and respect from Church members as the President of the Church. The President is the PROPHET and, as such, is revered by the members of the Church. He is the only person in the Church who may direct and authorize all uses of the KEYS OF THE PRIESTHOOD. He is the chief administrative officer in the Church, assisted by his counselors in the FIRST PRESIDENCY and the members of the QUORUM OF THE TWELVE APOSTLES. They direct the work of other GENERAL AUTHORITIES and the lay leaders of the Church serving in hundreds of callings.

The Doctrine and Covenants specifies that the President's duty is "to be like unto Moses" (D&C 107:91–92; 28:2), relaying the will of God to his people and teaching them the gospel. His work is somewhat analogous to that of PETER, who presided over the APOSTLES and the early Christian Church. In response to Peter's affirmation that Jesus was the son of God, Jesus pointed out that the testimony had been divinely revealed to Peter, saying, "Thou art Peter, and upon this rock I will build my church" (Matt. 16:13–20). Latter-day Saints understand the "rock" to be the divine REVELATION through which ancient and modern prophets have directed the membership of Christ's Church (TPJS, p. 274).

Latter-day Saints believe that there is need for revealed knowledge from God to direct the affairs of the Church and provide insight into God's will today just as there was anciently. Revelations to the President of the Church may include declaration or clarification of doctrines or direction concerning theological issues, organizational matters, moral conduct, and practical administration. The unity of the Church worldwide is enhanced by the prophet of the Church as God's spokesperson. As such, the President may speak authoritatively on such matters as scriptural interpretation, spiritual concerns, and temporal issues. His official statements in his time may take precedence over revelations in scripture pertinent to other times or over statements by previous presidents of the Church, though in fact these rarely are in conflict (cf. Benson, pp. 27–28).

The President possesses the inspired capacity to discern between truth and error for the Church. Consequently, he may recognize and denounce

This painted tin sign (4″ × 14″) marked the office of Joseph Smith in his Red Brick Store in Nauvoo, Illinois, 1842–1844. It reads "Joseph Smith's Office. President of the church of JESUS Christ of LATTER day Saints." The Church President is trustee of the Church's worldwide activities, involving extensive Church services, charitable and missionary activities, financial interests, and concern for the well-being of all Church members.

mistaken beliefs and movements within the Church and in the world. While it is understood that he may at times speak or act as a private person outside his calling as prophet (*TPJS*, p. 278), the general view is that the counsel of the President of the Church is always to be taken seriously.

Whenever new doctrines are to be introduced, they are first presented by the President to his counselors and then to the Quorum of the Twelve Apostles in a meeting of the COUNCIL OF THE FIRST PRESIDENCY AND THE QUORUM OF THE TWELVE APOSTLES. If unanimously approved, they are then presented to the membership of the Church at a general conference for a sustaining vote.

Latter-day Saints are counseled that following the prophet is wise, even in personal matters (*see* FOLLOWING THE BRETHREN). The President of the Church, as prophet, will never be allowed by the Lord to lead members of the Church into apostasy or error (D&C, Official Declaration—1).

The President of the Church is the only person on earth who directs the use of all the keys of the priesthood, though these keys are held also by the ordained apostles and are directed by their quorum upon the death of the President and until a new First Presidency is organized. This means that the President holds the power and authority to govern and direct all of the Lord's affairs on earth in the Church. All worthy males in the Church who are twelve years of age or older may also be given privileges and powers appropriate to various offices of the priesthood, but every act performed under this AUTHORITY must be exercised in the

proper way. The power to direct these acts at any level is called the keys of the priesthood. Although all the keys are exercised by the President alone, he delegates the use of some of them to other leaders under his direction. The authority to perform ordinances and teach the gospel comes from the Lord, but the orderly use thereof is regulated by those holding keys given to Joseph Smith and passed on to his successors (D&C 1:38; 28:2; *see also* MELCHIZEDEK PRIESTHOOD: RESTORATION OF).

Instituted through revelation, the position or calling of President of the Church has developed together with the ORGANIZATION of the Church as a whole. Prior to the official ORGANIZATION OF THE CHURCH in 1830, Joseph Smith held the central leadership role as prophet of the RESTORATION. In a revelation given on May 15, 1829, Joseph Smith was instructed that he and Oliver COWDERY should be ordained the first and second ELDERS when the Church was formally organized (JS—H 1:72). This took place on April 6, 1830.

During the organizational meeting, Joseph Smith received a revelation in which he was given the titles of seer, translator, prophet, apostle of Jesus Christ, and elder of the Church of Jesus Christ. He was also told how to lay the foundation of the Church (D&C 21:1–2). Those present at the first meeting voted unanimously to accept Joseph Smith as first elder and prophet. At this meeting the fundamental precedent for Church government was established: Callings, including that of prophet, require that the mind and will of God be made manifest and that the will and consent of the people to abide by it be indicated through a sustaining vote (see COMMON CONSENT).

While the Church was in its early years, Joseph Smith, Oliver Cowdery, and a small group of elders met quarterly and made basic policy decisions for the Church. In September 1830 the uniqueness of Joseph Smith's position in the Church was affirmed when Hiram Page, a member of the Church, claimed to have received revelations for the Church. Joseph Smith inquired of the Lord and received a clarifying revelation that he alone was to receive commandments and revelations for the entire Church (D&C 28:2, 11–14).

In January 1832, at a small conference of elders in Amherst, Ohio, Joseph Smith was sustained as President of the High Priesthood and ordained to that office by Sidney RIGDON. In March of that same year, the office of President of the Church was further elaborated by the announcement of the organization of a Presidency to consist of a President and counselors (D&C 81:1–3). On April 26, 1832, a general conference of the Church was held in Jackson County, Missouri, where Joseph Smith was sustained and acknowledged as President of the High Priesthood.

Presidents of the Church serve for life and are not released because of age or health. The authority to designate a successor, after receiving revelation from the Lord, rests in the hands of the Twelve, who meet for that purpose after the death of the President. Once a new president has been designated and approved by the unanimous vote of the apostles, he selects his counselors, who are also sustained by the Twelve. These actions are then sustained by the Church membership at the next general conference.

The procedures of SUCCESSION IN THE PRESIDENCY have developed gradually since the organization of the Church. After the Prophet Joseph Smith was assassinated, some members thought his counselor, or even his son, should be his successor; but the Twelve knew that they held the keys and that the senior apostle should preside. Accordingly, Brigham Young, the president of the Quorum of the Twelve Apostles, led the Church from that position for three and a half years until he was installed and sustained with counselors as a First Presidency. The next two Presidents were also ordained after about the same lapse of time; but since 1898 the succession process has been invoked without delay after the death of a President.

BIBLIOGRAPHY

Allen, James B., and Glen M. Leonard. *The Story of the Latter-day Saints.* Salt Lake City, 1976.

Benson, Ezra Taft. "Fourteen Fundamentals in Following the Prophet." In *1980 Devotional Speeches of the Year.* Provo, Utah, 1981.

Esplin, Ronald K. "Joseph, Brigham and the Twelve: A Succession of Continuity." *BYU Studies* 21 (Summer 1981):301–341.

Kimball, Spencer W. "We Thank Thee, O God, for a Prophet: The Privilege of Sustaining the Leaders of the Church." *Ensign* 3 (Jan. 1973):33–35.

Petersen, Mark E. "Follow the Prophets." *Ensign* 11 (Nov. 1981):64–66.

Tanner, N. Eldon. "The Administration of the Church." *Ensign* 9 (Nov. 1979):42–48.

J. LYNN ENGLAND
W. KEITH WARNER

PRESIDING BISHOPRIC

The Presiding Bishopric consists of three men, the Presiding Bishop and his two counselors, who comprise one of the presiding councils of The Church of Jesus Christ of Latter-day Saints. These GENERAL AUTHORITIES, who each hold the office of BISHOP, serve in their positions under the direct supervision of the FIRST PRESIDENCY. Since its formation, the Presiding Bishopric has been responsible for many of the temporal affairs of the Church. These have included involvement in receiving, distributing, and accounting for member tithes, offerings, and contributions; administration of programs to assist the poor and needy; design, construction, and maintenance of places of worship; and auditing and transferring records of membership (see BISHOP, HISTORY OF THE OFFICE; FINANCIAL CONTRIBUTIONS; RECORD KEEPING; WELFARE). Men chosen to be Presiding Bishops have been recognized for their business and management skills as well as their religious commitment. Historically, the Presiding Bishopric has presided over the AARONIC PRIESTHOOD. As General Authorities, members of the Presiding Bishopric regularly speak at general conferences, often specifically addressing the young men of the Church.

The Presiding Bishop is selected by the First Presidency and then approved by the QUORUM OF THE TWELVE APOSTLES. He chooses two men to serve as his counselors, who are also approved by the First Presidency and the Quorum of the

Twelve, and they are all then sustained by the Church membership. The Presiding Bishop and his counselors are set apart and empowered by the First Presidency and given the priesthood keys and authority to act in their respective offices. At first, Presiding Bishops held office for life, but in the twentieth century they have been released and replaced as circumstances and Church needs have dictated.

On February 4, 1831, the Prophet Joseph Smith called Edward Partridge to serve as the first bishop of the Church. Bishop Partridge was to spend the majority of his time managing the receipt, control, and disposition of the consecrated properties and of donations received by the Church (*see* CONSECRATION; FAST OFFERINGS; TITHING). He was to care for the poor and needy and to store surplus items for the future needs of the Church. After Bishop Partridge was called, it was revealed to Joseph Smith that other bishops would be chosen. On December 4, 1831, Newel K. Whitney was also called, by revelation (D&C 72:8), to serve as a bishop. The two bishops had different jurisdictions, Whitney in Ohio and Partridge in Missouri. In Nauvoo they both had a general jurisdiction but also supervised donations and the caring for the poor in a particular city WARD. In 1847, Newel K. Whitney was designated the first Presiding Bishop.

Throughout the history of the Church, the First Presidency has assigned Presiding Bishoprics extensive but varying responsibilities with the Aaronic Priesthood and the youth of the Church. In 1873 President Brigham Young assigned the Presiding Bishopric to organize full Aaronic PRIESTHOOD QUORUMS of priests, teachers, and deacons throughout the Church. In 1876 he clarified the Presiding Bishop's position as general president of the Aaronic Priesthood. In 1937 the Presiding Bishopric was assigned responsibility for the Young Men's Mutual Improvement Association, and in 1946 for the Young Women's Mutual Improvement Association. These programs were designed to provide a balance of religious study, social skills, community awareness, and physical development for LDS youth (*see* YOUNG MEN; YOUNG WOMEN). Since 1977 the First Presidency has administered the Aaronic Priesthood programs directly through a Young Men's presidency called from the Quorums of the Seventy.

Prior to 1847, Bishops Partridge, Whitney, and Partridge's replacement, George Miller,

The Presiding Bishopric in 1947 (from left): first counselor Joseph L. Wirthlin, presiding bishop LeGrand Richards, and second counselor Thorpe B. Isaacson. Under the energetic leadership of Richards, the Presiding Bishopric improved record-keeping, youth programs, ward teaching, and management of Church properties and temporal affairs.

served as general bishops to the Church. Presiding Bishops and their terms of service after 1847 have been Newel K. Whitney (1847–1851), Edward Hunter (1851–1883), William B. Preston (1884–1907), Charles W. Nibley (1907–1925), Sylvester Q. Cannon (1925–1938), LeGrand Richards (1938–1952), Joseph B. Wirthlin (1952–1961), John H. Vandenberg (1961–1972), Victor L. Brown (1972–1985), and Robert D. Hales (from 1985).

Until recent times, these men visited wards and stakes, conducted training sessions for bishops at general conferences, and published bulletins and training materials for bishops and local priesthood quorums. At the present time the Presiding Bishopric does not directly supervise other bishops or preside over local wards of the Church.

By scriptural designation the Presiding Bishopric, the First Presidency, and the Quorum of the Twelve Apostles constitute the Council on the Disposition of Tithes (D&C 120). This council monitors receipt of tithes and controls expenditure of funds. It meets periodically to consider matters of financial importance and to authorize budgets for Church organizations and departments (*see* FINANCES OF THE CHURCH). Members of the Presiding Bishopric, as appointed by the First Presidency, additionally serve on various other administrative, executive, and policy-determining committees and councils, such as the Appropriations Committee, General Welfare Services Committee, Priesthood Executive Council, Temple and Family History Executive Council, and the Missionary Executive Council (*see* ORGANIZATION: CONTEMPORARY).

In 1977 a major organizational restructuring took place within the Church under the direction of the First Presidency. With the significant growth in Church membership the Presiding Bishopric was assigned much broader responsibilities for temporal administration throughout the world. Under the direction of the Presiding Bishopric, directors for temporal affairs were sent to a number of international locations to supervise the administration of the construction of meetinghouses and temples, the maintenance of membership records, and the preparation and distribution of scriptures and other curriculum materials. Departments at Church headquarters responsible for temporal operations were also assigned to the Presiding Bishopric for their direction. Since that time, the Presiding Bishopric has appointed managing directors for the various departments that support activities of the directors of temporal affairs, which include finance and records, LDS FOUNDATION, printing services, distribution of curriculum materials, purchasing, scripture and curriculum translation, temple clothing production, transportation, information systems and communications, security, investments, temples and special project construction and remodeling, real estate acquisitions and sales, meetinghouse construction, welfare production and processing, LDS SOCIAL SERVICES, and property management.

In 1986 the First Presidency called AREA PRESIDENCIES to give supervision to ecclesiastical activities within defined geographical areas of the world. These area presidencies presently give direct supervision to directors for temporal affairs in international areas and to welfare and physical facilities activities in the United States and Canada. The Presiding Bishopric, along with headquarters departments, provides training, evaluation, manpower planning, technical support, and program design to assist area presidencies in their roles.

BIBLIOGRAPHY

Cowan, Richard O. *The Church in the Twentieth Century*, pp. 140, 270, 297, 406–407, 420. Salt Lake City, 1985.

Palmer, Lee A. *Aaronic Priesthood through the Ages*, pp. 321–31. Salt Lake City, 1964.

Widtsoe, John A. *Priesthood and Church Government*, rev. ed., pp. 277–79. Salt Lake City, 1954.

H. DAVID BURTON
WM. GIBB DYER, JR.

PRESIDING HIGH PRIEST

"Presiding high priest" is a phrase sometimes used in The Church of Jesus Christ of Latter-day Saints to refer to the priesthood officer in charge of a particular unit of Church organization (e.g., D&C 106:1). When used without qualification, it ordinarily refers to the PRESIDENT OF THE CHURCH.

Local congregations or WARDS are presided over by a BISHOP, who may also be spoken of as the presiding high priest in his ward. Similarly, a STAKE PRESIDENT presides over a STAKE, and an AREA president presides over the stakes of a major geographical area. All of these preside as ordained high priests, even though the bishop and area president function on the basis of an additional ordination as a bishop or seventy, respectively.

Only the President of the Church, by right of his ordination to this office, is designated the presiding high priest of the whole Church (D&C 107:91). His calling includes being "President of the High Priesthood of the Church; or, in other words, the Presiding High Priest over the High Priesthood of the Church" (D&C 107:65–66). In 1832 the Prophet Joseph SMITH was sustained as President of the High Priesthood and ordained to that office by Sidney RIGDON. An 1835 revelation further directed that a FIRST PRESIDENCY of three men be chosen, "appointed and ordained to that office, and upheld by the confidence, faith, and prayer of the church" (D&C 107:22). The President's counselors may preside in his absence, and are also called presiding high priests (D&C 107:22), but do not function independently in this role.

ROY W. DOXEY

PRESS, NEWS MEDIA, AND THE CHURCH

Early press coverage of The Church of Jesus Christ of Latter-day Saints was shaped by the traditions of the partisan press. Some journalists treated the Latter-day Saints with a degree of fairness, but the more common approach was ridicule and hostility. Outside media took a rather dim view of the Church, and when the LDS media were confrontational, non-Mormon media responded with a hostility that increased as the nineteenth century continued. Joseph SMITH's arrest and martyrdom grew partly out of the Nauvoo City Council's suppression of the *Nauvoo Expositor*, an opposition press. In the latter part of the century, developing technology and urbanization fostered unprecedented big-city newspaper circulation battles and the rise of yellow journalism. Among those vilified were the Latter-day Saints, particularly their practice of PLURAL MARRIAGE.

The press's perception of the Church began to change slowly after the practice of polygamy was officially suspended in 1890 and Utah was granted statehood in 1896. Then in the early twentieth century press coverage continued to improve as the Church began to be recognized as an influential American institution, and the public began listening to MORMON TABERNACLE CHOIR BROADCASTS. Still later, Latter-day Saints in government and business such as George Romney, governor of Michigan; Ezra Taft BENSON, secretary of agriculture in the Eisenhower cabinet; and J. Willard Marriott, president of the Marriott Corporation, also helped the press view the Church with an air of greater approval and commendation. The creation of the Church's PUBLIC COMMUNICATIONS OFFICE in 1970 has further helped with media relations throughout the world. Although there are still occasional flare-ups of sensational news about the Church and individual members, the general view of Mormons provided by the mainstream media in the last decades of the twentieth century has been more accurate and better balanced.

BIBLIOGRAPHY

Mulder, William, and A. Russell Mortensen, eds. *Among the Mormons: Historic Accounts by Contemporary Observers*. New York, 1969.

Lythgoe, Dennis Leo. "The Changing Image of Mormonism in Periodical Literature." Ph.D. diss., University of Utah, 1969.

PAUL ALFRED PRATTE

PRESS AND PUBLICATIONS

[*From its beginning, The Church of Jesus Christ of Latter-day Saints was frequently attacked and abused by the press. For a concise statement on the relationship of the press and the Church, see* Press, News Media and the Church. *At the same time, the Church has used the printed word to convey its message to the world. For a fuller study of the Church's use of the printed word to produce books, pamphlets, broadsides, newspapers, and magazines, see* Publications. *For a listing of the periodicals and newspapers published by the Church, see* Magazines; *and* Newspapers, LDS. *For separate articles on several different publications see* Almanacs; Bible, LDS Publication of; Bulletin; Conference Reports; Journal of Discourses; Juvenile Instructor; Liahona the Elders' Journal; Messenger and Advocate; Millennial Star; Nauvoo Neighbor; New Era; Relief Society Magazine; Times and Seasons; Utah Genealogical and Historical Magazine; Woman's Exponent; *and* Young Woman's Journal.]

PRIDE

In an address drawing together Book of Mormon and other scriptural teachings regarding pride, President Ezra Taft BENSON called it "the universal sin, the great vice" (1989, p. 6). He characterized its central feature as "enmity—enmity toward God and enmity toward our fellowmen" and defined "enmity" as "hatred toward, hostility to, or a state of opposition." He observed that "pride is essentially competitive in nature," arising when individuals pit their will against God's or their intellects, opinions, works, wealth, and talents against those of other people (p. 4). He warned that "pride is a damning sin in the true sense of that word," for "it limits or stops progression" and "adversely affects all our relationships" (p. 6).

The scriptures abound with admonitions against pride. "Pride goeth before destruction" (Prov. 16:18). Pride felled Lucifer (cf. Moses 4:1–3; 2 Ne. 24:12–15; D&C 29:36; 76:28) and destroyed the city of Sodom (Ezek. 16:49–50). In the closing chapters of the Book of Mormon, the prophet Mormon wrote, "Behold, the pride of this nation, or the people of the Nephites, hath proven their destruction" (Moro. 8:27). Three times in the Doctrine and Covenants the Lord uses the phrase "beware of pride," including warnings to Oliver COWDERY, the second elder of the Church, and to Emma SMITH, the wife of Joseph Smith (D&C 23:1; 25:14; 38:39). The Lord has said that when he cleanses the earth by fire, the proud shall burn as stubble (3 Ne. 25:1; D&C 29:9; Mal. 4:1).

While most consider pride a sin of the rich, gifted, or learned looking down on others, President Benson warned that it is also common among those looking up—"faultfinding, gossiping . . . living beyond our means, envying, coveting, withholding gratitude . . . and being unforgiving and jealous" (1989, p. 5).

God has commanded the Saints to "seek to bring forth and establish the cause of Zion" (D&C 6:6). When ZION is established, its people will be "of one heart and one mind" and will dwell together in righteousness (Moses 7:18). But "pride is the great stumbling block to Zion" (Benson, 1989, p. 7). Pride leads people to diminish others in the attempt to elevate themselves, resulting in selfishness and contention.

The proud love "the praise of men more than the praise of God" (John 12:42–43) and fear the judgment of men more than that of God (cf. D&C 3:6–7; 30:1–2; 60:2). They do not receive counsel or correction easily but justify and rationalize their frailties and failures, making it difficult for them to repent and receive the blessings of the Atonement. They have difficulty rejoicing in their blessings, because they are constantly comparing them to see whether they have more or less than someone else. Consequently, they are often ungrateful.

The antidote for pride is humility, "a broken heart and a contrite spirit" (3 Ne. 9:20, 12:19). Men can choose to do those things that will foster the growth of humility: they can choose to confess and forsake their sins, forgive others, receive counsel and chastisement, esteem others as themselves, render service, love God, and submit to his will (Benson, 1989, p. 7). By yielding "to the enticings of the Holy Spirit," the prideful individual can become "a saint through the atonement of Christ" and become "as a child, submissive, meek, humble" (Mosiah 3:19; cf. Alma 13:28).

BIBLIOGRAPHY

Benson, Ezra Taft. "Cleansing the Inner Vessel." *Ensign* 16 (May 1986):4–7.

———. "Beware of Pride." *Ensign* 19 (May 1989):4–7.

Burton, Theodore M. "A Disease Called Pride." *Ensign* 1 (Mar. 1971):26–29.

REED A. BENSON

PRIEST, AARONIC PRIESTHOOD

Priest is the highest office of the AARONIC PRIESTHOOD to which young male members of the Church may be ordained. To receive this office the candidate must be sixteen or older; most priests are between the ages of sixteen and nineteen.

Priests in the restored Church are empowered to "preach, teach, [and] expound" the doctrines and the covenants of the Church and to "visit the house of each member, and exhort them to pray . . . and attend to all family duties" (D&C 20:46–47). Priests fulfill these duties in Church meetings and in visits to members as HOME TEACHERS. They also have AUTHORITY to baptize, to administer the SACRAMENT, to ordain other priests, TEACHERS, and DEACONS under the direction of their BISHOP, to preside at meetings when NO ELDER is present, and to perform all duties of deacons and teachers.

Historically the term "priest" has been used to describe a variety of offices and functions. From the time of AARON until the ministry of JOHN THE BAPTIST, priests in the Aaronic order taught the LAW OF MOSES, offered sacrifices, officiated or performed in numerous temple functions and priesthood ordinances, and thereby mediated between the people and God. Only the lineal descendants of Aaron could be priests. Christ's sacrifice and atonement fulfilled the "law of carnal commandments," thereby ending for Christians the priests' role as officiators in Mosaic ordinances.

In the New Testament, Jesus Christ is named the great "high priest" and as such is seen as the everlasting mediator by whom all men may come unto God (Heb. 5:1–10; 9:24–26). For Latter-day Saints, HIGH PRIEST is an office in the MELCHIZEDEK PRIESTHOOD. While most English-speaking Christian traditions use the word priest to refer both to the ancient Levitical roles and to the presbyters (elders) of the early Christian churches who had responsibilities to preside over and instruct congregations, the two offices are separated in the LDS Church in that priests are of the Aaronic Priesthood and perform basic ordinances and otherwise assist the elders and high priests of the Melchizedek Priesthood.

Because there were no descendants of Aaron among the Nephites or Lamanites, priests in the Book of Mormon held the Melchizedek Priesthood and thus engaged both in the sacrificial functions and in broader presiding and teaching functions (Alma 18:24; 45:22).

Joseph SMITH and Oliver COWDERY received the Aaronic Priesthood from John the Baptist on May 15, 1829 (see D&C 13; *see* AARONIC PRIESTHOOD: RESTORATION OF). They subsequently ordained the first priests in this dispensation on June 9, 1830.

Today, priests in each ward are organized into quorums of forty-eight or fewer members. The ward bishop presides over this quorum, with two priests called to assist him, and another as secretary. An adult adviser is also assigned by the bishopric to teach and assist quorum members. As in all of the offices of the Aaronic Priesthood, members of this PRIESTHOOD QUORUM receive instruction to prepare them for ordination as elders in the Melchizedek Priesthood and for missionary service. Each priest is expected to emulate the example of Jesus Christ.

In addition to performing their priesthood duties, priests participate together in a variety of educational, recreational, and social activities (*see* YOUNG MEN). For example, the priests in a ward in the United States participate as a group in the Explorer program of the Boy Scouts of America (*see* SCOUTING). In social and service activities they often join with the Laurels, who are sixteen- to eighteen-year-old members of the YOUNG WOMEN organization of the Church.

BIBLIOGRAPHY

Abba, R. "Priests and Levites." In *The Interpreter's Dictionary of the Bible*, Vol. 3, pp. 876–89. Nashville, Tenn., 1962.

Palmer, Lee A. *The Aaronic Priesthood Through the Centuries.* Salt Lake City, 1964.

Shepherd, M. H., Jr. "Priests in the New Testament." In *The Interpreter's Dictionary of the Bible*, Vol. 3, pp. 889–91. Nashville, Tenn., 1962.

W. LADD HOLLIST

PRIESTCRAFT

The Book of Mormon says, "Priestcrafts are that men preach and set themselves up for a light unto the world, that they may get gain and praise of the world; but they seek not the welfare of Zion. . . . But the laborer in Zion shall labor for Zion; for if they labor for money they shall perish" (2 Ne. 26:29, 31). Inherent in this definition is the concern that Church leaders must labor to build ZION into the hearts of the people, and not for their personal aggrandizement or reward. When leaders "make merchandise" of men's souls (2 Pet. 2:3), they turn religion into a business, and pride, materialism, and unrighteous dominion follow.

Both in scripture and in literature priestcraft is condemned. Peter cursed Simon the sorcerer, who wanted to purchase the priesthood for money (Acts 8:14–24). Dante's Peter castigates several popes and priests for not serving freely and for making a sewer of the sepulcher of Peter by selling priesthood appointment (*Paradiso* 27:22–57). Chaucer observed that greed for personal gain and glory often replaced genuine priesthood service ("General Prologue" and "Introduction to the Pardoner's Tale," *Canterbury Tales*). Milton's lines from *Lycidas* condemning a clergy who "for their bellies' sake, / Creep and intrude, and climb into the fold" (ll. 114–15) sum up the evil of priestcraft: "The hungry sheep look up, and are not fed, / But swoln with wind and the rank mist they draw, / Rot inwardly, and foul contagion spread" (ll. 125–27).

CHARLES D. TATE, JR.

PRIESTHOOD

[*Other articles dealing with various aspects of the priesthood are* Aaronic Priesthood; Authority; Brotherhood; Clergy; Godhood; Keys of the Priesthood; Lay Participation and Leadership; Levitical Priesthood; Magnifying One's Calling; Melchizedek Priesthood; Men, Roles of; Oath and Covenant of the Priesthood; Presidency, Concept of; Presiding High Priest; Priesthood Councils; *and* Priesthood Quorums.

On the specific offices of the priesthood, see Apostle; Bishop; Deacon, Aaronic Priesthood; Elder; High Priest; Patriarch; Priest, Aaronic Priesthood; Priesthood Offices; Prophet; Seventy; Teacher, Aaronic Priesthood.

For discussions of various priesthood ordinances, see Baptism; Baptismal Prayer; Children: Blessing of Children; Confirmation; Dedications; Father's Blessing; Laying on of Hands; Ordinances; Ordination to the Priesthood; Patriarchal Blessing; Priesthood Blessings; Rebaptism; Sacrament Prayers; Sealing; Setting Apart; Sick, Blessing the; Temple Ordinances.]

THE SOURCE OF PRIESTHOOD POWER. Jesus Christ is the great High Priest of God; Christ is therefore the source of all true priesthood authority and power on this earth (Heb. 5–10). Man does not take such priesthood power unto himself; it must be conferred by God through his servants (Heb. 5:4; D&C 1:38).

Before the world was created, Jesus Christ, the great JEHOVAH and firstborn of God the Father in the spirit world, covenanted to use the power he had obtained from the Father to implement God's program for the eternal happiness of all God's children (cf. *TPJS*, p. 190). The actual name of the

Restoration of the Melchizedek Priesthood, by Gary E. Smith (1980, oil on canvas, 36″ × 42″). The apostles Peter, James, and John bestowed the Melchizedek Priesthood upon Joseph Smith and Oliver Cowdery. Courtesy Blaine T. Hudson.

priesthood is "the Holy Priesthood after the Order of the Son of God"; but to avoid the too-frequent repetition of the name of deity, it is called by other names, particularly the Melchizedek Priesthood; i.e., it is the same authority held by that righteous king and high priest (Gen. 14:18; Heb. 5:6; Alma 13:6, 17–19; D&C 107:1–4; 124:123).

As the divine Savior, Mediator, and Redeemer, Jesus sets the example for all priesthood performance. "Therefore, what manner of men ought ye to be?" Jesus asked his Nephite disciples whom he had ordained: "Verily I say unto you, even as I am" (3 Ne. 27:27).

DEFINITIONS. Joseph SMITH defined priesthood as "an everlasting principle, [which has] existed with God from eternity, and will to eternity, without beginning of days or end of years, . . . holding the keys of power and blessings. In fact, [the Melchizedek] Priesthood is a perfect law of theocracy" (*TPJS*, pp. 157, 322). It is the power and AUTHORITY by which The Church of Jesus Christ of Latter-day Saints is organized and directed.

The word "priesthood" has several meanings for Latter-day Saints:

1. Priesthood is *power*, the power of God, a vital source of eternal strength and energy delegated to men to act in all things for the well-being of mankind, both in the world and out of it (*DS* 3:80; Romney, p. 43).

2. Priesthood is *authority*, the exclusive right to act in the name of God as his authorized agents and to perform ORDINANCES for the purpose of opening certain spiritual blessings to all individuals.

3. Priesthood is the right and responsibility to *preside* within the organizational structure of the Church, but only in a manner consistent with the agency of others.

4. Sometimes the word priesthood is used to refer to the men of the Church in general (as in "the priesthood will meet in the chapel").

Priesthood power may be exercised only under the direction of the one holding the right, or KEYS, to authorize its use. Priesthood power functions in accord with the characteristics and attributes of God himself, namely persuasion, long-suffering, gentleness, meekness, love unfeigned, righteousness, virtue, knowledge, justice, judgment, mercy, and truth (D&C 121:41; *Lectures on Faith* 4). It ceases to exist in a man who uses it to obtain the honors of the world, or to gratify pride, or to cover sin or evil, or to exercise unrighteous dominion (D&C 121:33–37).

Priesthood embraces all forms of God's power. It is the power by which the cosmos was ordered, universes and worlds were organized, and the elements in all their varied structures and relationships were put into place. Through the priesthood, God governs all things. By this power, the gospel is preached and understood, and the ordinances of exaltation for both the living and the dead are performed (*see* PLAN OF SALVATION). Priesthood is the channel for obtaining REVELATION, the channel through which God reveals himself and his glory, his intents and his purposes, to mankind: The priesthood holds "the key of the mysteries of the kingdom, even the key of the knowledge of God" (D&C 84:19–20; cf. *TPJS*, pp. 166–67). It conveys the mind and will of God; and, when employed by his servants on his errand, it functions as if by the Lord's own mouth and hand (D&C 1:38).

Thus, the LDS doctrine of priesthood differs from all other views. Priesthood is not vocational or professional (*see* CLERGY). It is not hereditary, passed by inheritance from father to son (even the LEVITICAL PRIESTHOOD was conferred by ordination). It is not offered for money (see PRIEST-CRAFT). It is not held by a group of specialists who are separated from the community (all worthy Latter-day Saint men are eligible to be ordained to the priesthood). And yet it is not a "priesthood of all believers," as in the Protestant conception (ER 11:529).

HISTORY, ORDERS, AND OFFICES OF THE PRIESTHOOD. Whenever the government of God has existed on the earth, it has functioned through this priesthood power, held by righteous men chosen of God, as were Aaron (Heb. 5:4) and Joshua (Num. 27:18–19). In times of APOSTASY and wickedness, God has not permitted his servants to confer the priesthood on the unworthy, and it has been lost from the earth. When necessary, the priesthood has been restored with each new DISPENSATION of the gospel.

Following the ascension of Jesus Christ and the death of his apostles, apostasy occurred in the Christian church and priesthood authority was taken from the earth. However, after preparation by God through the lives of earnest and sincere reformers and seekers, mankind again received priesthood authority from angelic ministers who held the keys to this power. Beginning on May 15, 1829, heavenly messengers conferred priesthood authority upon Joseph Smith and Oliver COWDERY in a series of visitations (see AARONIC PRIESTHOOD: RESTORATION OF; MELCHIZEDEK PRIESTHOOD: RESTORATION OF; DOCTRINE AND COVENANTS: SECTION 110). These restorations included the Aaronic Priesthood (D&C 13), the Melchizedek Priesthood (D&C 27), the keys of the gathering of Israel (D&C 110:11), the keys of the fulfillment of the Abrahamic covenant (D&C 110:12), the keys of the binding and sealing power (D&C 110:13–16), and the keys of all dispensations of the gospel "from Michael or Adam down to the present time" (D&C 128:21). These keys of presiding authority have been in turn conferred upon each succeeding prophet and President of the Church. All priesthood power and authority function today under the direction of the PRESIDENT OF THE CHURCH, who holds all priesthood keys and powers (see FIRST PRESIDENCY; QUORUM OF THE TWELVE APOSTLES; SUCCESSION IN THE PRESIDENCY).

"There are three grand orders of priesthood referred to [in the Epistle to the Hebrews]" (TPJS,

p. 322–23; HC 5:554–55)—the Melchizedek, the Patriarchal, and the Aaronic:

1. The Melchizedek Priesthood is the "higher priesthood" that incorporates all priesthoods within itself (TPJS, p. 180). It holds "the right of presidency, and has power and authority over all the offices in the church in all ages of the world, to administer in spiritual things" (D&C 107:8). This order of ordination is an unchanging order that has been present in all dispensations (cf. Matt. 10:1; 16:19; John 20:23; Eph. 4:11; Heb. 7:24; see also HEBREWS, EPISTLE TO THE). From Adam to Moses, all major prophets held the Melchizedek Priesthood; Joseph Smith taught that the prophets after the death of Moses and before the time of Christ held this same priesthood and were "ordained by God himself" (TPJS, p. 181). This authority is superior to the lesser or Aaronic Priesthood that functioned under the law of Moses. The Nephites held the Melchizedek Priesthood and observed the law of Moses under that authority (cf. Alma 13:6–18).

2. The PATRIARCHAL ORDER OF THE PRIESTHOOD is the right of worthy priesthood-holding fathers to preside over their descendants through all ages; it includes the ordinances and blessings of the fulness of the priesthood shared by husbands and wives who are sealed in the temple (see SEALING: TEMPLE SEALINGS).

3. The Aaronic Priesthood, including the Levitical Priesthood, was instituted under the LAW OF MOSES at the time when Israel rejected the greater powers, blessings, and responsibilities of the Melchizedek Priesthood. God gave them a "lesser priesthood" comprising specific areas of authority dealing with sacrifices and temporal concerns of salvation (Ex. 20:19; JST Ex. 34:1–2). This authority was granted as a right to Aaron and his lineal descendants forever. Levitical Priesthood refers to certain duties within the Aaronic Priesthood that were delegated to worthy male members of the tribe of Levi (see PRIESTHOOD IN BIBLICAL TIMES).

Within the Melchizedek and Aaronic Priesthoods, men may be ordained to various offices. Those who hold certain offices may then be called and set apart to particular positions of Church service. Beginning at age twelve young men, if they are worthy and desire it, may have the Aaronic Priesthood conferred upon them and be ordained to the office of deacon; they may be ordained a

First Presidency and Quorum of the Twelve Apostles (in 1884). Top Row: George Q. Cannon, President John Taylor, Joseph F. Smith. Apostles (second row) Wilford Woodruff, Lorenzo Snow, Erastus Snow, Franklin D. Richards, (third row) Brigham Young, Jr., Albert Carrington, Moses Thatcher, Francis Marion Lyman, (fourth row) John Henry Smith, George Teasdale, Heber J. Grant, John W. Taylor.

teacher at age fourteen, and a priest at age sixteen. At the age of eighteen, they may have the Melchizedek Priesthood conferred upon them and be ordained to the office of elder. Later, as need and calling dictate, they may be ordained to other offices in the Melchizedek Priesthood. The office of BISHOP is an appendage to the Melchizedek Priesthood (D&C 84:29), but its function is to preside over the Aaronic Priesthood (D&C 107:87–88). The office of PATRIARCH is an office in the Melchizedek Priesthood.

All faithful and worthy Latter-day Saint men may be ordained to the priesthood and be authorized to act and participate in any of the offices, powers, blessings, and authorities of priesthood (*see* ORDINATION TO THE PRIESTHOOD; DOCTRINE AND COVENANTS: OFFICIAL DECLARATION—2). Ordination to each different priesthood office is by the authority and under the direction of the presiding priesthood officer in the ward, branch, stake, or mission of the Church where the person resides, by the laying on of hands by one holding appropriate priesthood office and designated to so act.

For all holders of the Melchizedek or Aaronic Priesthood, activity, training, service, and fellowship occur in PRIESTHOOD QUORUMS, organized according to priesthood office with appropriate presiding officers (see D&C 20; 107).

PRIESTHOOD AND THE FAMILY. The priesthood achieves its highest function in the family. In the family, the husband and father presides in righteousness and uses his priesthood to bless the lives of his family members, teaching by example and by counsel, giving righteous advice and decisions, openly expressing love and concern, and bestowing priesthood blessings by the laying on of hands when appropriate for the direction, healing, and comfort of his family. As the presiding priesthood bearer in his home, he is accountable to the Lord: Both the husband and wife are accountable to God for their respective responsibilities over the spiritual and temporal well-being of their family.

Exaltation and eternal life in the highest degree of the CELESTIAL KINGDOM are achieved only as the fulness of the priesthood is attained through building and achieving an eternal marriage (*see* MARRIAGE: ETERNAL MARRIAGE). The highest intellectual and spiritual development of both male and female is to become as God is. Both male and female are in the image of God (Gen. 1:27); GODHOOD cannot be achieved by male or female

alone. Everyone in the PREMORTAL LIFE was begotten as a spirit child of Heavenly Parents before being born into mortality by earthly parents, and life on earth is part of the progression of men and women toward becoming like their Heavenly Parents. Only through the sealing ordinances of the holy priesthood, performed in the temples of the Lord, and through faithful, righteous living can male and female join in an eternal marriage unit wherein they may attain a fulness of the priesthood and exaltation together.

Fulness of the priesthood, which is the highest order of priesthood, is attained only through an eternal union of male and female, sanctified by the sealing ordinances in a temple of the Lord and ratified by the HOLY SPIRIT OF PROMISE (D&C 132:18–19). Those so united, who honor their covenants with each other and the Lord, will in the Resurrection inherit EXALTATION and ETERNAL LIFE, consisting of an eternal union together and an eternal family, including ETERNAL INCREASE, spirit children, and the creation and possession of worlds and universes.

Thus, all blessings, benefits, and inheritances of the priesthood are equally shared and achieved by husband and wife alike if they carry out their respective responsibilities in faith, love, harmony, and cooperation in the Lord. The apostle Paul stated, "Neither is the man without the woman, neither the woman without the man, in the Lord" (1 Cor. 11:11).

In the temples of the Lord, sacred priesthood ordinances (e.g., washings, anointings, clothings) are administered to men by men and to women by women who have received the endowments of the priesthood in the temple (*TPJS*, p. 337) and have been given that specific priesthood responsibility. Women thus may act in priesthood power when called, set apart, and authorized by those who hold the keys; however, women officiators are not ordained to the priesthood or to an office in the priesthood to do this work.

THE POWER OF GOD UNTO EXALTATION. Joseph Smith said: "I advise all to go on to perfection. . . . A man can do nothing for himself unless God direct him in the right way; and the Priesthood is for that purpose" (*TPJS*, p. 364). Perfection is attained by obedience to the principles and ordinances of the gospel. Without priesthood authority, no ordinances—no matter how, when, where, or by whom performed—are valid, ratified by the Holy

Ghost, or recorded in heaven (D&C 132:7). The sealing power, the power to bind on earth and in heaven (Matt. 16:19; 18:18; D&C 132:46), belongs solely to the priesthood of God; and proper BAPTISM, the GIFT OF THE HOLY GHOST, the holy ENDOWMENT, eternal marriage, and family sealings come only through the authorized servants of the Lord. Through these powers and authorities of the holy priesthood, the work of salvation proceeds as it was planned in the grand councils of heaven before the world was.

Under the direction and authority of the priesthood in this last dispensation, the Dispensation of the Fulness of Times, the work of the priesthood includes proclaiming the gospel, perfecting the Saints, and performing ordinances for the redemption of the dead. Priesthood bearers are charged to teach the gospel to all nations and peoples, to proclaim the knowledge of salvation. Doing this missionary work is a responsibility of all members of the Church, and a particular obligation for bearers of the priesthood. They are also charged to watch over the Saints everywhere, to labor to increase faith, understanding, and testimony, and to improve the spiritual welfare and physical comfort of all who will receive them. Priesthood bearers are further charged to "redeem the dead" through the sealing power of the priesthood (D&C 128:14–18). Latter-day Saints are taught and encouraged to seek out the names and records of their dead progenitors, to actively engage in genealogical research, to turn their hearts to their ancestors, that every individual may be sealed by sacred temple ordinances in eternal families and ultimately in the family of Adam, which becomes the family of Jesus Christ (D&C 39:4–6; 42:52).

Essentially and eternally, the work of the priesthood is the work of Christ delegated to righteous servants. "This is my work and my glory," the Lord said to Moses, "to bring to pass the immortality and eternal life of man" (Moses 1:39). The work of priesthood is to assist in bringing souls to Christ and thereby to exaltation in the kingdom of the Father.

Achieving the fulness of the priesthood of the Son of God is the great goal of all faithful Latter-day Saints, because it is the power of God unto salvation and eternal lives. It is the power by which mortal bodies will be resurrected immortal, to be possessed forever by the spirits who dwelt in them, glorified by God according to their works while in mortality. It is the power by which eternal joy may be attained, but always and only through obedience to the laws and principles of righteousness as exemplified and taught by the Savior.

BIBLIOGRAPHY

Kimball, Spencer W., et al. *Priesthood*. Salt Lake City, 1981.

McConkie, Bruce R. "The Doctrine of the Priesthood." *Ensign* 12 (May 1982):32–34.

Romney, Marion G. "Priesthood." *Ensign* 12 (May 1982):43.

Smith, Joseph F. *GD*. Salt Lake City, 1919.

Taylor, John. *The Gospel Kingdom*. Salt Lake City, 1964.

Widtsoe, John A. *Priesthood and Church Government*. Salt Lake City, 1939.

Young, Brigham. *Discourses of Brigham Young*, ed. John A. Widtsoe, pp. 130–51. Salt Lake City, 1954.

RICHARD G. ELLSWORTH
MELVIN J. LUTHY

PRIESTHOOD IN BIBLICAL TIMES

Throughout the biblical period, God called prophets and other servants to direct his work and to be his authorized representatives by sharing his power or PRIESTHOOD with them. Through that priesthood, God administered his spiritual and temporal kingdom on earth, taught redeeming gospel truths, and provided saving ORDINANCES in all generations (D&C 84:17–21). An understanding of the priesthood in biblical times facilitates an appreciation of the contemporary LDS priesthood, since it represents a RESTORATION of priesthood authority in the latter days.

The priesthood or authority to act for God is governed by KEYS, which open God's greatest blessings, including the "privilege of receiving the mysteries of the kingdom of heaven, . . . [and] the communion and presence of God the Father, and Jesus" (D&C 107:19). These divinely bestowed powers came down in an unbroken line from Adam to Moses (D&C 84:6–17; 107:14–52), but the titles of priesthood officers changed periodically along with the type of social and religious structures that they administered.

PATRIARCHAL PRIESTHOOD AND MELCHIZEDEK. From Adam to Jacob, the main office of God's priesthood was that of patriarch. Adam, Enoch,

Noah, and Abraham administered the Lord's work, established covenants between God and the faithful, recorded their teachings and prophecies, and gave special PRIESTHOOD BLESSINGS. A patriarch could bless his offspring by calling upon the powers of heaven. As he gave the birthright blessing to one of his sons, for instance, the keys and powers of the priesthood were extended to the next generation. In the patriarchal order, under the law of primogeniture, these priesthood rights normally were to be given to the eldest son; from Abraham to EPHRAIM the birthright blessing went to younger sons because of their righteousness (Gen. 21, 27–28, 48–49).

MELCHIZEDEK, one of the most important biblical priesthood bearers, remains something of a mystery in the Bible because the precise lineage of his priesthood is not noted. He is simply identified as "priest of the most high God" (Gen. 14:18); a revelation to Joseph Smith adds that Melchizedek received the priesthood "through the lineage of his fathers, even till Noah" (D&C 84:14). Melchizedek not only blessed Abraham and gave him the priesthood after the order of the Son of God, but he was such a righteous high priest that the "greater" priesthood was named the MELCHIZEDEK PRIESTHOOD after him (D&C 84:19; 107:1–4; Alma 13:1–19). Jesus also was identified as a priest "after the order of Melchisedec" (Heb. 5:6). The Prophet Joseph SMITH observed, "All priesthood is Melchizedek, but there are different portions or degrees of it. That portion which brought Moses to speak with God face to face was taken away; but that which brought the ministry of angels remained. All the prophets had the Melchizedek Priesthood and were ordained by God himself" (TPJS, pp. 180–81).

Although little is known from the Bible about these patriarchs, their righteousness set a pattern referred to in later generations (e.g., Ps. 110:4; 1 Kgs. 18:36). The books of Abraham and Moses in the PEARL OF GREAT PRICE reveal more of the visions, revelations, ordinations, and divine experiences of many of these ancient priesthood holders than the Bible does.

AARON AND THE LEVITICAL PRIESTHOOD. With Moses, a new social and religious order with special priesthood offices was established among the Israelites. The priesthood emphasis shifted from patriarchs presiding over extended families to a designated tribe of Levitical priesthood holders, who served Israel for centuries. Under the Lord's direction, Moses ordained his older brother, AARON, to preside over the tribe of Levi, which served all the people (Lev. 8:1–13; Num. 8:13–22; Heb. 5:4). Over time, Aaron became exemplary in his priesthood service and the "lesser" priesthood was named the AARONIC PRIESTHOOD after him (Heb. 7:11; D&C 84:18, 26; 107:13–16). The major priesthood offices were the priests, including a "high" (Hebrew "great") priest, and the Levites.

Priests were worthy male descendants of Aaron. The high priest was designated from among the first-born descendants of Aaron. His office was responsible for the annual Day of Atonement rituals (Lev. 16) and for all the tithes and offerings of the Israelites (see TITHING). The priests supervised the system of worship and sacrifices at the holy sanctuary and helped regulate the religious affairs and holy days of Israel.

The Levites included all male descendants of Levi. They assisted the priests in collecting and distributing the tithes and offerings, in the elaborate system of animal and food sacrifices, in teaching the law, in singing, and in building and maintaining places of worship, especially the tabernacle and the temple.

Prophets in Old Testament times held the Melchizedek Priesthood, as noted above (TPJS, p. 181); and some of them held special priesthood keys for the gathering of Israel (see ISRAEL: GATHERING OF ISRAEL) and the SEALING powers of eternal ordinances (D&C 132:38–39). In an extension of their mortal ministries, Moses and Elijah delivered these keys to Jesus' apostles on the MOUNT OF TRANSFIGURATION (Matt. 17:1–8) and, along with ELIAS, delivered them also to Joseph Smith in the Kirtland Temple in 1836 (D&C 110). In general, however, the various PRIESTHOOD OFFICES of the Aaronic and Melchizedek priesthoods were not held by Israelite men from the time of Moses to the New Testament period.

Although the Melchizedek Priesthood was limited to those prophets specially called and commissioned, the Aaronic Priesthood continued "with the house of Aaron among the children of Israel" from Aaron to JOHN THE BAPTIST (D&C 84:26–27; TPJS, p. 319). However, after MALACHI (c. 400 B.C.), political corruption occurred involving the office of high priest. Persian, Greek, and Roman rulers sought to control the Jewish priesthood office by making the high priest a political appointee of the state rather than a true and righteous descendant of Aaron. This political manipulation led to rival claimants to priesthood offices and authority, with particular opposition between the Sadducees of Jerusalem and the Essenes of Qumran.

CHRIST'S MINISTERS. John the Baptist was a priesthood bridge between the Old and New Testament periods. Being of priestly descent through both parents, he was a legal administrator of the LAW OF MOSES, yet he received additional blessings and keys to usher in Christ's ministry, being set apart to this power by an angel of God when he was eight days old (D&C 84:28).

As Jesus organized his Church, he established a religious order with new priesthood leaders. While he retained features of the earlier structures such as the Twelve (cf. Num. 1:4, 44; Ezra 8:24–30) and the SEVENTY (cf. Ex. 24:1–11), he gave new titles and ordained new offices, especially the apostles, who served as special witnesses of his ministry and resurrection. Upon the foundation of apostles and prophets, Christ's Church was administered by EVANGELISTS, seventies, ELDERS, BISHOPS, priests, TEACHERS, and DEACONS (Eph. 4:11–16; 1 Cor. 12:12–28; see also ORGANIZATION OF THE CHURCH IN NEW TESTAMENT TIMES).

As part of the RESTORATION OF ALL THINGS (Acts 3:21; cf. Moses 6:7), The Church of Jesus Christ of Latter-day Saints received elements from all the biblical priesthood periods, with the greater part coming from the pattern and offices of Christ's New Testament Church. Under the direction of modern prophets, priesthood holders of both the Melchizedek and Aaronic orders officiate today in a variety of offices and callings, continuing God's pattern of administering to his children's needs.

BIBLIOGRAPHY

De Vaux, Roland. *Ancient Israel*, Vol. 2. New York, 1965.

Palmer, Lee A. *Aaronic Priesthood Through the Centuries*. Salt Lake City, 1964.

Smith, Joseph Fielding. *DS* 3:80–90.

Sperry, Sidney B. *Doctrine and Covenants Compendium*, pp. 388–93, 567–70. Salt Lake City, 1960.

Tvedtnes, John A. *The Church of the Old Testament*, pp. 30–44. Salt Lake City, 1980.

Widtsoe, John A. *Priesthood and Church Government*, pp. 1–25. Salt Lake City, 1939.

VICTOR L. LUDLOW

PRIESTHOOD BLESSINGS

Priesthood blessings are pronounced in connection with most of the essential ORDINANCES of the gospel: blessing and naming children; CONFIRMATION; ORDINATION TO THE PRIESTHOOD; SETTING APART; and other occasions. In addition, any person may request a blessing at the hands of a worthy Melchizedek Priesthood bearer at any time. The person who does so is usually seeking inspired counsel and asking for official prayer and blessing under the hands of one who is authorized and discerning.

In The Church of Jesus Christ of Latter-day Saints, the PRIESTHOOD is not a centralized elite. Ideally, the priesthood is held by every husband and father. The home is viewed as his constant and most important ministry, regardless of the offices he may hold in the Church. One who seeks a priesthood blessing is encouraged to approach father or brother, BISHOP or HOME TEACHERS rather than prominent Church authorities. In principle and in practice, this recognizes the diversity of spiritual gifts, the individual heritage of faith, and the shared sanctity of priesthood service.

Priesthood blessings are usually conferred by LAYING ON OF HANDS, which is seen as the New Testament pattern. Exceptions are found in administering the SACRAMENT and in apostolic blessings given to a congregation (see *HC* 2:120; 5:473).

All priesthood blessings are given in the name of Jesus Christ and by authority of the MELCHIZEDEK PRIESTHOOD (so named to avoid the too frequent repetition of its sacred title [D&C 107:4]). The blessing process may vary according to circumstance and individual need: e.g., the extent of preparation, the use of consecrated OIL, involvement of other persons as participants or witnesses, recording or writing the blessing (often the counsel is to "write it in your heart"), and whether and when further blessings may be appropriate. Blessings given by a father to his wife are known as husband's blessings, to his children as father's blessings; those given by a PATRIARCH, as PATRIARCHAL BLESSINGS; when related to a personal crisis or need, as comfort blessings; those given in response to illness or injury, as administration to the sick.

Priesthood blessings are to be "spoken with care, and by constraint of the Spirit" (D&C 63:64). To refuse to give a blessing when one is called or to attempt to give a blessing when one is unworthy is to "trifle with [sacred] things" (D&C 8:10).

In giving blessings, priesthood bearers are constantly admonished to seek the Spirit. The Prophet Joseph SMITH taught, "The Holy Ghost is God's messenger to administer in all those priesthoods" (TPJS, p. 323). The officiator strives for the promptings and impressions of the HOLY GHOST, and these may not be what he anticipated or planned. By fasting and prayer, by experience in the things of God, and by patience, he learns to distinguish authentic inspiration from subjective factors that distort or mislead. He strives during the blessing to use appropriate language to express the ideas that impress his mind by the Spirit. The process is often strenuous: Jesus felt virtue go out of him at the touch of the woman of faith (Mark 5:25–34). Similarly, one who seeks to serve in blessing others "is liable to become weakened" (TPJS, p. 281).

Recipients are charged to unite their faith in God and Christ with the faith of others present, and to bring contrite and teachable hearts. Concentration and communion are required for both receiving and understanding blessings. As blessings are pronounced, the recipients are to take to heart the counsel offered, and adjust their lives accordingly. In cases where the recipients are unconscious, infirm, or out of touch, the main burden of faith is upon the person pronouncing the blessing, and other concerned persons present.

The efficacy of priesthood blessings is not presumed to be automatic or formulaic, or simply a matter of saying the right words. Priesthood authority does not entitle one to act independently of God, but rather bestows the right to seek the mind and will of God and then to transmit it through the priesthood blessing. Neither can a blessing be given with intent to infringe on the recipient's own agency but "only by persuasion, by long-suffering, by gentleness and meekness, and by love unfeigned" (D&C 121:41). These are called "the principles of righteousness" (D&C 121:36). Unless they are complied with, the blessing "is of no use, but withdraws" (TPJS, p. 148).

Latter-day Saints cherish priesthood blessings as a vital source of grace in facing the crossroads, crises, setbacks, anxieties, and decisions of life. Those who give and receive blessings at the hands of the priesthood in this spirit are lifted up and sustained, and healed in mind, body, and spirit.

BIBLIOGRAPHY

"Performing Priesthood Blessings and Ordinances." Melchizedek Priesthood Personal Study Guide, 1988, pp. 151–55.

J. ELLIOT CAMERON

PRIESTHOOD COUNCILS

The concept of a council in The Church of Jesus Christ of Latter-day Saints embodies both a philosophy of administrative behavior and an organizational body or unit. There are formally constituted councils, such as the Council of Twelve Apostles (see QUORUM OF THE TWELVE APOSTLES), stake HIGH COUNCILS, and councils consisting of PRIESTHOOD QUORUM and AUXILIARY OFFICERS who work together as WARD COUNCILS or stake councils. To these latter councils concerned representatives (athletic, single adult, etc.) are sometimes added. Church councils coordinate and schedule activities, gather information, plan future programs or events, and make decisions and resolve problems for their units.

At the most basic level of organization—the FAMILY—a family council ideally exemplifies both the spirit and function of the whole concept of Church councils. In a family council, family members meet regularly to discuss plans, decisions, and problems that affect them individually and as a whole. Family councils reinforce shared commitment to the well-being of each individual and effective management of group activities.

The philosophy of a council is what sociologist Thomas O'Dea called a "democracy of participation" in Mormon culture (The Mormons [Chicago, 1964], p. 165). At periodic council meetings both individual and organizational needs are considered. Recognizing the unique circumstances surrounding a particular unit, geographical area, or set of individuals, the council identifies the programs and activities that need to be planned and correlated. (The council does not have final decision-making power; this resides with the unit leader, such as the STAKE PRESIDENT or BISHOP.)

Councils are more than operational coordinating mechanisms. They also serve as vehicles for family, WARD, STAKE, REGION, AREA, or general Church teaching and development. As members participate in councils, they learn about larger organizational issues. They see leadership in action, learning how to plan, analyze problems, make de-

Council room in the Salt Lake Temple where the First Presidency and the Quorum of the Twelve Apostles and other General Authorities meet each Thursday.

cisions, and coordinate across subunit boundaries. Participation in councils helps prepare members for future leadership responsibilities.

Church councils are also convened for DISCIPLINARY PROCEDURES. Such councils, which may be held at the ward, stake, or general Church level, consider serious infractions where individuals may need institutional help in the REPENTANCE process beyond the personal counseling of a leader or where excommunication or other disciplinary action may be necessary. Individual circumstances are considered by the council and the final decision is made by the bishop or president, with council ratification. Disciplinary councils are set up to protect both the individual and the Church by assigning council members to represent the interests of both parties (D&C 102:15).

J. BONNER RITCHIE

PRIESTHOOD EXECUTIVE COMMITTEE, STAKE AND WARD

The WARD priesthood executive committee (PEC) consists of the leaders of key ward organizations. The PEC generally meets weekly under the direction of the BISHOP and his counselors to direct and coordinate ward PRIESTHOOD programs that have been designed to promote the spiritual and temporal welfare of each individual and family in the ward. This committee includes leaders of MELCHIZEDEK PRIESTHOOD quorums, who administer welfare (physical and material well-being), temple, missionary, and family history (genealogy) activities, and leaders responsible for youth priesthood programs. A ward executive secretary prepares each meeting's agenda, and the ward clerk records its minutes. The PEC also coordinates ward efforts to activate its members not regularly participating in the Church.

The PEC thus provides a forum for ward priesthood officers to foster the well-being of ward members; discuss applications of Church policy; participate in and sponsor leadership training; and report their stewardship concerns to the bishop, including problems discovered through monthly home teaching visits to congregation members.

The STAKE PRESIDENCY and HIGH COUNCIL compose the Stake Priesthood Executive Committee. They oversee the administration of all Church programs in the stake; consider issues that affect all wards in the stake; and approve nominations of members to be called for service in ward BISHOPRICS, stake priesthood quorums, and stake AUXILIARY ORGANIZATIONS. The stake PEC usually meets twice a month. The stake president presides and conducts. The stake executive secretary and stake clerk assist the stake presidency with the agenda and minutes of the meeting. Both the ward and stake priesthood executive committees are augmented periodically by leaders of the PRIMARY, YOUNG WOMEN, and RELIEF SOCIETY organizations to form two additional councils.

[*See also* Home Teaching; Ward Council.]

DAVID C. BRADFORD

PRIESTHOOD INTERVIEW

The Church has developed a system of regularly scheduled priesthood interviews for effective overseeing of delegated responsibilities. Commonly used in HOME TEACHING accountability (referred to as Home Teaching Interviews) and in other Church programs, these private meetings between a priesthood leader and a member who reports to him are designed to increase communication, resolve concerns, maintain accountability, build spirituality, and empower members to fulfill their responsibilities.

The interview typically begins with a prayer about the issues at hand, and the first few minutes are spent following up on assignments generated during the previous session. When assignments have not been completed, plans are made to ensure completion before the next meeting. Although the format for the remainder of the interview varies to fit the needs and circumstances, it might include the following: discussion and resolution of administrative or organizational problems; training in administrative and management skills; resolution of interpersonal problems; sharing information on what is happening in the organization, including success experiences; identification of individual and organizational needs; and discussion of personal problems as appropriate. The last matter on the agenda of a priesthood interview is often a review of new assignments generated during the meeting, ensuring mutual understanding and verifying the accuracy of the notes recorded.

The priesthood interview is widely used as an administrative procedure between levels of Church organization and assists Church leaders to "organize [themselves] and appoint every man his stewardship; that every man may give an account . . . of the stewardship which is appointed unto him" (D&C 104:11–12). Interviews are often scheduled on a monthly or quarterly basis at the initiative of the priesthood leader.

Research shows that applying the principles of interviews to secular organizations in the private and public sectors can produce a number of benefits. Employed by either religious or nonreligious organizations, such interviews can increase the quantity and quality of communication, build higher levels of trust, improve the organizational climate and group effectiveness, and prevent regression that normally follows team-building meetings. Managers also report that regular interviews consistently save them time by reducing unscheduled interruptions.

BIBLIOGRAPHY

Boss, R. Wayne. "Team Building and the Problem of Regression: The Personal Management Interview as an Intervention." *Journal of Applied Behavioral Science* 19 (1983):67–83.

———. "Just Between You and the Boss." *Training and Development Journal* 39 (Nov. 1985):68–71.

Faust, James E. "These I Will Make My Leaders." *Ensign* 10 (Nov. 1980):34–37.

R. WAYNE BOSS

PRIESTHOOD OFFICES

Priesthood offices are appointments or CALLINGS in The Church of Jesus Christ of Latter-day Saints to serve in specified areas of PRIESTHOOD responsibility. Each priesthood office includes a specific set of rights and duties, in addition to responsibilities shared by all bearers of the priesthood. These offices provide needed service to the Church and its members and give priesthood bearers opportunities to learn and serve. Both are important in a church operated by LAY PARTICIPATION and LEADERSHIP.

All priesthood offices derive their AUTHORITY from the priesthood itself, which is greater than any of those offices. Hence, ORDINATION to an office does not increase an individual's authority or power, but rather focuses the individual's service in particular functions. When a person receives the priesthood by the LAYING-ON OF HANDS, he first has the priesthood *conferred* upon him, after which he is *ordained* to a specific office in the priesthood.

The four offices in the AARONIC PRIESTHOOD are DEACON, TEACHER, PRIEST, and BISHOP. The offices in the MELCHIZEDEK PRIESTHOOD include ELDER, HIGH PRIEST, PATRIARCH, SEVENTY, and APOSTLE. The general title "elder" is applied to all bearers of the Melchizedek Priesthood.

Hierarchy of priesthood authority is associated more with presiding PRIESTHOOD QUORUMS and presidencies and less with the offices of the Melchizedek Priesthood themselves. For example, although an elder and an apostle have different rights and responsibilities, they both hold the same priesthood (cf. 1 Pet. 5:1, in which the apostle Peter refers to himself as an elder).

Scriptural records show that priesthood offices were established in ancient as well as modern times, although it is not known in some cases what duties these officers had in earlier dispensations. MELCHIZEDEK was ordained to the office of high priest (JST Gen. 14:26–27; JST Heb. 7:3; Alma 13:14–18; D&C 84:14). MOSES consecrated AARON and his sons to minister "in the priest's office" (Ex. 28:1, 41). Elders and seventies officiated in ancient Israel (Ex. 24:9–11; Num. 11:16). The Book of Mormon indicates that teachers, priests, and elders were ordained among the NEPHITES, and that a high priest presided over the Church (Mosiah 23:16–18; Alma 4:7; 5:3). The New Testament records that Church organization included priesthood offices such as apostles, teachers, seventies, bishops, deacons, priests, and high priests (Luke 10:1, 17; Eph. 4:11–16; 1 Tim. 3:1–13; *see* ORGANIZATION OF THE CHURCH IN NEW TESTAMENT TIMES).

Following the RESTORATION of priesthood authority in modern times, Joseph SMITH and Oliver COWDERY were ordained elders on April 6, 1830 (*HC* 1:60–61, 75–78). Other ordained offices were instituted as the growth and needs of the Church required. The first ordinations to the offices of bishop and high priest took place in 1831 (D&C 41:9; *HC* 1:176). The first apostles and seventies were called in 1835 (*HC* 2:187, 201–02). In the Aaronic Priesthood, the first priests and teachers were ordained in 1830, and the first deacons in 1831. (*See* ORGANIZATION: ORGANIZATIONAL AND ADMINISTRATIVE HISTORY.)

All priesthood bearers belong to a quorum corresponding to their priesthood office, either within local WARDS and STAKES (deacons quorum, high priests quorum, etc.) or in the general Church ORGANIZATION (the QUORUM OF THE TWELVE APOSTLES, etc.).

In addition to ordained priesthood offices, administrative positions in the priesthood, such as the presidency of a quorum, are sometimes referred to as offices. In this sense, the members of the FIRST PRESIDENCY, who preside over the entire Church, are sometimes spoken of as PRESIDING HIGH PRIESTS. Individuals are installed in these offices by SETTING APART rather than by ordination. Such a setting apart bestows upon the individual the rights and blessings pertaining to the leadership of that quorum.

BIBLIOGRAPHY

Lowrie, Walter. *The Church and Its Organization in Primitive and Catholic Times: An Interpretation of Rudolph Sohm's Kirchenrecht.* New York, 1904.

Palmer, Lee A. *The Aaronic Priesthood Through the Centuries.* Salt Lake City, 1964.

Widtsoe, John A. *Priesthood and Church Government.* Salt Lake City, 1939.

BRUCE T. HARPER

PRIESTHOOD QUORUMS

All bearers of any given priesthood office in The Church of Jesus Christ of Latter-day Saints are organized into priesthood quorums. A male member is ordained to a specific priesthood office when he receives the priesthood and may subsequently be ordained to other offices as he grows older and receives new Church callings.

STRUCTURE AND PURPOSE. In WARDS and BRANCHES where there are sufficient AARONIC PRIESTHOOD bearers, the young men twelve to eighteen are organized into three quorums: DEACONS (ages twelve to fourteen), TEACHERS (ages fourteen to sixteen), and PRIESTS (ages sixteen to eighteen). All MELCHIZEDEK PRIESTHOOD bearers residing in a ward or branch who hold the office of ELDER are organized into an elders quorum. The maximum number of members for each of these quorums is set by revelation: twelve deacons, twenty-four teachers, forty-eight priests, and ninety-six elders (D&C 107:85–89). All Melchizedek Priesthood bearers living within a stake who hold the office of HIGH PRIEST are members of the high priests' quorum of that stake, which is presided over by the stake presidency. The high priests' quorum is divided into high priests' groups at the ward level. In most parts of the world, priesthood quorums and groups meet every Sunday.

The BISHOP is president of the Aaronic Priesthood in his ward. He also is president of the priests' quorum; two priests serve as assistants and one as a secretary. The bishop's first and second counselors in the BISHOPRIC oversee the activities of the teachers and deacons quorums, respectively. Each of these quorums has a president, two counselors, and a secretary, who are members of the quorum. Adult men, called to serve as quorum advisers, guide and help the Aaronic Priesthood quorum presidencies and members. Advisers do not preside over the quorums; they assist the presidencies in building a properly functioning priesthood quorum. In addition, advisers are expected to watch over and teach quorum members, build quorum leadership, and fellowship young men of quorum age.

Melchizedek Priesthood quorums and groups are responsible to assist quorum members, their families, and single women members in their temporal and spiritual needs. The purposes of priesthood quorum and group meetings at the local level are to conduct priesthood business, teach members their duties, study the gospel, and encourage members to use their priesthood to serve and bless others. They also provide opportunities for per-

The leading priesthood quorums of the Church are the First Presidency and the Quorum of the Twelve Apostles (shown here as of 1934). First Presidency: J. Reuben Clark, Jr., President Heber J. Grant, David O. McKay. Apostles: (second row) Rudger Clawson, Reed Smoot, George Albert Smith, George F. Richards, (third row) Joseph Fielding Smith, Stephen L Richards, Richard R. Lyman, Melvin J. Ballard, (fourth row) John A. Widtsoe, Joseph F. Merrill, Charles A. Callis, Alonzo A. Hinckley.

sonal growth and leadership experiences; most members are called to serve in quorum or group leadership positions from time to time. Quorum presidencies are responsible for planning and conducting quorum meetings and activities, teaching quorum members their duties, and extending fellowship and support to each quorum member (*see* LAY PARTICIPATION AND LEADERSHIP).

Three other priesthood quorums preside over the entire Church. The highest is the Quorum of the FIRST PRESIDENCY, composed of the PRESIDENT OF THE CHURCH and his counselors. The second is the QUORUM OF THE TWELVE APOSTLES, composed of twelve APOSTLES, or special witnesses, who form a quorum "equal in authority and power" to the Presidency (D&C 107:23–24); however, that power is exercised fully only with the dissolution of the First Presidency, which occurs upon the death of the President. The third quorum of priesthood bearers who have Churchwide responsibilities and authority is the SEVENTY. Seventies are organized into quorums that do not exceed seventy members each.

ORIGINS OF QUORUM ORGANIZATION. Shortly after being chosen and ordained, the Twelve Apostles gathered in Kirtland, Ohio, on March 28, 1835, before departing to the eastern states on missions. They asked the Prophet Joseph SMITH to inquire of the Lord concerning their duties. In response, the Lord gave an important revelation on the priesthood and the relationship of the respective quorums to each other and to the Church (*see* DOCTRINE AND COVENANTS: SECTION 107).

As years passed and circumstances changed, the need arose for a reorganization of the priesthood. In 1877, Brigham Young effected such a reorganization (Hartley, 1979). Some of the main results of this historic action included (1) moving members of the Quorum of the Twelve Apostles out of stake presidencies into full-time service as General Authorities; (2) making stakes independent of one another and placing them under their own locally supervised priesthood quorums; (3) modifying the role of then-existing seventies quorums; (4) filling up elders quorums; and (5) filling Aaronic Priesthood quorums with youth. Later (1908–1922), under the direction of presidents Joseph F. SMITH and Heber J. Grant, a specially appointed General Priesthood Committee instituted Churchwide priesthood changes and reorganization that eventually led to the present system (Hartley, 1973).

BIBLIOGRAPHY

Backman, Milton V., Jr. "Church Policies, Programs, and Administration." In *The Heavens Resound: A History of the Latter-day Saints in Ohio, 1830–1838*, pp. 237–61. Salt Lake City, 1983.

Hartley, William. "The Priesthood Reform Movement, 1908–1922." *BYU Studies* 13 (Winter 1973):137–56.

———. "The Priesthood Reorganization of 1877: Brigham Young's Last Achievement." *BYU Studies* 20 (Fall 1979):3–36.

Roberts, B. H. *CHC* 1:371–86.

SHERMAN N. TINGEY

PRIMARY

The Primary is an organized program of religious instruction and activity in The Church of Jesus Christ of Latter-day Saints for children from eighteen months of age until their twelfth birthdays. Its purpose is to teach children the gospel of Jesus Christ and help them learn to live it.

ORIGINS. In the summer of 1878, Aurelia Spencer ROGERS, a Farmington, Utah, mother, who felt the need for a united effort to help parents teach their children the gospel, voiced her concerns to Eliza R. SNOW, president of the RELIEF SOCIETY of the Church: "Could there not be an organization for little boys, and have them trained to make better men?" (Rogers, p. 208). Sister Snow presented the matter to President John TAYLOR, and he authorized establishment of the organization.

Under the direction of local Church leaders, the first Primary was organized on August 11, 1878, with Aurelia Rogers as president. On August 25, the first Primary meeting was held in Farmington, where 224 boys and girls met to be taught obedience, faith in God, prayer, punctuality, and good manners. The girls were included to make the singing "sound as well as it should" (Rogers, p. 209).

EARLY PRIMARIES. Within a short time, more Primaries were organized throughout the territory. By the mid-1880s, a Primary group had been organized in nearly every LDS settlement. The women of the Church were given the responsibility to organize and administer the Primary program. The bulk of the weekly program was devoted to songs, poems, and activities presented by children. Primary general officers did not take a controlling leadership role until the 1890s, and curricular materials were few, although most Pri-

The general officers of the Primary, 1896–1905. Louie B. Felt, president (center); Aurelia S. Rogers (standing, left); May Anderson, secretary (standing, right); Lillie T. Freeze, first vice president (front, left); Josephine R. West, second vice president (front, right).

maries used a hymnbook, a tune book, and a catechism of Old and New Testament questions and answers prepared by Eliza R. Snow in 1881. In many localities, children remained in Primary through their early teens and often served as Primary secretaries.

1890–1939. During this period, Primary general officers assumed the leading role in Primary development. Louie B. Felt (1880–1925), the first Primary general president, and her counselor and successor, May Anderson (1925–1939), sought professional training in education. Exposed to the ideas of progressive education, they initiated curriculum development and teacher training. General officers encouraged local Primaries to establish age-graded classes with lessons appropriate to the children's development. They began publication of the CHILDREN'S FRIEND (1902), at first with lessons and instructions for leaders and, within a few years, with stories, handiwork, and music for children. In 1913 the Primary established a children's ward in the Grove's Latter-day Saint Hospital in

Salt Lake City, the first in a series of Primary efforts to provide pediatric hospital care. When religion classes, instituted in 1890 for weekday religious instruction for children, were discontinued in 1929, the Primary assumed greater responsibility for children's spiritual education. Lessons were scheduled three weeks each month, and activities were reduced to one per month, except during the summer program. Stake boards held monthly training meetings for ward leaders; general board members visited regularly.

1940–1974. Spiritual education remained the focus of Primary programs under presidents May Green Hinckley (1940–1943) and Adele Cannon Howells (1943–1951). Mission lessons were written for the growing number of Primaries in Church missions throughout the world and, during World War II, for the hundreds of home and neighborhood Primaries developed because of wartime travel restrictions. Under President LaVern Watts PARMLEY (1951–1974), the Primary lessons were made applicable to all units in the growing

Louie B. Felt (1850–1928), first general president of the Church organization for children, the Primary Association. She was sustained in 1880 and served for forty-five years. She initiated the *Children's Friend* magazine in January 1902, established a hospital fund in 1911, and oversaw the construction of a hospital for children in 1922. Courtesy Utah State Historical Society.

Church, including mission Primaries. When a comprehensive Church correlation program was begun in the 1960s, responsibility for Primary lesson materials was transferred to priesthood leaders and professional departments.

The Primary Children's Hospital, authorized by Church leaders in 1949, was completed in 1952, and President Parmley became the first chair of the hospital's board of trustees (*see* HOSPITALS). While the majority of patients were from the intermountain region, others came from many areas of the world. Children of all races and creeds were welcomed. Patients' families usually paid for their medical costs, but charitable funds assisted many. The hospital, transferred to private ownership in

1975, made possible some of the most important contributions that the Primary has made to the lives of individual children.

In 1952 the Primary was given responsibility for Cub Scouting for LDS boys eight, nine, and ten years of age and Boy Scouting for eleven-year-old boys. Since that time, a close working relationship has existed between the Primary and the Boy Scouts of America. Primary is also involved with Scouts in Canada, throughout the United Kingdom, and in New Zealand.

Until 1952, women could serve only as den mothers in Cub Scouting. That year the Primary obtained permission from the National Scout Committee for women to serve as leaders of the eleven-year-old Scouts. Since then, women have become registered Scouters and serve on local and national boards.

1974–1990.   With the growth of a more geographically widespread Church, annual general conferences of Church auxiliaries were discontinued in 1975. Under presidents Naomi M. Shumway (1974–1980), Dwan J. Young (1980–1988), and Michaelene P. Grassli (1988–), communication with local leaders continued through materials prepared for regional conferences, a *Primary Handbook*, information published in the BULLETIN, and periodic visits to regional training sessions. Responsibility for planning lesson concepts for Primary manuals was returned to the Primary General Board in 1977.

In the consolidated Sunday meeting schedule (1980), Primary meetings were moved from midweek to Sunday, junior Sunday Schools were discontinued, and Primary was given responsibility for all formal religious classroom instruction of children in the Church. With that change, callings to teach in the Primary began to be extended to men as well as women, although only women serve in Primary presidencies. Weekday activities involving all Primary children were reduced to four per year, and spiritual education was further emphasized. Children were encouraged to read the scriptures regularly, and Primary lessons taught gospel principles from their scriptural foundations. Music and activities culminating in the yearly children's sacrament meeting presentation (e.g., "The Book of Mormon—A Witness of Jesus Christ," 1988; "I Am a Child of God," 1989; and "I Belong to The Church of Jesus Christ of Latter-day Saints," 1990) focused on scriptures and gospel principles.

This group from the South Davis Stake, located a few miles north of Salt Lake City, were Trail Builders, the forerunners of today's Valiant B and Blazer classes, Primary boys of ages nine through eleven (photo, c. 1940).

CURRENT STRUCTURE. As of 1990, Primaries serve over a million and a half children with lessons taught in many languages. Primary meetings are held each Sunday for approximately an hour and a half. A nursery program is provided for children between eighteen months and three years of age. Children between the ages of three and eleven meet as a group under the direction of the ward Primary presidency. The children offer prayers, read from the scriptures, and give short gospel-related talks. They learn gospel principles through role playing, readers' theaters, choral readings, buzz sessions, panel discussions, and other activities. They also learn and sing music selected from a children's songbook.

The children divide according to age for small group classroom sessions. Age-appropriate lesson materials are selected to help children grow in understanding gospel principles; learn that the Heavenly Father and Jesus love them; and prepare to be baptized, receive the HOLY GHOST, and keep their BAPTISMAL COVENANTS. Classroom presentations and discussions help girls prepare to fulfill their roles as righteous young women and to live lives of service. Classes help boys prepare to receive the PRIESTHOOD and be worthy to use this power to bless the lives of others.

In addition to Sunday Primary meetings, twice-a-month weekday activities are held for ten-

and eleven-year-old boys and girls. In some countries, eleven-year-old boys use Scouting activities for their weekday activities. A quarterly activity is

The Primary Children's Hospital in Salt Lake City was completed in 1953, and its size was doubled in 1966. Construction of the hospital culminated a series of Primary efforts to provide pediatric hospital care begun in 1913. Annual "Penny Days" and contributions by Primary children on their birthdays supported charity care at the facility. The Church transferred ownership of its hospitals to a private nonprofit organization in 1975. Courtesy University of Utah Libraries.

Children in the Trollhätten, Sweden, Primary (1990). Singing time is a standard part of Primary meetings. Songs are usually selected from the *Children's Songbook* or the Church hymnal. While most have gospel themes, some are just for fun. Courtesy Peggy Jellinghausen.

held for all Primary children. The weekday and quarterly activities encourage children to interact with each other and have wholesome fun involving them in physical, creative, cultural, and service activities.

Children with disabilities are nurtured in Primary and are given opportunity to participate in the full program. Leaders assess their needs individually and tailor programs to meet specific needs. They are integrated into the regular program whenever possible by giving additional support and training to their teachers, leaders, and peers.

Church leaders call and set apart lay officers and teachers to oversee the Primary; and Primary general officers and Church curriculum committees prepare handbooks, teaching guides, visual aids, lesson manuals, and a variety of training videos for their use. Monthly in-service lessons help teachers improve their teaching skills and relate appropriately to children. Periodically, the Primary general presidency and board members conduct multistake or regional training sessions. Leaders and teachers seek and receive inspiration in their Primary service.

Michaelene P. Grassli served as second counselor in the general presidency of the Primary from 1980 until she was sustained as president in 1988.

The Primary's mission, the impetus for its historical development, and the purpose for its current structure are summarized in the scripture that has become the Primary's theme: "All thy children shall be taught of the Lord; and great shall be the peace of thy children" (3 Ne. 22:13).

[*See also* Auxiliary Organizations; Children, Roles of.]

BIBLIOGRAPHY

Madsen, Carol Cornwall, and Susan Staker Oman. *Sisters and Little Saints*. Salt Lake City, 1979.

Primary Handbook. Salt Lake City, 1985.

Rogers, Aurelia A. *Life Sketches*. Salt Lake City, 1898.

NAOMI M. SHUMWAY

PROBATION

See: Disciplinary Procedures

PROCLAMATIONS OF THE FIRST PRESIDENCY AND THE QUORUM OF THE TWELVE APOSTLES

In performance of their calling as apostles, prophets, seers, revelators, and spokesmen for The Church of Jesus Christ of Latter-day Saints, the First Presidency and the Quorum of the Twelve Apostles have from time to time issued formal written proclamations, declarations, letters, and various public announcements. These have been addressed sometimes to the members of the Church (as a type of general epistle) and sometimes to the public at large. All such declarations have been solemn and sacred in nature and were issued with the intent to bring forth, build up, and regulate the affairs of the Church as the kingdom of God on the earth. Subject matter has included instruction on doctrine, faith, and history; warnings of judgments to come; invitations to assist in the work; and statements of Church growth and progress.

Only a few of the many formal declarations have been labeled "Proclamations." Others have been characterized "Official Declarations," "Doctrinal Expositions," or "Epistles." Some have the signature of the First Presidency, some of the First Presidency and the Twelve, and some of the Twelve only. This article considers four documents: (1) Proclamation of the First Presidency on January 15, 1841, at Nauvoo, Illinois; (2) Proclamation of the Twelve Apostles on April 6, 1845, in New York City, and on October 22, 1845, in Liverpool, England; (3) Proclamation of the First Presidency and the Twelve Apostles on October 21, 1865, in Salt Lake City, Utah; and (4) Proclamation from the First Presidency and the Quorum of the Twelve Apostles, April 6, 1980, issued from Fayette, New York.

1. A Proclamation of the First Presidency of the Church to the Saints Scattered Abroad (January 15, 1841, Nauvoo, Illinois)

[*This document, signed by Joseph Smith, Sidney Rigdon, and Hyrum Smith, reviews the progress of the Church in spite of hardships and persecution, and speaks at length on the prospects of the settlement of Nauvoo, as the following excerpts illustrate.*]

BELOVED BRETHREN:—The relationship which we sustain to The Church of Jesus Christ of Latter-day Saints, renders it necessary that we should make known from time to time, the circumstances, situation, and prospects of the Church, and give such instructions as may be necessary for the well being of the Saints, and for the promotion of those objects calculated to further their present and everlasting happiness.

We have to congratulate the Saints on the progress of the great work of the "last days," for not only has it spread through the length and breadth of this vast continent, but on the continent of Europe, and on the islands of the sea, it is spreading in a manner entirely unprecedented in the annals of time. This appears the more pleasing when we consider, that but a short time has elapsed since we were unmercifully driven from the state of Missouri, after suffering cruelties and persecutions in various and horrid forms. . . .

It would be impossible to enumerate all those who, in our time of deep distress, nobly came forward to our relief, and, like the good Samaritan, poured oil into our wounds, and contributed liberally to our necessities, and the citizens of Quincy *en masse*, and the people of Illinois, generally, seemed to emulate each other in this labor of love. . . .

We would likewise make mention of the legislators of this state, who, without respect to parties, without reluctance, freely, openly, boldly, and nobly, have come forth to our assistance, owned us as citizens and friends, and took us by the hand, and extended to us all the blessings of civil, political, and religious liberty, by granting us, under date of December 16, 1840, one of the most liberal charters, with the most plenary powers ever conferred by a legislative assembly on free citizens, "The City of Nauvoo," the "Nauvoo Legion," and the "University of the City of Nauvoo." . . .

The name of our city (Nauvoo) is of Hebrew origin, and signifies a beautiful situation, or place, carrying with it, also, the idea of rest; and is truly descriptive of the most delightful location. It is situated on the east back of the Mississippi river, at the head of the Des Moines rapids, in Hancock county, bounded on the east by an extensive prairie of surpassing beauty, and on the north, west, and south, by the Mississippi. . . .

Having been instrumental, in the hands of our heavenly Father, in laying a foundation for the gathering of Zion, we would say, let all those who appreciate the blessings of the Gospel, and realize the importance of obeying the commandments of heaven, who have been blessed with the possession of this world's goods, first prepare for the general gathering; let them dispose of their effects as fast as circumstances will possibly admit, without making too great sacrifices, and remove to our city and county; establish and build up manufactures in the city, purchase and cultivate farms in the county. This will secure our permanent inheritance, and prepare the way for the gathering of the poor. This is agreeable to the order of heaven, and the only principle on which the gathering can be effected. Let the rich, then, and all who can assist in establishing this place, make every preparation to come on without delay, and strengthen our hands, and assist in promoting the happiness of the Saints. . . .

The Temple of the Lord is in process of erection here, where the Saints will come to worship the God of their fathers, according to the order of His house and the power of the Holy Priesthood, and will be so constructed as to enable all the functions of the Priesthood to be duly exercised, and where instructions from the Most High will be received, and from this place go forth to distant lands. Let us then concentrate all our powers, under the provisions of our *magna charta* granted by the Illinois legislature, at the "City of Nauvoo" and surrounding country, and strive to emulate the action of the ancient covenant fathers and patriarchs, in those things which are of such vast importance to this and every succeeding generation. . . .

The greatest temporal and spiritual blessings which always flow from faithfulness and concerted effort, never attended individual exertion or enterprise. The history of all past ages abundantly attests this fact. In addition to all temporal blessings, there is no other way for the Saints to be saved in these last days [than by the gathering], as the concurrent testimony of all the holy Prophets clearly proves, for it is written—"They shall come from the east, and be gathered from the west; the north shall give up, and the south shall keep not back." "The sons of God shall be gathered from far, and His daughters from the ends of the earth."

It is also the concurrent testimony of all the Prophets, that this gathering together of all the Saints, must take place before the Lord comes to "take vengeance upon the ungodly," and to be glorified and admired by all those who obey the Gospel." The fiftieth Psalm, from the first to the fifth verse inclusive, describes the glory and majesty of that event.

The mighty God, and even the Lord hath spoken, and called the earth from the rising of the sun unto the going down thereof. Out of Zion, the perfection of beauty, God hath shined. Our God shall come and shall not keep silence; a fire shall devour before Him, and it shall be very tempestuous round about Him. He shall call to the heavens from above, and to the earth (that He may judge the people). Gather my Saints together unto me; those that have made covenant with me by sacrifice.

We might offer many other quotations from the Scriptures, but believing them to be familiar to the Saints, we forbear.

We would wish the Saints to understand that, when they come here, they must not expect perfection, or that all will be harmony, peace, and love; if they indulge these ideas, they will undoubtedly be deceived, for here there are persons, not only from different states, but from different nations, who, although they feel a great attachment to the cause of truth, have their prejudices of education, and, consequently, it requires some time before these things can be overcome. . . . Therefore, let those who come up to this place be determined to keep the commandments of God, and not be discouraged by those things we have enumerated, and then they will be prospered—the intelligence of heaven will be communicated to them, and they will eventually, see eye to eye, and rejoice in the full fruition of that glory which is reserved for the righteous.

In order to erect the Temple of the Lord, great exertions will be required on the part of the Saints, so that they may build a house which shall be accepted by the Almighty, in which His power and glory shall be manifested. Therefore let those who can freely make a sacrifice of their time, their talents, and their property, for the prosperity of the kingdom, and for the love they have to the cause of truth, bid adieu to their homes and pleasant places of abode, and unite with us in the great work of the last days, and share in the tribulation, that they may ultimately share in the glory and triumph.

We wish it likewise to be distinctly understood, that we claim no privilege but what we feel cheerfully disposed to share with our fellow citizens of every denomination, and every sentiment of religion; and therefore say, that so far from being restricted to our own faith, let all those who desire to locate themselves in this place, or the vicinity, come, and we will hail them as citizens and friends, and shall feel it not only a duty, but a privilege, to reciprocate the kindness we have received from the benevolent and kind-hearted citizens of the state of Illinois.

Joseph Smith,
Sidney Rigdon,
Hyrum Smith,
Presidents of the Church
[*HC* 4:267–73].

2. Proclamation of the Twelve Apostles of The Church of Jesus Christ of Latter-day Saints (April 6 and October 22, 1845)

[*The Proclamation of 1845 was issued by the Twelve only, because at that time there was no First Presidency due to the martyrdom of the Prophet Joseph Smith on June 27, 1844, and a new First Presidency was not organized until December 1847. The Proclamation was apparently made in response to a revelation given January 19, 1841 (D&C 124:1–11). It was first printed in a sixteen-page pamphlet in New York City on April 6, 1845, and again in Liverpool, England, October 22, 1845. It was addressed to the rulers and people of all nations. This document was an announcement that God had spoken from the heavens and had restored the gospel of Jesus Christ to the earth. It spoke of blessings and of punishments to come, issued a warning voice, and invited all who were interested to assist in the building of the kingdom of God on the earth in preparation for the Savior's second coming. On October 3, 1975, President Ezra Taft Benson, president of the Quorum of the Twelve Apostles, spoke of this Proclamation and quoted portions of it in his general conference address (Ensign 15 [Oct. 1975]:32–34).*

Extracts from the 1845 Proclamation follow.]

TO ALL THE KINGS OF THE WORLD, TO THE PRESIDENT OF THE UNITED STATES OF AMERICA; TO THE GOVERNORS OF THE SEVERAL STATES, AND TO THE RULERS AND PEOPLE OF ALL NATIONS.

Greeting.

Know ye that the kingdom of God has come, as has been predicted by ancient prophets, and prayed for in all ages; even that kingdom which shall fill the whole earth, and shall stand for ever. . . .

Therefore we send unto you, with authority from on high, and command you all to repent and humble yourselves as little children before the majesty of the Holy One; and come unto Jesus with a broken heart and a contrite spirit, and be baptized in his name for the remission of sins (that is, be buried in the water, in the likeness of his burial, and rise again to newness of life in the likeness of his resurrection), and you shall receive the gift of the Holy Spirit, through the laying on of the hands of the apostles and elders, of this great and last dispensation of mercy to man.

This Spirit shall bear witness to you of the truth of our testimony, and shall enlighten your minds, and be in you as the spirit of prophecy and revelation; it shall bring things past to your understanding and remembrance, and shall show you things to come. . . .

By the light of this Spirit, received through the ministration of the ordinances—by the power and authority of the Holy Apostleship and Priesthood, you will be enabled to understand, and to be the children of light; and thus be prepared to escape all the things that are coming on the earth, and so stand before the Son of Man.

We testify that the foregoing doctrine is the doctrine or gospel of Jesus Christ in its fulness; and that it is the only true, everlasting, and unchangeable gospel; and the only plan revealed on earth whereby man can be saved. . . .

And we further testify that the Lord has appointed a holy city and temple to be built on this continent, for the endowment and ordinances pertaining to the priesthood; and for the Gentiles, and the remnant of Israel to resort unto, in order to worship the Lord, and to be taught in his ways and walk in his paths; in short, to finish their preparations for the coming of the Lord. . . .

The Latter-day Saints, since their first organization in the year 1830, have been a poor, persecuted, abused, and afflicted people. They have sacrificed their time and property freely, for the sake of laying the foundation of the kingdom of God, and enlarging its dominion by the ministry of the gospel. They have suffered privation, hunger, imprisonment, and the loss of houses, lands, home, and political rights for their testimony.

And this is not all. Their first founder, Mr. Joseph Smith, whom God raised up as a prophet and apostle, mighty in word and in deed, and his brother Hyrum, who was also a prophet, together with many others, have suffered a cruel martyrdom in the cause of truth, and have sealed their testimony with their blood; and still the work has, as it were, but just begun.

A great, a glorious, and a mighty work is yet to be achieved, in spreading the truth and kingdom among the Gentiles—in restoring, organizing, instructing, and establishing the Jews—in gathering, instructing, relieving, civilizing, educating, and administering salvation to the remnant of Israel on this continent—in building Jerusalem in Palestine, and the cities, stakes, temples, and sanctuaries of Zion in America; and in gathering the Gentiles into the same covenant and organization—instructing them in all things for their sanctification and preparation, that the whole Church of the Saints, both Gentile, Jew and Israel, may be prepared as a bride for the coming of the Lord. . . .

Again, we say, by the word of the Lord, to the people as well as to the rulers, your aid and your assistance is required in this great work; and you are hereby invited, in the name of Jesus, to take an active part in it from this day forward.

Open your churches, doors, and hearts for the truth; hear the apostles and elders of the Church of the Saints when they come into your cities and neighbourhoods; read and search the scriptures carefully, and see whether these things are so; read the publications of the Saints, and help to publish them to others; seek for the witness of the Spirit, and come and obey the glorious fulness of the gospel, and help us to build the cities and sanctuaries of our God. . . .

To this city [Zion or New Jerusalem], and to its several branches or stakes, shall the Gentiles seek, as to a standard of light and knowledge; yea, the nations, and their kings and nobles shall say— Come, and let us go up to the Mount Zion, and to the temple of the Lord, where his holy priesthood stand to minister continually before the Lord; and where we may be instructed more fully, and receive the ordinances of remission, and of sanctification, and redemption, and thus be adopted into the family of Israel, and identified in the same covenants of promise. . . .

The city of Zion, with its sanctuary and priesthood, and the glorious fulness of the gospel, will constitute a *standard* which will put an end to jarring creeds and political wranglings, by uniting the republics, states, provinces, territories, nations, tribes, kindred, tongues, people, and sects of North and South America in one great and common bond of brotherhood; while truth and knowledge shall make them free, and love cement their union.

The Lord also shall be their king and their lawgiver; while wars shall cease and peace prevail for a thousand years. . . .

We say, then, in life or in death, in bonds or free, that the great God has spoken in this age.—*And we know it.*

He has given us the holy priesthood and apostleship, and the keys of the kingdom of God, to bring about the restoration of all things as promised by the holy prophets of old.—*And we know it.*

He has revealed the origin and the records of the aboriginal tribes of America, and their future destiny.—*And we know it.*

He has revealed the fulness of the gospel, with its gifts, blessings, and ordinances.—*And we know it.* . . .

He has commanded us to gather together his Saints, on this continent, and build up holy cities and sanctuaries.—*And we know it.*

He has said, that the Gentiles should come into the same gospel and covenant, and be numbered with the house of Israel, and be a blessed people upon this good land for ever, if they would repent and embrace it.—*And we know it.* . . .

He has said, that the time is at hand for the Jews to be gathered to Jerusalem.—*And we know it.*

He has said, that the ten tribes of Israel should also be revealed in the north country, together with their oracles and records, preparatory to their return, and to their union with Judah, no more to be separated.—*And we know it.*

He has said, that when these preparations were made, both in this country and in Jerusalem, and the gospel in all its fulness preached to all nations for a witness and testimony, he will come, and all the Saints with him, to reign on the earth one thousand years.—*And we know it.*

He has said, that he will not come in his glory and destroy the wicked, till these warnings were given, and these preparations were made for his reception.—*And we know it.* . . .

Therefore, again we say to all people, repent, and be baptized in the name of Jesus Christ, for remission of sins, and you shall receive the Holy Spirit, and shall know the truth, and be numbered with the house of Israel. . . .

New York, April 6th, 1845

TO THE ENGLISH READER.

It will be borne in mind that the foregoing was written in the United States of America, therefore the language, which we have not altered, will be understood as emanating from thence. . . .

W. WOODRUFF.

Liverpool, October 22nd, 1845 [Liverpool pam-

phlet, BYU Library, Provo, Utah: see also *MFP* 1:252–66].

3. Proclamation of the First Presidency and the Twelve Apostles (October 21, 1865)

[*This document was issued to members of the Church to correct certain theories about the nature of God that had been published by one of the Twelve in official Church literature, without having those statements cleared and verified by the First Presidency and the Twelve.*

An apparent major purpose of this Proclamation was to emphasize the established order of the Church, that new doctrine is to be announced only by the First Presidency. A paragraph near the end of the Proclamation states:]

It ought to have been known, years ago, by every person in the Church—for ample teachings have been given on the point—that no member of the Church has the right to publish any doctrines, as the doctrines of the Church of Jesus Christ of Latter-day Saints, without first submitting them for examination and approval to the First Presidency and the Twelve. There is but one man upon the earth, at one time, who holds the keys to receive commandments and revelations for the Church, and who has the authority to write doctrines by way of commandment unto the Church. And any man who so far forgets the order instituted by the Lord as to write and publish what may be termed new doctrines, without consulting with the First Presidency of the Church respecting them, places himself in a false position, and exposes himself to the power of darkness by violating his Priesthood (*MFP* 2:239).

[*The Proclamation is signed by Brigham Young, Heber C. Kimball, Orson Hyde, John Taylor, Wilford Woodruff, George A. Smith, Amasa M. Lyman, Ezra T. Benson, Charles C. Rich, Lorenzo Snow, Erastus Snow, Franklin D. Richards, George Q. Cannon (MFP 2:235–40).*]

4. Proclamation of the First Presidency and the Quorum of the Twelve Apostles of The Church of Jesus Christ of Latter-day Saints (April 6, 1980)

[*This document was put forth in commemoration of the 150th anniversary of the organization of the Church. On Sunday, April 6, 1980, a portion of the Sunday morning session of General Conference was broadcast from the newly reconstructed Peter Whitmer, Sr., home in Fayette, New York. President Spencer W. Kimball spoke briefly of the organization of the Church that had occurred on that very spot of ground. He then announced that the Church had a proclamation to declare. President Kimball's concluding words were:*

Now, my brothers and sisters, with the future before us, and sensing deeply the responsibilities and divine mission of the restored Church on this sacred occasion, the First Presidency and the Quorum of the Twelve Apostles declare to the world a proclamation. We have felt it appropriate to issue this statement from here, where the Church began. Accordingly, I shall ask Elder Gordon B. Hinckley of the Quorum of the Twelve Apostles, to speak in my behalf and in behalf of my brethren, to read this proclamation to you and to the world (CR, Apr. 1980, p. 74).

Elder Gordon B. Hinckley then read the Proclamation from the Whitmer home in Fayette, New York, which was broadcast by satellite to the Tabernacle in Salt Lake City, and published in the April 12, 1980 Church News, in the May 1980 Ensign, and in the April 1980 Conference Report. The full text of the proclamation follows.]

The Church of Jesus Christ of Latter-day Saints was organized 150 years ago today. On this sesquicentennial anniversary we issue to the world a proclamation concerning its progress, its doctrine, its mission, and its message.

On April 6, 1830, a small group assembled in the farmhouse of Peter Whitmer in Fayette Township in the State of New York. Six men participated in the formal organization procedures, with Joseph Smith as their leader. From that modest beginning in a rural area, this work has grown consistently and broadly, as men and women in many lands have embraced the doctrine and entered the waters of baptism. There are now almost four and a half million living members, and the Church is stronger and growing more rapidly than at any time in its history. Congregations of Latter-day Saints are found throughout North, Central, and South America; in the nations of Europe; in Asia; in Africa; in Australia and the islands of the South Pacific; and in other areas of the world. The gospel restored through the instrumentality of Joseph Smith is presently taught in forty-six languages and in eighty-one nations. From that small meeting held in a farmhouse a century and a half ago, the Church has grown until today it includes nearly 12,000 organized congregations.

We testify that this restored gospel was introduced into the world by the marvelous appearance of God the Eternal Father and His Son, the resurrected Lord Jesus Christ. That most glorious manifestation marked the beginning of the fulfillment of the promise of Peter, who prophesied of "the times of restitution of all things, which God hath spoken by the mouth of all his holy prophets since the world began," this in preparation for the coming of the Lord to reign personally upon the earth (Acts 3:21).

We solemnly affirm that The Church of Jesus Christ of Latter-day Saints is in fact a restoration of the Church established by the Son of God, when in mortality he organized his work upon the earth; that it carries his sacred name, even the name of Jesus Christ; that it is built upon a foundation of Apostles and prophets, he being the chief cornerstone; that its priesthood, in both the Aaronic and Melchizedek orders, was restored under the hands of those who held it anciently: John the Baptist, in the case of the Aaronic; and Peter, James, and John in the case of the Melchizedek.

We declare that the Book of Mormon was brought forth by the gift and power of God and that it stands beside the Bible as another witness of Jesus the Christ, the Savior and Redeemer of mankind. Together they testify of his divine sonship.

We give our witness that the doctrines and practices of the Church encompass salvation and exaltation not only for those who are living, but also for the dead, and that in sacred temples built for this purpose a great vicarious work is going forward in behalf of those who have died, so that all men and women of all generations may become the beneficiaries of the saving ordinances of the gospel of the Master. This great, selfless labor is one of the distinguishing features of this restored Church of Jesus Christ.

We affirm the sanctity of the family as a divine creation and declare that God our Eternal Father will hold parents accountable to rear their children in light and truth, teaching them "to pray, and to walk uprightly before the Lord" (D&C 68:28). We teach that the most sacred of all relationships, those family associations of husbands and wives and parents and children, may be continued eternally when marriage is solemnized under the authority of the holy priesthood exercised in temples dedicated for these divinely authorized purposes.

We bear witness that all men and women are sons and daughters of God, each accountable to him; that our lives here on earth are part of an eternal plan; that death is not the end, but rather a transition from this to another sphere of purposeful activity made possible through the Atonement of the Redeemer of the world; and that we shall there have the opportunity of working and growing toward perfection.

We testify that the spirit of prophecy and revelation is among us. "We believe all that God has revealed, all that He does now reveal; and we believe that He will yet reveal many great and important things pertaining to the Kingdom of God" (Articles of Faith 1:9). The heavens are not sealed; God continues to speak to his children through a prophet empowered to declare his word, now as he did anciently.

The mission of the Church today, as it has been from the beginning, is to teach the gospel of Christ to all the world in obedience to the commandment given by the Savior prior to his ascension and repeated in modern revelation: "Go ye into all the world, preach the gospel to every creature, acting in the authority which I have given you, baptizing in the name of the Father, and of the Son, and of the Holy Ghost" (D&C 68:8).

Through the Prophet Joseph Smith the Lord revealed these words of solemn warning:

> Hearken ye people from afar; and ye that are upon the islands of the sea, listen together. For verily, the voice of the Lord is unto all men, and there is none to escape; and there is no eye that shall not see, neither ear that shall not hear, neither heart that shall not be penetrated. And the rebellious shall be pierced with much sorrow; for their iniquities shall be spoken upon the housetops, and their secret acts shall be revealed. And the voice of warning shall be unto all people, by the mouths of my disciples, whom I have chosen in these last days [D&C 1:1–4].

It is our obligation, therefore, to teach faith in the Lord Jesus Christ, to plead with the people of the earth for individual repentance, to administer the sacred ordinances of baptism by immersion for the remission of sins and the laying on of hands for the gift of the Holy Ghost—all of this under the authority of the priesthood of God.

It is our responsibility to espouse and follow an inspired program of instruction and activity, and to build and maintain appropriate facilities for the accomplishment of this, that all who will hear and accept may grow in understanding of doctrine and develop in principles of Christian service to their fellowmen.

As we stand today on the summit of 150 years of progress, we contemplate humbly and gratefully the sacrifices of those who have gone before us, many of whom gave their lives in testimony of this truth. We are thankful for their faith, for their example, for their mighty labors and willing consecrations for this cause which they considered more precious than life itself. They have passed to us a remarkable heritage. We are resolved to build on that heritage for the blessing and benefit of those who follow, who will constitute ever enlarging numbers of faithful men and women throughout the earth.

This is God's work. It is his kingdom we are building. Anciently the prophet Daniel spoke of it as a stone cut out of the mountain without hands, which was to roll forth to fill the whole earth (see Dan. 2:31–45). We invite the honest in heart everywhere to listen to the teachings of our missionaries who are sent forth as messengers of eternal truth, to study and learn, and to ask God, our Eternal Father, in the name of his Son, the Lord Jesus Christ, if these things are true.

> And if ye shall ask with a sincere heart, with real intent, having faith in Christ, he will manifest the truth of it unto you, by the power of the Holy Ghost. And by the power of the Holy Ghost ye may know the truth of all things [Moro. 10:4–5].

We call upon all men and women to forsake evil and turn to God; to work together to build that brotherhood which must be recognized when we truly come to know that God is our Father and we are his children; and to worship him and his Son, the Lord Jesus Christ, the Savior of mankind. In the authority of the Holy Priesthood in us vested, we bless the seekers of truth wherever they may be and invoke the favor of the Almighty upon all men and nations whose God is the Lord, in the name of Jesus Christ, amen [*CR*, Apr. 1980, pp. 75–77; see also *Ensign* 10 (May 1980):51–53].

BIBLIOGRAPHY

Messages of the First Presidency, James R. Clark, comp., 5 vols. Salt Lake City, 1965–1975.

ROBERT J. MATTHEWS

PROCREATION

Latter-day Saints have an exceptionally positive view of procreation. After God commanded Adam and Eve to "multiply and replenish the earth" (Gen. 1:28), he pronounced all of his creation, including the power of procreation, "very good" (Gen. 1:31). President Joseph F. SMITH noted, "The lawful association of the sexes is ordained of God, not only as the sole means of race perpetuation, but for the development of the higher faculties and nobler traits of human nature, which the love-inspired companionship of man and woman alone can insure" (*IE* 20:739).

Mankind existed in a premortal life as spirit children of God (*see* FIRST ESTATE). This earth was created to provide physical life and experience in a SECOND ESTATE. The divine plan of procreation provides physical bodies for premortal spirits. Thus, "children are an heritage of the Lord" (Ps. 127:3). To beget and bear children is central to God's plan for the development of his children on earth. The powers of procreation therefore are of divine origin. An early LDS apostle, Parley P. Pratt, noted that the desires and feelings associated with procreation are not evil, but are ordained of God for sacred purposes:

> The fact is, God made man, male and female; he planted in their bosoms those affections which are calculated to promote their happiness and union. That by that union they might fulfill the first and great commandment . . . "To multiply and replenish the earth, and subdue it." From this union of affection, springs all the other relationships, social joys and affections diffused through every branch of human existence. And were it not for this, earth would be a desert wild, an uncultivated wilderness [Pratt, pp. 52–54].

Procreation is a divine partnership with God, and Church leaders counsel husbands and wives to seek his inspiration as they use their AGENCY to bring children into the world even in difficult situations and circumstances (*see* BIRTH CONTROL). The responsibilities of procreation include providing for the child's temporal well-being (1 Tim. 5:8), as "children have claim upon their parents for their maintenance until they are of age" (D&C 83:4). By seeking spiritual guidance and by following other divine laws, such as TITHING and making FAST OFFERINGS, parents are blessed of the Lord to provide the daily necessities for their children (cf. Mal. 3:3–10).

The abuse of the divine privilege and power of procreation in licentious indulgence has serious consequences. First is the loss of the Spirit to direct one's life (cf. Ex. 20:14; Prov. 6:32; D&C 42:22–24; 63:14–16). In addition, when the creative powers are prostituted, they become a detriment to one's emotional, physical, social, and spiritual well-being (*see* ABORTION; ABUSE, SPOUSE AND CHILD; ADULTERY; CHASTITY).

Using the power of procreation does not alienate one from God. Rather, properly used, it enables mortals to become cocreators with him in the divine PLAN OF SALVATION, which stretches across the eternities and includes the opportunity for the faithful to participate in family life and eternal increase (*see* ETERNAL LIVES).

BIBLIOGRAPHY

Barlow, Brent A. "They Twain Shall Be One: Thoughts on Intimacy in Marriage." *Ensign* 16 (Sept. 1986):49–53.

Packer, Boyd K. "Why Stay Morally Clean." *Ensign* 2 (July 1972):111–13.

Pratt, Parley P. *The Writings of Parley P. Pratt*, ed. Parker P. Robison. Salt Lake City, 1952.

BRENT A. BARLOW

PROFANITY

GENERAL AUTHORITIES of the Church have defined profanity to include the following: (1) blasphemy (irreverent use of the Lord's name); (2) swearing; (3) vulgarity (coarse jokes, foul stories, lewd words); (4) use of the Lord's name without proper authority; and (5) any type of filthiness in speech that is degrading and soul-destroying.

Profanity has become a common practice among both young and old, both male and female, in today's society. Some may be inclined to say that the commandment "Thou shalt not take the name of the Lord thy God in vain" (Ex. 20:7) is outdated. However, the wide use of profanity in contemporary society does not excuse Latter-day Saints from using any form of profanity or other blasphemous speech: "The Lord will not hold him guiltless that taketh his [God's] name in vain" (Ex. 20:7). President Spencer W. KIMBALL told the Church, "We, as good Latter-day Saints . . . do not use foul language. We do not curse or defame. We do not use the Lord's name in vain" (1981, p. 5).

To strip profanity and vulgarity from one's vocabulary not only is commendable and a mark of refinement but it is also a commandment from God. Early members of the Church were told in a general epistle that "the habit . . . of using vulgarity and profanity . . . is not only offensive to all

well-bred persons, but it is a gross sin in the sight of God, and should not exist among the children of the Latter-day Saints" (*MFP* 3:112–13). Profanity makes the holy profane, the sacred commonplace, the serious flippant, and the precious cheap.

To refrain from profane and vulgar speech also shows self-control. H. Burke Peterson, of the Seventy and former First Counselor in the PRESIDING BISHOPRIC, said, "We might consider vulgarity in a couple of ways: first, *as an expression* of personal weakness, and second, *as a contribution to* personal weakness" (Peterson, p. 38). Similarly, President Kimball described profanity as "the effort of a feeble brain to express itself forcibly" (1974, p. 7).

Instead of using profane speech, Latter-day Saints should "enlighten, edify, lift, motivate, elevate, build and uplift" others through their words (Brewerton, p. 73). By doing so, they will not forfeit the multitude of blessings promised them if they "bridle [their] tongues" (James 1:26).

BIBLIOGRAPHY

Brewerton, Ted E. "Profanity and Swearing." *Ensign* 13 (May 1983):72–74.

Kimball, Spencer W. "God Will Not Be Mocked." *Ensign* 4 (Nov. 1974):4–9.

———. "President Kimball Speaks Out on Profanity." *Ensign* 11 (Feb. 1981):5.

Peterson, H. Burke. "Purify Our Minds and Spirits." *Ensign* 10 (Nov. 1980):37–39.

GRANT VON HARRISON

PROHIBITION

Partly because belief in the WORD OF WISDOM supported abstinence from alcoholic beverages, Prohibition was an important political and moral issue for LDS leaders and members in the early twentieth century. Although LDS voters were naturally inclined to support legislation that limited the consumption of liquor, Utah, the state most affected by LDS votes, differed little from other western states in its position on Prohibition, with a variety of moral, political, and social issues influencing the position.

In 1908, when four states had already passed statewide prohibition laws, 600 saloons were operating in Utah. That year the national Anti-Saloon League began to recruit Prohibition supporters among the Protestant clergy and LDS General Authorities in the state. Heber J. GRANT, then an apostle, became the leader among Latter-day Saints in lobbying for Prohibition. Utah Republican leader Senator Reed Smoot, also an apostle, was concerned that support for Prohibition might alienate non-Mormon Republican supporters. President Joseph F. SMITH was also torn between his desire for Prohibition and his desire for defeat of the American Party, an anti-Mormon third party in the state. With many views affecting its vote, the 1909 state legislature narrowly defeated a statewide prohibition bill, and Governor William Spry later vetoed a local option bill that would have given cities authority to ban alcoholic beverage sales.

In 1910 President Smith instructed the Quorum of the Twelve to ignore statewide prohibition and work for local option. After a local option bill passed the state legislature in March 1911, Church leaders encouraged members to vote their communities "dry" in statewide elections. Most communities did so, but Salt Lake City, Ogden, and other cities with large non-LDS populations continued to allow the sale of alcohol.

Statewide prohibition again became a major political issue in 1915, with Elder Grant leading the supporters. Although Senator Smoot was no longer opposed to Prohibition, Governor Spry was. A prohibition bill easily passed the Utah legislature, but not in time to avoid the governor's pocket veto. During 1916 many LDS leaders were chagrined that Utah had not yet voted for Prohibition, particularly since Idaho, Colorado, Arizona, Washington, and Oregon had already done so.

Utah joined the ranks of the "dry" states on February 8, 1917, when newly elected Governor Simon Bamberger signed a law making Utah the twenty-third state to adopt statewide prohibition. In 1919 Utah joined other states in ratifying the Eighteenth Amendment to the federal Constitution, making Prohibition national in scope.

After the depression began in 1929, anti-Prohibition forces gained strength in Utah and the rest of the country. Nevertheless, led by Grant, who had become President of the Church in 1918, LDS leaders continued to support national Prohibition. Despite this support, the citizens of Utah voted in November 1933 for both national and state repeal. One month later Prohibition ended in Utah and the rest of the nation.

BIBLIOGRAPHY

Thompson, Brent G. "Standing Between Two Fires: Mormons and Prohibition, 1908–1917." *Journal of Mormon History* 10 (1983):35–52.

BRENT G. THOMPSON

PROLONGING LIFE

Medical science has made it possible to sustain physical life by artificial support systems under circumstances where functional and productive life may be no longer feasible. Prolonging life in these situations presents a moral and ethical dilemma for the medical profession and the family of the afflicted individual. On the one hand is the emotion of hope for recovery of useful function in a situation where the science of prognosis is imperfect and based to a certain extent on probability analysis, while on the other hand is the reality that physical death is imminent without life-support measures. Members of the medical profession deal with this dilemma by calculated evaluation of the data presented in the clinical situation and may present recommendations to the family and other concerned individuals as regards prognosis and what should be done. The family must analyze these recommendations in a situation clouded by the intense emotion of anticipated separation from a loved one.

Latter-day Saints are sustained during these trying times by their faith in Jesus Christ, whose teachings provide the strength, reason, and hope to guide one in making difficult decisions regarding life and death. "He that heareth my word, and believeth on him that sent me, hath everlasting life, and shall not come into condemnation; but is passed from death unto life" (John 5:24).

Jesus Christ presented himself as the Savior of mankind through the atonement and the resurrection: "I am the resurrection, and the life: he that believeth in me, though he were dead, yet shall he live: And he that liveth and believeth in me shall never die" (John 11:25–26).

Belief in everlasting life after mortal death should allow faithful Latter-day Saints to make wise and rational decisions regarding artificially prolonging life when medical means to restore useful and functional existence have been exhausted. This is reflected in Church policy regarding prolonging life:

When severe illness strikes, Church members should exercise faith in the Lord and seek competent medical assistance. However, when dying becomes inevitable, death should be looked upon as a blessing and a purposeful part of an eternal existence. Members should not feel obligated to extend mortal life by means that are unreasonable. These judgments are best made by family members after receiving wise and competent medical advice and seeking divine guidance through fasting and prayer [*General Handbook of Instruction*, 11-6].

BIBLIOGRAPHY

General Handbook of Instructions. Salt Lake City, 1989.

DONALD B. DOTY

PROMISED LAND, CONCEPT OF A

In the Book of Mormon, the prophet LEHI spoke of a particular promised land as "choice above all other lands; a land which the Lord God hath covenanted with me should be a land for the inheritance of my seed" (2 Ne. 1:5). Because the earth belongs to the Lord (Ps. 24:1), those who inherit a promised land must covenant to "serve the God of the land," who will then keep them "free from bondage, and from captivity" (Ether 2:12); otherwise they will "be swept off" (Ether 2:10; cf. Deut. 27–28).

From the beginning, the Lord has reserved choice lands for righteous followers. They include the GARDEN OF EDEN for Adam and Eve (Gen. 2:9), a "land of promise" for Enos (Moses 6:17), and Zion for Enoch and his people (Moses 7:19). Notably, God received up Zion's inhabitants (Moses 7:69), who will return to earth to the NEW JERUSALEM during the LAST DAYS (Moses 7:62–64; Rev. 21:2). Moreover, God gave the land of Canaan "unto [Abraham's] seed . . . for an everlasting possession" if "they hearken to [God's] voice" (Abr. 2:6). This promise was partially fulfilled when Moses led the Israelites out of Egypt to Canaan.

The BOOK OF MORMON PEOPLES, including the family of Lehi and the JAREDITES, were given a promised land in the hemisphere now called the Americas, on condition of keeping God's commandments (1 Ne. 2:20; Ether 1:42–43). The prophet MORONI₂ warned future inhabitants of this land: "Behold, this is a choice land, and whatso-

ever nation shall possess it shall be free . . . if they will but serve the God of the land, who is Jesus Christ" (Ether 2:12). This admonition applies to all lands that the Lord has promised to any of his peoples.

Latter-day Zion, a "promised land" for members of The Church of Jesus Christ of Latter-day Saints, includes the city New Jerusalem that will be built in the Americas (A of F 10) and, in another sense, the STAKES of the Church in all the world. Members also believe that the New Jerusalem is where the "lost ten tribes" will first come (D&C 133:26).

Through the Prophet Joseph SMITH, the Lord promised in 1831 to lead the Saints to a "land of promise" (D&C 38:18; cf. Ex. 3:8). Because of persecution by enemies and sin among Church members, Joseph Smith was unsuccessful in establishing a permanent community (D&C 101:1–8). After his death, the Saints migrated to the Rocky Mountains, "a land of peace" (D&C 136:16), and still anticipate fulfillment of the Lord's promises to open the way for building New Jerusalem in the designated place (D&C 42:9; 57:1–5; 101:9–22).

BIBLIOGRAPHY

Davies, William D. "Israel, the Mormons, and the Land." In *Reflections on Mormonism*, ed. T. Madsen, pp. 79–87. Provo, Utah, 1978.

CLARISSA KATHERINE COLE

PROPHECY

Latter-day Saints believe in both ancient and modern prophecy; indeed, continuing prophetic guidance is held to be a characteristic or SIGN OF THE TRUE CHURCH. These concepts were an integral part of the LDS Church's origin and restoration, and they continue to distinguish the Church from many other religious movements.

The term "prophecy" encompasses the entire range of divinely inspired utterances of a PROPHET, both as a "forth-teller" and as a "foreteller." The predominant assumption by many readers is that this term in the scriptures refers usually to foretelling—the prophetic power to reveal events in the future—but it is not so limited. Prophecy is a diverse spiritual gift bestowed by the HOLY GHOST (2 Pet. 1:21; 1 Ne. 22:2; Moro. 10:8; D&C 20:26; 68:4). Prophecy is firmly grounded in history, and prophets as spokespersons for the Lord have the power to reveal things relevant to the past, present, and future. The gift of prophecy, as demonstrated by Miriam, Deborah, Huldah, and others, is not limited to any special ordination in the priesthood (*AF*, pp. 228–29) but can be given to all as Moses understood when he cried: "Would God that all the Lord's people were prophets, and that the Lord would put his spirit upon them!" (Num. 11:29; cf. 1 Cor. 14:1–5, 29, 31, 39). In the restored Church all are baptized, confirmed, and provided with the gift of the Holy Ghost, through which all can enjoy prophetic gifts pertinent to their STEWARDSHIPS.

The possession of spiritual gifts, including the gift of prophecy, is one of the vital means of guiding the true Church (A of F 7; *see* GIFTS OF THE SPIRIT). Paul elaborated upon the gift of prophecy in the early Church (1 Cor. 12, 14). Moroni₂ similarly explained, "All these gifts of which I have spoken, which are spiritual, never will be done away, even as long as the world shall stand, only according to the unbelief of the children of men" (Moro. 10:8–19); and the Lord included the gift of prophecy among the spiritual gifts in the restored Church as declared in a revelation to Joseph SMITH (D&C 46:7–29).

Through his prophets the Lord reveals the plan of salvation and the gospel, full appreciation of which requires a correct understanding of significant events from the past as well as the present and future. Thus, prophetic guidance provides the eternal perspective necessary for individuals to understand their roles in the time in which they live and urges all to repent and prepare for what lies ahead. It is when people need hope that prophets become predictive.

Because knowledge of God's gracious plan of redemption has been so helpful to all mortals, all of the prophets have spoken about the coming of Christ (Luke 24:44–48; Jacob 4:4; Mosiah 13:33; D&C 20:26), and ancient prophecies demonstrate that people before his advent had a detailed knowledge of the events of the mission of Christ as well as a profound doctrinal understanding of his atonement (2 Ne. 2, 9; Mosiah 3; Alma 34; *see also* JESUS CHRIST: PROPHECIES ABOUT JESUS CHRIST). Enoch, for example, foresaw the coming of the Messiah, his death on the cross, and his resurrection and ascension into heaven (Moses 7:53–59); Isaiah described Christ as a suffering servant (Isa. 53; cf. Abinadi's explanation in Mosiah 14–15);

Lehi saw Christ's coming and noted the meaning of his baptism (1 Ne. 10:4–11); Nephi₁ prophesied that Christ's mother would be a virgin from Nazareth (1 Ne. 11:13–20); and both king Benjamin and Alma₂ noted that her name would be Mary (Mosiah 3:7; Alma 7:10). In addition, Nephi cited prophecies of Zenos, Zenock, and Neum, ancient prophets whose works are not extant in the Old Testament, giving details of the Crucifixion and Resurrection and the events that would accompany his death along with a foretaste of the atoning benefits to humankind wrought thereby (1 Ne. 19:10–21).

Many biblical prophets, including Isaiah, Jeremiah, Ezekiel, Malachi, and Christ himself, foresaw events in fulfillment of the Lord's plan for the latter days. The Pearl of Great Price and the Book of Mormon contain prophecies from the biblical and Book of Mormon periods specifically preserved to give hope and guidance in later times. For example, "The Lord showed Enoch all things, even unto the end of the world" (Moses 7:67), including the restoration of the gospel, the building of Zion, the coming of Christ, and the ushering in of the Millennium (Moses 7:62–66); Nephi and Moroni foresaw the spiritual conditions of pride, wickedness, unbelief, and false doctrine prevalent in the world at a time propitious to the restoration of the gospel, with the coming forth of the Book of Mormon as an instrument in the ensuing conversion and gathering of Israel (2 Ne. 26–30; Morm. 8–9).

The Doctrine and Covenants, like the ancient scriptures, contains divine admonitions, instructions, and reproofs, and also gives guidance through many prophetic predictions of events yet to transpire. A prophecy of civil war in the United States and of ultimate worldwide strife has already been partly fulfilled (D&C 87; 130:12–13; *see also* CIVIL WAR PROPHECY). Other prophecies still to be fulfilled include predictions of the signs of ultimate times (D&C 29:14–21; 45:16–47; 88:86–93), the preparatory preaching of the gospel to all nations, the latter-day gathering of Israel (D&C 133), the building of Zion (D&C 84:1–5), the second coming of Christ (D&C 45:48–53; 133:17–25), the Millennium (D&C 63:49–52; 101:22–31), and the resurrection of the dead and final judgment (D&C 29:22–30; 76; 88:95–116). The stated purposes of such prophecies are to warn and inform the inhabitants of the earth of the urgent need to repent and to share the gospel in all the earth and thus: "Be prepared in all things against the day when tribulation and desolation are sent forth" (D&C 29:8); therefore, "labor ye, labor ye in my vineyard for the last time—for the last time call upon the inhabitants of the earth" (D&C 43:28–29; cf. 133:4–5).

The scriptures address the problem of distinguishing true and false prophecies (Matt. 7:15–20; *TPJS*, p. 365). The Old Testament criterion, "If the thing follow not, nor come to pass, that is the thing which the Lord hath not spoken" (Deut. 18:22), is of course not always a practicable test for the prophet's contemporaries to discern the validity of the call and message.

Joseph Smith noted that "a prophet [is] a prophet only when he [is] acting as such" (*TPJS*, p. 278), and Brigham Young taught that the responsibility of discernment lies with individual members of the Church (*JD* 9:150). When Nephi's brothers wanted to know the truth of his prophecies, he told them that the Lord says, "If ye will not harden your hearts, and ask me in faith, believing that ye shall receive, with diligence in keeping my commandments, surely these things shall be made known unto you" (1 Ne. 15:11). These modes of evaluating a prophet's teachings are still valid. Jesus promised his disciples, "When he, the Spirit of truth, is come, he will guide you into all truth . . . and he will shew you things to come" (John 16:13). These prophetic gifts of the Holy Ghost have been restored and are available to all worthy individuals. Paul wrote to the Corinthians, "No man can say that Jesus is the Lord, but by the Holy Ghost" (1 Cor. 12:3). Indeed, the SPIRIT OF PROPHECY was, and is, "the testimony of Jesus" (Rev. 19:10). Moroni$_2$ promised all who will believe and partake of the spiritual gifts available that the truthfulness of spiritual things can be ascertained through serious intent, study, reflection, and prayer: "And by the power of the Holy Ghost ye may know the truth of all things" (Moro. 10:3–5; 1 Ne. 10:17–19; Moro. 7:12–18; D&C 9). The validity and value of prophetic teachings, past and present, may thus be known.

BIBLIOGRAPHY

Heschel, Abraham J. *The Prophets*. New York, 1962.

McConkie, Joseph F. *Prophets and Prophecy*. Salt Lake City, 1988.

Nibley, Hugh. *The World and the Prophets*. CWHN, Vol. 3.

Wilson, Robert R. *Prophecy and Society in Ancient Israel*. Philadelphia, 1980.

DAVID R. SEELY

PROPHECY IN BIBLICAL TIMES

From Adam (Moses 6:8) to John the Revelator, the Lord has revealed his word to prophets: "The Lord God will do nothing, but he revealeth his secret unto his servants the prophets" (Amos 3:7; cf. Num. 12:6–8; Jer. 23:18). Prophecy refers to God's word received by prophets acting as authorized intermediaries between God and humans.

The Lord called men from the course of their normal lives to be prophets and revealed his word in various ways: by face-to-face encounters, his voice alone, divine messengers, dreams, and inspiration. Often prophets received the Lord's word through symbolic object lessons, visions of councils in heaven and scenes of judgment, and views of past, present, and future events, and hence, they were also called "foretellers" and "forth-tellers." Occasionally expressed poetically, biblical prophecy is rich in imagery, metaphor, symbolism, allusion, and other literary figures. Besides the prophecies in the Bible, others from the biblical period are preserved in the Pearl of Great Price, the Book of Mormon, and the Doctrine and Covenants.

Biblical prophets acted frequently as mediators of covenants. Prophets such as Adam, Enoch, Noah, the BROTHER OF JARED, Abraham, and Moses acted as agents through whom the Lord established his COVENANTS among men and women. These prophets proclaimed the gospel and called their contemporaries to repent and join in a covenantal relationship with the Lord, providing inspired descriptions of future blessings and cursings that depended on obedience to the conditions of the covenants. Prophets who followed, such as Lehi, Ether, Isaiah, Jeremiah, King Benjamin, and John the Baptist, renewed the covenant and warned the covenant people, in varying states of apostasy, that they must repent and keep their covenantal obligations or face the consequences of disobedience—judgment, destruction, and scattering.

Biblical prophets often addressed the present by looking into the future, and prophecies of destruction were balanced by those of hope. Prophets foresaw apostasy and RESTORATION, the scattering and gathering of Israel, the coming of Jesus Christ and his atonement (Jacob 4:4; Mosiah 13:33; D&C 20:26), and times of tribulation preceding his return (Acts 3:21). Along with their indictments of COVENANT ISRAEL, many prophets delivered oracles directed to foreign nations, affirming the universal scope of their message (Amos 9:7). Most prophets in biblical times directed their unpopular message of repentance toward individuals or the community, thus placing the prophet in opposition to the prevailing social, political, and religious values, practices, and institutions of his time and place. Some prophets were killed or persecuted by those whose beliefs and behavior they condemned.

From the beginning, the Lord has set no limit on his ability to send prophets at his discretion. "And I do this that I may prove unto many that I am the same yesterday, today, and forever; . . . and because that I have spoken one word ye need not suppose that I cannot speak another; for my work is not yet finished; neither shall it be until the end of man, neither from that time henceforth and forever" (2 Ne. 29:9). Biblical prophecy did not end with MALACHI but continued with the coming of John the Baptist (Matt. 13:57; Luke 7:39; 1 Ne. 10:4). In addition, the prophetic tradition continued in the Western Hemisphere until the destruction of the NEPHITES around A.D. 400. Joel prophesied the future restoration of prophecy: "I will pour out my spirit upon all flesh; and your sons and your daughters shall prophesy, your old men shall dream dreams, your young men shall see visions" (Joel 2:28). The fulfillment of this prophecy was acknowledged by PETER on the day of Pentecost (Acts 2:16–18) and again by the angel MORONI to the Prophet Joseph SMITH (JS—H 1:41).

Latter-day scriptures cite, interpret, and allude to ancient prophecy, emphasizing its relevance to the restored Church. For example, important prophecies not in the biblical canon, such as those of JOSEPH OF EGYPT (2 Ne. 3) and ZENOS (Jacob 5), are preserved in the Book of Mormon. NEPHI$_1$ (e.g., 1 Ne. 20–22; 2 Ne. 11–24), JACOB (2 Ne. 7–8), ABINADI (Mosiah 14–15), and Christ (3 Ne. 20–25) cite Isaiah extensively and provide inspired interpretation (*see* ISAIAH: TEXTS IN THE BOOK OF MORMON). In the Doctrine and Covenants, Joseph Smith addressed specific questions about Isaiah 11 (D&C 113) and the book of Revelation (D&C 77) and through revelation confirmed the fulfillment of several biblical prophecies in the latter days, including Daniel's vision of "the stone which is cut out of the mountain without hands" as the restoration of the gospel (D&C 65:2) and the coming of ELIJAH in Malachi 4:5–6 by his appearance in the KIRTLAND TEMPLE in 1836 (D&C 110).

BIBLIOGRAPHY

Jackson, Kent, ed. *Studies in Scripture*, Vol. 4. Salt Lake City, 1991.

Lindblom, Johannes. *Prophecy in Ancient Israel*, 2nd ed. Oxford, 1978.

Sperry, Sidney B. *The Voice of Israel's Prophets*. Salt Lake City, 1952.

DAVID R. SEELY

PROPHECY IN THE BOOK OF MORMON

The Book of Mormon reports prophecies made during a thousand-year period concerning the future of the NEPHITES and LAMANITES, the earthly ministry of Jesus Christ, his visit to the Western Hemisphere, the future RESTORATION of the gospel to the GENTILES, and related events of the LAST DAYS. While this record includes the fulfillment of some prophecies, Latter-day Saints see fulfillment of other prophecies in the restoration of the gospel through the Prophet Joseph SMITH and expect yet others to be fulfilled in the future.

Messianic prophecies include the number of years until Jesus' birth (1 Ne. 10:4; Hel. 14:2), conditions surrounding his birth (1 Ne. 11:13–21), his mother's identity (Mosiah 3:8), the manner and location of his baptism by John the Baptist (1 Ne. 10:7–10), his miracles and teachings (1 Ne. 11:28–31), and his atonement, resurrection, and second coming. PROPHETS foretold details concerning Christ's crucifixion and his atoning sacrifice, one stating that "blood cometh from every pore, so great shall be his anguish for the wickedness and the abominations of his people" (Mosiah 3:7). Furthermore, he would rise on the third day (2 Ne. 25:13) and appear to many (Alma 16:20). SAMUEL THE LAMANITE prophesied specific signs of Christ's birth and death to be experienced among BOOK OF MORMON PEOPLES (Hel. 14).

During his visit to the Americas, the risen Jesus attested to the authenticity of these prophecies by stating that "the scriptures concerning my coming are fulfilled" (3 Ne. 9:16). Later, he reminded NEPHI$_3$ of a prophecy of his resurrection, the fulfillment of which had not been recorded. The details were promptly added to Nephite records (3 Ne. 23:6–13; cf. Hel. 14:25).

The Book of Mormon relates the fulfillment of other prophecies foretelling events among Book of Mormon peoples. Besides many Messianic prophecies, examples include ALMA$_2$ prophesying that the Nephites, dwindling in unbelief, would eventually become extinct (Alma 45:9–14; Morm. 6:11–

15) and ABINADI forecasting the destiny of his captors and their descendants (Mosiah 11:20–25; 17:15–18). Other prophecies anticipated more immediate events. For example, on the eve of Jesus' birth, when lives of believers were threatened by unbelievers, Nephi₃ received divine assurance that "on the morrow" the signs of Christ's birth would be seen (3 Ne. 1:9–15).

Book of Mormon prophets also forecast events of the latter days. They foretold the European exploration of America (1 Ne. 13:12–15), the American Revolution (1 Ne. 13:16–19), and the gathering of Israel (1 Ne. 22; 3 Ne. 20–22). They warned of deceptive practices among religionists, including priestcraft, secret combinations, and neglect of the poor. They foretold the impact of the Book of Mormon on latter-day people and the destruction of the wicked. The prophecies of MORONI₂ included admonitions addressed to those who would live in the last days: "Behold, I speak unto you as if ye were present, . . . behold, Jesus Christ hath shown you unto me, and I know your doing" (Morm. 8:35).

Under inspiration, prophets in the Book of Mormon frequently quoted previous prophets in support of their teachings. They warned that in rejecting the living prophet's witness, their hearers were rejecting the testimonies of such revered prophets as Isaiah, Moses, and ZENOS (Hel. 8: 11–20).

Prophesying falsely was viewed as a crime among the Nephites (W of M 1:15–16). Agreement with past prophets was a test of a prophet's authenticity. For instance, during a debate, JACOB exposed Sherem as a false prophet by showing that his testimony contradicted previous prophecy. Jacob then demonstrated that his own teachings agreed with former prophets, thus sealing Sherem's conviction as a false prophet (Jacob 7: 9–12).

Prophecy sometimes came in dreams or visions after pondering and prayer. Lehi and NEPHI₁ were caught up in the Spirit (1 Ne. 1:7–8, 11:1). King BENJAMIN and Samuel the Lamanite were visited by angels (Mosiah 3:2; Hel. 13:7). Prophecy was delivered variously, as in a psalm by Nephi₁ (2 Ne. 4:20–35), in Zenos' allegory (Jacob 5), or in Jacob's chastisements (2 Ne. 9:30–38).

Besides their service to God, as his messengers, prophets served as religious leaders (ALMA₁), kings (Benjamin; MOSIAH₂), military leaders (Helaman₁), and historians (Nephi₃). They were also social and moral critics of their society. Jacob denounced wickedness among his people not only because of its effects on that generation but also for wounds inflicted on the next (Jacob 2–3). Samuel the Lamanite foretold dire future consequences of the Nephites' lifestyle, criticizing their state of degradation (Hel. 13).

The presence of prophets and of contemporary prophecies were important to the Book of Mormon people. MORMON testified, "I also know that as many things as have been prophesied concerning us . . . have been fulfilled, and as many as go beyond this day must surely come to pass" (W of M 1:4).

BIBLIOGRAPHY

Nibley, Hugh W. *The Prophetic Book of Mormon.* In *CWHN* 8. Salt Lake City, 1989.

Parsons, Robert E. "The Prophecies of the Prophets." In *First Nephi, the Doctrinal Foundation*, ed. M. Nyman and C. Tate. Provo, Utah, 1988.

CAMILLE FRONK

PROPHET

[*This entry consists of two articles*: Prophets *presents the LDS belief in prophets, both past and present, as an integral part of the Church, and* Biblical Prophets *discusses the phenomenon of prophets and prophecy as a distinctive feature of biblical religion.*]

PROPHETS

A belief in prophets and their messages lies at the heart of LDS doctrine (A of F 4, 5, 6, 7, 9). Latter-day Saints recognize the biblical and Book of Mormon prophets, as well as latter-day prophets, as servants of Jesus Christ and accept as scripture the Bible, the Book of Mormon, the Pearl of Great Price, and the Doctrine and Covenants. They believe that Joseph SMITH and all subsequent PRESIDENTS OF THE CHURCH were and are prophets and representatives of Jesus Christ.

The word "prophet" comes from the Greek *prophetes*, which means "inspired teacher." Although neither the Greek term nor its Hebrew equivalent, *nabi*, initially required the function of foretelling (Smith, p. 3), all prophecy looks to the future. Since the Lord has chosen some of his servants to be foretellers—to disclose, sometimes in specific terms, momentous events that are to occur—the predictive element often overshadows other implications of the word in the minds of some (*see* REVELATION; JESUS CHRIST: PROPHECIES ABOUT).

But the gift of prophecy is not restricted to those whose words have been recorded in scripture. By scriptural definition, a prophet is anyone who has a testimony of Jesus Christ and is moved by the Holy Ghost (Rev. 19:10; cf. *TPJS*, pp. 119, 160). Moses, voicing his approval of two men who had prophesied, exclaimed, "Would God that all the LORD's people were prophets, and that the LORD would put his spirit upon them!" (Num. 11:26–29). Schools of prophets and "sons" (followers) of prophets, some false and some true, existed in large numbers in Old Testament times. In modern times, speaking of Brigham YOUNG, Elder Wilford WOODRUFF said, "He is a prophet, I am a prophet, you are, and anybody is a prophet who has the testimony of Jesus Christ, for that is the spirit of prophecy" (*JD* 13:165; *see* SPIRIT OF PROPHECY). It follows that this spirit does not operate in every utterance of its possessor. The Prophet Joseph Smith explained that "a prophet [is] a prophet only when he [is] acting as such" (*HC* 5:265).

In 1820 a passage in James (1:5) led to Joseph Smith's First Vision (JS—H 1:11–20). Three years later the angel-prophet-messenger MORONI₂, while instructing Joseph Smith, quoted from the prophets Malachi, Joel, and Isaiah, who told of the forthcoming mission of the Messiah and of the role of prophets, including Elijah, in the latter-day RESTORATION of the gospel. Subsequent revelations given to Joseph Smith make frequent reference to the prophets of the Old and New Testaments. Most frequently cited, in addition to those mentioned above, are Enoch, Noah, Abraham, Isaac, Jacob, Moses, Peter, James, John, and John the Baptist. In April 1836, the prophets Moses, Elias, and Elijah appeared to Joseph Smith and Oliver COWDERY and committed to them the KEYS OF THE PRIESTHOOD (see D&C 110:11–16). Other angelic messengers, all prophets, had been instrumental in restoring the Aaronic and Melchizedek priesthoods, beginning in 1829 (JS—H 1:68–73).

Joseph Smith had the spirit of prophecy after he and Oliver Cowdery were baptized in May 1829 (JS—H 1:73–74), and his prophetic office was officially recognized when the Church was organized on April 6, 1830. A revelation to him says, "Thou shalt be called a seer, a translator, a prophet, an apostle of Jesus Christ, an elder of the church . . .

being inspired of the Holy Ghost to lay the foundation thereof" (D&C 21:1–2). In March 1836, under the prophetic leadership of Joseph Smith, the membership of the Church sustained the FIRST PRESIDENCY and the QUORUM OF THE TWELVE APOSTLES as PROPHETS, SEERS, AND REVELATORS (*HC* 2:417). Their successors have been similarly sustained.

An unbroken series of prophets have led the Church since the death of Joseph Smith in 1844: Brigham YOUNG (1844–1877); John TAYLOR (1877–1887); Wilford Woodruff (1887–1898); Lorenzo SNOW (1898–1901); Joseph F. SMITH (1901–1918); Heber J. GRANT (1918–1945); George Albert SMITH (1945–1951); David O. MCKAY (1951–1970); Joseph Fielding SMITH (1970–1972); Harold B. LEE (1972–1973); Spencer W. KIMBALL (1973–1985); and Ezra Taft BENSON (1985–). Since 1847, these prophets have administered the affairs of the Church from Church headquarters in Salt Lake City. They have dedicated themselves to their appointed mission of helping the people of the world prepare for eternal life, and for the second coming of Jesus Christ. They have provided leadership for the international missionary program of the Church and for the building of temples. The living prophet continues to receive revelations, select and ordain leaders by the spirit of prophecy, and serve as the principal teacher of the Church, instructing its members in doctrine and in righteous living.

Prophets and their messages have occupied a central place in God's dealings with his children from the beginning. Elder Bruce R. McConkie, an apostle, has written that a foreordained prophet has stood at the head of God's church in all dispensations of the gospel from the time of Adam (see Moses 5:9, 10) to the present, including, for example, Noah, Abraham, Moses, Peter, and Joseph Smith (*A New Witness for the Articles of Faith*, Salt Lake City, 1985, p. 2).

Prophets are always witnesses of Jesus Christ, a fact that is particularly evident in the Book of Mormon. The experience common to all its prophets is the witness they bore of Jesus Christ, the Messiah—of his divine sonship and his earthly mission. A number of them, including Lehi, Nephi₁, Jacob, Benjamin, Abinadi, Alma₂, and Samuel the Lamanite, foretold his coming (1 Ne. 1:19; 10:4; 19:7–8; Jacob 4:4–5; Mosiah 3:5–8). They foresaw his atoning sacrifice and his resurrection (Mosiah 3:10–11; 15). Nephi wrote earlier of ancient prophets, Zenos, Neum, and Zenock (1 Ne. 19:10; 3 Ne. 10:14–16), who also foretold the visitation of Jesus Christ to the Americas after his resurrection (3 Ne. 11–26). Because Latter-day Saints identify Jesus Christ as Jehovah, they recognize that Old Testament prophets bore this same witness (see JEHOVAH, JESUS CHRIST).

The Book of Mormon, apart from its function as history, is essentially a record of the dealings of God with a long series of prophets, from Lehi, in the sixth century before Christ, to Moroni₂, a thousand years later. As witnesses of Jesus Christ, all were called to be teachers of righteousness. Though their teachings were all based in the gospel of Jesus Christ and they taught the same essential things, the record we have preserves some individual points of emphasis: ABINADI stressed living the Mosaic law with the proper spirit (Mosiah 12, 13); Nephi₁ and Alma₂ preached baptism and repentance (2 Ne. 31; Mosiah 18), as did Alma's sons (Alma 17–29). Many, including Nephi₁, Enos, Ether, and Moroni, were prompted to write and speak of faith and the gift of the Holy Ghost (e.g., 2 Ne. 26:13; 32:2–3). In counsel to his son Jacob, Lehi taught the principles of "opposition in all things" and of agency (2 Ne. 2). King Benjamin urged his people to serve God by serving one another (Mosiah 2:17). He and other Book of Mormon prophets, like their Old Testament counterparts, warned against vanity, greed, sexual immorality, materialism, and similar sins; but they also counseled love, kindness, patience, humility, and all peaceable things.

The Hebrew prophets spoke for God for many centuries until the post-apostolic era, from the second to the nineteenth centuries, when faith in continuing prophecy had vanished in that part of the world and when people assumed, even as did some in Jesus' day, that the prophets were dead (John 8:53) and their offices abolished. To believe that God had spoken to people of one's own time was "the test that Christ's generation could not pass" (CWHN 3:7).

"He that prophesieth," wrote Paul, "speaketh unto men to edification, and exhortation, and comfort" (1 Cor. 14:3)—such a person teaches, admonishes, and gives assurance of God's love. The prophets have proclaimed those God-given messages in many ways and with varying emphases. Their messages, though timeless in import, have been relevant to the immediate life of communities and nations. Some have combined their functions as prophets with other activities, such as being judges, military leaders, historians, poets, and church and civic administrators.

Some prophets have been popular figures and charismatic leaders—Moses, Samuel, and ALMA₂, for instance. But many have suffered abuse and betrayal. For every prophet who has been honored during earth life, many have suffered persecution and even martyrdom (2 Chr. 36:15–16; Matt. 5:11–12; Mosiah 17:20; D&C 135). Clearly, prophetic messages have not been designed to gain popular favor. A fundamental, common theme in all these messages is the call to repentance. Though prophets have counseled mercy, brotherhood, and humility, and though they have promised life and joy to those who have sought to love God and to receive his love, they have foreseen sorrow and despair as the unavoidable consequences of immorality, greed, idolatry, malice, pride, and other sins. They have yearned for peace, but they have condemned false prophets who have cried, "Peace, peace; when there is no peace" (Jer. 6:14). Unwarranted complacency, obsessive materialism, and the worship of other gods were main attributes of false prophets and their followers.

The messages of the prophets have taken many forms. Foremost are direct instructions and commandments from God to his children, as in much of the Pentateuch and the Doctrine and Covenants. Many have come as sermons and covenant renewal ceremonies, such as those of Moses and Joshua (Deut. 4–11; Josh. 24). Important truths are found in the counsel of the prophets to their own families, as in the words of LEHI and Alma₂ to their children (2 Ne. 1–4; Alma 36–42). Some prophetic messages have been recorded in letters, such as the epistles of Paul, James, Peter, and John in the New Testament and those of Joseph Smith in Doctrine and Covenants 127 and 128. Some are expressed as prayer—such as David's prayer of thanksgiving (2 Sam. 7:18–29)—and some are couched in symbol and poetry: the symbolism of Ezekiel and John the Revelator, the songs of David, the poetic passages of Isaiah and Jeremiah, the figurative language of Paul (Eph. 6:10–18), and such poetic utterances as the "new song" in Doctrine and Covenants 84:98–102.

No true prophets, ancient or modern, have ever called themselves to their positions. Some, such as Moses, Amos, and Jeremiah, have even accepted the calling reluctantly. Some, including John the Baptist, Samuel, Nephi₁, and Joseph Smith, were called in childhood or youth.

The calls made to individual prophets and God's further communications with and through them have been accomplished in various ways: through the ministering of angels; in dreams; in day or night visions; by prophetic inspiration, an intense conviction verified by subsequent events; by the literal voice of God; and in face-to-face visitations such as those experienced by Moses (Ex. 33:11), Enoch (Moses 7:4), and Joseph Smith (JS—H 1:17). Sometimes the call has come with blinding intensity, as in those of Paul and ALMA₂; sometimes, as with Elijah, the prophet has heard "a still small voice" (1 Kgs. 19:12). God has often spoken to his prophets in answer to prayer, but true prophets have not been mystics who try to make contact with the unseen by self-induced trances or similar means.

The calling of a prophet has always been made, and his messages have been written or spoken, through the power of the Holy Ghost, sometimes called the Spirit of the Lord (Acts 2:1–4, 37–42). Ananias put his hands on Paul that he might receive his sight and be filled with the Holy Ghost. "And straightway he preached Christ . . . that he is the Son of God" (Acts 9:17–20). So, too, did the prophets before Paul, and so have all of them since. In close conjunction with the gift of the Holy Ghost is the priesthood power that has been exercised by God's representatives throughout all dispensations.

BIBLIOGRAPHY

Madsen, Truman G. *Joseph Smith the Prophet*. Salt Lake City, 1989.

Nibley, Hugh W. *The World and the Prophets*. Vol. 3 of *CWHN*.

Smith, J. M. Powis. *The Prophets and Their Times*. Chicago, 1925.

Welch, John W. "The Calling of a Prophet." In *The Book of Mormon: First Nephi, The Doctrinal Foundation*, ed. M. Nyman and C. Tate, pp. 35–54. Provo, Utah, 1988.

RALPH A. BRITSCH
TODD A. BRITSCH

BIBLICAL PROPHETS

The phenomenon of PROPHECY is a distinctive feature of biblical religion. In its fully developed character, it sets biblical religion apart from other religions of the ancient Near East. As in other related matters, such as worship, sacrifice, ethical principles, and practices, ISRAEL shared much with its neighbors. But often, and specifically in matters of religion, the people of the Bible formed and forged something distinctive and different from all that came before or continued side by side. And this is particularly true of biblical prophecy.

With few exceptions the surviving materials of pagan antiquity command now only marginal academic interest—quaint reminders of a distant past—whereas the prophets of the Bible speak across the centuries with words, and out of experiences, that have direct bearing on modern lives and meaning for modern civilization.

Prophets in the Bible claim to be both foretellers and forth-tellers and base their claims upon their private access to the God of Israel, who is the ruler of history—past, present, and future. Prophecy as an essential part of Israel's theopolitical structure and the prophetic movement as an actual historical phenomenon had their beginnings with Samuel and his band of followers in the eleventh century B.C., at the point of transition from the era of the judges to the beginnings of the monarchy with the installation of Saul as royal head of the Israelite Confederation, or League of Tribes. Prophets, beginning with Samuel, played a significant, if not decisive, part in establishing but also censuring the monarchy and remained an integral part of Israelite society as long as the monarchy survived, and even beyond, when there was still thought or hope of restoring the kingship of the house of David. While God generally speaks to prophets through VISIONS, auditions, and even dreams, with MOSES he spoke face to face (Deut. 34) or mouth to mouth (Ex. 33). And whereas other prophets often only sense the presence of deity, Moses saw his actual form and person (Num. 12; cf. Ex. 33–34).

From the biblical records of the prophets and their experiences, one can piece together a picture of prophets and their calling.

THE CALL. The divine call and commission mark the beginning of the prophet's career. In all recorded cases, the details are striking and distinctive; no two prophetic situations are exactly the same, although all share important elements. We have sufficient data for people like Moses, Samuel,

Elisha (but not ELIJAH), and the great literary prophets such as Amos, Hosea, ISAIAH, JEREMIAH, and EZEKIEL to fill out a composite picture. But we lack information about the call of such prophets as Nathan and Ahijah. Typically, the call is initiated by God and is often accompanied by one or more visions, along with some unusual or miraculous occurrence (e.g., the burning bush). It is the combination of circumstances that persuades the prophet (or prophetess) that he (or she) is not hallucinating but is having contact with the living God.

THE COMMISSION. The call is always accompanied by a commission. The purpose is to enlist or draft the prophet to carry out a mission or duty—to do something in response to the call. Some prophets are reluctant to take on such responsibility, and therefore make excuses or otherwise try to evade their calling (e.g., Moses, Jeremiah, and, above all, Jonah). Other prophets are eager to carry out their task and hasten to do so (e.g., Isaiah, Ezekiel, perhaps Hosea). The basic rules for the prophet—the marching orders, as it were—are given succinctly and eloquently in the book of Jeremiah: "Wherever I send you you shall go, and what I tell you, you shall say" (Jer. 1:7 [author translation]). In brief, the prophet is the ambassador or messenger of God, and his (or her) sole duty is to deliver the message as given.

THE MESSAGE. In most cases, the message is for others and especially for the nation, its leaders, and the people generally. Often it contains warnings and threats, sometimes promises and encouragement. Inevitably there is a predictive element, as messages are mostly oriented to the future but rooted in the past. For the most part, predictions are morally conditioned, based upon the COVENANT between God and Israel, offering the choice between life and death, with success as the result of obedience and failure as the consequence of disobedience and defiance. Occasionally the oracles are pronounced absolutely, guaranteeing the future, whether of destruction or restoration. Occasionally they are timebound—that is, within a specified period the events described will occur, but often no time frame is specified. Even when moral or temporal conditions are not articulated, they may be implied by the speaker or inferred by the hearers. A notable case is the flat prediction by Micah (Micah 3:12) that Jerusalem will be destroyed. A century later, Jeremiah quotes the passage not to show that the prophecy was unfulfilled (Jerusalem had not been destroyed and was still standing), or much less to indict Micah as a false prophet, but rather to argue that as a result of the prophecy, the king (Hezekiah) and the people repented, and hence Yahweh (Jehovah) forgave them and spared the city (Jer. 26:16–19). It was the prophet's message that produced the result, and therefore both he and his message were vindicated as coming from God.

THE PROPHET AS WONDER-WORKER. MIRACLES are clearly and strongly associated with prophets such as Moses, Samuel, and especially Elijah and Elisha—as well as Isaiah among the so-called writing prophets—but there are many prophets with little or no such connection (e.g., Jeremiah, Amos, Hosea, Micah, etc.). Miracles seem to be attached to unusual charismatic individuals who were also prophets but not necessarily to the role or office of prophet. In the case of Moses, they were designed to strengthen and confirm his claims to have received an authentic and authoritative message from God, and they served to augment the function and purpose of visions and similar experiences of other prophets.

SUCCESS AND FAILURE. On the whole, the results of the prophetic experience are themselves unpredictable, and success or failure on the part of individual prophets hardly affects their status as true prophets of God. Prophets such as Samuel and Elisha are reported to have met with much success in carrying out their missions. With Elijah and perhaps Isaiah, the results are mixed, as also with Amos, Hosea, and Micah. Ultimately, they were all recognized as true prophets, not because the leaders and the people heeded their words (often they did not), but because they faithfully reported what they heard from the mouth of God, regardless of consequences for themselves or the people to whom they delivered the message. The survival of the nation was seen to be at stake, and it was of the greatest importance to distinguish true from false prophets. This was no mere academic exercise, but required the best judgment of leaders and people alike.

TESTS OF TRUE PROPHETS. The book of DEUTERONOMY offers rules of procedure to decide the issue of truth and falsehood. There are two basic principles, both practical and applicable: (1) if the prophet speaks in the name of, and delivers messages from, another god or other gods, then he is automatically condemned for APOSTASY and must be put to death (Deut. 13:1–5); (2) if the prophet makes a prediction and in due course the prediction is not fulfilled—that is, what is predicted does not come to pass—then the prophet is judged to be false and is to be executed (Deut. 18:20–22).

But the Deuteronomic rules will not work in many situations, and the jury is thrown back on other resources. In the end, the decision cannot wait until all the evidence is in, and must be based on other factors. The chief factor (after the basic test of orthodoxy: in the name of which god does the prophet speak?) must be the impact the prophet makes on his audience: his honesty, his courage, his reliability—the ability to make real to the listeners the experience of God and his messages to the prophet and through him to the people. Later there can be confirmation and vindication.

THE PROPHET AS CUSTODIAN OF COVENANT AND COMMUNITY. From beginning to end, the emphasis in prophetic utterance is on the ethical dimension of biblical religion and how it affects the well-being of the nation and its individual members. In contrast to the cultic concerns of the priests, the prophets stress the moral demands of deity and the ethical requirements of the covenant. The survival and success of the community depend more on the righteousness of the nation than on either the cultic activities of the priests or the military, political, social, and economic exploits of the king and his coterie. The battle against idolatry and apostasy was waged unremittingly through the whole biblical period, and the leaders in the struggle were the prophets. Second to that and equally difficult and important was the obligation to one's neighbor and to the community as a whole. On these two foundations, the prophetic message was constructed, and the prophets never ceased to propound the elementary and basic truths about biblical religion and the relationship of God to his people.

PROPHETS AND UNIVERSALISM. With the great prophets of the eighth and following centuries B.C., there was an important shift, although the basic truths remained untouched. The same requirements and the same standards were upheld and applied even more sharply to an Israel prone to defection and default. With the appearance of the great world powers—Assyria in the eighth and seventh centuries B.C. and Babylonia toward the end of the seventh and on into the sixth—the question of the survival of the little kingdoms of Israel and Judah (and their neighbors) became acute. The prophets raise the issue sharply and in a new way for the first time since the time of the patriarchs, with a larger perspective on the world scene and the role of Yahweh in ruling over the nations. The place of Israel and Judah in the larger picture is defined, and a theory of world order and time frame is foreshadowed. The implications of a single God ruling the universe but with special ties to one small nation (or two kingdoms) are developed. The danger and threats to the people of God are defined more sharply, but so also are the hopes and promises of the future. Ultimately, the God of the world, who is also the God of his particular way, and a restored and revealed Israel will take their place among the nations in a harmonious resolution of conflicts—to form the Peaceable Kingdom. The ultimate vision encompasses all nations and peoples, with a special place for Israel, still obligated by essential covenant stipulations, but a leader and model for all the others. Personal FAITH and morality are at the core of prophetic religion, but the implications and ramifications are social, national, and ultimately worldwide.

THE PROPHET AS SPOKESMAN FOR THE PEOPLE OF GOD. Normally one thinks of the priests as offering up prayers and sacrifices to God in behalf of the people, and especially of the role of the High Priest on the Day of Atonement. In the same manner, prophets may exercise the role of intercessor, but in a different context. Jeremiah mentions two intercessors, Moses and Samuel, while confirming that God himself has denied that role to Jeremiah. The most dramatic case is that of Moses in the episode of the golden calf (Ex. 32). Only Moses has the audacity and the closeness to God to demand a change of heart and mind on the part of the deity. Only Moses can command REPENTANCE on the part of God (but see JST, Ex. 32:14). And he succeeds, as the text reports. Israel is spared. A different poetic version of the same event is Psalm 90:13. It is not accidental or incidental that this is the only psalm in the Bible directly attributed to Moses.

Moses remains the unique model of a prophet of Israel because of his inspiration, his leadership, and ultimately his intercessory powers. The closing words of the book of Deuteronomy reflect this singularity: "Not has arisen a prophet in Israel like Moses, whom God knew face to face" (Deut. 34:10 [author translation]; cf. Ex. 33:11). And Yahweh would talk to Moses face to face, as men and women talk to their companions (cf. also Num. 12:8): "Mouth to mouth I speak to him . . . and the shape of Yahweh he beholds" (author translation).

BIBLIOGRAPHY

Friedrich, Gerhard, ed., and Geoffrey W. Bromiley, ed. and trans. *Theological Dictionary of the New Testament*, Vol. 6, pp. 781–861. Grand Rapids, Mich., 1964–1974.

Nibley, Hugh. *The World and the Prophets.* CWHN 3.

Sawyer, John F. A. *Prophecy and the Prophets of the Old Testament.* Oxford, 1987.

DAVID NOEL FREEDMAN

PROPHET JOSEPH SMITH

[*Joseph Smith, Jr., Prophet and first President of The Church of Jesus Christ of Latter-day Saints, is the primary subject of several entries and is mentioned prominently in many more. For a brief biography and articles on his teachings and writings, see* Smith, Joseph: The Prophet. *See also* History of the Church: c. 1820–1831 *and* c. 1831–1844 *and numerous articles relating to Joseph Smith cross-referenced there. For a history of Joseph Smith's prophetic ministry prepared under his direction, see* History of the Church.

Regarding Joseph Smith's early prophetic experiences, see First Vision; Moroni, Visitations of; *and* Sacred Grove. *During one of Moroni's visits in 1827, Joseph Smith received the* Gold Plates *from which he translated by the "gift and power of God" the* Book of Mormon; *see* Book of Mormon Translation by Joseph Smith. *For other visions and visitations, see* Visions of Joseph Smith.

In company with Oliver Cowdery, *Joseph Smith received divine authority; see* Aaronic Priesthood: Restoration of, *and* Melchizedek Priesthood: Restoration of. *Thus authorized, they proceeded with the* Organization of the Church, 1830. *Numerous* Revelations *given through Joseph Smith guided the infant organization; see* Book of Commandments *and* Doctrine and Covenants. *For other scripture that came through the Prophet Joseph Smith, see* Book of Abraham; Book of Mormon; Book of Moses; Joseph Smith Translation of the Bible (JST); *and* Pearl of Great Price.

Joseph Smith's mission focused on the Restoration of the Gospel of Jesus Christ, *including the* First Principles of the Gospel *and its* Ordinances; *he encouraged the* Gathering *of the Saints and laid the foundation for the establishment of* Zion *and the* New Jerusalem *in preparation for the Second Coming of Christ. The* Articles of Faith *provides a summary statement of some of the principal doctrines of the gospel.*]

PROPHET, SEER, AND REVELATOR

"Prophet, seer, and revelator" is the threefold title applied to all who have received the fulness of the KEYS of the MELCHIZEDEK PRIESTHOOD associated with the apostleship. Ordinarily, those to whom this title applies are members of the FIRST PRESIDENCY or the QUORUM OF THE TWELVE APOSTLES. All members of these two governing bodies are sustained as prophets, seers, and revelators by the Latter-day Saints in a public congregational vote (*see* COMMON CONSENT).

Though there are technical distinctions between the functions of a PROPHET, a SEER, and a revelator (cf. Mosiah 8:12–18), this threefold term is applied in its entirety to describe all these leaders. It was applied to Hyrum SMITH when he was made Assistant President of the Church and Patriarch to the Church, and to Joseph SMITH in his role as President of the Church (D&C 124:94). Also, at the dedication of the Kirtland Temple in 1836, Joseph Smith invited the members of the Church to acknowledge the Twelve Apostles as prophets, seers, and revelators (*TPJS*, p. 109).

LEWIS R. CHURCH

PROTESTANTISM

Christian Protestantism may be viewed as the product of late medieval "protests" against various elements of the Roman Catholic church. Though there were always persons within Catholicism pressing for reforms, the beginning of the Protestant Reformation is usually dated to 1517 when Martin Luther (1483–1546), an Augustinian monk in Wittenberg, Germany, published his ninety-five theses against papal indulgences. The theses challenged the authority of the pope and by extension of the Roman Catholic church. Protestants since that time are generally considered to be those Christians who are neither Roman Catholics nor Eastern (or Russian) Orthodox.

Although Protestant theology is varied today, it can be characterized by four basic beliefs: (1) the

Bible is the Word of God and all authority resides within its pages as it bears witness to Jesus Christ; (2) the Bible should be in the language of the people, who, by the power of the HOLY GHOST, can gain their own understanding of God's Word; (3) all church members hold the priesthood and should be involved in the total life of the church, meaning that no mediatorial priesthood is necessary; and (4) people are saved by their faith, through the grace of God, and not by any works they may do apart from or in addition to faith.

While Latter-day Saints share with Protestants a conviction of the importance of the scriptures, an extensive lay priesthood (but given only by the LAYING ON OF HANDS by those having proper priesthood authority), and the primacy of faith in Jesus Christ as Lord and Savior as the first principle of the gospel, they differ from them by affirming a centralized authority headed by a latter-day PROPHET and by a number of other doctrines unique to the Church, i.e. temple ordinances for the living and the dead, and the eternal nature of the marriage covenant. Despite some important differences, Latter-day Saints actually share much in doctrine, heritage, and aspiration with Roman Catholics, Eastern Orthodox, and Protestants. Even so, they view themselves as embodying an independent Christian tradition standing on its own apart from these other traditions. The Church of Jesus Christ of Latter-day Saints is not a *reformation* of a previously existing ecclesiastical body but is instead a RESTORATION through heavenly ministrations of authority and of truths, structures, and scriptures that God returned to the earth through the Prophet Joseph Smith and his successors.

BIBLIOGRAPHY

Dillenberger, John, and Claude Welch. *Protestant Christianity*. New York, 1954.

JOHN DILLENBERGER
ROGER KELLER

PROTESTANT REFORMATION

The sixteenth-century Reformation was a major religious upheaval that has had repercussions to the present day. When Martin Luther challenged the Catholic doctrine of the sacraments, boldly declaring that salvation comes not by human works but by the grace of God alone through faith in Jesus Christ, he set in motion a complex series of events that not only broke the religious stronghold of the Catholic church but also had a profound impact on political, social, and cultural events as well.

LDS perspective regards the Protestant Reformation as a preparation for the more complete restoration of the gospel that commenced with Joseph SMITH. Thus, the Protestant Reformation initiated a return to pure Christianity, a work that could not be completed without divine revelation and restoration. The leaders of the Reformation are honored as inspired men who made important progress, but without direct revelation they could not recover the true gospel or the priesthood authority to act in God's name. That was the mission of the Prophet Joseph Smith.

Perhaps the greatest legacy of the Reformation was the increased attention to freedom, one's own freedom more than that of others. This concern eventually grew into religious toleration and the desire for greater political self-determination. The ending of the single, "universal" church and the proliferation of new churches and sects had echoes in the political arena, most notably in the independence of the United States of America. A great many factors contributed to the establishment of the United States, but the political and religious heritage of the Protestant reformers was certainly among them.

The restoration of the gospel through Joseph Smith took place within the context of this post-Reformation world. Yet Joseph Smith is not considered a successor to the reformers in the sense of building on their teachings. He claimed to receive his knowledge and priesthood authority directly by revelation, not by the study of other writers, thus initiating a new dispensation of the gospel rather than a continuation of the Reformation.

The religious environment of early-nineteenth-century America was predominantly Protestant. That environment encouraged religious differences and resulted in many rival churches. Among the characteristics of that religious revivalism was an emphasis on the Bible and Bible reading, a feature that was first promoted by the sixteenth-century humanists and reformers. The Bible used by Joseph Smith and others of his day was the English King James Version of 1611. It was his own reading of the Bible (in particular James

1:5–6) that led Joseph Smith to his first personal encounter with God.

The Reformation legacy is also seen in the frontier emphasis on congregational religion, emphasizing the right and ability of individual congregations to organize themselves as autonomous religious bodies, conducting their own worship services and generally governing their own affairs. Congregationalism grew out of the sixteenth- and seventeenth-century English Calvinist tradition in particular, but it was also practiced by other groups.

Especially important in relation to the Restoration was the concept that religion is personal, a one-on-one relationship between God and the individual worshiper. This was a key feature of the Reformation Anabaptists, who believed, much as Latter-day Saints do, in personal revelation and individual responsibility. The Anabaptists rejected infant baptism, teaching instead that baptism was a cleansing covenant with God, entered into only after the exercise of faith and repentance. Many other Anabaptist doctrines are remarkably similar to Latter-day Saint beliefs, including the concept of restoration itself, which the Anabaptists called Restitution—meaning the restitution of the apostolic Church of the New Testament.

Not as many specific doctrines are shared with mainline Protestants, but Latter-day Saints do have in common a devoted faith in Jesus Christ as Redeemer of the world and as personal Savior. This faith was the moving force in the actions of Martin Luther and other early reformers, and was central to the life and work of the Prophet Joseph Smith. It remains today a central tenet of the Church.

BIBLIOGRAPHY

Grimm, Harold J. *The Reformation Era, 1500–1650*, 2nd ed. New York, 1965.

Jensen, De Lamar. *Reformation Europe: Age of Reform and Revolution*, 2nd ed. Lexington, Mass., 1981.

Spitz, Lewis W. *The Protestant Reformation, 1517–1559*. New York, 1985.

DE LAMAR JENSEN

PSALMS, MESSIANIC PROPHECIES IN

The Psalms are a rich source of messianic prophecy; indeed Psalms 2, 22, 69, and 110 are cited or partially quoted as messianic prophecies in the NEW TESTAMENT. The Prophet Joseph SMITH appreciated the messianic and prophetic nature of the Psalms, revising under inspiration several verses to make them even more emphatically prophetic of the messianic message (*see* JOSEPH SMITH TRANSLATION OF THE BIBLE [JST]). Included in the revisions are Psalms 10, 11, 12, and 24.

Citations from Psalms contribute 116 of the 283 Old Testament quotations in the New Testament. Of these, a number are clearly messianic. For instance, Psalm 2:7 is referred to in Acts 13:33; and Hebrews 1:5 and 5:5 specifically apply the affirmation "Thou art my Son" to Jesus. Nearing death on the cross, Jesus himself quoted Psalm 22:1 (Matt. 27:46) and much of the rest of that Psalm characterizes his suffering. His disciples recalled the zeal mentioned in Psalm 69:9 during Jesus' cleansing of the temple (John 2:17); and the same verse is applied to Christ by Paul in Romans 15:3. Jesus credits the HOLY GHOST with inspiring David in Psalm 110:1, and applies the passage to himself (Mark 12:35–37; Luke 20:41–44). Hebrews 5:6 quotes Psalm 110:4 concerning Christ and the MELCHIZEDEK PRIESTHOOD.

The JST revision of Psalm 10:15–16 alludes to the kingly role of the MESSIAH: "O Lord, thou wilt break the arm of the wicked. . . . And the Lord shall be king . . . for the wicked shall perish out of his land."

Psalm 11:1–5 similarly becomes more messianic by specifying the LAST DAYS rather than a contemporary Davidic event: "In that day thou shalt come, O Lord; and I will put my trust in thee. Thou shalt say unto thy people . . ." (JST Psalm 11:1). Referring to the Messiah's overcoming of evil, verse 3 is changed to read, "But the foundations of the wicked shall be destroyed, and what can they do?" The JST also casts verse 4 into the future, emphasizing a future deliverance from evil and speaking of the Lord "when he shall come into his holy temple." Verse 5 is doubled in length and adds a key messianic clause, "and he shall redeem the righteous."

JST Psalm 12:1–8 begins with a sentence not found in the King James Version—that underscores divine assistance: "In that day thou shalt help, O Lord, the poor and the meek of the earth." Other verses—2, 4, 5, 6, and 8—have been recast into the future tense. Verse 5 (JST) is messianic, beginning, "Therefore, thus saith the Lord, I will arise in that day, I will stand upon the earth and I will judge the earth for the oppression of the poor."

JST Psalm 24:7–10 proclaims a future redeemer. Verse 8 reads, "And he will roll away the heavens; and will come down to redeem his people; to make you an everlasting name; to establish you upon his everlasting rock." The future redeemer is also noted in verse 10: "Even the king of glory shall come unto you; and shall redeem his people, and shall establish them in righteousness."

Latter-day Saints may thus see more messianic prophecies in the Psalms because Joseph Smith revealed a more messianically oriented Psalter than was found in his King James text. They also accept a tradition of prophecy during the Israelite period and its fulfillment either with the coming of Christ or with the latter-day RESTORATION of the gospel in preparation for the Messiah's millennial reign.

[*See also* Jesus Christ: Prophecies About Jesus Christ.]

BIBLIOGRAPHY

McConkie, Joseph F. "Joseph Smith and the Poetic Writings." In *The Joseph Smith Translation*, ed. M. Nyman and R. Millet. Provo, Utah, 1985.

GERALD E. JONES

PSEUDEPIGRAPHA

See: Apocrypha and Pseudepigrapha

PUBLICATIONS

From its inception in 1830, The Church of Jesus Christ of Latter-day Saints has been a diverse and prolific publisher of the printed word. The varied publications have included scriptures, doctrinal treatises, missionary tracts, newspapers, magazines, histories, accounts of persecutions and petitions for redress, proclamations and warnings to the world, hymnals and books of poetry, and replies to anti-Mormon attacks. While the history of the Mormon press is unique, it does fit into the context of American religious printing in general. The period from 1800 to 1865 saw the printing of religious literature in America reach a high point—the result of the Second Great Awakening and the activities of various interdenominational Bible and tract societies. It was in this environment of vigorous printing activity that the Church emerged and grew.

Church publishing in the years 1830–1844 is best described as informal and quasi-official because the Prophet Joseph SMITH was occupied with more pressing concerns and left much of the business of printing and disseminating literature to others. After 1844, President Brigham YOUNG and the QUORUM OF THE TWELVE APOSTLES assumed more control over Church publishing. As the main body of Saints made their permanent move to the Great Basin (1846–1852), the responsibility for publishing Church literature moved to Great Britain until the late 1870s because of the unavailability of suitable presses and inexpensive paper in the intermountain area.

SCRIPTURES. To Latter-day Saints, the most important publications are the four STANDARD WORKS of scripture: the Bible, Book of Mormon, Doctrine and Covenants, and Pearl of Great Price. As Christians, Latter-day Saints accept the Holy Bible as sacred scripture from God (the Church endorses the King James Version for English-speaking members). However, they get their popular nickname, Mormons, from their acceptance of the Book of Mormon as additional scripture from God. Since its first printing (Palmyra, New York, 1830), the Book of Mormon has had scores of editions published in many languages. Subsequent English-language editions of significance include those printed in Kirtland, Ohio, 1837; Nauvoo, Illinois, 1840; Liverpool, England, 1841, and 1879; and Salt Lake City, Utah, 1871, 1920, and 1981.

The Doctrine and Covenants contains most of the important recorded revelations received by Joseph Smith. Many of these first appeared in the Church's early newspapers, the EVENING AND THE MORNING STAR (Independence, Missouri, 1832–1833) and *Latter Day Saints'* MESSENGER AND ADVOCATE (Kirtland, 1834–1838). The first collection of the revelations was to be published as the BOOK OF COMMANDMENTS (Independence, 1833). But the press was destroyed by a mob before the printing was completed, and a fuller collection was published in Kirtland, as the Doctrine and Covenants, in 1835 by the Kirtland Literary Firm (cf. D&C 72:20–21), the publications committee apparently then in charge of Church publications in Kirtland. Later editions of the Doctrine and Covenants were published in Nauvoo, 1844; Liverpool, 1845, 1879; and Salt Lake City, 1876, 1908, 1918, 1921, and 1981.

The fourth volume of LDS scripture is a compilation entitled the Pearl of Great Price, pub-

Latter-day Saints have a long and extensive publication history. This bold masthead of John Taylor's newspaper, *The Mormon*, printed in New York, expresses many LDS sentiments about the freedom of the press, including: "U.S. Constitution Given by the Inspiration of God"; "It is better to represent ourselves than to be represented by others," "Truth will prevail," and "Mormon creed, Mind your own business." *The Mormon* was published weekly from February 1855 until September 1857. Courtesy Rare Books and Manuscripts, Brigham Young University.

lished first in Liverpool in 1851, with other editions printed in Liverpool in 1879 and in Salt Lake City in 1878, 1902, 1921, 1976, and 1981.

PERIODICALS. Periodical literature has been used extensively by Church leaders to disseminate information to members. Early on, it was the pattern to publish two papers, one religious and the other secular. The first of these pairs, *The Evening and the Morning Star* and *The Upper Missouri Advertiser*, commenced publication in Independence, Missouri, in June 1832. The *Star* was printed monthly to provide members of the Church with appropriate reading material and included the text of many revelations given to the Prophet Joseph Smith. The *Advertiser* was a weekly single-sheet paper intended for the community. Both were printed from June 1832 to July 1833, when the press at Independence was destroyed. Other early periodicals include *Latter-day Saints' Messenger and Advocate* (Kirtland, Ohio, 1834–1837) and *The Northern Times* (Kirtland, c. 1835–1836); *Elders' Journal of the Church of Latter Day Saints* (Kirtland, Ohio, and Far West, Missouri, 1837–1838); *Times and Seasons*

(Nauvoo, 1839-1846) and *The Wasp* (1842–1843), which was replaced by *Nauvoo Neighbor* (1843–1846).

The longest-published periodical was the MILLENNIAL STAR (full name, *Latter Day Saints' Millennial Star*, Manchester, Liverpool, and London, England, 1840–1970). First issued for the fast-growing British membership, it later served American Saints as the most substantial Church periodical between their Nauvoo exodus in 1846 and the commencement of the weekly newspaper DESERET NEWS (Salt Lake City, 1850–); from 1850 to 1971, it continued as a substantial missionary periodical read worldwide. Another important periodical printed in England, JOURNAL OF DISCOURSES (Liverpool, 1854–1886), provided Latter-day Saints on both sides of the Atlantic with reports of sermons given at several places, including the Church's semiannual general conferences. After the Church formally announced the practice of PLURAL MARRIAGE in 1852, President Brigham Young assigned different brethren to establish periodicals in the large cities to counter the increased attacks on the Church that resulted from that announcement. The following journals were responses to his request: *The Seer* (Orson Pratt, ed.,

Washington, D.C., 1853–1854); *The St. Louis Luminary* (Erastus Snow, ed., 1854–1855); *The Mormon* (John Taylor, ed., New York, 1855–1857); and *The Western Standard* (George Q. Cannon, ed., San Francisco, 1856–1857). Much of what would eventually be published in book or pamphlet form was first issued in one of these journals.

After the Church became established in Utah Territory, other periodicals (issued from Salt Lake City unless otherwise noted) included: *Juvenile Instructor* (1866–1929), which became *The Instructor* (1929–1970); *Contributor* (1879–1896); *Young Woman's Journal* (1889–1929); *The Improvement Era* (1897–1970); *The Elders' Journal* (Chattanooga, Tennessee, 1903–1907), which became *Liahona the Elders' Journal* (Independence, 1907–1945); *The Children's Friend* (1902–70); *Utah Genealogical and Historical Magazine* (1910–1940); and *Relief Society Magazine* (1915–1970).

As the Church expanded into other lands, its missions often established periodicals in their respective languages. The earliest was the Welsh *Prophwyd y Jubili* (1846–1848), and the longest running was the Danish *Skandinaviens Stjerne* (1851–1956). Other early journals were *Der Stern* (German, 1869–), *Nordstjärnan* (Swedish, 1877–), and *De Ster* (Dutch, 1896–).

Current English language periodicals include three monthly magazines (published since 1971): *Ensign*, for adults (over 18); *New Era*, for young adults and youth (ages 12 to 18); and *The Friend*, for children (to 12). Selected articles from these periodicals are gathered into *International Magazines*, which in 1990 was printed with local additions in some twenty non-English languages. *BYU Studies* (1959–), a scholarly quarterly, is produced at Brigham Young University. (*For a fuller list of most of the major LDS periodicals, see* Appendix 3.)

DOCTRINAL WORKS. Following the formal organization of the Church on April 6, 1830, a rigorous missionary effort began that ultimately became the impetus for much early publishing in the Church. The successes of a number of Protestant tract societies in early nineteenth-century England and America provided LDS writers an effective model for disseminating the restored gospel through the printed word. A sizable portion of early LDS printing took the form of doctrinal and missionary tracts and pamphlets.

Early influential tracts of a doctrinal nature included Orson Hyde's *A Prophetic Warning to All the Churches, of Every Sect and Denomination*, published in Canada in 1836. Although only a short treatise, this broadside was the first tract to be used for proselytizing purposes. Elder Hyde, a member of the Quorum of the Twelve Apostles, suggested that the Christian world must prepare for the SECOND COMING of the Savior. He asserted the LDS claim that the New Testament prophecy of future apostasy from primitive Christianity had already occurred and that men and women need baptism performed by someone with proper authority from Jesus Christ.

Other early doctrinal works were written by several LDS writers. The Church's most notable early author was Parley P. Pratt, also an apostle, whose *A Voice of Warning* (New York, 1837) was arguably the most influential nineteenth-century nonscriptural book of LDS literature. Its descriptions of the unique doctrines of the Church would be repeated and imitated by others in many publications that followed. He also produced *Mormonism Unveiled* (New York, 1838), the first LDS tract responding to anti-Mormon criticisms; *The Millennium and Other Poems* (New York, 1840), a book of poetry expressing LDS ideas; and *Key to the Science of Theology* (Liverpool, 1855), the first comprehensive treatment of the doctrines of the Church.

Another writer who made significant doctrinal contributions in print was Orson Pratt, Parley's younger brother, also an apostle, whose important tracts include *A[n] Interesting Account of Several Remarkable Visions* (Edinburgh, Scotland, 1840); *A Series of Sixteen Pamphlets* (Liverpool, 1851) containing sixteen doctrinal tracts which formed a book later published under the title *Orson Pratt's Works* (1945); and a second series of tracts [*Eight Pamphlets on the First Principles of the Gospel*] (Liverpool, 1856–1857).

Yet other important early doctrinal works include Lorenzo SNOW's *The Only Way To Be Saved* (London, 1841); Orson Spencer's *Correspondence Between the Rev. W. Crowel, A.M., and O. Spencer, B.A.* (Liverpool, 1847), later known as *Spencer's Letters*; and Franklin D. Richards's *A Compendium of the Faith and Doctrines of the Church of Jesus Christ of Latter-day Saints* (London, 1857).

Examples of influential doctrinal works from the twentieth century include James E. Talmage's *Articles of Faith* (1899) and *Jesus the Christ* (1915), B. H. Roberts' *Seventy's Course in Theology* (5 volumes, 1907–1912), Joseph Fielding SMITH's compilation *Teachings of the Prophet Joseph Smith* (1938) and *Doctrines of Salvation* (3 volumes, 1954–1956), Bruce R. McConkie's *Mormon Doctrine* (1958), and Spencer W. KIMBALL's *Miracle of Forgiveness* (1969).

HISTORICAL WORKS. During the Church's early years, Latter-day Saints experienced intense and extensive religious persecutions, which resulted in forced moves for the entire Church on several occasions. Important published histories that document the Saints' difficulties in Missouri include John P. Greene's *Facts Relative to the Expulsion of the Mormons or Latter Day Saints, from the State of Missouri* (Cincinnati, 1839); Parley P. Pratt's *Late Persecution of the Church of Jesus Christ of Latter Day Saints* (Detroit, 1839; enlarged ed., New York, 1840); and Sidney RIGDON's *An Appeal to the American People* (Cincinnati, 1840). In Illinois the persecutions continued, culminating in the martyrdom of the Prophet Joseph Smith and his brother Hyrum. An important history of that dark day is William M. Daniels' *A Correct Account of the Murder of Generals Joseph and Hyrum Smith, at Carthage* (Nauvoo, 1845). Other nineteenth-century histories of note include *Biographical Sketches of Joseph Smith the Prophet* (Liverpool, 1853), by Joseph's mother, Lucy Mack SMITH, and *The Autobiography of Parley Parker Pratt* (New York, 1874).

Significant historical works published in the twentieth century include the seven-volume *History of the Church* (1901–1932, formerly referred to as the Documentary History of the Church), edited by B. H. Roberts, and his six-volume *A Comprehensive History of the Church of Jesus Christ of Latter-day Saints* (1930); Joseph Fielding Smith's *Essentials in Church History* (1922); John Henry Evans' *Joseph Smith, an American Prophet* (1933); Leonard J. Arrington's *Great Basin Kingdom* (1958); and James B. Allen and Glen M. Leonard's *The Story of the Latter-day Saints* (1976). The years 1960–1990 saw a virtual explosion of monographs and professional journal articles documenting the history of the Church. This same period saw the publication of several independent, non-Church periodicals, including *Dialogue* (1966–), *Journal of Mormon History* (1974–), *Sunstone* (1975–), and *This People* (1979–).

HYMNALS. Music and hymns have always been an important part of Latter-day Saint worship ser-

vices. As early as July 1830, Emma SMITH was instructed to select a group of hymns for publication. The first LDS hymnal, though dated 1835, was not published until March 1836 in Kirtland. Entitled *A Collection of Sacred Hymns, for the Church of the Latter Day Saints*, this first hymnal, that printed the texts of the hymns without music, served as a model for several subsequent editions compiled by Church members. Another early hymnal was the first British edition, *A Collection of Sacred Hymns, for the Church of Jesus Christ of Latter-day Saints, in Europe, Selected by Brigham Young, Parley P. Pratt, and John Taylor* (Manchester, 1840). This hymnal was the basis for more than a dozen subsequent editions. Other significant hymnals include the first Salt Lake City edition (1871), the first edition to add music to the texts (Salt Lake City, 1889), and revised editions in 1927 and 1948. The current 1985 edition was a major revision of the Church's hymnal.

OTHER PUBLICATIONS. The Church has also issued ALMANACS printed independently from 1845–1866, and by the Church since 1974. The Church also printed emigrant guidebooks, a multivolume biographical encyclopedia, and many historical works.

CURRENT PUBLICATIONS. In addition to official publications such as scriptures, hymnals, and monthly periodicals, the Church produces a large body of educational curriculum material, including instructional manuals for the study of the scriptures, doctrine, and Church history for all organizations within the Church—the priesthood, Relief Society, Sunday School, Young Men, Young Women, and Primary. The Church Education System produces materials for use in the secondary school seminaries and college and university institutes of religion.

In addition, numerous independent publishers serve the LDS market.

BIBLIOGRAPHY

For a comprehensive bibliographic listing of pre-1930 publications relating to the Church, see Chad J. Flake, *A Mormon Bibliography, 1830–1930* (Salt Lake City, 1978), and its companion volume, *Ten-Year Supplement* (Salt Lake City, 1989), compiled by Flake and Larry W. Draper. These two publications list approximately 12,000 books, pamphlets, and broadsides that contain discussions of LDS doctrine, history, and culture during the Church's first century. Lengthier discussions of specific early LDS publications include Peter Crawley, "A Bibliography of The Church of Jesus Christ of

Latter-day Saints in New York, Ohio, and Missouri" (*BYU Studies* 12 [Summer 1972]:465–537); David J. Whittaker, "Early Mormon Pamphleteering" (Ph.D. diss., Brigham Young University, 1982); Crawley and Flake, *A Mormon Fifty* (Provo, Utah, 1984); and Crawley and Whittaker, *Mormon Imprints in Great Britain and the Empire, 1836–1857* (Provo, Utah, 1987). For a bibliography listing more recent publications on LDS subjects, see "Mormon Bibliography," a serial article appearing in one issue annually of *BYU Studies* since 1960.

LARRY W. DRAPER

PUBLIC COMMUNICATIONS

The Public Affairs Department of The Church of Jesus Christ of Latter-day Saints was organized in 1972 in response to a long-felt need for channeling and coordinating information about the growing Church throughout the world. The department handles news-media relations, hosts visiting dignitaries, and maintains liaison with volunteer public communications representatives called to serve in STAKES and MISSIONS. Originally, the department also produced radio and television public service announcements and exhibits for TEMPLE SQUARE and other VISITORS CENTERS, but these functions were later transferred to the Missionary Department of the Church. In 1983 the department's name was expanded to Public Communications/Special Affairs after the original department merged with Special Affairs, the Church's government and community relations office.

Forerunners to the department were the Church Radio, Publicity, and Mission Literature Committee, organized in 1935 with recently returned missionary Gordon B. Hinckley (later an apostle and counselor in the FIRST PRESIDENCY) as its director, and the Church Information Service, organized in 1957 with Theodore Cannon as director. Wendell J. Ashton was the first managing director of the Public Communications Department. Subsequent managing directors have been Heber G. Wolsey (1978–1983), Richard P. Lindsay (1983–1989), and Bruce L. Olsen (1989–).

Divisions in the department include Media Relations; National News Placement; Community Relations; Field Publications Liaison; Hosting; and Administration. Area offices with full-time directors are situated in Washington, D.C.; Los Angeles; Toronto; London; Paris; Frankfurt; São Paulo; and Sydney. The headquarters staff in Salt Lake City coordinates the efforts of local public communications directors, designated to serve in the stakes, regions, and areas.

The department is responsible to, and counsels with, the Church's Special Affairs Committee, comprised of members of the Quorum of the Twelve Apostles and the Presidency of the Quorums of the Seventy. It maintains ongoing contacts with news media at local, national, and international levels. The staff prepares and distributes both print and electronic news and feature releases about the Church, its programs, events, and activities. Public-affairs radio and television programs are produced and distributed for the use of the media and community organizations; queries from the media and the public are answered; and news media representatives are hosted. Designated spokespersons convey Church policy statements on pertinent issues to the public via the media. Designated staff members monitor legislative issues affecting the Church, its operations, and its members, and keep the leaders of the Church apprised of such developments. In addition, designated members of the staff join with representatives of other Churches and national organizations committed to combat such things as pornography, alcohol abuse, gambling, and various other social problems.

ARCH L. MADSEN

PUBLIC RELATIONS

Many public relations programs, activities, and services exist in The Church of Jesus Christ of Latter-day Saints to support its public ministry. These efforts are coordinated by the Church Public Affairs Department and are grounded in Christ's instruction to his disciples, "Go ye therefore, and teach all nations" (Matt. 28:19). This instruction was repeated in revelations to the Prophet Joseph SMITH (D&C 1:4–5; 49:11–14; 71:1–2; 84:62).

Making Christ's gospel known throughout the world has been central to the Church's purpose from the beginning. Sharing the gospel requires Church members to reach out to others (*see* JOINING THE CHURCH; MISSION; TOLERANCE). Various approaches have been used over the years to attract interest and to introduce and explain the Church, its people, and their beliefs. Now, as at first, personal communication and distribution of printed materials, especially the Book of Mormon, are the principal methods of sharing the gospel. Joseph Smith's brother Samuel undertook the first formal missionary journey shortly after the Church was organized in April 1830. Soon, other missionaries went to the eastern United States, to Canada, and to England, taking with them the Book of Mormon as their primary teaching tool and preaching to local congregations and in homes and at street meetings. In 1831 the Church purchased a printing press and began producing newspapers, books, and broadsides (*see* MAGAZINES; PUBLICATIONS).

Organized missionary work is a major part of Church public relations. Since 1830, more than half a million members of the Church have served as full-time missionaries. As of 1990, they were serving in eighty-eight countries and twenty-two territories, teaching in sixty-seven languages and providing printed materials in more than fifty languages. In addition to scriptures, tracts, and other reading material, missionaries have added videotapes and other modern visual aids to their presentations.

The Mormon Tabernacle Choir, under the direction of Richard P. Condie, sang in Carnegie Hall, New York City, November 5, 1958, as part of an expanded public relations effort launched by the Church in the 1950s.

The Church fosters cultural and social relationships with the general public through concerts, theatrical performances, and making Church buildings available for civic and educational events. For example, before its own facility was built, the Utah Symphony used the Salt Lake Tabernacle for its performances free of charge for thirty-two years. Church buildings also have been used as polling places and for town meetings and other noncommercial gatherings.

The MORMON TABERNACLE CHOIR is prominent in the Church's public relations image. In early recognition of its appeal, the choir was invited to perform at the World's Columbian Exposition in 1893 (*see* EXHIBITIONS AND WORLD FAIRS). The choir's radio broadcast, presented weekly since 1929, is the longest-running network program in broadcasting history (*see* BROADCASTING). The choir has made more than 150 recordings, has performed at U.S. presidential inaugurations and world fairs, and has gone on many concert tours.

In 1935 the Church formed a Radio, Publicity, and Mission Literature Committee to develop ways to use the latest communications media in missionary work. The committee produced film strips, pamphlets, tracts, books, recordings, radio programs, and exhibits and supervised translations of the Book of Mormon. Under President David O. MCKAY, the Church began to use professional public relations consultants, who recommended that the Tabernacle Choir make recordings with the Philadelphia Symphony Orchestra and worked to obtain press coverage of the CUMORAH PAGEANT in New York. In 1957 the Church Information Service was begun, with a primary purpose to distribute accurate information about Church activities of interest to the general public.

In 1972 the Church formed a Department of Public Communications. In 1974 President Spencer W. KIMBALL stated: "When we have used the satellite and related discoveries to their greatest potential, and all the media—papers, magazines, television, radio— . . . to their greatest power, . . . then and not until then shall we approach the insistence of our Lord and Savior to go into all the world and preach the Gospel to every creature" ("When the World Will Be Converted," Regional Representatives' seminar, Apr. 4, 1974). Accordingly, the Public Affairs Department, headquartered in Salt Lake City (with smaller offices in twelve other cities), and staffed by full-time public-relations professionals, focuses on serving the media and effectively using modern communications technology.

The Church makes regular use of network and cable television, radio, telephones, print, and electronic exhibits for programming and public-service advertising in many countries.

Services to the media include recorded newscasts; radio, television, and print releases; features and interviews; magazine pieces; and broadcast-quality public affairs programs. Church news regarding doctrines and activities is available through official releases. Also, Church positions on public issues such as pornography, drugs, and parenting are announced.

The Public Affairs Department coordinates the volunteer service of 3,500 local public communications directors in the stakes and missions of the Church. These individuals, many of them business and professional leaders, interact with local media and arrange coverage of Church events of local interest. They report to the Church on public reactions in their local areas and, as directed, respond to commendations and criticism.

When the Church is criticized (see ANTI-MORMON LITERATURE) or involved in controversy, the Public Affairs Department may provide responses and position statements. The standard Church response to criticism is to deal respectfully but not to debate with critics. When controversy arises, the Church strives to keep its comments within the scope of its activities, so as not to interfere with the jurisdiction of other entities.

Under the direction of the Missionary Department, the Church maintains some thirty-seven volunteer-staffed VISITORS CENTERS and HISTORICAL SITES. Volunteers also conduct tours of new and remodeled TEMPLES before they are dedicated. About ten million people annually tour Church places of interest. Distinguished visitors to Church headquarters in Salt Lake City are hosted by volunteers who arrange tours, visits to members' homes, interviews with Church leaders or directors of WELFARE SQUARE, and visits to the FAMILY HISTORY LIBRARY, the Museum of Church History and Art (see MUSEUMS), and other sites.

In 1988 the Church became a charter member of the Vision Interfaith Satellite Network, a project of twenty-two faith groups. A milestone in interdenominational cooperation, VISN provides people of faith with original, value-based cable television programs. The Church's programs appear in the schedule fourteen or more times weekly.

BIBLIOGRAPHY

For a general overview, see Leonard Arrington and Davis Bitton, *The Mormon Experience: A History of the Latter-day Saints* (New York, 1979). The symposium on the Church and the public media in *Dialogue* 10 (Spring 1977), includes an interview with Wendell Ashton (then managing director of public communications) and articles on history, journalism, and the challenges of presenting a clear and appealing, but not misleading, image of the Church to a wide variety of public audiences.

ELIZABETH M. HAGLUND

PUBLIC SPEAKING

The Church of Jesus Christ of Latter-day Saints encourages its members at all ages to express publicly not only their FAITH and TESTIMONY but also their wisdom, humor, and gratitude. Anyone may be invited to speak in an LDS meeting, whether man, woman, or child. Children begin their public speaking experience by sharing two or three sentences learned at home; later, talks of original construction and longer duration are given. Subject matter may be assigned or left to the selection of the speaker. Although some Latter-day Saints write out and read their speeches aloud, that practice is less common as members mature in their gospel experience and become more confident in their speaking ability. Experienced speakers, such as Church officers, often "take no thought" beforehand (Matt. 10:19) as to precisely what they will say, but "study the word of the Lord" and then speak "as they [are] directed by the Spirit" (D&C 42:12–14). Thousands of young people who serve on MISSIONS for the Church become adept at public speaking.

Typically, an LDS speaker addresses the congregation as "brothers and sisters" and may introduce the topic by using a story, humorous event, or personal experience. The speaker then presents the substance of the speech, sometimes in traditional rhetorical form, giving general thesis statements with supporting data for each, and sometimes very informally. The information is usually based on observation, logic, authority of the SCRIPTURES, personal experience, writings of Church leaders, and sometimes comparative social or religious approaches (e.g., why Mormons may live longer than others). In summary, the speaker often declares faith in the principles discussed and testifies to their truthfulness, generally concluding the talk invoking the name of Jesus Christ and saying AMEN. The audience affirms agreement by uttering an audible "Amen."

Latter-day Saints believe that admission to the Kingdom of Heaven is achieved through obedience to ORDINANCES and the development of personal perfection. Such spiritual growth comes in part from individual enlightenment, which is reason to receive the spoken or written word. Inspiration often derives from hearing the oral testimony of others, for if people do not nourish the word, they "can never pluck of the fruit of the tree of life" (Alma 32:40).

Thus, public speaking is a basic LDS exercise, for "how shall they believe in him of whom they have not heard? and how shall they hear without a preacher?" (Rom. 10:14–17). As opportunity allows, a speaker introduces the restored gospel to others and, significantly, preaches the gospel in the Church's meetings. Speaking in church carries the responsibility of teaching and inspiring others. The speaker becomes a voice for GOD and is expected to prepare so that the word of God can effectively be expressed. The speaker is therefore admonished to use "great plainness of speech" (2 Cor. 3:12) and to speak as "moved upon by the Holy Ghost" (D&C 68:3).

Public speaking is periodically encouraged on a local level through speech festivals and contests. These events focus on the art of speaking, involve members in refining their speaking abilities in a Church context, and provide an appropriate arena for the enjoyment and appreciation of public speaking.

LAEL J. WOODBURY

PURPOSE OF EARTH LIFE

[*This entry consists of two articles:* LDS Perspective *discusses the Mormon understanding of life's purposes, and* Comparative Perspective *contrasts the LDS understanding with that of the major world religions.*]

LDS PERSPECTIVE

Latter-day Saint prophets have affirmed the purpose of life within the framework of three questions: (1) Whence did we come? (2) Why are we here? (3) What awaits us hereafter? The scriptural context of these questions is assurance of the eternal character of the SOUL and of the creation of the earth as a place for the family of God.

All men and women have lived as spirit beings in a premortal state, and all are the spiritual offspring of God (Abr. 3:21–22). In that world all the family of God were taught his plans and purposes. "At the first organization in heaven we were all present, and saw the Savior chosen and appointed and the plan of salvation made, and we sanctioned it" (*TPJS*, p. 181). All the spirit children of God developed various degrees of intelligence and maturity. Those who voluntarily subscribed to the conditions of mortality were embodied and made subject to the light of Christ "that lighteth every man that cometh into the world" (D&C 93:2). So that earth life may be a probation, a veil of forgetfulness has been drawn over the former life.

In mortality, at least six purposes are opened to mankind:

1. To be given a body, whose experiences and maturation, and eventual permanent resurrection, are essential to the perfecting of the soul. "We came to this earth that we might have a body and present it pure before God in the celestial kingdom" (*TPJS*, p. 181; *see* PHYSICAL BODY; RESURRECTION).

2. To grow in knowledge, and develop talents and gifts (*see* INTELLIGENCE). "If you wish to go where God is, you must be like God, or possess the principles which God possesses, for if we are not drawing towards God in principle, we are going from Him and drawing towards the devil" (*TPJS*, p. 216).

3. To be tried and tested. "We will prove them herewith," says the record of Abraham, "to see if they will do all things whatsoever the Lord their God shall command them" (Abr. 3:25). Through mortality one experiences contrasts and opposites—health and sickness, joy and sadness, blessings and challenges—and thus comes to know to prize the good. "Adam fell that men might be; and men are, that they might have joy" (2 Ne. 2:23). Such joy, as Elder B. H. Roberts of the Seventy wrote, can come only from "having sounded the depths of the soul, from experiencing all emotions of which mind is susceptible, from testing all the qualities and strength of the intellect" (Roberts, p. 439; *see* JOY; MORTALITY; SUFFERING IN THE WORLD).

4. To fill and fulfill the missions and callings that were conferred or preordained (*see* FOREORDINATION; PREMORTAL LIFE). Latter-day Saints often speak of earth life as a second estate and al-

lude to the promise given to and through Abraham that "they who keep their second estate [i.e., fulfill the purposes of mortality] shall have glory added upon their heads for ever and ever" (Abr. 3:26).

5. To exercise agency without memory of the premortal existence, thus to "walk by faith" and have the "realities anticipated in the spirit world renewed and confirmed" (*see* AGENCY; FAITH).

6. To establish the foundations of eternal family relationships, first as sons and daughters, then as fathers and mothers. The united family is the epitome of the fulfilled and saintly life (*see* MARRIAGE: ETERNAL).

The life to come is the extension and fulfillment of the mortal sojourn: to enter into and live forever in the presence of God. But probation does not end with death. Nor do opportunities to hear, accept, and apply the truths and powers of Christ. Indeed, Joseph SMITH taught that even for the faithful, "it is *not all* to be comprehended in this world; it will be a great work to learn our salvation *and exaltation even beyond the grave*" (*TPJS*, p. 348). He added that when the spirit is separated from the body, the process is somewhat impeded, hence the importance of using the time while in mortality, for redemption, and the folly of procrastination of repentance and renewal.

In all this, the continuity of the former life with this one, and in turn this life with the next, is clearly taught. The tendency of much religion, Eastern and Western—to divide life into two worlds and to hold that they are utterly distinct and unlike—is reversed. Life is change, transformation, and exaltation. Mortality is a dress rehearsal for the next world. There, light, glory, and dominion will be conferred in fulness on those who have fulfilled the words of eternal life in this world, and are therefore prepared for eternal life in the world to come.

BIBLIOGRAPHY

Roberts, B. H. "Modern Revelation Challenges Wisdom of Ages to Produce More Comprehensive Conception of the Philosophy of Life." *Liahona the Elders' Journal* 20 (May 8, 1923):433–39.

JAMES P. BELL

COMPARATIVE PERSPECTIVE

Religions tend to present life as meaningful when it conforms to a cosmic plan—a plan that is either intentionally instituted by God or is grounded in the nature of a cosmos that is divine in origin. For Latter-day Saints, the divinely ordered cosmos is the tenor of all scripture. Within this context, latter-day scripture affirms the interrelated themes of the crucial importance of the PHYSICAL BODY, of trials, of the experience of opposition, of the eternality of family, and of the vision of joy and glory in the likeness of God (*see* PURPOSE OF EARTH LIFE: LDS PERSPECTIVE).

Alternative views move in two directions. Some hold that if there is no God and if the ultimate end of all human life is personal annihilation, life has no meaning. This is the position, for example, of Arthur Schopenhauer. Existentialists, who generally assert that humans create their own meaning in a godless and objectively absurd universe, take a similar stance. Others, including some naturalists and humanists, hold that life is worthwhile even if the claims of supernatural religion are false. Marxists, for instance, hold that a purposive society, if not a meaningful cosmos, emerges as an objective entity through the inexorable processes of history.

Some thinkers affirm that life has purpose even if that purpose is shrouded in mystery. Hedonism typically maintains that questions of ultimate meaning cannot be answered and hence should be ignored in favor of calculating maximum pleasure and minimum pain. Confucianism tends not to speak to this issue. It asserts the existence of a spiritual order that is prior to, and superior to, the social order, but focuses on issues of a this-worldly character. Many strands of Judaism take the same approach, believing that the life to come is secondary to the task of establishing and maintaining a sanctified community in this world and looking to a day when, in the words of a venerable Hebrew prayer, "the world shall be perfected under the reign of the Almighty."

Latter-day Saints see life as a three-stage process—a premortal, mortal, and postmortal existence. All stages are essential to the unfolding and perfecting of the self, which is the work and glory of God. The process can be characterized as both this-worldly and other-worldly (*see* GOD: WORK AND GLORY OF; MORTALITY; PRE-EXISTENCE; RESURRECTION).

Plato's "myth of the cave" depicts the human condition as bondage to false beliefs and illusions, which the true philosopher aims to transcend. In the *Phaedo*, Socrates argues that the philosopher "is always pursuing death and dying." The wise man longs for the separation of his soul from his body; for freedom from illness, fatigue, and the deceptions of the senses; and for release into a realm of intuitive contemplation. Gnosticism, a movement akin to Platonism, shared the notion of the fall and hoped-for ascent of a divine soul, but frequently denied the goodness of both the physical universe and the deity who had made it. In the thirteenth century Thomas Aquinas offered a classical enunciation of the Catholic position that man's highest goal, even in this material world, is the "contemplative life," which will be perfected after death. The happiness of the saints will consist in an intellectual "seeing" of the divine essence, vision not in the eye but in the mind. Latter-day scripture affirms both the life of intelligence, defined as light and truth, and the redemption of the soul, defined as both spirit and body. The purpose of life is not escape but transformation—of man, of community, and of the cosmos.

In the major religious traditions of eastern and southern Asia, God (or the gods) sometimes has a marginal role. Hinduism teaches that the deepest human desire is for infinitude, for infinite being, knowledge, and joy. One must therefore seek *mukti*, liberation, from the finitude and limitations that seem to be humanity's natural condition. The word "seem" is crucial because Hinduism insists that behind individual and finite personalities lies Atman-Brahman, the Godhead itself. Men and women are already infinite; liberation consists simply—although it is not so simple!—in recognizing that fact. Buddhism, springing from Hindu soil and often considered a kind of reformation of the older religion, essentially concurs in this diagnosis of the human condition, although its nontheistic forms differ in the way it explains human nature. The Buddha (the title comes from a word meaning roughly "to be enlightened") held that the fundamental human problem is a desire to be separate and that life's purpose is the extinction of that desire, thus enabling men and women to overcome, in this or a series of lives, the selfish cravings that are the chief source of their sufferings and woe. LDS thought rejects both reincarnation and the theory of human suffering as illusory (*see* REINCARNATION; SUFFERING IN THE WORLD).

The notion of soul liberation as the purpose of life is not uncongenial to religions of the Abrahamic tradition, including that of the Latter-day Saints, although it has seldom if ever become the dominant paradigm. The declaration of the Hebrew scriptures that God pronounced the material cosmos "good" has remained normative. For this and other reasons, Jewish, traditional Christian, Muslim, and LDS thought unite in the view that the supremely good God is directly responsible for the general situation in which human beings find themselves. But no tradition emphasizes more than does the LDS that the conditions of mortality were "voluntarily subscribed to" by each individual (*TPJS*, p. 325; cf. D&C 93:30–31; *see also* THEODICY). Latter-day Saints likewise agree that eventual union with God implies no loss of finite individual identity, but rather a relationship with him.

A pervasive Christian view is expressed in the Westminster Shorter Catechism of 1647, which declares that "man's chief end is to glorify God, and to enjoy him forever." God created us to bring glory to himself—which was not vanity on his part, since he fully deserves that glory, whereas human beings do not—and will reward those whom he saves with the enjoyment of himself. This can be compared with the position of Islamic tradition that attributes to God the words "I was a hidden treasure but wished to be known, and therefore I created the world." The aim of human beings in Islam is therefore to submit (*aslama*) themselves to the will of God and to glorify him through their actions. Judaism and Islam are closely related in their emphasis upon law and right behavior and in their declaration that obedience to the commandments of God is the purpose of life. Judaism, however, differs from Islam in its belief that the full range of the divine commandments (*mitzvoth*) is incumbent only upon Jews, with non-Jews subject to the few basic "Noachian precepts." Islam, on the other hand, insists that God's demands are identical for all human beings. "I did not create the jinn and mankind," the Koran quotes Allah as saying, "except to serve me."

Some Protestant thinkers have affirmed that human beings exist to manifest the divine attributes, to embody in their own imperfect lives something of God's glory. A similar view occurs in the statement of the Catholic Baltimore Catechism that "God made us to show forth His goodness and to share with us His everlasting happiness in heaven." Latter-day scripture affirms that God will share not only his gifts and blessedness but also his divine nature (*see* DEIFICATION). Catholic and Protestant forms of Christianity, however, part company; the former holds that God's aims for mankind are ideally realized in a life of sacramental and liturgical worship, whereas the latter emphasizes acceptance of the free grace of Christ. Latter-day Saints affirm that saintly life is impossible without access to the grace of Christ; freely chosen obedience to divinely given covenants, laws, and ordinances in which the atonement and grace of Christ are manifest; and then the giving of oneself in whole-souled discipleship.

BIBLIOGRAPHY

Palmer, Spencer J., and Roger R. Keller. *Religions of the World: A Latter-day Saint View.* Provo, Utah, 1989.

Romney, Thomas C. *World Religions in the Light of Mormonism.* Independence, Mo., 1946.

DANIEL C. PETERSON
HUSTON SMITH

Q

QUORUM OF THE TWELVE APOSTLES

Twelve men ordained to the MELCHIZEDEK PRIESTHOOD office of APOSTLE constitute the Quorum of the Twelve Apostles, the second-highest presiding quorum in the government of The Church of Jesus Christ of Latter-day Saints. The highest presiding quorum is the FIRST PRESIDENCY, three HIGH PRIESTS who have generally been apostles who hold all keys (AUTHORITY) pertaining to the spiritual and temporal affairs of the Church. The Twelve serve under the direction of the First Presidency. Latter-day Saints sustain these fifteen men as PROPHETS, SEERS, AND REVELATORS for the Church, who receive "a special spiritual endowment in connection with their teaching of the people. . . . Others of the General Authorities are not given this special spiritual endowment and authority covering their teaching" (J. Reuben Clark, Jr., *Church News* [July 31, 1954]:9).

Several titles refer to the body of the twelve apostles: the Quorum of the Twelve, the Council of the Twelve, or simply the Twelve. The designation Quorum of the Twelve is the scriptural title and the formal name used by the First Presidency in presenting the Twelve to Church members for their sustaining vote. The designation Council of the Twelve is used commonly in Church publica-tions and in communicating with persons of other faiths.

HISTORY. The first members of the Quorum of the Twelve in modern times were ordained on February 14, 1835. This type of quorum has its roots in New Testament precedent (Matt. 10:1) and in modern REVELATION (D&C 18:26–39). After the ZION'S CAMP expedition of 1834, the Prophet Joseph SMITH called together in 1835 those who had participated and revealed that "it was the will of God that those who went to Zion, with a deter-mination to lay down their lives, . . . should be ordained to the ministry" (*HC* 2:182). He then directed the three witnesses of the Book of Mormon (Oliver COWDERY, David WHITMER, and Martin HARRIS) to prayerfully choose the Twelve in harmony with an earlier revelation (D&C 18:37). The Presidency then laid hands on the Three Witnesses, empowering them to make the selection (*HC* 2:186–87). Those chosen were Thomas B. Marsh, David W. Patten, Brigham YOUNG, Heber C. Kimball, Orson Hyde, William E. McLellin, Parley P. Pratt, Luke S. Johnson, William B. Smith, Orson Pratt, John F. Boynton, and Lyman E. Johnson. These twelve men were then ordained apostles by the Three Witnesses and given the keys pertaining to their holy calling. The First Presidency also laid their hands on them and con-firmed these blessings and ordinations (*T&S* 2

Quorum of the Twelve Apostles (1944): Front (left to right): George Albert Smith, George F. Richards, Joseph Fielding Smith, Stephen L Richards, John A. Widtsoe, Joseph F. Merrill. Back (left to right): Charles A. Callis, Albert E. Bowen, Harold B. Lee, Spencer W. Kimball, Ezra Taft Benson, Mark E. Petersen. Courtesy University of Utah.

[Apr. 15, 1845]:868). Oliver Cowdery then gave to the Twelve a charge to "preach the Gospel to every nation" (*HC* 2:195).

A month later, the Twelve requested further divine guidance as they prepared to preach. The response was a revelation that defined their duties and the duties of the newly formed Quorum of the Seventy (see D&C 107:21–39). Primary duties of the Quorum of the Twelve are to be "special witnesses of the name of Christ in all the world," "to officiate in the name of the Lord, under the direction of the Presidency of the Church," "to build up the Church, and regulate all the affairs of the same," and "to open the door [of all nations] by the proclamation of the gospel of Jesus Christ" (D&C 107:23, 33, 35; cf. 112:16–21; 124:128).

Joseph Smith assigned the members of the Quorum of the Twelve to regulate the scattered branches of the Church. Later, he sent them on proselytizing missions to foreign lands. In 1840–1841 nine of the Twelve served special missions to the British Isles. When they left Great Britain after twelve months, more than 4,000 new members had joined the Church. These nine brethren also established procedures for a continuing program of immigration of the British convert Saints to America (*see* BRITISH ISLES, THE CHURCH IN; MISSIONS OF TWELVE TO BRITISH ISLES.)

Missionary success in Britain bonded members of the Twelve into a united quorum under the leadership of the quorum president, Brigham Young, who was appointed January 19, 1841. When they returned to Church headquarters at Nauvoo, Illinois, Joseph Smith expanded their duties to include regulating the affairs of the STAKE there.

In late March 1844, Joseph Smith conferred on the Quorum of the Twelve all of the ORDINANCES, keys, and authority that he possessed. Describing this event, Wilford WOODRUFF said Joseph Smith "lived until every key, power and principle of the holy Priesthood was sealed on the Twelve and on President Young, as their President." He further quoted the Prophet's explanation and injunction to the Twelve: "I have lived until I have seen this burden, which has rested on my shoulders, rolled on to the shoulders of other men; . . . the keys of the kingdom are planted on the earth to be taken away no more for ever. . . . You have to round up your shoulders to bear up the kingdom. No matter what becomes of me" (*JD* 13:164).

After a mob assassinated Joseph Smith on June 27, 1844, and the First Presidency was dissolved, the Church faced the question of SUCCESSION IN THE PRESIDENCY for the first time.

The resulting confusion was resolved when the Quorum of the Twelve, as the next highest presiding quorum, stepped forward and was sustained to succeed the First Presidency. From June 1844 to December 1847, the Twelve governed the Church under their president, Brigham Young. In their presiding capacity, they published an 1845 proclamation to the kings of the world and the President of the United States of America (*see* PROCLAMATIONS OF THE FIRST PRESIDENCY AND THE QUORUM OF THE TWELVE APOSTLES). President Young was sustained as PRESIDENT OF THE CHURCH on December 5, 1847, by the Twelve and by the Saints in conference on December 27, 1847.

This transition of leadership established the precedent and order that have been followed in all subsequent reorganizations of the First Presidency. Upon the death of a Church President, the First Presidency is dissolved and the Quorum of the Twelve becomes the presiding council of the Church. The President of the Twelve who is the senior apostle on the earth becomes the presiding officer of the Church and remains in that capacity until a new First Presidency is organized.

An event that was highly significant to the Twelve occurred at the close of the administration of President Lorenzo SNOW in 1901. For more than five decades preceding this time, the Twelve had spent less time taking the gospel to other nations because of the need to preside over the Saints at home. Also, U.S. government prosecution of polygamists had driven some of them into exile. Shortly before the October 1901 General Conference, President Snow reminded the Twelve that they had a scriptural duty to preach the gospel to all the world; presiding over the STAKES was not sufficient (*Juvenile Instructor* 36 [Nov. 1901]:689–90.)

At the final session of that conference, President Snow defined the duties of the apostles, seventies, high priests, and ELDERS. The Twelve were "to look after the interests of the world" (*CR* [Oct. 1901]:61). President Snow died four days after the conference, but the Twelve recognized the impor-

Quorum of the Twelve Apostles (October 1988): Front row (left to right): Howard W. Hunter, Boyd K. Packer, Marvin J. Ashton, L. Tom Perry. Back row (left to right): David B. Haight, James E. Faust, Neal A. Maxwell, Russell M. Nelson, Dallin H. Oaks, M. Russell Ballard, Joseph B. Wirthlin, Richard G. Scott.

The room in the Salt Lake Temple (1991) where the Quorum of the Twelve Apostles meets regularly to plan, pray, and take counsel together. Quorum action requires unanimity.

tance of his instruction. The Quorum president, Joseph F. SMITH, wrote that "we accept what [President Snow said] on the duties of the Twelve . . . as the word of the Lord to us all" (*Juvenile Instructor* 36 [Nov. 1901]:690). Consequently, the Twelve renewed their international missionary effort. Since that time, by direction of the First Presidency, the Twelve have dedicated many nations for preaching the gospel and continue to supervise missionary work throughout the Church.

APPOINTMENT.   A member of the Quorum of the Twelve is selected by the First Presidency, which may consider several candidates. The Presidency then chooses one person by revelation and calls him to the position. This involves essentially the same principles as the selection of Matthias to fill the vacancy that resulted from the death of Judas Iscariot (Acts 1:15–26).

When a new appointment to the Quorum is to be announced (usually at a general conference), a member of the First Presidency presents the names of GENERAL AUTHORITIES, including the new apostle, and other general Church officers to be sustained by Church members. The sustaining complies with the principle of COMMON CONSENT (D&C 26:2).

After Church members sustain the newly called person, the First Presidency and Quorum of the Twelve ordain him to the office of apostle and give him all the keys of the holy apostleship. These are the same keys Jesus Christ conferred on the Twelve he called in New Testament times, and also the same keys restored by Peter, James, and John to Joseph Smith and Oliver Cowdery in this dispensation. The keys given to the new apostle include the authority to preach the gospel in all the world and to seal ordinances on earth that will be sealed eternally (Matt. 16:19; 28:19–20; John 20:22–23).

Callings to the Quorum of the Twelve are for life. The date on which a person becomes a member of the Quorum (usually the date he is sustained as an apostle) establishes his position of seniority in the Quorum relative to other quorum members. Seniority within the Quorum determines who will be the next President of the Church, for that office passes to the senior apostle. This divinely revealed order identifies the most experienced apostle as the future president and prevents any striving for office or vying for power or position (*see* SUCCESSION IN THE PRESIDENCY).

DUTIES.   Consistent with earlier revelations, the Twelve today are commissioned to open the nations of the world to the preaching of the gospel (D&C 107:35). By assignment from the First Presidency, members of the Twelve meet with heads of state to obtain official permission for the Church to teach the gospel consistent with the laws of those countries.

When the Twelve act under direction of the First Presidency, they have authority to receive revelation for their assignments, which include supervising the Seventy, overseeing the stakes, and training leaders (D&C 107:33). Only the President of the Church, however, has the right and authority to receive revelation for the whole Church (D&C 28:2–3).

Members of the Twelve serve on committees established by the First Presidency and those within the Quorum. Committee assignments are rotated periodically.

The Quorum of the Twelve directs the work of the Seventy. The Twelve are to "call upon the Seventy, when they need assistance . . . instead of any others" (D&C 107:38). The presidents of the Quorums of the Seventy report to the Twelve.

The Twelve meet in the SALT LAKE TEMPLE, usually weekly, to transact all business that requires decisions by the Quorum. The Quorum normally brings the decisions it reaches to its meetings with the First Presidency. These two bodies together constitute the Council of the First Presidency and the Quorum of the Twelve Apostles. This council takes final action on all matters that affect the Church, including new Church leadership callings; establishment of policies, procedures, and programs; creation, division, and reorganization of missions and stakes. Church PRIESTHOOD QUORUMS strive for unanimity in their decisions, in accordance with revelation (D&C 107:27). Until agreement is reached, the Quorum of the Twelve takes no action. Instead, the President of the Twelve usually defers the matter for reconsideration. Unanimity among the presiding quorums of the Church provides Church members with an assurance that "the united voice of the First Presidency and the Twelve" will never "lead the Saints astray or send forth counsel to the world that is contrary to the mind and will of the Lord" (Joseph Fielding Smith, *Ensign* 2 [July 1972]:88).

The First Presidency assigns members of the Twelve and other General Authorities to speak at semiannual general conferences of the Church, but normally does not assign a topic. Members of the First Presidency and the Twelve speak at every general conference; other General Authorities speak periodically as assigned. Church members regard messages of the First Presidency and the Twelve as inspired (D&C 68:4).

Each stake has semiannual stake conferences. A General Authority or a Regional Representative usually presides at one of these conferences each year, as assigned by the President of the Quorum of the Twelve. Because of the large and increasing number of stakes, members of the Twelve are generally assigned to attend stake conferences only to organize new stakes, divide existing stakes, or reorganize STAKE PRESIDENCIES.

The President of the Quorum also assigns Quorum members to attend conferences where several stakes meet together. These multiregional conferences give Church members a more frequent opportunity to see and hear members of the First Presidency and the Twelve.

Members of the Twelve are "special witnesses" of the name of Jesus Christ in all the world; they possess a KNOWLEDGE, by revelation, of the literal RESURRECTION of Christ and a knowledge that he directs the affairs of his Church today. That shared conviction unites the Twelve in a bond of unity and love.

BIBLIOGRAPHY

Allen, James B., and Malcolm R. Thorp. "The Mission of the Twelve to England, 1840–41: Mormon Apostles and the Working Classes." *BYU Studies* 15 (Summer 1975):499–526.

Esplin, Ronald K. "The Emergence of Brigham Young and the Twelve to Mormon Leadership, 1830–1841," pp. 427–512. Ph.D. diss., Brigham Young University, 1981.

Larsen, Dean L. "Apostle and Prophet: Divine Priesthood Callings." *Priesthood*, pp. 38–47. Salt Lake City, 1981.

McConkie, Bruce R. "Succession in Presidency." *Church News* (Mar. 23, 1974):7–9.

Smith, Joseph Fielding. "The Holy Apostleship." *DS*, Vol. 3, pp. 144–59.

———. "The Twelve Apostles." *IE* 59 (Nov. 1956):786–88.

———. "The First Presidency and the Council of the Twelve." *IE* 69 (Nov. 1966):977–79.

Talbot, Wilburn D. "The Duties and Responsibilities of the Apostles of The Church of Jesus Christ of Latter-day Saints, 1835–1945." Ph.D. diss., Brigham Young University, 1978.

WILLIAM O. NELSON

R

RACE, RACISM

The Church of Jesus Christ of Latter-day Saints teaches that all humans are literally the spirit offspring of the eternal Heavenly Father (Acts 17:26, 29). The concept of race refers to populations identifiable by the frequency with which a selected number of genetically determined traits appear in that population. While all human groups belong to the same species (*Homo sapiens*), they may be differentiated into various races by such traits as skin pigmentation, hair color, head shape, and nose form. A negative concept of racism implies that one set of racial characteristics is superior to others. The Church denounces this viewpoint.

In 1775, Johann Friedrich Blumenbach established five human races differentiated by skin color. Later anthropologists used other characteristics of the human body and arrived at a different number of racial subdivisions, from a minimum of two to a maximum of several dozen. By limiting criteria, most anthropologists now agree on the existence of three distinct groups: the Caucasoid, the Mongoloid, and the Negroid.

The apostle Paul taught in the New Testament that God "hath made of one blood all nations of men for to dwell on all the face of the earth" (Acts 17:26). In the sight of God, race, color, and nationality make no difference, an idea stressed in the Book of Mormon: "He inviteth them all to come unto him and partake of his goodness; and he denieth none that come unto him, black and white, bond and free, male and female; and he remembereth the heathen; and all are alike unto God, both Jew and Gentile" (2 Ne. 26:33).

Spencer W. KIMBALL, in speaking of race and racism as President of the Church, said: "We do wish that there would be no racial prejudice. . . . Racial prejudice is of the devil. . . . There is no place for it in the gospel of Jesus Christ" (pp. 236–37).

Latter-day Saints believe that Jesus Christ came to earth to die for all mankind and to teach them how to live. He taught two great commandments: first, to love God with all one's heart, might, mind, and strength; second, to love one's fellow men as one loves oneself (Matt. 22:36–39). Throughout his life, Jesus showed how to obey these two commandments.

Prior to June 1978, priesthood denial to blacks within the Church aroused both concern about, and accusations of, racism in the Church, especially during the civil rights movement of the 1960s in the United States. For more than a century Presidents of the Church had taught that blacks were not yet to receive the priesthood, for reasons known only to God, but would someday receive it. As made clear in Official Declaration—2 (appended to the Doctrine and Covenants in September 1978), there had long been an anticipation that the priesthood would be made available to all worthy men—an anticipation realized and announced June 9, 1978.

In the October 1978 Semiannual General Conference of the Church, President Spencer W. Kimball restated to the world that he had received a revelation making all worthy male members of the Church eligible for the priesthood without regard for race or color (*see* DOCTRINE AND COVENANTS: OFFICIAL DECLARATION—2).

BIBLIOGRAPHY

Bush, Lester E., Jr., and Armand L. Mauss, eds. *Neither White Nor Black.* Midvale, Utah, 1954.

Hunter, Howard W. "All Are Alike Unto God." *Ensign* 9 (June 1979):72–74.

Kimball, Spencer W. *The Teachings of Spencer W. Kimball,* ed. Edward L. Kimball. Salt Lake City, 1982.

LeBaron, Dale E. *All Are Alike Unto God.* Salt Lake City, 1990.

RITA DE CASSIA FLORES
ENOC Q. FLORES

RAISING THE DEAD

God has the power to raise the dead. This truth is confirmed by ancient scripture and reaffirmed by revelations in the RESTORATION OF THE GOSPEL in this dispensation. When asked if the "Mormons" could raise the dead, the Prophet Joseph SMITH replied, "No, . . . but God can raise the dead, through man as an instrument" (*TPJS,* p. 120).

Raising the dead is the act of restoring to life one whose eternal spirit has departed from its mortal body. Restoration to mortal life, however, is not to be equated or confused with resurrection of the body from death to immortality. A person raised from the dead is not thereby made immortal; in such cases, the individual becomes mortal a second time and must die again before being raised in the resurrection to immortality (Bruce R. McConkie, *Doctrinal New Testament Commentary,* Vol. 1, p. 256, Salt Lake City, 1965).

The scriptures report that on three separate occasions during his mortal ministry Jesus raised individuals from the dead. The daughter of Jairus was called back to life within hours of her death (Mark 5:22–43). The lifeless body of the widow's son in the village of Nain was being carried to the cemetery when Jesus intervened and commanded him to arise, "and he that was dead sat up, and began to speak" (Luke 7:11–17). The body of Lazarus had been dead four days, prepared for burial, and entombed when Jesus commanded, "Lazarus, come forth. And he that was dead came forth" (John 11:1–46). During his ministry in the Western Hemisphere, the resurrected Jesus again performed many miracles, including raising a man from the dead (3 Ne. 26:15).

Jesus gave his twelve apostles power to raise the dead (Matt. 10:8). He also gave this power to his disciples in the Western Hemisphere, and they "did heal the sick, and raise the dead" (4 Ne. 1:5).

Elijah raised the widow's son (1 Kgs. 17:17–24). Elisha restored to life the son of a Shunammite woman (2 Kgs. 4:18–37). Peter raised Tabitha and "presented her alive to her friends" (Acts 9:36–42). Paul raised Eutychus (Acts 20:7–12). Nephi$_3$ restored his brother Timothy to life after he had suffered a violent death (3 Ne. 7:19; 19:4).

The priesthood authority by which miracles were performed in ancient times by the servants of God has been restored and is functional in the latter days. The power to raise the dead, if the Lord wills, is inherent in the exercise of priesthood authority by righteous priesthood holders and in the restoration of the gospel of Jesus Christ.

BIBLIOGRAPHY

Cowley, Matthew. *Matthew Cowley Speaks,* p. 247. Salt Lake City, 1971.

Romney, Thomas C. *The Life of Lorenzo Snow,* pp. 406–419. Salt Lake City, 1955.

DENNIS D. FLAKE

REASON AND REVELATION

LDS teaching affirms the supreme authority of divine REVELATION. However, revelation is not understood as an impediment to rational inquiry but as the framework within which the natural human desire to know can most vigorously and fruitfully be exercised. In traditional Judaism and Islam, revelation is mainly seen as law, and the orthodox life of pious obedience is incompatible with the questioning spirit of philosophic life (*see* WORLD RELIGIONS [NON-CHRISTIAN] AND MORMONISM). The Christian view of religion as belief or FAITH and of revelation as teachings or DOCTRINE has encouraged a perennial interest in reconciling the authority of revealed religion with that of reason. Thus, among revealed religions, Christianity has been the most open—and the most vulnerable—to the claims of reason.

The theological tradition of medieval Christianity viewed the Gospels as a supernatural fulfillment of the brilliant but partial insights of natural reason as represented by Greek philosophers, especially Plato and Aristotle. The Christian philosophers Augustine and Aquinas agreed with their pagan predecessors that reason is the noblest natural human faculty, but argued that it cannot reach God, its true end, without the aid of revelation. Thus, revelation was held to be superior, but even this superiority was to some extent defined by a view of the good inherited from pre-Christian PHILOSOPHY.

The founders of the Protestant tradition attacked this alliance between classical philosophy and the gospel, and tended to limit reason to an instrumental status. So limited, however, the Protestants viewed the exercise of reason as redounding to the glory of God. In this way, the Reformation laid the foundation for the later alliance between faith and technological science.

The LDS understanding of this issue rests upon foundations equally distinct from Protestant and Catholic traditions. LDS doctrine emphasizes the continuity between the natural and the divine realms, a continuity founded in part on the eternal importance of human understanding. But Latter-day Saints do not see the dignity of the mind as the sole basis of this continuity. Rather, they look to the exaltation of the whole person—not only as a knower of truth but also as a servant of the Lord and a source of blessings to one's fellow beings and one's posterity. In contrast to other Christian and Jewish traditions, moreover, LDS teaching emphasizes the necessity of present and future revelation, both to the individual and to the Church, in the pursuit of all these ends.

Warnings against the arrogance of human reason are common and founded in scripture. Thus, the Book of Mormon prophet Jacob decries "the vainness, and the frailties, and the foolishness of men! When they are learned they think they are wise, and they hearken not unto the counsel of God, for they set it aside, supposing they know of themselves, wherefore, their wisdom is foolishness and it profiteth them not. And they shall perish. But to be learned is good if they hearken unto the counsels of God" (2 Ne. 9:28–29). He thus announces a theme—the goodness of learning—that is almost as prominent in LDS teaching as the necessity of revelation, especially in the Doctrine and Covenants, where the Saints are enjoined to pursue learning of all kinds by "study" as well as by "faith" (D&C 88:78–79, 118).

Though one purpose of rational inquiry is to enhance missionary work (D&C 88:80), the goodness of learning transcends any practical applications. Indeed, this intellectual goodness is linked directly and intrinsically with the exaltation of the individual, whose nature must conform to the "conditions" or "law" of the kingdom he or she attains: "For intelligence cleaveth unto intelligence; wisdom receiveth wisdom; truth embraceth truth; virtue loveth virtue; light cleaveth unto light" (D&C 88:38–40). Such perfections also pertain to natural human faculties, directed and aided by general and personal revelation, for ultimately the light that "enlighteneth your eyes" and "quickeneth your understandings" is the "light of Christ," the "light of truth . . . which is in all things" (D&C 88:6, 7, 11, 13; cf. Moro. 7:16–25).

Revealed light and natural light are not completely distinct categories. Revelation engages natural reason and indeed may build upon it. It is sometimes described in LDS teaching as "a still voice of perfect mildness" able to "pierce unto the very soul" (Hel. 5:21–31) or as a spirit that resonates with the mind to produce a feeling of "pure intelligence" or "sudden strokes of ideas" (*TPJS*, p. 151). It is thus appropriate to seek and prepare for revelation by the effort of reason: "You must study it out in your mind; then you must ask me if it be right" (D&C 9:8).

LDS teaching encourages a distinct openness to the intrinsic as well as instrumental goodness of the life of the mind, an openness founded on the continuity between the human and divine realms. The full exercise of human reason under the direction of revelation holds a high place among the virtuous and praiseworthy ends to be sought by the Saints (A of F 13), for the scripture promises that "whatever principle of intelligence we attain unto in this life, it will rise with us in the resurrection," and the more "knowledge and intelligence" one gains through "diligence and obedience," the greater "the advantage in the world to come" (D&C 130:18–19). This emphasis on intellectual development in human progress toward GODHOOD accords with the fundamental doctrine that is the official motto of Brigham Young University—

namely, that "the glory of God is intelligence" (D&C 93:36).

Equated with "light and truth," such intelligence by nature "forsake[s] that evil one" (D&C 93:37). It cannot be simply identified with conventional measures of "intelligence" or with the Greek philosophic idea of a pure, immaterial, and self-directed intelligence, a concept that was very influential in medieval theology. For Latter-day Saints, the attainment of INTELLIGENCE must be integrated with the labor of shaping the material world and binding together families and generations, for "the elements are eternal, and spirit and element, inseparably connected, receive a fulness of joy" (D&C 93:33). To the doctrine that "the glory of God is intelligence," one must add God's statement to Moses that "this is my work and my glory—to bring to pass the immortality and eternal life of man" (Moses 1:39).

BIBLIOGRAPHY

Etienne Gilson's *Reason and Revelation in the Middle Ages* (New York, 1938) provides an excellent discussion from a Thomistic standpoint. Hugh W. Nibley, in "Educating the Saints" (in *Nibley on the Timely and the Timeless*, edited by T. Madsen, Provo, Utah, 1978), cites quotations from former Church President Brigham Young to praise intellectual improvement as essential both to individual salvation and to building the kingdom of God. For an interesting attempt to set forth LDS revelation as harmonious with the evidence of reason, see Parley P. Pratt's *Key to the Science of Theology* (Salt Lake City, 1973). Though somewhat confined by the categories of nineteenth-century science, Pratt exhibits much of the distinctive potential of Mormon belief for engagement with scientific cosmology. Leo Strauss, in "Jerusalem and Athens: Some Preliminary Reflections" (in *Studies in Platonic Political Philosophy*, ed. T. Pangle, pp. 147–73, Chicago, 1983), emphasizes the difference between the life of rational inquiry and the life of pious obedience.

RALPH C. HANCOCK

REBAPTISM

Once a person joins The Church of Jesus Christ of Latter-day Saints, circumstances requiring rebaptism are unusual. In current policy and practice, a person would be rebaptized only in two cases: (1) if membership records were irretrievably lost and no other proof of membership could be established; or (2) if an excommunicated person qualified for reentry into the Church. As members partake of the SACRAMENT weekly, repenting of sin, their baptismal COVENANTS are renewed and rebaptism is unnecessary.

One enters into membership in the Church only through BAPTISM by immersion for the REMISSION OF SINS by one holding the appropriate priesthood, regardless of any prior baptism or initiation ordinance. Latter-day scriptures refer to baptism as a NEW AND EVERLASTING COVENANT. It is the ordinance received by one who accepts the gospel of Jesus Christ, with the promise that proper baptism opens onto the path that leads to eternal life. But baptisms performed outside the framework of the restored priesthood are of no avail for one who wishes to enter in at the strait gate and onto that path (D&C 22:1–2).

Rebaptism is rare among Latter-day Saints in modern times. Historically, however, many members were rebaptized as an act of rededication. This was first practiced in Nauvoo and was continued in the Utah Territory. Rebaptism served as a ritual of recommitment but was not viewed as essential to salvation. Members often sought rebaptism when called to assist in colonization or to participate in one of the UNITED ORDERS. On some occasions, the Saints were rebaptized as they prepared for marriage or entrance into the temple. Early members also rebaptized some of the sick among them as an act of healing. Because of misuse by some Church members, all such practices of rebaptism were discontinued in 1897.

H. DEAN GARRETT

RECORD KEEPING

The keeping of records is done in response to a direct commandment from the Lord and is considered a sacred trust and obligation. "The matter of record keeping is one of the most important duties devolving on the Church," said Elder Joseph Fielding SMITH (p. 96). Indeed, the very day the LDS Church was organized, the Prophet Joseph SMITH received a revelation: "Behold, there shall be a record kept among you" (D&C 21:1). This requirement apparently has been the same in every DISPENSATION. The Pearl of Great Price states that a BOOK OF REMEMBRANCE was first kept in the ADAMIC LANGUAGE, and Adam's children were taught to read and write, "having a language that was pure and undefiled"; therefore, it was given unto many "to write by the spirit of inspiration" (Moses 6:5–6). ENOCH, seventh in descent from ADAM and the father of Methuselah, also kept a record and commented upon the divine prototype of it: "For a book of remembrance we have written among us, according to the pattern given by the finger of God" (Moses 6:46). Abraham continued the practice, affirming that "records of the fathers" had come into his hands and stating, "I shall endeavor to write some of these things upon this record, for the benefit of my posterity that shall come after me" (Abr. 1:31). Such records are of three types: (1) accounts of God's dealings with his children (the scriptures, for example); (2) records of religious ORDINANCES; and (3) histories of nations and peoples, including personal histories.

SCRIPTURES. Prophets have been commanded to write scripture. For example, Moses in his time received a great revelation concerning the creation of heaven and earth with the divine imperative, "Write the words which I speak" (Moses 2:1). Those words are largely preserved in Genesis in the Bible. During Jeremiah's difficult mission a king desecrated a scroll containing some of God's revelations and the word of the Lord came to Jeremiah saying, "Take thee again another roll, and write in it all the former words that were in the first roll" (Jer. 36:27–32). Jeremiah and his scribe did so, and those words are in the book of Jeremiah.

Near the time of Jeremiah's vicissitudes, the Book of Mormon prophet LEHI took his family and fled from Jerusalem into the wilderness in 600 B.C. He was commanded by the Lord to send his sons back to Jerusalem to obtain certain plates of brass that had been kept by his forebears. The plates were engraved with the genealogy of Lehi's family, the five books of Moses, and writings of the prophets down to Jeremiah (1 Ne. 5:11–14). LAMAN and NEPHI$_1$, two of the sons of Lehi, tried to get Laban, the keeper of the plates, to give them the plates or to exchange them for certain other treasures, but Laban refused and sought to kill Lehi's sons. Eventually Laban himself was condemned of the Lord and slain (*see* SWORD OF LABAN), for "it is better that one man should perish than that a nation should dwindle and perish in unbelief" (1 Ne. 4:12–13). Thus the plates were procured and preserved, and they provided the cultural and spiritual foundation of the Nephite civilization in their promised land in the Western world (Mosiah 1:3–5; *DS* 2:198).

A page from Wilford Woodruff's journal (1837). From the earliest days of the Church, members have been exhorted to keep historical and personal records. One of the most prodigious journal writers was Wilford Woodruff, who kept copious journals for over sixty-five years.

After his resurrection at Jerusalem, Jesus Christ appeared to the Nephites and personally emphasized the importance of record keeping. He provided them some of the revelations given to MALACHI. The Lord then commanded NEPHI$_3$ (the record keeper at the time of Jesus' advent and a descendent of the first Nephi) to bring out the records kept by the Nephites. He examined them and reminded Nephi that Samuel, a Lamanite prophet, had testified that he (Christ) should arise from the dead and prophesied that at Christ's resurrection others would also arise and appear to many. Jesus then inquired, "How be it that ye have not written this thing . . . ? And it came to pass that Jesus commanded that it should be written; therefore it was written according as he commanded" (3 Ne. 23:11, 13).

RELIGIOUS ORDINANCES. Just as the doctrines and commandments from God must be recorded, so also must the responses and actions of the children of God be written. Prophetic scriptures warn that God's children will be judged out of sacred records kept both on earth and in heaven. Those responsible for keeping the records on earth are charged to make them as accurate as possible. Ordinances such as baptisms, confirmations, ordinations to the priesthood, patriarchal blessings, endowments, and sealings—all should be precisely recorded. Financial records of donations are especially carefully preserved, such as the TITHING record. Earthly and spiritual conduct is to be measured by the things written (Mal. 3:16–18; Rev. 20:12). The Prophet Joseph Smith affirmed, "Our acts are recorded, and at a future day they will be laid before us, and if we should fail to judge right and injure our fellow-beings, they may there, perhaps, condemn us; there they are of great consequence, and to me the consequence appears to be of force, beyond anything which I am able to express" (*TPJS*, p. 69).

To qualify for eternal blessings, each person must come unto God through Christ, make commitments and covenants through certain ordinances, and have them properly recorded. Those who have died without hearing the gospel of Jesus Christ must have the ordinances of salvation and exaltation performed in their behalf (*see* BAPTISM FOR THE DEAD), and record keeping is vital for all such ordinances performed in the Church. Vicarious ordinances can be performed only for individuals properly identified through dependable records. The Church sponsors programs to locate and microfilm family records worldwide and make them available to members and others in their genealogical research and FAMILY HISTORY work. Many members are involved in such research and in vicarious service in the TEMPLES of the Church in behalf of the dead. It is all done in the faith that whatsoever is done by proper authority, in the name of the Lord, truly and faithfully, and with accurate records kept, is established on earth and in heaven, and cannot be annulled, according to the decrees of the great Jehovah (cf. D&C 128:9).

HISTORIES. Church members are counseled to include personal histories among the records they keep. All such records are valuable in the preservation and transmission of culture within each family, and they often have an impact broader than anticipated by those who write them. Nephi₁, who wrote a history of his people as commanded by God, did anticipate its benefit to others, saying, "I write the things of my soul. . . . For my soul delighteth in the scriptures, and my heart pondereth them, and writeth them for the learning and the profit of my children" (2 Ne. 4:15).

President Spencer W. KIMBALL offered this challenge: "Get a notebook . . . a journal that will last through all time, and maybe the angels may quote from it for eternity. Begin today and write in it your goings and comings, your deepest thoughts, your achievements and your failures, your associations and your triumphs, your impressions and your testimonies" (1975, p. 5). Parents may not see, in the present moment, the potential value of what they write in a personal journal, nor can they predict the response of their descendants to it, but anyone who holds the journal of an ancestor can testify of the joy in possessing it. Minimally, parents should record accurately special events such as dates of birth, marriages, ordinations, and deaths. While it is not necessary to write everything that occurs each day, things of a spiritual nature and other happenings that arouse poignant feelings should be recorded (*see* JOURNALS). One parent recounted with regret, "I remembered [a] . . . spiritual experience I had had years earlier, just before my baptism. I hadn't written that in my journal, . . . and now I couldn't remember enough details of the story to retell it. I wanted to share that event with my son—and because I hadn't recorded it, I could not" (Espinosa, p. 24). President Kimball promised: "As our posterity read of our life's experiences, they, too, will come to know and love us. And in the glorious day when our families are together in the eternities, we will already be acquainted" (1980, p. 61).

Record keeping has resulted in the creation of sacred scriptures of incalculable value; records of ordinances done and covenants made will have eternal significance; and the histories of nations and individuals have helped throughout the ages in the developments of civilization.

[*See also* Genealogical Society of Utah; Granite Mountain Record Vault; Historians, Church; World Conferences on Records.]

BIBLIOGRAPHY

Espinosa, Luis V. "The Voice Spoke Spanish." *Ensign* 7 (Jan. 1977):24.

"Eternal Implications of the Gospel: Life Everlasting, Family Records, Temple Blessings." *Ensign* 7 (Jan. 1977):2–75.

Kimball, Spencer W. "The Angels May Quote from It." *New Era* 5 (Oct. 1975):4–5.

———. "President Kimball Speaks Out on Personal Journals." *Ensign* 10 (Dec. 1980):61.

Smith, Joseph Fielding. *Church History and Modern Revelation*, pp. 96–97, 99. Salt Lake City, 1946.

BEVERLY J. NORTON

REDEEMER

See: Jesus Christ, Names and Titles of

REFORMATION, PROTESTANT

See: Protestant Reformation

REFORMATION (LDS) OF 1856–1857

A reform movement initiated by Church leaders in 1856–1857 to rekindle faith and testimony throughout the Church has long been known as the Mormon Reformation. Motivations for reform had as much to do with the lofty expectations of Church leaders as with the spiritual complacency or deficiency of the Saints. The Reformation occurred in a period of optimism and anticipation, as Church leaders hoped to create the unified society viewed as a necessary precursor to the MILLENNIUM. With the Saints now secluded in their Rocky Mountain retreat, a reemphasis of basic principles seemed especially appropriate.

The Mormon Reformation commenced in early September 1856, when President Brigham YOUNG sent his counselor Jedediah M. Grant to preach reform in settlements north of Salt Lake City. While speaking to assembled Saints, Grant was prompted to commit them to reform and to instruct them to signify that commitment through REBAPTISM. Grant's success had a contagious effect, and within days Saints in other settlements were also rebaptized.

Early reform efforts, influenced by President Grant's unbridled enthusiasm, were somewhat spontaneous. The revivalistic spirit, the anxious confession, and the mass rebaptisms, however, gradually gave way to more judicious and ordered reform. The reform became especially systematic at Church headquarters, where a policy was established to have two home missionaries assigned to each WARD. Equipped with a twenty-seven-question catechism to help measure the worthiness of the Saints, the home missionaries assisted families with everything from hygiene and church attendance to obeying the Ten Commandments. Only after some months of missionary-member visits were Saints in the Salt Lake City wards rebaptized

in early spring of 1857. In Salt Lake City, rebaptism generally marked the formal end of the Reformation, though reform fervor continued until mid-1858.

Under instructions from President Young, the Reformation was carried to settlements and missions throughout the world. While procedures differed somewhat in areas away from Utah, rebaptism was a requirement for all faithful Saints. It symbolized both forgiveness of sin and a recommitment to obey commandments. Those who refused to be rebaptized might lose their membership in the Church. In Britain, zealous application of Reformation principles resulted in trimming from Church rolls a large number of the less-committed.

The era of the Reformation is often regarded as a controversial period. Some critics have claimed that BLOOD ATONEMENT was practiced at this time. While President Young did preach that forgiveness for certain sins could come only through the sinner's shedding his blood, such comments reflect his style more than his intent. Many of Brigham Young's utterances were rhetorical and designed to encourage (or even frighten) Saints into gospel conformity. While publicly he threatened, privately he instructed Church leaders to forgive those who expressed sorrow for sin and repented.

For many Latter-day Saints, the Reformation was a period of spiritual rejuvenation. Attending meetings, paying tithing and other free-will offerings, and showing other outward indicators of renewal increased dramatically. The Reformation also had the effect of separating "wheat from chaff." Some members were disconcerted by the processes and the effects of reform and chose to leave LDS settlements. Perhaps the most damaging legacy from the point of view of Latter-day Saints was the grist the Reformation provided anti-Mormon writers who for decades would inaccurately characterize the period as a "reign of terror" (*see* ANTI-MORMON PUBLICATIONS).

It may be that both critics and apologists have claimed too much for the Reformation. Certainly the reform impulse was on the whole more structured and restrained than has often been believed. Conversely, it appears that the major impact was of short duration and only moderate consequence—perhaps because the UTAH EXPEDITION and impending armed conflict abruptly ended the main thrust of the movement less than a year after it began.

BIBLIOGRAPHY

Larson, Gustive O. "The Mormon Reformation." *Utah Historical Quarterly* 26 (Jan. 1958):45–63.

Peterson, Paul H. "The Mormon Reformation of 1856–1857: The Rhetoric and the Reality." *Journal of Mormon History* 15 (1989):59–87.

PAUL H. PETERSON

REGION, REGIONAL REPRESENTATIVE

Regions are intermediate geographic units positioned between the STAKE and the general AREA levels of administration in The Church of Jesus Christ of Latter-day Saints. In 1990, 447 regions around the world consisted of two to six stakes per region in close geographical proximity, each stake being comprised of between four and ten local WARDS of 200 to 700 members each. Groups of ten to forty regions are organized into areas determined by geographic and administrative convenience. Each area is presided over by three seventies who constitute the area presidency.

Regional Representatives are part-time lay officers of the Church that are called by the First Presidency, receive general instructions from the Quorum of the Twelve Apostles, and serve under the direction of the area presidency. Because Regional Representatives do not preside as line officers, they serve without counselors, and stake presidencies report directly to area presidencies. A Regional Representative may preside at a stake conference when assigned.

The principal responsibility of a Regional Representative is to train stake leaders. This training may take place through personal visits, regional council meetings consisting of the stake presidencies in the region, stake CONFERENCES, or other leadership meetings. A Regional Representative has no authority to call local leaders or to counsel individual members in connection with personal matters, but serves as an organizational link providing information and feedback between local Church officers and the General Authorities at area or Church headquarters.

A Regional Representative serves for a period determined by the First Presidency, typically five years. The first Regional Representatives were called in October 1967, and with the growth of the Church, the number has increased steadily.

With the approval of the area presidency, the regional council may organize occasional conferences, special training, athletic competitions, or other events. For members who might otherwise be somewhat isolated or limited by circumstance, such occasions provide perspective, motivation, and exposure to other members and to Church leaders.

[*See also* Organization: Contemporary.]

DOUGLAS L. CALLISTER
GERALD J. DAY

REINCARNATION

Reincarnation refers to a theory that one SPIRIT (life or soul) passes from one material body to another through repeated births and deaths, usually of the same species, often with ethical implications; thus the present life is viewed as only one of many. This theory is rejected by The Church of Jesus Christ of Latter-day Saints.

The idea of repeated return or of a continuing, exacting wheel of rebirth is based on the Eastern doctrine of karma. Karma literally means "deeds" or "actions" and, in a limited sense, may refer to a system of cause and effect. According to this belief, all inequalities of birth, society, race, and economic being are products of one's individual karma created by an accumulation of previous behavior. Karma is also seen as a cosmic law of justice. It is an eternally moving wheel of rebirth. Experience is repeatable. An individual spirit can live again and again in a wide variety of guises and forms in the mortal estate.

In Latter-day Saint doctrine, mankind is on the road to IMMORTALITY and ETERNAL LIFE. One moves from one type of existence to another along the way. But this teaching is distinguishable from reincarnation on several counts:

1. In Latter-day Saint belief, there is only one physical death for any one person (Heb. 9:27). Amulek, in the Book of Mormon, taught that man can die only once (Alma 11:45). Reincarnation posits many deaths, but in Latter-day Saint thought, the RESURRECTION (incarnation) follows death (cf. D&C 29:24–25).

2. In LDS theology, the PHYSICAL BODY is sacred, and its elements are imperishable. The body is prerequisite to becoming like God. In reincarna-

tion, the present physical body is of little or no consequence.

3. In LDS theology, mortality is a time to be tested and proved "to see if [people] will do all things whatsoever the Lord their God shall command them" (Abr. 3:25). In reincarnation, there are many future lives, so there is no urgent need to repent now. Reincarnation contradicts Amulek's admonition that "this life is the time for men to prepare to meet God" (Alma 34:32). The Prophet Joseph SMITH said that transmigration of souls (spirits) was not a correct principle (*TPJS*, pp. 104–105).

4. In LDS theology, there is one single, unique historical act of redemption made by Jesus Christ. Through it, Christ becomes the only name under heaven "whereby man can be saved" (D&C 18:23). Reincarnation denies the absolute centrality of Christ's atonement by affirming the theoretical existence of an abundance of equally miraculous deities, who appear in a variety of forms, born again and again.

BIBLIOGRAPHY

Palmer, Spencer J., and Roger R. Keller. *Religions of the World: A Latter-day Saint View.* Provo, Utah, 1990.

SPENCER J. PALMER

RELIEF SOCIETY

The Relief Society is the official adult women's organization of The Church of Jesus Christ of Latter-day Saints and is an essential part of the structure of the Church at general, STAKE, and WARD levels. The organization provides opportunities for association, leadership, COMPASSIONATE SERVICE, and education. Through the Relief Society, "women of the Church are given some measure of divine authority particularly in the direction of government and instruction in behalf of the women of the church" (J. F. Smith, p. 5).

The motto "Charity Never Faileth" expresses the commitment of Relief Society members to love and nurture one another and to minister graciously to the needs of Church members and others. The binding sense of SISTERHOOD that characterizes the Relief Society is founded upon the women's common faith and enhanced by the lessons, activities, and interpersonal involvements that consti-

tute the Relief Society program. Current lesson materials for a weekly Sunday class focus twice a month on spiritual themes; the other two weeks have lessons on compassionate service and on home and family education. Lessons on cultural refinement and varied interests provide an optional midweek activity for interested sisters. Once a month, a midweek homemaking meeting features instructions for visiting teachers, a short home management lesson, and miniclasses emphasizing homemaking arts, WELFARE SERVICES projects, and individual and family development. Members especially appointed as "visiting teachers" are expected to make regular contacts with each woman once a month in her home, or more often if needed.

When the Prophet Joseph Smith organized the Female Relief Society of NAUVOO in 1842, he stated that the restored Church of Jesus Christ

Joseph and Emma Smith, by Florence Hansen (1978, cast bronze), Nauvoo Monument to Women, LDS Church Visitors Center, Nauvoo, Illinois. Joseph Smith is shown giving a five-dollar gold piece to Emma Smith, his wife and the first general president of the Relief Society. When he organized the society, he stated: "All I have to give to the poor I shall give to this society" (Minutes, Mar. 17, 1842, p. 13).

could not be perfect or complete without it. Elder Joseph Fielding SMITH later confirmed that "the Relief Society was revealed to the Prophet Joseph Smith as a fundamental part of the gospel" (J. F. Smith, p. 4). As an integral part of the Church organization, the Relief Society functions in close connection with, rather than independent of, the ecclesiastical priesthood structure. Ward Relief Society presidents work with BISHOPS, stake Relief Society presidents, with stake presidents, and the general Relief Society presidency, with designated GENERAL AUTHORITIES in what has been described as "a companionship relationship—not inferior or subordinate, but companion, side-by-side" (B. B. Smith, p. 11). Final decision-making responsibility rests with priesthood leaders.

ORIGINS 1842–1844. In 1842 a small group of women met at the home of Sarah M. KIMBALL in Nauvoo to organize a sewing society to aid NAUVOO TEMPLE workmen. When they sought the Prophet's endorsement for their proposed constitution, he praised their efforts but proffered an alterna-

tive: he would "organize the sisters under the priesthood after a pattern of the priesthood" ("Story of the Organization of the Relief Society," p. 129). Meeting with twenty women on March 17, 1842, he organized the Female Relief Society of Nauvoo. The women elected Emma SMITH president, and like presidents of priesthood quorums, she selected two counselors. The three presiding officers were SET APART for their callings by the LAYING ON OF HANDS by priesthood leaders. Joseph Smith explained that the decisions of this presidency, together with minutes of society proceedings, would serve as the group's constitution. A secretary and treasurer were appointed, and the presidency could appoint other officers as necessary. New members were admitted individually when standing members voted to give them full fellowship. By 1844, there were 1,341 members.

The Female Relief Society of Nauvoo brought women into the formal structure of the Church and gave them significant responsibility and authority. They contributed to the Nauvoo Temple, supported moral reform, and petitioned the governor

Relief Society general board in 1916. President Emmeline B. Wells (center, seated), with counselors Clarissa S. Williams (left) and Julina L. Smith (mother of Joseph Fielding Smith, right). Courtesy Utah State Historical Society.

of Illinois on behalf of Joseph Smith. Primarily occupied with "looking to the wants of the poor," society members donated cash, commodities, housing, and labor. In July 1843 a visiting committee of four was appointed in each ward to assess needs, solicit contributions from Church members, and distribute necessities. Visiting teachers have remained part of the Relief Society's basic organizational structure ever since (see VISITING TEACHING).

Joseph Smith further charged members with the responsibility to "save souls." He personally instructed them in the same gospel principles he taught the men, with particular emphasis on humility, charity, and unity. He also introduced them to sacred doctrines related to TEMPLE WORSHIP. This instruction set the precedent for meetings in which women could discuss religious principles and testify of their faith in the restored gospel, a continuing aspect of the Relief Society.

1844–1866. The Nauvoo society held its last recorded meeting on March 16, 1844, apparently unable to maintain unity of purpose during the factious events preceding the June 1844 martyrdom of Joseph Smith. Brigham YOUNG, the next President of the Church, did not initially encourage women to resume formal meetings, nor did the organization function during the Saints' westward trek and early settlement of Utah, though women continued their charitable works and gathered as friends to support and minister to one another through prayer, testimony, and the exercise of the gifts of the spirit. The Female Council of Health, organized in Salt Lake City in 1851 for midwives and others interested in healing by faith and herbs, preceded the 1854–1857 renewal of collective effort.

In early February 1854, sixteen women in Salt Lake City responded to President Young's exhortation to befriend and aid the Indians by organizing "a society of females for the purpose of making clothing for Indian women and children." This charitable Indian Relief Society elected its own officers and met weekly until June 1854, when President Young explicitly encouraged women to "form themselves into societies" and meet "in their own wards" to make clothing for the LAMANITES (the Indians). Members of the initial group later disbanded to join their respective ward organizations. During 1854, some twenty-two Indian Relief Societies were organized in Salt Lake City and outlying

LDS settlements, and their members contributed enough bedding and clothing to meet the demand for such goods. Many of these societies remained organized for the long-range goal of assisting the poor within their wards, as well as for short-range projects such as meetinghouse carpets and clothing and bedding for destitute HANDCART COMPANIES.

The 1857 UTAH EXPEDITION resulted in a widespread disorganization of wards that greatly diminished Relief Society operations for several years. There had been strong local leadership in a number of the wards, but the guiding central organization that would become a permanent and stabilizing feature of Relief Society was lacking.

1866–1887. In 1866 President Young initiated Churchwide reorganization of the Relief Society, appointing Eliza R. SNOW to assist bishops in establishing the organization in each ward. The minutes that she had recorded in Nauvoo became the common "constitution" for all local units, providing continuity of name, purpose, and organizational pattern. Though not formally called and set apart as general president until 1880, Eliza R. Snow directed Relief Society work from 1867 until her death in 1887. She was aided by her counselors Zina D. H. YOUNG and Elizabeth Ann Whitney and by the RETRENCHMENT SOCIETY, which served informally as a central board.

By 1880, the Relief Society had 300 local units, and each one cared for the suffering and needy within its ward boundaries, using an expanded corps of visiting teachers to collect and distribute donations. Ward Relief Societies managed their own financial resources, and many of them built their own meeting halls.

The Relief Society engaged in a number of bold and innovative economic activities spurred by the Church's movement for economic self-sufficiency. Ward societies initiated cooperative enterprises for making and marketing homemade goods, raised silk (see SILK CULTURE), established a grain storage program with local granaries, and helped finance the medical training of midwives and female doctors. With the support of ward units, the central board established the DESERET HOSPITAL (1882–1895). Assuming a new political role, the Relief Society sponsored a series of "indignation meetings" to voice women's opposition to proposed antipolygamy legislation. After Utah women were enfranchised in 1870, the Relief Society encouraged women to vote. Then they actively cam-

The headquarters of the Relief Society in Salt Lake City, located between the Salt Lake Temple and the Church Office Building, was dedicated in 1954. Sheaves of wheat, symbolic of preparing for times of need, feeding the hungry, and serving others, ornament the building.

paigned for woman suffrage after they were disfranchised by the federal government in 1887.

The Relief Society helped to organize and nurture the Young Ladies' Retrenchment Association (later YOUNG WOMEN) and the PRIMARY. Though separate general presidencies were appointed for these groups in 1880, President Eliza R. Snow served as their general head, and she and her board visited local congregations in Utah and Idaho to instruct all three groups. Local visits and conferences, the appointment of stake Relief Society presidents and boards (beginning in 1877), and publication of the semimonthly *Woman's Exponent* (1872–1914) strengthened women's sense of sisterhood. In assuming new responsibilities at ward, stake, and general levels, hundreds of LDS women entered the public sphere, simultaneously strengthening the community and developing their individual talents.

1888–1921. Economic and political activity continued during the administration of Zina D. H. Young (1888–1901). During the 1895 debate over the proposed constitution for the new state of Utah, Relief Society members successfully campaigned for a provision assuring women's right to vote and hold public office. Committed to cooperating with non-Mormons for the advance of women and later for international peace, the Relief Society affiliated with the National Woman Suffrage Association and the International Council of Women (1888). It was a charter member of the National Council of Women (1891) and, as such, became incorporated in October 1892 as the National Woman's Relief Society, establishing a twenty-three-member board of directors or general board composed of its general presidency and stake Relief Society presidents. Many ward units were also incorporated to facilitate management of property.

The Relief Society's political and economic involvement in the western United States did not displace its primary concern of spiritually nurturing its members and caring for the poor. These purposes united women across cultures, as members attested at their 1892 Relief Society Jubilee celebration. "Whether the language spoken is the English, French, German, Hawaiian or whatever tongue . . . they are all partakers of the same Spirit" ("The Jubilee Celebration," p. 133).

The increase in Relief Society membership and geographical spread that accompanied Church growth prompted greater centralization to assure continuity and unity. Annual dues for members, introduced in 1898, helped to defray the general board's traveling and operating expenses. Under the direction of President Bathsheba W. SMITH (1901–1910), the general presidency and board published its initial handbook (1902) and established its first official headquarters in the newly constructed Bishop's Building in Salt Lake City (1909).

The physical housing of the Relief Society and Church AUXILIARIES with the PRESIDING BISHOPRIC was one manifestation of emerging efforts to correlate a larger and more complex Church. The building of separate stake and ward Relief Society halls was likewise discouraged, though some local units maintained their own halls into the 1940s. Effective correlation required greater communication and interdependence between priesthood and Relief Society leaders, and they began meeting together more regularly to discuss common concerns such as charity and community work.

The nineteenth-century format for local Relief Society meetings—based on charity work, sewing, testimony bearing, and scripture study—made way in the twentieth century for a more varied and extensive educational program. As the society's membership aged, leaders attempted to meet the needs of these older women as well as of the younger ones of a new generation. Mothers classes, introduced in 1902, featured a widely varied curriculum prepared by each stake. During the administration of President Emmeline B. WELLS (1910–1921), the general board introduced new standardized lessons in the *Relief Society Bulletin* (1914) and the next year commenced publication of the RELIEF SOCIETY MAGAZINE through which it regularly issued standardized monthly lesson plans on theological, cultural, and homemaking topics, designating a week each month for each topic, while still reserving time for "work" (charity projects) and testimonies. This monthly format of rotating topics has been maintained, though subject matter has varied with changing interests and needs.

The most long-lived of the society's economic enterprises was the grain storage program directed initially by Sister Wells in 1876 and continued until the close of World War I (1918), when the Relief Society sold 205,518 bushels of their storage wheat to the U.S. government at its request. The sale capped the Relief Society's intensive involvement in the war effort. A "Wheat Trust Fund" was then established that made possible the purchase and storage of more wheat in 1941. Responsibility for the wheat continued until 1978, when the Relief

The Relief Society logo is an intertwined RS, surrounded by the organization's motto, "Charity never faileth," from 1 Cor. 13:8. Completing the circle are "1842," when the society was founded in Nauvoo, Illinois, and two sheaves of wheat.

Society transferred 266,291 bushels of wheat and nearly 2 million dollars in assets to the First Presidency for use in the welfare program. In 1920 the general board terminated another longstanding enterprise, and closed its Nurse School as adequate professional schools were then in place.

1921–1945. Relief efforts and community involvement reached a high point during these years. Under the innovative and businesslike administration of President Clarissa S. WILLIAMS (1921–1928), the Relief Society enlarged the professional component of its traditional charity work and increased cooperation with public and private welfare agencies. The Relief Society Social Services Department, established in 1919 by general secretary-treasurer Amy Brown LYMAN, served as the Church's professional link with other welfare agencies and trained Relief Society workers in modern methods of family casework. Between 1920 and 1942, more than 4,000 women participated in its intensive two- and six-week "institutes," returning to their wards and stakes to aid Relief Society and priesthood leaders in welfare work. The department also provided an employment bureau for women and girls and served as the Church's licensed agency for child placement until 1963.

Beginning in 1921, at a time of national concern over high rates of maternal and infant mortality, stake and ward societies used interest from the Wheat Trust Fund to sponsor hundreds of health clinics for expectant mothers, babies, and preschool children. Two stake Relief Societies established and operated maternity hospitals, the Cottonwood (Utah) Maternity Hospital (1924–1951) and the Snowflake (Arizona) Maternity Hospital (1939–1960). Branches attached to the European missions prepared "maternity chests" for needy mothers and home deliveries.

The worldwide depression of the 1930s at first intensified the direct-aid efforts of Relief Society officers, particularly in the United States, where they cooperated with county and later with federal agencies in dispensing temporary relief to the unemployed and needy. As a new system of permanent federal aid was established, Church leaders developed their own comprehensive Church Welfare Plan (1936), in which the Relief Society had a supportive role. Priesthood leaders directed the new program, but the society was represented on the governing committees and took the main re-

"Benevolence Panel" on the *Relief Society Centennial Memorial*, by Avard T. Fairbanks (cast bronze, 1942), on Temple Square, Salt Lake City. One aspect of Relief Society membership is compassion and service. The star on this commemorative sculpture symbolizes the love of Christ. The central figure is a strong, mature woman giving encouragement to a young mother, to a youth, and to an aged sister. The women bearing clothing and food extend physical, mental and spiritual comfort, guided by the inscription, "Through love serve one another."

sponsibility for preserving food, providing clothing and bedding, and teaching welfare principles to the sisters.

The Relief Society's own traditional relief efforts through the visiting teachers gradually phased out and finally terminated in 1944 when visiting teachers stopped collecting charity funds. Since 1921, ward presidents rather than visiting teachers have been assessing family needs and distributing relief to the needy, under the direction of their respective bishops. Underscoring the high degree of interdependence of the Relief Society president's and the ward bishop's two offices, Elder Harold B. LEE said in 1939, "The bishop is the father of his ward; the Relief Society is the mother" (p. 526). Ward Relief Society presidents also supervise other charitable work, such as caring for the sick, termed "compassionate service" to distinguish it from "welfare service."

President Louise Y. ROBISON (1928–1939), who led the Relief Society through these institutional changes, made other innovations. She started MORMON HANDICRAFT (1938) in Salt Lake City to help women at home earn money by selling their handiwork on consignment. She also encouraged the formation of stake and ward Relief Society choruses known as Singing Mothers.

During World War II, President Amy Brown Lyman (1940–1945) guided the Relief Society's efforts to limit meetings, simplify activities, and strengthen homes fragmented by the demands of war. In the United States, Canada, Hawaii, New Zealand, and Australia, members sewed projects on workday for the Red Cross as well as for welfare assignments. They gave blood, saved animal fats, refurbished clothing, kept lists of registered nurses, and took nursing and first aid courses. As in World War I, some local ward Relief Societies became Red Cross units. In war-torn Europe, members shared their meager supplies, struggled to do their visiting teaching with makeshift transportation, and comforted each other. Recognizing that some of its curriculum was not relevant outside the United States, the general board began providing alternative lesson materials for the units in other countries.

The Relief Society played an important part in the Church's postwar emergency aid to the Saints in Europe, sending through the Church welfare program clothing, food, and thousands of quilts that had been made and stored by sisters in the United States and Canada. Sisters in Hawaii sent similar help to Japan.

1945–1974. By the end of 1945, Relief Society membership had reached 102,000. In the years that followed, its membership has kept pace with the accelerating worldwide growth of the Church. The first Relief Societies in Japan were organized in 1949; membership in the Far East increased from 439 in 1950 to 7,400 in 1969. Rapid growth in Mexico and South America led to the printing of the *Relief Society Magazine* in Spanish (1966). By the 1970s, most members were using the same lesson materials and learning to appreciate each other's cultures through monthly cultural refinement lessons.

President Belle S. SPAFFORD traveled widely, both as general president of the Relief Society (1945–1974) and as a two-year president of the U.S. Council of Women (1968–1970). She further professionalized the Relief Society Services Department and directed expansion of its services to include programs for INDIAN STUDENT PLACEMENT SERVICES and youth guidance. The department was housed in Salt Lake City in the Relief Society Building, which had been built in 1956 from contributions from LDS women and matching funds from the Church.

During President Spafford's long administration, the Relief Society moved toward fuller correlation within the larger Church structure. Under the comprehensive Church correlation program, the reporting and financing systems, magazine and lesson materials, and social services once managed by the Relief Society became the responsibility of priesthood leaders and professional departments, such as the new LDS SOCIAL SERVICES Department. After September 1971, Relief Society membership automatically included all LDS women and soon exceeded a million.

1974–1990. As the movement for women's liberation called into question women's traditional work as homemakers and volunteers, the Relief Society increased its support for the vital roles of women in their home and Church responsibilities. The Relief Society Building became a resource center for stake and ward officers, offering ideas, materials, and training for their Relief Society work. President Barbara B. Smith (1974–1984) joined Church officials in opposing passage of the proposed Equal Rights Amendment to the U.S. Constitution, which they were convinced would not help women. The Relief Society promoted scholarly study of women's concerns by helping to establish the Women's Research Center at Brigham Young University (1978) and rallied its members worldwide to contribute to a visible symbol of honor for women, the Monument to Women at Nauvoo, a garden park with thirteen bronze statues portraying the many-faceted contributions of women (1978).

The rapid worldwide growth of Relief Society membership encouraged accommodation for diversity. Stake boards expanded to meet a variety of options for young, single, and working women. The Church's college sorority, Lambda Delta Sigma, was incorporated into the Relief Society

structure. In 1978, under the direction of President Spencer W. KIMBALL, the first general women's fireside was held. This has become an annual event called the General Women's Meeting and is broadcast worldwide; it has also become a model for women's conferences subsequently held by stake Relief Societies.

CURRENT ADMINISTRATION. Increased simplification and correlation with priesthood leaders characterized the administration of President Barbara W. Winder (1984–1990). Her first general board had seventeen fewer members than the preceding board. And stake Relief Society boards were released. Ward Relief Society presidencies attended the quarterly (instead of monthly) stake leadership training meetings and carried the training to their own ward boards. The general board maintained contact with stake officers, while members of the general presidency visited stakes on speaking assignments; however, the focal point of Relief Society action subtly shifted to the local

Elaine L. Jack, born in Cardston, Canada, became general president of the Relief Society in March 1990, after serving on the general boards of the Relief Society and Young Women and as a counselor in the general presidency of the Young Women.

level. In the wards and branches, members continued to find the opportunities for service, learning, sisterhood, and spiritual growth.

As President Elaine L. Jack (1990–) moved Relief Society toward a sesquicentennial consideration of its Nauvoo legacy, membership reached 2,784,000. Though the Relief Society's programs have changed substantially over its 150-year history in an effort to meet the changing needs of women and the Church, its basic organizational structure and essential mission have not varied significantly. Emphasis on simplification, diversity, and worldwide sisterhood in the 1970s and 1980s resulted in a basic standard format for Relief Society that affirms common goals and programs for women around the world. Through its changes and growth, Relief Society has exemplified its motto. Sister Jack stated, "It is no minor thing that the motto of the Relief Society is 'Charity Never Faileth'" (p. 74), for "charity is the pure love of Christ, which endureth forever" (Moro. 7:47).

BIBLIOGRAPHY

Cannon, Janath R.; Jill Mulvay-Derr; and Maureen Ursenbach Beecher. *Women of Covenant: A History of Relief Society*. Salt Lake City, 1991.

General Board of the Relief Society. *History of Relief Society, 1842–1966*. Salt Lake City, 1966.

Jack, Elaine L. "The Mission of Relief Society." *Ensign* 21 (Jan. 1991):74.

"The Jubilee Celebration." *Woman's Exponent* 20 (March 15, 1892):132–33.

Lee, Harold B. "The Relief Society in the Welfare Plan." *Relief Society Magazine* 26 (Aug. 1939):526–27.

Smith, Barbara B. "A Conversation with Sister Barbara B. Smith, Relief Society General President." *Ensign* 6 (Mar. 1976):7–12.

Smith, Joseph Fielding. "The Relief Society Organized by Revelation." *Relief Society Magazine* 52 (Jan. 1965):4–6.

"Story of the Organization of the Relief Society." *Relief Society Magazine* 6 (Mar. 1919):127–42.

JANATH RUSSELL CANNON
JILL MULVAY DERR

RELIEF SOCIETY MAGAZINE

The *Relief Society Magazine* was the official monthly publication of the women's Relief Society of The Church of Jesus Christ of Latter-day Saints from 1915 to 1970. It preserves the history of the Relief Society for those years, with reports of each annual general Relief Society conference held in the Salt Lake Tabernacle, and with the talks of General Authorities and the Relief Society presidencies given at those conferences. It also contains articles of particular interest to the women of the Church, such as gospel topics, prose and poetry, housekeeping aids, recipes, pictures, and descriptions of Relief Society activities from near and far. Some space each month was devoted to the progress of women worldwide. It also published the Relief Society lessons, which were written by authorities in various fields such as the scriptures, art, architecture, social sciences, economics, the Constitution of the United States, world governments, and literature.

In its first issue, President Joseph F. SMITH expressed his hope that the magazine would be "entrenched about by the bulwarks of worthy and

The Relief Society Magazine, the official monthly magazine of the Relief Society from 1915 to 1970, published lessons, reports of annual Relief Society Conferences, and articles of particular interest to women. This cover portrays the organization of the society in 1842 and carries Joseph Smith's statement: "I now turn the key to you in the name of God and this society shall rejoice, and knowledge and intelligence shall flow down from this time."

capable endeavor and enduring truth." The magazine was owned and operated by the General Board of the Relief Society for all of its fifty-six years. Originally a forty-four-page, black and white publication, it evolved into an eighty-page journal with liberal use of color. Its readers liked its small size, which let it fit neatly into a woman's purse. In 1966 the *Magazine* added a Spanish edition for its 6,000 Spanish-speaking subscribers.

Editors of the *Relief Society Magazine* looked upon their assignments as mission calls to further the work of Relief Society and strengthen the testimonies of its members. Its first editor, Susa Young Gates (1914–1922), was followed by Alice Louise Reynolds (1923–1930), Mary Connelly Kimball (1930–1937), Belle S. Spafford (1937–1945), and Marianne Clark Sharp (1945–1970). Vesta P. Crawford was associate editor (1947–1970).

From 1872 to 1914 Relief Society matters were disseminated in the *Woman's Exponent*, a privately owned and edited women's journal, which ceased publication in 1914 with the announcement of the official Church magazine for women.

The *Relief Society Magazine* had 301,000 subscribers in 1970, when it was incorporated into the *Ensign*, the Church magazine for adults. Relief Society lessons are now published in a manual each year.

[*See also* Ensign; Relief Society; Woman's Exponent.]

BIBLIOGRAPHY

Sharp, Marianne C., and Irene Woodford, eds. *History of Relief Society—1842–1966*. Salt Lake City, 1966.

MARIANNE CLARK SHARP

This plate depicts the organization meeting of the Relief Society on March 17, 1842. The Prophet Joseph Smith, who formally organized the twenty women present into a society, stated: "The Church was never perfectly organized until the women were thus organized." Emma Smith was the first president, with Sarah M. Cleveland and Elizabeth Ann Whitney as counselors, and Eliza R. Snow as secretary. Church Museum of History and Art.

RELIEF SOCIETY IN NAUVOO

Organized in 1842, the Female Relief Society of NAUVOO differed from other contemporary women's church groups in that it was organized under the PRIESTHOOD direction of the Prophet Joseph SMITH.

The society began as a response to the need for provisions, clothing, and supplies for builders of the NAUVOO TEMPLE. On her own initiative, Sarah M. Granger KIMBALL invited a group of women to her home on March 4, 1842, to discuss the possibility of organizing a sewing society to aid the workers. Eliza R. SNOW drafted possible by-laws and a constitution for the group and submitted them to Joseph Smith. He told her that there was something better for them than a written constitution and that he would organize the women of the Church as the priesthood was organized. He added that the Church would never be perfectly organized until the women were organized.

Minutes of the charter meeting name twenty women and three men who were present in the upper story of Smith's red-brick store on March 17, 1842. Emma SMITH, elected president, chose Sarah M. Cleveland and Elizabeth Ann Whitney as counselors, Eliza R. Snow as secretary, and Elvira A. Cowles as treasurer.

At the first meeting, the Prophet redefined and expanded the object of the society. The women were to look to the needs of the poor, to search after those in need and administer to their wants, and to assist in correcting the morals and strengthening the virtues of the community. He later added the charge to save souls. During a particularly significant address on April 28, 1842, he cited 1 Corinthians 13, from which later members took their motto, "Charity Never Faileth." He then pronounced the much-quoted sentence, "I now turn the key to you in the name of God and this Society shall rejoice and knowledge and intelligence shall flow down from this time" ("Minutes of the Female Relief Society").

The society grew quickly. During its first season, 1,189 women became members. The society received and dispersed money, clothing, provisions, and services to the needy. Its meetings were held first in the upper room and then, for lack of space there, outdoors in "the Grove" until September 28, 1842. When the society reconvened in the following spring, the presidency divided the membership into four WARDS, which then met separately. Each ward had its "necessity committee," forerunner of the present visiting teachers, who canvassed their area in search of people in need (see VISITING TEACHING). Meetings again ceased for the winter of 1843–1844, but presumably the charitable works continued.

Beset with differences between its president and Church leaders—differences related to the introduction of PLURAL MARRIAGE—the society ceased to function formally after the meetings of March 1844. Aspects of its operation, however, continued through the last days of Nauvoo and the exodus of 1846–1847 in the acts of charity, the sisterly bonding, the gatherings of women in prayer meetings, and the persistence of spiritual manifestations. The leaders of a revived RELIEF SOCIETY in Utah, which President Brigham YOUNG authorized Churchwide beginning in 1867, conscientiously adhered to the patterns established in Nauvoo and resolutely maintained a continuity of operation.

BIBLIOGRAPHY

Kimball, Sarah M. "Early Relief Society Reminiscences." In "The Relief Society Record, 1880–1892." Relief Society General Offices, Salt Lake City.

"Minutes of the Female Relief Society of Nauvoo." LDS Church Historical Department, Salt Lake City.

Sharp, Marianne C., and Irene Woodford, eds. *History of Relief Society, 1842–1966.* Salt Lake City, 1966.

BARBARA W. WINDER

RELIGIOUS EXPERIENCE

In the gospel of Jesus Christ, personal religious experience is the foundation, vitality, and culmination of religious life. As in the biblical book of Acts, LDS religious experience is varied and owes as much to firsthand experience as to texts and traditions. Latter-day Saints may recognize as a religious experience feelings or impressions that build faith in Christ, show that God hears and answers prayer, manifest what is good and right, enhance personal conviction of truth, or confirm that one's life is approved of God. The sum of one's religious experiences is sometimes called a "testimony." Interpretations of these experiences are derived from cumulative personal experience, which language is often inadequate to describe. The frequency, intelligibility, coherence, and shareability of these phenomena among Latter-day Saints are relatively unique.

Regardless of individual differences in age, culture, and language, such experiences enhance the underlying unity of the members of the Church, enabling them to feel one with each other and with the prophets. They recognize familiar religious experiences in one another's words and actions and in the scriptures. While the transmission of these experiences is often oral (as in testimony meetings, classes, conversations), many are also preserved in diaries, journals, and family histories. Some of these have become widely familiar and almost normative.

At the core of a Latter-day Saint's life is CONVERSION to the gospel. First impressions are often crucial. Converts frequently testify to feeling a divine assurance, unexpected and unheralded, that truth is to be found in the Book of Mormon and in the teachings of the Church. They also commonly speak of feeling clean, of being washed of their sins, and of being spiritually reborn with an infusion of new life, peace, joy, light, warmth, and fire (see BAPTISM OF FIRE AND OF THE HOLY GHOST). The experience of finding oneself, though a sinner, accepted by the Lord, often becomes the foundation of a lifetime commitment to God, because maintaining this feeling is desired above all else. Classic examples of this are found in the conversions of Alma$_2$ (Mosiah 27; Alma 36) and Joseph Smith (*PJS* 1:5–8).

Latter-day Saints believe that the divine love they receive in individual religious experience should be reflected to others as CHARITY (Mosiah

2:17–21; 5:2; Moro. 7:46). Rendering service to others in the name of Christ produces feelings of joy and happiness that Latter-day Saints treasure as religious experiences.

Baptized members are given the GIFT OF THE HOLY GHOST by the laying on of hands, entitling them to the companionship of the Holy Ghost. President Lorenzo Snow described his reception of this gift as "a tangible immersion in the heavenly principle or element, the Holy Ghost" (*Biography and Family Record of Lorenzo Snow* p. 8, Salt Lake City, 1884), saying that he "tasted the joys of eternity in the midst of the power of God" (Journal, p. 3, Church Archives, Salt Lake City). Alfred D. Young said it was "as if warm water was poured over me coming on my head first. I was filled with light, peace and joy" [*Autobiography (1808–1842)*, BYU Special Collection].

Individual Latter-day Saints speak of being shown righteous courses of action by the Holy Ghost, being warned of dangers and evils, and being otherwise inspired and guided. One sister, reflecting on her life, wrote that the Holy Ghost "warns, counsels, reproves, commends, instructs, and when necessary commands" (YWJ 27 [Nov. 1916]:691–92). Motivational changes are chronicled, as are infusions of energy, compassion, insight, healing power, and beauty, and also refinement of talents, faculties of communication, and Christlike love.

Impressions of the Holy Ghost often come after much preparation in FASTING, prayer, service, and study. At other times they come unbidden and arrive at unexpected moments as a "still, small voice" (1 Kgs. 19:12). The Prophet Joseph Smith observed that the word of the Lord "has such an influence over the human mind—the logical mind—that it is convincing without other testimony" (HC 5:526). Joseph Smith further remarked, "sudden strokes of ideas" from the Holy Ghost attend a flow of pure intelligence (TPJS, p. 151); "the answer comes into my mind with such a logical sequence of thought and ideas, and accompanied by such a burning feeling within, that I know it is of God" (cited in W. Berrett, "Revelation," address to seminary and institute faculty, Brigham Young University, June 27, 1956, p. 9).

Such influences and impressions of the Holy Ghost may come as inspiration amid duties in the home, at work, or in Church callings, as well as self-knowledge in the most menial of everyday tasks. Typical reported examples include a glimpse of celestial origins and destiny (Heber C. Kimball); impressions of impending events (Wilford Woodruff); guidance and reassurance in emotional crises such as the death of a loved one (Zina D. H. Young); or insight and strength in pressing practical needs or predicaments (Amanda Smith). Many members of the Church attest to receiving inspiration in creative processes, such as when writing religious poetry, drama, music, or scriptural commentary, or when seeking a solution to a scientific or genealogical research problem. Personal REVELATION is probably the most widely shared and unifying form of religious experience among Latter-day Saints. It also helps explain the confidence with which many Latter-day Saints make religious decisions.

Latter-day Saints may receive individual blessings from a priesthood bearer in which they seek the guidance of the Holy Spirit (*see* FATHER'S BLESSING; PATRIARCHAL BLESSING). Through such personal experiences most Latter-day Saints have received needed direction, restoration of spiritual and physical health, or other divine aid. One Church leader describes the giving and receiving of blessings as vitalizing and enlightening, through "an essence of force or power" inherent in the holy priesthood. Diaries commonly report experiences such as this: "He blessed me. I felt the influence and power of the Lord upon him and upon me. I have never forgotten that blessing from that day to this and I never shall" (Ezra T. Clark).

A wide range of manifestations of the Spirit—visions, dreams, visitations, contact with the dead, miraculous aid in answer to prayer—is known in every LDS community, though not generally publicly heralded (*see* GIFTS OF THE SPIRIT). For example, Karl G. Maeser reported experiencing the gift of interpretation where all language and cultural barriers were removed; Franklin D. Richards received the gift of prophetic dreams; James G. Marsh, the gift of visions; and Lucy Mack SMITH, the gift of faith.

LDS religious experience also includes pentecostal outpourings, dramatic and overwhelming spiritual manifestations, witnessed simultaneously by many people and recorded privately. Of the foundation experiences of the Restoration the most crucial were shared, witnessed, and recorded. Each conferral of divine priesthood authority was shared by at least two persons (*see* AARONIC PRIESTHOOD: RESTORATION OF; MELCHIZEDEK PRIESTHOOD: RESTORATION OF) and included visitations analogous to the appearance of Moses and Elijah on the Mount of Transfiguration (Matt. 17:2–4). Here the experience was no less objective than the deliverances of sense-experience. Several hundred experienced the outpouring of spiritual gifts in the KIRTLAND TEMPLE dedication (see Backman, pp. 284–309). Several thousand, including many children, witnessed the experience in Nauvoo when the "mantle" fell upon Brigham Young and he was providentially portrayed in Joseph Smith's likeness (*see* SUCCESSION IN THE PRESIDENCY). Approximately 63,000 participated in the dedicatory sessions of the SALT LAKE TEMPLE, and many reported seeing visions and hearing heavenly music.

LDS journals are replete with testimonies that the Spirit of the Lord enlivens all of the senses—seeing, hearing, smelling, tasting, and touching—and that one is more physically alive and aware when spiritually quickened. This illumination is more than an aid to physical perception; it is a medium of comprehension. Latter-day Saints sometimes speak of a "sixth sense," interrelated with the other senses, that apprehends spiritual things. All things "are revealed to our spirits precisely as though we had no bodies at all" (*TPJS*, p. 355). One may be lighted up "with the glory of [his] former home" (J. F. Smith, *GD*, p. 14) and be led to say with Eliza R. Snow, "I felt that I had wandered from a more exalted sphere" ("O My Father," *Hymns of The Church of Jesus Christ of Latter-day Saints*, no. 292, Salt Lake City, 1985).

Many Latter-day Saints record such experiences in the setting of TEMPLE ORDINANCES, sensing a oneness with departed friends and relatives—"they are not far from us, and know and understand our thoughts, feelings, and motions, and are often pained therewith" (*TPJS*, p. 326)—and "seeming to see" and "seeming to hear" the realms of the spirit world (J. Grant, *JD* 4:134–36).

LDS spiritual experiences are often related to scripture study. One convert had mastered the entire Bible in Hebrew, German, and English. After receiving the gift of the Holy Ghost, he found new meaning in familiar verses (O. Hyde, *JD* 8:23–24). Another who had memorized New Testament books found, after receiving the Holy Ghost, that "new light dawned upon" him in "bold relief," which the Book of Mormon clarified and confirmed: "Truths were manifested to me that I had never heard of or read of, but which I afterwards heard preached by the servants of the Lord" (C. Penrose, *JD* 23:351). Still another, praying

through his youth for some great manifestation, learned slowly and for a lifetime, "line upon line, precept upon precept," until he felt his whole being was a testimony of the truth (J. F. Smith, *GD*, pp. 501–550).

Today, psychological, positivistic, and existential thought raises questions about religious awareness. There is much preoccupation with criteria of meaning and with the logic of religious discourse. The sum of LDS religious experience, however, suggests that anyone may appeal to the way of the prophets: Look and see.

BIBLIOGRAPHY

Backman, Milton V., Jr. *The Heavens Resound*, pp. 284–309. Salt Lake City, 1983.

Madsen, Truman G. "Joseph Smith and the Ways of Knowing." BYU Extension Publications, Provo, Utah, 1962.

TRUMAN G. MADSEN

RELIGIOUS FREEDOM

[*Latter-day Saints have always been vigorous defenders of religious liberty and have frequently been the victims of religious persecution. For accounts of LDS beliefs concerning religious freedom see* Church and State; Constitution of the United States; *and* Politics: Political Teachings. *The history of the LDS struggle for freedom is summarized in* Legal and Judicial History of the Church *and in* Politics: Political History. *The efforts of the Church to be recognized and to enjoy religious liberty in new countries are explained in* Diplomatic Relations. *The underlying commitments to human liberty in LDS teaching are outlined in* Freedom. *Nephite traditions of religious liberty are described in* Book of Mormon, Government and Legal History in.]

REMISSION OF SINS

"Remission of sins" is the scriptural phrase that describes the primary purpose of BAPTISM: to obtain God's forgiveness for breaking his COMMANDMENTS and receive a newness of life. It is fundamental among the FIRST PRINCIPLES AND ORDINANCES OF THE GOSPEL: FAITH in the Lord JESUS CHRIST, REPENTANCE, BAPTISM by immersion for the remission of SINS, and LAYING ON OF HANDS for the GIFT OF THE HOLY GHOST. To grant pardon of sins is one manifestation of God's mercy, made possible by the ATONEMENT. It is the blessing sought by those who fervently prayed, "O have mercy, and apply the atoning blood of Christ that we may receive forgiveness of our sins, and our hearts may be purified" (Mosiah 4:2). Having one's sins remitted is a vital part of the developmental process that results in godhood and lies at the heart of the religious experience of a Latter-day Saint.

Baptism for the remission of sins is one of the most prominent themes of the scriptures, being both a requirement and a blessing associated with accepting Christ as the divine Redeemer and Savior of the world and joining his Church. According to LDS scriptures and teachings, the principles and ordinances of the gospel, including baptism for the remission of sins, were taught and practiced by all the PROPHETS from ADAM and ENOCH (Moses 6:52–60, 64–68; 7:10–11) to the present time. The doctrine was taught before the earthly ministry of Jesus by BENJAMIN (Mosiah 4:3–4) and John the Baptist (Mark 1:3–4). It was articulated by Christ himself to the twelve apostles in Jerusalem (Matt. 28:16–20; John 20:21–23) and to the Nephites (3 Ne. 12:2), preached by Peter following Christ's ascension (Acts 2:37–38), and commanded of the Church as part of the restoration (D&C 49:11–14; 84:64). Authority to administer the ordinance of baptism by immersion for the remission of sins is held by bearers of the AARONIC PRIESTHOOD (D&C 13; 107:20) as well as by those who hold the MELCHIZEDEK PRIESTHOOD (D&C 20:38–45).

God commands all but little children and the mentally incompetent to submit to the first principles and ordinances (Moro. 8:11; D&C 29:46–50; 68:27), not as acts of compliance with his sovereignty, but because uncleanliness (sinfulness) is incompatible with godliness. There is no alternative path to exaltation (1 Ne. 15:33; 3 Ne. 27:19; Moses 6:57). Thus, those who do not receive a remission of sins through baptism are not BORN OF GOD and exclude themselves from his kingdom (Alma 7:14–16; D&C 84:74). Remission includes the pardoning of sins by God, who releases sinners with the promise that "their sins and their iniquities will I remember no more" (Heb. 8:12). Remission also includes the repentant person's recognition of God's communication of that forgiveness. Such a realization is accompanied by peace of conscience and feelings of inexpressible joy (Mosiah 4:1–3, 20). Having been "washed [by] the blood of Christ" (Alma 24:13; 3 Ne. 27:19), one is granted relief from the unhappiness that accompanies wickedness (Alma 41:10; 36:12–21) and increases in love for God, knowing that forgiveness is made possible only by the Savior's atoning sacrifice (D&C 27:2; 2 Ne. 9:21–27).

Remission of sins is an achievement made possible through the Atonement and earned through genuine changes in spirit and a discontinuation of behavior known to be wrong. Enos described the process as a "wrestle . . . before God" (Enos 1:2). The essential experience is to recognize one's unworthiness, taste of Christ's love, stand steadfast in faith toward him (Mosiah 4:11), and with contrite heart acknowledge that he was crucified for the sins of the world (D&C 21:9; 3 Ne. 9:20–22). Thus committed to Christ and engaged in repentance, one keeps the commandments by submitting to baptism and receiving the gift of the Holy Ghost. The initial sense of repentance and forgiveness that leads one to the ordinances (3 Ne. 7:25; D&C 20:37) is amplified and confirmed through the BAPTISM OF FIRE administered by the Comforter (2 Ne. 31:17; D&C 19:31). This series of experiences forms the basis for a spiritual testimony of the truthfulness of the GOSPEL OF JESUS CHRIST and a lifelong commitment to Christian living and Church service.

Remission of sins can be lost through recurrent transgression, for "unto that soul who sinneth shall the former sins return, saith the Lord your God" (D&C 82:7). Benjamin therefore enjoins the forgiven to retain their state by righteous living: "For the sake of retaining a remission of your sins from day to day, that ye may walk guiltless before God . . . ye should impart of your substance to the poor, every man according to that which he hath, such as feeding the hungry, clothing the naked, visiting the sick and administering to their relief, both spiritually and temporally, according to their wants" (Mosiah 4:26).

BIBLIOGRAPHY

Kimball, Spencer W. *The Miracle of Forgiveness.* Salt Lake City, 1969.

WILLIAM S. BRADSHAW

REORGANIZED CHURCH OF JESUS CHRIST OF LATTER DAY SAINTS (RLDS CHURCH)

The RLDS church emerged during the 1850s from the conflict and schism that arose in Mormonism after the June 27, 1844, murder of Joseph SMITH, Jr., its founding PROPHET. From 1834 to 1844, Smith had indicated as many as eight possible modes of prophetic succession. One of these was a designation of his son Joseph III (1832–1914) to succeed him as prophet-president. He had not, however, chosen anyone to lead pro tempore until his son should be old enough to preside. During the decade following Smith's assassination, Mormonism split into more than a dozen factions. The main body of believers accepted the QUORUM OF TWELVE APOSTLES as their leaders. They remained headquartered at Nauvoo, Illinois, until 1846, when they fled to the Great Salt Basin of present-day Utah. Brigham YOUNG, the senior APOSTLE, who had been President of the Quorum of the Twelve since April 14, 1840, organized the westward trek and was sustained as President in the FIRST PRESIDENCY of The Church of Jesus Christ of Latter-day Saints in 1847 (*see* SUCCESSION IN THE PRESIDENCY).

Jason W. Briggs (1821–1899), leader of the Beloit, Wisconsin, branch, rejected Brigham Young's leadership in 1848 to affiliate with the faction led by James J. Strang (1813–1856). After Strang opted for polygamy in 1850, Briggs left to join a colony led by the slain prophet's younger brother, William B. Smith (1811–1893). Briggs left Smith in the fall of 1851 on learning that Smith was also a polygamist.

On November 18, 1851, Briggs sought and received what he felt to be divine revelation regarding the future of the church. His followers distributed copies of the record of Briggs's revelation to nearby branches. The four major thrusts of the document were to denounce other claimants to prophetic authority; to enjoin the elders to preach

The RLDS brick church in Lamoni, Iowa. Courtesy Library-Archives, Reorganized Church of Jesus Christ of Latter Day Saints.

against false doctrines that had overtaken the church; to instruct the elders to teach the original gospel law as found in the Bible, the Book of Mormon, and the Doctrine and Covenants; and to promise that from the lineage of Joseph Smith, Jr., would come the proper leader of the church. Zenas H. Gurley, Sr. (1801–1871), pastor of a church branch at Yellow Stone, Wisconsin, read the Briggs message to his people. Gurley had also rejected the leadership of Brigham Young, James Strang, and William Smith at about the same time as Briggs, his new ally. During the winter and spring of 1852 a nucleus of Saints in Wisconsin and northern Illinois began to effect what they felt to be a bona fide continuation of the original church.

The first formal conference of church elders of this emerging movement met on June 12–13, 1852, near Beloit, Wisconsin. The conference passed measures endorsing and enlarging on the sentiments expounded in the record of Briggs's revelation. The conference also ordered publication of a pamphlet supporting those measures and called for the convening of a second conference in October.

The October conference heard the pamphlet read, and authorized Jason Briggs to publish 2,000 copies of it as a means to inform the public of the basis of the emerging RLDS movement. In the publication process, three more pages were added condemning polygamy. A pivotal conference convened in April 1853, at which seven new apostles were chosen by a committee and ordained. This interim group presided over the church until the lineal successor to the founding prophet became available. The autumn conference of 1856 sent two representatives to the home of Joseph Smith III near Nauvoo, Illinois, to officially invite him to head the church. Smith firmly declined, but on the strength of later revelatory experiences, he accepted in early 1860. On April 6, 1860, Joseph Smith III became prophet-president of the RLDS church at its conference, at Amboy, Illinois. For early "reorganizers," the long-held conviction of lineal succession in presidency was now enacted.

Smith was both strongly opposed to polygamy and deeply convinced that his father could have had nothing to do with its inception in the church. He and other RLDS leaders, writers, missionaries, and members fought for decades to project the image of original Latter Day Saintism as non-polygamous. The public outcry against Utah Latter-day Saints for their polygamous doctrine and practice, however, together with the similarity of the two churches' names, greatly complicated the RLDS effort to mark itself as separate from Utah Mormonism.

Polygamy was the most clear-cut issue that RLDS people used to disassociate themselves from the LDS Church, and to arouse public antipathy against Utah Mormonism. Other issues, however, also placed Utah Mormonism and the RLDS church on opposite sides of an ideological boundary. Some of these stemmed from teachings Joseph Smith, Jr., had put in place in the Nauvoo setting (1839–1844). By the end of the century, the RLDS church was either repudiating them or taking a wait-and-see posture. Rejected were such doctrines as the political kingdom of God, militarism (i.e., military organizations such as the NAUVOO LEGION), the Adam-God theory (*see* YOUNG, BRIGHAM: TEACHINGS), plural gods, exclusion of blacks from priesthood offices, and absolute theocracy. In the wait-and-see category were the temple and its system of saving rituals for both dead and living (*see* SALVATION OF THE DEAD), the BOOK OF ABRAHAM, and strictly enforced restrictions on the use of coffee, alcohol, and tobacco (*see* WORD OF WISDOM).

In finding much of its nineteenth-century identity along this "Mormon boundary," the RLDS church marked out a difficult course of development. Missionaries working among Utah Mormons tried to convince their audiences that the RLDS church adhered to the "true Mormonism." When trying to persuade Protestant prospects, on the other hand, RLDS ministers were inclined to deemphasize aspects linking them with Mormonism and to focus on the common ground they shared with mainstream Christianity.

The resulting ambiguity within the RLDS church created recurring seasons of internal theological conflict. The church elders and leaders, until well into the twentieth century, tried to resolve much of that friction in the setting of their general conferences. Joseph Smith III and other leaders felt inclined to resolve only the most critical conflicts through revelatory fiat of the prophet. This means that for the most part the RLDS church has pursued a delicate, operational balance between the democratic and theocratic modes of church governance.

Joseph Smith III's early policy of restraining the scattered RLDS membership from gathering to one central location had a lasting effect on

The RLDS Auditorium, in Independence, Missouri. Groundbreaking ceremonies were held February 1, 1926, and the building was dedicated for church and community service in 1962. Courtesy Library-Archives, Reorganized Church of Jesus Christ of Latter Day Saints.

church development. Smith remembered the persecution the early Saints had suffered wherever they colonized en masse. He urged his followers to embody their Christian religion as fully as possible wherever they lived, widely dispersed as they were. From his headquarters office in Plano, Illinois, Smith repeatedly editorialized in the church periodical, *The True Latter Day Saints' Herald*, cautioning the widely scattered church branches to put down their roots where they were. He urged them to build solid foundations of Christian witness and community responsibility as a prerequisite to any ultimate recolonization to Independence, Missouri.

The "gathering" impulse within the membership, however, remained strong. In 1870 a group of men of means incorporated the "First United Order of Enoch." Under its charter, stockholders bought several thousand acres of land in Decatur County, Iowa, and began farming and related agribusiness enterprises. There they built up the town of Lamoni (a Book of Mormon name), which in 1881 became the church headquarters and home of the church press and of its editor in chief, President Joseph Smith III.

A number of Mormons either on the trail west through Iowa or newly arrived in the Great Salt Lake Basin left the West or the trail to unite with RLDS branches in southwest Iowa. By 1890 the center of RLDS church population (about 25,000) had shifted from Illinois to Iowa. Even Missouri, with rapidly expanding membership in and around St. Louis and Independence, had pulled ahead of Illinois. The church in 1895 founded Graceland College at Lamoni (its 1990 enrollment was more than 1,300).

Smith's death in December 1914 brought his son Frederick M. Smith (1874–1946), a counselor in the First Presidency since 1902, to the prophetic office. The primary emphases of Frederick M. Smith's thirty-one-year presidency were centralization of administrative control into a more theocratic mode; practical and theological training for the church's ministry; physical, cultural, and educational development of the "Center Place" in and around Independence, Missouri, as the new headquarters of the church (moved from Lamoni in 1920) and the primary place of Zionic witness; mobilization of the membership into stewardship communal enterprises, especially in and near the Center Place; and a heightened effort to streamline and expand the church's missionary effort.

Smith's plans for church expansion and development suffered from resistance to change within the church, both at the General Officer and local levels. Even more vexing were economic dislocations in the larger world. Two worldwide armed conflicts, the severe economic panic of 1920–1921, and the Great Depression of the 1930s deferred many of his hoped-for church goals. Several years of deficit spending brought the church to a financial crisis in 1931. An austere fiscal management policy designed by Presiding Bishop L. F. P. Curry (1887–1977) and his counselor, G. L. DeLapp (1895–1981), inspired the confidence of the members. Their sacrificial giving enabled liquidation of the nearly $2 million debt by January 1942. The membership ranks grew throughout F. M. Smith's presidency, from 74,000 in 1915 to nearly 133,000 at his death on March 20, 1946. One of his building enterprises, the vast Auditorium in Independence—headquarters and General Conference center—begun in 1926, was in use by 1928, but remained unfinished until 1962.

Israel A. Smith (1876–1958), brother of Frederick, became RLDS president in April 1946. During his twelve-year tenure, the church built financial reserves and greatly expanded its missionary forces. In Independence it founded Resthaven, a home for the elderly; the School of the Restoration, for education of church leaders and members; and the Social Service Center, a facility for various

helps to the needy. The church's hospital, with financial aid from the community at large, expanded greatly. This period was also a time of local church-building activity, with hundreds of branches either building new churches or expanding old ones. The church also added to its educational facilities at Graceland College.

William Wallace Smith (1900–1989), the third son of Joseph Smith III to serve as church president, was ordained to that office in October 1958. Utilizing the skills of many, he planted the RLDS church in more than twenty nations. This expansion has continued steadily in the years since his retirement in April 1978.

This recent crossing of cultural boundaries has stimulated much ideological and theological ferment within the church. Leaders soon realized that the task was more than merely extending an American church into other cultures. International diversity required the church to seek ways to magnify the Christian witness in other cultures in terms compatible with the life experiences and expectations of divergent peoples and worldviews. This quest prompted RLDS leaders to attempt to identify the "universal" aspects of the gospel that might find a place in other cultures while being adapted to indigenous values and needs. The church's General Officers then realized the necessity for pluralism, since what were earlier thought to be universals were now seen as particulars.

An urgently felt task issuing from this realization was the development of a theological base appropriate to a worldwide, multicultural church. This task required rigorous theological study, consultation, and synthesis. RLDS leaders participated in seminars on history, theology, evangelism, planning, Zionic concepts and procedures, higher education, and professional development. In the early stages of these programs, the First Presidency and the Council of Twelve Apostles in 1966 announced five new objectives to guide future church development. The first of these called the church to clarify its theology and unify the members in their faith. A special committee on basic beliefs, appointed years earlier, gained several new members who had pursued formal theological training. The newly constituted committee compiled essays explicating the various aspects of the faith. Its report, *Exploring the Faith*, issued in 1971, called the whole church to serious theological exploration and reflection.

As they entered into this complex process,

many RLDS leaders and members experienced considerable anxiety. The neo-orthodox Christian theological stances taken in *Exploring the Faith* and in many other works from the church's press in the 1960s and 1970s did not fit some of the more traditional views. For example, the fifth objective of 1966 called for an interpretation of Zion "in worldwide terms." As church leaders pursued this process, they began to speak and write of Zion, not only as a remnant colony of Saints in Missouri but also as a leavening process—a source of redemptive social change all over the world. This called the church to be a covenant people, transforming culture from within, wherever they lived.

A vocal minority of RLDS members viewed this concept and its implications as a total rejection of the early "remnant" image. They began to resist the church's pastoral, theological, educational, and programmatic efforts to nurture a wider, pluralistic application of the Zionic dimension. The resistance inhered in the fact that the expanding interpretation of Zion appeared to some to be a loss of loyalty by current leaders to the perpetual authority of the scriptures and to other statements of Joseph Smith, Jr., about the Zionic endeavor.

W. Wallace Smith's revelatory instruction of 1968 called the church to begin preparations for building a temple in Independence. This stirred much discussion, among both leaders and members, about the extent to which such an edifice would fit earlier temple purposes, either at Kirtland, Ohio (1834–1836) or Nauvoo (1840–1846). Very little along these lines was determined during W. Wallace Smith's tenure in office. The consensus was that the proposed temple was to have more in common with Kirtland's House of the Lord than with the Nauvoo Temple, in terms of educational and worship functions. The Temple School came into being in 1974, with a focus on leadership education related to the future temple. Graceland College president Dr. William T. Higdon (1929–), was called into the Council of Twelve Apostles at that time and assigned as president of Temple School. Clearly RLDS leadership was committed to a strong educational component as part of temple planning. Also during the late 1970s, the church took on a heavy financial and personnel commitment when it began to sponsor and operate Park College in Kansas City, Missouri.

Wallace B. Smith (1929–), son of W. Wallace Smith, became prophet of the RLDS church on April 5, 1978, having been chosen as "prophet and president designate" two years earlier. Leaving his practice of ophthalmology, Smith spent two years in rigorous theological studies to prepare for his presidency. The two most far-reaching leadership moves since his ordination are reflected in his revelatory instruction to the 1984 World Conference: section 156 of the RLDS Doctrine and Covenants.

Section 156:9–10 meant that the church would now move ahead with women's ordinations, a breakthrough foreshadowed by events dating back to 1970. Local pastors had been initiating priesthood calls for women since 1974, but no clear precedent permitted actual ordination. Now, the conference's approval of section 156 created the context for the ordination of women, the first ones being ordained November 17, 1985. This cluster of events led to intense conflict in scattered areas of the RLDS Church. An effort to rescind section 156 at the 1986 world conference failed decisively. Proponents of rescission continued to work to strengthen networks of resistance. Some formed what they call "independent branches," which defy the authority of the RLDS church on all matters. It is impossible to measure the extent of the disaffection, but it probably numbers about 3 percent of the 240,000 total membership.

Section 156:3–6 pointed the church in a new direction by setting forth the general purposes of the temple. The document declared that the primary purpose of the temple would be the "pursuit of peace, reconciliation, healing of the spirit." It would be built also to nurture "an attitude of wholeness of body, mind, and spirit." Furthermore, the temple would express the "essential meaning of the church as healing and redeeming agent, inspired by the life and witness of the redeemer of the world." Finally, the temple would require and enable new programs of leadership education in expansion of the ministries of all the priesthood and members of the church.

Section 156 also enjoined the church to redouble its efforts to finance and build the temple. Ground was broken for the temple at the 1990 World Conference, where it was also announced that more than $61 million had been pledged toward the $75 million needed for its completion and its supporting endowment fund.

As of 1990, the RLDS church stood at a new turning point in its history. More than 3,000 women ordained to all offices of priesthood except the General Officer category were adding new

Conference chamber inside the RLDS Auditorium, in Independence, Missouri, with choir and orchestra. Courtesy Library-Archives, Reorganized Church of Jesus Christ of Latter Day Saints.

styles and depths of caring ministries not before experienced in the church. The developing Temple School courses and the programs of the Temple Ministries Division have begun to create new life and energy in RLDS branches and members in many of the forty nations where the church is established. Since World War II, the RLDS church has also become much more ecumenical than at any previous time. A resolution passed at the 1990 World Conference requested the First Presidency to go beyond the bounds of the church for help. The specific intent was that the RLDS church would seek those whose experience and expertise would equip them to give valuable help to the forthcoming temple programs in the area of peace and justice.

The RLDS church seems intent on shedding many of the vestiges of its sectarian background of early Mormonism. To what extent it can discard these while retaining its identity as a recognizable part of Latter Day Saintism remains to be seen.

BIBLIOGRAPHY

Blair, Alma R. "The Tradition of Dissent—Jason W. Briggs." In *Restoration Studies I*, pp. 146–61. Independence, Mo., 1980.

Booth, Howard J. "Recent Shifts in Restoration Thought." In *Restoration Studies I*, pp. 162–75. Independence, Mo., 1980.

Davis, Inez Smith. *The Story of the Church*. Independence, Mo., 1969.

Edwards, F. Henry. *The History of The Reorganized Church of Jesus Christ of Latter Day Saints*, Vols. 5–8. Independence, Mo., 1970–1976.

Higdon, Barbara. "The Reorganization in the Twentieth Century." *Dialogue* 7 (Spring 1972):94–100.

Judd, Peter, and Bruce Lindgren. *An Introduction to the Saints' Church*. Independence, Mo., 1976.

Launius, Roger D. *Joseph Smith III: Pragmatic Prophet*. Chicago, 1988.

McMurray, W. Grant. "True Son of a True Father: Joseph Smith III and the Succession Question." In *Restoration Studies I*, pp. 131–45. Independence, Mo., 1980.

Newell, Linda King, and Valeen Tippetts Avery. *Mormon Enigma: Emma Hale Smith: Prophet's Wife, "Elect Lady," Polygamy's Foe, 1804–1879*. New York, 1984.

Smith, Joseph, III, and Heman C. Smith. *The History of The Reorganized Church of Jesus Christ of Latter Day Saints*, Vols. 1–4. Lamoni, Iowa, 1896–1903.

Vlahos, Clare D. "Images of Orthodoxy: Self-Identity in Early Reorganization Apologetics." In *Restoration Studies I*, pp. 176–88. Independence, Mo., 1980.

RICHARD P. HOWARD

REPENTANCE

Repentance is the process by which humans set aside or overcome sins by changing hearts, attitudes, and actions that are out of harmony with God's teachings, thereby conforming their lives more completely to his will. In the words of one latter-day prophet, repentance is "to change one's mind in regard to past or intended actions or conduct" (McKay, p. 14). Paul observes that "all have sinned, and come short of the glory of God" (Rom. 3:23). For this reason, the Lord "gave commandment that all men must repent" (2 Ne. 2:21; Moses 6:57). This means that repentance is required of every soul who has not reached perfection.

Repentance has been central to God's dealings with his children since they were first placed on the earth. Old Testament prophets constantly called the children of Israel individually and collectively to repent and *turn* to God and righteous living from rebellion, apostasy, and SIN. In New Testament times, the work of Jesus Christ on earth may be described as a ministry of repentance—that is, of calling on God's children to return to their God by changing their thinking and behavior and becoming more godlike. The Savior taught, "Be ye therefore perfect, even as your Father which is in heaven is perfect" (Matt. 5:48). Christ's apostles were called primarily to preach FAITH in Christ and to declare repentance to all the world

(Mark 6:12). In modern times, few topics occur in the Lord's revelations as pervasively as this one. He has given latter-day prophets and all messengers of his gospel repeated instructions to declare "nothing but repentance unto this generation" (D&C 6:9). The Prophet Joseph Smith identified repentance and faith in Jesus Christ as the two fundamental principles of the gospel (A of F 4). And the gospel itself has been called "a gospel of repentance" (D&C 13; 84:27).

In modern as in earlier times, the term "repentance" literally means a turning from sin and a reversing of one's attitudes and behavior. Its purposes are to develop the divine nature within all mortal souls by freeing them from wrong or harmful thoughts and actions and to assist them in becoming more Christlike by replacing the "natural man" (1 Cor. 2:14) with the "new man" in Christ (Eph. 4:20–24).

This process is not only necessary in preparing humans to return and live with God, but it enlarges their capacity to love their fellow beings. Those who have reconciled themselves with God have the spiritual understanding, desire, and power to become reconciled with their fellow beings. God has commanded all humans to forgive each other: "I, the Lord, will forgive whom I will forgive, but of you it is required to forgive all men" (D&C 64:10). As God shows his love by forgiving ("I will forgive their iniquity, and I will remember their sin no more"; Jer. 31:34), his children, as they forgive others, also reflect this love.

True repentance, while seldom easy, is essential to personal happiness, emotional and spiritual growth, and eternal SALVATION. It is the only efficacious way for mortals to free themselves of the permanent effects of sin and the inevitable attendant burden of guilt. To achieve it, several specific changes must occur. One must first recognize that an attitude or action is out of harmony with God's teachings and feel genuine sorrow or remorse for it. Paul calls this "godly sorrow" (2 Cor. 7:10). Other scriptures describe this state of mind as "a broken heart and a contrite spirit" (Ps. 51:17; 2 Ne. 2:7; 3 Ne. 9:20). This recognition must produce an inward change of attitude. The prophet Joel exhorted Israel to "rend your heart, and not your garments" (Joel 2:12–13), thereby bringing the inner transformation necessary to begin the process of repentance.

Some form of CONFESSION is also necessary in repentance. In some cases, the transgressor may need to confess to the person or persons wronged or injured and ask forgiveness; in other cases, it may be necessary to confess sins to a Church leader authorized to receive such confessions; in still other cases, a confession to God alone may be sufficient; and sometimes all three forms of confession may be necessary.

In addition, repentance requires restitution to others who have suffered because of the sin. Whenever possible, this should be done by making good any physical or material losses or injury. Even when this is not possible, repentance requires other, equally significant actions, such as apologies; increased acts of kindness and service toward offended persons; intensified commitment to, and activity in, the Lord's work; or all of these in concert.

Finally, for repentance to be complete, one must abandon the sinful behavior. A change of heart begins the process; a visible outward change of direction, reflected in new patterns of behavior, must complete it (Mosiah 5:2). Failure to alter outward actions means that the sinner has not repented, and the weight of the former sin returns (D&C 82:7; cf. Matt. 18:32–34).

One purpose of repentance is to bless people by affording through forgiveness the one and only way of relieving the suffering that attends sin: "For behold, I, God, have suffered these things for all, that they might not suffer if they would repent; but if they would not repent, they must suffer even as I" (D&C 19:16–17).

The Lord has repeatedly promised that all who repent completely shall find forgiveness of their sins, which in turn brings great joy. The parables of the lost sheep and the lost coin exemplify the joy in heaven over one sinner who repents (Luke 15:4–10); the parable of the prodigal son (or lost son) illustrates the joy in heaven and similar joy in the circle of family and friends and within the repentant son himself over his return from sin (Luke 15:11–32).

Though repentance is indispensable to eternal salvation and to earthly happiness, it is not sufficient by itself to reunite a person with God. Complete repentance first requires faith in the Lord Jesus Christ, which in turn generates strong motivation and power to repent. Both are necessary for, and thus must precede, BAPTISM, the reception of the GIFT OF THE HOLY GHOST, and MEMBERSHIP in the Lord's kingdom. After awakening faith in Christ in the hearts of his listeners on the day of Pentecost, Peter exhorted them to "repent, and be baptized every one of you in the name of Jesus Christ for the remission of sins and you shall receive the Holy Ghost" (Acts 2:38). Only with the requisite repentance, symbolized by a "broken heart and a contrite spirit" and the abandonment of former sinful deeds and thought patterns, is one prepared to be baptized, receive the Holy Ghost, and have all previous sins remitted. Through baptism, a repentant person enters the kingdom of God by making covenants to remember Christ always and keep his commandments. The REMISSION OF SINS comes "by fire and by the Holy Ghost" (2 Ne. 31:17; D&C 20:37).

Since repentance is an ongoing process in the mortal effort to become Christlike, the need for it never diminishes. It requires active, daily application as humans recognize and strive to overcome sin and error and in this way ENDURE TO THE END. For this reason, the Lord has instituted a means whereby each person who has repented and entered into the baptismal covenant may renew it by partaking of the SACRAMENT in remembrance of him. This time of self-examination allows one to reflect on the promises made at baptism, which were to take Christ's name upon oneself, to remember him always, and to keep his commandments. Thus, the process of repentance is kept alive by this frequent period of reflection as the participant partakes of symbols of Christ's body and blood in remembrance of his sacrifice to atone for human sin.

Scriptures inform us that "this life is the time for men to prepare to meet God" and that so-called deathbed repentance is usually not effective:

> Ye cannot say, when ye are brought to that awful crisis, that I will repent, that I will return to my God. Nay, ye cannot say this; for that same spirit which doth possess your bodies at the time that ye go out of this life, that same spirit will have power to possess your body in that eternal world. . . . If ye have procrastinated the day of your repentance even until death, behold, ye have become subjected to the spirit of the devil [Alma 34:32–35].

To return to God's presence, mortals must strive during this life to attain Christlike qualities, which can only be gained by turning from sin. To defer such efforts blocks the exercise of faith essential to repentance, prevents the operation of the Holy Ghost, and retards the development of the personal qualities reflected in the "broken heart and contrite spirit" necessary to live in God's presence.

Repentance is one of the most powerful redemptive principles of the restored gospel of Jesus Christ. Without it, there would be no eternal progression, no possibility of becoming Christlike, no relief from the burden of guilt that every human incurs in a lifetime. With it, there is the glorious promise uttered by Isaiah that even for grievous sins there might be forgiveness: "Though your sins be as scarlet, they shall be as white as snow; though they be red like crimson, they shall be as wool" (Isa. 1:18).

BIBLIOGRAPHY

Gillum, Gary P. "Repentance Also Means Rethinking." In *By Study and Also by Faith*, ed. J. Lundquist and S. Ricks, Vol. 2, pp. 406–37. Salt Lake City, 1990.

Kimball, Spencer W. *The Miracle of Forgiveness*. Salt Lake City, 1969.

———. *The Teachings of Spencer W. Kimball*, ed. Kimball, Edward L., pp. 80–114. Salt Lake City, 1982.

McKay, David O. *Gospel Ideals*, pp. 12–14. Salt Lake City, 1953.

JAMES K. LYON

RESTORATION OF ALL THINGS

The concept of a restoration of all things is biblical and is frequently spoken of in The Church of Jesus Christ of Latter-day Saints. Peter spoke of the anticipated "times of restitution of all things, which God hath spoken by the mouth of all his holy prophets since the world began" (Acts 3:21). Latter-day Saints understand this as a prophetic anticipation of a full and final restoration of the gospel in the development and fulfillment of the purposes of God in the LAST DAYS. The current era is therefore called the DISPENSATION OF THE FULNESS OF TIMES in which all things will be gathered together in Christ (Eph. 1:10; D&C 27:13). The Church teaches that every gospel truth and blessing, and all priesthood authority, keys, ORDINANCES, and COVENANTS necessary for mankind's eternal salvation have been, or will be, restored in this dispensation. In this manner, the blessings of DISPENSATIONS past will "flow into the most glorious and greatest of dispensations, like clear streams flowing into a mighty river" (DS 1:168).

The restoration spoken of in the scriptures involves more than a reestablishment of the

Church and the function of saving ordinances. Scattered Israel will be gathered, the SECOND COMING OF CHRIST will occur, the MILLENNIUM will begin, the kingdom of God will be established worldwide, and "the earth will be renewed and receive its paradisiacal glory" (A of F 10).

The Prophet Joseph SMITH testified that he was visited by divine messengers from former dispensations who conferred upon him priesthood powers and restored ordinances, doctrines, and blessings that existed in their dispensations. A brief outline follows:

1. God the Father and his Son Jesus Christ initiated the restoration when they appeared to Joseph Smith in the spring of 1820. He was told to join none of the churches of the day, and he was also taught important truths about the nature of the GODHEAD (see FIRST VISION).

2. The angel MORONI visited Joseph Smith, revealing the plates of the Book of Mormon, which Joseph Smith translated, restoring gospel knowledge that had been lost to the earth in the centuries since biblical times. Latter-day Saints believe that the canon of scripture is not closed and that God "will yet reveal many great and important things pertaining to the Kingdom of God" (A of F 9), including additional volumes of holy scripture.

3. On May 15, 1829, Joseph Smith and Oliver COWDERY were ordained to the AARONIC PRIESTHOOD under the hands of JOHN THE BAPTIST (D&C 13:1).

4. In 1829 or 1830, three New Testament apostles—Peter, James, and John—conferred the MELCHIZEDEK PRIESTHOOD, including the power of LAYING ON OF HANDS for the GIFT OF THE HOLY GHOST, upon Joseph and Oliver and ordained them "apostles and special witnesses" of Jesus Christ. This ordination restored to earth the same authority that existed in the Church during the Savior's ministry.

5. The restoration includes reestablishment of an organization to teach the gospel and administer its ordinances. The sixth Article of Faith states, "We believe in the same organization that existed in the Primitive Church, namely, apostles, prophets, pastors, teachers, evangelists, and so forth." Formal organization of the Church occurred on April 6, 1830, in FAYETTE, NEW YORK.

6. On April 3, 1836, the prophet MOSES came to Joseph Smith and Oliver Cowdery in the KIRTLAND TEMPLE in Ohio and conferred the "keys of the gathering of Israel from the four parts of the earth" (D&C 110:11).

7. The prophet ELIAS conferred the keys of the dispensation of the GOSPEL OF ABRAHAM (D&C 110:12), restoring the patriarchal order of marriage and the gifts and blessings given to Abraham and his posterity (DS 3:127; MD, p. 203).

8. ELIJAH restored authority to bind and seal on earth and in heaven, including the power to seal husbands and wives to each other, and children to their parents (Smith, p. 252). This fulfilled Malachi's prophecy that Elijah should be sent to "turn the hearts of the fathers to the children, and the children to the fathers, lest the whole earth be smitten with a curse" (Mal. 4:5–6; D&C 110:15). The genealogical research of the LDS Church and the TEMPLE ORDINANCES performed on behalf of the dead are integral parts of this process (see GENEALOGY).

The restoration will result in the culmination of all of God's purposes on the earth. The scriptures even speak of a reshaping of the land surfaces, with a coming together of the continents (D&C 133:23–24; cf. Gen. 10:25).

The fundamental purpose of the restoration is to prepare the Church and the world to receive their King, the Lord Jesus Christ. Latter-day Saints view the restoration of all things as the work of God preparatory to the time when all old things shall become new, with a new heaven and a new earth. The restoration will include RESURRECTION, regeneration, and renewal to all life upon the earth and the glorification of the earth itself, when it becomes a celestial sphere (Isa. 65:17; Matt. 19:28; Rev. 21:1; D&C 29:22–25; 88:17–20, 25–26). As explained by Alma, referring in particular to the resurrection, "the plan of restoration is requisite with the justice of God; . . . that all things should be restored to their proper order" (Alma 41:2).

BIBLIOGRAPHY

Hinckley, Gordon B. *Truth Restored.* Salt Lake City, 1947.

Matthews, Robert J. "The Fulness of Times." *Ensign* 19 (Dec. 1989):46–51.

Smith, Joseph Fielding. *The Restoration of All Things.* Salt Lake City, 1945.

CORY H. MAXWELL

RESTORATION OF THE GOSPEL OF JESUS CHRIST

When Latter-day Saints speak of the "restoration of the gospel of Jesus Christ" they refer primarily to the restoration that has occurred in the latter days, establishing the DISPENSATION OF THE FULNESS OF TIMES (Eph. 1:10; D&C 27:13). However, there have been a number of restorations of the gospel over the history of the earth.

"Restoration" means to bring back that which was once present but which has been lost. The introduction of the gospel of Jesus Christ on this earth began with Adam and Eve. In the GARDEN OF EDEN they partook of the fruit of the tree of knowledge of good and evil (Moses 4:12), and as a result they became fallen and mortal and were expelled from the garden. God then revealed to them that they could be redeemed through the Only Begotten (Moses 5:1–12) and gave Adam the PRIESTHOOD after the Order of the Son of God (cf. Abr. 1:3; Fac. 3, Fig. 3, Book of Abraham). Thereafter, they received the various ORDINANCES of the gospel, including a ceremonial ENDOWMENT, and entered into covenants of obedience to all of God's commandments (Fac. 3, Fig. 3, Book of Abraham).

After Adam and Eve became parents, they taught their children the gospel of Jesus Christ. But many of their posterity loved Satan more than God and from that time forth began to be "carnal, sensual, and devilish" (Moses 5:12–13). Eventually mankind substituted worldly interests in place of the commandments of God, and in time the gospel was distorted, fragmented, and lost from the earth.

Prophets have been called by God from time to time to *restore* the true covenants and gospel of Jesus Christ. One of the prophets was ABRAHAM (Abr. 3:22–25), who, having proved his faithfulness in numerous ways, was given a special covenant for himself, his descendants, and all who accept the gospel. This covenant extended to all future generations and nations of the earth (see ABRAHAMIC COVENANT). Another was MOSES, through whom the Lord restored the gospel for a short time, but because of the unwillingness of the people, the Lord instituted a preparatory law to help the people turn their hearts from idolatry to God (see LAW OF MOSES). Later God revealed his gospel to ELIJAH, ISAIAH, JEREMIAH, and EZEKIEL, among others, who urged the people to repentance and faithfulness. Many ancient prophets testified of a coming Messiah and of his crucifixion and resurrection. They also spoke of a subsequent long period of apostasy, but promised that there would be a restoration in the latter days, prior to the second coming of the Lord (cf. Amos 8–9).

The same gospel, covenants, and ordinances that had once been given to Adam, ENOCH, NOAH, Abraham, Moses, and the other ancient prophets, were restored to the earth during the MERIDIAN OF TIME when Jesus Christ lived on the earth. However, the Church that Jesus established in New Testament times was short-lived because of apostasy, which resulted in part from persecution and the eventual dispersion and death of the apostles. Hence, the authority of the priesthood, much of the gospel of Christ, and the ordinances and covenants were again lost to the earth. PETER, JOHN, and PAUL each spoke of this APOSTASY, which was already starting in their day, and prophesied that there would also be a restoration.

In the spring of 1820 a vision was given to Joseph SMITH, near Palmyra, New York, in response to his fervent prayer to know the truth concerning religion. In this experience, Joseph Smith was visited by God the Father and his Son Jesus Christ (JS—H 1:17; *see also* FIRST VISION). In subsequent visits, holy angels instructed, ordained, and prepared him to become a latter-day prophet and an instrument in God's hands in restoring the gospel of Jesus Christ for the last time and setting up the kingdom spoken of by Daniel (Dan. 2; D&C 27:13; 65:1–6).

As part of this restoration, The Church of Jesus Christ of Latter-day Saints was organized by revelation on April 6, 1830, "it being regularly organized and established agreeable to the laws of our country, by the will and commandments of God" (D&C 20:1). It has the same priesthood, doctrines, and ordinances, and the same "organization that existed in the Primitive Church, namely, apostles, prophets, pastors, teachers, evangelists, and so forth" (A of F 6). Eventually, all of the keys of the priesthood, which had been given to man from Adam's time onward, were restored. Prophets who held priesthood keys anciently came to Joseph Smith and conferred those keys upon him (D&C 128:18). These included JOHN THE BAPTIST (D&C 13), Peter, JAMES, and John (D&C 27:12), and Moses, ELIAS, and Elijah (D&C 110:11–16).

Thus, through the latter-day Prophet there has been a restoration of the gospel of Jesus Christ on the earth with the powers, authority, and ordinances as in ancient times. Other aspects of the restoration to occur are the gathering of Israel, the SECOND COMING OF CHRIST, and the MILLENNIUM.

[See also Dispensations of the Gospel; Restoration of All Things.]

BIBLIOGRAPHY

Smith, Joseph Fielding. *The Restoration of All Things*. Salt Lake City, 1945.

R. WAYNE SHUTE

RESTORATIONISM, PROTESTANT

Beginning about 1800, a religious movement known as the Second Great Awakening swept across the American frontier. The Church of Jesus Christ of Latter-day Saints emerged in this setting.

Many people in this period were seeking the original vitality of the New Testament Church, and those who espoused this point of view were called "restorationists." Protestant restorationism, as manifested in the early nineteenth century, followed the lead of the early reformers Martin Luther and John Calvin, who believed that the church should be firmly rooted in the scriptures. But even their theologies contained complexities that to the nineteenth century restorationists seemed far removed from day-to-day life. Men of differing persuasions, often unlettered, emerged to sound the cry for the restoration of biblical Christianity.

In New England, Elias Smith and Abner Jones, both Baptists, organized a "Christian church" in Portsmouth, New Hampshire. They sought the New Testament Church in its simple, nondenominational form and thus called themselves Christians. In Virginia and North Carolina, a similar movement developed under the leadership of James O'Kelly and Rice Haggard, both dissatisfied Methodist ministers. Their group was also to be known as Christians, and the Bible was to be their only creed. In 1811, the two groups united. William Kincaid, an illiterate frontiersman, converted at a revival meeting, led another group of Christians in Kentucky.

Barton W. Stone, a Presbyterian minister from Virginia and North Carolina, sought the experience of religion that he saw in the New Testament. He finally left the Presbyterian church in Kentucky to found a "Christian church." Thomas Campbell, a Presbyterian educated in Glasgow, Scotland, believed the church should be founded upon the Bible only, and his followers coined the slogan, "Where scripture speaks, we speak, and where scripture is silent, we are silent." In Pennsylvania he founded the Christian Association of Washington for the cultivation of piety. His son, Alexander, who influenced Sidney RIGDON, was the restorationist who founded the church known today as the Disciples of Christ.

Virtually all restorationists believed that the New Testament Church was to be restored, that there should be no CREEDS, that baptism should be by immersion, that salvation was through faith and repentance, and that there were a remission of sins and a gift of the Holy Ghost. They differed, however, in other points: whether the remission of sins and the gift of the Holy Ghost were a result of baptism, simply a product of faith, or conferred by the laying-on of hands; whether there had been a loss of authority; whether all things were to be restored, including New Testament miracles and gifts of the Spirit, or whether only some things would be restored; and whether religious experience was necessary.

Latter-day Saints were more comprehensively restorationist than any other group. The principal LDS beliefs that created the most discussion were that the authority of the priesthood was restored to Joseph Smith by heavenly messengers; that remission of sins follows baptism, which is essential to salvation; that all things (including miracles) are to be restored; that revelation is as requisite today as in the past; and that, as in the New Testament Church, the scriptural canon is not closed. The acceptance of these beliefs led Sidney Rigdon to break with Alexander Campbell and embrace the restored gospel as taught by Latter-day Saint missionaries.

BIBLIOGRAPHY

Bushman, Richard L. *Joseph Smith and the Beginnings of Mormonism*. Urbana and Chicago, 1988.

Garrison, Winfred Ernest. *Religion Follows the Frontier: A History of the Disciples of Christ*. New York, 1931.

JOHN DILLENBERGER
ROGER R. KELLER

RESURRECTION

Resurrection is the reunion of the SPIRIT with an immortal PHYSICAL BODY. The body laid in the grave is mortal; the resurrected physical body is immortal. The whole of man, the united spirit and body, is defined in modern scripture as the "soul" of man. Resurrection from the dead constitutes the redemption of the soul (D&C 88:15–16).

Although the idea of resurrection is not extensively delineated in the Old Testament, there are some definite allusions to it (e.g., 1 Sam. 2:6; Job 14:14; 19:26; Isa. 26:19; Dan. 12:2). And in the New Testament, the resurrection of Jesus Christ, as the prototype of all resurrections, is an essential and central message: "I am the resurrection and the life" (John 11:25).

The evidence of Christ's resurrection is measurably strengthened for Latter-day Saints by other records of post-Resurrection visitations of the Christ (see JESUS CHRIST: FORTY-DAY MINISTRY AND OTHER POST-RESURRECTION APPEARANCES). For example, in the 3 Nephi account in the Book of Mormon, an entire multitude saw, heard, and touched him as he appeared in transcendent resurrected glory. This is accepted by Latter-day Saints as an ancient sacred text. The tendency of some recent scholarship outside the Church to radically separate the "Jesus of history" and the "Christ of faith" and to ascribe the resurrection faith to later interpreters is challenged by these later documents and by modern revelation.

Ancient witnesses, including Paul, came to their assurance of the reality of the Resurrection by beholding the risen Christ. From like witnesses, Latter-day Saints accept the record that at the resurrection of Christ "the graves were opened," in both the Old World and the new, and "many bodies of the saints which slept arose" (Matt. 27:52; 3 Ne. 23:9–10). In the current dispensation, resurrected beings, including JOHN THE BAPTIST, PETER, JAMES, and MORONI₂ appeared and ministered to Joseph SMITH and Oliver COWDERY.

In the theology of Judaism and some Christian denominations resurrection has often been spiritualized—that is, redefined as a symbol for immortality of some aspect of man such as the active intellect, or of the soul considered to be an immaterial entity. In contrast, scientific naturalism tends to reject both the concept of the soul and of bodily resurrection. Latter-day Saints share few of the assumptions that underlie these dogmas. In

LDS understanding, the spirit of each individual is not immaterial, but consists of pure, refined matter: "It existed before the body, can exist in the body; and will exist separate from the body, when the body will be mouldering in the dust; and will in the resurrection, be again united with it" (TPJS, p. 207). Identity and personality persist with the spirit, and after the resurrection the spirit will dwell forever in a physical body.

Platonism and gnosticism hold that embodiment is imprisonment, descent, or association with what is intrinsically evil. In contrast, the scriptures teach that the physical body is a step upward in the progression and perfection of all. The body is sacred, a temple (1 Cor. 3:16; D&C 93:35). Redemption is not escape from the flesh but its dedication and transformation. Joseph Smith taught, "We came into this earth that we might have a body and present it pure before God in the celestial kingdom" (TPJS, p. 181). On the other hand, if defiled, distorted, and abused, the body may be an instrument of degradation, an enemy of genuine spirituality.

In contrast to the view that the subtle powers of intellect or soul must finally transcend the body or anything corporeal, the Prophet Joseph Smith taught that all beings "who have tabernacles (bodies), have power over those who have not" (TPJS, p. 190; 2 Ne. 9:8). At minimum, this is taken to mean that intellectual and spiritual powers are enhanced by association with the flesh. It follows that a long absence of the spirit from the body in the realm of disembodied spirits awaiting resurrection will be viewed not as a beatific or blessed condition, but instead as a bondage (D&C 45:17; 138:50). Moreover, "spirit and element [the spirit body and the physical body], inseparably connected, [can] receive a fulness of joy. And when separated, man cannot receive a fulness of joy" (D&C 93:33, 34).

In contrast to the view that the body when buried or cremated has no identifiable residue, Joseph Smith taught that "there is no fundamental principle belonging to a human system that ever goes into another in this world or the world to come" (HC 5:339). Chemical disintegration is not final destruction. The resurrected body is tangible, but when the flesh is quickened by the Spirit there will be "spirit in their [veins] and not blood" (WJS, p. 270; see also TPJS, p. 367).

Resurrection is as universal as death. All must die and all must be resurrected. It is a free gift to everyone. It is not the result of the exercise of faith or accumulated good works. The Book of Mormon prophet Amulek declares, "Now this restoration shall come to all, both old and young, both bond and free, both male and female, both the wicked and the righteous" (Alma 11:44; cf. *TPJS*, pp. 199–200, 294–297, 310–311, 319–321, 324–326).

Not all will be resurrected at the same moment, "but every man in his own order: Christ the firstfruits; afterward they that are Christ's at his coming" (1 Cor. 15:23). "Behold, there is a time appointed that all shall come forth from the dead," Alma writes, to stand embodied before God to be judged of their thoughts, words, and deeds (Alma 40:4).

"All men will come from the grave as they lie down, whether old or young" (*TPJS*, p. 199). And he who quickeneth all things shall "change our vile body, that it may be fashioned like unto his glorious body" (Philip. 3:21). "The body will come forth as it is laid to rest, for there is no growth nor development in the grave. As it is laid down, so will it arise, and changes to perfection will come by the law of restitution. But the spirit will continue to expand and develop, and the body, after the resurrection will develop to the full stature of man" (Joseph F. Smith, *IE* 7 [June 1904]:623–24).

The resurrected body will be suited to the conditions and glory to which the person is assigned in the day of judgment. "Some dwell in higher glory than others" (*TPJS*, p. 367). The Doctrine and Covenants teaches that "your glory shall be that glory by which your bodies are quickened" (D&C 88:28), and three glories are designated (D&C 76). Paul (1 Cor. 15:40) also mentioned three glories of resurrected bodies: one like the sun (celestial), another as the moon (terrestrial), and the third as the stars. In a revelation to Joseph Smith, the glory of the stars was identified as telestial (D&C 76). The lights of these glories differ, as do the sun, the moon, and the stars as perceived from earth. "So also is the resurrection of the dead" (1 Cor. 15:40–42).

In a general sense, the Resurrection may be divided into the resurrection of the just, also called the first resurrection, and the resurrection of the unjust, or the last resurrection. The first resurrection commenced with the resurrection of Christ and with those who immediately thereafter came forth from their graves. In much larger numbers, it will precede the thousand-year millennial reign, inaugurated by the "second coming" of the Savior

(D&C 45:44–45; cf. 1 Thes. 4:16–17). At that time, some will be brought forth to meet him, as he descends in glory. This first resurrection will continue in proper order through the MILLENNIUM. The righteous who live on earth and die during the Millennium will experience immediate resurrection. Their transformation will take place in the "twinkling of an eye" (D&C 63:51). The first resurrection includes the celestial and terrestrial glories.

The final resurrection, or resurrection of the unjust, will occur at the end of the Millennium. In the words of the apocalypse, "the rest of the dead lived not again until the thousand years were finished" (Rev. 20:5). This last resurrection will include those destined for the telestial glory and PERDITION.

Of his visionary glimpses of the Resurrection, the Prophet Joseph Smith remarked, "The same glorious spirit gives them the likeness of glory and bloom; the old man with his silvery hairs will glory in bloom and beauty. No man can describe it to you—no man can write it" (*TPJS*, p. 368). Referring to the doctrine of the Resurrection as "principles of consolation," he pled, "Let these truths sink down in our hearts that, we may even here, begin to enjoy that which shall be in full hereafter." He added, "All your losses will be made up to you in the resurrection, provided you continue faithful. By the vision of the Almighty I have seen it" (*TPJS*, p. 296).

The hope of a glorious resurrection undergirds the radiance that characterized the faith of New Testament Saints as well as those who have since kept that faith alive in the world, including the Saints of the latter days.

BIBLIOGRAPHY

Ballard, Melvin J. "The Resurrection." In *Melvin Ballard . . . Crusader for Righteousness*, ed. Melvin R. Ballard. Salt Lake City, 1966.

Nickelsburg, George W. *Resurrection, Immortality, and Eternal Life in Intertestamental Judaism*. Cambridge, Mass., 1972.

Smith, Joseph F. *GD*.

Talmage, James E. *AF*.

DOUGLAS L. CALLISTER

RETRENCHMENT ASSOCIATION

The retrenchment movement, conceived in 1869 by President Brigham YOUNG to encourage LDS women to "spend more time in moral, mental and spiritual cultivation, and less upon fashion and the vanities of the world" (*Woman's Exponent* 11 [Sept. 15, 1882]:59), spawned two similar but distinct organizations. Mary Isabella HORNE, appointed by President Young to head the initial movement, established semimonthly women's meetings in Salt Lake City to promote the "reformation." Shortly thereafter, Brigham Young organized his daughters into a Young Ladies Retrenchment Association as a model for similar organizations in each ward of the Church, appointing Emma Young Empey as president (*see* YOUNG WOMEN). Though the young women's retrenchment societies held independent ward meetings, the parent association, calling itself the Senior and Junior Cooperative Retrenchment Association, remained a single, overarching entity that superintended the subsidiary societies while pursuing its own agenda.

Despite its similarity to the RELIEF SOCIETY, the Retrenchment Association was unique among Church organizations. As an ad hoc auxiliary, it was attached to no ecclesiastical unit, had no geographic boundaries (its meetings were open to all LDS women), and functioned under no specific line of ecclesiastical authority. Conducted by President Horne or one of her six counselors, another innovation, the meetings were largely extemporaneous. Members of the congregation (sometimes numbering two hundred) expressed religious sentiments or spoke impromptu on themes suggested by the presiding officers. Timid members were urged to participate, for it was "as essential for the sisters to learn to preach as for the brethren" (Minutes, Feb. 6, 1875).

In its first decade, the Association's principal objectives were reform in "diet and dress" and avoidance of all forms of "worldliness." Affirming LDS distinctiveness from the world became an impassioned and persistent theme. HOME INDUSTRIES also fell within the stewardship of the Association. Before the organization of general and stake Relief Society boards, Eliza R. SNOW, general head of the Relief Societies, used the Retrenchment Association to coordinate the branches of home industry that Brigham Young had assigned to the ward Relief Societies in 1868. Committees were organized in the retrenchment meetings to implement and supervise silk manufacturing, grain storage, straw braiding, and women's commission stores, all part of President Brigham Young's de-

Caroline (Carlie) Partridge Young, a daughter of Brigham Young, is pictured in "retrenchment dress," the Retrenchment Association's prescribed clothing. The costume was intended to represent modesty and withdrawal from extravagant dress among LDS women beginning in the late 1860s. Courtesy Winnifred Cannon Jardine.

sign to develop a cooperative and self-sustaining economy. Recruiting women to study medicine (*see* MATERNITY AND CHILD HEALTH CARE), urging them to vote (Utah women were enfranchised in 1870), and soliciting contributors and subscribers to the WOMAN'S EXPONENT also found place on the Association's agenda. This initial task orientation brought LDS women firmly into visible kingdom building.

If retrenchment marked the Association's first decade, "circling the wagons" reflected the spirit of its second. Besieged by punitive ANTI-POLYGAMY LEGISLATION, women affirmed their commitment to the principle of PLURAL MARRIAGE, declared their acceptance of PERSECUTION as a refining process, and asserted their belief in God's overruling hand. The Association assuaged the family and religious dislocations imposed by the prolonged federal campaign and provided women an oasis of stability and mutual reassurance during a time of crisis.

In its final years the "ladies semimonthly meetings," as the gatherings were then called, became even more self-consciously faith-promoting. This focus was only briefly interrupted by a revived interest in home industries in response to a national economic slump and the loss of Church properties and funds mandated by the Edmunds-Tucker Act. The aging of first-generation Latter-day Saints prompted redoubled efforts to prepare a second generation of standard bearers. In fervent declarations of faith, affiliated women continued to evoke images of distinctiveness even as many of the elements that made them distinctive gave way to powerful federal and social forces.

This amorphous gathering endured for thirty-five years, mainly through the perseverance of a few devoted women, some of them the "leading sisters" or higher echelon of LDS female leadership. The Retrenchment Association served as an agent of orthodoxy to motivate and inspire and to provide a spiritual bulwark against an encroaching world. As first-generation Latter-day Saints, these women were self-appointed keepers of the faith, who by their own commitment sought to spur commensurate fidelity among all the Saints.

BIBLIOGRAPHY

Minutes of the Junior and Senior Cooperative Retrenchment Association, 1872–1876, LDS Church Archives, Salt Lake City.

Woman's Exponent, 1872–1904, Salt Lake City.

CAROL CORNWALL MADSEN

REVELATION

Receiving personal revelation is a vital and distinctive part of the LDS religious experience. Response to personal revelation is seen as the basis for true faith in Christ, and the strength of the Church consists of that faithful response by members to their own personal revelations. The purpose of both revelation and the response of faith is to assist the children of men to come to Christ and learn to love one another with that same pure love with which Christ loves them.

TYPES OF REVELATION. A DISPENSATION of the GOSPEL OF JESUS CHRIST is a series of personal revelations from God. These revelations may be direct manifestations from God, as in the following typical cases:

1. theophanies (seeing God face-to-face), as in the FIRST VISION of the Prophet Joseph SMITH, which came at the beginning of the present dispensation (JS—H 1:15–20)
2. revealed knowledge from the Father that Jesus is "the Christ, the Son of the living God" (Matt. 16:13–17; *see also* SPIRIT OF PROPHECY)
3. visitations of angelic persons, such as the appearance of the angel Moroni to Joseph Smith (JS—H 1:30–32)
4. revelations through the URIM AND THUMMIM, by which means Joseph Smith translated the BOOK OF MORMON
5. open visions, as when Joseph Smith and Sidney Rigdon were shown the kingdoms of the hereafter (*see* DOCTRINE AND COVENANTS: SECTION 76)
6. physically hearing the voice of God, as is recorded in 3 Nephi 11
7. receiving the still, small voice of the HOLY SPIRIT, as in the experience of Elijah (1 Kgs. 19);
8. receiving the GIFTS OF THE SPIRIT (D&C 46)
9. having a burning in the bosom as an indication of the will of God, as in the explanation given to Oliver Cowdery (D&C 9:8)
10. dreams (1 Ne. 8:2–32)
11. manifestations of the LIGHT OF CHRIST, by which all men know good from evil (Alma 12:31–32; D&C 84:46–48).

Such direct manifestations of the mind and will of God are known as gifts and are contrasted with SIGNS. Gifts always have a spiritual component, even when they have a physical aspect. Signs are physical manifestations of the power of God and are a form of revelation from God, though they may be counterfeited and misinterpreted. Signs may show that God is at work, but spiritual gifts are required to know how one should respond.

REVELATION TO THE CHURCH. In every dispensation, God appoints his PROPHET to guide his people. The prophet's purpose is not to be an intermediary between God and others, though a prophet

Stained-glass window depicting Joseph Smith's First Vision, donated to the Salt Lake City Seventeenth Ward in 1907 by Annie D. Watkins. It was created by Harry Kimball and made by glass artists in Belgium.

their leaders" that they would "settle down in a state of blind self-security," abandoning the responsibility to obtain their own revelation: "Let every man and woman know, by the whispering of the Spirit of God to themselves, whether their leaders are walking in the path the Lord dictates, or not" (JD 9:150).

Presiding quorums in the Church are entitled to revelation for the Church on matters of doctrine, policies, programs, callings, and disciplinary actions, as each might be appropriate to a given quorum. Decisions of these quorums are to be made only by the personal, individual revelation of God to each member of that quorum. "And every decision made by either of these quorums must be by the unanimous voice of the same; that is, every member in each quorum must be agreed to its decisions, in order to make their decisions of the same power or validity one with the other" (D&C 107:27).

The scriptures contain the inspired writings of God's appointed prophets and are provided to others for their edification (D&C 68:2–4). By this means, people have received the inspired words recorded in the Old and New Testaments. Through revelation, the Prophet Joseph Smith translated the Book of Mormon (see BOOK OF MORMON TRANSLATION BY JOSEPH SMITH) and received those things set forth in the DOCTRINE AND COVENANTS and the PEARL OF GREAT PRICE. Latter-day Saints anticipate that more prophetic scripture will yet be revealed and that scripture written by past prophets but now lost to the world will be restored (2 Ne. 29:11–14; D&C 27:6; see also SCRIPTURE: FORTHCOMING SCRIPTURE). The true meaning of all scripture is to be revealed by the power of the Holy Ghost to the individual reader or hearer (2 Pet. 1:20; D&C 50:17–24).

must often do so. His purpose is, rather, to assist others to receive from God the personal revelation that he, the prophet, has taught God's truth, which will show the way to Christ.

The prophet as head of The Church of Jesus Christ of Latter-day Saints and all other persons who preside in the Church, including General Authorities, stake presidents, bishops, general presidencies, and parents, may receive revelation for the benefit of those over whom they preside. These revelations can be passed on to the membership of the Church through conference and other talks and in personal counsel. But each individual is entitled to know by personal revelation that these messages given through presiding authorities are truly from the Savior himself. President Brigham Young expressed concern that the Latter-day Saints would "have so much confidence in

PERSONAL REVELATION. After baptism and confirmation, each member has the right, when worthy, to the constant companionship of the HOLY GHOST (see GIFT OF THE HOLY GHOST). Through that companionship all the gifts of the Spirit are revealed to faithful individuals, who accomplish their mortal works in righteousness through the gifts and power of God revealed to and through them (Moro. 10:25). The challenges of living by personal revelation include (1) distinguishing revelation from God through his Holy Spirit from personal thoughts and desires, and from the influences of Satan (see DEVIL); (2) following the teachings and directions of the living prophet of God; and (3) living by every word that proceeds from the mouth of God (Matt. 4:4; John 3:5–8; D&C 50:13–24; 98:11–13; Deut. 8:3).

In modern societies, the idea of divine revelation is widely discounted for many reasons, including the violent acts that some have perpetrated while claiming divine direction. But God has made it known through the RESTORATION OF THE GOSPEL that revelation is available to all who seek it and that failure to seek spiritual guidance and direction is itself a mistake and a form of wishful thinking. Humans have eternal spirits, and each person experiences the supernatural influences that work upon his or her own spirit. Better than to ignore the spiritual side of oneself is to study one's personal spiritual experiences until they make sense. Those who acknowledge spiritual experiences are called the "honest in heart," and they are candidates for the revealed riches of godliness (D&C 8:1; 97:8).

The fundamental revelation from God is the KNOWLEDGE of good through the light of Christ (John 1:9). The prophet Lehi taught his children that because of the choices made by Adam and Eve, their descendants receive supernatural knowledge of both good and evil, making a choice between the two necessary in fulfillment of the PURPOSE OF EARTH LIFE. After mortality God returns to each human being eternally the good or evil each chose in life (Alma 41:1–5; 2 Ne. 2:27).

But before any final judgment, each person will be taught the gospel of Jesus Christ by the power of the Holy Spirit. This gospel is the good news that the Son of God will assist all persons to stop doing evil and will save them from the consequences of all the evil they have done if they will believe in him and repent. Acting to accept this revelation constitutes faith in Jesus Christ, which, if it continues, may bring additional revelation from God: more instruction; the gifts of the Spirit; the knowledge imparted through saving ordinances of the NEW AND EVERLASTING COVENANT; angelic visitations; visions; the revelation to know God himself face to face; and finally, the revelation to be given the fulness of godhood, to be made joint-heirs with Christ (D&C 121:29).

The LDS concept of individual revelation as fundamental to all human experience helps explain other distinctive LDS teachings. The key to making the proper distinction between supernatural revelation and its counterfeit is that fundamental knowledge of good and evil. Individuals must experiment, being as honest in heart and mind as they can, until they can see clearly what is good and what is evil. Those who learn to distinguish good from evil in this life can then distinguish the good spirit from the evil spirit. They then can distinguish the true gospel of Jesus Christ from its counterfeits, the true path of righteousness from the byways of covenant breaking and bending, and the true and living God from the image of God produced by their own wishful thinking (Moro. 7:5–19).

Joseph Smith taught the Saints how to recognize and receive revelation:

A person may profit by noticing the first intimation of the spirit of revelation; for instance, when you feel pure intelligence flowing into you, it may give you sudden strokes of ideas, so that by noticing it, you may find it fulfilled the same day or soon; (i.e.) those things that were presented unto your minds by the Spirit of God, will come to pass; and thus by learning the Spirit of God and understanding it, you may grow into the principle of revelation, until you become perfect in Christ Jesus [*TPJS*, p. 151].

To learn to communicate with others by the gifts of that Holy Spirit makes it possible for one to be a prophet or prophetess of God. Latter-day Saints believe that through divine revelation every child of Christ may, and should, become a prophet or a prophetess to his or her own divinely appointed stewardship (Num. 11:29), holding fast to that which is good and rejecting that which is evil (1 Thes. 5:19–21).

Thus, the human problem is not to *get* revelation, but to *understand* the revelation one receives, to respond only to that which is good, and to minister only that which is good. The servants of Christ are counseled to look to him and to him only for light and TRUTH. They are told not to take counsel from any human being or to hearken to any person unless he or she speaks by the power of the Holy Spirit. Truth, light, righteous power, and salvation come from above, from God himself, through divine revelation, and not from human beings or from below (2 Ne. 28:30–31).

BIBLIOGRAPHY

Backman, Milton V., Jr. *The Heavens Resound*, pp. 284–309. Salt Lake City, 1983.

Oaks, Dallin H. "Revelation." In *Brigham Young University 1981–82 Fireside and Devotional Speeches*, pp. 20–26. Provo, Utah, 1982.

Packer, Boyd K. "Revelation in a Changing World." *Ensign* 19 (Nov. 1989):14–16.

Wright, H. Curtis. "The Central Problem of Intellectual History." *Scholar and Educator* 12 (Fall 1988):52–68.

CHAUNCEY C. RIDDLE

REVELATIONS, UNPUBLISHED

Not all revelations of God to his latter-day PROPHETS have been formally published, let alone accepted by the COMMON CONSENT of the Church as canonized scripture. Just as the compilers of the Bible had to decide which texts to include, similar decisions have been made in this DISPENSATION with respect to modern revelations. Initially this process was carried out by those assigned by the Prophet Joseph SMITH to gather the revealed materials, organize them, and, under his supervision, print the Book of Commandments (1833) and the Doctrine and Covenants (1835). They included those revelations that were relevant "for the establishment and regulation of the kingdom of God on the earth in the last days" (D&C [1981], "Explanatory Introduction"). Latter-day Saints believe that divine inspiration played a role in guiding these selections (*DS* 3:202).

Many revelations are not included in the STANDARD WORKS, however; for example, those given to specific individuals under particular circumstances containing personal instructions rather than doctrine for the Church. Many are published in the *History of the Church* or are found in collections of Church documents. Examples include a revelation calling John E. Page to go to Washington, D.C. (*HC* 6:82), and a revelation about the division of the United Firm (*Kirtland Revelation Book*, p. 111). Also excluded are temple ordinances and other sacred matters not published to the world.

The Church of Jesus Christ of Latter-day Saints regards its canon of scripture as open, and two earlier revelations were added to the canon in 1979 (D&C 137 and 138). Latter-day Saints believe that God "will yet reveal many great and important things pertaining to the Kingdom of God" (A of F 9).

Another example of revelation received but not published is the revelation underlying the announcement by the FIRST PRESIDENCY in June 1978 extending the priesthood to all worthy male members of the Church. Only an official statement concerning that revelation was published (*see* DOCTRINE AND COVENANTS: OFFICIAL DECLARATION—2). Other changes in the Church, such as the recent expanding of the role of the SEVENTY, accelerating temple building, and expanding missionary activity, are viewed by Latter-day Saints as manifestations of divine direction. The revealed basis of these changes is not always published, as it more often was in the early years of the Church. As Elder James E. Faust declared, "In our time God has revealed how to administer the Church with a membership of over six million differently than when there were just six members of the Church" (Faust, p. 8).

A few writers have attempted to collect and publish revelations that are attributed to prophets but not published in the scriptures. Some of these texts are based on credible sources; others come from sources that are suspect, if not invalid. When a so-called revelation contains statements and declarations that are clearly out of harmony with the standard works and official statements of the First Presidency, such materials are considered to be spurious.

In biblical times, false prophets sometimes spoke and wrote in the names of others and claimed revelations from God (cf. Deut. 18:20–22; Matt. 7:15). Today, some people similarly find journals or produce documents containing alleged revelations. The main guideline used for assessing these is as follows: "No one shall be appointed to receive commandments and revelations in this church excepting my servant Joseph Smith, Jun., for he receiveth them even as Moses . . . until I shall appoint . . . another in his stead" (D&C 28:2, 7). Latter-day Saints believe that the right to receive revelation for the entire Church is reserved for the PRESIDENT OF THE CHURCH.

BIBLIOGRAPHY

Cook, Lyndon W. *The Revelations of the Prophet Joseph Smith*. Provo, 1981.

Faust, James E. "Continuous Revelation." *Ensign* 19 (Nov. 1989):8–11.

C. MAX CALDWELL

REVERENCE

Latter-day Saints share with other religious people an inner yearning or inclination to venerate that which is holy. President David O. MCKAY emphasized this principle by saying, "The greatest manifestation of spirituality is reverence; indeed, reverence is spirituality. Reverence is profound respect mingled with love" (*Instructor* 101 [Oct. 1966]: 371). The supreme object of reverence is God the Father; his son Jesus Christ did the will of the Father by effecting the infinite ATONEMENT; and Latter-day Saints also equally revere him. They revere not only his personage but his name as well, for as Peter said, "there is none other name under heaven given among men, whereby we must be saved" (Acts 4:12; cf. 2 Ne. 25:20). Taking the name of the Lord, or of the Father, in vain is therefore a serious form of irreverence.

While taking pains to avoid any semblance of idolatry, Latter-day Saints revere or venerate all that proceeds from God. Knowledge that "the earth is the Lord's, and the fulness thereof" (Ps. 24:1) and his "very handiwork" (D&C 104:14) impels the Latter-day Saint to respect it. The meek, or the reverent, shall inherit it (Ps. 37:11; Matt. 5:5; D&C 88:17–18).

Certain buildings are set apart as places of worship, and in those places the attitude of reverence is particularly fostered. Written on the eastern facade of the most important of these edifices, the temples, are the words "Holiness to the Lord—The House of the Lord." Howard W. Hunter, an apostle, noted that "the temple where Jesus taught and worshipped in Jerusalem was built in such a way as to establish respect for and devotion to the Father. Its very architecture taught a silent but constant lesson of reverence. . . . It was intended to be a place of solace for men's woes and troubles, the very gate of heaven" (*Ensign* 7 [Nov. 1977]:52–53). Within the temple are revealed sacred symbols that intimately tie the Latter-day Saint to Christ and his atonement. Because of these vital links, the TEMPLE ORDINANCES are valued and revered and become treasures to be discussed only within the sacred walls. Indeed, only Latter-day Saints who are faithful may participate in temple worship.

Reverence is expected to pervade public places of worship as well. Because Latter-day Saints tend to be vibrant and sociable and because they often worship with their children, the Church leaders periodically emphasize the importance of reverence. Addressing the issue, President Gordon B. Hinckley stated, "We encourage the cultivation of friends with happy conversations among our people. However, these should take place in the foyer, and when we enter the chapel we should understand that we are in sacred precincts. . . . All who come into the Lord's house should have a feeling they are walking and standing on holy ground" (*Ensign* 17 [May 1987]:45).

Latter-day Saints hold as inimical to reverence the tendency of modern society to cynicism and LIGHTMINDEDNESS. They believe that honoring the sacred is necessary to ensure a stable relationship with God.

BIBLIOGRAPHY

Handy, Linda Lee. "Helping Children Listen." *Ensign* 12 (Mar. 1982):46–47.

"Reverence." *Seek to Obtain My Word* (Melchizedek Priesthood Personal Study Guide), pp. 139-44. Salt Lake City, 1989.

Romney, Marion G. "Reverence." *Ensign* 12 (Sept. 1982):3–5.

LYNN A. MCKINLAY

REYNOLDS V. UNITED STATES

Reynolds v. United States (98 U.S. 145 [1879]) was the first U.S. Supreme Court decision to interpret the "free exercise" language of the First Amendment to the U.S. Constitution. In giving an extremely narrow interpretation to that guarantee of religious freedom, the *Reynolds* decision opened the way for legal suppression of the Mormon practice of PLURAL MARRIAGE.

The Morrill Act (Act of July 1, 1862, 12 Stat. 501), which defined the crime of bigamy in U.S. territories, had been adopted for the express purpose of outlawing Mormon polygamous marriages. The First Amendment, however, expressly states that Congress shall "make no law . . . prohibiting the free exercise" of religion. The issue posed by the *Reynolds* case was whether a federal bigamy statute could constitutionally be applied to a person who practiced polygamy as a matter of religious duty. The Court held that it could.

George Reynolds, an English immigrant to Utah, private secretary to Brigham Young, and husband of two wives, was found guilty in March 1875 of violating the antibigamy provision of the Morrill Act. The conviction was overturned by the Utah Supreme Court on procedural grounds (*United States v. Reynolds*, 1 Utah 226 [1875]), but on retrial he was again convicted and was sentenced to two years in prison with a $500 fine. This conviction was upheld by the U.S. Supreme Court.

In applying the First Amendment's free exercise clause, Chief Justice Morrison R. Waite concluded that "Congress was deprived of all legislative power over mere opinion, but was left free to reach actions which were in violation of social duties or subversive of good order" (98 U.S. 164). This distinction between protected religious *belief* and unprotected religious *actions* was followed for several decades, and this specific holding regarding plural marriage is still the law. Since 1940, however, the Court has said that religious conduct also may fall within the free exercise guarantee (*Cantwell v. Connecticut*, 310 U.S. 296).

The Morrill Act was not an effective weapon against polygamy because of the difficulty of obtaining testimony to prove the plural marriages. Nevertheless, the *Reynolds* decision paved the way for other, more enforceable federal laws that penalized "unlawful cohabitation," disincorporated the Church, and forfeited its property. Ultimately at the direction of its Prophet, President Wilford Woodruff, the Church submitted to those laws and discontinued the practice of plural marriage.

[*See also* Antipolygamy Legislation; Manifesto of 1890.]

BIBLIOGRAPHY

Davis, Ray J. "Plural Marriage and Religious Freedom: The Impact of *Reynolds v. United States.*" *Arizona Law Review* 15 (1974):287–306.

Firmage, Edwin Brown. *Zion in the Courts*, pp. 151–59. Urbana, Ill., 1988.

ROBERT E. RIGGS

RICHES OF ETERNITY

Eternal riches come from God and are associated with wisdom and eternal life: "Seek not for riches but for wisdom; and behold, the mysteries of God shall be unfolded unto you, and then shall you be made rich. Behold, he that hath eternal life is rich" (D&C 11:7). Latter-day Saints believe that the "voice of glory and honor and the riches of eternal life" is one of the voices used by Jesus to gather his people (D&C 43:25) and that God adversely judges those who fail to seek earnestly the riches of eternity (D&C 68:31).

Although the phrase "the riches of eternity" occurs in scripture only in the Doctrine and Covenants (D&C 38:39; 67:2; 68:31; 78:18), the distinction between earthly and heavenly rewards is also biblical. The Psalms, for example, point out: "A little that a righteous man hath is better than the riches of many wicked" (Ps. 37:16). In the SERMON ON THE MOUNT, Jesus admonished his followers to "lay not up for yourselves treasures upon earth, . . . but lay up for yourselves treasures in heaven" (Matt. 6:19–20). In this life and in the world to come, the richest spiritual blessings come only from the eternal God.

These spiritual blessings include tangible as well as intangible gifts, for in the Lord's eyes "all things" are spiritual (D&C 29:34). As Orson PRATT stated, "Heavenly riches and earthly riches are of the same nature, only one is glorified and made immortal, while the other is in a fallen, unglorified state. If we are not willing to be governed by the law of equality in regard to that which is of the least value, who shall entrust us with all the riches of eternity?" (pp. 596–97).

Obtaining eternal riches can be equated with receiving and enjoying ETERNAL LIFE. "There is that maketh himself rich, yet hath nothing: there is that maketh himself poor, yet hath great riches. The ransom of a man's life are his riches" (Prov. 13:7–8). The word "ransom" (Hebrew *kofer*) refers to a payment made to redeem a person, suggesting to Latter-day Saints and other Christians that genuine riches are found in Christ's atoning redemption. Thus, Paul relates the winning of God's riches with repentance and eternal reward (Rom. 2:4–11), as well as with wisdom and knowledge (Rom. 11:33; Eph. 1:17–19). In Ephesians, Paul links them specifically to Christ: "Unto me . . . is this grace given, that I should preach among the Gentiles the unsearchable riches of Christ" (Eph. 3:8).

BIBLIOGRAPHY

Nibley, Hugh W. "How to Get Rich" and "But What Kind of Work?" In *CWHN* 9:178–201, 252–89.

Pratt, Orson. *Masterful Discourses and Writings of Orson Pratt*. Salt Lake City, 1946.

CATHERINE CORMAN PARRY

RICHMOND JAIL

When the Latter-day Saints at Far West, Caldwell County, Missouri, surrendered to the state militia in late October 1838, seven Church leaders—Joseph SMITH, Hyrum SMITH, Sidney RIGDON, Parley P. PRATT, Lyman Wight, Amasa Lyman, and George W. Robinson—were arrested (*see*

Joseph Smith Rebuking the Guards, by Danquart Weggeland (late nineteenth century, grisaille, 36″ × 46″). While incarcerated in Richmond, Missouri, in November, 1838, Joseph Smith was subjected to obscene jests, blasphemies, and boasts of rape and murder. Disgusted by their crude language, he commanded the guards in the name of Jesus Christ to be still. Parley P. Pratt wrote, "Dignity and majesty have I seen but *once*, as it stood in chains, at midnight, in a dungeon in an obscure village of Missouri." Church Museum of History and Art.

MISSOURI CONFLICT). They were first taken under guard to Independence, Jackson County, Missouri, and then to Richmond, the county seat of Ray County. They were confined on November 9, not in the county jail but in a small vacant house on the town square. Here they were imprisoned for three weeks to await a court inquiry into charges of treason, murder, arson, robbery, and perjury. Other Saints were also arrested and brought to Richmond for trial.

At the inquiry on November 28, the prisoners were bound over for trial, and Joseph Smith and five others were removed to a jail in Liberty, Clay County, Missouri, to await further hearings (*see* LIBERTY JAIL). Pratt and four others remained in the Richmond County Jail, some until late April 1839 and others until June 1839.

During the time Joseph Smith was incarcerated in Richmond, the prisoners were chained together under miserable conditions and constant harassment. One incident during the imprisonment has become a legend. Pratt recalled that Joseph Smith, chagrined at the verbal abuse, boasting, and obscenity by the guards, stood up in chains and commanded, "SILENCE, ye fiends of the infernal pit. In the name of Jesus Christ I rebuke you, and command you to be still; I will not live another minute and hear such language. Cease such talk, or you or I die this instant!" (p. 221). The tormenters reportedly fell silent.

The Richmond Jail no longer stands, and no marker designates its location.

BIBLIOGRAPHY

Gentry, Leland H. "A History of the Latter-day Saints in Northern Missouri from 1836 to 1839." Ph.D. diss., Brigham Young University, 1965.

LeSueur, Stephen C. "'High Treason and Murder': The Examination of Mormon Prisoners at Richmond, Missouri." *BYU Studies* 26 (Spring 1986):3–30.

Pratt, Parley P. *Autobiography of Parley Parker Pratt.* Salt Lake City, 1980.

HOWARD A. CHRISTY

RICKS COLLEGE

Ricks College is a private, two-year accredited college owned and operated by The Church of Jesus Christ of Latter-day Saints in Rexburg, Idaho, an agricultural community in the heart of the Upper Snake River Valley (less than 100 miles south of the Yellowstone/Grand Teton National Parks). With approximately 7,500 students and 300 faculty, Ricks is one of the largest private two-year colleges in the United States. It is a liberal arts college with a broad curriculum in the arts and sciences, and it is also noted for its career programs in technology, agriculture, nursing, and other disciplines.

Ricks College grants the associate degree in arts and sciences, emphasizing general education to students who plan to pursue bachelor's degrees at four-year colleges or universities, as well as degrees in specialized programs.

HISTORY. LDS settlers in the Rexburg area were faced with sending their children to public schools where sentiment was strong against them. In November 1888 the settlers established the Bannock Stake Academy, an elementary school with eighty-two students and three teachers, with Thomas E. Ricks, the president of the Bannock Stake, as Chairman of the Bannock Stake Academy Board of Education. In 1898 it was renamed the Fremont

The Manwaring Center houses the college bookstore, a cafeteria, and student union activities at Ricks College.

Stake Academy and high school courses were added. On October 1, 1903, the school was named Ricks Academy after Thomas E. Ricks. In 1915 college courses were first taught. During the Great Depression it was rumored that the school would be closed. The Church offered to give the college to the state of Idaho, but that offer was rejected, and the Church continued its operation. Under John L. Clarke, president of Ricks from 1944 to 1971, the college expanded from a student body of 200 to 5,150. In the late 1940s the Church Board of Education approved third and fourth college years, and for six years the college graduated students with four-year degrees. However, in 1956 Ricks discontinued its junior and senior years. Since 1984 the college has again experienced rapid growth, and in 1989 the Board of Trustees set the 7,500 enrollment ceiling.

MISSION. The mission of Ricks College is officially declared to (1) build testimonies of the restored GOSPEL OF JESUS CHRIST and encourage living its principles; (2) provide a high-quality education for students of diverse interests and abilities; (3) prepare students for further education and employment, and for their roles as citizens and parents; and (4) maintain a wholesome academic, cultural, social, and spiritual environment.

GENERAL EDUCATION. The Ricks College General Education program is designed to help students develop the ability to think and write clearly, maintain lifelong patterns of effective living, appreciate aesthetic and creative expressions of humanity, gain knowledge of the social and natural world, understand themselves and their relationship to God, and cultivate sensitivity to personal relationships, moral responsibilities, and service to society. Students seeking associate degrees study religion, English literature and composition, natural and physical science, social science, and health and physical fitness, and they must demonstrate proficiency in mathematics.

PHYSICAL PLANT, MATERIALS, AND EQUIPMENT. The Ricks College main campus is located on 255 acres at the south edge of Rexburg. In 1990, the main campus had forty-six buildings with about 1.6 million square feet of space and a replacement value of nearly $110 million. These buildings contained equipment valued at over $21 million.

The library, a building of 98,000 square feet, includes a serials collection of 750 titles and contains nearly 141,000 volumes, excluding bound periodicals and government publications.

The college owns a livestock center as part of its agricultural program on 140 acres, including 21 buildings, a few miles west of Rexburg. The college also owns a 160-acre outdoor learning facility on Badger Creek in Teton Valley.

RELATIONSHIP TO THE CHURCH.   The Ricks College Board of Trustees is composed of Church leaders and is chaired by the PRESIDENT OF THE CHURCH. The Church provides approximately 70 percent of the operating funds for the college. Student tuition and fees, campus auxiliary income, and gifts to the college provide the remainder of college operating funds.

Currently (1990) thirty-six student WARDS in four STAKES function at Ricks College. Students are required to take religion courses every semester. Graduates of Ricks consistently remark on the unique spirit of the college, the commitment of faculty to the progress of students, and the overall sense of community and caring they experienced there.

STUDENTS.   Ricks College has an open admission policy. Selectivity is used only as it applies to the Code of Honor, which each student must promise, in an ecclesiastical interview, to observe. Since Ricks has academic programs spanning a wide range of ability levels, the goal has been to admit any student who could benefit from the Ricks College experience.

Currently the Admissions Office admits 95 percent of those who apply. Of those admitted, approximately 80 percent actually enroll. Students from all fifty states and thirty foreign countries attend Ricks.

The attrition rate at Ricks is higher than at most two-year colleges because many Latter-day Saint students attend Ricks for one year and then serve a Church MISSION. Once they complete the mission, many desire to move to a university. In 1989–1990, Ricks College graduated 1,557 students.

BIBLIOGRAPHY

Jolley, JoAnn. "Rexburg and Ricks College." *Ensign* 14 (Jan. 1984):21–27.

SCOTT SAMUELSON

RIGDON, SIDNEY

Sidney Rigdon (1793–1876) was one of Joseph SMITH's closest friends and advisers. He was also a renowned early convert to the Church, its most persuasive orator in the first decade, and First Counselor in the FIRST PRESIDENCY from 1832 to 1844. Following the Prophet Joseph Smith's martyrdom, Rigdon became one of the Church's best-known apostates.

Rigdon was born February 19, 1793, on a farm in St. Clair Township, near Pittsburgh, Pennsylvania, the fourth child and youngest son of William and Nancy Briant Rigdon. In 1817, while supporting his widowed mother on the family farm, Rigdon experienced Christian conversion and a year later qualified himself to become a licensed preacher with the Regular Baptists. He moved to eastern Ohio to preach under the tutelage of Adamson Bentley, a popular Baptist minister, and in June 1820 he married Phebe Brooks, Bentley's sister-in-law. After ordination as a Baptist minister, Rigdon became pastor of the First Baptist Church in Pittsburgh in 1821. Famed for his dynamic preaching, Rigdon attracted listeners until his congregation became one of the largest in the city. One of his critics, William Hayden, described him as being of "medium height, rotund in form; of countenance, while speaking, open and winning, with a little cast of melancholy. His action was graceful, his language copious, fluent in utterance, with articulation clear and musical" (quoted in Chase, p. 24).

Throughout his early ministry, Rigdon kept looking for the pure New Testament church that practiced laying on of hands for the GIFT OF THE HOLY GHOST and healing the sick. Drawn to Alexander Campbell and Walter Scott, fellow ministers with similar views, Rigdon associated with leading members of the Mahoning Baptist Association, the forerunner of the restorationist Disciples of Christ movement (*see* RESTORATIONISM, PROTESTANT). In 1826 he became the pastor of a Grand River Association congregation in Mentor, Ohio. In 1830, however, Rigdon broke with Campbell and Scott, who went on to form the Disciples of Christ, while Rigdon established a communal "family" near Kirtland.

In late October 1830 four Mormon missionaries visited Rigdon in Ohio. One was Parley P. Pratt, whom Rigdon had converted to the reformed Baptists a year earlier. Pratt told Rigdon

Sidney Rigdon (1793–1876), formerly a Baptist-Campbellite minister, was one of the most important early converts to the Church. He served as counselor in the First Presidency, experienced revelations together with Joseph Smith, and was a gifted orator. Courtesy the Utah State Historical Society.

about the Book of Mormon and the RESTORATION OF THE GOSPEL through Joseph Smith. After two weeks of earnest investigation, Rigdon announced that he believed the new church to be the true apostolic church restored to the earth. In mid-November 1830 he was baptized and ordained an elder. More than a hundred members of his Kirtland congregation and common stock community followed him into the Church.

Rigdon, along with Edward Partridge, a young hatter who was interested in Mormonism, left almost immediately for Fayette, New York, to meet Joseph Smith. After their arrival, a REVELATION to Joseph commended Rigdon for his previous service, but called him to "a greater work," including that of scribe to the Prophet on his "new translation" of the Bible then under way

(D&C 35; see also JOSEPH SMITH TRANSLATION OF THE BIBLE [JST]). In December 1830, Smith, with Rigdon's help, worked on the manuscript that eventually became the seventh and eighth chapters of the BOOK OF MOSES in the Pearl of Great Price.

Rigdon's report of the harvest of souls in the Mentor-Kirtland area in Ohio may have encouraged Joseph to ask for guidance on moving the headquarters of the Church; in December 1830 a revelation commanded them to leave New York for Ohio (D&C 37; cf. 38). On February 1, 1831, Joseph and Sidney arrived in Kirtland, where they renewed their work on the inspired translation of the Bible.

In the summer of 1831, Joseph, Sidney, and other leaders journeyed to Independence, Missouri, which a revelation identified as the location of the latter-day ZION and the NEW JERUSALEM. Sidney was instructed to dedicate the land of Zion for the gathering of the Saints and to write a description of the country for publication (D&C 58:50). Upon their return to Ohio, Joseph and Sidney resumed the translation of the scriptures, and on February 16, 1832, they jointly received the vision of the degrees of glory that is now Doctrine and Covenants section 76. In March 1832 they were brutally attacked by a mob and tarred and feathered. Sidney received head injuries that occasionally affected his emotional stability for the rest of his life. His friend Newel K. Whitney said that thereafter he was "either in the bottom of the cellar or up in the garrett window" (Chase, p. 115).

In March 1833 Sidney Rigdon and Frederick G. Williams were formally set apart as counselors to Joseph Smith in the First Presidency. Sidney had already been called as a counselor to Joseph a year earlier, before there was a First Presidency. In 1833 Rigdon was also called to be a "spokesman" for the Church and for Joseph Smith. Rigdon was promised that he would be "mighty in expounding all scriptures" (D&C 100:11). At this same time, Joseph said of him, "Brother Sidney is a man whom I love, but he is not capable of that pure and steadfast love for those who are his benefactors that should characterize a President of the Church of Christ. This, with some other little things, such as selfishness and independence of mind . . . are his faults. But notwithstanding these things, he is a very great and good man; a man of great power of words, and can gain the friendship of his hearers very quickly. He is a man whom God will uphold, if he will continue faithful to his calling" (*HC* 1:443).

In 1834 Rigdon assisted in recruiting volunteers for ZION'S CAMP and, while Joseph was away on that undertaking, had charge of affairs in Kirtland, including the construction of the temple (*see* KIRTLAND TEMPLE). He was a leading teacher at the Kirtland school and helped arrange the revelations for publication in the 1835 edition of the Doctrine and Covenants (*see* SCHOOLS OF THE PROPHETS). Under the Prophet's direction, Sidney helped compose and deliver many of the doctrinally rich LECTURES ON FAITH. He often preached long, extravagant biblically based sermons, notably one at the dedication of the Kirtland Temple. In the persecution that followed the failure of the Kirtland Safety Society, Rigdon, along with Joseph Smith and other Saints, fled for their lives to Far West, Missouri, in 1838. There Rigdon delivered two famous volatile speeches, the Salt Sermon and the Independence Day oration, both of which stirred up fears and controversy in Missouri and contributed to the EXTERMINATION ORDER and the Battle of Far West (*see* MISSOURI CONFLICT). With Joseph and Hyrum Smith, Rigdon was taken prisoner and locked up in LIBERTY JAIL, but was released early because of severe apoplectic seizures.

Rigdon took an active part in the founding of Nauvoo and in 1839 accompanied Joseph Smith to Washington, D.C., to present the grievances of the Saints to the federal government. He was elected to the Nauvoo City Council and served also as city attorney, postmaster, and professor of Church history in the embryonic university projected for the city. Despite his many appointments, however, he was nearly silent during this time and often sick. He was accused of being associated with John C. Bennett and other enemies of the Church in their seditious plans to displace Joseph Smith, but this he always denied. He did not endorse the principle of plural marriage, although he never came out in open opposition to it. Joseph Smith eventually lost confidence in Rigdon and in 1843 wished to reject him as a counselor, but because of the intercession of Hyrum SMITH, retained him in office.

Early in 1844, when Joseph Smith became a candidate for president of the United States, Rigdon was nominated as his running mate and he established residence in Pittsburgh to carry on the campaign. He was there when news arrived of Joseph Smith's murder. He hastened to Nauvoo to offer himself as a "guardian of the Church," promising to act as such until Joseph Smith was resurrected from the dead. His claims were duly considered, but at a memorable meeting in Nauvoo on August 8, 1844, Church members rejected him as guardian (*see* SUCCESSION IN THE PRESIDENCY). The Twelve Apostles (*see* QUORUM OF THE TWELVE APOSTLES) were sustained as the head of the Church. When he undertook to establish a rival leadership, Rigdon was excommunicated in September 1844 and left with a few disciples for Pennsylvania, where they organized a Church of Christ. Acting erratically, he lost most of his followers in less than two years. In 1863, he made another effort, founding the Church of Jesus Christ of the Children of Zion, which continued into the 1880s. From 1847 to his death in 1876, Rigdon resided in Friendship, New York, usually in a state of emotional imbalance and unhappiness.

In 1834, in *Mormonism Unvailed*, Eber D. Howe attacked the authenticity of the Book of Mormon by adopting Philastus Hurlbut's argument that Sidney Rigdon purloined the "Manuscript Story" of Solomon Spaulding (*see* SPAULDING MANUSCRIPT), plagiarized it to compose the Book of Mormon, and gave it to Joseph Smith to publish under his name. During his lifetime Rigdon and members of his family consistently denied any connection with Spaulding, and after the discovery in 1885 of one of Spaulding's manuscripts, the story was discredited.

BIBLIOGRAPHY

Backman, Milton V., Jr. *The Heavens Resound: A History of the Latter-day Saints in Ohio, 1830–1838.* Salt Lake City, 1983.

Chase, Daryl. "Sidney Rigdon—Early Mormon." Master's thesis, University of Chicago, 1931.

McKiernan, F. Mark. *The Voice of One Crying in the Wilderness: Sidney Rigdon, Religious Reformer 1793–1876.* Lawrence, Kan., 1971.

BRUCE A. VAN ORDEN

RIGHTEOUSNESS

Righteousness comprises a broad group of concepts and traits. As with the biblical Hebrew *sedek* and the Greek *dikaiosune*, the English word "righteousness" describes the ideal of religious life, with Godlike behavior as the norm. Righteousness is right conduct before God and among mankind in all respects. The scriptures give the following perspectives:

Righteousness is ultimately synonymous with HOLINESS or godliness. Christ himself is known as "the Righteous" (Moses 7:45, 47) and as "the Son of Righteousness" (3 Ne. 25:2). His "ways are righteousness forever" (2 Ne. 1:19).

The state of righteousness is available to mankind through the redemption of Christ as one is BORN OF GOD: "Marvel not that all mankind, yea, men and women . . . must be born again; yea, born of God, changed from their carnal and fallen state, to a state of righteousness, being redeemed of God, becoming his sons and daughters" (Mosiah 27:25).

The terms "righteous" and "righteousness" also apply to mortals who, though beset with weaknesses and frailties, are seeking to come unto Christ. In this sense, righteousness is not synonymous with PERFECTION. It is a condition in which a person is moving toward the Lord, yearning for godliness, continuously repenting of sins, and striving honestly to know and love God and to follow the principles and ordinances of the gospel. Saints of God are urged to do "the works of righteousness" (D&C 59:23) and to "bring to pass much righteousness" (D&C 58:27).

Inherent in the meaning of righteousness is the concept of JUSTIFICATION. It is impossible for finite mortals to live in perfect obedience to God's laws or to atone infinitely for their sins. "For all have sinned," Paul wrote, "and come short of the glory of God" (Rom. 3:23). Christ's ATONEMENT mercifully reconciles the demands of justice (*see* JUSTICE AND MERCY), making it possible for repentant mortals to become "right" with God—"at one" with him.

When Saul of Tarsus saw the resurrected Christ on the road to Damascus, "he trembling and astonished said, Lord, what wilt thou have me to do?" (Acts 9:6). From that moment on, he sought to know the will of God and live accordingly. But he also lamented over mortal weaknesses: "For I know that in me, that is, in my flesh, dwelleth no good thing . . . only in Christ" (JST, Rom. 7:19). "There is none righteous, no, not one" (Rom. 3:10). Like all apostles and prophets, however, Paul also taught the glorious message that through the grace of Christ mortals can "put off . . . the old man"—their fallen and sinful selves—and "put on the new man, which after God is created in righteousness and true holiness" (Eph. 4:22, 24).

The scriptures abound in similar exhortations to flee wickedness, accept the Lord's grace, and come unto Christ in righteousness. "O wretched man that I am!" exclaimed Nephi. "Yea, my heart sorroweth because of my flesh; my soul grieveth because of mine iniquities." But recognizing the Savior as "the rock of [his] righteousness," Nephi cried: "O Lord, wilt thou redeem my soul? . . . Wilt thou make me that I may shake at the appearance of sin? . . . Wilt thou encircle me around in the robe of thy righteousness!" (2 Ne. 4:17-35).

Righteousness begins in the heart—the "broken heart." It begins when individuals see themselves where they really are: in a fallen state, as "unworthy creatures" who are unable to pull themselves out of their own sins. As they confront the monumental gulf between "the greatness of God, and [their] own nothingness," their hearts break and they "humble [themselves] even in the depths of humility, calling on the name of the Lord daily, and standing steadfastly in the faith" (Mosiah 4:11).

Righteous souls then seek to become right with the Lord, by asking sincerely for forgiveness. As the Lord blesses such with his grace, they desire to respond with even greater faithfulness, love, and obedience. Although they may not reach perfect righteousness in mortality, their lives are beyond reproach—"as becometh saints" (Eph. 5:3).

Scriptures provide a wealth of insight into the attitudes, behaviors, and beliefs that form the basis of a righteous life (e.g., 2 Pet. 1:4–8; D&C 4:5–6). Notably, in the Sermon on the Mount (Matt. 5–7; cf. 3 Ne. 12–14), Jesus revealed the meaning of righteousness—a pattern that he exemplified by his own life:

Those who seek righteousness become humble, poor in spirit. They reverence the Lord, acknowledging that "all things which are good cometh of God" (Moroni 7:12).

They mourn for their sins—and their "godly sorrow worketh repentance" (2 Cor. 7:10). They also compassionately "mourn with those that mourn; yea, and comfort those that stand in need of comfort" (Mosiah 18:9).

The righteous strive to be meek—kind and long-suffering, generous, sacrificing, patient, filled with love for their enemies, not "puffed up," and "not easily provoked" (1 Cor. 13:4–5).

Hungering and thirsting after righteousness, they continually seek the Lord through sincere

PRAYER, FASTING, SCRIPTURE STUDY, Sabbath WORSHIP, and service in the holy TEMPLES.

They seek to be merciful—to forgive as they would be forgiven, to judge as they would be judged, to love as they would be loved, to serve as they would be served (D&C 38:24–25).

They seek to be pure in heart—thinking no evil, envying not, and rejoicing not in iniquity but in the truth (1 Cor. 13:4–6). They are honest in their COVENANTS with God and in their dealings with their fellowmen. They are chaste and also virtuous.

Seekers of righteousness are peacemakers. They avoid contention, anger, and evil-speaking. They promote goodwill, brotherhood, and sisterhood; they seek to establish God's will and his kingdom on earth as it is in heaven.

When persecuted for righteousness' sake or when reviled or maligned for their allegiance to the Lord, they bear all things and endure all things (1 Cor. 13:7).

Such scriptural descriptions of righteousness are not to be reduced to lists that individuals self-righteously check off. They are constant reminders on the journey toward God, who has promised a Comforter—the HOLY GHOST—to give guidance and direction on that path (John 14:26).

The Lord delights "to honor those who serve [him] in righteousness" (D&C 76:5). At the last day, "the righteous, the saints of the Holy One of Israel, they who have believed in the Holy One of Israel, they who have endured the crosses of the world, and despised the shame of it, they shall inherit the kingdom of God, which was prepared for them from the foundation of the world, and their joy shall be full forever" (2 Ne. 9:18).

BIBLIOGRAPHY

Benson, Ezra T. "A Mighty Change of Heart." *Ensign* 19 (Oct. 1989):2–5.

McConkie, Bruce R. "The Dead Who Die in the Lord." *Ensign* 6 (Nov. 1976):106–8.

Scoresby, A. Lynn. "Journey Toward Righteousness." *Ensign* 10 (Jan. 1980):52–57.

MARVIN K. GARDNER

ROBISON, LOUISE YATES

Louise Yates Robison (1866–1946) succeeded Clarissa Williams to become the seventh general president of the RELIEF SOCIETY of The Church of Jesus Christ of Latter-day Saints in October 1928 and led that society through the difficult years of the Great Depression (1928–1939). She had previously served as second counselor to President Williams in the general presidency. These two women had become friends while they prepared surgical dressings for the Red Cross during World War I. Louise Robison's name rarely appears on lists of outstanding LDS women, an obscurity that would have pleased this unassuming, down-to-earth woman of plain appearance and quiet ways; nevertheless, she deserves recognition for several unique contributions to the Church and for the important principle of service she exemplified.

Born May 27, 1866, in the small rural town of Scipio, in south-central Utah, Louise grew up in a log house where she learned pioneer values from her parents, Thomas and Elizabeth Yates. Her early marriage to Joseph L. Robison and subse-

Louise Yates Robison (1866–1946), seventh general president of the Relief Society, served from 1928 to 1939. Photographer: Naylor Sisters.

quent rearing of six children shortened her studies at Brigham Young Academy, but her love of books and learning was lifelong. A six-month course in dressmaking at age fifteen helped prepare her for future service on the Relief Society General Board, where she directed the Temple and Burial Clothing Department.

As General President of the Relief Society, one of her practical responses to women's needs during the Depression of the 1930s was to establish MORMON HANDICRAFT in 1937. This shop enabled Relief Society women to sell homemade gift items on consignment. The shop reflected President Robison's appreciation both for the handiwork of women and for their role as mothers in the home. It flourished under the Relief Society until 1986, when management of the store was transferred to the DESERET BOOK COMPANY.

Louise Robison believed that burdens could be lightened with song. A daughter later remembered that she sang, or sometimes whistled, while doing her work at home. "A singing mother makes a happy home," she said when she named the popular Relief Society choral groups Singing Mothers in 1934.

Several modest historic achievements can be credited to President Robison. She was the first Relief Society general president to address a regular session of a General Conference (October 1929). She was the first to visit the Relief Societies in Great Britain, and on that trip she also served as a delegate to the Tenth World Congress of the International Council of Women, held in Paris. In 1933 she instigated the erection of a monument to the Relief Society on the site of its founding in NAUVOO, Illinois. Later relocated in the Monument to Women gardens, it is thought to be the first Church effort to mark its historic sites in Nauvoo.

WELFARE SERVICES was the greatest concern of President Robison's administration. Her longtime friend and coworker Belle SPAFFORD said that Louise Robison "stressed the volunteer compassionate services. 'Go where you're needed, do what you can'; that was her theme" (Spafford). She practiced what she preached, and the principle of personal service she exemplified was a needed counterpoint to the more structured Church welfare system.

After being released from service as Relief Society general president in 1939, Louise Robison lived in San Francisco with her daughter Gladys Winter. She died March 30, 1946.

BIBLIOGRAPHY

Gladys Robison Winter Collection. LDS Church Archives, Salt Lake City.

Mulvay-Derr, Jill, and Susan Oman. "These Three Women." *Ensign* 8 (Feb. 1978):66–70.

Spafford, Belle S. *Oral History Interview with Jill Mulvay-Derr*, November 1975–March 1976. LDS Church Archives, Salt Lake City.

JANATH R. CANNON

ROGERS, AURELIA SPENCER

Aurelia Spencer Rogers (1834–1922), the first PRIMARY president of the Church, was born October 4, 1834, in Deep River, Connecticut, to Catherine Curtis and Orson Spencer, a Protestant minister. When Aurelia was six years old, her parents joined the Church and traveled to Nauvoo, Illinois. Years later, Aurelia's suggestions helped establish the Primary Association, the Church organization for children.

"Aurelia came by her concern for children through a long apprenticeship in mothering" (Madsen, p. 1). At the age of twelve, she and her older sister, Ellen, cared for four younger siblings when their mother died and their father was called by Church leaders to head the missionary work in Great Britain. The children lived on their own in WINTER QUARTERS, Nebraska, with limited provisions and then made the arduous trek to the Great Salt Lake basin. Wilford Woodruff, a member of the Quorum of the Twelve Apostles, wrote their father that "although in childhood, their faith, patience, . . . longsuffering and wisdom . . . [were] such as would have done honor to a Saint of thirty years" (Rogers, pp. 103–104).

At age seventeen Aurelia married Thomas Rogers. Through the next twenty-two years, she gave birth to twelve children, of whom only seven survived infancy. When three infants died in succession, she despaired and nearly lost her faith and belief in God; but a letter from her father came to mind and helped her gradually overcome her malaise. Her travail through the loss of children heightened her sensitivity to the preciousness of life and to the importance of nurturing the young.

Aurelia Spencer Rogers (1834–1922), founder of the Primary Association. Arriving in Salt Lake City from Winter Quarters in September 1849, she raised ten children. She was a delegate to the Woman's Suffrage Convention in Georgia in 1894 and the National Council of Women in Washington, D.C., in 1895.

Thomas and Aurelia Rogers lived all their married life in Farmington, Utah, a community sixteen miles north of Salt Lake City. Observing the rowdiness of children on the street, Aurelia Rogers wondered if an organization could be formed to teach them better deportment and moral and spiritual values. She brought the matter to the attention of Eliza R. SNOW, president of the Relief Society, who shared her concern and subsequently gained the support of Church leaders.

On August 11, 1878, Aurelia Spencer Rogers was set apart as president of the Farmington Ward Primary, the first Primary in the Church. Her counselors, Louisa Haight and Helen M. Miller, helped her organize the children into age groups; and on August 25, 1878, they held the first Primary meeting, with 224 children present, beginning

what is today a fully developed curriculum for children.

Although Eliza R. Snow and her immediate associates organized most of the Primaries throughout Church settlements, important impetus came from the work of Rogers in the development of Primary in and near Farmington, for which she received many honors. In 1897, in recognition of her role in founding the Primary, the children of the Church raised the funds to publish her book, *Life Sketches* (1898).

In the winter of 1894–1895, Aurelia Rogers also served as one of three Utah suffragist delegates to the Woman's Suffrage Convention in Atlanta and attended the Second Triennial Congress of the National Council of Women in Washington, D.C.

Although she suffered ill health for much of her life, Aurelia Rogers often said, "Cheerfulness and pleasant thoughts help to produce longevity" (p. 298). She must have practiced this principle, as she lived to be eighty-seven. She died August 19, 1922.

BIBLIOGRAPHY

Madsen, Carol Cornwall, and Susan Staker Oman. *Sisters and Little Saints: One Hundred Years of Primary.* Salt Lake City, 1979.

Rogers, Aurelia Spencer. *Life Sketches of Orson Spencer and Others, and History of Primary Work.* Salt Lake City, 1898.

SHIRLEY A. CAZIER

RUTH

The heroine of the biblical book of Ruth has been both a formal and an informal model of ideal womanhood for members of The Church of Jesus Christ of Latter-day Saints: loyal, hard-working, converted, courageous, she makes the best of what is available and, not incidentally, is pleasing and desirable.

Individual Latter-day Saints and Church instructional manuals frequently cite as exemplary Ruth's departure from her Moabite customs, gods, and people in order to accompany her mother-in-law, Naomi, worshiping Jehovah in his land and adopting the ways of his people. While members have not traditionally emphasized cultural details of the story, they have considered important

Ruth's OBEDIENCE to Naomi and the resulting marriage to Boaz by which she—the foreigner and Moabite convert—becomes a great-grandmother of David, and therefore an ancestress of Jesus Christ.

From 1928 to 1972, Ruth and her gleaning were official models for Church women eighteen years and older in Gleaner classes of the Young Women's Mutual Improvement Association and its successor, the YOUNG WOMEN organization. By achieving spiritual, cultural, homemaking, and service goals, a woman could earn the Golden Gleaner award, counterpart of the Master M Man award for men. The names of these honors express historical conceptions of admirable female and male roles in the Church. Sheaves of wheat, the Gleaners' emblem, were represented on instructional manuals and cards, and on metal pins.

FRANCINE R. BENNION

S

SABBATH DAY

The Sabbath is a day set apart for rest and spiritual renewal. The importance of Sabbath observance, taught from the Creation and throughout religious history, is reconfirmed in modern scripture and in the teachings of LDS leaders. Fundamentals of Sabbath observance include prayer, gospel study, worship at Sabbath meetings, uplifting family activities, and service to others.

God set the pattern when, after six days of creation labors, he rested on the seventh (Gen. 2:2; Moses 3:2). Following the Exodus, Moses instructed the Israelites to gather double portions of manna on the day preceding "the rest of the holy sabbath unto the Lord" (Ex. 16:23). Indeed, the word "Sabbath" is derived from the Hebrew *shabbath*, meaning "to break off," "to desist," or "to rest." The Ten Commandments included the command, "Remember the sabbath day, to keep it holy. Six days shalt thou labour, and do all thy work: But the seventh day is the sabbath of the Lord thy God: in it thou shalt not do any work" (Ex. 20:8–10).

The New Testament is replete with references to the Sabbath. By then, some had lost the spirit of the law and hedged it in inflexible obedience. The Savior reproved them: "The Sabbath was made for man, and not man for the Sabbath. Wherefore the Sabbath was given unto man for a day of rest; and

also that man should glorify God, . . . For the Son of Man made the Sabbath day, therefore the Son of Man is Lord also of the Sabbath" (JST Mark 2:25–27). Following Jesus' earthly ministry, the early Christians gathered on the Lord's day, the first day of the week, in observance of his resurrection (cf. Acts 20:7; Rev. 1:10).

Since its beginning, the LDS Church has observed the Sabbath on the first, rather than the seventh, day of the week (for some exceptions in the Middle East, *see* SUNDAY). The key revelation giving the pattern, scope, and purpose of Sabbath observance came to Joseph Smith on August 7, 1831, a Sunday:

> And that thou mayest more fully keep thyself unspotted from the world, thou shalt go to the house of prayer and offer up thy sacraments upon my holy day;
>
> For verily this is a day appointed unto you to rest from your labors, and to pay thy devotions unto the Most High; . . .
>
> But remember that on this, the Lord's day . . . thou shalt do none other thing, only let thy food be prepared with singleness of heart that thy fasting may be perfect, or, in other words, that thy joy may be full [D&C 59:9–13].

Throughout LDS history, leaders have emphasized the importance of Sabbath observance, teaching that the Sabbath is a holy day of worship, on which the faithful renew their covenants with the Lord, meet and teach each other the things of the Spirit, visit and strengthen the weak and afflicted, and study and contemplate the word of the Lord. While they have avoided arbitrarily specific prohibitions, Church leaders have given clear guidelines, as in this instruction from President Spencer W. Kimball:

> The purpose of the commandment is not to deprive man of something. Every commandment that God has given to his servants is for the benefit of those who receive and obey it. . . .
>
> The Sabbath is not a day for indolent lounging about the house or puttering around in the garden, but is a day for consistent attendance at meetings for the worship of the Lord, drinking at the fountain of knowledge and instruction, enjoying the family, and finding uplift in music and song.
>
> The Sabbath is a holy day in which to do worthy and holy things. Abstinence from work and recreation is important, but insufficient. The Sabbath calls for constructive thoughts and acts, and if one merely lounges about doing nothing on the Sabbath, he is breaking it. To observe it, one will be on his knees in prayer, preparing lessons, studying the gospel, meditating, visiting the ill and distressed, writing letters to missionaries, taking a nap, reading wholesome material, and attending all the meetings of that day at which he is expected. . . .
>
> It is true that some people must work on the Sabbath. And, in fact, some of the work that is truly necessary—caring for the sick, for example—may actually serve to hallow the Sabbath. However, in such activities our motives are a most important consideration.
>
> When men and women are willing to work on the Sabbath to increase their wealth, they are breaking the commandments; for money taken in on the Sabbath, if the work is unnecessary, is unclean money. . . .
>
> Sabbath-breakers too are those who buy commodities or entertainment on the Sabbath, thus encouraging pleasure palaces and business establishments to remain open—which they otherwise would not do. If we buy, sell, trade, or support such on the Lord's day we are as rebellious as the children of Israel ["The Sabbath—A Delight," Ensign 8 (Jan. 1978):4–5].

The form of LDS Sabbath observance has evolved through the years, but the principles have remained the same. Of the Church's first conference meeting, on June 9, 1830, Joseph Smith wrote, "Having opened by singing and prayer, we partook together of the emblems of the body and blood of our Lord Jesus Christ. We then proceeded to confirm several who had lately been baptized, after which we called out and ordained several to the various offices of the Priesthood. Much exhortation and instruction was given" (HC 1:84). Singing, prayer, SACRAMENT, and teaching—those have remained the fundamentals of Latter-day Saint Sabbath meetings.

For many years, following the organization of the SUNDAY SCHOOL in 1849, Sabbath services consisted of Sunday School in the morning and SACRAMENT MEETING in the afternoon or early evening. Weekly ward PRIESTHOOD meetings were held on Monday evenings, and FAST AND TESTIMONY MEETING on the first Thursday of each month. In 1896, fast day was changed to the first Sunday to make attendance more convenient and less disruptive to members in their employment; in the 1930s, priesthood meeting was changed to Sunday mornings.

Another major change came in 1980 with consolidation of all Sunday meetings into a single time block—generally three hours, including RELIEF SOCIETY, YOUNG WOMEN, and PRIMARY meetings that formerly were held midweek. The change was instituted to save time, travel, and expense; to allow several wards to meet more conveniently in a single building; to strengthen the home by allowing families to spend more time together during the week; and to provide more time for Church members to devote to community service.

In announcing the change, the First Presidency reemphasized the Church's fundamental principles regarding the Sabbath: "A greater responsibility will be placed upon the individual members and families for properly observing the Sabbath day." They suggested that each family participate in a Sunday gospel study hour and in "other appropriate Sabbath activities, such as strengthening family ties, visiting the sick and homebound, giving service to others, writing personal and family histories, genealogical work, and missionary work" (Church News, Feb. 2, 1980, p. 3).

The Lord has promised blessings to those who observe the Sabbath as a holy day. In ancient times, he promised to send them rain in due season, help them overcome their enemies, give them peace, multiply them, and establish his covenant with them (Lev. 26:2–9). "And I will walk among you; and will be your God, and ye shall be my people" (v. 12; cf. Isa. 58:13–14). In modern times, he has reaffirmed these promises: "Inasmuch as ye do this, the fulness of the earth is yours" (D&C 59:16).

[*See also* Meetings, Major Church; Pioneer Life and Worship; Worship.]

BIBLIOGRAPHY

For a collection of articles treating LDS Sabbath observance, including perspectives on both doctrine and historical practice, see *Ensign* 8 (Jan. 1978).

WILLIAM B. SMART

SACRAMENT

[*This entry is in two parts:* Sacrament *and* Sacrament Prayers. *The first part explains the practice of partaking of the sacrament in The Church of Jesus Christ of Latter-day Saints, and the second part gives the history and contents of the sacrament prayers used in the administering of the sacrament.*]

SACRAMENT

The word "sacrament" is used by The Church of Jesus Christ of Latter-day Saints to refer almost exclusively to the Lord's Supper. The English word "sacrament" derives from the Old French *sacrement* by way of Middle English; the Old French noun in turn is based on the Latin *sacramentum*, which denotes a sum deposited by the two parties to a suit (so named probably from being deposited in a sacred place) binding an agreement, oath of allegiance, or obligation. Though the word never occurs in the Bible, the sacrament has come to have a major role in the practices of nearly all Christian denominations. In traditional Catholic and Protestant Christianity, the "sacrament of the Lord's Supper" is regarded as one of a group of sacraments, whose purpose is to serve both as conveyors of God's grace and as the outward signs that such grace has been bestowed. The definition of seven sacraments for the Roman Catholic church came at the Fourth Lateran Council, convened by Pope Innocent III in 1215. Protestant reformers, while rejecting most of the sacramental doctrines of the medieval church, retained the notion of sacraments with respect to baptism and the Eucharist.

In Latter-day Saint usage, sacrament designates that ordinance instituted by Jesus Christ as a means by which worthy Saints may renew their COVENANTS with their Redeemer and with God

the Father (cf. Mosiah 18:8–10; *JC*, pp. 596–97; *AF*, p. 175). On the eve of his trial and crucifixion in Jerusalem and surrounded by his closest associates, the twelve apostles, Jesus took bread, which he blessed and broke and then gave to them, saying, "Take, eat; this is my body." Jesus likewise took the cup, blessed it, and then gave it to them, "Drink ye all of it; For this is my blood of the new testament, which is shed for many for the remission of sins" (Matt. 26:26–28). The Book of Mormon records that the resurrected Jesus instituted this same ordinance in memory of his body and blood as he showed himself to the righteous of the Western Hemisphere after his ascension from Jerusalem (3 Ne. 18:7; 20:3; 26:13).

Paul notes that the Savior gave a commandment to perform this ordinance regularly, "As often as ye eat this bread, and drink this cup, ye do shew [i.e., testify of] the Lord's death till he come" (1 Cor. 11:26). The New Testament indicates that the injunction was observed in the early Christian Church (cf. Acts 2:42; 20:7). To the Saints at Corinth, Paul wrote in plainness of the simple ordinance which he had received from the Lord, stressing that it was done "in remembrance of [Jesus Christ]" (1 Cor. 11:19–26; cf. Luke 22:19; 3 Ne. 18:7).

The time and setting chosen by Jesus for administering the sacrament among his Jerusalem disciples tie this ordinance to the older observances of the Passover, including the bread and

A girl takes a small piece of bread from a sacrament tray. "Take, eat: this is my body, which is broken for you: this do in remembrance of me" (1 Cor. 11:24). Orem, Utah, 1982; courtesy Floyd Holdman.

wine he used, and to which he gave new symbolism (Matt. 26:26–28; Luke 22:15–20). Through his atonement Christ fulfilled the purpose of the ordinance of animal sacrifice found in the Old Testament, which was to prefigure the ultimate sacrifice of the Son of God. The new ordinance replaced the need for animal sacrifice with the sacrifice on the part of Christ's followers of a broken heart and contrite spirit (3 Ne. 9:18–20).

The sermon that Jesus delivered on the topic of the "bread of life" in the Gospel of John draws on the symbolism of the Lord himself as "the living bread which came down from heaven." It also prefigures the ordinance of the sacrament that he initiated later as a reminder to all that salvation comes only through "the living bread" and the "living water" (cf. John 6:48–58). In the postapostolic age, however, theologians transformed the symbolic nature of the sacrament of the Lord's Supper into the dogma of transubstantiation, thereby introducing the notion that those who partake of the bread and wine miraculously ingest the literal body and blood of Christ, although the outward appearance of the emblems (i.e., the accidentals) remain the same. The LDS Church rejects this dogma and holds that the sacrament is to help the Saints remember Jesus and that the transformation envisioned is a renovation of the human soul by the Spirit (D&C 20:75–79).

The sacrament in LDS belief does not serve primarily as a means of securing REMISSION OF SINS. It does, however, focus attention on the sacrifice for sin wrought by the Savior and on the need for all those who have been baptized to maintain their lives constantly in harmony with his teachings and commandments. For this reason, there are numerous scriptural injunctions concerning the need for compliance with God's commandments by those who partake of the sacrament (1 Cor. 11:22–23; 3 Ne. 18:28–29; D&C 46:4). Unbaptized children, however, being without sin, are entitled and expected to partake of the sacrament to prefigure the covenant they themselves will make at the age of accountability, age eight (see CHILDREN: SALVATION OF CHILDREN). In administering the sacrament, Christ himself used emblems readily at hand at the Last Supper—bread and wine. To Joseph SMITH the Lord declared "that it mattereth not what ye shall eat or what ye shall drink when ye partake of the sacrament, if it so be that ye do it with an eye single to my glory—remembering unto the Father my body which was laid down for you, and my blood which was shed for the remission of your sins" (D&C 27:2). In typical LDS practice, bread and water are used.

The ordinance of the sacrament is administered by "those having authority"—that is, by priesthood bearers. According to modern revelation, priests in the AARONIC PRIESTHOOD and any MELCHIZEDEK PRIESTHOOD holder may officiate at the sacrament table; in general practice, the table is prepared by teachers in the Aaronic Priesthood, and the bread and water are blessed by priests and passed to the members of the Church by deacons in the same priesthood.

The prayers spoken over these emblems are among the few that are scripturally prescribed exactly. Those who partake of the sacrament place themselves under covenant with the Lord to take upon them the name of Christ, to always remember him, and to keep his commandments. The Lord in turn covenants that they may always have his Spirit to be with them (D&C 20: 75–79; Moro. 4-5; John 6:54).

[See also Atonement; Communion; Last Supper.]

BIBLIOGRAPHY

Madsen, Truman G. "Christ and the Sacrament" and "The Sacramental Life." *Christ and the Inner Life*, pp. 39–42. Salt Lake City, 1981.

PAUL B. PIXTON

SACRAMENT PRAYERS

The sacrament prayers, which were revealed by the Lord to the Prophet Joseph SMITH, are among the few set prayers in the Church, and the only ones members are commanded to offer "often" (D&C 20:75). They are offered regularly during the administration of the ordinance of the sacrament in SACRAMENT MEETING, occupying a central place in the religious lives of Latter-day Saints. They originate in ancient practice and, with one exception (the current use of water instead of wine), preserve the wording of NEPHITE sacramental prayers:

> O God, the Eternal Father, we ask thee in the name of thy Son, Jesus Christ, to bless and sanctify this bread to the souls of all those who partake of it; that they may eat in remembrance of the body of thy Son, and witness unto thee, O God, the Eternal Father, that they are willing to take upon them the name of thy Son, and always remember him, and

keep his commandments which he hath given them, that they may always have his Spirit to be with them. Amen [Moroni 4:3].

O God, the Eternal Father, we ask thee, in the name of thy Son, Jesus Christ, to bless and sanctify this wine to the souls of all those who drink of it, that they may do it in remembrance of the blood of thy Son, which was shed for them; that they may witness unto thee, O God, the Eternal Father, that they do always remember him, that they may have his Spirit to be with them. Amen [Moroni 5:2].

The prayers, in turn, formalize language used by the resurrected Savior when he visited the Americas (3 Ne. 18:5–11; cf. D&C 20:75–79). Subsequent to a revelation in August 1830 (D&C 27) water has been used instead of wine.

No such exact wording of the prayers is included in the New Testament. However, one scholar has detected parallels between Latter-day Saint sacrament prayers and ancient eucharistic formulas (Barker, pp. 53–56). The JOSEPH SMITH TRANSLATION OF THE BIBLE (JST) confirms that key elements of the sacrament prayers were part of the original Last Supper: Jesus included covenantal obligations similar to those in the prayers (JST Matt. 26:25) and made clear that his action introduced a formal "ordinance" that they were to repeat often (JST Mark 14:24). Further, in the JST, Jesus does not say, "This is my body," and "This is my blood"—metaphors whose interpretation has historically divided Christians on the matter of "transubstantiation." He said instead, "This is in remembrance of my body," and "This is in remembrance of my blood" (JST Matt. 26:22, 24; cf. JST Mark 14:21, 23).

The sacrament prayers invite personal introspection, repentance, and rededication, yet they are also communal, binding individuals into congregations who jointly and publicly attest to their willingness to remember Christ. This shared commitment to become like Christ, repeated weekly, defines the supreme aspiration of Latter-day Saint life.

BIBLIOGRAPHY

Barker, James L. *The Protestors of Christendom.* Independence, Mo., 1946.

Tanner, John S. "Reflections on the Sacrament Prayers." *Ensign* 16 (Apr. 1986):7–11.

Welch, John W. "The Nephite Sacrament Prayers." *F.A.R.M.S. Update.* Provo, Utah, 1986.

JOHN S. TANNER

SACRAMENT MEETING

Sacrament meeting is the principal LDS worship service held on the Sabbath and is based on the commandment "Thou shalt go to the house of prayer and offer up thy sacraments upon my holy day" (D&C 59:9). The entire WARD membership, from infants to the elderly, attend the weekly sacrament meeting as families, and partake of the sacrament of the Lord's Supper together.

A sacrament meeting was held on the day the Church was organized, April 6, 1830. It is recorded, "The Holy Ghost was poured out upon us to a very great degree—some prophesied, whilst we all praised the Lord, and rejoiced exceedingly" (HC 1:78). In Church annals this primal worship service is called a "time of rejoicing," a time of "great solemnity," and "truly a refreshing season to spirit and body" (HC 2:430, 433, 480). At the time of entering the new land of Zion (in Missouri), a revelation was given concerning the Sabbath with the admonition that all should come to this meeting in the spirit of thanksgiving and should offer up "a sacrifice of a broken heart and a contrite spirit" (D&C 59:8). Hence, it is often referred to as a time for the renewing of covenants.

The sacrament meeting is led by the BISHOP of the ward or one of his counselors. To enhance the spirit of worship and fellowship, there are other participants: the organist, music director, and members of the ward preassigned to give talks and the invocation and benediction. From the earliest days of the Church, music has been essential in the worship of LATTER-DAY SAINTS. In the sacrament meeting, music is manifest in the singing of hymns such as "He Died! The Great Redeemer Died," "While of These Emblems We Partake," "In Memory of the Crucified," and "Reverently and Meekly Now." Each ward is encouraged to maintain a choir to periodically perform hymns and anthems. The orientation of all music is toward the classical tradition.

The two SACRAMENT PRAYERS—one on the bread, one on the water—are offered by priests, usually young men between the ages of sixteen and nineteen. They kneel in the presence of the congregation and ask that all present, by their partaking of the broken bread and the water, witness unto the Father their willingness "to take upon them the name of thy Son," Jesus Christ, to always remember him, to keep his commandments, and to seek his Spirit. These patterns are derived in part from the dramatic introduction of the sacrament in the Book of Mormon, where the Master teaches a multitude of men, women, and children, "And if ye shall always do these things blessed are ye, for ye are built upon my rock" (3 Ne. 18:12). And he promises, "And if ye do always remember me ye shall have my Spirit to be with you" (3 Ne. 18:7, 11).

During the passing of the bread and water to the congregation, silence prevails. The communion aspired to is embodied in statements of modern leaders: Hyrum SMITH spoke of the sacramental process as bestowing spiritual sustenance enough to "last a whole week." The ordinance was given, as President Brigham YOUNG taught, "in order that the people may be sanctified" (*JD* 19:91–92). "I am a witness," said Elder Melvin J. Ballard, "that there is a spirit attending the administration of the sacrament that warms the soul from head to foot; you feel the wounds of the spirit being healed" (Hinckley, p. 133).

The typical sacrament meeting is sixty to seventy minutes long and has the following components, with mild variations from week to week:

Organ prelude
Greeting by a member of the bishopric
Opening hymn sung by the congregation
Announcements and ward business
Invocation by a ward member
Sacramental hymn sung by the congregation
Administration and partaking of the sacrament
Musical selection
Speakers
Closing hymn sung by the congregation
Benediction by ward member
Organ postlude

The spoken messages in sacrament meetings are given by different members of the congregation each Sunday, or by visiting officers from the stake organization. All speak with the same purpose: to witness of Jesus Christ, to review gospel principles, to inspire, to uplift, to encourage, and to motivate the congregation to renewed efforts to live a Christlike life. Speakers frequently quote from the scriptures, and members, young and old, are encouraged to bring their own book of scriptures and to follow the cited references. The time is usually shared by several speakers. Sometimes entire families are assigned to develop a gospel topic, and each member contributes to the chosen

Sacrament meetings begin and end with the singing of a congregational hymn. This sacrament meeting is in Berlin (1990). Courtesy Peggy Jellinghausen.

theme. Youth speakers are likewise regularly invited to give sacrament meeting talks. Sometimes the bishop assigns topics, and sometimes he leaves the choice to the individual or family.

Sacrament meeting is periodically combined with the observance of special events such as Christmas, Easter, Mother's Day, and Father's Day. On such occasions, the meeting follows the usual pattern through the sacrament and then proceeds around the commemoration program.

On one Sunday a month, usually the first, sacrament meeting is a FAST AND TESTIMONY MEETING. After the sacrament, the final portion of the meeting is devoted to extemporaneous testimony bearing by members of the congregation.

BIBLIOGRAPHY

"Church Consolidates Meeting Schedule." *Ensign* 10 (Mar. 1980):73–78.

Hartley, William G. "Mormon Sundays." *Ensign* 8 (Jan. 1978):19–25.

Hinckley, Bryant S. *Melvin J. Ballard . . . Crusader for Righteousness.* Salt Lake City, 1966.

CRAWFORD GATES
GEORGIA GATES

SACRED GROVE

A grove of trees on the Joseph SMITH, Sr., farm near Palmyra, New York, is revered by Latter-day Saints as the vicinity where Joseph SMITH experienced his FIRST VISION, the divine manifestation of God the Father and his Son Jesus Christ that began the RESTORATION of the gospel in this DISPENSATION. For that reason, Latter-day Saints honor the place as sacred. The grove is part of the forest that once covered the Smiths' 100-acre farm in Manchester Township as well as much of western New York.

The forest was some 400 years old when the family of Joseph Smith, Sr., moved to the site in 1818 or 1819. The large trees of the forest—maple, beech, elm, oak, and hickory—reached heights of up to 125 feet and diameters of 6 feet or more. Beneath this natural canopy grew hop hornbeam, wild cherry, and ash. The woodland floor was carpeted with leaves, ferns, grasses, wildflowers, and clumps of chokecherry and dogwood.

The Smiths cleared the trees from sixty acres of their property. The Sacred Grove was part of a

In such a grove of towering beeches, maples, and other trees, about one-fourth mile west of the Smith family home near Palmyra, New York, fourteen-year-old Joseph Smith saw God the Father and Jesus Christ in the spring of 1820. Photographer: George E. Anderson, 1926.

fifteen-acre wooded tract at the farm's west end, reserved as a sugarbush, where trees were tapped for making maple syrup and sugar.

Subsequent owners of the farm maintained the grove, associating it with Joseph Smith's vision, although the exact location of the vision is unknown. In 1907 the Church purchased the farm and grove from William A. Chapman, and these sites formed the nucleus of the Church HISTORICAL SITES program, which at present includes properties from Vermont to Utah.

Through an ongoing professional maintenance program, the Church has retained much of the primeval beauty of the Sacred Grove. Trees that were mature at the time of Joseph Smith's boyhood still grace this forest. People from many lands visit the

Sacred Grove each year. In 1989 the number of visitors exceeded 36,000.

BIBLIOGRAPHY

Backman, Milton V., Jr. *Joseph Smith's First Vision*, 2nd ed. Salt Lake City, 1980.

Enders, Donald L. "A Snug Log House." *Ensign* 15 (Aug. 1985):14–23.

Jessee, Dean C. "The Early Accounts of Joseph Smith's First Vision." *BYU Studies* 9 (Spring 1969):275–96.

DONALD L. ENDERS

SACRIFICE

God requires sacrifice of his people both to make or renew COVENANTS with him and to test their ultimate loyalties (D&C 98:12–15). When the Lord drove Adam and Eve from the GARDEN OF EDEN, he gave them the law of sacrifice, whereby they were to offer the firstlings of their flocks to him (Moses 5:5). From the beginning, offerings to the Lord that involved the shedding of blood were in similitude of the future sacrifice of Jesus Christ, who would come to atone for the sins of mankind (Moses 5:6–8). The Book of Mormon includes accounts of Lehi's people making burnt offerings in compliance with the LAW OF MOSES (1 Ne. 5:9; Mosiah 2:3).

With the sacrifice of Jesus, "the performances and ORDINANCES of the Law of Moses" were fulfilled (4 Ne. 1:12), and his death ended the practice of sacrifices on an altar. To his disciples in the western continents, Jesus said that he would no longer accept burnt offerings, but that anyone who believes in him should offer a broken heart and a contrite spirit (3 Ne. 9:19–20; cf. D&C 59:8).

For members of The Church of Jesus Christ of Latter-day Saints, sacrifice is required of those who wish to become the Lord's people (D&C 64:23). All are invited to come to Christ—rather than to a sacrificial altar—with humble, teachable spirits and repentant hearts, willing to sacrifice all things for the Lord and for one another (cf. Mosiah 18:8–9). The Prophet Joseph SMITH taught that only a religion that requires total sacrifice has power sufficient to produce the faith necessary for salvation (*Lectures on Faith* 6:5–7). To appreciate the need to sacrifice, one need only recall Jesus' words to the rich young ruler: "Sell all that thou hast, and distribute unto the poor . . . and come, follow me" (Luke 18:22).

Covenants made by Church members embrace the commitment to sacrifice all for the KINGDOM OF GOD. Examples of willingness to sacrifice are legion among early Latter-day Saints who sacrificed homes, comforts, and even their lives for their beliefs. Prior to his martyrdom, Joseph Smith knew that he was going as "a lamb to the slaughter" (D&C 135:4). Sacrifices made by Mormon pioneers to establish the Church in the western United States have become legendary. And sacrifices are still required of Latter-day Saints. For instance, faithful members pay one-tenth of their income as TITHING to the Church, contribute financially to mission funds, and give FAST OFFERINGS for the poor. Missionaries spend one or two years preaching the gospel at their own or their families' expense while delaying education, employment, marriage, or retirement. Members serve their congregations—without pay—in assigned lay positions that make possible the operation of Church programs. It is service to others through formal callings and through personal concern for their welfare that leads Church members to know that "sacrifice brings forth the blessings of heaven" (Hymns, p. 27).

[*See also* Consecration, Law of; Sacrifice in Biblical Times.]

BIBLIOGRAPHY

Benson, Ezra Taft. "This Is a Day of Sacrifice." *Ensign* 9 (May 1979):32–34.

Hymns of The Church of Jesus Christ of Latter-day Saints. Salt Lake City, 1985.

Matthews, Robert J. "The Doctrine of the Atonement—The Revelation of the Gospel to Adam." In *Studies in Scripture*, ed. K. Jackson and R. Millet, Vol. 2, pp. 111–29. Salt Lake City, 1985.

GLORIA JEAN THOMAS

SACRIFICE IN BIBLICAL TIMES

The first commandments received by Adam and Eve after being driven from the Garden of Eden were to worship God and to offer the firstlings of their flocks and herds (Moses 5:5–6). Adam and Eve obeyed. Later, an angel explained to them the purpose for the law of sacrifice: it was made in similitude of the offering that the Son of God would make of his own life for all mankind (Moses 5:7). Each offering was to point to the necessity of the Savior's sacrifice. Thus, Adam and Eve knew that a future atonement was to be made by Jesus Christ and that only through him could fallen man be reconciled to God.

Latter-day Saints believe that to perform any ordinance, a man must hold the PRIESTHOOD, which includes the authority from God necessary to offer sacrifices after the pattern that Adam received. But because of an unwillingness to follow God, historically many turned away, worshiped falsely, and followed selfish practices for personal aggrandizement, as did Cain (Moses 5:18–31). For the faithful, because sacrifice promoted faith in the Lord and reliance on him, selfishness was superseded, for the best was not to be used for self but for God. Men and women could thus recognize that it was not the earth, sun, or idols that supplied necessities, but God.

From Seth to Jacob, God's people renewed their covenant relationship with him, apparently by offering two kinds of sacrifice: the burnt offering and slain offering. Through Moses, Israel received and practiced further ordinances to remind them daily of their duty toward God (Lev. 1–7; Mosiah 13:30). Types and symbols which were woven into the LAW OF MOSES taught God's people of the Savior's atoning sacrifice (2 Ne. 11:4; Mosiah 13:31; Alma 25:16).

The Book of Mormon prophet LEHI and his family brought the Mosaic sacrificial system to the western hemisphere. NEPHITES continued those sacrificial practices until the resurrected Savior appeared to them (3 Ne. 9:19–20).

The Lord specifically forbade human sacrifice (Lev. 18:21; Jer. 19:5; Morm. 4:14, 21). Thus, when God commanded Abraham to sacrifice Isaac, he was testing Abraham's faith and teaching him of the Redeemer to come (Gen. 22; Heb. 11:17–19; Jacob 4:5; John 3:16; Gal. 3:8). The trial proved that Abraham loved God unconditionally; therefore, he could be blessed unconditionally.

The Bible prophet MALACHI predicted a time when Levites would again offer sacrifice in righteousness (Mal. 3:3). Such offerings will not be of the Mosaic type, which were fulfilled in Christ. However, the sacrificial system that antedated Moses was not fulfilled in Jesus. The Prophet Joseph SMITH, taught that blood sacrifices similar to those revealed to Adam will once again be performed prior to Christ's second coming in order to complete the RESTORATION OF ALL THINGS (TPJS, pp. 172–73; DS 3:94–95). These may be undertaken for only a brief period and perhaps only by a selected group. In a very different sense sacrifice continues in modern LDS temples (D&C 124:38–39), for those laboring therein are modern equivalents of Levites, and performance of temple ordinances in behalf of the dead constitutes an offering of righteousness (D&C 128:24).

BIBLIOGRAPHY

DeVaux, Roland. Ancient Israel, Vol. 2, pp. 415–56. New York, 1965.

Draper, Richard D. "Sacrifices and Offerings: Foreshadowings of Christ." Ensign 10 (Sept. 1980):20–26.

McMullin, Phillip W. "Sacrifice in the Law of Moses: Parallels in the Law of the Gospel." Ensign 20 (Mar. 1990):37–41.

RICHARD D. DRAPER

SAINTS

The revealed name of the Church is The Church of Jesus Christ of Latter-day Saints (D&C 115:4), wherein the term "saints" is synonymous with "members." The Church has no "patron saints" and does not canonize or venerate the dead. The usage of the term follows biblical precedents in which "saints" refers to Israelites as the chosen people of God—that is, as a community of believers set apart from nonbelievers (cf. "the congregation of the saints," Ps. 89:5). The Hebrew and Aramaic usage of the term in the Old Testament and in the writings of the Essene community is qadosh and qaddish, respectively, meaning "separate, set apart, holy."

Paul used the term "saint" (Greek hagios also denotes "set apart, separate, holy") in referring to baptized members of the Church of his day (e.g., Phil. 1:1). The Book of Mormon also designates "saints of God" as all those who belong to the "church of the Lamb" (1 Ne. 14:12).

Used this way, the term today denotes all members of Christ's Church, who, through baptism, have expressed a desire to follow the Savior's counsel to become more Godlike, toward the ideal to be "even as your Father which is in heaven is perfect" (Matt. 5:48), and who, though imperfect, strive to live in a manner that will lead them toward that goal.

BIBLIOGRAPHY

Nelson, Russell M. "Thus Shall My Church Be Called." *Ensign* 20 (May 1990):16–18.

JAMES K. LYON

SALT LAKE CITY, UTAH

Between July 21 and 23, 1847, an advance party of LDS men under Orson Pratt, an apostle, entered the Salt Lake Valley, placed a dam across City Creek, and began plowing and planting. President Brigham YOUNG arrived on July 24, and four days later designated the spot on the valley floor between City Creek's two forks as a site for the Salt Lake Temple, establishing what was then thought of as the center of Salt Lake City.

The valley had been inhabited by Indians—particularly Ute, Shoshone, and Gosiute—and had been visited by explorers before the Latter-day Saints entered the valley. Reports by explorers such as John C. Frémont and the blazing of the 1846 Donner-Reed trail helped further the LDS migration.

The city grew rapidly. Dividing it into what became twenty ecclesiastical wards in the nineteenth century, the Mormon pioneers laid out ten-acre blocks. The business district developed southward from the temple block on Main Street. At first most people engaged in agricultural, industrial, and merchandising enterprises, but eventually Salt Lake City became principally a commercial, manufacturing, and governmental center. By 1870, only 16.1 percent of the heads of households were farmers, compared with 33.6 percent in 1850.

Dominated by the LDS population in the nineteenth century, the city's non-Mormon population began to grow after the construction of the Utah Central Railroad in 1870 and the subsequent boom in mining, milling, and smelting. The city owed much of its growth in the nineteenth century to European immigration. In 1870, more than 65 percent of the 12,800 people in the city had come from abroad—principally from the British Isles. After 1900, immigrants from southern and eastern Europe came in larger numbers.

City government changed over time. It operated at first with a mayor-council–alderman system. Until the February 1890 election, the Mormon People's party governed the city. With the division of the citizens of the two religion-based

Looking south on Main Street (c. 1869). Visible in this photograph are the Lion House (upper left), part of Temple Square (upper right), and the Heber C. Kimball block (foreground left). Photographer: C. W. Carter.

This panorama of Salt Lake City, looking southeast, shows the Wasatch Range of the Rocky Mountains in the background. The tall building at the left is the Church Office Building, with the six-spired Salt Lake Temple to the right of it. Courtesy Salt Lake Convention and Visitors Bureau.

parties (Mormon People's party and non-Mormon Liberal party) into both the national Republican and the Democratic parties, politics became much more like that of other American cities except for a brief period between 1905 and 1912, when the American party, organized by non-Mormons, controlled city government. The city commission system was adopted in 1911.

The city faced a number of problems in the nineteenth and early twentieth centuries, not the least of which was providing urban services. In general, private companies, such as those that operated street railways and provided electricity and telephone services, offered those services under franchise and expected to earn a profit. The city provided services not anticipated to pay their way, such as streets, water, and sewers.

During the 1920s, the city faced special problems of air pollution, zoning regulations, and budgetary concerns. Before these could be fully solved, the decade of the Great Depression arrived and was as difficult for citizens of Salt Lake City as for those elsewhere. In spite of economic problems, the city continued to play a dominant role as a key regional city in the Rocky Mountains. This was due in part to the planning of nineteenth-century LDS pioneers who had emphasized commercial, financial, educational, transportation, and religious activities, and in part to the admixture of non-Mormons. In April 1936, the Church announced its welfare plan, which, along with federal work programs, softened the blow of the Great Depression on city residents.

Strategic placement of military industries benefited Salt Lake City during World War II and brought some prosperity to the city. Fort Douglas, Kearns Army Air Base, Hill Air Force Base, Tooele Ordnance Depot, and other military facilities contributed to the economic vitality that was centered in the city.

Space industries based on rocket fuels and high technology gradually replaced defense-based employment after World War II. During the 1960s the Salt Lake City metropolitan area became one of the fastest-growing in the United States. The LDS Church, under the guidance of N. Eldon Tanner, a counselor in the First Presidency, became a major contributor to downtown development. Investment by Church-owned businesses helped in the building of the Salt Palace Convention Center, the Beneficial Towers, the ZCMI Mall, and the Crossroads Mall, some of the first downtown malls in the nation.

In 1979, a dispute in city government over administrative practices resulted in a vote by the public to change the commission form of government to a mayor-council form. This led the way for other Utah cities, and by 1986 all commission governments in the state had changed to the mayor-council form.

In 1983, Salt Lake City residents became nationally known for their volunteer efforts in controlling floodwaters through the city. A strong volunteer network and ethic grew in the city, which was later recognized when Salt Lake City was designated the United States bid city for the Winter Olympic Games by the United States Olympic Committee in 1989.

In 1990, Salt Lake City enjoyed renewed economic vitality after a period of recession in the mid-1980s. Though the city proper continues to lose population as younger people move to the suburbs, it remains the heart of the LDS community. The activities established by the pioneer founders continue to make Salt Lake City a vital and important Rocky Mountain center.

[*See also* Temple Square; "This Is the Place" Monument; Welfare Square.]

BIBLIOGRAPHY

Alexander, Thomas G., and James B. Allen. *Mormons and Gentiles: A History of Salt Lake City*. Boulder, Colo., 1984.

McCormick, John S. *Salt Lake City: The Gathering Place*. Woodland Hills, Calif., 1980.

Tullidge, Edward W. *History of Salt Lake City*. Salt Lake City, 1886.

THOMAS G. ALEXANDER
TED L. WILSON

SALT LAKE TEMPLE

The Salt Lake Temple is an impressive structure standing on the ten-acre TEMPLE SQUARE in the heart of Salt Lake City. For many years after its construction, the temple physically dominated the Salt Lake Valley. While other buildings now tower over it, the gray granite structure is still recognized as the religious symbol of The Church of Jesus Christ of Latter-day Saints worldwide. Millions of visitors annually have seen the building. Photographs of the temple have gone to scores of countries where people who have never personally

The Salt Lake Temple, begun in 1853 and dedicated in 1893. The granite structure, topped by a gilded copper statue of the angel Moroni on the east-central spire, is the heart of Temple Square. In the foreground is the Seagull Monument. Courtesy Utah State Historical Society.

Workers cut slabs of granite in Little Cottonwood Canyon (c. 1872), about twenty miles south-east of Salt Lake City, for use in building the Salt Lake Temple. In the early years, the granite was moved to the temple site by ox team, a four-day journey, and after twenty years, by railroad. Stereoscopic image. Photographer: C. W. Carter.

seen the structure identify its striking presence with the Church and the city.

SITE SELECTION. Several days after the LDS pioneers entered the Salt Lake Valley in July 1847, Brigham Young planted his walking stick at a certain point while traversing the ground with some associates and exclaimed, "Here we will build the temple of our God" (Gates, p. 104).

CONSTRUCTION. Construction on the temple began on February 14, 1853, with Brigham Young turning the first shovelful of dirt in ground-breaking ceremonies. That April 6, the cornerstones were laid, following the pattern established for temples by Joseph Smith (cf. *TPJS*, p. 183). By this date, Truman O. Angell and William Ward, architect and assistant, had completed plans for the foundation and part of the basement, and Brigham Young had approved them. Sandstone from nearby Red Butte Canyon provided the basic material for the foundation and footings. The great walls of the building were to be granite from a vast mountain deposit in Little Cottonwood canyon about twenty miles away.

The foundation was completed in 1855, and some granite blocks were assembled on the site. Then, in 1858, under threat of an approaching U.S. army unit (*see* UTAH EXPEDITION), the Saints evacuated Salt Lake City and temporarily moved southward. They buried the foundation of the temple, leaving the appearance of a plowed field.

Work on the temple was not resumed for several years. Some deterioration of the foundation was discovered when it was reexcavated, and replacements were made with stone of the best quality. The exterior walls from the ground up, eight feet thick at ground level and six feet thick at the top, were painstakingly prepared and fitted from solid granite.

Transporting the granite from the mountain quarry proved to be a severe challenge. The builders tried using a wooden railroad spur, a canal, special roads, and even a uniquely constructed wagon. Although it was less than forty miles, a round trip required four days. The arrival of the transcontinental railroad in 1869 and the later laying of a spur into the canyon for mining purposes resolved the transportation problem.

As many as 150 men worked on the temple at any given time. During the forty years from the beginning to the end of the project, they also completed the construction of the great domed Tabernacle, the Assembly Hall, the Temple Annex, and a 15-foot-high wall that, a century and a half later, still sequesters Temple Square from the city that surrounds it.

COMPLETION AND DEDICATION. The capstone was laid April 6, 1892, one year before the dedication, amidst a tremendous spiritual outpouring of appreciation and anticipation. After the large spherical capstone was put in place, the people unanimously adopted a resolution to complete and dedicate the building one year from that date. That afternoon, the 12-foot-high gold-leafed copper statue representing the angel Moroni was placed on the central eastern spire, anchored through the capstone with huge weights suspended into the tower below.

The temple was completed within the year, and the dedication was held on the appointed date—April 6, 1893—forty years after Brigham Young laid the cornerstone. More than 2,250 people crowded the large Assembly Room on the fourth floor of the temple for the first of twenty-three dedicatory sessions that continued over almost three weeks. Many reported having spiritual experiences at the dedications. President Wilford WOODRUFF offered the dedicatory prayer, and the HOSANNA SHOUT and original inspirational music were rendered (see DEDICATIONS). The sacred celebration was concluded with the singing of a special hymn saluting the sentiments of the people: the Hosanna Anthem.

INTERIOR DIVISIONS (DESIGN). Entrance to the temple for patrons is through an annex outside the main building. For the instructions and ordinances within, a processional plan is followed through several rooms, each signifying a stage in man's path of ETERNAL PROGRESSION. Each room is decorated with murals depicting that stage of the journey.

First is the Creation Room, where the creative periods of the earth are considered. Next, the events of Eden are the subject in the Garden Room. The World (or Telestial) Room depicts conditions following the expulsion of Adam and Eve from the Garden of Eden, providing a background for the atonement of Christ, the great apostasy, and the RESTORATION of the gospel.

In the Terrestrial Room, the requirements of the pure life and of complete commitment to the work of the Lord are taught. The path then leads through the veil of the temple to the Celestial Room, representing the "heaven of heavens," the glorious kingdom of God. On this level also are small rooms with altars for marriage and sealing ordinances.

The building also includes in the lower area a baptistry, and on other levels, a large assembly room, rooms where the leaders of the Church meet, lecture rooms, administrative offices, and dressing rooms.

SYMBOLISM. Notable among all LDS temples, the Salt Lake Temple includes significant symbolism in its architecture. The six major towers and finial spires signify the restoration of priesthood authority. Earth stones, sun stones, moon stones, star stones, cloud stones penetrated with rays of light, the all-seeing eye, the clasped hands, Ursa Major pointing to the North Star, and the inscriptions "The House of the Lord" and "I Am Alpha and Omega" all appear on its exterior.

UNIQUE FUNCTIONS. Notwithstanding the increasing availability of temples nearer to them offering the same religious experience, many members of the Church still travel long distances to receive their individual ENDOWMENT in the Salt Lake Temple or to be married or sealed as families in the same building in which parents or perhaps grandparents or other family members were married long ago.

This temple is also unique among LDS temples in that the highest quorums of the priesthood meet there. The First Presidency, the Quorum of the Twelve Apostles, and the Presidents of the Seventy gather separately as quorums weekly, and the First Presidency and Quorum of the Twelve also meet conjointly. All General Authorities meet there monthly.

It is also, as already noted, architecturally and artistically unique and is the most widely known and recognized building in the Church.

BIBLIOGRAPHY

Anderson, James H. "The Salt Lake Temple." *Contributor* 14 (Apr. 1893):243–303.

Gates, Susa Young. *The Life Story of Brigham Young.* New York, 1931.

McAllister, D. M. *The Great Temple* (pamphlet). Salt Lake City, 1935.

MARION D. HANKS

SALT LAKE THEATRE

The Salt Lake Theatre was built in downtown Salt Lake City in 1861–1862 at a cost of over $100,000. President Brigham YOUNG donated more than half of the funds because he believed the Saints needed a theater to bring recreation, relaxation, and additional unity to the pioneer community. Visitors from other areas were shocked and even a little scandalized by his support because the theatrical stage did not have a good reputation in the 1860s. However, a glance at his talk given at the dedication shows that President Young made very clear his expectations for good, moral theater (*JD* 9:242–45).

The Salt Lake Theatre, with a seating capacity of 1,500, was one of the finest buildings in pioneer Salt Lake City, comparing well to theaters worldwide. It was praised by many of the professional actors who performed in it, including such theatrical greats as Sarah Alexander, Julie Dean Hayne, E. L. Davenport, and John McCullough. "There was scarcely a 'star' of the American stage who did not make a Salt Lake Theatre appearance" (Walker and Starr, p. 73).

Salt Lake Theatre (1862–1929). Feeling that people needed amusement as well as religion, Brigham Young instructed a son-in-law, Hiram Clawson, to build this theatre. Completed in 1862, it seated 3,000. All performances were opened and closed with prayer, and the actors and actresses were expected to set a good example in the community. Photographer: C. R. Savage, c. 1913.

After more than half a century of significant productions, however, the financially troubled and aging playhouse was sold in 1928 to be razed for a commercial office building. But the elements of theater—music, dance, and drama—established by the Salt Lake Theatre by the Mormon pioneers through six decades of continuous operation could not be torn down or destroyed. In 1962 the Pioneer Memorial Theatre, commemorating the old Salt Lake Theatre, was dedicated on the University of Utah campus and has since played a full season each year (*see* DRAMA).

BIBLIOGRAPHY

Asahina, Roberta Reese. "Brigham Young and the Salt Lake Theater, 1862–1877." Ph.D. diss., Tufts University, 1980.

Maughan, Ila Fisher. *Pioneer Theatre in the Desert.* Salt Lake City, 1961.

Walker, Ronald W., and Alexander M. Starr. "Shattering the Vase: The Razing of the Old Salt Lake Theatre." *Utah Historical Quarterly* 57 (Winter 1989):64–88.

CHARLES L. METTEN

SALT LAKE VALLEY

In 1847 Brigham YOUNG, like a modern Moses, led the first pioneer Saints across a 1,300-mile stretch of "wilderness" into a large valley, surrounded by high mountain peaks and bordered on the northwest by a large lake of salty water, which gave the valley its name. Religious persecution of the 1830s and 1840s in the more populated eastern states necessitated the movement of the Latter-day Saints to the West, where they could be more isolated. The Prophet Joseph SMITH had designated Jackson County, Missouri, on the fringes of civilization, as the ZION of the latter days. However, continued persecution in Ohio, in Missouri, and later in Illinois caused the Latter-day Saints to seek a refuge in the Rocky Mountains, farther to the west, where they could worship God and practice their religious beliefs in the absence of religious bigotry, in land claimed by Mexico. To approximately 80,000 LDS pioneers who gathered from many nations and traveled across the great American desert by wagons before the advent in 1869 of the railroad, and to the thousands who followed afterward, the LDS presence in the Salt Lake Valley was compared to a fulfillment of Isaiah's prophecy of the latter days, the City of God, established in the top of the mountains where people from all nations could gather to the House of the Lord to learn his ways (Isa. 2:1–3). To the Latter-day pioneers, President Brigham Young's words expressed their feelings: "This is the place."

The seventeen-mile-wide by twenty-five-mile-long Salt Lake Valley is some 4,500 feet above sea level and is surrounded by towering mountain peaks of the Wasatch Range that rise to over 11,000 feet. The valley is part of the Great Basin, where river waters are kept from flowing into the Pacific Ocean by high mountains. Lake Bonneville once lay within the Great Basin, and geologists say that it measured 1,000 feet deep where SALT LAKE CITY is now located. The current Great Salt Lake is the evaporation remnant of that inland sea.

Though the valley floor was very dry and covered with sagebrush when the LDS pioneers arrived in July 1847, it did not take long for them to divert the clear, snow-fed mountain streams onto the parched soil and make a productive farming community. Fur trappers and traders, explorers, and Roman Catholic priests had "passed through," but the Latter-day Saints were in the valley to stay.

Salt Lake City, in the north end of the valley, became the "big city," the headquarters of the Church. But as immigrants gathered from far-flung countries to their Zion, numerous smaller towns were established in the valley along the mountain streams.

With the coming of the transcontinental railroad in 1869, Gentiles (non-Mormons) began to move into the valley, diluting the LDS population; but Latter-day Saints continued to be a majority. The railroad helped foster more manufacturing, mining, and commerce, and the valley took on a decided change. By 1870 modern houses were replacing the log and adobe brick cabins, and green trees lined the streets and roads. Farms were fenced and well groomed.

The 1880s saw the introduction of the telephone and electricity to Salt Lake City, and in 1893 the Salt Lake Temple was finished. In the early 1900s money from Utah's mining industry was being invested in the valley's first skyscrapers, and a modern capital city emerged with hospitals, colleges, business buildings, libraries, and thousands of homes. Salt Lake City had changed from the all-Mormon village of 1847 to a cosmopolitan city.

By 1990 the population within the formal city boundaries was 165,000, but the greater Salt Lake Valley population totaled over 715,000. With shopping malls, freeways, and employment opportunities scattered throughout the valley, the population shift away from the city became valleywide on both sides of the Jordan River, which flows north from Utah Lake to the Great Salt Lake. Mountains surrounding the valley have been extremely valuable. Mining in the west side Oquirrh Mountains has brought many jobs to the people of the valley and the world's largest open-pit copper mine is a major employer. The mountains to the east provide precious drinking water and are used chiefly for recreational purposes, especially for skiing in the winter.

As travelers drive down out of the mountains today, they view a beautiful tree-filled Salt Lake Valley below. The scene stirs feelings of gratitude for the labor of the pioneers, who, in many cases, were their forefathers. The faithful Saints may feel that Isaiah's words have literally been fulfilled, that "The wilderness and the solitary place shall be glad for them; and the desert shall rejoice, and blossom as the rose. . . . They shall see the glory of the Lord, and the excellency of our God" (Isa. 35:1–2).

BIBLIOGRAPHY

Alexander, Thomas G., and James B. Allen. *Mormons and Gentiles: A History of Salt Lake City.* Boulder, Colo., 1984.

McCormick, John S. "The Valley of the Great Salt Lake." Reprint of the *Utah Historical Quarterly* 27 (July 1959); rev. ed., 1963.

———. *Salt Lake City, the Gathering Place.* Woodland Hills, Calif., 1980.

LAMAR C. BERRETT

SALVATION

Salvation is the greatest gift of God (D&C 6:13). The root of the word means to be saved, or placed beyond the power of one's enemies (*TPJS*, pp. 297, 301, 305). It is redemption from the bondage of sin and death, through the ATONEMENT OF JESUS CHRIST. Some degree of salvation will come to all of God's children except the SONS OF PERDITION. Jesus said, "In my Father's house are many mansions: if it were not so, I would have told you. I go to prepare a place for you" (John 14:2). Paul said, "There is one glory of the sun, and another glory of the moon, and another glory of the stars. . . . So also is the resurrection of the dead" (1 Cor. 15:40–

42). Paul also explained that "as in Adam all die, even so in Christ shall all be made alive" (1 Cor. 15:22). The Latter-day Saint concept of salvation derives from the teachings of Jesus Christ and the revelations given to ancient and latter-day prophets. It is evident from such teachings that there are different degrees or levels of salvation in the afterlife (*see* DEGREES OF GLORY).

There are various levels of salvation because there are various levels of belief and works among people (D&C 76:99–101). The Prophet Joseph Smith observed, "If God rewarded every one according to the deeds done in the body the term 'Heaven' as intended for the Saints' eternal home, must include more kingdoms than one" (*TPJS*, pp. 10–11).

The gospel of Jesus Christ comprises fundamental principles and ORDINANCES that must be followed to obtain a fulness of salvation. The first steps are FAITH in the Lord Jesus Christ, REPENTANCE, BAPTISM by immersion for the remission of sins, and the LAYING ON OF HANDS by one who is in authority for the gift of the HOLY GHOST. Additional ordinances are administered in the TEMPLE. And finally, "he only is saved who endureth unto the end" (D&C 53:7).

The most sacred ordinances pertaining to the salvation of both the living and the dead are performed in the temples. These ordinances include the ENDOWMENT, the SEALING of husband and wife to form an eternal MARRIAGE, and the sealing of children to parents to form an eternal family. All the ordinances that are essential for the salvation of the living are likewise essential for the dead, beginning with proxy BAPTISM FOR THE DEAD. These can only be performed in a temple. Baptism is for entrance into the CELESTIAL KINGDOM; the endowment and the sealing ordinances are for EXALTATION in the celestial kingdom. In the mercy of God and his love for his children, the PLAN OF SALVATION provides for everyone to hear and respond to the gospel either in this life or in the SPIRIT WORLD so that all who will may be saved by obedience to the laws and ordinances of the gospel (D&C 137:7–9; *see also* SALVATION OF THE DEAD).

Salvation in a Latter-day Saint context includes activity and service in the kingdom of God for all eternity, unhampered by the effects of sin, death, physical pain, sickness, or other impediments to joy. The highest level of salvation is to become like God and involves a family unit. Lesser

degrees of salvation are correspondingly less glorious and have restrictions.

ALMA P. BURTON

SALVATION OF CHILDREN

See: Children: Salvation of Children

SALVATION OF THE DEAD

A distinctive doctrine of The Church of Jesus Christ of Latter-day Saints is that the dead as well as the living may receive the GOSPEL OF JESUS CHRIST. Every man, woman, and child who has ever lived or who ever will live on this earth will have full opportunity, if not in this life then in the next, to embrace or reject the gospel in its purity and fulness.

When this doctrine was first taught at NAUVOO, ILLINOIS, in 1842 (D&C 127; 128), the Prophet Joseph SMITH said it was the "burden of the scriptures" and that it exhibited "the greatness of divine compassion and benevolence in the extent of the plan of human salvation" (*TPJS*, p. 192). It is in harmony with the Jewish idea that the family is the instrument of holiness and redemption and that the dead may need atonement. It is also a Christian concept in the writings of Paul and Peter (*see* BAPTISM FOR THE DEAD). "[It] justifies the ways of God to man, places the human family upon an equal footing, and harmonizes with every principle of righteousness, justice, and truth" (*TPJS*, p. 223).

The Prophet posed the dilemma resolved by the doctrine: "One dies and is buried having never heard the gospel of reconciliation; to the other the message of salvation is sent, he hears and embraces it and is made the heir of eternal life. Shall the one become the partaker of glory and the other be consigned to hopeless perdition? . . . Such an idea is worse than atheism" (*TPJS*, p. 192).

Five fundamental principles underlie LDS understanding of salvation for the dead:

1. Life is eternal. Birth does not begin life nor does death end it. In each stage of existence there are ever-higher levels of divine enlightenment and blessedness.

2. Repentance is possible in the next life as well as this one. "There is never a time when the spirit

This replica of a temple baptismal font, in the South Visitors Center on Temple Square, is like those in LDS temples where baptisms by immersion are performed by proxy for the dead. The twelve oxen symbolize the twelve tribes of Israel.

is too old to approach God. All are within the reach of pardoning mercy, who have not committed the unpardonable sin" (*TPJS*, p. 191).

3. The family bonds extend beyond death. The family bonds that are formed on this earth and consecrated to God by sacred covenants and ordinances are indissoluble and extend into the SPIRIT WORLD. "They without us cannot be made perfect—neither can we without our dead be made perfect" (D&C 128:15; Heb. 11:39–40).

4. Ordinances may be performed for the dead. Through the holy priesthood, held by the prophets in the Church, Jesus Christ has authorized mortals to receive ordinances "of salvation substitutional" [that is, by proxy] and become "instrumental in bringing multitudes of their kindred into the kingdom of God" (*TPJS*, p. 191).

5. Temple ordinances are not "mere signs." They are channels of the Spirit of God that enable one to be BORN OF GOD in the fullest sense and to receive all the COVENANTS and blessings of Jesus Christ. The performing of earthly ordinances by proxy for those who have died is as efficacious and vitalizing as if the deceased person had done them. That person, in turn, is free to accept or reject the ordinances in the spirit world.

In harmony with these principles, Latter-day Saints identify their ancestors through FAMILY HISTORY research, build temples, and, in behalf of their progenitors, perform the ordinances that pertain to EXALTATION: BAPTISM; CONFIRMATION; ORDINATION TO THE PRIESTHOOD; WASHING AND ANOINTING; ENDOWMENT; and SEALING. Thus, "we redeem our dead, and connect ourselves with our fathers which are in heaven, and seal up our dead to come forth in the first resurrection . . . [we] seal those who dwell on earth to those who dwell in heaven" (*TPJS*, pp. 337–38). This is the chain that binds the hearts of fathers and mothers

The St. George Temple, the first temple dedicated in Utah, was also the first in which endowments were received by proxy for the dead, in 1877. Prior to that time, endowments for the living had been performed in the Nauvoo Temple and in the Endowment House. This temple was dedicated under the direction of Brigham Young, in his advanced age and failing health, shortly before he died. Photograph, 1982; courtesy Floyd Holdman.

to their children and the hearts of the children to their parents. And this sealing work "fulfills the mission of Elijah" (*TPJS*, p, 330; *see also* ELIJAH, SPIRIT OF).

When the Twelve Apostles chosen in Joseph Smith's day were instructed to initiate these ordinances in Nauvoo in 1842, they soon recognized that it was the beginning of an immense work and that to administer all the ordinances of the gospel to the hosts of the dead was no easy task. They asked if there was some other way. The Prophet Joseph replied, "The laws of the Lord are immutable, we must act in perfect compliance with what is revealed to us. We need not expect to do this vast work for the dead in a short time. I expect it will take at least a thousand years" (*Millennial Star* 37:66). As of 1991 vicarious temple ordinances have been performed for more than 113 million persons. The Prophet Joseph said, "It is no more incredible that God should save the dead, than that he should raise the dead" (*TPJS*, p. 191).

BIBLIOGRAPHY

Widtsoe, John A. "Fundamentals of Temple Doctrine." *Utah Genealogical and Historical Magazine* 13 (June 1922):129–35.

ELMA W. FUGAL

SAMUEL THE LAMANITE

Samuel the LAMANITE was the only Book of Mormon prophet identified as a Lamanite. Apart from his sermon at Zarahemla (Hel. 13–15), no other record of his life or ministry is preserved. Noted chiefly for his prophecies about the birth of Jesus Christ, his prophetic words, which were later examined, commended, and updated by the risen Jesus (3 Ne. 23:9–13), were recorded by persons who accepted him as a true PROPHET and even faced losing their lives for believing his message (3 Ne. 1:9).

Approximately five years before Jesus' birth, Samuel began to preach repentance in Zarahemla. After the incensed Nephite inhabitants expelled him, the voice of the Lord directed him to return. Climbing to the top of the city wall, he delivered his message unharmed, even though certain citizens sought his life (Hel. 16:2). Thereafter, he fled and "was never heard of more among the Nephites" (Hel. 16:8).

Samuel prophesied that Jesus would be born in no more than five years' time, with two heavenly signs indicating his birth. First, "one day and a night and a day" of continual light would occur (Hel. 14:4; cf. Zech. 14:7). Second, among celestial wonders, a new star would arise (Hel. 14:5–6). Then speaking of mankind's need of the ATONEMENT and RESURRECTION, he prophesied signs of Jesus' death: three days of darkness among the Nephites would signal his crucifixion, accompanied by storms and earthquakes (14:14–27).

Samuel framed these prophecies by pronouncing judgments of God upon his hearers. He spoke of a final devastation—four hundred years distant—that would end Nephite civilization because of its rebellion against God. This desolation would come through "the sword and with famine and with pestilence" (13:9; cf. Morm. 1:19). He spoke of curses from God on the land (13:17–20, 23, 30, 35–36), on property (13:18–19, 21, 31), and on the people themselves (13:19, 21, 32, 38). Such afflictions would arise because the Nephites would knowingly reject true prophets while accepting false ones, clamor for wealth, and refuse to acknowledge the blessings of God (13:19–34). Samuel reiterated the judgments of God against the Nephites (15:1–3, 17) and then emphasized the divine promises extended to the Lamanites—including assurances for "the latter times" of "restoration" (15:4–16).

S. MICHAEL WILCOX

SANCTIFICATION

Sanctification is the process of becoming a SAINT, holy and spiritually clean and pure, by purging all SIN from the SOUL. Latter-day Saint scriptures mention several factors that make sanctification possible.

First is the ATONEMENT of JESUS CHRIST (D&C 76:41–42; 88:18; Moro. 10:33; Alma 13:11). Christ's blood sanctifies God's repentant children by washing them clean in a way that extends beyond the REMISSION OF SINS at BAPTISM. This cleansing is given through GRACE to all who "love and serve God" (D&C 20:31). "For by the water ye keep the commandment; by the Spirit ye are justified, and by the blood ye are sanctified" (Moses 6:60; cf. 1 John 5:8).

Second is the power of the HOLY GHOST, the agent that purifies the heart and gives an abhorrence of sin (Alma 13:12; 3 Ne. 27:20).

Third is progression through personal RIGHTEOUSNESS (*see also* JUSTIFICATION). Faithful men and women fast; pray; repent of their sins; grow in HUMILITY, FAITH, JOY, and consolation; and yield their hearts to God (Hel. 3:35). They also receive essential ORDINANCES such as baptism (D&C 19:31) and, if necessary, endure CHASTENING (D&C 101:5). Thus, Latter-day Saints are exhorted to "sanctify yourselves" (D&C 43:11) by purging all their iniquity (*MD*, pp. 675–76).

King BENJAMIN's people in the Book of Mormon illustrate the sanctification process. They humbled themselves and prayed mightily that God would apply the atoning blood of Christ and purify their hearts. The Spirit came upon them and filled them with joy; a mighty change came into their hearts and they had "no more disposition to do evil, but to do good continually" (Mosiah 5:2).

Latter-day Saint scripture often states that no unclean thing can dwell in God's presence (e.g., 3 Ne. 27:19; Moses 6:57). Thus, the sanctification that Latter-day Saints seek is more than a physical or moral state; it is a perpetual spiritual life—an ongoing effort to be worthy and pure to live with God—to overcome the evils of one's life and lose "every desire for sin" (*TPJS*, p. 51).

C. ERIC OTT

SARAH

Sarah was the wife of ABRAHAM. Originally named Sarai (which possibly meant "contentions"), she was renamed Sarah ("princess") when, in her old age, God promised Abraham that she would bear a son. The fragmentary information available about her paints a picture of great faith manifested in sacrifices not easily made. Sarah shared equally in Abraham's trials; her experience permits a feminine perspective on the universal obligations of faith, hope, and sacrifice.

Childless until late in life, Sarah suffered years of travail. Barrenness was a heavy burden for any woman in Near Eastern cultures but would have been felt as a particularly searing inadequacy by a woman whose husband had received divine promises of endless posterity.

Against this backdrop, Sarah was twice thrust into situations where she had to feign being unmarried in order to protect Abraham—first with Pharaoh (Gen. 12) and then with Abimelech (Gen. 20). The book of Abraham makes it clear that this was not mere cowardice or prevarication on Abraham's part; it was obedience to divine direction (Abr. 2:22–25). But this did not simplify Sarah's dilemma. Already torn between commitment to sacred marriage vows and the apparent certainty of death if she did not play the allotted role, she was required to rely on God for protection during the very hours when his instructions seemed to place her in the jaws of destruction. As in the ultimate trial with Isaac, it was the joint faith of Sarah and Abraham that ultimately opened the path of deliverance.

In her old age, Sarah gave Hagar, her maid, to Abraham. Modern revelation indicates that Sarah thereby "administered unto Abraham according to the law" (D&C 132:65), and more recent scholarship has confirmed the widespread legal obligation of the childless wife in the ancient Near East to provide her husband with a second wife (Claus Westermann, *Genesis 12–36*, p. 239, Minneapolis, 1985). Tensions flared with Hagar and later Ishmael (Gen. 16:4–16; 21:8–10). In both cases, Hagar was driven away, first temporarily when pregnant, and then permanently, with her teenage son Ishmael. Significantly, in both cases, the Lord had Abraham place the resolution of these conflicts in Sarah's hands: "In all that Sarah hath said unto thee, hearken unto her voice" (Gen. 21:12; cf. Gen. 16:4–6).

The promise that she would bear a son, which had caused Sarah to "laugh . . . within herself" (Gen. 18:12), was fulfilled in the birth of Isaac. The scriptures do not indicate whether Sarah knew beforehand of the call to take Isaac to Moriah, but she had been prepared. Her experiences had carved out in her a reservoir of patient faith, and she was capable of complete trust in God. Sarah was human and real and sometimes even imperfect in wrestling with the burdens of obedience. Yet she endured. Ultimately, she entered with Abraham into the exaltation that her motherhood helped prepare for all the house of Israel (see D&C 132:37).

BIBLIOGRAPHY

Nibley, Hugh. "A New Look at the Pearl of Great Price, Part 11: The Sacrifice of Sarah." *IE* 73 (Apr. 1970):79–95.

LOUISE GARDINER DURHAM

SATANISM

The cult of Satanism has evolved over many years. At the present time, symbols related to Satan have become so prevalent that the warning voices of leaders in the Church have again been raised concerning some people's fascination with the power of evil. Latter-day Saints are admonished to avoid any contact with Satanism, even with the good intention of learning about it in order to warn others of its dangers.

The answer that Jesus Christ gave when Satan offered him the glories of the world if he would fall down and worship him could be a guide to Church members when confronted with similar temptations: "Get thee hence, Satan: for it is written, Thou shalt worship the Lord thy God, and him only shalt thou serve" (Matt. 4:10).

Bruce R. McConkie, an apostle, warned, "One of Satan's greatest aims, as he works his nefarious schemes among men, is to get them 'to worship him'" (*MD*, p. 193). From earliest times, many evil things have been done in the name of Satan worship (Moses 6:49). Satanism may claim to offer powers beyond those available to humans through righteous sources, but the worship of Satan leads only to destruction.

The forces of evil cannot overcome a person without some willingness on the part of the individual (1 Cor. 10:13). President Brigham YOUNG said, "You are aware that many think that the Devil has rule and power over both body and spirit. Now, I want to tell you that he does not hold any power over man, only so far as the body overcomes the spirit that is in a man, through yielding to the spirit of evil" (pp. 69–70).

BIBLIOGRAPHY

Cannon, George Q. *Gospel Truth*, ed. Jerreld L. Newquist. Salt Lake City, 1987.

Young, Brigham. *Discourses of Brigham Young*, ed. John A. Widtsoe. Salt Lake City, 1946.

JANET THOMAS

SATELLITE COMMUNICATIONS SYSTEM

Communications satellites, as here referred to, are small radio transmitters orbiting the earth. Typical geosynchronous orbits are 22,300 miles above the equator. These tiny man-made moons make possible transmission of voice, data, radio, and television signals to every point on the globe. The introduction of The Church of Jesus Christ of Latter-day Saints to satellite broadcasting came during the first satellite exchange between North America and Europe, which included a performance by the TABERNACLE CHOIR in front of Mount Rushmore, South Dakota. Since that time the Church has developed its own private satellite distribution system. In 1982 it purchased transponder capacity on Westar IV from the Public Broadcasting Service. Transmitting, or "uplink," facilities were built in City Creek Canyon near Salt Lake City from which signals from the TABERNACLE and elsewhere could be beamed into space. Receiving, or "downlink," antennas were installed at many STAKE centers across North America. The Church has global communication capabilities, enabling signals to reach cable operators, stake centers, and other satellite receiving facilities.

Programming sent by Church satellite includes CONFERENCES, educational and professional training, FIRESIDES and special religious programs, entertainment, and BRIGHAM YOUNG UNIVERSITY sports. Most important, this system brings the GENERAL AUTHORITIES closer to the Saints throughout the world.

Satellite communications systems allow for open as well as encoded transmissions. This flexibility permits Church use of the system for public as well as private communications. The private use holds the promise expressed by President Gordon B. Hinckley in a general conference address: "We are now expanding the miracle of satellite transmission . . . to develop the means whereby the membership of the Church, wherever they may be, can be counselled in an intimate and personal way by [the Lord's] chosen prophet. Communication is the sinew that binds the Church as one great family" (p. 5).

BIBLIOGRAPHY

Hinckley, Gordon B. "Faith: The Essence of True Religion." *Ensign* 11 (Nov. 1981):5.

Pace, Geoffrey L. "The Emergence of Bonneville Satellite Corporation: A Study of Conception and Development of a New Telecommunications Service." Master's thesis, Brigham Young University, 1983, pp. 12–79.

BRUCE L. CHRISTENSEN

SAVIOR

See: Jesus Christ: Names and Titles of

SCANDINAVIA, THE CHURCH IN

At the General Conference of the Church in Salt Lake City on October 6, 1849, Elder Erastus Snow, an apostle, and Peter Olsen Hansen were called to serve missions to Scandinavia. John Erik Forsgren asked that he might also be called to his native Sweden. They were joined by George Parker Dykes, who was already a missionary in England, and these four men formally introduced the Church into Scandinavia. Successful in finding converts from the beginning, the Church has had

LDS chapel in Ålborg, Denmark, c. 1937. The Danish Mission was first a part of the Scandinavian Mission organized in 1850. The Copenhagen Denmark Stake was organized in 1974, and the Århus Denmark Stake, including the Ålborg ward, in 1978. Photographer: Alma L. Petersen.

two very dynamic periods of growth there, from 1850 to 1870, and from 1947 to 1967. Emigration of Church members to the United States was particularly high between 1861 and 1891 and after World War II. By the end of 1990, the Church had over 20,000 members living in seven STAKES and 119 WARDS and BRANCHES throughout Scandinavia, served by a TEMPLE in Västerhaninge, Sweden. Records show that 57 percent of the LDS converts in Scandinavia have been women and 43 percent men.

EARLY CONVERTS. Hansen arrived first in Copenhagen on May 12, 1850, and immediately visited a Baptist congregation. The first Danish Mormon converts later came from that group. Elder Snow, Forsgren, and Dykes arrived on June 14, 1850.

Forsgren visited his family in Gävle, Sweden, and baptized his brother Peter Adolf Forsgren on July 26, 1850. This was the first LDS BAPTISM in Scandinavia. On August 12, eight men and seven women were baptized at Øresund, near Copenhagen. The first Danish branch of about fifty members was organized in Copenhagen a month later.

Dykes was sent to Ålborg in Jutland in northern Denmark, where he also contacted a Baptist congregation. The first converts in Ålborg included Hans Peter Jensen, a prominent Baptist, who owned an iron foundry employing over one hundred men, and his CONVERSION to the LDS Church became widely known. Within four months the branch in Ålborg included sixty members.

A Norwegian ship's captain named Svend Larsen first encountered the Church in Ålborg. He was taught by Elder Snow in Brother Jensen's home, and noted in his diary that an inner voice whispered to him that this was a man of God. Baptized in Ålborg on September 23, 1851, he became the first resident Norwegian to join the Church. Larsen gave important support to spreading the Church in Norway. On September 11, 1851, he brought Hans F. Peterson, the first LDS missionary, to Norway, who baptized master blacksmith John Olsen and his assistant Peter Adamsen on November 26 at Risør. With the help of missionaries from Denmark, the work was extended to Brevik and Fredrikstad. The first convert there was Svend Peter Larsen, a stepson of one of the leading Methodists in Fredrikstad. His wife, Berthine Randine, was baptized four days later. In spite of mob disturbances and occasional brief imprisonment of the missionaries, the Church grew. The first branch in Norway was organized in Risør on July 16, 1852. During the next six years branches were organized in Fredrikstad, Brevik, Christiania (Oslo), Drammen, Stavanger, Halden, Trondheim, and Bergen.

John Erik Forsgren's missionary work in Sweden ended quickly as he and Mikel Johnson were deported to Copenhagen. The first highly successful missionary in Sweden was Anders W. Winberg, who began his work in Skåne in April 1852, and organized the first branch in Skönabäck with thirty-six members on April 24, 1852. Soon thereafter branches were established in Malmö, Lomma, and Lund. On June 25, 1853, the Skåne Conference was organized.

The Church was introduced into Iceland by two young Icelanders, Thorarinn Halflidasson and Gumundur Gudmundsson, who were baptized in Denmark in 1851 and returned to their homeland to proselyte as instructed by Elder Snow. Benedikt Hanson and his wife were baptized, but when Halflidasson accidentally drowned on a fishing trip, no one was left with priesthood authority to baptize in Iceland. On April 10, 1853, Johan P. Lorenzen of the Copenhagen Branch arrived to continue the missionary work. He organized a branch in Iceland on June 19, 1853. The Church has had only moderate success in Iceland.

Thus by 1853 the Church had gained a foothold in all the Scandinavian countries except Finland. In 1876, Carl August and John E. Sundström of the Stockholm Conference were called to Finland. They organized a small branch in Larsmo, under difficult conditions because of the lack of religious freedom. After having been ruled by Sweden for 600 years, Finland was a Russian Grand Duchy from 1809 until 1917, and the authorities confiscated LDS books and tracts. Post offices in Finland opened packages containing *Nordstjärnan*, the LDS Swedish publication, and sent the empty wrappers to subscribers with the explanation that no Mormon literature would be allowed into the country. In 1903 Elder Francis M. Lyman, an apostle, dedicated Finland for the preaching of the gospel, but it was not until after World War II that missionary work showed any significant success. C. Fritz Johansson and Karl Lagerberg were sent to Finland in May 1946, and Elder Ezra Taft BENSON, an apostle, rededicated the country on July 16, 1946, at Larsmo, where the

small branch had been established earlier. Henry A. Matis became the first MISSION PRESIDENT of the Finnish MISSION in August 1947. At the end of 1990 Finland had two stakes and one mission of the Church.

EMIGRATION. Since 1852, many Scandinavian members have emigrated to the United States. Particularly in the nineteenth century, poverty, starvation, persecution, and hopelessness motivated people to seek a better life and, for Latter-day Saints, the spirit of GATHERING to the "PROMISED LAND" in Utah was strong. There they could enjoy religious freedom and practice their religion without ridicule or harassment.

The Church in Western America has been significantly augmented by these immigrants. From 1850 to 1950, 27,000 members of record emigrated from Scandinavia. If unbaptized children under eight years of age were counted, the total would be much higher. A little more than half of these emigrants were Danish, a third Swedish, and the balance Norwegians. Emigrating Icelanders amounted to less than one percent. A 1950 survey concluded that about 45 percent of the Church membership was at least partly of Scandinavian descent.

CLASH OF CULTURES. To understand the environment in which early missionaries to Scandinavia found themselves, it is necessary to know that a strong liberal movement prevailed there in the mid-1800s. On June 5, 1849, only months before the first LDS missionaries came to Denmark, King Frederik VII signed the new Danish Constitution, which guaranteed the people freedom of speech, press, and religion. In Norway a Dissenter Law guaranteeing religious freedom to all Christian denominations was passed as early as 1845. As soon as Mormon missionaries began to proselytize in Norway, some of the clergy and public officials questioned whether Latter-day Saints could be considered Christians. On November 4, 1853, the Supreme Court of Norway ruled that Mormons could not enjoy protection under the Dissenter Law, and missionaries were arrested and fined for preaching, baptizing, or administering the SACRAMENT. Unable to pay, they had to go to jail, where they studied the SCRIPTURES, sang hymns, and taught the gospel to the jailers, who often were sympathetic and provided them with the best cells. In Sweden limited religious freedom was granted by law in 1858, but it was not until 1952 that the Church was given full legal religious freedom. For Scandinavians, PLURAL MARRIAGE was a real problem. It took a long time after the 1890 Manifesto (*see* Official Declaration—1) to convince the public that Mormons who lived their religion were law-abiding and hard-working citizens with strict moral principles. The right to exercise full religious freedom has come slowly to the Latter-day Saints in Scandinavia. But the resentment long prevalent among Scandinavian public officials and clergy has gradually turned into respect and, in some instances, into admiration for the Church, which can now legally pursue full worship and perform all its ORDINANCES in all the Scandinavian countries.

LANDMARK TRANSLATIONS. Using the standard translations of the Bible, the missionaries in Copenhagen realized the pressing need to have the Book of Mormon translated into Danish. Peter Olsen Hansen and Elder Snow's translation was printed by F. E. Bordings Bogtrykkeri in May 1851. This was the first foreign language edition of the Book of Mormon.

Because the Norwegians could read the Danish translation, the Book of Mormon was not translated into Norwegian until 1950. The first Swedish translation was published in 1878, the Finnish in 1954. Selected passages were published in Icelandic in 1981. The Doctrine and Covenants and the Pearl of Great Price have also been printed in all Scandinavian languages.

LOCAL PUBLICATIONS. Peter Olsen Hansen also wrote the first Mormon tract published in Scandinavia, *En Advarsel til Folket* (*A Warning to the People*). When Elder Snow arrived in June 1850, he wrote *A Voice of Truth*, which Hansen translated as *En Sandheds Røst*, which has seen many reprintings. *Skandinaviens Stjerne* (*The Scandinavian Star*), published in 1851, was the first official periodical of the Church in Scandinavia. It later became *Den Danske Stjerne* (*The Danish Star*), presently *Stjernen*. Comparable Norwegian and Finnish MAGAZINES, *Lys Over Norge* (*Light over Norway*) and *Valkeus*, were published monthly in 1990. The Swedish journal is called *Nordstjärnan* (*The North Star*). March 1851 saw publication of the first Danish LDS book of HYMNS.

GENERAL AUTHORITIES BORN IN SCANDINAVIA. Three native-born Scandinavians have become GENERAL AUTHORITIES of the Church. Anthon H.

Lund, born in Ålborg, Denmark, became an apostle (1889) and counselor in the FIRST PRESIDENCY (1903-1921). John A. Widtsoe, born at Daløe, Island of Fröya, Norway, was an apostle (1921-1952). And Christian D. Fjeldsted from Sundbyvester, Copenhagen, Denmark, was a member of the SEVENTY (1884-1905).

ORGANIZATION OF MISSIONS AND STAKES. Copenhagen became the center for the Church in Scandinavia as communication from Salt Lake City went through the Scandinavian Mission office located there. As membership increased, branches were organized into conferences. In 1900 the Scandinavian Mission consisted of sixty organized branches in nine conferences: three in Denmark (Copenhagen, Århus, and Ålborg), three in Sweden (Stockholm, Göteborg, and Skåne), and three in Norway (Christiania, Bergen, and Trondheim). Even after thousands of Saints had emigrated, Church membership in Scandinavia totaled 4,535, with 165 American missionaries. The Swedish Mission was divided from the original Scandinavian Mission on July 1, 1905, and the Norwegian Mission was organized on April 1, 1920.

In the fall of 1939, the American missionaries were withdrawn from Europe, and local leaders were made acting presidents over the missions: Orson B. West in Denmark, Olaf Sønsteby in Norway, and C. Fritz Johansson in Sweden. Even though Denmark and Norway were occupied by Germany from 1940 until 1945, the local members were able to continue Church activity. When the new American mission presidents arrived in 1945–1946, they found the missions to be in good condition in spite of the ravages of war.

On February 15, 1946, Elder Ezra Taft Benson began administering a relief program of food and clothing to Latter-day Saints in Scandinavia. Many members emigrated to the United States after World War II, and most were educated people who left good jobs to go to Zion. Yet, recent growth of the Church in all of the Scandinavian countries has led to organized stakes. The first stakes organized in each country are: the Copenhagen Denmark Stake on June 16, 1974; the Stockholm Sweden Stake on April 20, 1975; the Oslo Norway Stake on May 22, 1977; and the Helsinki Finland Stake on October 16, 1977.

THE STOCKHOLM SWEDEN TEMPLE. In 1985, the Church dedicated a temple in Västerhaninge, Sweden, eighteen miles south of Stockholm, with John and Edna Fluge Langeland, Norwegian-Americans, as TEMPLE PRESIDENT AND MATRON. Scandinavian members who have TEMPLE RECOMMENDS perform sacred TEMPLE ORDINANCES in their own languages there. It was the first place in Europe where Latter-day Saints could receive TEMPLE SEALINGS for time and eternity without first being married by civil authority. With stakes and wards in their countries and the temple in Västerhaninge, Scandinavian Latter-day Saints can enjoy the full program of the Church.

BIBLIOGRAPHY

Haslam, Gerald M. *Clash of Cultures: The Norwegian Experience with Mormonism, 1842–1920.* New York, 1984.

Jenson, Andrew. *History of the Scandinavian Mission.* Salt Lake City, 1927.

Mulder, William. "Mormons from Scandinavia 1850–1905." Ph.D. diss., Harvard University, 1955.

———. *Homeward to Zion: The Mormon Migration from Scandinavia.* Minneapolis, 1957.

Zobell, Albert L., Jr. *Under the Midnight Sun: Centennial History of Scandinavian Missions.* Salt Lake City, 1950.

JOHN LANGELAND

James J. Strang (1813–1856) asserted the right to lead the Church shortly after Joseph Smith's assassination in 1844 and attracted a group of followers.

SCHISMATIC GROUPS

Like any large religious body, The Church of Jesus Christ of Latter-day Saints has had a number of variously disaffected members break away. Some have taken a group of members with them and started rival organizations, based on their interpretations of the teachings of Joseph SMITH. There have been about 130 such groups; only a few have existed for more than ten years.

The first was known as the Pure Church of Christ, founded in 1831 by Wycam Clark, Northrop Sweet, and others. Asserting that Joseph Smith was a false prophet, Clark claimed that he was the true leader of the Church. The group held only two or three meetings and died out.

The most prominent schismatic group organized during Joseph Smith's lifetime was the Church of Christ, established by Warren Parrish in Kirtland, Ohio, in 1837. A few months earlier Parrish was accused of embezzling funds from the Church's bank, the Kirtland Safety Society, and was excommunicated. Alleging that Joseph had fallen from his divine calling as leader of the Church, Parrish claimed the authority to lead it.

He gained the support of three members of the Quorum of the Twelve Apostles, some of the presidents of the Seventies, and several other influential leaders who had become alienated from Smith during the 1837–1838 economic crisis in Kirtland. That group broke up in less than a year (*CHC* 1:403–407).

The death of Joseph Smith in 1844 produced another flurry of new groups seeking to take advantage of the loss of the Church's leader. There were people in these organizations who agreed that Joseph Smith had been a true prophet, although many of them rejected or ignored some of the doctrines or practices he had established; the question in their minds was who was to take his place.

Joseph's counselor in the First Presidency, Sidney RIGDON, was one of the first to press his claim, telling the Saints that there could be no successor to Joseph Smith and that he should be named guardian of the Church, to watch over it in Joseph's name and build it up to the memory of the slain prophet. His claim was rejected by most members, who sustained Brigham YOUNG and the

Quorum of the Twelve Apostles. Rigdon was excommunicated, and he returned to Pittsburgh, Pennsylvania, where he established the Church of Christ, which lasted less than two years. In 1863 he organized the Church of Jesus Christ of the Children of Zion. This group lasted into the 1880s.

In August 1844, James J. Strang, converted only a few months before Joseph Smith's death, produced a letter supposedly from Joseph Smith appointing Strang to lead the flock (see FORGERIES), and claimed that an angel had appeared to him shortly after the martyrdom and ordained him to that calling. Strang was immediately excommunicated. A few weeks later, he moved with a group of converts to Voree, Wisconsin, the area he claimed as the new gathering place for the church. His followers included two apostles, John E. Page and William Smith (younger brother of Joseph Smith), and William Marks, former president of the Nauvoo Stake. For a short time, Martin HARRIS accompanied a Strangite leader on a mission to England.

Strang moved his group to Beaver Island, a small island in northern Lake Michigan, where in 1850 Strang was crowned king in an elaborate ceremony. There he established a theocracy that thrived for most of the decade with an estimated 3,000 members; he also continued the practice of PLURAL MARRIAGE. On June 16, 1856, two assassins, part of a larger conspiracy, shot Strang; he did not appoint a successor before he died eleven days later. His group was broken up by the combined action of federal and local forces, and the majority was forcibly exiled from the island. A small remnant of Strang's order, however, still exists in Wisconsin, Michigan, Colorado, and New Mexico (Van Noord, pp. 48–177, 233–66; Lewis, pp. 274–91).

A move toward creating a larger reorganization began early in the 1850s. Some former Strangites, including William Marks, Jason Briggs, and Zenas H. Gurley, met in 1850 to decide on a new leader. Briggs and Gurley had been members of William Smith's group, called the Church of Jesus Christ of Latter Day Saints, which had been organized in 1846 after the excommunication of William Smith from the Strangites. Marks, Briggs, and Gurley were convinced that succession in the presidency of the Church must be lineal, descending from father to son. In an intense proselytizing effort, they drew to them a number of other Mormons and former Mormons in the Midwest of the same idea. A group met in Beloit, Wisconsin, on June 12–13, 1852, to organize. In 1853 they held another conference and apostles were chosen. In 1859 Joseph Smith III formally accepted the call to become the new president and prophet, and in April 1860 the group formally incorporated under the name of the REORGANIZED CHURCH OF JESUS CHRIST OF LATTER DAY SAINTS. Most of Joseph Smith, Jr.'s immediate family joined this church in the early 1860s, and many descendants remain active members today (Launius, pp. 77–139).

Other groups broke away during Brigham Young's administration in Utah. One of the most significant was the Godbeites, organized in 1868 under the leadership of William S. Godbe. Several years earlier, Godbe had joined with E. L. T. Harrison, Edward W. Tullidge, Eli B. Kelsey, William H. Shearman, and other disaffected Mormon businessmen and intellectuals to protest the economic self-sufficiency policy of Brigham Young. Godbe and his group favored a less structured society, free trade inside Utah Territory, and open trade with the outside world. Their social protest soon developed into a thorough rejection of doctrine and practice. They discarded all of the Church's theological structure, claiming loyalty to no single prophet or set of scriptures. Instead, they proclaimed the universal brotherhood of man and the universal love of God. This led to involvement with the Spiritualist movement, popular in the nineteenth century. They participated in a number of séances, in the belief that they were speaking with deceased LDS Church leaders, Jesus Christ, and the ancient apostles. The Salt Lake Stake High Council excommunicated Godbe and Harrison on October 25, 1869. Others in the group eventually brought on their own excommunication. In 1870 they formally organized the Church of Zion, an openly anti-Mormon organization, both religiously and economically, which founded the *Salt Lake Tribune*. The movement failed to attract many new followers and died out by 1880 (Walker, 1974, 1982).

Other splinter groups have followed from time to time, especially following the termination of plural marriage in 1890 (for further discussion *see* FUNDAMENTALISTS).

BIBLIOGRAPHY

Anderson, C. LeRoy. *For Christ Will Come Tomorrow: The Saga of the Morrisites*. Logan, Utah, 1981.

Carter, Kate B. *Denominations That Base Their Beliefs on the Teachings of Joseph Smith*. Salt Lake City, 1969.

Launius, Roger D. *Joseph Smith III: Pragmatic Prophet.* Urbana, Ill., 1988.

Lewis, David Rich. "'For Life, the Resurrection, and the Life Everlasting': James J. Strang and Strangite Mormon Polygamy, 1849–1856." *Wisconsin Magazine of History* 66 (Summer 1983):274–91.

Morgan, Dale L. *Bibliographies of the Lesser Mormon Churches.* Salt Lake City, n.d.

Rich, Russell R. *Those Who Would Be Leaders: Offshoots of Mormonism.* Provo, Utah, 1959.

Shields, Steven L. *Divergent Paths of the Restoration: A History of the Latter Day Saint Movement,* 3rd ed. Bountiful, Utah, 1982.

Van Noord, Roger. *King of Beaver Island: The Life and Assassination of James Jesse Strang.* Urbana, Ill., 1988.

Walker, Ronald W. "The Commencement of the Godbeite Protest: Another View." *Utah Historical Quarterly* 42 (Summer 1974):216–44.

———. "When the Spirits Did Abound: Nineteenth-Century Utah's Encounter with Free-Thought Radicalism." *Utah Historical Quarterly* 50 (Fall 1982):304–324.

MARTIN S. TANNER

SCHOOLS

LDS theology places great importance on the acquiring of knowledge. This knowledge includes not only religious truth but truth in the sciences, arts, and humanities as well (*TPJS*, p. 217; D&C 131:6). Congruent with that value and throughout its history, the Church has established and operated numerous schools and universities to provide educational opportunities for its members.

Comprehensive higher education is offered at Brigham Young University (campuses at Provo, Utah; Laie, Hawaii; and Jerusalem, Israel) and Ricks College in Rexburg, Idaho. Correspondence study is also available at the secondary, college, and adult education levels through Brigham Young University. The LDS Business College in Salt Lake City offers postsecondary instruction in business and related fields. Full-time primary and secondary schools currently are owned and administered by the Church in the South Pacific and Mexico, providing education to approximately 10,000 students.

In the Pacific islands, two high schools, one large elementary school, and four meetinghouse elementary schools are operated in Samoa, two high schools in Tonga, one technical college and one elementary school in Fiji, one high school in Kiribati, and the Church College of New Zealand

Church College of New Zealand, in Hamilton (c. 1960), is one of the schools owned and administered by the Church.

in Hamilton. Initially established to provide an educational opportunity for the Maori people, the college in New Zealand presently is a high school with college preparatory courses. Local teachers are hired on a full-time basis, and in a few cases full-time missionary couples with educational experience also provide instruction.

In Mexico City, the Benemerito campus offers secondary education (the last two years are college preparatory) and is the largest of all primary and secondary schools in the Church (2,300 students). The Juarez Academy in Juarez, Mexico, provides a high school education, and is the only remaining academy of those established between 1875 and 1911 (*see* ACADEMIES).

The Church's schooling enterprises arose in response to concerns over the secularization of the schools, the need for trained teachers for public schools and trained leadership in the Church, LDS youth's participation in other denominational schools, and youth leaving home for their schooling. The establishment of schools, and subsequently an educational system, drew the Church into a relationship with state public school systems in the United States. This relationship divides into five periods:

ORIGINS (1830–1846). Educational efforts were hampered by frequent and difficult moves from New York to Kirtland, Ohio, to Missouri, to Nauvoo, Illinois, and finally, to the Great Basin. As was customary in the frontier, most education was provided at home by parents teaching their children the basic skills of literacy and a general understanding of the scriptures and religious values. As early as 1831 efforts were made to collect and write books for schools (D&C 55:4); subsequently, some formal schools were established. Most prominent among these was the SCHOOL OF THE PROPHETS, established first in KIRTLAND, OHIO, in 1833, involving fewer than twenty-five adults in instruction intended to prepare them for religious MISSIONS and other assignments. Subjects taught included geography, English grammar, Hebrew, literature, philosophy, politics, and theology. Later, in Illinois in 1841, a system of LDS common schools and the University of the City of Nauvoo were established under the direction of the University of Nauvoo Board of Regents. Tuitions and a basic child and adult curriculum were established, but the program's objectives were largely unrealized as persecution forced the families to move to the West.

EARLY UTAH PERIOD (1847–1869). The first schools in Utah were conducted in tents and log huts. At the outset, schools were taught by private teachers who advertised, charged fees, and gathered a few students around them. The UNIVERSITY OF DESERET was established in 1850 in Salt Lake City to train teachers for schools; however, it survived only two years because few could afford to pay tuition. For the next twenty years, schools throughout the state were held primarily in Church meetinghouses, loosely organized on ecclesiastical lines, sparsely financed by member tuition, and sometimes by Church supplements, or local tax funds in the late 1860s. Church leaders encouraged parents to send their children to school and pay the tuition, usually a few cents per week. The children, however, often worked with their families on farms and ranches and could attend classes only intermittently. Church–state relationships were not an issue because no government-sponsored territorial school system existed at the time. The curriculum reflected Church belief. Most materials, however, had to be imported from the East, and teachers generally lacked formal credentials. Often they were only slightly more knowledgeable than their students.

PROTESTANT–MORMON RIVALRY (1869–1890). The period was initiated with the establishment of St. Mark's Episcopal School in Salt Lake City in 1867. Catholics, Presbyterians, Methodists, Baptists, Lutherans, and Congregationalists soon followed with their own schools, especially after the completion of the railroad in 1869. Their object was not only to serve their own people but also to convert the Latter-day Saint children attending their schools, although few were converted. Many LDS students did attend, however, because the quality of education they offered was often superior to what Latter-day Saint residents could provide in their own schools. The establishment by non-LDS territorial school officials of a tax-supported public school system in 1890 with its prohibition of sectarian religious teaching and administration initiated the demise of de facto Church influence in most of the schooling. For a time afterwards, the Church sought to maintain its own school system by establishing secondary school academies modeled after the Brigham Young Academy. Eventually, however, other sources of education became available, the expense of providing education became prohibitive, and the Church relinquished its efforts to provide a comprehensive system of education for all its members.

ESTABLISHMENT OF SUPPLEMENTAL RELIGIOUS EDUCATION CLASSES (1890–1953). The Church initiated a policy of providing released time religious instruction concurrent with the regular offerings of the state public education system. Beginning in the 1920s, Church academies, or high schools, were either discontinued or turned over to the state. Some academies that had achieved junior college status were sold to the state in the 1930s.

GROWTH AND EXPANSION (1953–1990). During this period, seminaries and institutes were established in all fifty states and many foreign countries. Much of this growth was realized because of decisions not to build additional universities or junior colleges, and to endeavor to establish schools where educational opportunities could not be provided by the local government. Currently owned schools were maintained only until the time that local government could assume responsibility. Schools in Indonesia, Chile, Tahiti, American Samoa, and Mexico were closed as improved public school programs became more available to members of the Church in those countries. In 1965, the Church schools outside the United States administratively became part of the Unified Church School System. Presently, the schools are administered separately from the institutions of higher education.

BIBLIOGRAPHY

Arrington, Leonard J. "The Latter-Day Saints and Public Education." *Southwestern Journal of Social Education* 7 1977:9–25.

Bennion, Milton Lynn. *Mormonism and Education.* Salt Lake City, 1939.

Clark, James R. "Church and State Relationships in Education in Utah." Ph.D. diss., Utah State University, 1958.

Moffit, John C. *The History of Public Education in Utah.* Salt Lake City, 1946.

Palmer, Spencer J. "Educating the Saints." In *The Expanding Church.* Salt Lake City, 1978.

A. GARR CRANNEY

SCHOOLS OF THE PROPHETS

Between 1833 and 1884, Church leaders from time to time organized schools for instructing members in Church doctrine and secular subjects and for discussing political and social issues relevant to the Church's mission. Although they varied greatly in form and purpose, these schools were called Schools of the Prophets, or sometimes Schools of the Elders.

The first such school met on January 23, 1833, in Kirtland, Ohio, in response to a revelation (D&C 88:119–33) instructing the Church to prepare priesthood members to carry the gospel to the world. Following prayer and an outpouring of spiritual gifts, the Prophet Joseph SMITH invited each man present to receive the ordinance of washing of feet and a blessing. They ended their daylong fast by partaking of the Lord's Supper, after which they sang a hymn and were dismissed.

The School of the Prophets met in Kirtland through the winter and early spring of 1833, usually in a room above Newel K. WHITNEY'S STORE. Joseph Smith presided, and Orson Hyde was the instructor. Enrollment was limited to selected priesthood holders and probably never exceeded twenty-five. In accordance with the revelation about the school, members were initiated through the washing of feet, then reaffirmed their commitment and mutual goodwill by exchanging a formal salutation at the commencement of each class. School usually convened at sunrise and dismissed in late afternoon. Instruction focused on scripture and doctrine, though some time was devoted to secular topics such as grammar. During the February 27, 1833, meeting, Joseph Smith received the revelation known as the WORD OF WISDOM (D&C 89), which thereafter was binding upon members of the school.

The school ended in April 1833, when spring weather permitted active missionary work to begin, and never reconvened. Instead, a series of educational efforts expanded on the original idea and took on added responsibilities. Two of these later schools, known as the School of the Elders or School of the Prophets, convened in Jackson County, Missouri, during the summer of 1833 and in Kirtland, Ohio, from late fall to early spring in 1834–1835 and 1835–1836. These had larger enrollments than the first School of the Prophets and, in addition to the spiritual preparation of priesthood members, taught students an expanded secular curriculum, including penmanship, English, Hebrew, grammar, arithmetic, philosophy, literature, government, geography, and history. These later schools did not observe the earlier initiation rite and formalized salutation. Parley P. Pratt led the Missouri school, and Joseph Smith, Sidney Rigdon, Frederick G. Williams, and William E. McLellan taught in Kirtland. During the 1834–1835 school year, students in Kirtland heard the lectures later published in the Doctrine and Covenants as the LECTURES ON FAITH.

Following the closure of the School of the Elders in 1836, the School of the Prophets did not meet again until the Church moved west. In December 1867, President Brigham Young reorganized the School of the Prophets in connection with the University of Deseret. The Church's First Presidency presided over a theological class of ecclesiastical officers and selected priesthood holders that served as a forum for the discussion of questions related to the spiritual and temporal concerns of the Church. The class later separated from the University, and branch classes were established in major LDS communities throughout the Intermountain West. Total enrollment eventually exceeded 1,000 members. Locally elected priest-hood leaders presided over meetings of active priesthood members in discussions of religious, civic, and economic issues as well as of the spiritual and temporal concerns of the Church. Meetings were confidential, and admission was by tickets given to an invited membership.

President Brigham Young dissolved these branches of the Schools of the Prophets late in the summer of 1872 and then reorganized in November 1872 a Salt Lake City School of the Prophets for General Authorities and other invited priest-hood leaders. Participants numbering more than 200 discussed theology and also temporal concerns. This school helped introduce cooperative enterprises into LDS communities. When united order organizations were incorporated in the spring and summer of 1874 to facilitate economic cooperation, the Salt Lake City School of the Prophets dissolved and some of its functions were absorbed by local united orders.

President John Taylor, who succeeded Brigham Young as Church President, reconvened the School of the Prophets in the fall of 1883. Inviting Church General Authorities and a select group of other Church leaders to participate, President Taylor followed the ceremonies of the original school. A branch of the school was established in St. George, Utah, in December 1883. These schools probably ceased to operate in early 1884, with no subsequent attempt by the Church to organize further Schools of the Prophets.

BIBLIOGRAPHY

Backman, Milton V., Jr. *The Heaven's Resound: A History of the Latter-day Saints in Ohio 1830–1838.* Salt Lake City, 1983.

Cook, Lyndon W. *The Revelations of the Prophet Joseph Smith: A Historical and Biographical Commentary of the Doctrine and Covenants.* Provo, Utah, 1981.

Patrick, John R. "The School of the Prophets: Its Development and Influence in Utah Territory." Master's thesis, Brigham Young University, 1970.

STEVEN R. SORENSEN

SCIENCE AND RELIGION

Because of belief in the ultimate compatibility of all truth and in the eternal character of human knowledge, Latter-day Saints tend to take a more positive approach to science than do some people in other religious traditions who also claim a strong foundation in scripture. The LDS experience includes encounters between religious belief and the natural sciences in three broad areas. For the most part, LDS responses to discoveries in American antiquities and New World archaeology have been enthusiastic, but sometimes cautious, as these findings are thought to have some potential for expanding contemporary understanding of the ancient BOOK OF MORMON PEOPLES and BOOK OF MORMON GEOGRAPHY. Latter-day Saints have often been defensive toward, though they have not necessarily rejected, developments in geology and the biological sciences that bear on the nature of the Creation and the age of the earth (*see* EVOLUTION; ORIGIN OF MAN). The revelations to Joseph Smith of an Abrahamic ASTRONOMY and three creation accounts, having some variation, have also stimulated positive interest in astronomical and cosmological issues. In particular, these revelations affirmed the plurality of worlds and heliocentrism in the scriptural writings of ancient prophets. Historical, scientific, philosophical, and theological factors have tempered discussions of science and religion in the LDS context.

Conceptions of scientific knowledge have changed many times since Greek antiquity. Thus, for example, modern understanding of the nature of the cosmos has changed radically from Aristotle in early Greece; to Galileo, Descartes, and Newton in the seventeenth century; to Lyell and Darwin in the nineteenth century; and in the twentieth century to Einstein, Hubble, and Hawking. Science itself continues in a state of constant flux, so that the total collection of scientific ideas at any point in time could never be considered final truth. Consequently, scientific theories are forever tentative and are not likely to be fully compatible with revealed religion at any particular time.

Realizing this, scholars today recognize that older descriptions of "conflict" or open "warfare" between science and Christianity are often mistaken. Nor could LDS thinking about science be described in this way. The Church is distinguished by its acceptance of ongoing revelation and the view that divine revelation underlies its scriptures and teachings. Consequently, Latter-day Saints assume that ultimate truths about religious matters and about God's creations can never be in conflict, as God is the author of both. They look forward to a time when more complete knowledge in both areas will transcend all present perceptions of conflict.

As early revelations to Joseph Smith seemed to invite reflections on the nature of the universe and the place of human beings in it, Latter-day Saints came to reflect the kind of optimism about a future reconciliation of science and religion that characterized many of their contemporaries. As positive ideas and attitudes about the compatibility of science and religion emerged with growing confidence among Latter-day Saints, many began to use the theories and observations of science to support their religious beliefs. Two main reasons for this appear to be that (1) LDS THEOLOGY is philosophically committed to a positive conception of "true" science, and (2) Latter-day Saints could invoke science in partial support of the revealed world of the RESTORATION (true religion).

These LDS appeals to science are distinct from the traditional Christian efforts in natural theology, which assumed that science can lead to a theology of nature in which science and Christianity are compatible. While individual Latter-day Saints freely invoke philosophical arguments and scientific evidences to affirm religious claims, these have never been considered official or conclusive. Latter-day Saints tend to be dubious of natural theology because the existence and nature of God can be known only through revelation, not through speculative theology.

Several basic Church teachings combine to provide additional support for a positive attitude toward science. Because God governs his creations through the laws of nature, of which he is the author, science is perceived as one important means of gaining understanding of his governance. Furthermore, LDS scriptures teach that "the glory of God is intelligence, or, in other words, light and truth" (D&C 93:36) and that the knowledge and intelligence gained in this life will be an advantage in the next (D&C 130:18–19). Finally, Latter-day Saints also use pragmatic and empiricological methods as legitimate means of gaining knowledge. They believe God expects them to use all forms of knowledge, including the revelatory and the scientific. Yet, revelation is always primary, and there is little sympathy among Latter-day Saints for the emphasis on science that leads to a rejection of scripturally based understanding.

While LDS publications from 1832 to the Nauvoo exodus in 1846 occasionally examined scientific ideas, extensive use and discussion of scientific themes did not emerge until the 1850s. Early Latter-day Saint speculations on science were set forth occasionally in conference addresses and published in the *Journal of Discourses*, the *Millennial Star*, and in the writings of apostles Parley P. PRATT and Orson PRATT. For example, Orson Pratt, the first LDS science-philosopher, wrote in 1873 that "the great temple of science must be erected upon the solid foundations of everlasting truth; its towering spires must mount upward, reaching higher and still higher, until crowned with the glory and presence of Him, who is Eternal" (*Deseret News* 22 [1873]:586).

Beginning in the 1890s, positive LDS speculations on science generally, and specifically in such fields as astronomy, cosmology, evolution, geology, and paleontology, while not always harmonious, drew on the ideas of the first academically trained LDS scientists (and later General Authorities) James E. Talmage, John A. Widtsoe, Joseph F. Merrill, and Richard R. Lyman. All four of these highly influential apostles used their scientific expertise to further the view that "correct" science and revealed religion are in close harmony because the author of both is God. Thus, Talmage asked rhetorically, "What is the field of science?" His answer: "Everything. Science is the discourse of nature and nature is the visible declaration of Divine Will. . . . There is naught so small, so vast that science takes no cognizance thereof. . . . Nature is the scientist's copy and truth his chief aim" (c. 1895). "Among our young people," Talmage wrote elsewhere, "I consider scientific knowledge as second in importance only to that knowledge that pertains to the Church and Kingdom of God. . . . Nature, as we study it, is but the temple of the Almighty" (c. 1900).

In 1930, Widtsoe wrote:

> Science . . . is the recognition by the mind through human senses of the realities of existence. The mind of man is a noble instrument, a pre-eminent possession, by which he becomes conscious, not only of his own existence, but of the conditions of external nature. . . . The glory of physical conquests, of the sea and earth and air, have often dazzled men to such a degree that they have forgotten that back of all discovery and progress is the power of observation and thought. Without mind, there is no science, no progress, only extinction [*In Search of Truth* (Salt Lake City, 1930), pp. 36–37].

Later, in *Evidences and Reconciliations*, one of Widtsoe's most widely known books, he wrote, "The Church supports and welcomes the growth of science. . . . The religion of the Latter-day Saints is not hostile to any truth, nor to scientific search for truth" (Vol. 1, p. 129).

Other (non-scientist) Church authorities, principally Joseph Fielding SMITH, writing in the first half of the twentieth century, and later Bruce R. McConkie, vigorously criticized the ideas of some that the scriptures could be reconciled with scientific theories, in particular, evolutionary accounts of the origin of man.

Talmage, Widtsoe, and B. H. Roberts, writing in the first half of the twentieth century, probably have contributed more than any other LDS authorities—with the possible exception of the Pratt brothers—after the initial years of Church growth to scientific topics and their assumed general harmony with the gospel. That this attitude continues and is presently sustained within the larger Latter-day Saint culture, particularly among LDS scientists, is also supported by recent studies that suggest that the LDS community has produced more scientists per capita than most religious groups in twentieth-century America (*see* SCIENCE AND SCIENTISTS).

BIBLIOGRAPHY

The finest scholarly examination of the complex relation between the natural sciences and religion from the Middle Ages to the twentieth century can be found in David Lindberg and Ronald Numbers, eds., *God and Nature: Historical Essays on the Encounter Between Christianity and Science* (Berkeley, Calif., 1986). For a discussion of numerous issues dealing with science and the LDS Church by prominent LDS scientists and authorities, including Henry Eyring, Carl J. Christensen, Harvey Fletcher, Franklin S. Harris, Joseph F. Merrill, Frederick J. Pack, and John A. Widtsoe, see Henry Eyring et al., *Science and Your Faith in God* (Salt Lake City, 1958). For a discussion by LDS scientists affirming the compatibility of their faith and their fields of specialty, see Wilford M. Hess, Raymond T. Matheny, and Donlu D. Thayer, eds., *Science and Religion: Toward a More Useful Dialogue*, 2 vols. (Geneva, Ill., 1979). On the issue of American antiquities, see John Sorenson, *An Ancient American Setting for the Book of Mormon* (Salt Lake City, 1985). For a review of issues dealing with evolution and geology, respectively, see Duane E. Jeffery, "Seers, Savants and Evolution: The Uncomfortable Interface," *Dialogue* 8 (Autumn–Winter 1973):41–75, and Morris S. Petersen, "[Fossils and Scriptures]," *Ensign* 17 (Sept. 1987):28–29. For an extensive examination of science and cosmology and their relationship to LDS theology, see Erich Robert Paul, *Science, Religion, and Mormon Cosmology* (Champaign, Ill., 1991).

ERICH ROBERT PAUL

SCIENCE AND SCIENTISTS

In a world where science and religion have sometimes been at odds, Latter-day Saints stand out for their positive attitudes toward science and their high proportion of involvement in scientific careers. Active scientists are often called to positions of Church leadership, and a number of LDS scientists have been internationally recognized for scientific work. With Church sponsorship, Brigham Young University maintains sizable programs in most scientific fields of study and supports significant research in many of these. The positive attitude toward science is often attributed to distinctive theological beliefs.

In the nineteenth century, some Latter-day Saints showed great interest in science, but none were broadly known as practicing scientists. Their experience in those early decades included constantly moving from place to place, struggling with persecution and economic loss, carrying the message of the restored gospel to the nations of the earth, and establishing new communities on the American frontier. While this life afforded little opportunity to become professional scientists, several pursued their scientific interests as they were able, including Orson Pratt's early establishment of an observatory in Salt Lake City. Distinctive cultural factors present from the earliest years eventually led Latter-day Saints to pursue careers in science in large numbers.

Harvey Fletcher (1884–1981), physicist. Courtesy Stephen Fletcher.

The commitment to education and the pursuit of truth was reinforced by teachings of early Church leaders and specifically by revelations received by Joseph Smith. One statement based on revelation explains that "whatever principle of intelligence we attain unto in this life, it will rise with us in the resurrection" (D&C 130:18). Another scripture asserts that "all things are created and made to bear record of me, . . . things which are in the heavens above, and things which are on the earth, and things which are in the earth: . . . all things bear record of me" (Moses 6:63). Thus, for many Latter-day Saints, the pursuit of scientific knowledge is a religious quest.

Latter-day Saints also teach that God created all things using laws natural to his environment; that the natural world is a world of pattern, law, order, and meaning; and that men and women possess the ability to discover truth and to use that knowledge to improve the world in which they live. Because they believe that God works by law, the study of the world can also be seen as a study of the divine. From this perspective they see themselves as coworkers with God in improving the human condition. These same ambitions are reinforced by the instillation of the value of hard work and the idea that all men and women are responsible to the larger society as well as to their immediate families. Further support for scientific activity can be found in repeated encouragement to young people to work for long-term goals and to leave the world a better place than they found it. These indirect sources of encouragement for scientific endeavor are often supplements by LDS leaders teaching that God reveals certain truths through scientific research and not alone through prophets. President Brigham Young claimed that "God has revealed all the truth that is now in the possession of the world, whether it be scientific or religious. The whole world [is] under obligation to him for what they know and enjoy; they are indebted to him for it all" (JD 8:162).

As the LDS community stabilized and became part of mainstream America in the twentieth century, these attitudes began to bear fruit in scientific endeavor. A 1940 study established that Utah led all other states in the number of scientific men born there in proportion to the population (Thorndike, pp. 138–39). A thorough analysis of state-by-state contributions to science from 1920 to 1960 found that Utah led all other states by a wide margin in the proportion of its university graduates who eventually received doctoral degrees in sci-

Henry Eyring (1901–1981), chemist. Courtesy Special Collections Department, University of Utah Libraries.

ence (Hardy, p. 499). Unpublished research indicates that this high productivity continued through the 1970s, though Utah dropped to second place among the fifty. It is generally recognized that the high percentage of Latter-day Saints in Utah largely accounts for Utah's distinctiveness in these studies. Researchers find that the LDS beliefs described above correlate strongly with positive attitudes toward science, as they also distinguish Latter-day Saints in this regard from most other Christian groups.

A number of LDS apostles and other General Authorities have been scientists. Even in the earliest decades, Orson Pratt demonstrated exceptional interest and competence in his scientific avocations; his contributions were highly valued by the Mormon people. Later, in the frontier period, individual Latter-day Saints began to pursue formal scientific studies, first by correspondence courses, and later by traveling out of the state for enrollment in scientific institutions. James E. Talmage graduated from Lehigh University and studied at

Johns Hopkins University before completing a Ph.D. through correspondence work at Illinois Wesleyan University. He undertook pioneering geological studies on the Great Salt Lake before his call to the apostleship in 1911. John A. Widtsoe studied biochemistry at Harvard University and in 1899 received a Ph.D. in chemistry from Göttingen University in Germany. Joseph F. Merrill received his Ph.D. in physics from Johns Hopkins University in 1899. These three succeeded one another in the European mission presidency and contributed a great deal to the enthusiasm for scientific thinking among Latter-day Saints in the first half of the twentieth century. The rise of European ideologies that embraced science and technology while rejecting Christian values led them to a more cautious endorsement of scientific realism in later years.

Examples of prominent LDS scientists in the mid-twentieth century include chemist Henry Eyring and physicists Harvey Fletcher and Willard Gardner. Eyring pioneered the application of quantum mechanics to chemistry and developed the Absolute Rate Theory of chemical reactions, for which he received the National Medal of Science. He was elected president of the American Chemical Society (1963) and of the American Association for the Advancement of Science (1965). Fletcher directed research at Bell Labs, where he played a central role in the development of stereophonic reproduction. He was elected president of the American Physical Society (1945). The American Society of Agronomy cited Gardner as "the father of soil physics" for his descriptions of the movement of water through unsaturated soils by reference to capillary potential. The number of Latter-day Saints significantly involved in scientific pursuits continued to grow throughout the twentieth century.

Two apostles were called in the 1980s from careers in medicine and engineering. Russell M. Nelson, a prominent heart surgeon, received a Ph.D. in surgery from the University of Minnesota for his research on gram negative bacterial toxinemia. Richard G. Scott used his degree in mechanical engineering as a base for advanced studies at the Oak Ridge laboratory in Tennessee and a career in nuclear engineering.

Like people in other religious traditions, the Latter-day Saints have also discovered scriptural reasons for some ambivalence toward modern science. In some instances, prominent Church leaders have voiced strong skepticism about science in general and about certain theories of psychology, evolutionary biology, and astronomy in particular. Some have suggested that a number of these scientific ideas are incompatible with the scriptures and the basic doctrines of the Church. Others have proposed ways to reconcile these and have emphasized the ultimate compatibility of all truth, whether revealed to prophets or discovered by scientists.

The Church's governing councils have consistently refrained from being drawn into official discussions of such matters. Early-twentieth-century controversies over biological EVOLUTION did stimulate formal statements from the First Presidency. But these were carefully drawn to avoid dampening legitimate scientific activity while clearly articulating and defending basic doctrinal positions of the Church. Church leaders and scientists have repeatedly noted the essentially tentative character of scientific theorizing and experimentation and have emphasized the necessity of divine revelation for sure guidance in their lives. Similarly, scriptures have been frequently invoked to indicate that religious understanding also is incomplete and that additional revelation is both expected and necessary (D&C 101:32–34; A of F 9). Such statements have reminded Latter-day Saints that both science and revealed religion are continually building toward greater understanding of truth.

[See also Intellectual History; Matter; Metaphysics.]

BIBLIOGRAPHY

Eyring, Henry. The Faith of a Scientist. Salt Lake City, 1967.

Hardy, Kenneth R. "Social Origins of American Scientists and Scholars." Science 185 (Aug. 9, 1974):497–506.

Hess, Wilford M., and Raymond T. Matheny, eds. Science and Religion: Toward a More Useful Dialogue. Geneva, Ill., 1979.

Green, Paul R., comp. Science and Your Faith in God. Essays by Henry Eyring, Harvey Fletcher, and others. Salt Lake City, 1958.

Merrill, Joseph E. The Truth-Seeker and Mormonism: A Series of Radio Addresses. Independence, Mo., 1946.

Pack, Frederick J. Science and Belief in God. Salt Lake City, 1924.

Paul, Erich Robert. Science, Religion, and Mormon Cosmology. Champaign, Ill., 1991.

Rich, Wendell O. Distinctive Teachings of the Restoration. Salt Lake City, 1962.

Talmage, James E. "The Earth and Man." Speech printed in Deseret News, Nov. 21, 1931, pp. 7–8. Reprinted in Instructor 100 (Dec. 1965):474–77 and 101 (Jan. 1966):9–11, 15.

Thorndike, E. L. "The Production, Retention and Attraction of American Men of Science." *Science* 92 (Aug. 16, 1940):137–41.

Widtsoe, John A. *Joseph Smith as Scientist: A Contribution to "Mormon" Philosophy*, 2nd ed. Salt Lake City, 1920.

———. *In Search of Truth: Comments on the Gospel and Modern Thought*. Salt Lake City, 1930.

———. *Evidences and Reconciliations*, arr. by G. H. Durham, 3 vols. Salt Lake City, 1960.

ROBERT L. MILLER

SCOUTING

The Boy Scout movement began in England under the guidance of Lord Robert Baden-Powell in 1909. It appeared in the United States early in 1910 as the Boy Scouts of America (BSA), where a variety of churches used its programs as a part of their ministries to youth and families. After investigating the new scouting movement, the Young Men's Mutual Improvement Association (YMMIA) of The Church of Jesus Christ of Latter-day Saints organized the MIA Scouts on November 29, 1911, with the intent to provide worthwhile leisure time and athletic activities for its young men. On May 21, 1913, the MIA Scouts, upon invitation from the National Council, became part of the BSA.

Under YMMIA direction, this program moved rapidly forward in the Church. In 1928 Church leaders designated scouting as the activity program for the DEACONS and TEACHERS of the AARONIC PRIESTHOOD and transferred its administration to the PRESIDING BISHOPRIC.

In that same year the Vanguard program was developed by the Church for young men older than Boy Scout age. In 1949 Cub Scouting was officially adopted by the Church, and the PRIMARY

Mutual Improvement Association (MIA) Scout Band in front of the LDS Church Office Building, c. 1917. The Boy Scouts of America was organized in 1910. Inspired by this movement, the Church organized the MIA Scouts in 1911 and became one of the first sponsoring organizations of Boy Scouts of America in 1913. Courtesy Utah State Historical Society.

organization was asked to administer scouting for boys under twelve years of age, with boys eight to eleven as Cub Scouts and eleven-year-old boys as Boy Scouts of the Blazer Patrol. In 1959 the Vanguard program was replaced by the Explorer Scout program, designed by the Church for older boys and later adopted by BSA for use throughout the United States.

Over time the Church's scouting program for older boys was divided into the Explorer program, for young men age sixteen through eighteen, and the Venturer program, for those fourteen and fifteen. The Venturer program was eventually replaced with the nationwide BSA "Varsity Scout" program.

In 1977 responsibility within the Church for the scouting program was transferred from the Presiding Bishopric to the newly organized Young Men Presidency, which has operated since that time under the direction of the QUORUM OF THE TWELVE APOSTLES.

As scouting evolved, the Church adopted scouting programs in the United States that correspond with specific age groups and Aaronic PRIESTHOOD QUORUMS. Currently those programs include Boy Scouts for deacons quorum members,

An LDS sponsored scout troop at the Evergreen Boy Scout Camp, Uinta Mountains, Utah, 1986. The Church sponsors more Boy Scout units than any other single sponsor in the world. Courtesy Craig Law.

Varsity Scouts for teachers quorum members, and Explorer Scouts for PRIESTS quorum members. In each case, the scouting program serves as a part of the activity program for the Aaronic Priesthood quorum.

Although scouting has become an integral part of the Church's activity program for young men in the United States, it is less prominent in Church units in other countries. Many Scouting organizations throughout the world follow principles and policies incompatible with Church standards. As a result, the Church authorizes WARDS and BRANCHES to associate only with scouting programs affiliated with the World Scouting Organization. In countries where this organization operates, Church units are urged to affiliate with, and develop, full scouting programs. Because scouting institutions are rare in Western Europe, the Church there has developed its own scouting organization, known as Aaronic Priesthood Scouting, as part of the activity program for the Aaronic Priesthood.

Wards and branches in the United States sponsor scouting units as part of their Aaronic Priesthood program. As a result, the Church has for years led all other organizations, religious and otherwise, in the total number of scouting units sponsored by any one chartered organization. In 1990 the Church registered 24,560 scouting units with BSA. During that same year, the public schools sponsored 16,543 units; the United Methodist Church, 11,179 units; and the Roman Catholic Church and affiliations, 9,530. The public schools enrolled 1,096,914 scouts; the Roman Catholic Church, 298,997; and the United Methodist Church, 333,086. The Latter-day Saints enrolled 342,156 scouts and 139,557 adult leaders that year.

Church leaders have taken an active role in BSA affairs at the national level as well as in Church scouting. Most of the PRESIDENTS OF THE CHURCH since the time scouting was organized have been honored by the BSA, including George Albert SMITH, Heber J. GRANT, David O. MCKAY, Harold B. LEE, Spencer W. KIMBALL, and Ezra Taft BENSON, all of whom have received significant honors for their contribution to scouting on a national level. Most recently, President Ezra Taft Benson received the Bronze Wolf Award, given by the World Scouting Organization for distinguished service to scouting around the world. He also received the Silver Beaver and Silver Antelope awards from BSA in recognition of many years of service on a local and national level.

In addition to Church presidents, Thomas S. Monson, Vaughn J. Featherstone, Robert L. Backman, Marion D. Hanks, and others among the GENERAL AUTHORITIES, have also served in positions of distinction and leadership at the national level of the Boy Scouts and have been recognized for their contribution on behalf of the Church.

Both the program and the support service system of the BSA have been influenced by LDS volunteers, and many of the values, objectives, and goals of the Church for its young men are reflected in the expanding program of BSA.

When the BSA was first organized, certain religious principles were defined as the keystone of the organization, including (1) belief in God, (2) reverence for God, (3) fulfillment of religious duties, and (4) respect for beliefs of others. Because these principles have remained at the heart of scouting, the Church has embraced and promoted scouting as a major part of its program for young men.

The BSA and the Church have forged a close working relationship. In partnership with the Church, the BSA provides its programs, facilities, support, and training. The Church, in turn, provides youth, youth leaders, financial support, and promotion of its implicit values. This relationship has flourished because scouting continues to support wholesome leisure-time activities, to provide a spiritual view of life that is compatible with the Church's teachings, and to encourage boys and leaders to be loyal to the Church.

BIBLIOGRAPHY

Boy Scout Handbook. Irving, Tex., 1990.

Hillcourt, William. Baden-Powell: The Two Lives of a Hero. Irving, Tex., 1985.

Scouting, A handbook on relationships between The Church of Jesus Christ of Latter-day Saints and the Boy Scouts of America, published by the Church. Salt Lake City, 1985.

Strong, Leon M. "A History of the Young Men's Mutual Improvement Association, 1875–1938." Master's thesis, Brigham Young University, 1939.

Williams, John Kent. "A History of the Young Men's Mutual Improvement Association 1939 to 1974." Master's thesis, Brigham Young University, 1976.

LOWELL M. SNOW

SCRIPTURE

[*This entry consists of four articles*:

    Scriptures

    Authority of Scripture

    Words of Living Prophets

    Forthcoming Scripture

The origin and history of the Latter-day Saints is closely tied to scripture, ancient and modern. The article Scriptures *sets out the LDS view of scripture and the differences between it and other scriptural traditions and concepts.* Authority of Scripture *deals with the role of scripture in the beliefs and practices of Latter-day Saints. The essay* Words of Living Prophets *focuses on one of the distinctive features of LDS belief, that of divine revelation through modern prophets. The article* Forthcoming Scripture *treats the LDS expectation, rooted primarily in latter-day scripture, that other scriptures are yet to be revealed by God.*]

SCRIPTURES

Although "scripture" usually denotes written documents, in LDS sources it is also defined as "whatsoever [God's representatives] shall speak when moved upon by the Holy Ghost" (D&C 68:2–4; cf. 1:38; 2 Pet. 2:21; 2 Tim. 3:16). This broader understanding of the term is at once a comprehensive principle and a functional definition, taking into account both written and spoken modes of inspiration.

The corpus of LDS scripture is substantially larger than that of the traditional Protestant canon. It includes the Bible, the Book of Mormon (531 pages, 1981 English edition), the Doctrine and Covenants (294 pages, 1981 edition), and the Pearl of Great Price (61 pages, 1981 edition). From the outset, Latter-day Saints' commitment to the Bible and the Book of Mormon and their attempt immediately to formulate and standardize their teaching in relation to surrounding cultures made them a "bookish" people. By contrast, in Judaism, Christianity, and Islam the process of compiling and fixing sacred writings as "canonical" came comparatively long after their origins, and in each case the process resulted in a closed canon.

The Bible is accepted as the word of God by Latter-day Saints "as far as it is translated correctly" (A of F 8). They acknowledge that though the messages of scripture are divine in origin and impetus, the words in which they are clothed are from humans (cf. Morm. 8:16–17; Ether 12:23–27). The title page of the Book of Mormon says, "If there are faults they are the mistakes of men." For some such admissions strengthen rather than weaken the respect for true revelation (Stendahl, p. 100). This position avoids both the doctrine of verbal inerrancy and the naturalistic position that the Bible is a thoroughly human document, and an obsolescent one at that.

LDS scriptures are referred to as STANDARD WORKS. The word "canon" is used infrequently, in part because it connotes finality, completion, closure. In principle and in fact, additions, as well as occasional official clarifications and translations, are made to the standard works in the dual process of presentation through living leaders and, in accord with the law of COMMON CONSENT, acceptance by members of the Church. In this way, Latter-day Saints bind themselves by covenant to uphold them as scripture. The addition to the Doctrine and Covenants of both a REVELATION about the CELESTIAL KINGDOM received by Joseph Smith and a vision of the redemption of the dead received by President Joseph F. SMITH are modern examples (D&C 137, 138).

The perpetual unending character of the scripture, a corpus ever augmented by living witnesses in a setting of prophecy and TESTIMONY, is a sign and symbol of the inclusiveness of LDS faith (Davies, p. 61). Such a position is in contrast with finalist and minimalist views ("one canon is enough"). The Samaritans, for example, accorded scriptural status to the Pentateuch alone. For Latter-day Saints, scripture is not "final revelation." There is no unexpandable "circle of faith." No sacred texts, because of their acknowledged holiness, forbid the addition of more sacred texts. No document or collection is "all-sufficient" for redemption, for salvation, for complete enlightenment, or for the perfecting of the soul.

Two principles have emerged in defining what is to be regarded as scripture. First, one knows whether another is speaking with the authority of the Holy Ghost only by the influence of the Holy Ghost. Thus, in the last analysis, the burden of proof for scriptural status is placed upon the reader and hearer (cf. Brigham Young, JD 7:2). Latter-day Saints teach that all are entitled to this assurance and testimony. Second, the President of the Church and those associated with him as prophets, seers, and revelators have received a special spiritual endowment and jurisdiction. The President alone speaks or writes for the Church and to the Church as a whole. Others can function similarly, but only within their own offices and callings. Further, "a prophet was a prophet only when he was acting as such" (HC 5:265; 2:302; TPJS, p. 278). Those officially called and ordained to lead are, in LDS terminology, the "living oracles," and "Where the oracles of God are not there the Kingdom of God is not" (WJS, p. 156). Only the President of the Church has the responsibility and burden of exercising all the KEYS of scriptural presentation and declaration. These principles and practices are established to safeguard the sanctity, and vitalize the application, of inspired speaking and writing, both past and present.

Above the authority of the written record stands the authority of the living prophet and, beyond him, the supreme authority of the Lord himself. "You may hug up to yourselves the Bible," said Joseph Smith, "but except through faith in it you can get revelation for yourself, the Bible will profit you but little" (Osborne). Further, "the best way to obtain truth and wisdom is not to ask it from books, but to go to God in prayer, and obtain divine teaching" (TPJS, p. 191). Brigham Young asserted that "I would rather have the living oracles than all the writing in the books" (cited in CR, Oct. 1897, pp. 22–23). But living oracles and responsible laymen are not, in theory or in tradition, wholly independent of the written word. B. H. Roberts, an authoritative second-generation historian and a General Authority, wrote of the corpus of scripture:

> It fixes permanently the general truths which God has revealed. It preserves, for all time and for all generations of men, the great frame-work of the plan of salvation—the Gospel. There are certain truths that are not affected by ever-changing circumstances; truths which are always the same, no matter how often they may be revealed; truths which are elementary, permanent, fixed; from which there must not be, and cannot be, any departure without condemnation. The written word of God preserves the people of God from vain and foolish traditions, which, as they float down the stream of time, are subject to changes by distortion, by addition or subtraction, or by the fitful play of fancy in fantastic and unreliable minds. It forms a standard by which even the living oracles of God may instruct themselves, measure themselves, and correct themselves. It places within the reach of the people, the power to confirm the oral words, and the ministry of the living oracles, and thus to add

faith to faith, and knowledge to knowledge [*IE* 3 (May 1900):576–77].

In contrast, in Judaism the replacement of prophets by rabbis or scholars as custodians and interpreters of scripture was taken to the extreme: "Even if they [the sages] tell you that left is right and right is left—hearken unto their words" (*Midrash Siphre on Deut.* 17:10–11; cf. Jerusalem Talmud tractate *Horayoth* 1:1, 45d). Reassurance against error, even community error, was given on the ground that even the errors made in decisions of law are binding. In a dramatic case, Rabbi Eliezer claimed that a heavenly voice sanctioned his minority opinion. But Rabbi Joshua insisted that the Torah, or text of scripture, is not in heaven but on earth and that the majority view must prevail (*see also* Davies, *Paul and Rabbinic Judaism*, 1980, pp. 374, 212n). In traditional Christianity, ecclesiastical councils have sometimes assumed similar prerogatives.

In their doctrine of scripture, Latter-day Saints have reduced these and other tensions, such as those that exist between biblical and Talmudic Judaism (i.e., between the written and the oral law) or, as in the Roman and Eastern Christian traditions, between the biblical heritage and the claims of both tradition and the pronouncements of the creeds, or, as in Protestantism, between the original intent, coupled with the spirit of scripture, and the claim that individual interpretation is valid.

The idea of an open canon has meant historically a certain openness to other historical, apocryphal, and pseudepigraphical sources. Modern scripture assures Latter-day Saints that important records will yet come to light (cf. 2 Ne. 29:10–14; A of F 9). The Old Testament Apocrypha contains many things "that are true" but also many interpolations (D&C 91); "To those who desire it, should be given by the Spirit to know the true from the false" (*HC* 1:363). By analogy, other documents recently recovered (e.g., the Dead Sea Scrolls, the Nag Hammadi library, and related inscriptions and fragments) are viewed as instructive, though not canonical. In some cases, their teachings anticipate and echo authentic scriptural materials.

The importance of linguistic, contextual, historical, and literary approaches to scripture has been emphasized in the LDS Church in several ways: a SCHOOL OF THE PROPHETS was organized in the very infancy of the Church where Hebrew, Greek, and German were studied as biblical aids; the alternative Bible translations, including the revisions of the JOSEPH SMITH TRANSLATION OF THE BIBLE (JST), were used; official preference was given for the King James Version on the grounds of its literary style and its availability to other Christian groups, and others; various editions of biblical and latter-day scriptures, including critical texts, Bible dictionaries, and selective utilization of burgeoning efforts of worldwide biblical scholarship were utilized (*see* BIBLE SCHOLARSHIP).

A whole constellation of meanings attends the concept of the living word coming from a living prophetic voice. Moreover, the living voice is generally richer than any writing, which is at best a cryptosynopsis. On these grounds, Joseph Smith said, in effect, that one should never trust a letter to say what could be said in person. "No matter how pure your intentions may be; no matter how high your standing is, you cannot touch man's heart when absent as when present" (*Woman's Exponent* 3 [April 1, 1875]:162). The range of possible misunderstanding is significantly increased when one has only the written word.

In the history of canon, various stages or periods have witnessed exegesis, expansion, and the glosses and stylistic alterations that also change substance. One can argue that over the centuries this process has worked in the direction of textual improvement and power; but one can maintain equally that there have been departure and dilution and textual corruption. Latter-day Saints see both processes at work. "Ignorant translators, careless transcribers, or designing and corrupt priests have committed many errors" (*TPJS*, p. 327). On the other hand, the Bible and other texts are impressively preserved, with sufficient light to bless and condemn. For their part, Latter-day Saints ultimately trust the inspiration of the Spirit.

Latter-day Saints are not alone in this position. For instance, H. J. Schoeps shows that Jewish criticism of the ideas of temple and sacrifice were changed when the Bible was assembled (Davies, p. 61). And over the centuries, changes have often led away from, rather than toward, a refinement of original Christian norms and practices.

The revelatory power of scripture depends in part on its adaptive quality. Of modern scripture and, by implication, all earlier scripture the word of the Lord says, "These commandments are of me, and were given unto my servants in their weakness, after the manner of their language, that they might come to understanding" (D&C 1:24).

Plain meaning has also been a leading principle in LDS exegesis. "My soul delighteth in plainness," said the Book of Mormon prophet NEPHI₁ (2 Ne. 31:3). Nothing can override the plain meaning of the text (cf. Talmudic tractate *Shabbath* 63a). This position is neither a refusal to see subtle and layered meanings in the text nor a theologically a priori position that permits allegorical excess, as in the teachings of some early rabbis and Christian schoolmen. Deeper meanings cannot be superimposed on a text of scripture, but are to be found by divine aid in the intent and spirit of the original author (cf. 2 Pet. 1:20–21). For all their complexity and diversity, the scriptures are written in ordinary language; for instance, the working vocabulary of the Book of Mormon comprises fewer than 2,300 basic words.

In practice, Latter-day Saints view certain other texts with special respect, based on their use, each with its own measure of authority. For example, exact prayers are specified for baptism and for the sacrament (*see* BAPTISMAL PRAYER; PRAYER). Other authoritative texts and words—with differing levels of authority—include messages of the First Presidency, temple ordinances and covenants, patriarchal blessings, the hymnal, handbooks for priesthood and auxiliary organizations, and manuals for teaching in the various ward organizations.

A unity of the faith, often seen as remarkable, arises both from a unique openness to further revelation and from the Church's system of checks and balances. The Church's lay participation, which entails the sharing of responsibility, and the law of common consent operate together in the process of presenting, confirming, and accepting the inspired word.

For Latter-day Saints, the scriptures are not reducible to scientific history, sociology, or folklore; a simple set of fundamentals, commandments, and legal apparatus; charming parabolic accounts; esoteric and hidden names with mystical connections that have a power and life of their own. The scriptures are the result of an outpouring from on high whose present meaning and relevance to a person require painstaking study and direct inspiration.

Objecting to the views of the Torah as a closed world, Martin Buber wrote, "To you God is one who created once and not again; but to us God is He who 'renews the work of creation every day.' To you God is One who revealed Himself once and no more; but to us He speaks out of the burning thornbush of the present . . . in the revelations of our innermost hearts—greater than words" (p. 204). This statement captures much of the spirit of the LDS approach to scripture. Meaning and power rise against "hardening" traditions and sponsor trust in the living witness of the Spirit to illumine, clarify, and sanctify scripture as the "present truth."

BIBLIOGRAPHY

Buber, Martin. *Great Jewish Thinkers of the Twentieth Century*, ed. S. Noveck. Clinton, Mass., 1963.

Clark, J. Reuben, Jr. "When Are Church Leaders' Words Entitled to Claim of Scripture?" *Church News*, July 31, 1954, pp. 9–11.

Davies, W. D. "Reflections on the Mormon Canon." *Harvard Theological Review* 79 (1986):44–66. Reprinted in *Christians Among Jews and Gentiles*, ed. G. W. E. Nicklesburg and George W. MacRae, S.V., pp. 44–66. Philadelphia, 1986.

Osborne, D. *Juvenile Instructor* 27 (Mar. 15, 1892):173.

Stendahl, Krister. "The Sermon on the Mount and Third Nephi in the Book of Mormon." In *Meanings*, p. 100. Philadelphia, 1984.

Welch, John W., and David J. Whittaker. "Mormonism's Open Canon: Some Historical Perspectives on Its Religious Limits and Potentials." *F.A.R.M.S. Paper*. Provo, Utah, 1986.

W. D. DAVIES
TRUMAN G. MADSEN

AUTHORITY OF SCRIPTURE

For Latter-day Saints, the concept of scripture entails two complementary definitions—a broad definition that embraces all revelation from God as "scripture," and a narrower view that includes only the STANDARD WORKS as "the scriptures." Both categories are authoritative, since both are viewed as coming from God.

The first definition uses "scripture" as synonymous with such terms as "inspired" or "divinely revealed." Concerning those who have been called and ordained to proclaim God's word, a revelation in the DOCTRINE AND COVENANTS provides the foundation: "Whatsoever they shall speak when moved upon by the Holy Ghost shall be scripture, shall be the will of the Lord, shall be the mind of the Lord, shall be the word of the Lord, shall be the voice of the Lord, and the power of God unto salvation" (D&C 68:4). In this light, Latter-day

Saints hold in high regard the words of Church leaders at all levels. Especially authoritative are the official pronouncements of the FIRST PRESIDENCY and the QUORUM OF THE TWELVE APOSTLES, who are sustained by Church members as "prophets, seers, and revelators." Their writings and addresses—particularly in general conference—are cited frequently as guides for living and for authoritative interpretation of doctrine. Statements issued by the First Presidency represent the official position and policy of the Church.

Joseph SMITH taught that "a prophet was a prophet only when he was acting as such" (HC 5:265). Thus, the words of prophets carry the force of scripture only when they are uttered under the influence of the HOLY GHOST. Latter-day Saints freely acknowledge this divine influence in the teachings and counsel of leaders and deem it a privilege to be instructed by them. They consider this inspired direction to be "scripture" in the broad definition and endeavor to harmonize their lives with it.

The more restrictive view of what constitutes scripture would include only what is called "the scriptures"—that is, the four standard works: the Bible, the Book of Mormon, the Doctrine and Covenants, and the Pearl of Great Price. These constitute the canonized, authoritative corpus of revealed writings against which all else is measured. President Joseph Fielding SMITH taught, "My words, and the teachings of any other member of the Church, high or low, if they do not square with the revelations, we need not accept them. . . . We have accepted the four standard works as the measuring yardsticks, or balances, by which we measure every man's doctrine" (DS 3:203).

While the Church views its scriptures as a canon in a strict sense, they are not viewed as closed. The doctrine of continuing revelation is one of the fundamental beliefs of the Church. As was expressed by Joseph Smith, "We believe all that God has revealed, all that He does now reveal, and we believe that He will yet reveal many great and important things pertaining to the Kingdom of God" (A of F 9). While accepting "all that God has revealed," whether canonized in the scriptures or not, Latter-day Saints also believe that revelation continues to enlighten their leaders. Moreover, additional divine guidance is anticipated because God "will yet reveal many great and important things." Those future revelations will be scripture,

according to the broad definition, and it is likely that some of them will be added to the scriptures in due time.

BIBLIOGRAPHY

Jackson, Kent P. "Latter-day Saints: A Dynamic Scriptural Process." In The Holy Book in Comparative Perspective, ed. F. Denny and R. Taylor, pp. 63–83. Columbia, S.C., 1985.

———. "The Sacred Literature of the Latter-day Saints." In The Bible and Bibles in America, ed. E. Frerichs, pp. 163–91. Atlanta, Ga., 1988.

Talmage, James E. AF, pp. 236–313.

KENT P. JACKSON

WORDS OF LIVING PROPHETS

Any message that comes from God to man by the power of the HOLY GHOST is scripture to the one who receives it, whether in written or spoken form (MD, p. 682; cf. 2 Ne. 32:3). PAUL wrote to Timothy that "all [written] scripture is given by inspiration of God, and is profitable for doctrine, for reproof, for correction, for instruction in righteousness" (2 Tim. 3:16). Further, every person may receive personal revelation for his or her own benefit. God, however, has always designated prophets to speak for him, thus resulting in holy writ or scripture. When Aaron was called as a spokesman for Moses, the Lord said, "And he shall be thy spokesman unto the people: and he shall be . . . to thee instead of a mouth, and thou shalt be to him instead of God" (Ex. 4:15–16).

Members of The Church of Jesus Christ of Latter-day Saints believe in continuous REVELATION, especially to prophets who direct the Church. This doctrine was announced in a revelation received through the Prophet Joseph SMITH in November 1831: "And whatsoever [the Lord's servants] shall speak when moved upon by the Holy Ghost shall be scripture, shall be the will of the Lord, shall be the mind of the Lord, shall be the word of the Lord, shall be the voice of the Lord, and the power of God unto salvation" (D&C 68:4). Inspired utterances of the Prophet and PRESIDENT OF THE CHURCH have been and may in the future be added to the STANDARD WORKS by the COMMON CONSENT of the Church.

Latter-day Saints sustain the FIRST PRESIDENCY and the QUORUM OF THE TWELVE APOSTLES as PROPHETS, SEERS, AND REVELATORS. Since the prophet and President of the Church is sustained as *the* prophet, seer, and revelator, he is the official spokesman who speaks on behalf of the Lord to the Church (D&C 21:4–5; 28:2). These other prophets, seers, and revelators have the right, power, and authority to declare the mind and will of God to his people, subject to the presiding authority of the President (D&C 132:7).

The inspired utterances of the President of the Church become binding upon members of the Church whether formally accepted as part of the written CANON or not. The living prophet's inspired words supersede and become more important to Latter-day Saints than the written canon or previous prophetic statements (D&C 5:10). The salvation and exaltation of members of the Church depend upon their adherence to this divine INSPIRATION through the living prophet, which comes as a VOICE OF WARNING to the world (D&C 1:4–5).

This doctrine appears in the Old Testament. For example, people could be saved from the flood only by listening to the voice of God through his prophet NOAH. Likewise, the Israelites were expected to accept and be responsibly obedient to words of Moses as if the Lord himself had spoken them (Deut. 18:18–22). The Lord also taught that "if there be a prophet among you, I the Lord will make myself known unto him in a vision, and will speak unto him in a dream" (Num. 12:6).

Early Christian emphasis on the "living voice" can be found in the writings of Papias (c. A.D. 130): "If anyone chanced to come who had actually been a follower of the elders, I would enquire as to the discourses of the elders, what Andrew or Peter said, or what Philip or Thomas or James, or what John or Matthew or any other of the Lord's disciples . . . say. For I supposed that things out of books did not profit me so much as the utterances of a living and abiding voice" (Eusebius, *Ecclesiastical History* 3.39.4).

Latter-day Saints accept the doctrine that what God declares, "whether by [his] own voice or by the voice of [his] servants, it is the same" (D&C 1:38). On the other hand, prophets have the right to personal opinions; not every word they speak is therefore regarded as an official pronouncement or interpretation of scripture. Only when they are inspired to speak to the Church by the Holy Ghost do they speak scripture. In order for a hearer to determine whether a prophet speaks thus, the power of the Holy Ghost must testify to the individual that the message is divinely inspired. The

Holy Ghost is given to all to know the truth of all things (Moro. 10:5).

BIBLIOGRAPHY

Benson, Ezra Taft. "Fourteen Fundamentals in Following the Prophet." *BYU Speeches of the Year, 1977–80*, pp. 26–30. Feb. 26, 1980.

Church Educational System. *Teachings of the Living Prophets*, pp. 6–22. Salt Lake City, 1982.

Clark, J. Reuben, Jr. "When Are Church Leaders' Words Entitled to Claim of Scripture?" *Church News* (July 31, 1954):9–11.

Horton, George A., Jr. *Keys to Successful Scripture Study*, pp. 2–11. Salt Lake City, 1989.

A. GARY ANDERSON

FORTHCOMING SCRIPTURE

Latter-day Saints believe that God "will yet reveal many great and important things" (A of F 9), that the heavens are not closed, and that God continues to "pour down knowledge from heaven upon [their] heads" (D&C 121:23). Forthcoming revelations are expected to include both ancient truths restored and new truths uncovered.

The scriptures specifically foretell the restoration of many books that will make known plain and precious things taken away from the world (1 Ne. 13:39–40). These include the BOOK OF ENOCH (D&C 107:57); an additional account of the events on the Mount of Transfiguration (D&C 63:20–21); the fulness of the record of JOHN and of visions about the end of the world (1 Ne. 14:18–27; Ether 4:16; D&C 93:6, 18); the sealed portion of the Book of Mormon, which includes the vision of the BROTHER OF JARED (2 Ne. 27:7–11; Ether 3:25–27; 4:7); the brass plates (Alma 37:4–5; *see also* BOOK OF MORMON PLATES AND RECORDS); a more complete record of the teachings of Jesus Christ to the Nephites (3 Ne. 26:6–11); and records of the lost tribes of Israel (2 Ne. 29:12–13).

How or when these scriptures will come forth is unknown, beyond the general belief that further revelations will come in the Lord's time when people repent, exercise faith, and are prepared to receive them (2 Ne. 28:30; Ether 4:1–12). Latter-day Saints believe that the world has seen only the beginning of the great doctrinal and scriptural restoration whereby God will "gather together in one all things in Christ" (Eph. 1:10). Heavenly and earthly records of all DISPENSATIONS are to be gathered together (1 Ne. 13:41), and "nothing shall be withheld" (D&C 121:28).

BIBLIOGRAPHY

Maxwell, Neal A. "God Will Yet Reveal." *Ensign* 16 (Nov. 1986):52–59.

McConkie, Bruce R. "The Doctrinal Restoration." In *The Joseph Smith Translation*, ed. M. Nyman and R. Millet, pp. 1–22. Provo, Utah, 1985.

ROBERT A. CLOWARD

SCRIPTURE, INTERPRETATION WITHIN SCRIPTURE

The key to interpreting scriptural passages often lies in the body of scripture itself. For example, some passages from the Old Testament receive commentary and interpretation in the New Testament. Jesus Christ frequently taught from the Old Testament, not only giving interpretation—as in David's need to eat the temple shew bread (1 Sam. 21:1–6) as justification for his disciples plucking wheat on the Sabbath (Mark 2:23–26)—but also often emphasizing that the scriptures testify of himself as Messiah (Luke 4:18–21; John 5:39). The additional scriptures that Latter-day Saints accept—the BOOK OF MORMON, the DOCTRINE AND COVENANTS, and the PEARL OF GREAT PRICE—also cite and interpret the Bible. In fact, many of the clearest explications of doctrine arise from modern REVELATIONS or restored scripture.

In the Pearl of Great Price, the BOOK OF MOSES and the BOOK OF ABRAHAM augment the Old Testament Genesis account of the Creation (Moses 2–3; Abr. 4–5), affirm human AGENCY (Moses 3:17; 7:32), clarify the fall of Adam (Moses 4; Abr. 5), and explain the resulting need for a redeemer (Moses 6:59; cf. 4:1–2; 5:7–8). In addition, these two books add information on the claims of Satan and the choosing of Christ in the premortal world (Moses 4:1–4; Abr. 3:27–28) where all the spirits of mankind lived before their advent on the earth (*see* PREMORTAL LIFE).

In JOSEPH SMITH—MATTHEW, the Prophet Joseph Smith received clarification of the Savior's discussion in Matthew 24 of the events to precede the fall of Jerusalem and those to precede Jesus' latter-day coming. According to the JOSEPH SMITH—HISTORY, MORONI₂ quoted Malachi 4:6 to Joseph Smith differently from the Old Testament version, suggesting that the phrase "the fathers" refers to the patriarchs, especially ABRAHAM, with whom God made covenants pertaining to Abraham's posterity, who would bear priesthood ORDINANCES to the world for the exaltation of the human family (JS—H 1:39; D&C 27:9–10).

The Book of Mormon clarifies many of the writings of Old Testament prophets. The prophet NEPHI₁ quoted Isaiah 48–49 (1 Ne. 20–21) and then gave a plain commentary on the major points of those chapters in 1 Nephi 22, emphasizing that the NEPHITES were a remnant of scattered Israel, who would eventually be gathered with the aid of the GENTILES. In another example, about 148 B.C. the Nephite prophet ABINADI identified the "suffering servant" of Isaiah 53 as Jesus Christ (Mosiah 15:2–5) and enlarged on Isaiah's discussion of the Messiah's atonement (Mosiah 14–15).

The Book of Mormon also illuminates the SERMON ON THE MOUNT (Matt. 5–7). In a similar sermon given in the Western Hemisphere (3 Ne. 12–14), the resurrected Jesus said, "Blessed are the poor in spirit *who come unto me*" (3 Ne. 12:3; italics added). Such added words, plus the context of Jesus' address, indicate that one must come to the Savior through BAPTISM and righteousness to receive the blessings promised in the BEATITUDES.

The Doctrine and Covenants offers explication on several obscure points in the book of Revelation that pertain to events of the Last Days, such as the gathering of Israel and their receiving priesthood ordinances (D&C 77:8–9, 11). Elucidation of biblical passages that focus on latter-day signs to precede Jesus' second coming are found especially in Doctrine and Covenants 45 and 86. While pondering 1 Peter 3:18–20, President Joseph F. SMITH received a vision of the redemption of the dead (now D&C 138) that clarified and enlarged the Savior's redemptive work in the SPIRIT WORLD following his crucifixion.

Much modern revelation came to the Prophet Joseph Smith in response to questions arising from his work on the JOSEPH SMITH TRANSLATION OF THE BIBLE (JST). For example, while meditating on the resurrection to life or damnation mentioned in John 5:29, Joseph Smith and Sidney RIGDON received the revelation on the DEGREES OF GLORY in the resurrection (D&C 76). Joseph Smith recorded several instances in which, while pondering a passage of scripture (e.g., James 1:5, an invitation to ask the Lord for wisdom), he prayed and received additional scripture from the Lord that made the first more plain or confirmed its reality (JS—H 1:11–20). While translating from the Book of Mormon PLATES, Joseph Smith and Oliver COWDERY prayed after reading about baptism. In answer, JOHN THE BAPTIST came with authority and instructions on baptism (JS—H 1:68–72). After their baptisms, the Prophet described their being filled with the HOLY GHOST: "Our minds being now enlightened, we began to have the scriptures laid open to our understandings, and the true meaning and intention of their more mysterious passages revealed unto us in a manner which we never could attain to previously, nor ever before had thought of" (JS—H 1:74).

Nephi observed that having the SPIRIT OF PROPHECY is essential to grasping the correct understanding of scripture. He mentioned in particular Isaiah, "for because the words of Isaiah are not plain unto you, nevertheless they are plain unto all those that are filled with the spirit of prophecy" (2 Ne. 25:4). In chapters 25–30, Nephi provided prophetic insight into the teachings of Isaiah.

Modern revelation and restored scripture offer indispensable interpretations of the Bible, helping Latter-day Saints to understand the Bible more fully. Jesus rebuked those who had taken away the "key of knowledge" or the means whereby the biblical scriptures could be understood (JST Luke 11:53), thereby causing confusion in the interpretation of scripture. The Lord said, "Because that ye have a Bible ye need not suppose that it contains all my words; neither need ye suppose that I have not caused more to be written. . . . I shall speak unto the Jews and they shall write it; and I shall also speak unto the Nephites and they shall write it; and I shall also speak unto the other tribes of the house of Israel . . . and they shall write it. . . . And my word also shall be gathered in one" (2 Ne 29:10, 12, 14; cf. Ezek 37:16–20). Latter-day Saints interpret the Bible in the light of restored scripture and modern revelation because these have reestablished the lost key of knowledge.

BIBLIOGRAPHY

Gileadi, Avraham. "Isaiah: Four Latter-day Keys to an Ancient Book." In *Isaiah and the Prophets*, ed. M. Nyman. Provo, Utah, 1984.

McConkie, Bruce R. "The Bible, a Sealed Book." In *Supplement to a Symposium on the New Testament*, Church Educational System, pp. 1–7. Salt Lake City, 1984.

Rust, Richard Dilworth. "'All Things Which Have Been Given of God . . . Are the Typifying of Him': Typology in the Book of Mormon." In *Literature of Belief*, ed. N. Lambert. Provo, Utah, 1981.

M. CATHERINE THOMAS

SCRIPTURE STUDY

From childhood, Latter-day Saints are taught to read and study the scriptures in order to know Jesus Christ and his teachings. Those having faith will be able to read by the power of the Lord and hear the Lord's voice (D&C 18:35–36). They will be given power to expound scripture (D&C 25:7; 97:3–5; 100:11), which includes reasoning with people (D&C 68:1), unfolding and laying open the scriptures to them (Alma 12:1; 21:9; JS—H 1:74), responding to their questions (Alma 12:8–10), explaining what prompted the passage (*TPJS*, pp. 276–77), and likening the messages of the scriptures to their needs (1 Ne. 19:23). Latter-day Saints are to avoid disputation regarding the scriptures and are told particularly to avoid doctrinal contention (D&C 10:62–68; 19:31; 3 Ne. 11:28–40; *HC* 5:340). Missionaries are to read and preach from the scriptures (Alma 18:36; D&C 22:12–13). The resurrected Jesus read chapters of scripture and expounded all things, both great and small, to hearers in the Western Hemisphere (3 Ne. 23:6,14; 26:1).

Scripture study is central to the teaching activities of the Church and plays a major role in strengthening the spiritual life of the members and in helping them to acquire a TESTIMONY. Members are urged to read and examine the scriptures daily, both individually and as families (Kimball, pp. 2–5). They are instructed to ponder the messages of the scriptures, to pray concerning them, and to relate the teachings to their own lives. Members are cautioned that unless they teach their children the scriptures, they will "dwindle in unbelief"; hence, the Book of Mormon prophets treasured their scriptures and made great effort to obtain them and safeguard them in their travels (1 Ne. 4:5–18; Mosiah 1:4–5).

The current Church curriculum is based on the scriptures, and manuals include scriptural references to aid teachers, provide weekly reading assignments, and anchor learning on a scriptural foundation. The study of the scriptures is also enhanced by articles published in Church magazines, written by lay members, leaders, and scholars. Courses on the Bible, the Book of Mormon, the Doctrine and Covenants, and the Pearl of Great Price are offered through the Church educational system, and Brigham Young University helps coordinate scripture research and makes research reports available to the Church membership.

The 1979–1981 published edition of the scriptures aids readers in their scriptural study, making available extensive cross-references, maps, an index, a topical guide, and a Bible dictionary. Members may also examine alternative English or other translations in their study. Joseph SMITH once expressed appreciation for the Martin Luther German translation (*WJS*, p. 351) and the Greek and Hebrew versions: "My soul delights in reading the word of the Lord in the original" (*PWJS*, p. 161). In addition to the editions of the scriptures published by the Church in many languages, tape recordings of the scriptures and computer word-search programs are available as further study aids.

Religious research studies indicate that the more education Latter-day Saints receive, the more likely they are to study the gospel. Nearly half of the LDS college graduates surveyed in the United States and Canada regularly study gospel principles.

In Latter-day Saint scripture, the Lord urges all people to open their hearts and give ear to his word, to lay hold of it, to cling to it (1 Ne. 8:1–38), to ponder it, to search it, to feast upon it, and to treasure it (2 Ne. 32:3; 3 Ne. 23:1; D&C 84:85). With such receptiveness, one understands the word of the Lord in one's heart and mind, does not rebel against the Lord, lets go of prejudice, and is compassionate and caring (Mosiah 2:9; 3 Ne. 19:33; 2 Ne. 7:5; D&C 31:7; 75:25; 101:92; 109:56; 124:9). Those who study the scriptures with an open heart are promised that their tongues will be loosened and they will learn what to say with the convincing power of God (D&C 11:21–22; 23:2–3; 84:85; cf. Alma 17:2–3).

BIBLIOGRAPHY

Albrecht, Stan L., and Tim B. Heaton. "Secularization, Higher Education, and Religiosity." *Review of Religious Research* 26 (1984):42–58.

"Catalogue—A Scripture Research Library." F.A.R.M.S. Provo, Utah, published yearly.

Kimball, Spencer W. "How Rare a Possession—the Scriptures!" *Ensign* 15 (July 1985):2–5.

Packard, Dennis J., and Sandra Packard. *Feasting upon the Word.* Salt Lake City, 1981.

DENNIS J. PACKARD

SCULPTORS

The earliest LDS sculptors were English emigrant craftsmen who provided ornamentation for the Nauvoo and pioneer TEMPLES. A temple sunstone, one of the most distinctive surviving artifacts from

Avard T. Fairbanks, with his cast bronze model for the statue of the Angel Moroni on the Washington Temple (1970, now in LDS Church Collection, Museum of Church History and Art, Salt Lake City). Courtesy Nelson Wadsworth.

Nauvoo, is part of the collection of the Smithsonian Institution.

A tradition of creating public monuments that celebrate the history of the Latter-day Saints is now a century old. Contributors include Cyrus Dallin (1861–1944), who studied in Paris. He sculpted the angel MORONI$_2$ that caps the tallest tower of the SALT LAKE TEMPLE. This beaux arts sculpture has become the most recognized and copied piece in the LDS tradition. Most of Dallin's career was spent in Boston, where he sculpted John Winthrop, Paul Revere, and Massasoit. His life-sized bronze equestrian figures also grace Chicago, Kansas City, Philadelphia, and Vienna.

A grandson of Brigham YOUNG, Mahonri Young (1877–1957), also studied in Paris, where he was strongly influenced by Rodin. "THIS IS THE PLACE" MONUMENT, which marks the entry of the pioneers into the SALT LAKE VALLEY, is one of his major religious works, the largest sculptured monument in Utah.

Avard Fairbanks (1897–1987), who created the Department of Fine Arts at the University of Utah, is well known in the Church for his elaborate frieze around the Hawaii Temple, his statue of the restoration of the AARONIC PRIESTHOOD, and the WINTER QUARTERS Cemetery Monument. He was knighted by King Paul of Greece after sculpting "Lycurgus the Lawgiver."

On TEMPLE SQUARE (Salt Lake City) stands a monument to the dramatic epic of the pioneer trek, the Mormon HANDCART COMPANIES, sculpted by Torlief Knaphus (1881–1965), a convert from Norway.

The Mormon Arts Festival, held at Brigham Young University since the early 1970s, has displayed religious pieces produced by Franz Johansen (1929–) and Trevor Southey (1940–) that are now in the Museum of Church History and Art. The Monument to Women sculpture garden in Nauvoo displays life-sized bronze statues of women. Most of the pieces are done by Dennis Smith (1942–), but the sculpture of Joseph and Emma Smith was created by Florence Hansen (1920–).

The last quarter of the twentieth century has produced many LDS sculptors, including some with roots in cultures that reflect the international presence of the Church. Representative sculptors are Epanaia Christy (1921–) and Mataumu Alisa (1942–) from Polynesia; Native Americans Lowell

Florence Hansen created this model for her statue *Teaching with Love*, a life-sized bronze now part of the Nauvoo Monument to Women (1978), at the LDS Church Visitors Center in Nauvoo, Illinois.

Talishoma (1950–), Oreland Joe (1958–), and Harrison Begay (1961–); Victor de la Torres (c. 1935–) of Venezuela; and Mae Cameron (n.d.) from Australia.

[*See also* Architecture; Historical Sites; Kirtland Temple; Museums, Latter-day Saint; Symbols, Cultural and Artistic.]

BIBLIOGRAPHY

Gibbs, Linda Jones. *Masterworks*. Salt Lake City, 1984.

Olpin, Robert S. *Dictionary of Utah Art*. Salt Lake City, 1980.

Oman, Richard G. "Sculpting: An LDS Tradition." *Ensign* 20 (Oct. 1990):38–43.

Swanson, Vern G. *Sculptors of Utah*. Springville, Utah, n.d.

RICHARD G. OMAN

SEAGULLS, MIRACLE OF

The first LDS PIONEERS entered the SALT LAKE VALLEY in July 1847 (*see* PIONEER DAY). Nearly 2,000 made the journey that year, with another 2,400 emigrants arriving in 1848. From the beginning, having so many dependent on first harvests from an untried land with an unknown growing season produced concern. That first summer, pioneers observed Indians harvesting "millions" of crickets for winter food. The crickets were driven into fires and roasted, and then stored in baskets and bags. Survival—individual and group survival—was clearly on the minds of these first Mormon settlers as they watched the Indians prepare to endure the winter.

During the first year in the Great Basin, most Latter-day Saint settlers resided in the Salt Lake Valley, although small settlements were also begun to the north at Kaysville, along the Weber River, and at Bountiful. Through the summer and fall of 1847, they planted 2,000 acres of winter wheat near the main settlement. A mild winter and thaw permitted plowing in early 1848, making it possible to plant more wheat and another 3,000 to 4,000 acres in corn and garden vegetables by spring.

As spring arrived, pioneer farmers reported with pride that their crops appeared to be doing very well. But April and May frosts leveled some of the crops, and late May brought another devastation—hordes of insects began to destroy the crops. These insects, later dubbed "Mormon crickets," were as large as a man's thumb. Not a true cricket but a member of the katydid family, the Mormon cricket has only small wings and cannot fly. Pioneer diarists reported the invaders in the fields as early as May 22. Some described them as numbering in the millions; John Steele wrote that they appeared by the "thousands of tons." For more than a month, the crickets devastated the fields, devouring the new corn, beans, wheat, pumpkins, squash, cucumbers, melons, and other crops. Farmers battled the crickets with a variety of defensive measures but had little success.

By early June, relief arrived in the form of the seagull. The appearance of gulls was described in a letter of June 9 to Brigham YOUNG in the following manner: "The sea gulls have come in large flocks from the lake and sweep the crickets as they go; it seems the hand of the Lord is in our favor" (Hartley, p. 230). For the next three weeks, gulls ap-

The Seagull Monument (1985), on Temple Square in Salt Lake City, by Mahonri M. Young, a grandson of Brigham Young. Completed in 1913, the monument commemorates the miraculous work of the gulls that saved crops of the early pioneers. The spires of the Assembly Hall are visible in the background. The seagull is the state bird of Utah. Courtesy Floyd Holdman.

peared daily. They fed on the crickets, drank water, and then regurgitated before eating more crickets. There would be a harvest that year, after all.

Some 1848 pioneer journals mention the problems of frost, crickets, and drought without mentioning the gulls. However, several autumn accounts credited the counterinvasion by the gulls for the scanty crops that survived and acknowledged the hand of God in the event.

Ornithologists have noted that gulls, whose spring and summer habitat centers on the shores of the Great Salt Lake, regularly return to the valleys of the Great Basin to devour crickets, grasshoppers, and other insects, and that the 1848 appearance of the gulls was therefore not unusual. Some skeptics thus saw the 1848 activities of both crickets and gulls as simply natural phenomena. On the other hand, many Latter-day Saints, with faith in a God whose hand is in history and who often acts through "natural" events, believed that their crops had been saved in part by God's intervention. Over time, the 1848 "cricket war," now called "the miracle of the gulls," became a prominent part of the Saints' collective memory. In honor of this occasion, the indigenous California gull became the Utah state bird, and in 1913 the Seagull Monument on TEMPLE SQUARE was dedicated to commemorate the birds' role in the 1848 crisis.

In the Salt Lake Valley, crickets, frost, and lack of water played havoc on the harvest of 1848, and crop losses were severe. But the losses would have been much worse without the appearance of the gulls, which was thus a significant factor in the survival of Utah's pioneer settlers.

BIBLIOGRAPHY

Hartley, William G. "Mormons, Crickets, and Gulls: A New Look at an Old Story." *Utah Historical Quarterly* 38 (Summer 1970):224–39.

RICHARD W. SADLER

SEALING

[*This entry consists of three articles:*

    Sealing Power

    Temple Sealings

    Cancellation of Sealings

The first article, Sealing Power, *explains the meaning of sealing in the Church and the authority required to perform an ordinance so it will be considered sealed; what is a temple sealing and how it is obtained is presented in the second article,* Temple Sealings; *and the third article,* Cancellation of Sealings, *is a brief statement on who may cancel a sealing.*]

SEALING POWER

Signets and seals have been used from early antiquity to certify AUTHORITY. The word "seal" appears many times in the scriptures. Jesus Christ was "sealed" by God the Father (John 6:27), and Paul reminded ancient Saints that God had anointed and sealed them (2 Cor. 1:21–22) and told others they "were sealed with that holy Spirit of promise, which is the earnest [assurance] of our inheritance until the redemption" (Eph. 1:13–14). John spoke of the servants of God being sealed in their foreheads (Rev. 7:3). In the apocryphal Acts of Thomas (verse 131), Thomas prayed that he and his wife and daughter "may receive the seal" and "become servants of the true God." Even today licenses, diplomas, legal documents, and the like bear seals that officially attest to their authenticity.

For Latter-day Saints, the ultimate sealing power is the priesthood power given to authorized servants of the Lord to perform certain acts on earth and have them recognized (sealed) or validated in heaven. They believe it is this authority the Lord Jesus Christ described when he said to Peter, "I will give unto thee the keys of the kingdom of heaven: and whatsoever thou shalt bind on earth shall be bound in heaven: and whatsoever thou shalt loose on earth shall be loosed in heaven" (Matt. 16:19).

The President of the Church holds and exercises the KEYS of sealing on earth. When a man is ordained an APOSTLE and set apart as a member of the QUORUM OF THE TWELVE APOSTLES, sealing is one of the powers bestowed upon him. Other GENERAL AUTHORITIES of the Church, the presidencies of temples, and a limited number of officiators in each temple receive this sealing power during their tenure. After one is approved by the FIRST PRESIDENCY to receive the sealing power, the President of the Church, one of his counselors, or a member of the Twelve Apostles specifically designated by the President confers the sealing power upon him by the LAYING ON OF HANDS. This is the specific authority to perform the temple sealing ORDINANCES.

This is the authority by which "all covenants, contracts, bonds, obligations, oaths, vows, performances, connections, associations, or expectations" can be "made and entered into and sealed by the Holy Spirit of promise" and receive "efficacy, virtue, or force in and after the resurrection of the dead" (D&C 132:7).

In this DISPENSATION OF THE FULNESS OF TIMES, the sealing power was restored by ELIJAH, the last prophet of the Old Testament period to hold it (*TPJS*, pp. 339–40). He bestowed that authority on Joseph Smith and Oliver COWDERY in the Kirtland Temple on April 3, 1836 (D&C 110). As each man who has been President of the Church was ordained an apostle and became a member of the Quorum of the Twelve, he had the sealing power bestowed upon him, and thus it has been transmitted to the present (D&C 110:13–16; 128:11).

What might be called the general sealing power is also vested in the President of the Church. Everyone who receives the PRIESTHOOD obtains this general sealing power to a degree. For example, as Elder Bruce R. McConkie said, "All things that are not sealed by this power have an end when men are dead. Unless a baptism has this enduring seal, it will not admit a person to the celestial kingdom. . . . All things gain enduring force and validity because of the sealing power" (MD, pp. 615–616).

BIBLIOGRAPHY

Packer, Boyd K. The Holy Temple. Salt Lake City, 1980.

Smith, Joseph Fielding. "Elijah: His Mission and Sealing Power." DS, Vol. 2, pp. 115–28. Salt Lake City, 1955.

DAVID H. YARN, JR.

TEMPLE SEALINGS

A "sealing," as a generic term, means the securing, determining, or establishment of a bond of legitimacy. Among members of the Church sealing refers to the marriage of a husband and wife and to the joining together of children and parents in relationships that are to endure forever. This special type of sealing of husband and wife in MARRIAGE is referred to as "eternal marriage" or "celestial marriage." It contrasts with civil and church marriages, which are ceremonies recognized only by earthly authority and are only for the duration of mortal life.

The sealing together of husband, wife, and children in eternal family units is the culminating ORDINANCE of the PRIESTHOOD, to which all others are preparatory. It must be performed by one holding the SEALING POWER and today in an LDS TEMPLE dedicated to God. The Savior referred to this sealing power when he gave his apostle Peter the KEYS of the kingdom of heaven, saying that "whatsoever thou shalt bind on earth shall be bound in heaven" (Matt. 16:19). In modern times this sealing authority was restored to the earth in the Kirtland Temple on April 3, 1836, by the prophet ELIJAH, who was the ancient custodian of this power (D&C 110:13–16).

Both ancient and modern prophets have observed that if families are not sealed together in eternal units—if the hearts of the children and the fathers are not turned to each other (as alluded to in Malachi 4:5–6)—then the ultimate work and glory of God are not attained and the highest purposes of the creation of the earth are not achieved. "For we without them [ancestors or progenitors] cannot be made perfect; neither can they without us be made perfect" (D&C 128:16–18).

To Latter-day Saints, the SPIRIT WORLD is as real as this world. By divine mandate, temple sealings are not only available to living persons, but are extended also to the deceased progenitors of a family through proxy ordinances performed in the temples. This process is known as SALVATION OF THE DEAD. Children born to parents who have been sealed in the temple are BORN IN THE COVENANT and thus are bonded to their parents for eternity without a separate ordinance of sealing.

To receive temple sealing ordinances, Church members must receive a TEMPLE RECOMMEND from a proper Church authority attesting that they are living prescribed Church standards. They then visit a temple and receive initiatory ordinances and the blessing referred to as the temple ENDOWMENT. This entails the receipt of instruction and being put under COVENANT to obey eternal laws set forth by God, which, as observed, will ensure a superior standard of morality, marriage, and family life. The sealing ordinances can then be administered, the full benefit of which can be secured only by continued obedience to the divine laws set forth in the gospel of Jesus Christ.

A sealing ceremony is an inspiring and solemn ordinance performed in specially designated and dedicated rooms of a temple. The couple to be married or the family to be sealed kneel at an altar. The officiator is one who has received the sealing power under the highest priesthood authority in the Church (see PROPHET, SEER, AND REVELATOR; SEALING POWER).

For members of the Church, sealings endow life with greater purpose and give marriage a sense of divine partnership with spiritual safeguards. Bringing children into the world becomes a divinely inspired stewardship. Sealings can sustain a family in life and console them in death. They establish continuity in life, here and hereafter.

BIBLIOGRAPHY

Derrick, Royden G. In Temples in the Last Days, chap. 3. Salt Lake City, 1988.

Smith, Joseph Fielding. *DS* 2:119. Salt Lake City, 1954–1956.

Talmage, James E. *The House of the Lord*, pp. 84–91. Salt Lake City, 1976.

PAUL V. HYER

CANCELLATION OF SEALINGS

The KEYS of the kingdom of heaven, conferred upon Peter by the Lord Jesus Christ (Matt. 16:19) and restored to the earth in recent times (D&C 110) by the prophet ELIJAH, who was custodian of this power anciently (see Mal. 4:5–6), include the AUTHORITY to "bind and loose" on earth, with corresponding effect in heaven. Currently this power is held and exercised only by the PRESIDENT OF THE CHURCH and others upon whom it is conferred by him or at his direction. Once a sealing ORDINANCE is performed, only the First Presidency can approve a change in sealing status, including the cancellation of a sealing (*General Handbook of Instructions*, 6-5 through 6-7).

The First Presidency may cancel temple sealings when the circumstances of a request for cancellation warrant it.

BIBLIOGRAPHY

General Handbook of Instructions. Salt Lake City, 1989.

RONALD E. POELMAN

SECOND COMFORTER

See: Jesus Christ, Second Comforter

SECOND COMING OF JESUS CHRIST

[*The second coming of Jesus Christ refers to his return to the earth in glory to reign as King of Kings, as contrasted to his first coming as an infant in Bethlehem. Articles relevant to this topic are* David, Prophetic Figure of Last Days; Dispensation of the Fulness of Times; Jesus Christ: Second Coming of Jesus Christ; Marriage Supper of the Lamb; Messiah: Messianic Concept and Hope; Millennium; Parables; Restoration of All Things.

Both the first and second appearances were foretold in the scriptures, with the second advent to be accompanied by earthshaking events of worldwide consequence. See Armageddon; Joseph Smith—Matthew; Last Days; Malachi, Prophecies of.]

SECOND ESTATE

"Second estate" is a Latter-day Saint term that refers to mankind's mortal existence on this earth. In scripture it occurs only in the writings of ABRAHAM (Abr. 3:26), but the preearth life of spirits is called "their first estate" in Jude 1:6. Latter-day Saints believe that through the process of BIRTH, the spirit children of God who kept their FIRST ESTATE (premortal) enter into their second estate by receiving a PHYSICAL BODY with additional opportunities for experience and development. MORTALITY is then a probationary period in which individuals "prepare to meet God" (Alma 12:24). In the final JUDGMENT all MANKIND will "be judged of their works . . . which were done by the temporal body in their days of probation" (1 Ne. 15:32; cf. Alma 12:14). All who receive the saving principles and ORDINANCES of the GOSPEL OF JESUS CHRIST (including FAITH, REPENTANCE, BAPTISM, the GIFT OF THE HOLY GHOST, ordination to the PRIESTHOOD for men, ENDOWMENT, and eternal MARRIAGE) and seek to live righteous and useful lives, embracing the FULNESS OF THE GOSPEL, will obtain the complete blessings of the ATONEMENT of Jesus Christ. All who had no opportunity to do so during earth life will have it in the postmortal spirit world (1 Pet. 3:18–19; 4:6; D&C 138:36–37). Every person who has lived on the earth will be resurrected with perfected corporeal bodies, and those who have kept the commandments will enter into ETERNAL LIFE, and "have glory added upon their heads for ever and ever" (Abr. 3:26).

ALEXANDER L. BAUGH

SECRET COMBINATIONS

In latter-day scriptures, secret combinations are groups of conspirators who plot and initiate "works of darkness" for evil and selfish purposes. Secret combinations have existed since the days of Cain (Moses 5:51). Satan is their author (2 Ne. 26:22), power and gain are their motives (Ether 8:15, 25), and conspiracy is their method of operation (Hel. 6:22–24). Secret combinations may be brotherhoods, groups, societies, or governments. They operate in secrecy to perform evil acts for the purpose of gaining power over the minds and actions of people.

As the enemies of honest men and women governed by the rule of law, such secret combinations seek to subvert public virtue and legally constituted authority. They defile, defraud, murder, deceive, and destroy the elements of good government, religious or secular. Their goal is to seize power and to rule over all the people (3 Ne. 6:27–30), which results in the destruction of human freedom and agency and the paralysis of peaceful and just communities.

Secret combinations and their practices have a scriptural and historic tradition that extends from the days of Cain's secret covenant with Satan to modern times. Members of these Satanic combinations are bound by secret oaths and covenants. The DEVIL proclaims, initiates, and sustains these combinations and their conspiratorial practices (Moses 5:29–33, 47–52).

In the Book of Mormon, several secret combinations challenged governments ruled by the "voice of the people" or by righteous kings. They were a continuing threat to the Jaredites, who succumbed eventually to their power. Later, they were a threat to the Nephite and Lamanite nations when the Gadianton combinations, over a period of many years, challenged the constituted authorities and eventually seized power. The concerted effort of the whole populace later defeated the Gadiantons, but others rose in their place. The Book of Mormon details the tactics and strategies of the Gadiantons, mentions a variety of countermeasures, and shows that a secret combination was responsible for the final downfall of the Nephites (Hel. 2:13–14; Ether 8:21; see also BOOK OF MORMON: HELAMAN and BOOK OF MORMON: 3 NEPHI).

In the contemporary world, secret combinations take various forms and operate at different levels of society. They are expressed in organized crime and in religious, economic, and political conspiracies. The Lord has warned that secret combinations will be present in modern society (D&C 38:29; Ether 8:20–25). They threaten freedom everywhere. However, Latter-day Saints believe that secret combinations and their practices can be overcome, but only through righteous living and full support of honest government.

Secret combinations are often referred to in latter-day scripture, particularly in the book of Moses and the Book of Mormon. In the Doctrine and Covenants, this term describes those who have conspired against the Saints (D&C 42:64). It does not appear in the Bible, but the equivalent "conspiracy" is used at least ten times.

BIBLIOGRAPHY

Hillam, Ray C. "The Gadianton Robbers and Protracted War." BYU Studies 15 (Winter 1975):215–24.

Meservy, Keith H. "'Gadiantonism' and the Destruction of Jerusalem." In The Pearl of Great Price: Revelations from God, ed. H. D. Peterson and C. Tate, pp. 171–95. Provo, Utah, 1989.

Peterson, Daniel C. "The Gadianton Robbers as Guerrilla Warriors." In Warfare in the Book of Mormon, ed. S. Ricks and W. Hamblin, pp. 146–73. Salt Lake City, 1990.

"Secret Combinations." F.A.R.M.S. Update (Oct. 1989).

RAY C. HILLAM

SECT

In ordinary usage the word "sect" refers to any body of followers or adherents, ranging from the main religions of the world to small groups of heretics. "Sect" derives from the Latin sequi, to follow. In sociological terminology, a sect is a separately organized religious group that meets specified criteria. Technically, this term does not adequately describe The Church of Jesus Christ of Latter-day Saints.

As defined by social scientists, three criteria are central in determining whether a religious group is a sect: (1) a sect is organizationally simple; (2) it stands in high tension with the dominant society (typically because sect members view themselves as a "faithful remnant" of the pure religion that has been rejected by society); and (3) it views itself as uniquely legitimate, the sole source of salvation. Applying these criteria to The Church of Jesus Christ of Latter-day Saints is not always easy. With respect to these factors, the organizational structure of the LDS Church is obviously complex and international in scope. While the nineteenth-century commitment to building a literal political and economic kingdom and the practice of plural marriage placed the LDS Church in tension with its host societies, neither of these practices sociologically characterize the twentieth-century Church. In fact, the Church has always embraced many values central to the dominant value systems of the United States and other host countries, including an emphasis on family, hard work, and national loyalty. Nevertheless, moderate tension remains, partly because of the Church's claim of unique legitimacy.

"Churches" and "denominations" in sociological terminology differ from sects in that both of the former are organizationally complex and have positive relationships with society. Denominations accept the legitimacy claims of other religious groups, while churches do not (Roberts, pp. 181–202). There are several problems in classifying The Church of Jesus Christ of Latter-day Saints according to this typology. Its claim to unique legitimacy makes it something other than a denomination, while its lack of societal dominance makes it something other than a church (except in Utah and certain other locations).

To explain unclear cases like this, sociologists developed an additional classification—the "established sect" (Yinger, pp. 266–73). An established sect is organizationally complex while retaining moderate tension with society and the claim to unique legitimacy. While the LDS Church meets these criteria, social scientists increasingly argue that it deviates sufficiently from conventional religious traditions to warrant even further classification outside of the church-denomination-sect typology. They argue that the term "new religion" is perhaps the most accurate and that modern-day Mormonism is on the verge of becoming a major new world religion (Stark, pp. 11–12).

[See also Cult.]

BIBLIOGRAPHY

Roberts, Keith A. Religion in Sociological Perspective, 2nd ed. Belmont, Calif., 1990.

Stark, Rodney. "How New Religions Succeed: A Theoretical Model." In The Future of New Religious Movements, ed. D. Bromley and P. Hammond, pp. 11–29. Macon, Ga., 1987.

Yinger, J. Milton. The Scientific Study of Religion. New York, 1970.

LAWRENCE A. YOUNG

SEED OF ABRAHAM

The "seed of Abraham" are those who, through righteousness, inherit the blessings promised Abraham through the covenant he made with the Lord and who themselves are a promised blessing to Abraham (Gen. 12:1–5; 13:16; 17; Abr. 2:6–11). The phrase also has messianic overtones: Abraham saw the days of the Messiah and rejoiced (John 8:56). Jesus Christ is of the seed of Abraham (Gal. 3:16).

In a lineal sense, two groups are called the "seed of Abraham" in scripture. The first comprises the literal descendants of Abraham through Isaac (Gen. 26:1–4) and Jacob (Gen. 28; 35:9–13), who are thus the twelve tribes of Israel. The second comprises the descendants of Ishmael and the many other children of Abraham.

In addition to those who are of lineal descent, all who are not of Abrahamic lineage but who become adopted by their acceptance of the gospel of Jesus Christ and continued obedience to God's commandments are heirs of all the blessings of the Abrahamic covenant (TPJS, pp. 149–50). Adoption is completed by the gospel ordinances, including baptism and confirmation; ordination to the PRIESTHOOD, and magnifying one's calling in the priesthood; the TEMPLE ENDOWMENT; and eternal MARRIAGE, through which husbands, wives, and families share "all the blessings of Abraham, Isaac, and Jacob." Modern REVELATION assures that these people will have a fulness of blessings, even "all that [the] Father hath" (D&C 84:38). They are "sanctified by the Spirit unto the renewing of their bodies," and they become "the seed of Abraham" (D&C 84:34).

[See also Abrahamic Covenant; Gospel of Abraham.]

ALLEN C. OSTERGAR, JR.

SEER

In ancient usage, "seer" is an alternative term for PROPHET (1 Sam. 9:9). A seer is a person endowed by God with a special gift for seeing spiritually. In the modern Church, members of the FIRST PRESIDENCY and the QUORUM OF THE TWELVE APOSTLES serve as seers. These fifteen apostolic officials are designated PROPHETS, SEERS, AND REVELATORS who direct the Church by means of divine REVELATION, with the President of the Church being the only one in whom the keys are fully active at any one time. Though all three titles describe revelatory capacity, the terms are not fully synonymous. A "prophet" is one who speaks for GOD; the office of "seer" extends that divine endowment to a capacity for envisioning future and past. The Book of Mormon teaches that a "seer is greater than a prophet," because a seer is "a revelator and a prophet also"; seers are unique among prophets in that they "can know of things which are past, and also of things which are to come, and by them shall all things be revealed" (Mosiah 8:15–17).

In the Doctrine and Covenants, the Prophet Joseph SMITH refers to the spiritual process of seership. He describes "being in the Spirit" along with Sidney RIGDON, and "by the power of the Spirit our eyes were opened and our understandings were enlightened, so as to see and understand the things of God" (76:11–12; cf. JS—H 1:74).

The office of seer is often associated with the use of revelatory instruments, particularly the URIM AND THUMMIM, sometimes called SEER STONES. The Book of Mormon suggests that "whosoever has these things is called seer, after the manner of old times" (Mosiah 28:16).

Visionary prophets of the Bible, such as Isaiah, Jeremiah, Peter, and John the Revelator, clearly functioned as seers. In the Book of Mormon, LEHI refers to Joseph of Egypt as a seer who foresaw that in modern times God would raise up from among his descendants yet another "choice seer" (2 Ne. 3:6). The ancient calling of seer remains active through modern times. A seer is "one who sees with spiritual eyes. He perceives the meaning of that which seems obscure to others. . . In short, he is one who sees, who walks in the Lord's light with open eyes" (Widtsoe, p. 205).

BIBLIOGRAPHY

Sperry, Sidney B. *The Voice of Israel's Prophets.* Salt Lake City, 1952.

Widtsoe, John A. *Evidences and Reconciliations*, Vol. 1. Salt Lake City, 1943.

STEVEN C. WALKER

SEER STONES

Joseph SMITH wrote that in 1823 an angel told him about "two stones in silver bows . . . fastened to a breastplate . . . the possession and use of [which] constituted 'seers' in ancient or former times" (JS—H 1:35). Joseph used these and other seer stones that he found in various ways (occasionally referred to by the biblical term URIM AND THUMMIM) for several purposes, primarily in translating the Book of Mormon and receiving revelations (see *HC* 1:21–23, 33, 36, 45, 49; 3:28; 5:xxxii; *CHC* 6:230–31).

Historical sources suggest that effective use of the instruments required Joseph to be at peace with God and his fellowmen, to exercise faith in God, and to exert mental effort (*CHC* 1:128–33). Otherwise, little is said authoritatively about their operation. Occasionally, people have been deceived by trying to use stones to receive revelation, the best-known latter-day example in the Church being Hiram Page (D&C 28:11–12).

While useful in translating and receiving revelation, seer stones are not essential to those processes. Elder Orson Pratt reported that Joseph Smith told him that the Lord gave him the Urim and Thummim when he was inexperienced as a translator but that he later progressed to the point that he no longer needed the instrument ("Two Days' Meeting at Brigham City," *Millennial Star* 36 [1874]:498–99).

RICHARD E. TURLEY, JR.

SELF-SUFFICIENCY (SELF-RELIANCE)

The term "self-sufficiency" refers to a principle underlying the LDS program of WELFARE SERVICES, and to an ideal of social experience. Self-sufficiency is the ability to maintain one's self and relates to women and men being agents for themselves. Independence and self-sufficiency are critical keys to spiritual and temporal growth. A situation that threatens one's ability to be self-sufficient also threatens one's confidence, self-esteem, and freedom. As dependence is increased, the freedom to act is decreased.

Church writings often use the terms self-sufficiency and "self-reliance" interchangeably. Teachings pertaining to Welfare Services emphasize and place considerable importance on both individual and family independence. Six principles form the foundation of the infrastructure of the welfare program. Three of these principles emphasize responsibility to care for one's own needs: work, self-reliance, and stewardship; the other three focus on responsibility to others: love, service, and consecration (Faust, p. 91).

President Spencer W. KIMBALL defined Welfare Services as the "essence of the Gospel . . . the Gospel in action" (Kimball, p. 77). Within the context of welfare, the term self-sufficiency also includes an emphasis on prevention, temporary assistance, and rehabilitation. Self-sufficiency is helping oneself to the point of reliance. Welfare, a program based on self-sufficiency, helps individuals to help themselves. Home industry, gardening, food storage, emergency preparedness, and avoidance of debt reflect the applications of self-sufficiency (*Welfare Services Resource Handbook*, p. 21).

Since the inauguration of Welfare Services in 1936 by President Heber J. GRANT, self-sufficiency has continued to be refined and clarified by Church leaders. This focus has remained as the Church has expanded to countries outside the United States and Canada, and most recently to developing countries of the world. While the Church responds to crises and natural disasters abroad, it is still in a planning stage regarding the tremendous cross-cultural challenges pertaining to the principle of self-sufficiency (*International Welfare Services*, p. 1).

As a social ideal, self-sufficiency includes spiritual, intellectual, and emotional dimensions. Just as the world is economically interdependent, agricultural communities and enterprises have been interdependent; families, farms, and other units have specialized in a product or service with the intent to engage in trade for the additional necessities of life. Self-sufficiency is central to such interdependence and is necessary for one to be in a position to assist others, beginning with one's own family, neighbors, and ward. A universal concern of individuals can be personal integrity and identity within the larger social systems. A responsible, productive, and integrated life in a varied and changing world is desirable and exemplified by Christ and others of integrity discussed in the scriptures.

New Testament teachings conceive of liberty as a person's relationship to God and others (Buttrick, p. 121). Christ gave his followers sacred charge and opportunity to serve the poor, needy, sick, and afflicted. Rather than looking on God as the only one able to provide, individuals as self-sufficient beings work together in mutual responsibility, compassion, gentleness, and love.

Perspective on the balance between an individual person's being totally self-sufficient and also needing assistance comes from the understanding that everyone is self-reliant in some areas and dependent in others. Latter-day Saints accept the observation that everyone is flawed and imperfect; everyone experiences human limitation or poverty. Scriptures recognize that poverty resides in both temporal or spiritual matters. In fact, all are "beggars" for a remission of sins (Mosiah 4:20). Nevertheless, a certain equality emerges from human interdependence, noted in the counsel to be equal in both heavenly and earthly things: "For if ye are not equal in earthly things ye cannot be equal in obtaining heavenly things" (D&C 78:6). From one's strengths, each should endeavor to help another; on the other hand, one should accept the help of another. "If a man be overtaken in a fault, ye which are spiritual, restore such an one in the spirit of meekness; . . . bear ye one another's burdens, and so fulfill the law of Christ" (Gal. 6:1–2). Interdependence, then, creates the opportunity to participate in the sanctifying experience of giving and receiving (Romney, p. 91).

In a gospel sense, there exists an interdependence between those who have and those who have not. The process of sharing lifts the poor, humbles the rich, and sanctifies both. The poor are released from bondage and limitations of poverty and are able to rise to their full potential, both temporally and spiritually. The rich, by imparting of their surplus, participate in the eternal principle of sharing. A person who is whole or self-sufficient can reach out to others, and the cycle of equality and giving repeats itself.

Without self-sufficiency it is difficult to exercise these innate desires to serve. Food for the hungry cannot come from empty shelves; money to assist the needy cannot come from an empty purse; support and understanding cannot come from the emotionally starved; teaching cannot come from the unlearned. Most important of all, spiritual guidance only comes from the spiritually strong. Indeed, self-sufficiency forms the basis to bear one another's burdens and to live interdependently.

BIBLIOGRAPHY

Buttrick, George A., ed. "Liberty." In *The Interpreter's Dictionary of the Bible*, Vol. 3, pp. 122–23. New York, 1962.

Faust, James E. "Establishing the Church: Welfare Services Missionaries Are an Important Resource." *Ensign* 12 (Nov. 1982):91–93.

International Welfare Services. Salt Lake City, 1981.

Kimball, Spencer W. "Welfare Services: The Gospel in Action." *Ensign* 7 (Nov. 1977):76–79.

Romney, Marion G. "The Celestial Nature of Self-Reliance." *Ensign* 12 (Nov. 1982):91–93.

Welfare Services Resource Handbook. Salt Lake City, 1980.

VAL DAN MACMURRAY

SEMINARIES

Seminaries are that part of the CHURCH EDUCATIONAL SYSTEM which provides weekday religious instruction for youth, usually from the ages of fourteen to eighteen, to balance their secular secondary education with study in the SCRIPTURES, religious teachings, and moral values of their faith. To accomplish this objective, four year-long courses are offered: OLD TESTAMENT, NEW TESTAMENT, DOCTRINE AND COVENANTS/ Church HISTORY, and the BOOK OF MORMON. These courses are designed in three basic formats: released-time, early-morning, and home-study.

Released-time seminaries operate during the regular school day in Church-owned facilities near junior and senior high schools. The courses are taught by professionally trained teachers. At the request of parents, students are "released" by the school district to attend one class period a day in a seminary course. This allows the students to receive the moral, character, and scriptural educa-tion available through Church-related instruction along with regular public school education in a nearby facility. The constitutionality of released-time religious education has been tested and upheld in the courts in cases involving Catholic and Protestant programs (with some LDS participation as *amicus curiae*). The legality of the LDS approach has also been resolved in various western U.S. states to allow released-time classes, but not to permit transfer of high school credit for those classes (*see* LEGAL AND JUDICIAL HISTORY OF THE CHURCH). It is common for enrollments in released-time seminaries to exceed 80 percent of the total number of LDS youth attending the high school.

Early-morning seminaries provide weekday religious instruction in areas where local public school laws do not grant released-time or where the LDS population does not warrant the establishment of a released-time seminary program. These classes generally meet before the regular school day begins, usually in an LDS MEET-

The first graduating seminary class, Granite High School, 1927, where the first released-time classes began in 1912–1913. After the Church closed its stake academies in the 1920s, it began building a staff of centrally directed religion instructors to teach high school students during public school hours. Courtesy Department of Special Collections, University of Utah Libraries.

INGHOUSE convenient to the high school. The instructors are generally local members appointed on a part-time or volunteer basis. Typically, between 50 to 70 percent of eligible LDS youth are enrolled where early-morning seminary classes function.

Home-study seminaries are provided to meet the needs of LDS youth living where distance or other problems make participation in a daily class impossible or inadvisable. Curriculum materials based on the four regular courses have been developed for students to study daily at home. Home-study students generally meet once each week in a class taught by an appointed teacher. Average enrollment levels in home-study seminary programs are usually a lower percentage of the LDS youth of an area than that of the early-morning and released-time seminaries.

ADMINISTRATION. Seminaries are directly administered by the office of Religious Education and Elementary and Secondary Schools of the Church Educational System, which is governed by the Church Board of Education. The FIRST PRESIDENCY of the Church presides over this board, with board members appointed from among the QUORUM OF TWELVE APOSTLES and other general church officers, including the presidents of the women's RELIEF SOCIETY and the YOUNG WOMEN organization. Professional educational administrators responsible to the central administrator of Religious Education in the Salt Lake office are appointed to supervise the day-to-day operation of the high school seminary program throughout the world. STAKE PRESIDENTS also assist in local administration, especially in encouraging registration of the youth of their STAKES.

HISTORICAL BACKGROUND. Shortly after the LDS PIONEERS arrived in the Salt Lake Valley in 1847, the leaders of the Church directed the establishment of SCHOOLS to provide education for its members. In the last quarter of the nineteenth century, each STAKE was encouraged to establish an ACADEMY to offer secondary educational instruction. Classes in religion were an essential component of this Church-sponsored school system.

In the early 1900s, when Utah public high schools became more fully established, Church leaders decided to close their academies and to support the public high schools, thus eliminating

the need for Church members to fund both Church-owned and public schools.

To supplement secular public education with religious instruction, the first Latter-day Saint seminary was established in 1912 adjacent to Granite High School in Salt Lake City. When this released-time seminary program proved to be effective, it was quickly adopted in other communities with a high ratio of LDS youth. In 1990 released-time seminaries were operating in Utah, Idaho, Wyoming, Arizona, Oregon, and some parts of Colorado. From 1950 to 1970, early-morning seminaries had been established throughout California and other western states. With the home-study adaptation, the Church has essentially established seminary programs of one variety or another in all fifty states. Graduation from seminary is accomplished by students completing all four courses and living lives which reflect the moral teachings of their faith.

In the fall of 1970, when the Church Board of Education determined that the seminary program should reach the membership of the Church throughout the world, the seminary program was internationalized, with course materials translated into sixteen languages. In 1990, the seminary program was operating in more than ninety countries and territories with more than 300,000 students enrolled.

BIBLIOGRAPHY

Berrett, William E. *A Miracle in Weekday Religious Education.* Salt Lake City, 1988.

Quinn, D. Michael. "Utah's Educational Innovation: LDS Religion Classes, 1890–1929." *Utah Historical Quarterly* 43 (Fall 1975):379–89.

Widtsoe, John A. "The Church School System." *IE* 26 (1923):863–69.

JOE J. CHRISTENSEN

SENIOR CITIZENS

The Church of Jesus Christ of Latter-day Saints has always had concern for the well-being of its older members. "Mormon attitudes toward old age were influenced by Joseph Smith and other Church leaders, and by scriptural injunctions to honor the elderly" (Reeves, p. 150). Latter-day Saints view aging as an important part of God's plan and believe that completing one's mortal probation and

Old Folks outing, c. 1898. Photographer: Ebenezer Beesley.

ENDURING TO THE END are essential in the plan of salvation.

While programs for the youth of the Church currently are better known than programs for the elderly, the reverse was true during the nineteenth century. The best example is the Old Folks movement, founded as a private initiative by Charles R. Savage, which began with annual excursions to various Utah locations in 1875 and continued until the turn of the century, when stake presidencies and ward bishoprics were instructed by the First Presidency to organize stake and ward Old Folks committees. They were to entertain the elderly in their wards and stakes twice a year, a function which continued in some wards and stakes through the 1960s.

The elderly in the Church have often immersed themselves in genealogical and temple work. As early as 1951, Church leaders urged older people also to become more involved in missionary work. Today, many of them serve effectively as full-time missionaries.

Conference addresses of General Authorities are replete with advice to, and about, the elderly.

Two dominant themes in the first half of this century were that children should care for their aging parents and that old people should avoid government doles. More recently, Church President Ezra Taft BENSON identified eight areas in which he urged the elderly of the Church to be involved: (1) to serve often in the temple (*see* TEMPLE WORSHIP); (2) to collect and write FAMILY HISTORIES; (3) to render MISSIONARY service or give support to the missionaries; (4) to provide leadership by building family togetherness (*see* FAMILY ORGANIZATION); (5) to accept and fulfill Church CALLINGS; (6) to plan for a sound financial future; (7) to render Christlike service; and (8) to stay physically fit, healthy, and active (*Ensign* 19 [Nov. 1989]:4–6).

Research comparing older Mormons with other senior citizens is limited. One study (Peterson) found that older Mormons are more family-oriented, more active in their religion, and more conservative in religious beliefs; however, it also concluded that older Mormons are like the general population in matters of health-consciousness and contentedness. Perhaps the most comprehensive study of aging Mormons within a family context is the *LDS Family Longitudinal Study*, sponsored by Brigham Young University. This projected twenty-year study was initiated in 1983 with approximately 1,200 individuals from 133 three-generation families. It suggests that most older Church members are doing rather well; however, individual conditions and challenges vary considerably.

BIBLIOGRAPHY

Peterson, Evan T. "A Comparative Analysis of Elderly Mormons and Non-Mormons." Annual Meeting of the Association for the Sociology of Religion, Chicago, Aug. 14–16, 1987.

Reeves, Brian D. "Hoary-headed Saints: The Aged in Nineteenth-Century Mormon Culture." Master's thesis, Brigham Young University, 1987.

EVAN T. PETERSON

SERMON ON THE MOUNT

The Sermon on the Mount (Matt. 5–7) is for Latter-day Saints, as well as for all other Christians, a key source for the teachings of Jesus and of Christian behavior ethics. The fact that parallel accounts appear in the BOOK OF MORMON (3 Ne. 12–14) and the JOSEPH SMITH TRANSLATION OF THE BIBLE (JST Matt. 5–7) offers both the opportunity for a better understanding of the Sermon and the obligation to refute notions of mere plagiarism by the Prophet Joseph SMITH. A careful comparison of the texts reveals significant differences that are attributable primarily to the specific setting of the Book of Mormon sermon.

In the Book of Mormon account, the resurrected Jesus appeared to the more righteous survivors of a fierce storm and major earthquake in the Western Hemisphere who had gathered at the temple in the land called Bountiful. The setting includes the performance of ordinances, for the people prepared for baptism, first that of water by twelve men whom Jesus had ordained, followed by that of fire from the Lord himself (3 Ne. 12:1). The sermon at the temple thus provides the assembled multitude with an understanding of their duties and obligations. It also introduces them to the fulness of the gospel that Jesus established among them because he had fulfilled the law "that was given unto Moses" (3 Ne. 15:4–10) under which they had lived. Obedience to Jesus' gospel gave

the Book of Mormon people two hundred years of peace and harmony as it became established throughout their lands (4 Ne. 1:17–23). Since Jesus himself observes that he had given a similar sermon in Palestine before he ascended to his Father (3 Ne. 15:1), Latter-day Saints have no doubt that the Sermon on the Mount reflects a unified presentation that the Savior possibly gave on several occasions (JST Matt. 7:1–2, 9, 11) and not merely a collection brought together by Matthew or his sources. As in many speaking situations, a speaker can repeat the basic message with appropriate alterations to fit the specific audience.

SETTING OF THE SERMONS. While much of the text in 3 Nephi 12–14 is identical to Matthew 5–7, there are numerous and significant differences. Most of the differences stem from the specific setting of the Book of Mormon sermon. First, the risen Jesus opened his Book of Mormon sermon with three additional BEATITUDES that underscore its purpose as an address to believers: "Blessed are ye if ye shall give heed unto the words of these twelve whom I have chosen; . . . blessed are ye if ye shall believe in me and be baptized; . . . more blessed are they who shall believe in your words . . . and be baptized . . . [and] receive a remission of their sins" (3 Ne. 12:1–2). Further, the Book of Mormon account is post-Resurrection, and the emphasis is on the fact that the Lord has completely fulfilled his mission of salvation. Thus, Jesus can summarize the series of antitheses recorded in 3 Nephi 12:21–45: "Those things which were of old time, which were under the law, in me are all fulfilled" (3 Ne. 12:46). Furthermore, rather than instructing the people "Be ye therefore perfect, even as your Father which is in heaven is perfect" (Matt. 5:48), Jesus in meaningfully modified words told them, "I would that ye should be perfect even as I, or your Father who is in heaven is perfect" (3 Ne. 12:48). In place of the open-ended "one jot or one tittle shall in no wise pass away from the law, till all be fulfilled" (Matt. 5:18), the Book of Mormon passage replaced the phrase "till all be fulfilled" with "but in me it hath all been fulfilled" (3 Ne. 12:18).

Other changes reflect both the Book of Mormon setting and the absence of antipharisaic statements that figure prominently in Matthew's account. Two examples of the former are the replacement of the "farthing" (Matt. 5:26) with the "senine" (3 Ne. 12:26), which was the smallest Nephite measure of gold (Alma 11:3, 15–19), and the lack of reference to the swearing "by Jerusalem . . . the city of the great King" (Matt. 5:35). Similarly, the sermon at the temple in Bountiful does not mention surpassing the righteousness of the scribes and Pharisees, as in Matthew 5:20, or that of the publicans who are loved by their friends (Matt. 5:46–47). In place of the references to the scribes and Pharisees (Matt. 5:20), the Lord told the Nephites: "Except ye shall keep my commandments, which I have commanded you at this time, ye shall in no case enter into the kingdom of heaven" (3 Ne. 12:20). Also, the Book of Mormon account does not contain the references to self-mutilation found in Matthew 5:29–30, or the qualifying phrase "without a cause" in Matthew 5:22 (cf. 3 Ne. 12:22).

CLARIFICATIONS. A further type of difference consists of additions to the Sermon on the Mount text that often provide sensible clarifications. Several examples are found in the Beatitudes. The Book of Mormon version noted that it is "the poor in spirit *who come unto me*" who inherit the kingdom of heaven (3 Ne. 12:3; Matt. 5:3; emphasis added). At the end of 3 Nephi 12:6 (cf. Matt. 5:6), one finds "blessed are all they who do hunger and thirst after righteousness, for they shall be filled *with the Holy Ghost*" (emphasis added). While these might seem to be small changes, they nonetheless enhance understanding of Jesus' meaning.

For Latter-day Saints, the message of the Sermon on the Mount centers on its normative value. As a covenant-making people, they take upon themselves the obligation to emulate the Savior in their personal lives and to work toward the ultimate goal of becoming like him. Although the demands are substantial, they are provided an incentive to strive to become like their divine model (cf. 2 Ne. 31:7–10, 16; 3 Ne. 27:27). The simple words and teachings that Jesus gave to his followers in Palestine and to the Book of Mormon survivors are still applicable to his Saints today.

[*See also* Lord's Prayer.]

BIBLIOGRAPHY

Stendahl, Krister. "The Sermon on the Mount and Third Nephi." In *Reflections on Mormonism*, ed. T. Madsen, pp. 139–54. Provo, Utah, 1978.

Thomas, Catherine. "The Sermon on the Mount: The Sacrifice of the Human Heart." In *Studies in Scripture*, ed. K. Jackson and R. Millet, Vol. 5, pp. 236–50. Salt Lake City, 1986.

Welch, John W. *The Sermon at the Temple and the Sermon on the Mount.* Salt Lake City, 1990.

ROBERT TIMOTHY UPDEGRAFF

SETH

Seth was the son of Adam and Eve, a high priest, a patriarch, and one chosen to fill the birthright promise of the covenant seed. While the Bible devotes only seven verses to Seth (Gen. 4:25–26; 5:3–4, 6–8), Latter-day scripture adds substantial detail, underscoring his importance in a manner reminiscent of other ancient texts. According to LDS sources, Seth was born after numerous other children (Moses 5:2–3), was ordained at age sixty-nine by Adam, and became patriarchal leader after the death of his father (D&C 107:41–42).

Following the murder of ABEL, Seth inherited the birthright of the patriarchal order of the high priesthood because of his righteousness (D&C 107:40–43), taking Abel's place (Gen. 4:25; Moses 6:2). "The order of this priesthood was confirmed to be handed down from father to son, and rightly belongs to the literal descendants of [Seth's] chosen seed, to whom the promises were made . . . in the days of Adam, and came down by lineage . . . from Adam to Seth, who . . . received the promise of God by his father, that his posterity should be the chosen of the Lord, and that they should be preserved unto the end of the earth" (D&C 107:40–42). At ADAM-ONDI-AHMAN, before his death, Adam bestowed a "blessing upon seven of his [descendants]—Seth, Enos, Jared, Canaan, Mahalaleel, Enoch, and Methuselah" (Durham, p. 64).

Seth was obedient and righteous under the tutelage of Adam so that "he seemed . . . like unto his father in all things," and was called "a perfect man" (D&C 107:43), as were NOAH and others (Gen. 6:9; Job 1:1). He "offered an acceptable sacrifice, like unto his brother Abel," with the result that "God revealed himself unto Seth" (Moses 6:3). Apocryphal texts, seeking patterns for the ministry of the expected MESSIAH, focus on notions of Seth's leadership in the premortal life, his complete obedience, and his role as father and patriarch of the covenant race (Brown, p. 278).

BIBLIOGRAPHY

Brown, S. Kent. "The Nag Hammadi Library: A Mormon Perspective." In *Apocryphal Writings and the Latter-day Saints*, ed. C.W. Griggs. Provo, Utah, 1986.

Charlesworth, James H. *The Old Testament Pseudepigrapha*, 2 vols. Garden City, N.Y., 1983–1985.

Woodruff, Wilford. *Discourses of Wilford Woodruff*, comp. G. Homer Durham. Salt Lake City, 1969.

L. LAMAR ADAMS

SETTING APART

"Setting apart" is a priesthood ordinance that is performed by the LAYING ON OF HANDS, authorizing a man or woman to serve in a Church CALLING. It occurs after one has been sustained by COMMON CONSENT to perform certain duties and responsibilities in a specific calling in a geographical or organizational part of the Church. It is performed by, or under the direction of, the one in AUTHORITY over that unit. One is "ordained" to priesthood offices, but is "set apart" to preside or serve. In the setting apart, one is given the authority and charged to act; he or she is also counseled, instructed, and blessed. The blessings are conditional upon faithful performance.

The meaning of being set apart to service in the Church is symbolically a setting apart (a separation) from the world to act on a higher plane (Lev. 20:26; Num. 8:14; Ezra 8:24; Rom. 1:1). The act of setting apart is referred to in the Bible in a number of places, though not always using the same terminology. Moses was told to "put some of thine honour" upon Joshua that the Israelites might be obedient to him (Num. 27:20). Seven men of honest report were "set before the apostles," who laid their hands on them to take charge of temporal matters in the early church (Acts 6:6). The early Twelve were told to "separate me Barnabas and Saul for the work whereunto I have called them" (Acts 13:2). The Book of Mormon writers appear to use the terms "consecrate" and "appoint" to describe a setting apart (Mosiah 6:3).

Settings apart concern both the Church unit and the person. When men and women are set apart as presidents of Church organizations, they are given the authority as well as the obligations and responsibilities to act in their offices. The president is always set apart before the counselors, since counselors are set apart as counselors to the specific person serving as president.

In the early days of the Church, the words "ordain" and "set apart" were often used interchangeably for both ordination and setting apart. Therefore, the Doctrine and Covenants speaks of men being ordained high councilors and women being ordained to preside over auxiliaries (D&C 20:67; 25:7). In modern usage, both these would be instances of being set apart.

BIBLIOGRAPHY

Allred, Rex. "Where Does the Church's Practice of Setting Apart Come From?" *Ensign* 13 (Mar. 1983):67–68.

DENNIS L. THOMPSON

SEVENTY

[*This entry contains three articles:*

Overview

First Council of the Seventy

Quorums of Seventy

The first article identifies the office of Seventy in The Church of Jesus Christ of Latter-day Saints. Then it discusses the biblical precedents in Old and New Testament times. It then describes the establishment of the priesthood office of seventy by Joseph Smith in the 1830s and the subsequent development of that office at greater length. The second article discusses the organization of General Authority seventies before the reorganization of 1975, when its functions and officers were incorporated into the current quorums of the Seventy. The third article describes the contemporary constitution and function of seventies in The Church of Jesus Christ of Latter-day Saints. The bibliography for all the articles follows the first entry. See also General Authorities; Melchizedek Priesthood; Organization: Contemporary; Priesthood Quorums.]

OVERVIEW

Seventy is a PRIESTHOOD OFFICE in the Melchizedek Priesthood reserved since 1986 for General Authorities called to assist the FIRST PRESIDENCY and QUORUM OF THE TWELVE APOSTLES in the administration of the Church worldwide. The organization and assignments of seventies have undergone numerous changes as the Church organization has developed.

On February 28, 1835, at Kirtland, Ohio, the organization of the Seventy commenced with individuals selected from among the participants in ZION'S CAMP. The Prophet Joseph Smith recorded that they were "ordained and blessed at that time, to begin the organization of the first quorum of Seventies, according to the visions and revelations which I have received. The Seventies are to constitute traveling quorums, to go into all the earth, whithersoever the Twelve Apostles shall call them" (*HC* 2:201–202). In a March 1835 revelation the role of the Seventy was further clarified: "The Seventy are also called to preach the gospel, and to be especial witnesses unto the Gentiles and in all the world—thus differing from other officers in the church in the duties of their calling" (D&C 107:25). Further, they are to act in the name of the Lord and under the direction of the Quorum of the Twelve Apostles "in building up the church and regulating all the affairs of the same in all nations, first unto the Gentiles and then to the Jews" (verse 34). Finally, the Seventy are to be "traveling ministers" to Gentiles and Jews (verse 97).

BIBLICAL BACKGROUND.   God instructed Moses to take seventy of the elders of Israel up onto the holy mount, where "they saw God, and did eat and drink" (Ex. 24:1, 9–11). On another occasion, Moses was told to gather seventy men of the elders of Israel to the tabernacle of the congregation. There the Lord put his spirit upon them, empowering them to assist Moses in bearing the burdens of the people (Num. 11:16–17, 24–25). Many Jewish writers have read this as an account of the divine origin of their Sanhedrin, a body of seventy-one or seventy-two elders that regulated many of their affairs, particularly at the time of Jesus Christ.

Luke recorded the Lord's appointment of the seventy whom he sent "two and two before his face into every city and place, whither he himself would come" (Luke 10:1). Of their return he wrote, "And the seventy returned again with joy, saying, Lord, even the devils are subject unto us through thy name" (Luke 10:17). Some regard Luke's statement that "the Lord appointed other seventy also" to be an indication that more than one group of seventies served the Lord during his ministry (Luke 10:1). Latter-day Saints see these seventy as an important part of the ORGANIZATION OF THE CHURCH IN NEW TESTAMENT TIMES.

IN THE MODERN CHURCH.   The first quorums of the Seventy in the RESTORATION were organized in 1835–1836 in Kirtland, Ohio. Their members participated in the momentous events surrounding the dedication of the Kirtland Temple in 1836. On occasions, most notably in the temple dedicatory services, the Prophet referred to members of the Seventy broadly as APOSTLES and special witnesses to the nations in assisting the Twelve (*HC* 2:418). In 1838 the First Quorum of the Seventy organized and led the Kirtland Camp, consisting of 529 people, in their march from Kirtland to Far West and Adam-ondi-Ahman in Missouri.

In Nauvoo the number of seventies rapidly expanded, in part because of a decision that all elders under the age of thirty-five become seventies. To provide leadership for the newly established quorums, the sixty-three members of the First Quorum who were not in its presidency were divided into nine presidencies of seven and assigned to preside over the next nine quorums. The seven presidents who remained in the First Quorum presided over all seventies. These men were designated the First Council of the Seventy and were sustained as General Authorities of the Church. In December 1844 the Seventies' Hall was dedicated in Nauvoo in imposing ceremonies that continued for a week. A famous LDS hymn, "The Seer," written in honor of the recently martyred Prophet, was prepared for these services. The quorums of the Seventy then numbered fifteen. By the time of the exodus from Nauvoo, the number of seventies quorums had increased to thirty-five. These quorums were independent of geographical wards. When one was made a member of a quorum, it was presumed to be for life.

When the Saints arrived in Utah and began to spread throughout the territory, members of a quorum were dispersed geographically, making it impossible for them to meet together as a quorum. Disarray and confusion persisted into the 1880s. Efforts were made to identify and motivate seventies throughout the Church. In 1882 a revelation came to President John Taylor calling on the Twelve to assist the seventies and increase service among the Lamanites (American Indians). This revelation appeared to be a response to the organizational woes of the seventies quorums, but little success resulted from the change. In 1883 the First Presidency prepared instructions on the organization of the Seventy, and President Taylor received a revelation affirming that what they had written "is [God's] will, and is acceptable unto [him]" (Hartley, p. 70). The instructions established the First Quorum of the Seventy, consisting of its seven presidents (the First Council of Seventy) and the senior presidents of the sixty-four oldest quorums. While this action answered the appeal of many to reorganize the First Quorum, this new quorum never met or functioned as a body—perhaps because of the increasing pressures from federal ANTIPOLYGAMY LEGISLATION.

The headquarters and records of the numbered quorums were then redistributed throughout the wards and stakes of the Church, under the direction of the First Council of Seventy, as the numbers residing in each locality justified. Counsel was given for all seventies in good standing to join the quorum located in their district. Quorum presidents were released if they did not live in the boundary of their quorum and, where possible, were sustained in new quorums where they were residing. Some found it difficult to give up the membership and seniority they enjoyed in their original quorums. Nevertheless, by April 1884 there were 76 quorums; by 1888 there were 101.

By October 1904, the number of quorums had reached 146 with some 10,000 members. President Joseph F. Smith said that their special duty was "to respond to the call of the Apostles to preach the Gospel, without purse or scrip, to all the nations of the earth. They are minute men" (CR, Oct. 6, 1904, p. 3). Their chief function was to serve as MISSIONARIES for the Church. But, since the quorums were now geographical, stake and ward officers gradually utilized seventies in the common duties of the Church. For several years the Seventy had their own course of study, but in 1909 they began to use the study manuals followed by other Melchizedek Priesthood quorums. In 1912, in Salt Lake City's Granite Stake, the program of stake missions was initiated with the seventies as the major participants. This program expanded with occasional adjustments into the 1980s. Every stake had its "stake mission," largely under supervision of the seventies.

As the Church expanded, the demands upon its General Authorities determined much of the future role the seventies would be given. The presiding offices of the Church established by the revelations consisted only of the quorums of the First Presidency, the Twelve, and the Seventy. In every revelation, the Seventy are subordinate to, and under the direction of, the other two. Over time, the First Presidency and the Quorum of the Twelve Apostles have introduced many changes affecting the seventies that have proven to be appropriate responses to expanding needs of the Church. Decisions affecting the Seventy in the last three decades have been especially substantial and rapid.

In 1961 the members of the First Council of the Seventy were ordained high priests by the First Presidency. President David O. McKay stated, "The members of the First Council of the Seventy are now given the authority of high priests to set in order all things pertaining to the stake and the wards, under the direction of the Twelve Apostles" (IE 65 [Jan. 1962]:42). On January 12, 1964, the seven members of the First Council of Seventy were given the sealing authority. On March 29, 1974, the First Presidency authorized stake presidents to ordain seventies approved by the First Council. On October 3, 1974, all previous seventies units were replaced by quorums in each stake and were designated with the name of the stake, rather than a number.

President Spencer W. KIMBALL organized the First Quorum of the Seventy on October 3, 1975, and called three new General Authorities as members of that quorum, in addition to the seven presidents. Unlike the stake quorums, members of this quorum would be General Authorities. On October 1, 1976, twenty men previously sustained as ASSISTANTS TO THE TWELVE were added to the First Quorum of the Seventy and the titles First Council of the Seventy and Assistant to the Twelve were dropped. The First Presidency also announced that the seven presidents would not be determined by tenure of service and would be rotated periodically. In the October 1978 general conference, emeritus status was announced for several designated members of the First Quorum of the Seventy whose age and health prevented their full participation. In the April 1984 general conference, six new members of the Seventy were sustained for a period of three to five years—rather than for life, as before. In the general conference held on October 4, 1986, all stake quorums of seventy were discontinued, and all seventies in those quorums were directed to affiliate with the elders quorums in their wards.

In the April 1989 general conference, the Second Quorum of the Seventy was organized, with General Authorities called to temporary service. As additional General Authorities are required to administer the growing worldwide organization, it is assumed that additional quorums of seventy will be formed "until seven times seventy, if the labor in the vineyard of necessity requires it" (D&C 107:95–96). The First Quorum of Seventy consists of members called for lifetime service or until granted emeritus status. The Presidency of the First Quorum of Seventy presides over both quorums of seventies, as their assignments are not distinguished by quorum.

BIBLIOGRAPHY

Brown, S. Kent. "The Seventy in Scripture." In *By Study and by Faith*, ed. J. Lundquist and S. Ricks, Vol. 1, pp. 25–45. Salt Lake City, 1990.

Hartley, William G. "The Seventies in the 1880s: Revelations and Reorganizing." *Dialogue* 16 (Spring 1983):62–88.

Ivins, Antoine R. "The Seventy and the First Council." *IE* 59 (Nov. 1956):792–93.

Roberts, B. H. *The Seventy's Course in Theology: Outline History of the Seventy and a Survey of the Books of Holy Scripture*, 2nd ed., pp. 3–31. Salt Lake City, 1944.

"Stake Seventies Quorums Discontinued." *Ensign* 16 (Nov. 1986):97–98.

Tuttle, A. Theodore. "The Calling of the Seventy." *IE* 73 (Dec. 1970):84, 86.

Young, Levi Edgar. "The Divine Call of the Seventies." *IE* 56 (Dec. 1953):952, 954.

Young, S. Dilworth. "The Seventies, A Historical Perspective." *Ensign* 6 (July 1976):14–21.

ALAN K. PARRISH

FIRST COUNCIL OF THE SEVENTY

The First Council of the Seventy, comprised of the first seven presidents of the First Quorum of Seventy, was organized on February 28, 1835, at Kirtland, Ohio, by Joseph Smith in response to revelation regarding the organization of priesthood offices. Later, when it was determined that five high priests had been ordained seventies, the First Council was reorganized in April 1837, using only priesthood members who were seventies (*HC* 2:476).

As outlined in Doctrine and Covenants 107:93–98, the Seventy "should have seven presidents to preside over them, chosen out of the number of the seventy." Other seventies could be called as needed, but the first seven presidents (First Council of the Seventy) were to preside over all the additional seventies as well as the First Quorum.

Through the years the role of the First Council of the Seventy and their specific function as General Authorities have been modified in such areas as the seventy's missionary role, their ability to preside and ordain, and their position as "especial witnesses" (Madsen, pp. 299–300).

By 1936 the various seventies quorums scattered throughout the Church were placed under stake supervision. In 1961 members of the First Council of Seventy were ordained high priests with their primary calling being missionaries, but they also had the authority to act as administrators and direct the affairs of the Church in various parts of the world, under the direction of the First Presidency and the Quorum of the Twelve Apostles. On October 3, 1975, the First Quorum of the Seventy was reconstituted as an entity, and on October 1, 1976, the members of the First Council of the Seventy and the Assistants to the Quorum of the Twelve Apostles were released and added to the First Quorum of the Seventy. A new presidency of the First Quorum of the Seventy was sustained. Additional men were selected to be members of the First Quorum and to act as General Authorities to assist in the expanded functions of Church leadership (*Ensign* 6 [Nov. 1976]:9–10). In 1984 Gordon B. Hinckley, counselor in the First Presidency, announced that in order to infuse "new talent and a much widened opportunity for men of ability and faith to serve" as General Authorities, new members of the First Quorum were to be called to act for a period of three to five years (*CR*, Apr. 1984, p. 4). This policy was redefined on April 1, 1989, when the Second Quorum of Seventy was organized, comprised of men who would be called to serve for a period of five years (*CR*, Apr. 1989, p. 22). President Hinckley later indicated that members of the First Quorum would serve until "factors of age and health" made them candidates for emeritus status (*Ensign* 20 [Jan. 1990]:10). The leaders of the Seventy were identified as the "Presidency of the Seventy."

BIBLIOGRAPHY

Cowan, Richard O. *The Church in the Twentieth Century*. Salt Lake City, 1985.

Madsen, Truman G. *Defender of the Faith: The B. H. Roberts Story*. Salt Lake City, 1980.

Roberts, B. H. *The Seventy's Course in Theology*. Salt Lake City, 1931.

RICHARD C. ROBERTS

QUORUMS OF SEVENTY

The quorums of Seventy consist of general Church officers, ordained to the Melchizedek Priesthood office of seventy, who, under the direction of the FIRST PRESIDENCY and the QUORUM OF THE

TWELVE APOSTLES, carry major responsibility for administering the affairs of The Church of Jesus Christ of Latter-day Saints throughout the world. The First Quorum of Seventy constitutes a third presiding quorum over the Church after the First Presidency and the Quorum of the Twelve Apostles (D&C 107:24; *see also* ORGANIZATION: CONTEMPORARY). A presidency of seven, all seventies and members of the First Quorum, presides over the quorums of Seventy, conducts quorum meetings, and instructs the members in their specific duties.

Members of the Seventy are called from the membership of the Church by the First Presidency. Generally they are HIGH PRIESTS of considerable experience in Church leadership within their own wards and STAKES who have distinguished themselves in their service. Like all LDS leaders, they are not professional clergy but come from many vocations and professions (*see* LAY PARTICIPATION AND LEADERSHIP). Each one is presented to the general membership of the Church for a sustaining vote at a general conference. Then he is ordained a seventy and set apart by the First Presidency of the Church, receiving the authority and powers that pertain to his calling as a GENERAL AUTHORITY. The Seventy have all of the authority necessary to officiate in any capacity assigned to them by the First Presidency and the Quorum of the Twelve Apostles: "The Seventy are to act in the name of the Lord, under the direction of the Twelve . . . in building up the church and regulating all the affairs of the same in all nations" (D&C 107:34).

Some members of the quorums of Seventy are assigned to serve in groups of three as AREA PRESIDENCIES and preside over large geographical subdivisions of the Church. In this capacity, they supervise MISSIONS, stakes, districts, wards, and branches and are responsible for the effective implementation of Church policies and programs in their areas.

For example, as of 1990, the continent of South America included three such areas, continental Europe was designated as another, and the United States and Canada were divided into nine areas. The seventies who preside over these areas administer all the affairs of the Church within their jurisdictions, including MISSIONARY work and all functions designed to enhance the spiritual and temporal welfare of Church members. These seventies make regular visits to missions and stakes within their area to train local leaders in their duties and to counsel and instruct Church members in conference meetings. They also administer the financial affairs of the Church and supervise the construction and maintenance of Church buildings. Those assigned outside North America live within their area and travel to Church headquarters for the general conferences in April and October of each year. Seventies assigned to an area within the United States and Canada generally reside in or near Salt Lake City, close to Church headquarters, and travel at regular intervals to their area. These seventies also administer headquarters departments of the Church, such as operations related to Church history, curriculum, priesthood and auxiliary organizations, temples, family history, missionary work, and correlation. These assignments, as well as those that pertain to area supervision, are made under the direction of the First Presidency and the Quorum of the Twelve Apostles, with recommendations from the presidency of the quorums. All these assignments of the Seventy are rotated periodically. The members of the presidency of the First Quorum of Seventy serve as executive directors of Church headquarters departments.

Members of the quorums of Seventy who are located at Church headquarters meet weekly under the direction of the presidency of the First Quorum of Seventy. These meetings provide instruction for quorum members in Church doctrine and procedure. Seventies who are assigned to international areas meet together regularly as area presidencies within their own assigned territories. Twice a year, during the annual and semiannual general conferences, all the General Authorities meet in Salt Lake City for about two weeks for an intensive review of, and instruction in, Church policies and programs. They report on Church progress and growth in all parts of the world and assess Church programs as they apply to various nationalities and cultures. All who assemble receive spiritual instruction and are given renewed vision and direction by the First Presidency and the Quorum of the Twelve Apostles.

In accordance with the revelation that mandates that the Seventy are to act under the direction of the Twelve, the seven presidents of the First Quorum of Seventy meet regularly with the Twelve to receive instruction and to coordinate the work assigned to them. Such coordination is essential to comply with one of the provisions in the revelation: "And every decision made by either of these quorums must be by the unanimous voice of the same; that is, every member in each quorum must be agreed to its decisions, in order to make their decisions of the same power or validity one with the other" (D&C 107:27).

Because the function of the Seventy in the administrative affairs of the Church remains flexible, future adjustments to accommodate changing situations may be expected.

DEAN L. LARSEN

SEX EDUCATION

Latter-day Saints are instructed that parents have the divinely appointed responsibility and privilege of teaching their children moral and eternal values associated with human SEXUALITY and reproduction. Except in unusual cases, they cannot ignore or shift the ultimate responsibility for educating their children about sex to any other person or entity.

The scriptures define the union of the spirit and the body as the soul of man (D&C 88:15) and declare that MARRIAGE and FAMILY in the highest degree of heavenly glory are eternal (D&C 131:2; 132:19). Therefore, LDS discussion about sex respects the PHYSICAL BODY, life, marriage, family, the intentions of God the Creator, and the shared creative powers he has entrusted to a heterosexual husband and wife (see PROCREATION). The spirit of the Lord's law of love and righteousness requires one to keep sacred and appropriate all sexual desires and all related behaviors. All people are admonished to remain chaste before marriage and totally faithful in marriage (see ADULTERY; CHASTITY).

At an early age, children begin to recognize sexual differences. The Church encourages parents to establish open communication by providing their children correct information and by being aware of each individual child's readiness for specific instruction so that children will feel free to talk with their parents about sex differences and functions.

Parents are counseled to help their adolescent and older children understand the need to stay in control of their emotions and behaviors relative to

physical desire and to teach them how to make personal decisions about sexual behavior based on moral awareness, with the realization that virtue and moral cleanliness lead to strength of character, peace of mind, lifelong happiness, and a fulness of love. LDS scriptures counsel, "See that ye bridle all your passions, that ye may be filled with love" (Alma 38:12).

A Parent's Guide was developed by the Church to provide information and suggest teaching methods to parents. It helps parents teach children in the home about sacred and personal matters appropriate to each age through all the stages of childhood, adolescence (see DATING AND COURTSHIP), and marriage. President David O. McKAY taught, "The home is the best place in the world to teach the child self-restraint, to give him [or her] happiness in self-control, and respect for the rights of others" (*IE* 62 [Aug. 1959]:583). Latter-day Saints view the home as the proper place for teaching children about care for the body, gender roles, sexuality, changing physical and emotional needs, prevention of sexual abuse, and enjoyment of proper and virtuous intimacies.

Where schools have undertaken sex education courses and programs, the Church believes the materials used should advocate abstinence from sex before marriage and should teach correct principles that will produce long-term happiness. Thus, the Church believes that public education should in no way promote or encourage sexual promiscuity, a lifestyle that is unhealthy, immoral, and fraught with potentially serious consequences. The Church takes the position that when sex education is taught in the schools, the teacher and the course materials should encourage parental involvement in sex-educational discussions to foster respect for the family, human life, and natural differences between the sexes. When educators teach about human sexuality, they should feel that they have been entrusted by the parents of their students with the privilege of discussing and teaching a subject that has eternal significance to the family and family members.

BIBLIOGRAPHY

"Sex Education." *General Handbook of Instruction*, 11-5. Salt Lake City, 1989.

A Parent's Guide. Salt Lake City, 1985.

DARLENE CHIDESTER HUTCHISON

SEXUALITY

In LDS life and thought, sexuality consists of attitudes, feelings, and desires that are God-given and central to God's plan for his children, but they are not the central motivating force in human action. Sexual feelings are to be governed by each individual within boundaries the Lord has set. Sexuality is not characterized as a need, or a deprivation that must be satisfied, but as a desire that should be fulfilled only within marriage, with sensitive attention given to the well-being of one's heterosexual marriage partner. As the offspring of God, humans carry the divine LIGHT OF CHRIST, which is the means whereby the appropriate expression of sexual desires can be measured. Depending on whether men and women are true or false to this light, they will be the masters or the victims of sexual feelings. Such desires are to be fulfilled only within legal heterosexual marriage, wherein sexual involvement is to be an expression of unity, compassion, commitment, and love. Mutuality and equality are to be the hallmark of a married couple's physical intimacy.

The purposes of appropriate sexual relations in marriage include the expression and building of joy, unity, love, and oneness. To be "one flesh" is to experience an emotional and spiritual unity. This oneness is as fundamental a purpose of marital relations as is procreation. President Spencer W. KIMBALL stated:

> The union of the sexes, husband and wife (and only husband and wife), was for the principal purpose of bringing children into the world. Sexual experiences were never intended by the Lord to be a mere plaything or merely to satisfy passions and lusts. We know of no directive from the Lord that proper sexual experience between husbands and wives need be limited totally to the procreation of children, but we find much evidence from Adam until now that no provision was ever made by the Lord for indiscriminate sex [1975, p. 4].

Furthermore, as Paul noted, "Let the husband render unto the wife due benevolence: and likewise also the wife unto the husband. The wife hath not power of her own body, but the husband: and likewise also the husband hath not power of his own body, but the wife" (1 Cor. 7:3–4). Thus, physical intimacy is a blessing to married couples when it is an expression of their mutual benevolence and commitment to each other's well-being,

an affirmation of their striving to be emotionally and spiritually one. The key in sexual matters is unselfishness. Self-centered pursuit of physical desire is destructive of the unity and love that characterize healthy marital relations. Such love or charity is long-suffering, kind, not envious, does "not behave itself unseemly, seeketh not [one's] own, is not easily provoked, thinketh no evil" (1 Cor. 13:4–5), and is compatible with the light of Christ, which directs all in the ways of righteousness.

Bringing children into a loving home is considered a sacred privilege and responsibility of husbands and wives. Given that context, BIRTH CONTROL is a matter left to the prayerful, mutual decisions of a righteous couple, with the counsel that husbands must be considerate of their wives, who experience the greater physical and emotional demands in bearing children. A woman's health and strength are to be preserved in childbearing; thus, wisdom should govern how a husband and wife carry out the responsibility to become parents and to care for their offspring.

Sexual feelings in the mature man or woman are relatively strong and constant, and they are not evil. An early apostle of this dispensation, Parley P. Pratt, noted:

> Some persons have supposed that our natural affections were the results of a fallen and corrupt nature, and that they are "carnal, sensual, and devilish," and therefore ought to be resisted, subdued, or overcome as so many evils which prevent our perfection, or progress in the spiritual life. . . . Our natural affections are planted in us by the Spirit of God, for a wise purpose; and they are the very main-springs of life and happiness—they are the cement of all virtuous and heavenly society—they are the essence of charity, or love. . . . There is not a more pure and holy principle in existence than the affection which glows in the bosom of a virtuous man for his companion [p. 52].

As with any appetite or passion, physical desire can be distorted, overindulged, or misused. Spencer W. Kimball observed that, as in all other aspects of marriage, there are virtues to be observed in sexual matters: "There are some people who have said that behind the bedroom doors anything goes. That is not true and the Lord would not condone it" (Kimball, 1982, p. 312).

The Church prohibits sexual involvement except between a man and woman who are lawfully married to each other. Latter-day Saints are expected to abstain from sexual intercourse prior to marriage and to honor the marriage covenant by confining sexual relations to the spouse only (*see* CHASTITY; PREMARITAL SEX). Sexual morality also requires abstention from activities that arouse desires not expressible until marriage. Sexual abstinence prior to marriage is considered not only right and possible but also beneficial. Abstinence is not viewed as repression, nor are there any particular negative consequences to so living.

Parents have the obligation to teach their children both the goodness—the sacredness—of the power to create life (*see* PROCREATION) and the principles of maturation and sexual development. Church leaders encourage parents to discuss sexuality openly with their children, answering their questions straightforwardly and contrasting the Lord's plan for his children—which includes their eventual ability to produce children themselves—with the ways this power to create life can be profaned or abused. Children are to be prepared while young and, according to appropriate stages of development, are to be taught regarding human reproduction and the emotional and spiritual meanings of the procreative power and sexual desires that will grow within them (*see* SEX EDUCATION). Parents are expected to teach correct principles and to be examples of what they teach, treating each other with compassion and charity and living in a relationship of absolute fidelity.

Fundamental to all parental instruction is a parent-child relationship of love and trust. Youth are vulnerable to sexual enticements both because of the strength of their developing desires and because they are still growing in understanding and responsibility. Full comprehension of the consequences—to themselves and to succeeding generations—of the failure to abstain sexually may not come simultaneously with their sexual interests. Trust and respect for parents can help insulate adolescents from temptation while their capacity to exercise full rights and responsibilities matures.

Parents' responsibility to educate children sensitively and directly should not be delegated to the public schools or other agencies outside the home. When public sex-education programs are offered, LDS parents are counseled to assure that such programs adequately acknowledge the sanctity of marriage and promote family-oriented values and standards. When such agencies undertake sex education, LDS parents should have prepared and taught their children in such a way that school

programs will at best be a supplement to the foundations of understanding established in the family circle.

The standard of sexual morality endorsed by the Church applies equally to men and women. Given that the power to create life is central to God's plan for his children, sexual transgression is most serious (*see* ADULTERY). Those who violate the law of chastity may be subject to Church DISCIPLINARY PROCEDURES, designed to help them cease their transgressions and restore them to full fellowship. Whether it is adultery, fornication, sexual abuse, incest, rape, perversion, or any other unholy practices, such behavior is to be addressed vigorously by local Church authorities, who seek the repentance of perpetrators and the protection of any victims. Homosexual relationships are prohibited (*see* HOMOSEXUALITY). In such cases, the Church affirms that such distortions in sexual feelings or behavior can, with the Lord's help, be overcome. A compassionate interest in the well-being of transgressors and the healing of relationships should motivate Church interest and action. Sexual wrongdoing is not to be condoned, ignored, or addressed casually. Transgressors themselves can be forgiven, but only by repenting and coming unto Christ (*see* REPENTANCE) and, through his ATONEMENT, turning away from their destructive beliefs and practices.

Victims of rape or incest often experience trauma and feelings of guilt, but they are not responsible for the evil done by others, and they deserve and need to be restored to their sense of innocence through the love and counsel of Church leaders.

Practically speaking, the benefits of living a chaste life prior to marriage and of observing a relationship of fidelity after marriage apply to every dimension of marriage and family relationships. By remaining chaste before marriage and totally faithful to one's spouse in a heterosexual marriage, one can avoid some physically debilitating diseases, extramarital pregnancies, and venereal infections passed on to offspring. The sense of trust, loyalty, love, and commitment essential to the ideal of oneness in marriage and family life is not damaged or strained. Furthermore, one's relationship to and confidence in God are strengthened. By governing the power to create life, one sets the stage for the exercise of these desires, not whimsically, but with a reverence for the sacredness of the divine powers of creation.

BIBLIOGRAPHY

Foster, Lawrence. *Religion and Sexuality: Three American Communal Experiments of the Nineteenth Century.* New York, 1981.

Kimball, Spencer W. "The Lord's Plan for Men and Women." *Ensign* 5 (Oct. 1975):2–5.

———. *The Teachings of Spencer W. Kimball*, ed. Edward L. Kimball. Salt Lake City, 1982.

Pratt, Parley P. *Writings of Parley Parker Pratt*, ed Parker P. Robison. Salt Lake City, 1952.

Rytting, Marvin. "On Sexuality." *Dialogue* 7 (Winter 1972): 102–104.

"Sexuality and Mormon Culture." *Dialogue* 10 (Autumn 1976): 9–93. Entire issue on sexuality.

TERRANCE D. OLSON

SICK, BLESSING THE

Latter-day Saints are committed to the reality of healing through faith in Jesus Christ, to a health code (the WORD OF WISDOM) that is a form of preventive medicine, and to the proper use of modern medical skills.

Latter-day Saints believe that Christ ordained and sent his disciples, in ancient and modern times, with the promise that through faith they might heal. The gift of healing is one of the gifts of the Spirit, a gift that may be present both in the

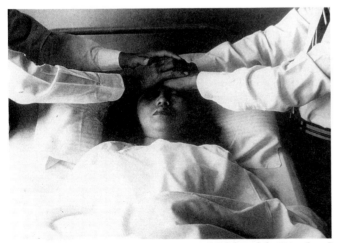

A young woman receives a Melchizedek Priesthood blessing of comfort and, if it is God's will, healing. The elders anoint the sick with consecrated olive oil (*see* James 5:14). Photograph, 1986; courtesy Floyd Holdman.

one who administers and the one who receives. The admonition of James is reenacted in LDS practice. "Is any sick among you? let him call for the elders of the church; and let them pray over him, anointing him with oil in the name of the Lord: And the prayer of faith shall save the sick, and the Lord shall raise him up; and if he have committed sins, they shall be forgiven him" (James 5:14–15; cf. D&C 42:43–44).

It is clear from modern REVELATION that even though not all have this gift of faith, they may still have faith in Christ and the gospel. In many LDS homes there is exercise of the gift of healing through administrations of the father's priesthood. Blessings of the sick are generally given by two MELCHIZEDEK PRIESTHOOD bearers. There are no prescribed prayers for this kind of blessing, but one of the priesthood bearers anoints the head of the sick person with a little consecrated olive oil and says in substance: "In the name of Jesus Christ and by authority of the Holy Melchizedek Priesthood, I lay my hands upon your head and anoint you with this consecrated oil, which has been dedicated for the blessing of the sick." Additional words may be said in harmony with, and under the guidance of, the Spirit.

Following this anointing, two or more priesthood bearers lay their hands upon the head of the sick person, and one being spokesman calls the person by name and says in substance, "In the name of Jesus Christ and by the authority of the holy Melchizedek Priesthood, we seal and confirm upon you this anointing with which you have been anointed to the end that . . . " He then voices a prayer of supplication and of blessing as the Spirit directs. The ORDINANCE concludes in the name of Jesus Christ. If two priesthood bearers are not available for the ceremony, one may perform both parts of the blessing.

In the temples of the Church throughout the world, frequent prayers are offered for those who are sick, bereaved, or in need. The names of those afflicted may be placed upon a temple prayer roll by request of family or friends. This practice derives from abundant scriptural counsels regarding unity in prayer—"Be agreed as touching all things ye shall ask" (D&C 27:18)—and the conviction that the modern temple, as anciently, is a house of prayer (D&C 109:8). United prayer and fasting, sometimes by an entire WARD or STAKE and in some historic instances by the full world membership of the Church, is occasionally advocated. This is the fulfillment of a divine admonition: "If ye are not one ye are not mine" (D&C 38:27).

Historically, miraculous healings have followed spiritual administrations to the sick for every kind of affliction, in every generation, and in every part of the Church. The promise is that the blind may receive sight, the deaf hear, the paralytic regain the use of limbs. Illustrative scriptural references are: "He that hath faith in me to be healed, and is not appointed unto death, shall be healed" (D&C 42:48). And those who "have not faith to be healed, but believe, shall be nourished with all tenderness" (verse 43).

Three scriptural cautions apply to the principle of blessing the sick. First, worthiness is to be cultivated by all. At any time, men or women may face the crisis of disease or injury and be asked to exercise faith in behalf of themselves or loved ones. Second, blessings are not to be given as signs for the skeptical, to satisfy curiosity, or to "consume it upon their lusts" (D&C 46:9). Faith in Christ is the prerequisite, not the consequence, of blessing the sick. Third, the resulting relief, healing, and fulfillment are not to be boasted about or heralded, but rather to "be spoken with care, and by constraint of the Spirit" (D&C 63:64; 84:73; 105:24). This is consistent with the plea of the Master in the New Testament after many of his miraculous healings: "See thou tell no man!" (Matt. 8:4; cf. D&C 50:33).

NEPHI K. KEZERIAN

SIGMA GAMMA CHI

See: LDS Student Association

SIGNS

[*Signs mark, indicate, represent, symbolize, give direction, or point to other things beyond themselves, and are sometimes miraculous or extraordinary in nature. The scriptures speak of God's "signs and wonders" by which his work, power, and wisdom are made known or recognized by people in the earth (Ex. 7:3–5). True signs provide objective evidence that an event can reasonably be expected, such as the new star in the east being a sign of Christ's birth (Matt. 2:1, 2) or certain dark clouds heralding a storm (Matt. 16:1–4). False or counterfeit signs are deceptive and give a false hope of security if accepted (Ex. 7:11–12; 8:7; D&C 63:7–9.*

Articles pertaining directly to this subject are Sign Seeking; Signs as Divine Witnesses; Signs of the Times; Signs of the True Chruch. *Related articles are* Jesus Christ: Birth of Jesus Christ; Miracles; *and* Second Coming of Jesus Christ.]

SIGNS AS DIVINE WITNESS

Signs have been given by the Lord to manifest his power "both in heaven and in earth" (Jacob 7:14); to witness that Jesus Christ shall come (Jacob 7:14; D&C 39:23; 68:10); to strengthen the faith of believers (D&C 35:8; 58:64; 84:65); and to ratify the condemnation of unbelievers (D&C 63:11).

In revealing his power in the heavens and on earth, God has used numerous signs and wonders. He "hath given a law unto all things, by which they move in their times and their seasons; and their courses are fixed, even the courses of the heavens and the earth, which comprehend the earth and all the planets, . . . and any man who hath seen any or the least of these hath seen God moving in his majesty and power" (D&C 88:42–47). Miracles performed by the power of God are signs of his might and majesty (cf. Ex. 7:3). He parted the Red Sea for the children of Israel after bringing the ten plagues upon the Egyptians (Ex. 7–12; 14:1–31). He confirmed Gideon's divine call by several signs (Judg. 6:17–23, 36–40).

During his mortal ministry the Lord filled empty nets with fish after the disciples had fished all night but caught nothing (Luke 5:6). He healed the sick, raised the dead, caused the lame to walk and the blind to see, and calmed the storm (*see* MIRACLES). The foregoing, and with hundreds of other instances, attest to the power and might of God, both in heaven and on earth.

Signs strengthen the faith of believers and therefore are beheld by those who already believe in Christ as confirmations of their belief. Jesus Christ revealed to the Prophet Joseph SMITH, "I will show miracles, signs, and wonders, unto all those who believe on my name" (D&C 35:8) and "he that believeth shall be blest with signs following, even as it is written" (D&C 68:10). Signs that follow faithful believers are many. They "shall heal the sick, . . . cast out devils, and shall be delivered from those who would administer . . . deadly poison," and if occasion warrants, they could even "raise the dead" (D&C 124:98–100; cf. Mark 16:17–18). In addition, faithful Saints have a comforting assurance, which comes to those who recognize the signs, that God's plans will not be frustrated (D&C 3:1; 10:43)

In addition to manifesting God's power, signs have been given as a witness of the coming of Christ to earth. Latter-day Saints believe that signs were given to prepare the people for his coming in the MERIDIAN OF TIME. King BENJAMIN declared, "And many signs, and wonders, and types, and shadows showed he unto them, concerning his coming" (Mosiah 3:15). MORMON reports that among the Book of Mormon people, signs and wonders abounded prior to the birth of Christ in the Holy Land (3 Ne. 1:4–22) and before his visit to the Western Hemisphere (3 Ne. 8–10).

Of particular interest in the present DISPENSATION OF THE FULNESS OF TIMES are signs pertaining to the second coming of Christ (see SECOND COMING OF JESUS CHRIST). The Lord has revealed the SIGNS OF THE TIMES (1 Thes. 5:1–2) to guide the faithful in their preparation for the "great and dreadful day of the Lord" (D&C 110:14)—that is, for Christ's second coming to the earth. Thus, the faithful watch for the signs so that when the hour comes, it will be great, but not dreadful to them (cf. 1 Thes. 5:2–4).

Elder Bruce R. McConkie noted at least fifty-one different signs, many of which pertain to natural phenomena, that have been foretold, pointing to the second coming of Christ. These include earthquakes, famines, depressions, economic turmoil, strikes, anarchy, violence, disasters, calamities, disease, plague, and pestilence. At the same time, both worldly knowledge and gospel knowledge increase, holy temples are built throughout the earth, Israel is gathered, and the true gospel is preached in all the world (*MD*, pp. 715–34).

BIBLIOGRAPHY
Smith, Joseph. *TPJS*, pp. 160, 198, 224, 262.

R. WAYNE SHUTE

SIGN SEEKING

Signs are greeted by the faithful with reverence and appreciation (see SIGNS AS DIVINE WITNESS). On the other hand, a sign can become a condemnation to an unbeliever (D&C 63:7–11). Skeptics may rationalize the signs as aberrations of nature,

harden their heart, and not recognize or acknowledge God's "hand in all things" (D&C 59:21). When an unbeliever seeks for a sign he is tempting God and subjects himself to possible condemnation and the WRATH OF GOD. Two vivid Book of Mormon cases illustrating the consequences of unholy sign seeking are Sherem (Jacob 7:13–14) and Korihor (Alma 30:43–56). Furthermore, Jesus said to the Jewish rulers, "a wicked and adulterous generation seeketh after a sign" (Matt. 16:4). And in the latter days, Jesus explained that "he that seeketh signs shall see signs, but not unto salvation" (D&C 63:7). There is a great difference between signs to confirm or reward faith and the seeking of signs as an excuse for not exercising faith or as a substitute for faith.

BIBLIOGRAPHY
Smith, Joseph. *TPJS*, pp. 157, 278.
Smith, Joseph Fielding. *Church History and Modern Revelation*, p. 4. Salt Lake City, 1948.

R. WAYNE SHUTE

SIGNS OF THE TIMES

The phrase "signs of the times" was used by Jesus Christ when he reproved certain antagonists for not recognizing earlier prophecies relative to his second advent. He said they understood signs pertaining to the weather, but did not understand the "signs of the times" (Matt. 16:3). Recognizing such signs will enable discerning individuals to understand the unfolding of prophetic events in the final phase of the earth's history. Prophets before and after Christ have prophesied that there would be signs pertaining to events occurring prior to Christ's second coming (Joel 2:30–31; Amos 8:11–12; 2 Thes. 2:1–3; *TPJS*, pp. 286–87).

These signs include the coming of false Christs and false prophets and the deception of many who believe in them (Matt. 24:11, 23–24). Included also are wars, rumors of wars, famines, earthquakes, pestilence, and other natural calamities (Matt. 24:6, 27; Mark 13:5–8). Latter-day revelation provides additional insights concerning these eschatological catastrophes and the consequences of them for those who are unprepared (D&C 29:13–21; 45:25–45). The gospel of Jesus Christ will be preached throughout the earth as a sign that the Lord's coming draws near (JS—M

1:31), and for those who believe and obey, his coming will be glorious. Even though no one on earth knows the exact time of Jesus' return (D&C 49:7), those who recognize the signs and prepare themselves by "treasuring up [his] word, shall not be deceived" (JS—M 1:37). These shall be as the "wise virgins" of Jesus' parable and shall profit from the signs of the times (Matt. 25:1–13; D&C 45:56; 53:54).

[*See also* Jesus Christ: Second Coming of Jesus Christ.]

DAVID F. BOONE

SIGNS OF THE TRUE CHURCH

The New Testament shows that in the MERIDIAN OF TIME Jesus Christ established his Church with definite doctrines, principles, and ordinances, and specifically ordained officers, giving the Church recognizable features by which it could be known. Many of the signs or essential features evident in Christ's New Testament Church are also recognizable in the Church he restored to the earth through the Prophet Joseph SMITH.

FAITH, REPENTANCE, BAPTISM, AND THE HOLY GHOST. One sign of Christ's Church is its insistence on the basic principles and ordinances of the gospel. Membership in the New Testament Church was obtained by faith in the Lord Jesus Christ, repentance from sin, baptism in water, and the LAYING ON OF HANDS for the GIFT OF THE HOLY GHOST (Acts 2:37–38). Baptism was by immersion administered by one having authority, just as Jesus was baptized in the Jordan River by John the Baptist (Matt. 3:11–16). Jesus said, "Except a man be born of water and of the Spirit, he cannot enter into the kingdom of God" (John 3:5).

The gift of the Holy Ghost was bestowed through the laying on of hands by one having authority, as exemplified at Samaria when Peter and John encountered some newly baptized persons: "For as yet [the Holy Ghost] was fallen upon none of them: only they were baptized in the name of the Lord Jesus. Then laid they their hands on them, and they received the Holy Ghost" (Acts 8:16–17). The same procedure is demonstrated by Paul at Ephesus (Acts 19:1–6). These same ordinances are required for membership in the Church today (cf. A of F 4).

CHURCH ORGANIZATION. Certain presiding officers, such as APOSTLES and PROPHETS, are characteristic of the Church of Jesus Christ. Paul states that Christ "gave some, apostles; and some, prophets; and some, evangelists; and some, pastors and teachers; for the perfecting of the saints, for the work of the ministry, for the edifying of the body [church] of Christ" (Eph. 4:11–12; cf. 2:20). The Church of Jesus Christ was restored to the earth in the early nineteenth century through the Prophet Joseph Smith with "the same organization that existed in the Primitive Church, namely, apostles, prophets, pastors, teachers, evangelists, and so forth" (A of F 6; *see also* ORGANIZATION OF THE CHURCH IN NEW TESTAMENT TIMES; QUORUM OF THE TWELVE APOSTLES; SEVENTY).

MIRACLES AND GIFTS OF THE SPIRIT. Jesus and the apostles performed miracles by faith and the power of God. Latter-day Saints believe that where there are apostles and prophets the gifts and signs of the Spirit will be present (Matt. 11:5). Where there is true faith, there will be miracles, and God's power will be manifest (Morm. 9:7–25). Bruce R. McConkie, an apostle, wrote, "Miracles wrought by the power of God are the perfect proof of pure religion. They are always . . . without fail, found in the true Church. Their absence is conclusive, absolute, and irrefutable proof of apostasy" (pp. 374–75).

CONTINUED REVELATION. The New Testament Church of Jesus Christ experienced frequent revelation, such as the visits of angels (Acts 4:5–19; 10:3; 27:23), visions (Acts 9:3–8), and the workings of the Holy Ghost (cf. John 15:26–27; 16:7–15). Through these means, knowledge was received from heaven. Continued revelation from God is necessary for the leaders of the Church and its members to learn the mind and will of the Lord and how to proceed from day to day. This view of revelation is stated thus in the latter-day Church: "We believe all that God has revealed, all that He does now reveal, and we believe that He will yet reveal many great and important things pertaining to the Kingdom of God" (A of F 9).

PERSECUTION. The New Testament shows that true followers of Jesus Christ were inevitably persecuted. Jesus said to his apostles, "If ye were of the world, the world would love his own, . . . but I have chosen you out of the world, therefore the world hateth you" (John 15:19). Paul said that "all that will live godly in Christ Jesus shall suffer persecution" (2 Tim. 3:12). Hence, a sign or characteristic of the true Church is rejection and persecution by the wicked (see WORLDLINESS).

SEALING POWER. Jesus gave his apostles the power to bind or seal on earth and in heaven. He said, "Verily I say unto you, Whatsoever ye shall bind on earth shall be bound in heaven: and whatsoever ye shall loose on earth shall be loosed in heaven" (Matt. 18:18). This SEALING power is a feature of the latter-day Church (D&C 128:8–10).

SALVATION OF THE DEAD. The true Church of Jesus Christ promulgates the doctrines and ordinances that provide for SALVATION OF THE DEAD. Evidence thereof is seen in 1 Corinthians 15:29 and 1 Peter 3:18–20 and 4:6. Christ's mission would not be complete without such a provision, because so many persons die without even hearing the name of Jesus Christ, and without either knowledge or understanding of the gospel (see BAPTISM FOR THE DEAD).

TEMPLES. Jesus called the temple in Jerusalem "my father's house" (John 2:16). A temple is a facility necessary for the total implementation of the laws and ordinances of the Church of Jesus Christ; therefore, the latter-day Church builds temples for the benefit of the people. From the days of Adam to the present, whenever the Lord has had a people on earth, temples and temple ordinances have been a crowning feature of their worship. In a revelation to the Prophet Joseph Smith regarding temples, endowments, and sacred ordinances, the Lord explained that these have been associated with the people of God in every dispensation (D&C 124:39–40; cf. MD, p. 780).

NAME OF THE CHURCH. Christ's Church bears his name, and believers in Jesus Christ take upon themselves his name by baptism (see JESUS CHRIST: TAKING THE NAME OF, UPON ONESELF). When the Nephites asked the Lord what the name of his Church should be, Jesus said, "How be it my church save it be called in my name? For if a church be called in Moses' name it be Moses' church; or if it be called in the name of a man then it be the church of a man; but if it be called in my name then it is my church, if it so be that they are built upon my gospel" (3 Ne. 27:8). The name of The Church of Jesus Christ of Latter-day Saints is symbolic of its author and ideal.

MISSIONARY ACTIVITY. Jesus commanded his disciples to go into all the world to teach his gospel and baptize those who believe (Matt. 28:18–20). Extensive missionary activity characterized the New Testament Church, as with Paul, Barnabas, Philip, and others. This characteristic is considered urgent by the Church today (D&C 58:64; see also MISSIONS).

LOVE. True faith and obedience bring the fruits of the Spirit, the greatest of which is love. Jesus said, "By this shall all men know that ye are my disciples, if ye have love one to another" (John 13:35; cf. 1 Cor. 13).

BIBLIOGRAPHY

Lee, Harold B. "Signs of the True Church." In Stand Ye in Holy Places, pp. 312–15. Salt Lake City, 1974.

McConkie, Bruce R. Doctrinal New Testament Commentary, Vol. 2, pp. 374–75. Salt Lake City, 1970.

LEON R. HARTSHORN

SILK CULTURE

President Brigham YOUNG conceived sericulture in the Great Basin as an important component in economic stability. He regarded locally produced silk as a practical textile and as a light industry that could be maintained at home by women and children, requiring less intensive labor and capital outlay than cotton, flax, or wool. He planted the first mulberry trees in Deseret, which were imported from France in 1855.

In 1856, Elizabeth Whitaker produced cocoons from worms that her husband brought from England as eggs; in 1858, Nancy Barrows planted mulberry seeds, feeding her worms on lettuce leaves until the mulberry trees matured. She reeled thread, wove it into fabric, and made the first silk dress in the territory of Deseret in 1859. In 1863, Octave Ursenbach and his wife exhibited 3,000 cocoons they had produced in Salt Lake City. Paul and Susanna Cardon produced silk in Cache Valley during the early 1860s, and Paul A. Schettler and his family set up a loom for weaving silk in 1867 and began raising cocoons in Salt Lake City.

In 1867, President Young offered free eggs and mulberry leaves to any persons willing to "undertake the work" of hatching, tending, and feed-

At the General Conference in April 1868, Brigham Young encouraged the cultivation of silk. Using the tools shown here, women and children in nearly 150 communities raised millions of silkworms and harvested, spun, and wove silk for dresses, draperies, and other fine articles. The enterprise was disbanded by the end of the century.

ing the worms. He called George D. Watt to promote silk culture throughout the territory and Zina D. H. YOUNG, of the newly reorganized RELIEF SOCIETY, to head the silk project. She traveled widely over the territory, delivering speeches, and organizing and teaching classes.

Carolyn Jackson raised the first silk in St. George in 1869. In Ogden Mariana Comb Bens was independently producing silk before the Relief Society took it on. By 1870, most ward Relief Societies produced silk, and by 1880 every Relief Society in the territory had a silk project. Important promoters of silk culture were A. K. Thurber in Spanish Fork, Daniel Graves in Provo, and Anson Call and Mary Carter in Layton. Susan B. Anthony and Mrs. Rutherford B. Hayes both enjoyed gifts of silk articles.

The silk industry continued moderately healthy through most of the 1880s, but a lull marked the late 1880s and the early 1890s. The last surge of Utah's silk works began when officials decided to feature silk at the state exhibit at the 1893 World's Fair. The exhibit was a stunning success, and the attention it received resulted in renewed activity.

Headed by Zina D. H. Young, the Utah Silk Commission was established by the state legislature in 1896 to replace the older Deseret Silk Association, simultaneously authorizing payment of a bounty of twenty-five cents per pound for cocoons produced in the state. During 1897–1904, bounties were paid on 4,769, 7,493, 6,479, and 8,647 pounds of cocoons. Although production nearly doubled during these years, the crop was never profitable. In 1905, the legislature could not justify renewing the cocoon bounty, and except for individuals scattered throughout the state who maintained silk culture as a hobby, sericulture ended in Utah in 1905.

BIBLIOGRAPHY

Arrington, Chris Rigby. "The Finest of Fabrics: Mormon Women and the Silk Industry in Early Utah." *Utah Historical Quarterly* 46:376–96.

Arrington, Leonard J. "The Economic Role of Pioneer Mormon Women." *The Western Humanities Review* 9(2):145–64.

Potter, Margaret Schow. "The History of Sericulture in Utah." Master's thesis, Oregon State College, 1949.

ELIZABETH H. HALL

SIN

Sin is willful wrongdoing. James indicates that it can also be the willful failure to do right: "Therefore to him that knoweth to do good, and doeth it not, to him it is sin" (4:17). Sin is transgression of the law (1 Jn. 3:4), but one is not held responsible for sins against a law that one has not had opportunity to know. Orson F. Whitney, an apostle, explained:

> Sin is the transgression of divine law, as made known through the conscience or by revelation. A man sins when he violates his conscience, going contrary to light and knowledge—not the light and knowledge that has come to his neighbor, but that which has come to himself. He sins when he does the opposite of what he knows to be right. Up to that point he only blunders. One may suffer painful consequences for only blundering, but he cannot commit sin unless he knows better than to do the thing in which the sin consists. One must have a conscience before he can violate it [pp. 241–42].

God does not hold one responsible for wrong done in ignorance or harm done to others unintentionally, because such actions do not constitute sin. One's ignorance, immaturity, or even recklessness may injure others, and individuals may be accountable for the consequences they help to bring about. But in such situations, where there is no ill intent, there is no sin. This does not mean that people who do wrong in ignorance do not suffer, perhaps physically or in their relationships with others. Moreover, when one becomes aware of having contributed to problems, it usually would be considered sin to avoid making amends or to refuse to help correct the difficulties created.

The Greek verb used in the New Testament meaning "to sin" is *hamartanein*. This word invokes the imagery of the archer, and can mean "to miss the mark." When people sin, they look "beyond the mark" toward inferior or selfish goals. The scriptures define mankind's high mark or calling as "that they might have joy" (2 Ne. 2:25). God, who experiences a fulness of joy (cf. 3 Ne. 28:10),

may be trusted to know the proper way to bliss. He offers to his children all that he has. He sent his Son to "save his people from their sins" (Matt. 1:21). To sin knowingly is to transgress or overstep the borders of the way to peace and happiness, and to reject the mission of the Savior.

All mortals inherently possess hearts that can be attuned to depths of love, peace, and purity (cf. Moro. 7:14–18). But through sin (intentionally doing wrong), humans obliterate joy and foster hatred, violence, and misery (see 2 Ne. 2:26–27; Mosiah 3:19; Hel. 14:30–31). Sin wastes, corrupts, saddens, and destroys. It extinguishes the "perfect brightness of hope" offered by Christ (2 Ne. 31:20) and replaces it with despair (Moro. 10:22). Its sting does not enliven or gladden the heart, but awakens "a lively sense of . . . guilt" (Mosiah 2:38), which is an unwished-for but inescapable consequence for the unrepentant.

The first taste of sin is bitter. As children mature, "sin conceiveth in their hearts, and they taste the bitter" (Moses 6:55). However, experimentation with sin is deceptively addictive. Even as a person's spiritual sensitivities dim; the sting may seem to diminish in time. Things are not as they seem to one in sin. It is as though one sleeps. The repetition of sin (known in the scriptures as wickedness) clouds one's view, and the effects of sin are more bitter with the progressive passing of life. Isaiah compares it to "when an hungry man dreameth, and, behold, he eateth; but he awaketh, and his soul is empty" (Isa. 29:8). And PAUL noted, sinners "being past feeling have given themselves over unto lasciviousness, to work all uncleanness with greediness" (Eph. 4:19).

Sin includes the willful breaking of covenants with God. It ruptures family and social relationships, creates disorder and mistrust, and encourages the selfish pursuit of one's own ends to the detriment of the community. Covenants give a sense of stability and permanence—they signal what to expect from one another. But sin creates uncertainty and instability. It never leads to the happiness expected, but to disappointment. As Jacob testified, breaking covenants creates suffering for the innocent: "Ye have broken the hearts of your tender wives . . .; and the sobbings of their hearts ascend up to God against you. . . . Many hearts died, pierced with deep wounds" (Jacob 2:35).

Sins are expressions of living in resistance to God and the things of the spirit. "A man being evil cannot do that which is good" (Moro. 7:10), because his behavior springs from a hard or bitter heart. One can quit "being" evil only through a change of heart; it is not just a modification or control of external actions (cf. Mosiah 5:2–15). The truth is either received or resisted. When the woman of Samaria who talked with the Savior at the well reported her conversation to others, she said, "Come, see a man, which told me all things that ever I did" (John 4:29). What the Savior told her included her current sins—"and he whom thou now hast is not thy husband" (John 4:18). Yet, she received his declarations; she accepted his testimony that he was the Christ and invited her friends to see for themselves (John 4:25–26, 29). Had she been hard-hearted, or had she clung to her sins, she would not have accepted his statements about her, or his testimony of his own divinity. She would not have come to the road of repentance and forgiveness.

To escape the effects of sin, mankind must both accept the ATONEMENT and repent. AMULEK, a Book of Mormon prophet, explains that the Atonement saves men *from* their sins, not *in* them (Alma 11:37). It is in large measure one's own sins that produce feelings of affliction and despair, perhaps more than what one suffers from the wrongs received from others. Mortals are punished *by* their sins rather than *for* them. This condition is described in the scriptures as the "bondage of sin" (D&C 84:49–51; Morm. 8:31).

Those in this bondage live in opposition to the two great commandments upon which hang all the law and the prophets: "Thou shalt love the Lord thy God with all thy heart, and with all thy soul, and with all thy mind," and "thou shalt love thy neighbor as thyself" (Matt. 22:37, 39). If these are the greatest of commandments, then perhaps the most debilitating sin is a refusal to love. Selfishness, greed, envy, pride, self-righteousness, resentment, hostility, smugness, self-pity, and lust are all ways of refusing to love. The allowance often asked for by sinners regarding these may contribute more to negative family relationships or even the level of crime in a society than supposed. Discourtesy can escalate to hostility, which in turn can escalate to violence.

Sinners are offended by the truth and find it a burden, as when LAMAN and Lemuel, after having the plan of salvation rehearsed to them by their brother NEPHI₁, complained, "Thou hast declared unto us hard things, more than we are able to

Sinner Fleeing Judgment (1977, acrylic on masonite, 18″ × 24″) was painted by LDS artist James Christensen (b. 1942). The fantasy work depicts an anxious figure whose investment in worldly treasure—represented by luxurious clothing—has woven a varicolored trap that slows flight and leaves no escape. Courtesy Museum of Fine Arts, Brigham Young University.

bear" (1 Ne. 16:1). Those refusing to live the truth rationalize and justify their wrongdoing. Cain, already having committed murder, responded to the Lord's inquiry about Abel's whereabouts by lying ("I know not"), and then hypocritically challenging God: "Am I my brother's keeper?" (Gen. 4:9; Moses 5:34).

Sin blinds one to the truth in any given situation. Nathan the prophet told king David a story of a man who possessed many flocks of sheep, but who, nevertheless, slaughtered the pet ewe lamb of a poor family to feed a guest. David was incensed. He judged that such a man should restore to the wronged family fourfold and be executed. Nathan declared: "Thou art the man" (2 Sam. 12:7). Spiritually blinded by his adultery with Bathsheba and the murder of her husband Uriah (2 Sam. 11), David no longer saw himself as he was seen by the prophet or, apparently, by anyone willing to examine the situation on the basis of the Lord's commandments.

"If we say that we have fellowship with him [Christ], and walk in darkness, we lie, and do not the truth: . . . If we say that we have no sin, we deceive ourselves, and the truth is not in us" (1 Jn. 1:6, 8). When a truth is not lived, it is seen falsely. Even personal guilt for sin is seen by the unrepentant as having been placed on them by someone else, and not as a symptom of their own hardness against the truth. Whether the sin be "great," such as murder, adultery, or embezzlement, or "small," as in pride, harshness, or jealousy, its effects are manifest in predictable patterns of behavior. These patterns commonly include being burdened by, blind to, or excusing oneself from, what one knows to be true.

Rarely do the scriptures give a detailed catalog of sins. Usually they give illustrative examples (cf. Alma 1:32; 16:18; Hel. 4:12). President Ezra Taft BENSON described the attitudes associated with the universal sin of pride: "Our enmity toward God takes on many labels, such as rebellion, hard-heartedness, stiff-neckedness, unrepentant, puffed up, easily offended, and sign seekers" (Benson, p. 4). King Benjamin noted, "I cannot tell you all the things whereby ye may commit sin; for there are divers ways and means, even so many that I cannot number them. But this much I can tell you, that if ye do not . . . continue in the faith of what ye have heard concerning the coming of our Lord, even unto the end of your lives, ye must perish. And now, O man, remember, and perish not" (Mosiah 4:29–30).

To be spiritually born of God is to be awakened, to be released from the burdens of sin (see FORGIVENESS; NATURAL MAN; REPENTANCE). The Book of Mormon records the history of a people who, for a time, overcame the bondage of sin. Of them it says, "And it came to pass that there was no contention in the land, because of the love of God which did dwell in the hearts of the people. And there were no envyings, nor strifes, nor tumults, nor whoredoms, nor lyings, nor murders, nor any manner of lasciviousness; and surely there could not be a happier people among all the people who had been created by the hand of God" (4 Ne. 1:15–16).

To overcome sin and be forgiven are to forsake ungodliness, to acknowledge dependence on God, and to seek to do his will. God's help is indispensable to abandoning sin: "He changed their hearts; . . . he awakened them out of a deep sleep, and they awoke unto God" (Alma 5:6). Those who abandon sin have "received his image in [their] countenances" and exercise faith in the redemption of Christ (cf. Alma 5:14–19); they are full of love (Mosiah 3:19; John 13:35; 15:10).

From an eternal perspective, there is no tragedy except in sin. Mortals are not on earth to prove themselves to one another but to God. This earth life is a probationary time, a test to see whether mankind will "do all things whatsoever the Lord their God shall command them" (Abr. 3:25; cf. Alma 34:34). Those whose "hearts are set . . . upon the things of this world, and aspire to the honors of men," or who cover their sins, gratify their pride, nurture vain ambition, or seek to control and dominate others "in any degree of unrighteousness" grieve the Spirit of the Lord (D&C 121:35, 37).

Escaping sin is a simple but not an easy matter. Repentance requires deep suffering, the uttermost farthing, all that one is capable of doing: "none but the truly penitent are saved" (Alma 42:24; cf. D&C 19). "We are saved [by grace] after all we can do" (2 Ne. 25:23). Those who abandon sin are characterized by going "forward with a steadfastness in Christ, having a perfect brightness of hope, and a love of God and of all men" (2 Ne. 31:20).

BIBLIOGRAPHY

Benson, Ezra Taft. "Beware of Pride." *Ensign* 19 (May 1989): 4–6.

Kimball, Spencer W. *The Miracle of Forgiveness.* Salt Lake City, 1969.

———. *The Teachings of Spencer W. Kimball,* ed. Edward L. Kimball, pp. 80–114. Salt Lake City, 1982.

Whitney, Orson F. *Saturday Night Thoughts.* Salt Lake City, 1927.

BRUCE L. BROWN
TERRANCE D. OLSON

SINGLE ADULTS

The Church is generally perceived to be a family church; but for various reasons many Church members become or remain single adults. Thirty percent of North American Latter-day Saint adults are currently widowed, divorced, separated, or have never married (1981 Church Membership Survey). Because of concern for their welfare, the Church has focused attention on the needs of single members and has organized activities and programs targeted to meet these needs.

Results of a demographic study indicated that among LDS single adults, 23 percent were divorced or separated, 13 percent were widowed, and 63 percent had never married. Children were present in 16 percent of single-adult households.

LDS SINGLE ADULTS IN U.S. AND CANADA
1990

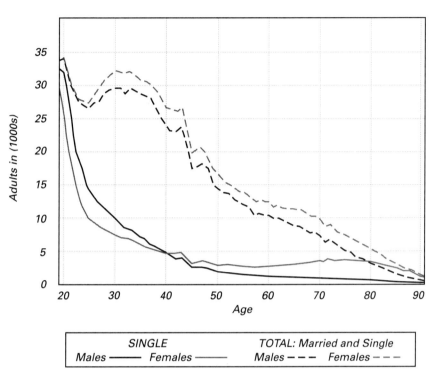

	SINGLE		TOTAL: Married and Single	
Males ———	Females ———		Males – – –	Females – – –

Estimates of marital experiences indicate that only 3 percent of LDS men and women between eighteen and thirty in 1981 would never marry by age sixty. Thus while most Latter-day Saints eventually marry, singleness is a relatively common experience for LDS adults. Only 51 percent of women and 64 percent of men between eighteen and thirty in 1981 are expected to be in an intact first marriage by age sixty. The others will have experienced some period of singleness due to having been divorced, widowed, or never married. If these trends continue, one-third of adult Church members will divorce at some time before age sixty (Goodman and Heaton, pp. 92–93, 96).

Poverty is a real threat to LDS single women, especially when children are present. When LDS households have equal numbers of members, those headed by females are 2.5–5.5 times as likely to be living below the poverty level as those headed by a married couple (Goodman and Heaton, p. 101). Church WELFARE SERVICES and the RELIEF SOCIETY seek to address both the immediate needs and the long-term problems of these women and families.

The ratio of single LDS men to single LDS women indicates a high number of women. In 1981, "for every 100 LDS women in the prime marriage ages (20–29 years) there are 89 LDS men" (Goodman and Heaton, p. 90). The ratio of weekly church attenders is even more out of balance: "For all singles over 30 there are 19 active men [who attend church weekly] for every 100 active women" (Goodman and Heaton, p. 91).

Furthermore, single LDS men and women are "mismatched on salient demographic characteristics. Single women over 30 have higher levels of education, occupation, and Church activity than single men. For example, never-married women over 30 are more likely to have four years of college (42 percent compared to 18 percent for never-married men) and professional occupations (70 percent compared to 38 percent)" (Goodman and Heaton, pp. 90–91). Goodman and Heaton conclude that "marriage to an active male is demographically impossible for many active single females over 30. And even when there are available males, they may possess other characteristics that rule them out as potential mates. Obviously, marriage is not a universal solution to singleness if the only acceptable marital option is marriage to an active LDS partner" (p. 91).

For instructional and activity programs, single adults in the Church are divided into two groups: young single adults, aged eighteen through thirty; and single adults, aged thirty-one and above. Wards, stakes, and regions of the Church sponsor a broad range of activities aimed at meeting the needs of these groups. Activities include young single adult Sunday School classes, FAMILY HOME EVENING groups, service projects, socials, recreational events, and conferences.

For five years (1972–1977), in response to the increasing number of single adults and a concomitant concern with addressing their needs, the Melchizedek Priesthood Mutual Improvement Association developed a uniform organizational program throughout the Church. Its purposes were to identify the needs of singles, to increase awareness of their contribution to the Church, to provide program and activity suggestions, and eventually to incorporate responsibility for the singles into the PRIESTHOOD QUORUMS and RELIEF SOCIETY, which is the situation at present. Each ward now has a committee for single adults that includes one member from the bishopric, the Relief Society presidency, and the elders quorum presidency; a mature married couple to serve as advisers to young single adults; and elders quorum and Relief Society representatives from both the young single adult and single adult groups. Each stake has a similarly composed committee with responsibility for responding to the needs of singles at the stake level. Regional and sometimes multiregional committees are formed on an ad hoc basis to meet the needs of singles by bringing together greater numbers for various social and spiritual activities.

Some stakes have established wards or branches for single adults in areas where there is a high concentration of single members. Single wards have been organized to provide more leadership opportunities for singles and increased social experiences within the Church setting. In general, ward members must reside within the geographic stake boundaries and be a young single adult (ages eighteen to thirty). In areas with significant college student populations, membership may be limited to students. With the exception of the bishop, who is married, positions in the ward are normally staffed by the single adult members.

Church curricula and publications have also addressed the issue of singleness. Numerous articles dealing with challenges encountered by single adults and the place of single adults in the Church have appeared in the official Church magazine, the ENSIGN. In recent years, priesthood and Relief Society lesson manuals have also responded to singles' concerns and have suggested that teachers relate instructional material to single adults in the class.

Latter-day Saints have always placed a high value on marriage and family life. Consequently, the increasing number of single adult members presents a special challenge on how best to blend these single members into the Church community. A 1981 Church Membership Survey provides evidence suggesting that married members of the Church currently have greater opportunities for institutional involvement. Specifically, the survey notes that "singles score higher on the forms of religious involvement that are private, such as prayer and tithing, than on public involvement such as having a calling" (Van Leer). In other words, when leaders consider two equally devout individuals for a Church calling where one is single and one is married, they are more likely to extend the calling to the married individual. In particular, single men traditionally have been excluded from main leadership positions within the wards and stakes of a predominantly married population. Clearly, all of these matters are issues that require special Church attention for the future.

Emphasis on temple marriage and family has grown over time within the Church (Shepherd and Shepherd, p. 76). President Ezra Taft BENSON reaffirmed the emphasis placed on marriage in his counsel to LDS single adults (Benson, May and Nov. 1988), reiterating the Church's position concerning temple marriage: To "obtain a fullness of glory and exaltation in the celestial kingdom, one must enter into this holiest of ordinances" (Benson, May 1988). Stressing the importance of marriage, he encouraged singles not to lose sight of the sacred goal of marriage and not to postpone or forego marriage for education and career. He also presented differing models of the responsibility single adults have toward temple marriage, with men having an active responsibility and women placed in a more passive role. In an article addressed to single Latter-day Saint men, President Benson warned single men that they were in danger of losing eternal blessings by failing to marry

(Benson, May 1988). On the other hand, he recognized that some women may not have the opportunity for temple marriage in this life. In a later article addressed to single Latter-day Saint women, he noted the Lord's promise that if their lives are "worthy and [they] endure faithfully . . . [they will] be assured of all blessings" (Benson, Nov. 1988, p. 97), if not in this life, then in the eternities.

BIBLIOGRAPHY

Benson, Ezra Taft. "To the Single Adult Brethren of the Church." *Ensign* 18 (May 1988):51–53.

———. "To the Single Adult Sisters of the Church." *Ensign* 18 (Nov. 1988):96–97.

Goodman, Kristen L., and Tim B. Heaton. "LDS Church Members in the U.S. and Canada: A Demographic Profile." *AMCAP* 12, no. 1 (1986):88–107.

Shepherd, Gordon, and Gary Shepherd. *A Kingdom Transformed: Themes in the Development of Mormonism.* Salt Lake City, 1984.

"Single Adult Programs Change, New Guide Issued for Singles Wards." *Ensign* 16 (May 1986):105–106.

Van Leer, Twila. "Singleness Becoming More Common." *Church News,* Nov. 6, 1983, p. 4.

LAWRENCE A. YOUNG

SISTERHOOD

Sisterhood, like BROTHERHOOD, is rooted in the gospel of Jesus Christ that views God as the actual father of the immortal and eternal SPIRITS of earthly women and men. President Barbara B. Smith of the RELIEF SOCIETY, said in 1976, "We look upon ourselves as being part of the family of the Lord, and so our sisterhood is one that has a deep understanding of this relationship" (Smith, pp. 7–8). Sisterhood in this broad sense includes all women in the world.

The title "Sister" also has a more special meaning in reference to the women of the Church. Every Latter-day Saint woman is appropriately called "sister." The term does not relate to a woman's profession or ecclesiastical calling, as it does in some religious and professional groups. Members of The Church of Jesus Christ of Latter-day Saints often refer to women members collectively as "the sisterhood of the Church," "sisters in the gospel," or simply as "the sisters."

"The sisterhood of the Church" may refer specifically to members of the Relief Society, organized by the Prophet Joseph SMITH in 1842, which includes all adult women of the Church—over two

million in 1990. Lucy Mack SMITH, the Prophet's mother, expressed the sisterly quality of the society in a classic statement: "This institution is a good one," she told the women assembled in their second meeting. "We must cherish one another, watch over one another, comfort one another, and gain instruction, that we may all sit down in heaven together" (Relief Society Minutes of Nauvoo, Mar. 24, 1842, LDS Church Archives). A later prophet would speak of "a society of sisters," and refer to "the loving fellowship" of the Relief Society VISITING TEACHING program, which from the beginning has been a channel for sisterly concern (Kimball, p. 2).

The organizational network of the Church promotes sisterhood by providing women opportunities to work and study together, to share religious convictions, and to serve others in charitable ways. Like Dorcas in the early Christian church (Acts 9:36), LDS sisters have traditionally sewn clothing for the needy. In the late nineteenth century they worked together in producing silk, saving grain, and managing retail stores. Later they held nurse training classes and sponsored maternal and child health clinics. They have also extended their service through cooperation with the Red Cross and other community agencies. The nature of the tasks has changed with time, but the sisterhood itself continues.

Several publications have helped to expand this network of concern. The sisters published *Woman's Exponent* from 1872 to 1914, *Relief Society Bulletin* in 1914, and *Relief Society Magazine* from 1915 to 1970. Currently, the *Ensign,* the Church's monthly magazine for adults, carries articles by and about women, messages from women leaders, and reports of women's CONFERENCES. The international MAGAZINES carry much of the same material in translation, keeping the sisters of the Church in touch worldwide.

Contributions from sisters in many nations financed two major projects in the 1950s and 1970s: the Relief Society headquarters building in Salt Lake City and the Monument to Women statuary gardens in NAUVOO, Illinois. At the dedication of the latter in 1978, some twenty thousand women celebrated their sisterhood at the place where their society had begun. In 1984, the Relief Society Building also became the headquarters of the PRIMARY (for children) and of the YOUNG WOMEN (girls twelve to eighteen), enabling the general women leaders of the Church to work closely together in their mutual concern for nurturing the young.

Since the early days of the Church, women's service in the TEMPLES of the Church has contributed a profound religious dimension to their sisterhood. By participating in TEMPLE ORDINANCES, in which they minister by divine commission to their "sisters in the gospel," worthy LDS women can help ensure the eternal nature of family ties and create friendships in the process.

The sisters also sustain each other in personal ways. Like RUTH and Naomi, the women of the early LDS Church who left homes and friends to live in a strange land found comfort in each other's loving support. Women who join the Church today often need the same kind of support as do those who are uprooted in an increasingly mobile society. To an elderly woman living alone, sisterhood may mean the assurance that she is not forgotten but has friends and significant work to do with them, perhaps in a nearby temple. To a young mother it can mean practical help in her home and empathetic sharing of problems in a Relief Society class.

Although LDS sisterhood includes a rich diversity of cultures, and occasional disagreements over local issues, its most important aspect is still the bonding relationship of a common FAITH. As one sister said of that faith, "It is a bond that connects women with women and with the Savior across generations" (Peterson, p. 79).

Bathsheba Wilson Bigler Smith (1822–1910), fourth general president of the Relief Society, served from 1901 to 1910. Courtesy Special Collections Department, University of Utah Libraries.

BIBLIOGRAPHY

Mulvay-Derr, Jill. "'Strength in Our Union': The Making of Mormon Sisterhood." In *Sisters in Spirit*, ed. M. Beecher and L. Anderson. Urbana, Ill., 1987.

Kimball, Spencer W. "Relief Society: Its Promise and Potential." *Ensign* 6 (Mar. 1976):2–5.

Peterson, Grethe B. "BYU Women's Conference Draws Thousands." *Ensign* 10 (Apr. 1980):79.

Smith, Barbara B. "A Conversation with Sister Barbara B. Smith, Relief Society General President." *Ensign* 6 (Mar. 1976):7–8.

JANATH RUSSELL CANNON
JILL MULVAY DERR

SMITH, BATHSHEBA BIGLER

Bathsheba Wilson Bigler Smith (1822–1910) was the fourth general president of the RELIEF SOCIETY, matron of the SALT LAKE TEMPLE, woman suffrage leader, and member of the Deseret Hospital Board of Directors.

Bathsheba was the eighth of nine children born to Mark and Susannah Ogden Bigler at Shinnston, Harrison County, Virginia, on May 3, 1822. She was reared in a genteel, upper South culture. The Biglers provided a substantial living for the family on their 300-acre plantation. Bathsheba was trained in management, hospitality, handiwork, and art, and was a cheerful, dignified, and prayerful woman.

At the age of fifteen, Bathsheba and her family joined The Church of Jesus Christ of Latter-day Saints. One of the missionaries serving in the area, George A. Smith, later to be the youngest member called to the QUORUM OF THE TWELVE APOSTLES, became acquainted with this tall, sophisticated southern belle; before he left Virginia, they pledged that "with the blessings of the Almighty in preserving us, in three years from this time, we will be married."

The Bigler family gathered with the Saints in Nauvoo in 1839. Following his return from a mission in England, George and Bathsheba were married on July 25, 1841. While in Nauvoo, they became parents of two children, George A., Jr., and Bathsheba. Their son was killed in 1860 by Indians while serving a mission.

From the time of her marriage, her life was closely intertwined with the Church's movements and programs. She was one of the twenty founding members of the Female Relief Society. She received the ordinance of anointing from Emma SMITH and, with her husband, received the ENDOWMENT under the direction of the Prophet Joseph SMITH. Her relationship with the Smiths provided Bathsheba with a solid conviction of the prophetic calling of Joseph Smith.

Bathsheba was a diversely talented woman. She studied portraiture with William W. Major, a British convert, and carried her paintings of her husband, her parents, and Joseph and Hyrum SMITH in a covered wagon to Utah. She was a full participant in the heritage of leadership prescribed to LDS women; she gave blessings to the sick, washed and anointed women in confinement prior to childbirth, and served in leadership positions in the Church and community. A loyal and committed friend, she exchanged names with a childhood girlfriend surnamed Wilson, adding that name to her established signature.

During the early 1870s, Bathsheba made frequent trips with her husband, then first counselor to President Brigham YOUNG, through settlements north and south of Salt Lake City on preaching and pioneering tours. After the death of her husband in 1875, Bathsheba pursued with customary vigor her commitments to civic and ecclesiastical affairs. Representative of such verve, at a women's meeting in 1870 she made the motion "that we demand of the Governor the right of franchise." This proposal was subsequently signed into law, making the Territory of Utah one of the first places in the nation to give women the right to vote.

In addition to her service as a ward and stake Relief Society leader, and as second counselor and later general president of the Relief Society, Bathsheba also officiated in each of the temples constructed during her lifetime: Nauvoo, Logan, Manti, St. George, and Salt Lake. For seventeen years, she also participated with Eliza R. SNOW in conducting sacred ceremonies in the ENDOWMENT HOUSE.

As general president of the Relief Society (1901–1910), President Smith maintained the forward pace of women. She sent representatives to national and international women's meetings, sponsored nurses' training and free services for the poor, and organized lessons for Relief Society classes. She promoted funding for construction of the Women's Building, from which the programs for the women of the Church were directed. It was this building that Church leaders later elected to rename the Bishops' Building, to accommodate the offices of both the PRESIDING BISHOPRIC and the women's organizations.

Bathsheba Smith died on September 20, 1910, in Salt Lake City. Her funeral was held in the Salt Lake Tabernacle.

BIBLIOGRAPHY

Horne, Alice M., ed. *Autobiography of Bathsheba Smith*. Salt Lake City, 1901.

Mulvay-Derr, Jill, and Susan Oman. "The Nauvoo Generation: Our First Five Relief Society Presidents." *Ensign* 7 (Dec. 1977):40–42.

Whitney, Orson F. *History of Utah*, Vol. 4, pp. 578–80. Salt Lake City, 1901–1904.

HARRIET HORNE ARRINGTON

SMITH, EMMA HALE

Emma Hale Smith (1804–1879), wife of the Prophet Joseph SMITH, was born July 10, 1804, in the Susquehanna Valley in HARMONY township (now Oakland), Pennsylvania, to Isaac and Elizabeth Lewis Hale, the first permanent settlers in the valley. As the seventh of nine children, Emma spent a happy childhood learning to ride horses and to canoe on the Susquehanna with her brothers, while honing her quick wit among her other siblings. She attended school whenever opportunity permitted, including a year beyond the common grammar school education of her brothers and sisters. Tall and gangly as a youth, she grew to be a stately, handsome, dark-haired woman.

Emma met Joseph Smith when he and his father arrived in Harmony to work for an acquaintance of the Hales, Josiah Stowell (sometimes spelled Stoal). During the two years he worked in the area, Joseph twice asked Isaac Hale for permis-

Genealogy of Emma Hale Smith

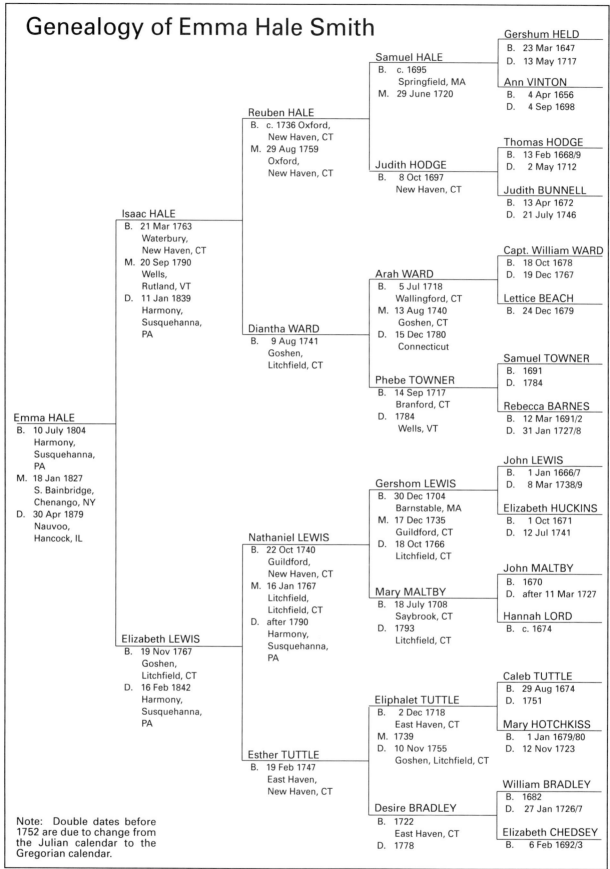

Emma HALE
B. 10 July 1804
    Harmony,
    Susquehanna,
    PA
M. 18 Jan 1827
    S. Bainbridge,
    Chenango, NY
D. 30 Apr 1879
    Nauvoo,
    Hancock, IL

Isaac HALE
B. 21 Mar 1763
    Waterbury,
    New Haven, CT
M. 20 Sep 1790
    Wells,
    Rutland, VT
D. 11 Jan 1839
    Harmony,
    Susquehanna,
    PA

Elizabeth LEWIS
B. 19 Nov 1767
    Goshen,
    Litchfield, CT
D. 16 Feb 1842
    Harmony,
    Susquehanna,
    PA

Reuben HALE
B. c. 1736 Oxford,
    New Haven, CT
M. 29 Aug 1759
    Oxford,
    New Haven, CT

Diantha WARD
B. 9 Aug 1741
    Goshen,
    Litchfield, CT

Nathaniel LEWIS
B. 22 Oct 1740
    Guildford,
    New Haven, CT
M. 16 Jan 1767
    Litchfield,
    Litchfield, CT
D. after 1790
    Harmony,
    Susquehanna,
    PA

Esther TUTTLE
B. 19 Feb 1747
    East Haven,
    New Haven, CT

Samuel HALE
B. c. 1695
    Springfield, MA
M. 29 June 1720

Judith HODGE
B. 8 Oct 1697
    New Haven, CT

Arah WARD
B. 5 Jul 1718
    Wallingford, CT
M. 13 Aug 1740
    Goshen, CT
D. 15 Dec 1780
    Connecticut

Phebe TOWNER
B. 14 Sep 1717
    Branford, CT
D. 1784
    Wells, VT

Gershom LEWIS
B. 30 Dec 1704
    Barnstable, MA
M. 17 Dec 1735
    Guildford, CT
D. 18 Oct 1766
    Litchfield, CT

Mary MALTBY
B. 18 July 1708
    Saybrook, CT
D. 1793
    Litchfield, CT

Eliphalet TUTTLE
B. 2 Dec 1718
    East Haven, CT
M. 1739
D. 10 Nov 1755
    Goshen, Litchfield, CT

Desire BRADLEY
B. 1722
    East Haven, CT
D. 1778

Gershum HELD
B. 23 Mar 1647
D. 13 May 1717

Ann VINTON
B. 4 Apr 1656
D. 4 Sep 1698

Thomas HODGE
B. 13 Feb 1668/9
D. 2 May 1712

Judith BUNNELL
B. 13 Apr 1672
D. 21 July 1746

Capt. William WARD
B. 18 Oct 1678
D. 19 Dec 1767

Lettice BEACH
B. 24 Dec 1679

Samuel TOWNER
B. 1691
D. 1784

Rebecca BARNES
B. 12 Mar 1691/2
D. 31 Jan 1727/8

John LEWIS
B. 1 Jan 1666/7
D. 8 Mar 1738/9

Elizabeth HUCKINS
B. 1 Oct 1671
D. 12 Jul 1741

John MALTBY
B. 1670
D. after 11 Mar 1727

Hannah LORD
B. c. 1674

Caleb TUTTLE
B. 29 Aug 1674
D. 1751

Mary HOTCHKISS
B. 1 Jan 1679/80
D. 12 Nov 1723

William BRADLEY
B. 1682
D. 27 Jan 1726/7

Elizabeth CHEDSEY
B. 6 Feb 1692/3

Note: Double dates before
1752 are due to change from
the Julian calendar to the
Gregorian calendar.

sion to marry Emma, but was twice refused, because he was "a stranger." At age twenty-two, Emma Hale married Joseph Smith on January 18, 1827, in South Bainbridge, New York, without her father's permission, and moved to Manchester, New York, to make her home with Joseph's parents. That experience marked the beginning of a warm, supportive, and enduring relationship between Emma and her mother-in-law, Lucy Mack SMITH. Returning briefly to Harmony to collect her belongings, Emma and Joseph were told the Hales's door would always be open to them, despite her father's continuing reservations about the man she had chosen to marry.

In the fall of 1827, Joseph, accompanied by Emma, finally obtained the gold plates from which he was to translate the Book of Mormon. Though never permitted to see the plates, Emma handled them frequently within their protective cover and helped hide them against the violent intrusion of townspeople in New York who sought the plates for the fortune they represented. Harmony offered refuge to Joseph and Emma, and so the young couple fled there, where Joseph hoped to translate the plates without disturbance. He bought a small farm from his father-in-law and engaged in sporadic farming. Emma became the first of several scribes who assisted in the translation. On June 15, 1828, she gave birth to their first child, a boy, who lived only a few hours. When the threats of Harmony residents began to hinder the work there, Emma and Joseph moved to Fayette, New York, where in June 1829 the translation was completed. In March 1830 the work was published in Palmyra, New York, as the Book of Mormon.

On April 6, 1830, Joseph Smith formally organized the Church of Christ, as The Church of Jesus Christ of Latter-day Saints was first known. Emma was baptized at Colesville, New York, on June 28, 1830, but before she could be confirmed a member of the Church the following day, Joseph was arrested "for being a disorderly person and setting the country in an uproar by preaching the Book of Mormon." He was vilified by his captors and subjected to two spurious trials, but was finally released. For the remainder of his life, Joseph would seldom be free of such encounters, and Emma would never again, during her husband's lifetime, know more than temporary respite from the anxiety she felt on that occasion.

Returning to Harmony in July 1830, Emma was the subject of a revelation received by Joseph

Emma Hale Smith, wife of Joseph Smith, was the seventh of nine children. She was a tall, attractive young woman, dark-complexioned, with brown eyes and black hair. Courtesy Utah State Historical Society.

but addressed specifically to Emma (D&C 25). In it she was designated the "Elect Lady," which Joseph would later explain means one elected "to preside." She was told that her calling was to be a support and comfort to her husband, to continue to act as his scribe, and "to expound scriptures and to exhort the church." She was also commissioned to prepare a hymnal for the Church, which was published five years later. Emma received her long-awaited confirmation in August 1830, almost two months after her baptism.

In August, Joseph and Emma moved back to Fayette, living there until January 1831, when they moved to Kirtland, Ohio. Like many other early converts, Emma was never to see her parents again, nor was she able to effect a lasting reconciliation between her father and husband.

On April 30, 1831, three months after moving to Kirtland, Emma gave birth to twins, both of whom died within hours. Nearby, a friend, Julia Clapp Murdock, wife of John Murdock, died after also giving birth to twins. Unable to care for them alone, her husband asked the bereft Joseph and Emma to raise his twins as their own. This they gladly did, naming the infants Joseph and Julia.

Emma faced continued difficulties during her eight-year residence in Kirtland. To the alarm of original settlers, Latter-day Saint converts swelled the community, inflating land values and creating hardship and dissension both within and outside the Church (see KIRTLAND ECONOMY). Scarcity of goods plagued the new residents. Emma witnessed again both the abuse and the fierce loyalty her husband and his work engendered. On March 24, 1832, she saw him dragged from the John Johnson house in the night and tarred and feathered by an angry mob. Five days later, she mourned the death of her adopted son, Joseph, from exposure to the cold as a result of mob action. Enduring her husband's frequent absences on Church business, Emma was obliged to support herself and her children by taking boarders into her already crowded quarters, an expedient that she would frequently employ throughout her life.

When the Saints in Missouri, like those in Kirtland, began experiencing the hostility of earlier settlers, Emma helped gather supplies for the men of Zion's Camp, who accompanied Joseph to Missouri to assist the beleaguered members there. She also provided room and board for builders of the temple in Kirtland and shared her means with new converts flooding into the area. With the assistance of William W. Phelps, she completed the first edition of the hymnal before the dedication of the Kirtland Temple in 1836, fulfilling the charge given her by revelation in 1830. She also gave birth to two more sons, Joseph (later known as Joseph III), born November 6, 1832, and Frederick Granger Williams, born June 20, 1836, both of whom lived to manhood.

In 1838, as relations with their Kirtland neighbors deteriorated and the Church experienced increasing internal difficulties, Emma followed her husband and other members to Missouri to consolidate the Church in one central location. Emma, Joseph, and their three children joined the settlement in Far West, the new center of the Church, and Emma gave birth to another son, Alexander Hale, on June 2, 1838. Missourians, however, continued to resist the LDS incursion, resentful of their growing political power. When feelings

Emma with her son David Hyrum Smith, born in November 1844, five months after the martyrdom of Joseph Smith.

erupted into widespread violence and an order from the governor expelled the Mormons, they turned eastward to Illinois, leaving their Prophet imprisoned in Liberty Jail (see MISSOURI CONFLICT). While her husband languished there through the winter of 1838–1839, Emma, with two babies in her arms and two at her skirts, walked across Missouri, finally crossing the frozen Mississippi to refuge in Quincy, Illinois, carrying the manuscript of her husband's translation of the Bible hidden in pockets in her clothing. From there she wrote to her husband of the trials she had endured, but vowed that she was "yet willing to suffer more if it is the will of kind heaven" (Joseph Smith Letterbook, Mar. 7, 1839, HDC).

While Emma suffered physical deprivation, harassment, and mob violence in New York, Pennsylvania, Ohio, and Missouri, the emotional and spiritual challenges she experienced in Nauvoo, Illinois, where the Church finally established itself, had more than personal ramifications. She and Joseph moved into a small house near the southern edge of the new town, later building a home they called the Mansion House, which also served as an inn or hotel for travelers. During the next five years, Emma gave birth to three more sons, losing one at birth and a second at eighteen months to a fever. Her last child, David Hyrum, was born November 17, 1844, five months after her husband's murder.

At the inception of the Female RELIEF SOCIETY of Nauvoo in 1842, Emma was elected president of the organization. As the Elect Lady, she was to preside "during good behavior" and "as long as [she] shall continue to fill the office with dignity" (Record of the Female Relief Society of Nauvoo). From March until October, Emma presided regularly and Joseph frequently attended, counseling the women on the charitable mission of the society and how they would "come in possession of the privileges, blessings, and gifts" associated with the priesthood (HC 4:602). Emma pressed for vigilance in watching over the morals of the community and diligence in succoring the poor. She saw the organization grow from a charter membership of twenty women to more than 1,100 at the end of the first year.

The following year, Emma became the first woman to receive the endowment, an ordinance that would later be administered to all worthy members in the temple then under construction in Nauvoo. Joseph Smith had earlier introduced these ordinances to some of his closest associates, and before his death as many as sixty-five men and women would receive them, with Emma officiating for the women. Joseph did not live to see the completion of the temple, and Emma chose not to participate during the brief period when temple ordinances were administered there before the Saints' exodus from Nauvoo in 1846.

The suspension of the Relief Society in 1844, only two years after its organization, was later attributed by John Taylor to Emma's opposition to PLURAL MARRIAGE or polygyny (more commonly, polygamy) and concern over her use of the society to preach against it ("Minutes of the General Meeting," [of the Retrenchment Association], July 17, 1880, reported in the Woman's Exponent 9 [Sept. 1, 1880]:53–54). The practice had been privately disclosed as a Church principle in 1840, and Emma's ambivalence enabled her husband to act on her brief acceptance of the doctrine long

enough to take additional wives. But her rejection of the principle soon became paramount. Loyal to her husband for seventeen years through all the vicissitudes that his mission had entailed, Emma Smith was unable, at the end, to make the sacrifice that the doctrine of plural marriage required. She struggled between her faith in her husband's prophetic role and her aversion to a principle that he, as Prophet, had been instructed to institute.

After Joseph's martyrdom in June 1844, Emma unfortunately became a symbol of the dissension within the Church. Unable to condone continuation of the practice of plural marriage or the leadership of Brigham YOUNG, who supported it, and ambivalent about the proper line of succession to her husband, Emma made her first priority after her husband's death the preservation of an inheritance for her five living children. Distinguishing Joseph's personal property from that of the Church defied easy solution, however, and involved Brigham Young and Emma Smith in a series of complex and often bitter legal entanglements. Brigham Young, as president of the Quorum of the Twelve Apostles and steward of the Church, claimed all that he felt rightfully belonged to its members. Emma Smith, as guardian of Joseph's children, just as vigorously claimed their share, to which she had contributed throughout her marriage to Joseph. Unable to reach an amica-

Emma Smith, the Elect Lady, by Theodore Gorka (1981, oil on canvas, 7' × 10'). Emma Smith often cared for the sick, as when a malaria epidemic struck Commerce (later Nauvoo), Illinois. Her son Joseph Smith III wrote, "I remember that Mother filled her house with the sick who were brought to her from near and far, giving them shelter, treatment, and nursing care."

ble solution and unwilling to accept plural marriage even in principle, Emma elected to remain in Nauvoo with her family while Brigham Young led the majority of Church members to the Rocky Mountains in 1846. On December 23, 1847, Emma Smith married Lewis Bidamon, a non-Mormon, further estranging her from the Church, to which she had once been known as the Elect Lady. Bidamon assisted Emma in raising her five children and remained her companion until her death in 1879 in Nauvoo.

In 1860, Emma's eldest son, Joseph Smith III, after four years of refusal, accepted the invitation to serve as prophet and first president of the REORGANIZED CHURCH OF JESUS CHRIST OF LATTER DAY SAINTS. It was offered by a group of men who formerly had been members of the Church, many of whom had left to follow James J. Strang for a time. As a group they chose not to go west with the body of the Church. Emma, who had heretofore rejected connection with any of the splinter Mormon groups, was admitted into membership in 1860. In his acceptance speech, Joseph III firmly rejected polygamy as a practice of the new church, and Emma denied that her husband had participated in the practice.

Still devoted to her mother-in-law, Emma cared for her until Lucy died in 1856. The Prophet's mother had always admired Emma. "I have never seen a woman in my life, who would endure every species of fatigue and hardship, from month to month, and from year to year," she wrote, "with that unflinching courage, zeal, and patience, which she has ever done" (Smith, pp. 190–91).

Emma Smith Bidamon's final years in Nauvoo were family-focused and private. She shared the Nauvoo House, her final home, with relatives and friends and basked in the love and care of her children and grandchildren. She continued to live her life with genteel qualities, meeting adversity and difficulty with grace and equanimity. She was polite to the "Utah Mormons" who occasionally visited, but was firm in her decision to remain apart from them.

Though Emma was publicly criticized by Church leaders for her failure to remain faithful to her husband's mission, she was sympathetically remembered by some of her former Nauvoo friends. Many of them, unlike Emma, had found the courage to accept the doctrine of plural marriage. "I know it was hard for Emma, and any woman to enter plural marriage in those days,"

wrote Emily Partridge Young, a plural wife, "and I do not know as anybody would have done any better than Emma did under the circumstances" (*Woman's Exponent* 12 [Apr. 1, 1884]:165).

In 1892 at the jubilee celebration in Salt Lake City of the founding of the Nauvoo Relief Society, a motion to hang a life-size portrait of Emma Smith in the Tabernacle brought mixed responses from the Relief Society board members. To settle the question, Relief Society president Zina D. H. Young took the matter to Church President Wilford Woodruff, who replied that "anyone who opposed it [hanging the portrait in the Tabernacle] must be very narrow minded indeed" (Emmeline B. Wells Diary, March 11, 1892, HDC). Fifty years had softened bitter memories, and Emma Smith could once again be honored as a leader of women and remembered for the essential part she had played in the restoration of the gospel and the support she gave her Prophet-husband through the difficult years of his ministry.

BIBLIOGRAPHY

Newell, Linda King, and Valeen Tippetts Avery. *Mormon Enigma: Emma Hale Smith*. Garden City, N.Y., 1984.

Smith, Lucy Mack. *History of Joseph Smith*. Salt Lake City, 1958.

Youngreen, Buddy. *Reflections of Emma, Joseph Smith's Wife*. Orem, Utah, 1982.

CAROL CORNWALL MADSEN

SMITH, GEORGE ALBERT

George Albert Smith (1870–1951), the eighth president of the Church, was born April 4, 1870, in Salt Lake City, the son of John Henry Smith and Sarah Farr. His grandfather, George A. Smith, was an APOSTLE and counselor to President Brigham YOUNG, and his father, John Henry Smith, was an apostle and counselor to President Joseph F. SMITH. His mother was a daughter of Lorin Farr, the pioneer founder and early mayor of Ogden, Utah. On May 25, 1892, George Albert Smith married Lucy Emily Woodruff, the daughter of Wilford Woodruff, Jr., and Emily Jane Smith. They had three children: Emily (Mrs. Robert M. Stewart), Edith (Mrs. George O. Elliott), and George Albert, Jr. George Albert Smith was ordained an apostle at thirty-three years of age on October 8, 1903, by President Joseph F. Smith.

George Albert Smith (1870–1951), eighth President of the Church, was ordained an apostle in 1903, at age 33. Courtesy Utah State Historical Society.

In his youth he worked in the ZCMI factory and as a salesman, traveling by wagon throughout Utah. He attended Brigham Young Academy and the University of Deseret (later the University of Utah). When he was on a railroad surveying job in eastern Utah, the glare of the sun permanently impaired his eyesight. In 1896 he declared for the Republican party and campaigned for William McKinley, which won him appointment in 1897 as receiver for the Land Office in Utah, a position to which he was reappointed in 1902 by Theodore Roosevelt.

At the time of his call to the apostleship in 1903, George Albert Smith was president of the Young Men's Mutual Improvement Association (YMMIA; see YOUNG MEN) in the Salt Lake Stake, with some forty WARDS to supervise. In 1891 he had undertaken a short mission for the Church among the young people in Juab, Millard, Beaver, and Parowan stakes, and in June 1892, a week after his marriage, he was called to the Southern States

Mission under President J. Golden Kimball. Elder Smith was soon appointed mission secretary. His wife joined him, and they served in the mission office until June 1894.

His call to the apostleship entailed continual weekly visiting to the established STAKES of the Church, organizing new wards and stakes, and supervising the missions of the Church. His travels averaged 30,000 miles yearly, and his attendance at meetings averaged more than ten per week.

Under this pressure, his already frail health broke, and his life became a constant struggle against physical weakness. Through his remaining years he guarded his energies and rationed them to fulfill his responsibilities. His illness was diagnosed only at end of life as lupus erythematosus, a disease that produces chronic weakness.

President Smith was a master of the art of making friends. Wherever he went he especially cultivated the acquaintance and companionship of the leaders of the people. Whether it was the President of the United States or the Lord Mayor of London, he established a friendship. His friends were legion, throughout the Church and around the globe.

Some of his finest work was done with youth. Over a lifetime he served in every capacity in the YMMIA, and shortly after becoming an apostle, he was called to the YMMIA General Board, serving from 1904 to 1921. As general superintendent of that organization from 1921 to 1935, he was influential in setting policies, establishing programs, and directing youth activities throughout the Church.

President Smith gained international prominence as a scout. When scouting came to the United States in 1910, he recommended its incorporation into the YMMIA program, where it came under his leadership. Beginning in 1931, he served on the advisory board of the National Council of Boy Scouts of America. At this time Utah and the Church came to lead the world in the percentage of boys registered as scouts and explorers. In 1932 he was awarded the Silver Beaver, and in 1934, the Silver Buffalo, two of scouting's highest awards.

As president of the European Mission (see MISSION PRESIDENT) from June 1919 to July 1921, he won the love and admiration of the missionaries and the Saints and made many friends for the Church. As World War I had just ended, a major task was to reestablish missionary work and help the Saints adjust. President Smith inaugurated friendly relations with governments and visited missionaries and Saints in Ireland, Scotland, France, Switzerland, Norway, Denmark, Sweden, and Germany. Between January and July 1938, he and Rufus K. Hardy of the First Council of the Seventy visited the missions of the Pacific Ocean area: Hawaii, the Fiji Islands, New Zealand, Australia, Tonga, and the Samoa Islands.

Throughout his life George Albert Smith maintained intense personal interests rooted in his pioneer family and Church heritage. He carried on his father's interest in irrigation, dry farming, and reclamation. Between 1913 and 1918 he attended the meetings of the International Irrigation Congress, the International Dry-farm Congress, and their successor, the International Farm Congress. At each of these congresses he was elected either a vice-president or president, increasing his friendships throughout the United States and Canada.

He had a keen interest in identifying and marking HISTORIC SITES. He was at Sharon, Vermont, for the 1905 dedication of the monument noting the centennial anniversary of the birth of the Prophet Joseph SMITH. In June 1907 he and others negotiated for the purchase of the Joseph Smith, Sr., farm in Manchester, New York. In 1937 he took the initiative in organizing the Utah Pioneer Trails and Landmarks Association, whose first purpose was to erect a monument at the mouth of Emigration Canyon to honor the arrival of the pioneers of 1847, a project realized in July 1947 with the "THIS IS THE PLACE" MONUMENT. More than a hundred historic monuments and markers were erected by the association, from Nauvoo to Utah and throughout the West.

Proud of his American patriot ancestry, President Smith affiliated with the Sons of the American Revolution. He was active in the Utah chapter and was elected a trustee of the national society.

His appreciation for his Smith family heritage included cordial relations with his cousins, the descendants of Joseph Smith III, and with other leaders of the REORGANIZED CHURCH OF JESUS CHRIST OF LATTER DAY SAINTS.

President George Albert Smith both taught and lived the two great commandments to "love the Lord thy God" and to "love thy neighbour as thyself" (Matt. 22:37–39). To him, all people were the children of God, and he could in no way hurt a child of God. "All the people of the earth are our Father's children, . . . regardless of race, creed, or color, all men are our brothers." He taught that

"men cannot approach the likeness of God except by the practice of love to their fellow men. Only by love can peace and joy be made to cover the earth." Other recurring themes and aphorisms in his teachings include: "This is our Father's work." "Keep on the Lord's side of the line." "Seek ye first the Kingdom of God and his righteousness." "There is only one aristocracy that God recognizes, and that is the aristocracy of righteousness" (Papers, Box 96). He preached of honest work, thrift, self-reliance, good homes, education, and progress. He gave comfort and cheer, praise and encouragement, without offense and without guile. He was the apostle of kindness and love. There was no room in his heart for hatred, anger, envy, resentment, or fear. "To him have been given many of the qualities which can only be described as being Christlike" (John D. Giles, *IE* 48 [July 1945]:388).

President Smith exemplified these qualities in all aspects of his personal life. He measured his life by the yardstick of service and was happiest when

George Albert Smith was a strong supporter of Boy Scouting. He was awarded the silver beaver and silver buffalo, two of scouting's highest honors. Courtesy Utah State Historical Society.

assisting the poor, the widows, and the fatherless, or visiting the sick among his neighbors or in hospitals. He was always polite, gentlemanly, tactful, forgiving, and kind, a man of peace who cultivated goodwill among all people. He lifted the burdens from the shoulders of both friends and strangers, planted hope in the human heart, and restored confidence. He practiced the divine law of love.

Upon the death of Elder Rudger Clawson on June 21, 1943, George Albert Smith was selected president of the QUORUM OF THE TWELVE APOSTLES, which office he held for two years. When President Heber J. GRANT died, George Albert Smith was sustained PRESIDENT OF THE CHURCH, May 21, 1945, at the age of seventy-five.

World War II ended that summer, and President Smith led a group to Washington, D.C., to facilitate the sending of Church welfare goods to Church members in war-devastated Europe. During the weeks that followed, the Church shipped 133 railroad carloads of food, clothing, and bedding, along with thousands of individual eleven-pound packages.

During President Smith's administration, he asked Spencer W. KIMBALL, an apostle, to assist in supervising the Navajo-Zuni Indian Mission, and he himself headed a delegation to the nation's capital to initiate plans to help NATIVE AMERICANS.

Missionary work was revitalized throughout the world after cutbacks during World War II. New stakes and missions were organized. The number of missionaries rose to more than 5,000, and the number of wards and branches increased from 1,273 to 1,492, and stakes from 149 to 179. Some 200 new MEETINGHOUSES were built. New hospitals were constructed and old ones enlarged. Microfilming of vital records was accelerated so that by February 1950 a total of 24,579 microfilm records had been catalogued. On September 23, 1945, President Smith dedicated the Idaho Falls Temple.

President George Albert Smith died on April 4, 1951, on his eighty-first birthday, leaving as his chief legacy an example of Christlike living.

BIBLIOGRAPHY

Pusey, Merlo J. *Builders of the Kingdom: George A. Smith, John Henry Smith, George Albert Smith*, pp. 203–364. Provo, Utah, 1981.

Smith, George Albert. Papers, Folders 1–4, Box 96. Special Collections, University of Utah Library, Salt Lake City.

Stubbs, Glen R. "A Biography of George Albert Smith, 1870–1951." Ph.D. diss., Brigham Young University, 1974.

S. GEORGE ELLSWORTH

SMITH, HYRUM

Among early Mormon leaders, Hyrum Smith (1800–1844) stands next to his brother the Prophet Joseph SMITH in the esteem of many Latter-day Saints. Although nearly six years older than his prophet brother, Hyrum became Joseph's closest adviser and confidant. When he died a martyr with Joseph on June 27, 1844, Hyrum was Associate President of the Church, second in authority.

Hyrum was born to Joseph SMITH, Sr., and Lucy Mack SMITH on February 9, 1800, in Tunbridge, Vermont. During his childhood, the family moved to eight different locations near the Connecticut River while the father struggled as a farmer, storekeeper, and tenant farmer. At age eleven, Hyrum was sent to Moor's Charity School, associated with Dartmouth College. About two years later, a severe epidemic of typhoid fever broke out and Hyrum returned home ill to find several siblings ill as well. Joseph, Jr., was stricken with the dreaded disease, which developed into osteomyelitis in his left leg. Hyrum, who was already recognized for his tender and compassionate nature, became young Joseph's nurse, developing an enduring bond between the brothers.

After the family moved to New York, Hyrum and the other Smith brothers helped the family finances by hiring out as farm laborers, coopers, and masons, in addition to clearing their own land for farming. On November 2, 1826, Hyrum married Jerusha Barden (1805–1837).

After Joseph received the plates and started translating the Book of Mormon, Hyrum journeyed to Harmony, Pennsylvania, in 1828, and again in May 1829, to learn how the work was progressing. Joseph sought a revelation at Hyrum's earnest request in which Hyrum learned that after he had prepared himself by studying the Bible and the teachings soon to come forth in the Book of Mormon, he was called to "assist to bring forth my work" and to preach "nothing but repentance" (D&C 11:9, 22). Early in June 1829, Hyrum was baptized in Seneca Lake, New York. Toward the end of June, he became one of the Eight Witnesses, examining and "hefting" the plates of gold

The Two Martyrs, an engraving of Hyrum (left) and Joseph Smith (right). John Taylor, who was a witness to their martyrdom, wrote, "In life they were not divided, and in death they were not separated" (D&C 135:3). Courtesy Utah State Historical Society.

(*see* BOOK OF MORMON WITNESSES). He served as Oliver COWDERY's bodyguard as he delivered a few pages of the Book of Mormon manuscript each day to the printer in Palmyra.

When the Church was organized under New York state law on April 6, 1830, Hyrum was the oldest at age thirty of the six men who signed their names as charter members (*see* ORGANIZATION OF THE CHURCH, 1830). He was told, "Thy duty is unto the church forever" (D&C 23:3), a duty he faithfully fulfilled. Hyrum became one of the first preachers of the Church in surrounding communities in New York, baptizing some of the earliest converts. When a substantial branch of the Church was formed in Colesville, Hyrum was called as its presiding officer.

In 1831 Hyrum Smith moved, along with most Church members, to Kirtland, Ohio. Be-

tween 1831 and 1833 he served three proselytizing missions to Missouri and Ohio. In 1834 he helped recruit members for Zion's Camp and served as Joseph Smith's chief aide in that military march. Upon his return, Hyrum became foreman of the stone quarry for the rising Kirtland Temple. Having proved his ability and faithfulness, Hyrum was ordained an Assistant President of the Church in December 1834. His responsibilities were further increased in November 1837 when he became Second Counselor in the First Presidency with Joseph Smith and Sidney RIGDON, and with Oliver Cowdery as Associate President.

In Missouri in October 1838, when the Latter-day Saints clashed with their neighbors, Joseph, Hyrum, Sidney Rigdon, and several other Mormons were arrested on false charges of treason, murder, arson, and stealing. They were taken to Richmond, Missouri, for trial, while the rest of the Saints were driven from the state (*see* MISSOURI CONFLICT). After a preliminary hearing in November, Joseph and Hyrum were bound over for trial. For nearly five more months, they and three others shared a jail cell in the village of Liberty, Missouri, while state officials deliberated on their fate. On April 16, 1839, during a second change of venue, they were allowed to escape.

In the Saints' new home along the Mississippi in Illinois, Hyrum Smith was ordained to two prominent positions in the Church: Presiding PATRIARCH, in place of his deceased father (D&C 124:91), and Associate President of the Church, in place of Oliver Cowdery (D&C 124:95). When Joseph Smith traveled to Washington, D.C., to seek redress from federal officials for the Saints' Missouri grievances, Hyrum served as Acting President of the Church in Nauvoo. Hyrum pronounced hundreds of patriarchal blessings upon the members of the Church, including numerous converts arriving from Britain. He was a founding leader of the Nauvoo Masonic lodge. In 1842 he clarified that "hot drinks" in the Word of Wisdom (D&C 89:9) referred to tea and coffee (*T&S* 3:800), a point that had been controversial. He was also the chairman of the Nauvoo Temple Building Committee and stood close to the Prophet Joseph, acting "in concert" with him in all leadership capacities (D&C 124:95).

Latter-day Saints revered their "Prophet Joseph" and "Patriarch Hyrum"; enemies of the Church despised both them and the power they represented. As events led toward Joseph's assassination in Carthage, Hyrum refused to leave him, even though Joseph requested that Hyrum flee with his family to Cincinnati. He went with Joseph to Carthage in June 1844 and was charged with riot and treason, along with his brother. When a mob stormed the jail where they were confined awaiting trial, Hyrum, standing to hold the door shut, was the first to die from gunfire through the door. Joseph and Hyrum became dual martyrs. Like many of "the Lord's anointed in ancient times," they sealed their works with their own blood; "in life they were not divided, and in death they were not separated" (D&C 135:3; *see also* CARTHAGE JAIL; MARTYRDOM OF JOSEPH AND HYRUM SMITH).

Hyrum Smith is credited in Church history with being an astute organizer who gave ecclesiastical leadership to the emerging Church. As a person, he was considered a man without guile. One scripture concerning him reads, "I, the Lord, love him because of the integrity of his heart" (D&C 124:15). With a love for Hyrum that was stronger than death, Joseph once described him as possessing "the mildness of a lamb, and the integrity of a Job, and in short, the meekness and humility of Christ" (*HC* 2:338). When John Taylor looked upon Hyrum's slain body, he reflected, "He was a great and good man, and my soul was cemented to his. If ever there was an exemplary, honest, and virtuous man, an embodiment of all that is noble in the human form, Hyrum Smith was its representative" (*HC* 7:107).

Hyrum and his first wife, Jerusha, had four daughters and two sons. After Jerusha's death, he married Mary Fielding in 1837, and she bore him a son and a daughter. When Joseph Smith introduced PLURAL MARRIAGE to him, Hyrum at first

Hyrum Smith's home in Kirtland, Ohio.

opposed the idea, but when converted to the principle, he became one of its staunchest advocates.

Many of Hyrum's descendants have played significant roles in Church history. A son, Joseph F. SMITH, became the sixth President of the Church, and a grandson, Joseph Fielding SMITH, became the tenth President. Four of the six Patriarchs to the Church since 1845 have been descendants of Hyrum Smith.

BIBLIOGRAPHY

Corbett, Pearson H. *Hyrum Smith, Patriarch.* Salt Lake City, 1963.

Smith, Joseph Fielding. "The Martyrs." *IE* 47 (June 1944):364–65, 414–15.

BRUCE A. VAN ORDEN

SMITH, JOSEPH

[*This entry is divided into four parts:*

> The Prophet
> Teachings of Joseph Smith
> Writings of Joseph Smith
> Legal Trials of Joseph Smith

The Prophet *is a biography of Joseph Smith;* Teachings of Joseph Smith *sketches his thought and teachings;* Writings of Joseph Smith *examines his personal writings and the body of scripture, revelations, and history resulting from his ministry; and* Trials of Joseph Smith *recounts his legal and judicial history. See also* Visions of Joseph Smith.

Historical overviews of LDS history during the Joseph Smith period are History of the Church: c. 1820–1831; c. 1831–1844. *For entries dealing with his prophetic calling consult* Prophet Joseph Smith. *For Joseph Smith's family background, see* Smith Family *and* Smith Family Ancestors; *see also entries for his mother,* Lucy Mack Smith; *his father,* Joseph Smith, Sr.; *his brother* Hyrum Smith, *and his wife,* Emma Hale Smith.]

THE PROPHET

Joseph Smith, Jr. (1805–1844), often referred to as the Prophet Joseph Smith, was the founding PROPHET of The Church of Jesus Christ of Latter-day Saints. Latter-day Saints call him "the Prophet" because, in the tradition of Old and New Testament prophets, he depended on REVELATION from God for his teachings, not on his own learning. They accept his revelations, many of them published as the DOCTRINE AND COVENANTS and

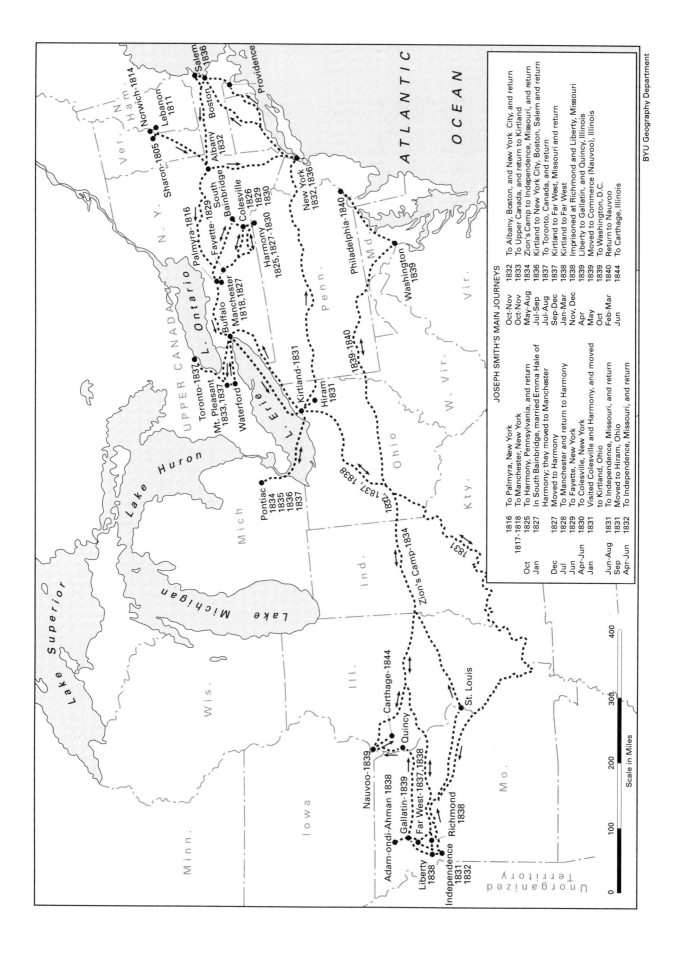

JOSEPH SMITH'S MAIN JOURNEYS

	1832	To Albany, Boston, and New York City, and return	Oct–Nov
	1833	To Upper Canada, and return to Kirtland	Oct–Nov
	1834	Zion's Camp to Independence, Missouri, and return	May–Aug
	1836	Kirtland to New York City, Boston, Salem and return	Jul–Sep
	1837	To Toronto, Canada, and return	Jul–Aug
	1837	Kirtland to Far West, Missouri and return	Sep–Dec
	1838	Kirtland to Far West	Jan–Mar
	1838	Imprisoned at Richmond and Liberty, Missouri	Nov, Dec
	1839	Liberty to Gallatin, and Quincy, Illinois	Apr
	1839	Moved to Commerce (Nauvoo), Illinois	May
	1839	To Washington, D.C.	Oct
	1840	Return to Nauvoo	Feb–Mar
	1844	To Carthage, Illinois	Jun

	1816	To Palmyra, New York	
	1817–1818	To Manchester, New York	
Oct	1825	To Harmony, Pennsylvania, and return	
Jan	1827	In South Bainbridge, married Emma Hale of Harmony; they moved to Manchester	
Dec	1827	Moved to Harmony	
Jul	1828	To Manchester and return to Harmony	
Jun	1829	To Fayette, New York	
Apr–Jun	1830	To Colesville, New York	
Jan	1831	Visited Colesville and Harmony, and moved to Kirtland, Ohio	
Jun–Aug	1831	To Independence, Missouri, and return	
Sep	1831	Moved to Hiram, Ohio	
Apr–Jun	1832	To Independence, Missouri, and return	

BYU Geography Department

1332

Joseph Smith, by Alvin Gittens (1959, oil on canvas, 31″ × 39″). Prophet, Seer, and Revelator, first elder and President of The Church of Jesus Christ of Latter-day Saints. His inspiration and genius single him out among the great spiritual leaders of all time.

as the PEARL OF GREAT PRICE, as scripture to accompany the Bible. As a young man, Joseph Smith also translated a sacred record from ancient America known as the BOOK OF MORMON. These revelations and records restored to the earth the pure gospel of Christ. Joseph Smith's role in history was to found the Church of Jesus Christ based on this restored gospel in preparation for the second coming of Christ.

Little in his background pointed toward this momentous life. Joseph Smith's ancestors were ordinary New England farm people. His Smith ancestors emigrated from England to America in the seventeenth century and settled in Topsfield, Massachusetts, where they attained local distinction. His grandfather Asael Smith, unable at the time to pay the debts on the family farm, sold the farm, liquidated the debts, and migrated in 1791 to

Tunbridge, Vermont, where he purchased enough land to provide for his sons. Joseph Smith's Mack ancestors, from Scotland, settled in Lyme, Connecticut, prospered for a while, and then fell on hard times. Joseph's grandfather Solomon Mack attempted various enterprises in New England and New York, with little financial success. One of the Mack sons moved to Tunbridge, and through him Lucy Mack met Joseph Smith, Sr., one of Asael's sons. The pair married in 1796. They had eleven children, nine of whom lived to adulthood. Joseph Smith, Jr., born December 23, 1805, in Sharon, Vermont, was the third son to live and the fourth child.

Young Joseph had little formal schooling. His parents lost their Tunbridge farm in 1803 through a failed business venture and for the next fourteen years moved from one tenant farm to another. In 1816 they migrated to Palmyra, New York, just north of the Finger Lakes, where in 1817 they purchased a farm in Farmington (later Manchester), the township immediately south of Palmyra. Clearing land and wresting a living from the soil left little time for school. "As it required the exertions of all that were able to render any assistance for the support of the Family," Joseph wrote in 1832, "we were deprived of the bennifit of an education suffice it to say I was mearly instructid in reading writing and the ground rules of Arithmatic which constuted my whole literary acquirements" (Jessee, 1989–, 1:5). His mother described him as "much less inclined to the perusal of books than any of the rest of the children, but far more given to meditation and deep study" (Smith, p. 84). His knowledge of the Bible and his biblical style of writing suggest that much of his early education came from that source.

One subject he pondered was religion. His parents had been reared under the influence of New England Congregationalism but, dissatisfied with the preachers around them, they were not regular churchgoers. Both parents had deep religious experiences and an intense longing for salvation, without having a satisfactory way to worship. A few years after settling in Palmyra, Lucy Smith and three of the children joined the Presbyterians; Joseph, Sr., and the others stayed home, Joseph, Jr., among them. Young Joseph was deeply perplexed about which church to join, and the preach-

←——Joseph Smith's main journeys, 1805–1844.

ing of the revival ministers in the area intensified his uncertainty.

In the spring of 1820, when he was just fourteen, Joseph turned directly to God for guidance. The answer was astonishing. As he prayed in the woods near his house, the Father and the Son appeared to him. Assuring him that his sins were forgiven, the Lord told him that none of the churches were right and that he should join none. Latter-day Saints call this Joseph Smith's FIRST VISION, the initial event in the RESTORATION OF THE GOSPEL. At the time, it made little impression on the people around Joseph Smith. He told a minister about the vision and was rebuffed. Believing the Bible sufficient, ministers were skeptical of direct revelation. The scorn upset Joseph, who had only tried to report his actual experience, and alienated him still further from the churches.

After three years with no further revelations, Joseph wondered if he still was in favor with God and prayed again for direction and forgiveness. The vision he received on September 21, 1823, set the course of his life for the next seven years. An angel appeared and instructed him about a sacred record of an ancient people. This angel, MORONI$_2$, told Joseph that he was to obtain the record, written on GOLD PLATES, and translate it. He also told him that God's covenant with ancient Israel was about to be fulfilled, that preparation for the second coming of Christ was about to commence, and that the gospel was to be preached to all nations to prepare a people for Christ's millennial reign. In a vision Joseph saw the hill near his home where the plates were buried. When he went the next day to get the plates, the angel stopped him. He was told that he must wait four years to obtain the plates and that, until then, he was to return each year for instructions. On September 22, 1827, he obtained the plates from which he translated the Book of Mormon (see MORONI, VISITATIONS OF).

The discovery of gold plates in a hillside resonated strangely with other experiences of the Smith family. Like many other New Englanders, they were familiar with searches for lost treasure by supernatural means. Joseph Smith's father was reputed to be one of these treasure-seekers, and Joseph Smith himself had found a stone, called a SEER STONE, which reportedly enabled him to find lost objects. Treasure-seekers wanted to employ him to help with their searches. One, a man named Josiah Stowell (sometimes spelled Stoal), hired Joseph and his father in 1825 to dig for a supposed Spanish treasure near HARMONY, PENNSYLVANIA. The effort came to nothing, and the Smiths returned home, but the neighbors continued to think of the Smiths as part of the treasure-seeking company. Joseph Smith had to learn, in his four years of waiting, to appreciate the plates solely for their religious worth and not for their monetary value. The angel forbade Joseph to remove the plates on his first viewing because thoughts of their commercial worth had crossed his mind. Joseph had to learn to focus on the religious purpose of the plates and put aside considerations of their value as gold.

While working in Harmony in 1825, Joseph Smith met Emma Hale at the Hale home where he and his father boarded. He continued seeing her through the next year while working at other jobs in the area, and on January 18, 1827, they married. She was tall, straight, slender, and dark-haired; he stood over six feet tall with broad chest and shoulders, light brown hair, and blue eyes. After the wedding they went to live with the Smith family in Manchester, close to the hill Cumorah where the plates still lay buried.

On September 22, 1827, Joseph Smith went to the hill for the fifth time. This time the angel permitted him to take the plates, with strict instructions to show them to no one. Designing people tried strenuously to get the plates, however, and he was not left in peace to begin translation. Eventually he and Emma were compelled to move, for their safety, to Harmony, near Emma's family.

For the next three years, Joseph's work depended on the support of a few loyal friends who came to his aid and helped buffer him from troublesome inquirers. His open manner inspired confidence, and his candor in simply narrating what had happened to him disarmed skepticism. His brother later wrote that Joseph's youth, his lack of education, and his "whole character and disposition" convinced the family that he was incapable of "giving utterance to anything but the truth" (*William Smith on Mormonism*, Lamoni, Iowa, 1883, pp. 9–10). By the time the translation was completed and the Book of Mormon published, three or four dozen people believed in his mission and divine gifts.

Martin HARRIS, a prosperous Palmyra farmer, was one of these friends. He helped Joseph move to Harmony and then moved there himself to help with the translation. To enable him to translate,

Joseph received with the plates a special instrument called interpreters or URIM AND THUMMIM. As he dictated, Martin Harris wrote (*see* BOOK OF MORMON TRANSLATION BY JOSEPH SMITH). In the spring of 1828, after three months of work, Martin Harris took the 116 pages of the translation home to show his wife, and they were lost or stolen. This interrupted the translation and left Joseph desolate. Soon after, he received a scathing rebuke in a revelation (D&C 3). About this time, Joseph and Emma's firstborn son died on the day of his birth, June 15, 1828, wrenching Joseph's feelings even further.

Translation resumed in the fall of 1828, continuing intermittently until the spring of 1829. Then Oliver COWDERY, a schoolteacher who learned of the plates from Joseph's parents, believed in Joseph and agreed to take dictation. From April to June 1829 they labored together. When the two friends prayed on May 15 for an understanding of baptism, a messenger who announced himself as John the Baptist appeared, conferred priesthood authority upon them, and instructed them to baptize each other (*see* AARONIC PRIESTHOOD: RESTORATION OF). Oliver later wrote: "These were days never to be forgotten—to sit under the sound of a voice dictated by the inspiration of heaven, awakened the utmost gratitude of this bosom" (JS—H 1:71n).

Oliver was not the only additional witness to the revelations. When opposition began to build in Harmony, Oliver and Joseph moved in June 1829 to FAYETTE, NEW YORK, to the family home of Oliver's friend David WHITMER. Here again Joseph received needed support from people who believed in him. Once the translation was completed, Joseph was told that others would be allowed to see the plates, which until that time only he had viewed. The angel Moroni appeared to Martin Harris, Oliver Cowdery, and David Whitmer and showed them the gold plates while a voice from heaven declared that the translation was done by the power of God and was true (*see* BOOK OF MORMON WITNESSES). Joseph's mother reported that Joseph came into the house after this revelation and threw himself down beside her, exclaiming that at last someone else had seen the plates. "Now they know for themselves, that I do not go about to deceive" (Smith, p. 139). His words suggest the pressure he felt in being the only witness of his remarkable experiences.

In March 1830 the Book of Mormon was pub-

The Joseph Smith homestead in Nauvoo (c. 1930). The Prophet and his family lived here from 1839 to 1843. About 1856 the Prophet's son Joseph Smith III added the larger part of the building to the west.

lished, ending one phase of Joseph's life but not his divine mission. Revelations in 1829 instructed him to organize a church. On April 6, 1830, at the Whitmers' house in Fayette, New York, the Church of Christ was organized with Joseph Smith and Oliver Cowdery as first and second elders (*see* ORGANIZATION OF THE CHURCH, 1830).

Leadership of the Church set Joseph Smith's life on a new course. Up to this time he had been a young man with a divine gift and a mission to translate the Book of Mormon; now, without any previous organizational experience, he was responsible for organizing a church and leading a people. He had to rely on revelation. Over the next six years, he received many revelations, 90 of which fill 190 pages in the Doctrine and Covenants. They range from instructions on mundane details of administration to exalted depictions of life hereafter. Typically, when problems had to be solved, whether administrative or doctrinal, the Prophet sought divine guidance and by virtue of this help led the Church.

The course the revelations laid out for the new Church was extraordinarily challenging. The Prophet received instructions for ventures reaching halfway across the continent and involving a reorganization of society. At the core of the instruction was the establishment of ZION. Book of Mormon teachings of Christ made reference to a NEW JERUSALEM, a city of Zion that would be established in America (3 Ne. 20:22). Later revelations outlined the nature of the new order. The central concept was the GATHERING of the pure and honest from among the nations into communities where they could learn to live in unity and love under divine direction, and where temples could be built to administer the sacred ordinances of salvation.

In September–October 1830, missionaries were called to teach Native Americans who resided near the western boundary of Missouri (*see* LAMANITE MISSION). These missionaries were told that the city of Zion would be located somewhere in that region. Later revelations called for a gathering to Missouri to organize Zion, and a new economic order designed to enable the Saints to live together in unity (*see* CONSECRATION). Joseph and other leading figures in the Church journeyed to Jackson County, Missouri, in the summer of 1831, and there learned by revelation that the city was to be constructed and a temple built near Independence, Missouri (*see* MISSOURI: LDS COMMUNITIES IN JACKSON AND CLAY COUNTIES). The gathering was to commence immediately.

When it is remembered that Joseph Smith was not yet twenty-six, and five years earlier was an uneducated farmer notable only for his spiritual gifts, the daring of these plans is hard to comprehend. The magnitude of his conceptions never troubled him. "I intend to lay a foundation that will revolutionize the whole world," he later remarked (*HC* 6:365). He acted in the certainty that the directions were from God and that the Church would triumph against all odds.

In the spring of 1831 virtually all Latter-day Saints left New York for Ohio. Joseph and Emma settled in KIRTLAND, OHIO, near a body of new converts, and for the next six years this was Church headquarters. The other focal point of Church life until 1838 was Missouri, first Independence, the site of the future city of Zion, then northern Missouri. As Latter-day Saints migrated to Missouri, tensions with old settlers increased. In Jackson County, in 1831–1833, and again in Caldwell County, in 1836–1838, efforts to establish Zion aroused violent opposition to what non-Mormons perceived as a threat to their way of life (*see* MISSOURI CONFLICT).

Joseph Smith also made efforts to realize his vision of Zion during the seven years that the Latter-day Saints were in Ohio. He organized the first STAKES and set up the presiding priesthood structure of the Church. The Prophet established a bank, a newspaper, and a printing office; he super-

vised the building of the Church's first temple, and initiated extensive missionary work in the United States, Canada, and England. His revelations, including a law of health (*see* WORD OF WISDOM), tutored the Saints in the conduct of daily life. He made a translation of the Bible (*see* JOSEPH SMITH TRANSLATION OF THE BIBLE). He introduced a school system to prepare the Saints for leadership and missionary roles and was himself a student of Hebrew in the school. The high point of the Kirtland years was the dedication of the temple. Although Joseph Smith had received priesthood authority several years earlier, in 1836, in the KIRTLAND TEMPLE, he received important additional KEYS of authority from Moses, Elias, and Elijah pertaining to the gathering of ISRAEL and the eternal SEALING of families.

Opposition had beset the Prophet from the time he first told people about his visions. In 1832 he was tarred, feathered, and beaten by a mob who broke into the house where he was staying at Hiram, Ohio, an intrusion that led to the death of a child. At Kirtland, dissent arose within the Church over the nature of the new society and the Prophet's involvement in economics and politics; some accused him of attempting to control their private lives and labeled him a fallen prophet. By early 1838, opposition, especially among Ohio leadership, grew to the point that the Prophet and loyal members moved to Missouri.

Joseph Smith arrived with his family at Far West, Caldwell County, Missouri, in March 1838, where he sought once again to establish a gathering place for the Saints and to build a temple (*see* MISSOURI: LDS COMMUNITIES IN CALDWELL AND DAVIESS COUNTIES). But, as before, the influx of outsiders with differing social, religious, and economic practices was unacceptable to the old settlers. Opposition flared into violence at Gallatin, Daviess County, on August 6, 1838, when enemies of the Church tried to prevent Latter-day Saints from voting. The ensuing fight produced injuries on both sides. A subsequent misunderstanding with a local justice of the peace led to charges against the Prophet. As rumors spread, citizens of several counties, then militias, mobilized to expel the Latter-day Saints (*see* MISSOURI CONFLICT; EXTERMINATION ORDER).

The crisis came to a head on October 31, 1838, when Joseph Smith and several others, expecting to discuss ways to defuse the volatile situation, were arrested—it was the beginning of five months of confinement. A November court of inquiry at Richmond, Ray County, accused the Prophet and others with acts of treason connected with the conflict and committed them to LIBERTY JAIL to await trial. Meanwhile, the Saints were driven from the state.

Harsh imprisonment made worse by forced separation from his family and the Church left Joseph time to reflect on the meaning of human suffering. His writings from prison contain some of the most sublime passages of his ministry. Excerpts from his letters were added to the collection of his revelations (see DOCTRINE AND COVENANTS: SECTIONS 121–23). Acknowledging all that he had experienced, one of the revelations reminded him that however great his sufferings, they did not exceed the Savior's: "The Son of Man hath descended below them all. Art thou greater than he?" (D&C 122:8).

The following April, while being taken under guard to Boone County, Missouri, for a change in venue, the Prophet and his fellow prisoners were allowed to escape. Within a month of rejoining family and friends at Quincy, Illinois, Joseph Smith had authorized the purchase of land on the Mississippi River near Commerce, Hancock County, Illinois, and had moved his family into a two-room log cabin. During the summer of 1839, the Saints began settling their new gathering place, which they named NAUVOO.

Like many areas along the river bottoms, Nauvoo was at first poorly drained and disease-infested. During a malaria epidemic, the Prophet gave up his home to the sick and lived in a tent. Witnesses reported miraculous healing under his administration. "There was many sick among the saints on both sides of the river and Joseph went through the midst of them taking them by the hand and in a loud voice commanding them in the name of Jesus Christ to arise from their beds and be made whole" (Wilford Woodruff Diary, July 22, 1839, Ms., LDS Church Archives). Deaths were so frequent that a mass funeral was held.

Late in 1839 the Prophet traveled to Washington, D.C., to seek redress from the federal government for losses sustained by his people in Missouri. While there he obtained interviews with President Martin Van Buren and prominent congressmen, but came away frustrated and without relief.

Nauvoo was soon incorporated under the state-authorized NAUVOO CHARTER. Within the next few years the city grew to rival Chicago as the largest in Illinois. Joseph served on the city council and eventually became mayor. As mayor he also served as presiding judge of the municipal court and as registrar of deeds. With the rank of lieutenant general, he led the NAUVOO LEGION, or municipal militia. He was also proprietor of a merchandise store and became editor and publisher of the newspaper *Times and Seasons*.

The relative security of Nauvoo provided Joseph Smith with an opportunity to move forward the work of the kingdom with renewed vigor. He sent the Quorum of the Twelve Apostles to Great Britain, where they expanded missionary work and launched an emigration program that provided a stream of immigrants into the new place of gathering (see MISSIONS OF THE TWELVE TO BRITAIN). At Nauvoo the Prophet organized the first WARDS, the basic geographical units of the Church. He expanded the ecclesiastical authority of the Twelve to include jurisdiction within stakes, placing them for the first time in a position of universal authority over the Church under the First Presidency. He supervised the building of the NAUVOO TEMPLE and established the Female RELIEF SOCIETY of Nauvoo.

The Prophet faced a dilemma as he began to restore long-lost divine principles. Prompted by forebodings that his remaining time was short, he wished to hasten his efforts, but because many did not understand his mission and opposed him, he had to move slowly. "I could explain a hundred fold more than I ever have of the glories of the kingdoms manifested to me . . . were the people prepared to receive them," he wrote in 1843 (*HC* 5:402). To resolve this dilemma, the Prophet presented some principles privately to a small number of faithful members, intending to plant the seeds before he died. As early as 1841, he introduced PLURAL MARRIAGE, a necessary part of the restoration of the ancient order of things, to members of the Twelve and a few others. Although he had understood the principle since 1831 and apparently had married one plural wife several years earlier, he married his first recorded plural wife, Louisa Beaman, in 1841. During his remaining years, he married at least twenty-seven others.

In May 1842 the Prophet introduced the full ENDOWMENT, religious ordinances subsequently observed in all LDS temples, to a small group in the upper room of his Nauvoo store. A year later he performed the first SEALINGS of married couples for time and eternity. In addition, he taught the Saints important doctrines pertaining to the nature of God and man (see KING FOLLETT DISCOURSE). In March 1844 he organized the COUNCIL OF FIFTY, the political arm of the kingdom of God. By the time of his death three months later, he had completed all that he felt was essential for the continuation of the kingdom. By then he had transferred to the Twelve the keys of authority, confident that the program he had initiated would now continue regardless of what befell him (see SUCCESSION IN THE PRESIDENCY).

Teaching these principles privately to a small circle enabled Joseph Smith to fulfill his mission but complicated the situation at Nauvoo and unleashed forces that eventually led to his death. Some Saints had difficulty in accepting these unusual teachings. Upon being taught plural marriage, Brigham YOUNG said it was the first time in his life that he had desired the grave. Joseph's wife Emma at one point became "very bitter and full of resentment" ["Statement of William Clayton," *Woman's Exponent* 15 (June 1, 1886): 2]. As knowledge of the private teachings leaked into the community, speculation and distorted rumors proliferated.

While the Prophet pursued his objectives, forces outside the Church organized against him. Missouri authorities tried three times to extradite him from Illinois, resulting in lengthy periods of legal harassment. Because of the loss of property in earlier persecutions, he was unable to pay his debts and had to fend off creditors. When Illinois political leaders turned against the Latter-day Saints and no national leaders would champion their cause, the Prophet declared his candidacy for president of the United States, gaining a platform from which to discuss the rights of his people (see NAUVOO POLITICS).

By April 1844, dissenters openly challenged Joseph Smith's leadership by organizing a reform church and publishing a newspaper, the NAUVOO EXPOSITOR, for the purpose of denouncing him. Perceiving the *Expositor* as a threat to the peace of the community, the Nauvoo city council, with Joseph Smith presiding as mayor, authorized him to order the destruction of the press—an act that ignited the opposition. On June 12 the Prophet was charged with riot for destruction of the press. After a flurry of legal maneuvers, Joseph submitted to arrest at nearby Carthage, the county seat, under the governor's pledge of protection. Joseph had premonitions of danger, and the vocal threats of hotheads in adjoining towns gave substance to his

fears. On June 27, 1844, while in CARTHAGE JAIL awaiting a hearing, Joseph Smith and his brother Hyrum were killed when a mob with blackened faces stormed the jail (see MARTYRDOM OF JOSEPH AND HYRUM SMITH). The next day the brothers' bodies were returned to Nauvoo, where ten thousand Latter-day Saints gathered to mourn the loss of their Prophet.

Despite the adversity that dogged him from youth until death, Joseph Smith was not the somber, forbidding person his contemporaries generally envisioned in the personality of a prophet. An English convert wrote that Joseph was "no saintish long-faced fellow, but quite the reverse" [John Needham to Thomas Ward, July 7, 1843, *Latter-Day Saints' Millennial Star* 4 (Oct. 1843):89]. It was not uncommon to see him involved in sports activities with the young and vigorous men of a community. He is known to have wrestled, pulled sticks, engaged in snowball fights, played ball, slid on the ice with his children, played marbles, shot at a mark, and fished. Tall and well built, Joseph Smith did not hesitate to use his strength. Once in his youth he thrashed a man for wife-beating. In 1839, as he was en route to Washington, D.C., by stagecoach, the horses bolted while the driver was away. Opening the door of the speeding coach, the Prophet climbed up its side into the driver's seat, where he secured the reins and stopped the horses.

Joseph was also deeply spiritual. His mother said of him that in his youth he "seemed to reflect more deeply than common persons of his age upon everything of a religious nature" (Lucy Smith, Biographical Sketches of Joseph Smith, preliminary manuscript, p. 46, LDS Church Archives). When he was just twelve, as he later wrote, his mind became "seriously imprest with regard to the all important concerns for the wellfare of my immortal Soul" (*PJS* 1:5). Years after he began receiving revelations, he continued to seek spiritual comfort. In 1832 while on a journey, he wrote of visiting a grove "which is Just back of the town almost every day where I can be Secluded from the eyes of any mortal and there give vent to all the feelings of my heart in meaditation and prayr" (*PWJS*, p. 238). Clearly he spoke from the heart in declaring that "the things of God are of deep import: and time, and experience, and careful and ponderous and solemn thoughts can only find them out" (*HC* 3:295).

Joseph Smith deeply loved his family, and his personal writings are filled with prayerful outpourings of tenderness and concern. "O Lord bless my little children with health and long life to do good in this generation for Christs sake Amen" (*PWJS*, p. 28). His family consisted of eleven children, including adopted twins. Of these, four sons and a daughter died in infancy or early childhood; five were living when their father was killed, and a sixth, a son, was born four months after his death. Occasional glimpses into his family life show him sliding on the ice with his son Frederick, taking his children on a pleasure ride in a carriage or sleigh, and attending the circus.

He was also a loyal friend and cared deeply about others. He repeatedly extended a forgiving hand to prodigals, some of whom had caused him pain and misery. "I feel myself bound to be a friend to all . . . wether they are just or unjust; they have a degree of my compassion & sympathy" (*PWJS*, p. 548). One observer noted that the Prophet would never go to bed if he knew there was a sick person who needed assistance. He taught that "love is one of the leading characteristics of Deity, and ought to be manifested by those who aspire to be the sons of God. A man filled with the love of God, is not content with blessing his family alone but ranges through the world, anxious to bless the whole of the human family" (*PWJS*, p. 481). One Church member who stayed at the Smith home and witnessed the Prophet's "earnest and humble devotions . . . nourishing, soothing, and comforting his family, neighbours, and friends," found observation of his private life a greater witness of Joseph Smith's divine calling than observing his public actions (*JD* 7:176–77).

Joseph Smith spent his life bringing forth a new dispensation of religious knowledge at great personal cost. He noted that "the envy and wrath of man" had been his common lot and that "deep water" was what he was "wont to swim in" (D&C 127:2). A little more than a year before his death he told an audience in Nauvoo, "If I had not actually got into this work and been called of God, I would back out. But I cannot back out: I have no doubt of the truth" (*HC* 5:336). He lived in the hope of bringing that truth to life in a society of Saints, and died the victim of enemies who did not understand his vision.

BIBLIOGRAPHY

Anderson, Richard L. *Joseph Smith's New England Heritage.* Salt Lake City, 1971.

Brodie, Fawn M. *No Man Knows My History.* New York, 1946.

Bushman, Richard L. *Joseph Smith and the Beginnings of Mormonism.* Urbana, Ill., 1984.

Ehat, Andrew F., and Lyndon W. Cook. *The Words of Joseph Smith: The Contemporary Accounts of the Nauvoo Discourses of the Prophet Joseph.* Provo, Utah, 1980.

Gibbons, Francis M. *Joseph Smith: Martyr, Prophet of God.* Salt Lake City, 1982.

Hill, Donna. *Joseph Smith, The First Mormon.* Garden City, New York, 1977.

Jessee, Dean C., ed. *The Personal Writings of Joseph Smith.* Salt Lake City, 1984.

———. *The Papers of Joseph Smith.* Salt Lake City, 1989– .

Millet, Robert L., ed., *Joseph Smith: Selected Sermons and Writings.* New York, 1989.

Porter, Larry C., and Susan Easton Black, eds. *The Prophet Joseph: Essays on the Life and Mission of Joseph Smith.* Salt Lake City, 1988.

Smith, Lucy. *Biographical Sketches of Joseph Smith the Prophet.* Liverpool, 1853.

RICHARD L. BUSHMAN
DEAN C. JESSEE

TEACHINGS OF JOSEPH SMITH

The written and spoken words of the revelations to Joseph Smith are clear, direct, and unequivocal, yet his teachings are difficult to characterize or summarize, since they do not fit easily into traditional theological categories, and they always presuppose that more can, and probably will, be revealed by God. Audiences eagerly listened to the Prophet's bold proclamations and reasoning on hundreds of topics, although his was not a work of systematic analysis or synthesis. His teachings, sayings, counsels, instructions, blessings, responses, and commentaries from 1820 to 1844 are scattered over thousands of pages of revelations, scriptures, histories, journals, letters, and minute books (see JOSEPH SMITH: WRITINGS OF JOSEPH SMITH).

The teachings of Joseph Smith may be approached in many ways. Some collections arrange them topically; other commentaries focus on the historical settings of his revelations and discourses; still others compare published versions with recorded recollections of his sayings. In any case, one finds continuity and consistency rather than conspicuous breaks or reversals.

The record shows that Joseph Smith's access to sources and his own understanding entailed growth processes. He said in 1842, two years before his death, that he had "the whole plan of the kingdom" before him (*HC* 5:139). But it is not clear how early in his life the "whole plan" reached maturity in his mind.

Some of his teachings now have scriptural status; others are authoritative but not sustained as scripture. As he himself explained, a prophet is not always a prophet, but "only when he was acting as such" (*TPJS*, p. 278). Careful scholarship will distinguish original utterances of the Prophet from later accretions; also, some statements that he did not make or endorse have been published under his name. The following sketch treats his revelations, his scriptural translations, and his most characteristic sayings as comprising his teachings.

Joseph Smith never claimed to establish a new religion but to initiate a new beginning, a RESTORATION of the everlasting GOSPEL OF JESUS CHRIST. "The fundamental principles of our religion are the testimony of the Apostles and Prophets, concerning Jesus Christ, that He died, was buried, and rose again the third day, and ascended into heaven; and all other things which pertain to our religion are only appendages to it" (*TPJS*, p. 121). He anticipated "a whole and complete and perfect union, and welding together of dispensations, and keys, and powers, and glories . . . from the days of Adam even to the present time" (D&C 128:18). This restoration would encompass "all the truth the Christian world possessed" (*TPJS*, p. 376)—including much that had been lost or discarded—and, in addition, revelations "hid from before the foundation of the world" (*TPJS*, p. 309). His teachings were often in contrast to postbiblical additions, subtractions, and changes. He said that he intended "to lay a foundation that will revolutionize the whole world" (*TPJS*, p. 366).

The following are selected from among the dozens of topics and insights that typify the teachings of the Prophet Joseph Smith:

GOD AND DIVINITY. Joseph Smith taught that God is properly called Father. He is a glorified, exalted person, with personal attributes. Jesus Christ is the mediator between man and God. He is not identical with God, but has become like the Father. This strips away the mystery of many classical creeds. This doctrine is refined anthropomorphism, and it permeates ancient and modern scriptures.

Because God is the preeminent person, he may be approached, encountered, and known. He is subject to, and involved in, man's struggles. He can be trusted to move, act, respond, love, serve, and give. From the presence of God and his Son proceeds forth a Spirit that gives light to everyone who comes into mortality. This light is in all things, gives life to all things, and is the law by which all things are governed, even the power of God (D&C 88:13).

TRUTH. Experience points to a plural universe. The highest knowledge is of things, existences, in all their varieties (D&C 93:24–25). The revelations to Joseph Smith speak of independent spheres of existence and an array of glorious degrees (D&C 76; cf. 88:37). Thus, any mystical thrust toward metaphysical union in which individuality is lost is abandoned.

SCRIPTURE. The Prophet taught that the scriptures are the written records of revelatory experiences. He rejected equally the dogmas of verbal inerrancy, of "merely human" origin, and of allegorical excess in interpreting the scriptures. The limits of the canon are fluid, as they were originally in early Judaism and Christianity. Scripture, spoken or written, is light to those who are quickened by divine life and light. The need for living prophets to supplement, clarify, and apply the written sources to contemporary needs is continual. "I told the brethren that the Book of Mormon was the most correct of any book on earth, and the keystone of our religion, and a man would get nearer to God by abiding by its precepts, than by any other book" (*TPJS*, p. 194).

CREATION AND COSMOS. Joseph Smith's teachings have been characterized by the word "eternalism": "Every principle that proceeds from God is eternal" (*TPJS*, p. 181). The "pure principles of element" and of intelligence coexist eternally with God: "They may be organized and re-organized, but not destroyed" (*TPJS*, p. 351). God created the universe out of chaos, "which is Element and in which dwells all the glory" (*WJS*, p. 351). "The elements are the tabernacle of God" (D&C 93:35). God is related to space and time, and did not create them from nothing. Change occurs through intelligence. The universe is governed by law. There were two creations: All things were made "spiritually" before they were made "naturally" (Moses 3:5). Through his Son, God is the Creator of multiple WORLDS. God is the Father of the human SPIRITS that inhabit his creations. His creations have no end.

NATURE OF MAN. As eternal intelligence, "man was in the beginning with God" (D&C 93:29-30). But his unfolding from grace to grace is dependent on the nurture of God. Because of the gospel and the Atonement, the children of God are heirs of all the Father has and is, and can become gods themselves (D&C 76:58–61; 84:35–39; 88:107).

Spirit is refined matter. Individual spirits "existed before the body, can exist in the body; will exist separate from the body, when the body will be mouldering in the dust; and will in the resurrection be again united with it" (*TPJS*, p. 207). Thus, extreme dualism between spirit and matter is rejected.

Man is free to resist or to embrace either the powers of God or those of evil. God, man, Satan, and his hosts are independent. One cannot force another.

PLAN OF SALVATION. Finding himself in the midst of spirits and glory, God saw fit to institute laws whereby his children might advance like himself and have glory upon glory (*see* PLAN OF SALVATION). "At the first organization in heaven we were all present, and saw the Savior chosen and appointed and the plan of salvation made, and we sanctioned it" (*TPJS*, p. 181). Like embraces like (D&C 88:40); harmonies are restored: knowledge replaces ignorance, sanctity replaces sin, and life replaces death.

FALL. The Prophet rejected the traditional theory of ORIGINAL SIN and returned to the doctrine of man's innocence before the Fall. ADAM and EVE transgressed, as planned, to open the way for the contrasting experiences of mortality. The Fall was not inevitable, but free. All men and women are, in their infant state, innocent before God. It follows that INFANT BAPTISM is unnecessary, that ACCOUNTABILITY comes later (at the age of eight), and that accountability for sin is personal, not inherited (D&C 68:25–27; 93:38). One becomes what one chooses to become.

God himself has a body "as tangible as man's" (D&C 130:22), and the human BODY is a temple. "The great principle of happiness consists in having a body" (*TPJS*, p. 181, 297). Redemption is of the whole soul, meaning spirit and body.

ATONEMENT. The power of redemption is the ATONEMENT of Jesus Christ, the Son of God. In the unfolding drama, the Son inherited the fulness of the Father; he was not "eternally begotten," nor were two absolutely unlike natures inherent in the person of Christ.

The atonement of Jesus Christ was necessary to reconcile the demands of JUSTICE AND MERCY. Christ responded to this need in a voluntary act, a descent in order to ascend (D&C 88:6).

Christ could not have known, except by experience, the depths of compassion. He suffered pains and afflictions and temptations "that his bowels might be filled with compassion according to the flesh," for only thus could he "succor his people according to their infirmities" (Alma 7:12). GETHSEMANE was the place and time of his most intense suffering for mankind; the CROSS was its final hour (D&C 19:16–20; JST Matt. 27:54).

Christ saves men from their SINS, not in them. He does not impute righteousness where there is none. One who seeks to become a law unto himself and abides in sin cannot be sanctified unless he repents (D&C 88:35).

The infinite atonement is intended to bring life and redemption to all the children of the Eternal Father, including those of other worlds who "are saved by the very same Savior of ours" (*T&S* 4:82–85).

KNOWLEDGE. Intelligence, as light and truth, is the glory of God (D&C 93:36). Mind is eternal, with access to the vast reaches of the eternities, and knowledge is essential to salvation: "One is saved no faster than he gets knowledge" (*TPJS*, p. 217); and he gains knowledge of the truths of the gospel no faster than he is saved—that is, no faster than he receives Christ into his life. "Knowledge through our Lord and Savior Jesus Christ is the grand key that unlocks the glory and mysteries of the kingdom of heaven" (*TPJS*, p. 298). "God hath not revealed anything to Joseph, but what He will make known unto the Twelve, and even the least Saint may know all things as fast as he is able to bear them" (*TPJS*, p. 149).

Knowledge of God and divine things comes through the Spirit. Revelation includes the visible presence, VISIONS, dreams, the visitations of angels and spirits, impressions, voices, prophetic flashes of inspiration and light, and the flow of pure intelligence into mind and heart. Such direct communications are essential to the religious life of every person. At least one GIFT OF THE SPIRIT is given to each person of faith. "It is impossible to receive the Holy Ghost and not receive revelation" (*TPJS*, p. 256). "No man can know that Jesus is the Lord but by the Holy Ghost" (*WJS*, p. 115). "No generation was ever saved or destroyed upon dead testimony neither can be; but by living" (*WJS*, p. 159). Within limits, these experiences can be verbalized and communicated.

PURPOSE OF LIFE: JOY. "Happiness is the object and design of our existence" (*TPJS*, p. 255). "We came to this earth that we might have a body and present it pure before God in the celestial kingdom" (*TPJS*, p. 181). Glorified bodies have powers and privileges over those who have not, and to be denied or separated from the body is bondage. The combination of spirit body and physical body can maximize joy (D&C 93:33–34).

God's glory is to work for the benefit of other beings. Likewise, man cannot find himself until he loses himself in the Christlike desire to elevate, benefit, and bless others (*PWJS*, p. 483). Even in mortality, members of the family of God may begin to experience the joy that will be in full hereafter (*TPJS*, p. 296).

TRIALS AND AFFLICTION. EVIL and pain are real, losses are real, temptation is real, overcoming is real. Both risk and reward attend the mortal experience. These are the conditions of soul growth. God's purpose is to lift his children, but he cannot do so without their cooperation; nor can he intervene in a way that removes the need for experience, even bitter experience.

Life is a trial, a probation: "All these things shall give thee experience" (D&C 122:7). Abraham's willingness to sacrifice Isaac was a similitude of the Father's sacrifice of his Only Begotten Son. One cannot attain the heirship of the Son without being willing to sacrifice all earthly things. The overcoming of such trials is the foundation of perfected LOVE, and until one has perfect love, one is liable to fall (*TPJS*, p. 9). The view that all suffering in the world is punishment for sin is "an unhallowed principle" (*TPJS*, p. 162). The Saints must expect to wade through much tribulation, but afflictions may be consecrated to their gain.

PRIESTHOOD. PRIESTHOOD is AUTHORITY and power centered in Christ. It is conferred only by tangible ORDINATION, by the laying on of hands of one having authority. Joseph Smith taught the importance of priesthood KEYS: Jesus Christ "holds the keys over all this world" (TPJS, p. 323). John the Baptist, Peter, James, John, Moses, Elijah, and Elias held various keys of priesthood functions and restored them to the earth by conferring them upon Joseph Smith and Oliver COWDERY.

Priesthood is not indelible; it can be lost. It is not infallible; only under the influence of the Spirit can one speak for and with the approval of God.

The opportunity for the fulness of priesthood blessings is conferred on both men and women when they make and keep unconditional covenants with Jesus Christ and then with each other as husband and wife (*see* FATHERHOOD; MOTHERHOOD).

In The Church of Jesus Christ of Latter-day Saints, Joseph Smith explained and established the roles of apostles, prophets, bishops, evangelists, pastors, teachers, and so on, in analogue to their New Testament functions. He dissolved the distinction between laity and a priestly class: All priests, teachers, and administrators are lay people, and all worthy laymen are priesthood holders.

ORDINANCES. Joseph Smith restored and taught a progressive series of ORDINANCES that confer spiritual enlightenment and power. These ordinances were "instituted in the heavens before the foundation of the world" (*TPJS*, p. 308). "Being born again comes by the Spirit of God through ordinances" (*TPJS*, p. 162). All essential ordinances, from BAPTISM to temple MARRIAGE, involve prayer, covenant making, and divine ratification.

TEMPLES. Some ordinances pertain to the holy TEMPLE, where "the power of godliness is manifest" (D&C 84:20). Temples embody and manifest sacred truths, "the mysteries and peaceable things" (D&C 42:61). They will enable the children of God to overcome the corruptible elements of their lives and enter the realms of light and fire, the presence of the Father and the Son. All of the temple functions and powers are reestablished today, with the authority of the high priesthood: BAPTISM FOR THE DEAD, the holy ENDOWMENT, and the SEALING of families are their essence. "We need the Temple more than anything else," Joseph Smith taught (*Journal History*, May 4, 1844).

All temple ordinances point to Christ. The temple is presently, as it was anciently, his sanctuary, endowed with his glory, blessed with his name and ultimately with his presence. Christ is a living temple, and through him one may become a living temple (D&C 93:35; cf. Rev. 21:22).

MARRIAGE, FAMILY, AND HOME. Reversing the Augustinian tradition that celibacy is preferable to marriage in this life and universal in the next, the Prophet taught that the Christlike life reaches its zenith in marriage and parenting. The greatest prophets and prophetesses are also patriarchs and matriarchs. The highest ordinance is marriage, when king and queen begin their eternal family kingdom: The symbols are ordination, coronation, and sealing.

SOCIAL, ECONOMIC, AND POLITICAL THOUGHT. In the earthly government of God, a theodemocracy is contemplated: a covenant kingdom led by Jesus Christ, the benevolent King of Kings. The KINGDOM OF GOD on earth is to become like Enoch's city of ZION, with utopian thought and culture realized in a community of the pure-hearted.

Joseph taught a law of STEWARDSHIP and CONSECRATION. All the earth is the Lord's; property in Zion is, in effect, held in trust for the establishment of Zion. In the infancy of the Church, the Saints tried to live this economic system and failed, foundering on what it was designed to overcome: greed, covetousness, jealousy. Consequently, the Prophet was instructed to substitute the law of TITHING to prepare the Saints to live this higher law.

"The Constitution of the United States is a glorious standard; it is founded in the wisdom of God" (TPJS, p. 147). The protections of constitutional government should extend to all (see POLITICS: POLITICAL TEACHINGS). Wilford WOODRUFF recalled Joseph Smith's saying "that if he were the Emperor of the world and had control over the whole human family he would sustain every man, woman and child in the enjoyment of their religion" (Journal History, Mar. 12, 1897). This would allow, without compulsory means, the growth of a kingdom of God eventually to be administered in two world capitals, JERUSALEM in the East and the NEW JERUSALEM in the West.

The Church is the body of members who have entered the covenant and formed a community for the perfecting of its individual members. The living prophets, seers, and revelators are the authority nucleus of the kingdom of God, but the Church performs its work in intimate communities: families, WARDS, and STAKES.

RESURRECTION. Eternal family life is perfected only in the highest degree of God's CELESTIAL KINGDOM. In the RESURRECTION and JUDGMENT, each body with few exceptions (see SONS OF PERDITION) will receive a DEGREE OF GLORY. One's identity in both spirit and body is secure and eternal. God's celestial being, perfected and glorified, is the ideal. The earth itself, having been baptized by water and then by fire, will die, be resurrected, glorified (D&C 88:25–26), and rolled back into the presence of God. The beauty, glory, perfection, and powers of a glorified resurrected body are unspeakable: "No man can describe it to you—no man can write it" (TPJS, p. 368). "All your losses will be made up to you in the resurrection provided you continue faithful. By the vision of the Almighty I have seen it" (TPJS, p. 296).

ESCHATOLOGY. Joseph Smith uttered many prophetic statements about the future. His eschatology is extensive and inclusive. The gospel will be taught to all mankind, either on this earth or in the world of the spirits, so that all may receive it. The family of ABRAHAM, which has permeated all races of men, will be united. The families of Judah and Joseph will join hands in redemptive fulfillment. Many of these expectations and realizations are beyond the power of man to achieve or to impede. The work is "destined to bringing about the destruction of the powers of darkness, the renovation of the earth, the glory of God, and the salvation of the human family" (TPJS, p. 232).

BIBLIOGRAPHY

Burton, Alma P., comp. Discourses of the Prophet Joseph Smith, 3rd ed. Salt Lake City, 1968 (arranged topically).

Ehat, Andrew F., and Lyndon W. Cook, eds. The Words of Joseph Smith: The Contemporary Accounts of the Nauvoo Discourses of the Prophet Joseph. Provo, Utah, 1980 (excerpts from 173 addresses).

Roberts, B. H. Joseph Smith: The Prophet Teacher. Salt Lake City, 1908; rep., Princeton, N.J., 1967.

Smith, Joseph Fielding, comp. Teachings of the Prophet Joseph Smith. Salt Lake City, 1938 (arranged chronologically).

Widtsoe, John A. Joseph Smith: Seeker After Truth, Prophet of God. Salt Lake City, 1957.

TRUMAN G. MADSEN

WRITINGS OF JOSEPH SMITH

The Prophet Joseph Smith's writing career began at age twenty-two when he commenced translation of the Book of Mormon. At his death seventeen years later, in 1844, he had left a substantial archive for the study of his life and the church he was instrumental in founding. In addition to the Book of Mormon, his papers include diaries covering intermittently the period 1832–1844; correspondence; reports of discourses; more than 130 revelations, published as the Doctrine and Covenants; a record of Abraham; a Bible revision, including some restored writings of Enoch and Moses; and the beginnings of a multivolume documentary HISTORY OF THE CHURCH based upon his papers.

Several factors influenced and initially limited the extent of Joseph Smith's writings and the literary style of his prose. Because of the indigent circumstances of his family, his formal schooling was very little, the basics of reading, writing, and arithmetic constituting, so he said, his entire scholastic preparation. Some who heard him noted that he seemed to have little native talent or training as a speaker. He felt inadequate as a writer, referring on one occasion to "the little narrow prison almost as it were total darkness of paper, pen, and ink."

But whatever the Prophet lacked in formal rhetorical training was compensated for by his message. Beginning in his early life, religious experiences inspired him with a strong sense of mission that propelled him onto the stage of public controversy. He saw his mission as laying a foundation that would revolutionize the whole world, not by sword or gun but by "the power of truth." The articulation of that truth was the impetus of his writings. Many who heard him were awed by his ability to make plain the way of life and salvation. Many outsiders found his views striking and magnetic. His writings carry the same sense of purpose and conviction.

A study of early Mormon sources indicates that only a fraction of Joseph Smith's writings and teachings were preserved. This was the result of

JOSEPH SMITH'S WRITINGS

Writings	Dates	Scribes*

Book of Mormon MSS
    Original MS
    Printer's MS
	1827–1829	Oliver Cowdery and others

Diaries	1832–1844	William Clayton, Oliver Cowdery, Warren A. Cowdery, James Mulholland, Warren Parrish, Parley P. Pratt, Willard Richards, Sidney Rigdon, George W. Robinson, Joseph Smith, Sylvester Smith, and others

Revelations
    Kirtland revelation book
    Unbound revelations
    Bible revision
    Book of Abraham
	1828–1844	William Clayton, Oliver Cowdery, Warren A. Cowdery, Orson Hyde, James Mulholland, Edward Partridge, William W. Phelps, Sidney Rigdon, Joseph Smith Sr., John Whitmer, Newel K. Whitney, Frederick G. Williams, and others

Correspondence
    Letter Bk. 1
    Letter Bk. 2
    Bound correspondence
	1829–1844	Thomas Bullock, William Clayton, Howard Coray, Oliver Cowdery, Warren A. Cowdery, James Mulholland, Willard Richards, Sidney Rigdon, James Sloan, Joseph Smith, Robert B. Thompson, John Whitmer, Frederick G. Williams, and others

Egyptian MSS	1835?–1841	Oliver Cowdery, Warren Parrish, William W. Phelps, Joseph Smith, Willard Richards
Autobiographical/historical writings	1832–1844	Oliver Cowdery, Warren A. Cowdery, James Mulholland, Warren Parrish, William W. Phelps, Willard Richards, Joseph Smith, Robert B. Thompson, Frederick G. Williams, and others

*Known scribes for Joseph Smith with life dates (in parenthesis) and approximate years of their clerical involvement: Thomas Bullock (1816–1885), 1843–1844; William Clayton (1814–1879), 1842–1844; Howard Coray (1817–1908), 1840–1841; Oliver Cowdery (1806–1850), 1829–1838; Warren A. Cowdery (1788–1851), 1836–1838; Orson Hyde (1805–1878), 1833–1836; James Mulholland (1804–1839), 1838–1839; Warren Parrish (1803–1887), 1835–1837; William W. Phelps (1792–1872), 1831–1844; Willard Richards (1804–1854), 1841–1844; Sidney Rigdon (1793–1876), 1830–1838; George W. Robinson (1814–1878), 1836–1840; James Sloan (1792–?), 1840–1843; Sylvester Smith (c.1805–?), 1834–1836; Robert B. Thompson (1811–1841), 1839–1841; John Whitmer (1802–1878), 1829–1838; Newel K. Whitney (1795–1850), 1831–1838; Frederick G. Williams (1787–1842), 1832–1839.

haphazard record-keeping procedures during his early lifetime; the incompetence or untimely death of some of his clerks; long imprisonments; vexatious and repeated lawsuits; poverty; and disruptive conditions that forced the migration of the Latter-day Saints across two-thirds of the American continent.

Joseph Smith's dependence upon others to write for him also complicates the record. His philosophy was that "a prophet cannot be his own scribe." Hence, most of his writings were dictated, and some ghostwritten, but approved and accepted by him. While the presence of clerical handwriting in his papers helps date the source material, it does obscure his own image and necessitates a careful look at the sources for those who would distinguish the Prophet's mind and personality from those who assisted him.

Joseph's writings are characterized by long, unbroken sentences connected by conjunctions, descriptive images, and an astute narrative sense.

Page of a letter from Joseph to his wife Emma in his own handwriting, written when Joseph was in chains in Richmond, Missouri, November 12, 1838. "Oh my affectionate Emma, I want you to remember that I am a true and faithful friend to you; and the children, forever, my heart is entwined around you[r]s forever and ever; oh, may God bless you all."

As a keen student of the scriptures, his prose is interspersed with biblical word forms and examples, and breathes a positive tone, reflecting a sense of vitality and love. His writing style and personality show up most clearly in his holograph writings. These show a conversational style, in contrast to the more formal manner of associates like Sidney RIGDON. Typical of his handwritten prose is this extract from an 1838 letter to his wife Emma written while in jail at Richmond, Missouri:

. . . Brother Robison is chained next to me he ~~he~~ has a true heart and a firm mind, Brother Whight, is next, Br. Rigdon, next, Hyram, next, Parely, next Amasa, next, and thus we are bound together in chains as well as the cords of everlasting love, we are in good spirits and rejoice that we are counted worthy to be per = secuted for christ sake, tell little Joseph, he must be a good boy, Father loves him <With > a per = fect ~~t~~love, he is the Eldest must not hurt those that <Are > smaller then him, but cumfor < t > them tell little Frederick, Father, loves him, with all his heart, he is a lovely boy. Julia is a lovely little girl, I love hir also She is a promising child, tell her Father wants her to remember him and be a good girl, tell all the rest that I think of them and pray for them all, . . . little ~~baby~~ Elexander is on my mind continuly Oh my affectionate Emma, I want you to remember that I am <a > true and faithful friend, to you and the children, forever, my heart is intwined around you[r]s forever and ever, oh may God bless you all amen ~~you~~ I am your husband and am in bands and tribulation &c— [Jessee, 1984, p. 368].

BIBLIOGRAPHY

Works by Joseph Smith

Ehat, Andrew F., and Lyndon W. Cook., comps. and eds. *The Words of Joseph Smith: The Contemporary Accounts of the Nauvoo Discourses of the Prophet Joseph.* Provo, Utah, 1980. A compilation of original reports of Joseph Smith's discourses during the Nauvoo years (1839–1844) of his life.

Faulring, Scott H., comp. and ed. *An American Prophet's Record: The Diaries and Journals of Joseph Smith.* Salt Lake City, 1987. A compilation of Joseph Smith's diaries, but missing his 1842 journal, one of his largest.

Jessee, Dean C., comp. and ed. *The Personal Writings of Joseph Smith.* Salt Lake City, 1984. A compilation of all of Joseph Smith's known holograph writings and core dictated material.

———. *The Papers of Joseph Smith,* Vol. 1, *Autobiographical and Historical Writing.* Salt Lake City, 1989. The first volume of a comprehensive edition of Joseph Smith's papers.

Smith, Joseph, ed. *History of the Church of Jesus Christ of Latter-day Saints.* Period 1. History of Joseph Smith, the Prophet, by Himself. Introduction and notes by B. H. Roberts. 2nd ed., 6 vols., Salt Lake City, 1964. Written in the form of a first-person daily journal, using the text of Joseph Smith's diaries interspersed with his correspondence and other documents, this work is the most extensive publication of the Prophet's papers to date. Its main limitation is the outdated editorial treatment of the sources.

Smith, Joseph Fielding, comp. and ed. *Teachings of the Prophet Joseph Smith*. Salt Lake City, 1938. A compilation of excerpts from sermons, letters, and other writings of Joseph Smith taken almost exclusively from *History of the Church* and arranged in chronological order.

Secondary Literature

Jessee, Dean C. "The Writing of Joseph Smith's History." *BYU Studies* 11 (Summer 1971):439–73.

King, Arthur Henry. *The Abundance of the Heart*. Salt Lake City, 1986.

Partridge, Elinore H. "Characteristics of Joseph Smith's Style." Task Papers in LDS History, No. 4, 1976. Typescript, LDS Church Archives.

Searle, Howard C. "Early Mormon Historiography: Writing the History of the Mormons 1830–1858." Ph.D. diss., UCLA, 1979.

DEAN C. JESSEE

LEGAL TRIALS OF JOSEPH SMITH

Joseph Smith believed that his enemies perverted legal processes, using them as tools of religious persecution against him, as they had been used against many of Christ's apostles and other past martyrs. Although he often gained quick acquittals, numerous "vexatious and wicked" lawsuits consumed his time and assets, leading to several incarcerations and ultimately to his martyrdom. Beginning soon after his ministry began and continuing throughout his life, Joseph Smith was subjected to approximately thirty criminal actions and at least that many civil suits related to debt collection or failed financial ventures.

The first charge of being a "disorderly person" involved treasure hunting for hire, brought against him at SOUTH BAINBRIDGE, NEW YORK, in 1826 by a disgruntled Methodist preacher related to Josiah Stowell, Joseph's employer. When Stowell refused to testify against him at the trial, Joseph was discharged. In July 1830 in the same venue, Joseph was tried and acquitted by another magistrate on charges of "being a disorderly person, of setting the county in an uproar by preaching the Book of Mormon, etc." (*HC* 1:88). The trial ended at midnight. The next day, he was seized and tried in neighboring Broome County on the same charges, as well as charges of casting out a devil and using pretended angelic visitations to obtain property

from others. Following a twenty-three-hour trial involving some forty witnesses, Joseph was again acquitted (*HC* 1:91–96).

After the Church moved to KIRTLAND, OHIO, in 1831, several religious-based charges were prosecuted against Smith and other LDS leaders, but were dismissed on the grounds listed following each charge: assault and battery (self-defense), performing marriages without a valid license (one was procured), attempted murder or conspiracy (lack of evidence), and involuntary servitude without compensation during the ZION'S CAMP military crusade to Missouri (won on appeal). In turn, Church leaders successfully instituted charges and recovered damages for assaults occurring while they were acting in a religious capacity. However, the financial Panic of 1837 swamped the Prophet and others with civil debt-collection litigation. Worse still were suits for violating Ohio banking laws when the Kirtland Safety Society Anti-Banking Company (*see* KIRTLAND ECONOMY) failed soon after it was organized in 1836 without a state charter. Charges of fraud and self-enrichment were raised but not proven; a jury conviction was appealed, but Joseph Smith left Ohio for Missouri before it was heard.

In Missouri, most actions against the Latterday Saints were extralegal, brought by non-Mormon vigilantes prejudiced against the Saints' opposition to slavery, their collective influx, and Smith's religious teachings concerning modern revelation and the territorial establishment of ZION in Jackson County. Civil magistrates routinely refused to issue peace warrants for Mormons or to redress their personal injuries or property damage. For example, despite being beaten and tarred and feathered and having the printing office destroyed, the LDS printer was awarded less than his legal fees and the Presiding Bishop received "one penny and a peppercorn." All three branches of state government seemed paralyzed or supportive of mob action, as the Saints were repeatedly dispossessed and expelled from county to county.

Finally, election-day violence between Mormons and non-Mormons erupted at Gallatin in Daviess County, Missouri, on August 6, 1838. Joseph Smith and others called on Justice of the Peace Adam Black to obtain an "agreement of peace" from Black to support the law and not attach himself to any mob. This resulted in Joseph Smith's and Lyman Wight's being arrested, based on an affidavit alleging riot and assault by them, while obtaining the writs from Black (*HC* 3:61).

Smith and Wight appeared before Judge Austin King and were ordered to appear at the next hearing of the grand jury in Daviess County (*HC* 3:73).

On October 25, 1838, Moses Rowland, a Missouri state militiaman, was killed at the Battle of Crooked River in a clash with a company of Saints who were attempting to rescue three kidnapped brethren. Upon hearing of this engagement, coupled with other reports, Governor Lilburn W. Boggs issued his infamous EXTERMINATION ORDER. Joseph and other leading Saints were arrested, and received a preliminary court hearing before Judge Austin King in Richmond, Missouri, on November 12–29, 1838. Joseph Smith and some other defendants were confined for four and a half months in LIBERTY JAIL pending a grand jury indictment on such charges as murder, arson, theft, rebellion, and treason. While en route to stand trial in a more impartial venue, Joseph and others were allowed to escape, thereby preventing widespread official embarrassment on the part of the state.

In 1838–1839 the Saints settled in NAUVOO, ILLINOIS, after their wrongful expulsion from Missouri. To avoid the "legal" persecutions suffered in earlier states, they obtained a liberal city charter for Nauvoo, which granted broad habeas corpus powers to local courts. These helped to free Joseph Smith and other Latter-day Saints when they were sought on writs by arresting officers from outside of Nauvoo. In 1841 state judge Stephen A. Douglas set aside a Missouri writ to extradite Joseph for charges still pending there, and in 1843 a federal judge did the same for a similar requisition after the alleged shooting of then ex-governor Boggs. However, the increasing use of the writ of habeas corpus by Nauvoo magistrates, preempting even state and federal authority, escalated distrust among non-Mormons who felt that Joseph Smith considered himself above the law.

The Prophet's final use of habeas corpus came after his arrest in June 1844 by a county constable for inciting a "riot" by ordering suppression of the NAUVOO EXPOSITOR. This action climaxed a series of lawsuits between the Prophet and several apostates, who had charged him with perjury and adultery; he had countercharged with perjury, assault, defamation, and resisting arrest. After a subsequent trial on the merits and his acquittal in Nauvoo, the governor persuaded the Prophet to let himself be arrested and tried again for the "riot," this time in Carthage, where he was incarcerated

Martyrdom of Joseph and Hyrum, by Gary E. Smith (1980s, oil on canvas, 48″ × 60″). On June 27, 1844, Joseph Smith, age 38, and his loyal brother Hyrum were shot in the Carthage Jail by a mob. Courtesy Blaine T. Hudson.

without bail on a new charge of "treason" for declaring martial law and ordering out the Nauvoo militia to keep peace. Joseph Smith's enemies charged that he was going on the offensive against citizens of Illinois. Two days later, he and his brother Hyrum were killed by a mob in disguise.

Even after death, legal trials involving the Prophet continued. Of sixty potential assassins named before a grand jury, nine were indicted and five stood trial at Carthage for the murder of Joseph (a separate trial was to follow for the murder of Hyrum). After a six-day trial, all defendants were acquitted in June 1845 for insufficient evidence. The final legal indignity to Joseph Smith and the Church in Illinois was a series of federal court decrees in 1851 and 1852 that liquidated all remaining personal and Church assets held by Joseph Smith during his lifetime, in order to discharge an 1842 default judgment. He had guaranteed a promissory note to the federal government in an early Nauvoo business transaction; when the note was unpaid, a succession of lawsuits followed, forestalling his efforts in bankruptcy and prompting charges of fraud and misconduct. Although plagued by bad advice and misfortune in business matters, the Prophet was never found guilty of any misconduct.

BIBLIOGRAPHY

Firmage, Edwin B., and Richard C. Mangrum. *Zion in the Courts: A Legal History of the Church of Jesus Christ of Latter-day Saints, 1830–1900.* Urbana, Ill., 1988.

Gentry, Leland H. "A History of the Latter-day Saints in Northern Missouri from 1836 to 1839," pp. 167–85, 352–401. Ph.D. diss., Brigham Young University, 1965.

History of the Church, Vol. 1, pp. 88–96, 377, 390–493; Vol. 2, pp. 85–450; Vol. 3, pp. 55–465; Vol. 4, pp. 40–430; Vol. 5.

Madsen, Gordon A. "Joseph Smith's 1826 Trial: The Legal Setting." *BYU Studies* 30 (Spring 1990):91.

Oaks, Dallin H. "The Suppression of the Nauvoo Expositor." *Utah Law Review* 9 (Winter 1965):862–903.

Oaks, Dallin H., and Joseph I. Bentley. "Joseph Smith and Legal Process: In the Wake of the Steamboat *Nauvoo.*" *BYU Law Review* 3 (1976):735–82; repr. *BYU Studies* 19 (Winter 1979):167.

Oaks, Dallin H., and Marvin Hill. *Carthage Conspiracy.* Urbana, Ill., 1975.

Walters, Wesley P. "Joseph Smith's Bainbridge, N.Y., Court Trials." *Westminster Theological Journal* 36 (Winter 1974):123–55.

JOSEPH I. BENTLEY

SMITH, JOSEPH, III

See: Reorganized Church of Jesus Christ of Latter Day Saints

SMITH, JOSEPH, SR.

Joseph Smith, Sr. (1771–1840), father of the Prophet Joseph SMITH, believed in the religious experiences of his son and supported him from the time of his FIRST VISION. He later received significant callings in the newly formed Church. Joseph, Sr., died following the expulsion of the Latter-day Saints from Missouri and was considered a martyr for the cause.

Joseph Smith, Sr., was born in Topsfield, Massachusetts, July 12, 1771, the third of eleven children born to Asael and Mary Duty Smith (*see* SMITH FAMILY ANCESTORS). As a young man, he moved with his parents to Tunbridge, Vermont, where he met Lucy Mack (*see* Lucy Mack SMITH). They were married January 24, 1796, in Tunbridge (*see* SMITH FAMILY).

The couple began married life as part owners in the Asael Smith farm and received a $1,000 wedding present from Lucy's brother Stephen and his business partner, John Mudget. Joseph and Lucy's finances declined, however, after they opened a mercantile store in Randolph and invested in ginseng, a root that grew wild in Vermont and was prized in China as a medicine. A failed exporting venture required them to sell their farm and sacrifice their wedding gift to pay their debts. Now tenants instead of landowners, they moved from one rented farm to another in Vermont and New Hampshire. After three successive crop failures in Norwich, Vermont, they moved to Palmyra, New York, in 1816.

Like his father, Joseph, Sr., was a religious man, but, remained aloof from conventional religion. From 1811 to 1819 he had seven dreams that reflected his yearnings for redemption and may have prepared him to believe in his son Joseph's VISIONS, despite the fierce opposition that they aroused among others who heard of them.

The Smiths purchased a 100-acre farm in Manchester, New York, soon after their arrival from Vermont in 1816, but lost it in 1825 when they were unable to make the final yearly payment of $100. In an effort to raise the money, Joseph, Sr., and his son Joseph joined Josiah Stowell in a venture to dig for purported treasure in Harmony, Pennsylvania. Critics of the Smith family have used this incident as evidence of their interest in money digging. While the practice of seeking buried treasure was common at that time in the Northeast and Joseph, Sr., may have participated in searching for it, his digging for Stowell was a desperate attempt to earn money to meet a mortgage payment. After they lost their farm, the Smiths again became tenant farmers.

In 1829 a revelation to Joseph SMITH, Jr., called his father to participate in the "marvelous work" about to be accomplished (D&C 4), and soon thereafter, Joseph, Sr., became one of the Eight Witnesses to the Book of Mormon and saw and held the GOLD PLATES (*see* BOOK OF MORMON WITNESSES). He was present when the Church was organized on April 6, 1830, and was baptized on the same day (*see* ORGANIZATION OF THE CHURCH, 1830). He was ordained the first PATRIARCH TO THE CHURCH in 1833 and in that office gave blessings of comfort and inspiration throughout the remainder of his life. In Kirtland, Ohio, in 1834 he was called also as a member of the high council.

Joseph, Sr., and Lucy moved with the Church from New York to Ohio, Missouri, and finally Nauvoo, Illinois. They operated a farm in Kirtland, Ohio, and a boardinghouse in Far West, Missouri.

In 1839, they assisted hundreds of Saints fleeing from Missouri to Quincy, Illinois (*see* MISSOURI CONFLICT).

Father Smith, as Church members came to call him, suffered more than his share of life's vicissitudes. In 1830 he was arrested in New York and spent a month in jail because of a $14 debt. In Ohio in 1837 he was charged with riot in connection with a confrontation with apostates in the KIRTLAND TEMPLE. He also suffered a serious illness in Ohio and was healed through a blessing given him by Joseph, Jr.

During the Missouri persecutions in the fall of 1838, Joseph, Sr., again became ill. He made the forced exodus from Missouri to Illinois in 1839 in cold and rain, and illness continued to plague him in Nauvoo, where he died on September 14, 1840. Before his death, he called his children to his bedside to give them final blessings. He assured his son Joseph that he would live to finish his work. In his final moments, Smith said he saw Alvin, a son who had died nearly seventeen years earlier.

BIBLIOGRAPHY

Anderson, Richard L. *Joseph Smith's New England Heritage.* Salt Lake City, 1971.

Bushman, Richard L. *Joseph Smith and the Beginnings of Mormonism.* Urbana, Ill., 1984.

Skinner, Earnest M. "Joseph Smith, Sr., First Patriarch to the Church." Master's thesis, Brigham Young University, 1958.

Smith, Lucy Mack. *History of Joseph Smith.* Salt Lake City, 1958.

A. GARY ANDERSON

SMITH, JOSEPH, VISIONS OF

See: Visions of Joseph Smith

SMITH, JOSEPH F.

Joseph F. Smith (1838–1918), sixth PRESIDENT OF THE CHURCH of Jesus Christ of Latter-day Saints (1901–1918), led the Church in the first two decades of the twentieth century and helped it win increasing respect in American society. He was a son of Hyrum SMITH and Mary Fielding SMITH and a nephew of the Prophet Joseph SMITH.

Joseph Fielding Smith (his full name) was born in Far West, Missouri, on November 13,

Joseph F. Smith (1838–1918) was ordained an apostle and counselor to Brigham Young at age 27 in 1866. He served in the First Presidency with Presidents Taylor, Woodruff, and Snow. He became the sixth President of the Church in October 1901, serving for a combined total of 52 years. He was an authority on Church doctrine. Selections from his sermons and writings are collected in *Gospel Doctrine*, a standard reference work. From an ambrotype, processed by Nelson Wadsworth.

1838, during one of the most strife-torn years in the Church's history. He was named after his uncle, the Prophet, and a maternal uncle, Joseph Fielding. Less than two weeks earlier, Joseph and Hyrum Smith had been arrested by the Missouri militia during the Battle of Far West (*see* MISSOURI CONFLICT). Mary Fielding, a Canadian convert to the Church who married Hyrum after the death of Jerusha Barden Smith, was severely ill when she gave birth to Joseph, her firstborn. Fortunately, Mary's sister Mercy Fielding Thompson, already nursing a five-month-old daughter, was able to nurse Joseph. One day soon after his birth, hostile men entered the house and ransacked the family's valuables. In the commotion, they threw bedding on the baby Joseph, and he nearly suffocated.

In January 1839, Mary and her two-month-old son visited Hyrum in LIBERTY JAIL and in February fled Missouri with other Latter-day Saints to refuge in Quincy, Illinois. In May, after Hyrum escaped from Missouri authorities, the Smith family moved to the new gathering spot of the Church in Nauvoo, Illinois. Joseph, although only five and a half years old when his father and Joseph Smith were murdered in 1844, retained many impressions of the two men in Nauvoo.

In 1846 Mary Fielding Smith left Nauvoo for the West with Joseph and three other children. Another son, John, met her in Iowa. Mary had only two children herself, Joseph and Martha Ann, but she was also mothering the five children of Hyrum and his deceased first wife, Jerusha. Although only seven, young Joseph drove a team of oxen across Iowa. From the fall of 1846 to the spring of 1848, the fatherless family endured the privations of WINTER QUARTERS, Nebraska, where many of the Saints suffered from sickness and some 359 died. Several of the family's horses and cattle, which Joseph tended, also died. At age nine he drove his mother's wagon across the plains to the valley of the Great Salt Lake.

In the early years in the Salt Lake Valley, Joseph tended cattle and sheep, cut wood, and hired out at harvest time. In 1852, when he was thirteen, his mother died from overwork and malnutrition. Throughout his long life, Joseph never forgot her example of faith and integrity and frequently told stories about her. Her death made him a substitute father to his sister, Martha Ann. While the two children were attending school in the winter of 1853–1854, a harsh schoolmaster took out a leather strap to punish the little girl. "Don't whip her with that," Joseph cried. Later he explained, "At that he came at me and was going to whip me; but instead of whipping me, I licked him, good and plenty" (Gibbons, pp. 26–27). During his youth, he struggled with a fiery temper before he eventually conquered it.

This incident both ended Joseph's short formal education and launched his long ecclesiastical career. In the next general conference he was called at age fifteen to serve in the Church's mission in the Sandwich Islands (Hawaii). Parley P. Pratt, an APOSTLE, set Joseph apart and promised that he would master the Hawaiian language by study and the gift of the Spirit. Joseph served a remarkably successful mission, which lasted nearly four years. While in Hawaii, he served as conference president on the islands of Maui and Hawaii. He also overcame his own attacks of "island sick-ness" and became well known for his gifts of healing and of casting out evil spirits.

Immediately upon his return to Salt Lake City in 1858, Joseph joined the NAUVOO LEGION, Utah Territory's militia, and started with an expedition of a thousand men to intercept Johnston's army. From his return until the end of the war in June he was almost constantly in the saddle, patrolling the region between Echo Canyon, in Utah, and Fort Bridger, in Wyoming. Upon the peaceful settlement of the Utah War, Joseph assisted his relatives in returning to Salt Lake City from the southern settlements where they had gone in anticipation of the invading army (see UTAH EXPEDITION).

In April 1859 twenty-one-year-old Joseph married his sixteen-year-old cousin Levira, daughter of Samuel Harrison Smith. With Levira's permission Joseph then married Julina Lambson in PLURAL MARRIAGE. Later, he also married Sarah Ellen Richards, Edna Lambson, Alice Ann Kimball, and Mary Taylor Schwartz. He eventually was the father of forty-three children, thirteen of whom preceded him in death. Joseph was known as a kind and loving husband and father among members of his family.

Joseph served a mission in Great Britain from 1860 to 1863 and returned briefly to Hawaii in 1864 to help straighten out irregularities in Church affairs. While in Hawaii, he selected the site for a Church plantation on Oahu at Laie, presently the location of the Hawaii Temple, Brigham Young University—Hawaii Campus, and the Polynesian Cultural Center. Returning to Salt Lake City, he began work in 1865 as a clerk in the Church Historian's office. He was elected to the Territorial House of Representatives in 1865 and to the Salt Lake City Council in 1866. Later he served several consecutive terms in the Utah legislature. He was also a member of the Salt Lake Stake high council.

In 1866 Brigham YOUNG ordained the twenty-seven-year-old Joseph an apostle. In 1867 he accompanied Abraham O. Smoot, former mayor of Salt Lake City, and fellow apostles John TAYLOR and Wilford WOODRUFF to Provo, Utah, where they acted as civic officials in an effort to suppress and redirect some "rowdy elements" that had arisen in the town's citizenry. He returned to Salt Lake City in 1869, resumed his duties in the Historian's office, and began officiating in ordinances in the ENDOWMENT HOUSE.

In 1874, now known as President Smith, he presided over both the European and British missions. Upon his return in late 1875, he was called as stake president over the Saints in Davis County, Utah, and was also president of the Davis County Cooperative Company, one of a chain of Church cooperatives established during the United Order era, initiated by Brigham Young in 1874. In April 1877, Elder Smith was again sent to Great Britain to preside over the European Mission. The death of Brigham Young in August 1877 interrupted this call. Elder Smith returned to Salt Lake City to help with the settlement of President Young's estate, putting in long hours and painstakingly going over financial records and correspondence in this complicated matter.

Joseph F. Smith's labors in the Church took a significant turn in October 1880 when, at age forty-one, he was set apart as second counselor to John Taylor in the FIRST PRESIDENCY. The first counselor was George Q. Cannon, a close friend for many years. The two men also served as counselors to Presidents Wilford Woodruff and Lorenzo SNOW. Both were experienced missionaries and Church administrators, well versed in Church history and doctrine.

In the 1870s and 1880s, mass rallies throughout the United States protesting the Church's practice of plural marriage were adding impetus to the federal government's increasingly stern antipolygamy crusade. Rather than submit to what they considered unjust laws, President Taylor and his counselors chose civil disobedience. Joseph spent much of 1883 and 1884 in seclusion, and in 1885, when a warrant was issued for the arrest of the members of the First Presidency, he went into hiding in Hawaii under the assumed name of J. F. Speight. Over the next two and a half years, he grieved that he could do little to provide for his wives and children. In June 1887 he was called back to Utah to the deathbed of President Taylor, who died on July 25.

Continuing to serve in his position as a member of the Twelve Apostles during the period from President Taylor's death to the sustaining of Wilford Woodruff as President of the Church, Joseph fulfilled an assignment as the chief lobbyist for the Church in Washington, D.C., during the terms of Congress in 1888 and 1889. The First Presidency was reorganized in April 1889, with Joseph called as second counselor to President Woodruff.

The new presidency continued further political negotiations concerning the principle of plural marriage in an effort to lift the burdens imposed by the federal government. These negotiations were inconclusive, but a revelation to President Woodruff, known as the MANIFESTO OF 1890, advised the Saints to refrain from contracting plural marriages where such were forbidden by law. The Manifesto gradually achieved the desired effect: prosecution of polygamists ceased, Church property was returned, and Utah obtained statehood. Joseph sought and obtained amnesty from U.S. President Benjamin Harrison and was able, for the first time in nearly a decade, to mingle openly in society and resume a normal life. After the Manifesto, Joseph continued to care for each of his wives and to have children by them.

He also took an active role in politics. The Church had been criticized for dominating politics in Utah through the People's party. In 1891 the People's party disbanded, and its members were encouraged to join the two national parties. To make sure of genuine diversity, the First Presidency asked Joseph F. Smith to join the Republican party, then the less popular of the two parties because of its leading part in the antipolygamy campaign. To strengthen the Republicans, in 1892 he published a pamphlet, *Another Plain Talk: Reasons Why the People of Utah Should Be Republicans*.

Following the death of Wilford Woodruff, Joseph continued as Second Counselor in the First Presidency from 1898 to 1901 while Lorenzo Snow was President. President Snow died on October 10, 1901, and at the next regular meeting of the Twelve in the temple on October 17, the First Presidency was reorganized, with sixty-two-year-old Joseph F. Smith as President and John R. Winder and Anthon H. Lund as counselors.

President Smith vigorously assumed the reins of leadership, determined to improve public opinion of the Church and its members. For half of his seventeen years as Church President, he was frustrated in this goal. He was forced to endure grueling interrogation before the U.S. Senate during the SMOOT HEARINGS, local editorial attacks from the *Salt Lake Tribune*, and diatribes from some of the nation's leading magazine editors. Gradually, however, partly through his genuine charity and his grandfatherly image, tension between the Church and the federal government and society diminished. President Smith labored indefatigably to strengthen the Church and improve its image by careful spending and getting out of debt; by purchasing and developing significant HISTORICAL

Joseph F. Smith and family (c. 1901). He and his wives had forty-eight children. His wives were Levira Annett Clark (m. 1859; no children; died 1888); Julina Lambson, on his right (m. 1866; 13 children, including Joseph Fielding Smith top row center); Sarah Ellen Richards, on his left (m. 1868; 11 children); Edna Lambson, second on his right (m. 1871; 10 children); Alice Ann Kimball, second on his left (m. 1883; 7 children); and Mary Taylor Schwartz, third on his right (m. 1884; 7 children).

SITES, such as Joseph Smith's birthplace in Vermont, the Smith farm in New York, important sites in Missouri, and CARTHAGE JAIL in Illinois; by completing the Church Administration Building, the LDS Hospital, a Church visitors bureau, and the Hotel Utah in Salt Lake City; and by promoting the expansion of the Church's missionary and educational systems.

One of Joseph F. Smith's legacies was through his exposition of various Church doctrines and of principles of priesthood government. He felt strongly that Church members should be taught "sound doctrine." Following his death in 1918, some of his voluminous teachings, recorded during five decades of instructing the Saints as a General Authority, were published under the title *Gospel Doctrine*. Possibly President Smith's most significant doctrinal contribution was his "Vision of the Redemption of the Dead," which he received on October 3, 1918, just six weeks prior to his death on November 19. In it he saw the world of departed spirits and many individuals who reside there, including ancient and modern prophets, and he viewed the visit of Jesus Christ to the spirit world, where Jesus declared liberty to the righteous and organized a mission to preach the gospel to the wicked spirits. In 1981 his account of this vision was added to the Doctrine and Covenants as section 138.

BIBLIOGRAPHY

Gibbons, Francis M. *Joseph F. Smith: Patriarch and Preacher, Prophet of God.* Salt Lake City, 1984.

Smith, Joseph F. *GD.*

Smith, Joseph Fielding. *Life of Joseph F. Smith.* Salt Lake City, 1969.

BRUCE A. VAN ORDEN

SMITH, JOSEPH FIELDING

Joseph Fielding Smith (1876–1972), the tenth President of the Church, was born July 19, 1876, in Salt Lake City, the firstborn son of Joseph F.

SMITH, an apostle who would become the sixth President of the Church, and Julina Lambson, the first of his six plural wives. His grandfather was the Patriarch Hyrum SMITH. Under the tutelage of his parents, Joseph Fielding, as he became known in the Church, grew up with a deep affection for the Prophet Joseph SMITH and his teachings. Upon learning to read, he constantly studied Church magazines, pamphlets, and other publications, reading the Book of Mormon twice by age ten. A few years later, he read the lengthy history of the Church, published in the *Millennial Star*. In his late teens he studied the New Testament in transit to and from his merchandizing job at ZCMI (Zion's Cooperative Mercantile Institution), the Church department store. He built the lasting scholarship on this foundation of constant learning that later distinguished his prolific writings.

He married Louie Emily (Emyla) Shurtliff in the Salt Lake Temple on April 26, 1898. One year later, he accepted a two-year mission call in the Nottingham conference of the British Mission (1899–1901). Upon his return, he secured employment in the Church Historian's office. In April 1906 he was appointed an assistant Church historian.

As antipolygamy sentiment raged in the early 1900s, Joseph Fielding felt the injustice of the attacks upon the Church and the men whom he knew and loved, such as his father. Some of his first publications were defenses of historical Church doctrine and practice, including *Blood Atonement and the Origin of Plural Marriage* (1905) and *Origin of the "Reorganized" Church: The Question of Succession* (1907).

In March 1908 his wife, Louie, died leaving him with two daughters. That November he married Ethel Georgina Reynolds, who bore him five sons and four daughters. Ethel died in August 1937, and he married Jessie Ella Evans in April 1938. She died on August 3, 1971, one year before President Smith.

Family influence powerfully shaped Joseph Fielding Smith's feeling about religion and his understanding of the gospel. In his later years he often commented that he had been tutored by his father, who was called to preside over the Church when Joseph Fielding was only twenty-five. "I have a great love for my father," he said. "It was marvelous how the words of living light and fire flowed from him" (remarks at Smith family reunion, Nov. 13, 1970; copies in family possession).

Joseph Fielding Smith (1876–1972), ordained an apostle in 1910, was well known for his gospel writings. He served as Church Historian for many years, publishing a selection of the teachings of the Prophet Joseph Smith. He wrote many "Answers to Gospel Questions" and articles that were collected in three volumes called *Doctrines of Salvation*. Courtesy Utah State Historical Society.

"In all my life," he continued, "whenever I have been tempted, one thought has always come to me. 'What would my father think of that?'" A year later, dramatizing the impact of his father on his own gospel scholarship, he said, "I feel a closeness to my father, and my grandfather, and my granduncle the Prophet [Joseph Smith] himself, and to the other early brethren of this dispensation. I believe what they believed and am sure that in large measure I think as they thought" (fireside speech to Latter-day Saint Student Association, Nov. 21, 1971, LDS Institute of Religion, University of Utah).

Family influences in turn became the molding forces in the lives of Joseph Fielding's children, who tell of his constant efforts to teach them. At meals, in family gatherings, while walking children to school or church, and later in letters to those in the military and on missions, he was always instructing his children in gospel principles. His letters, like his sermons, were filled with scriptural quotations, often interpreting world events or family activities in terms of what the scriptures said. Through these constant teachings he earned what he considered to be one of life's greatest blessings: all of his children remained faithful Latter-day Saints. Each married in the temple, and each of his sons served a mission for the Church. Following Joseph Fielding's death, Harold B. LEE, his successor as President of the Church, said, "Truly, the greatest monument to him is the great posterity which he has given to the world" (Letter to the Joseph Fielding Smith family, July 14, 1972, Salt Lake City, Historical Department of the Church [HDC]).

When Joseph Fielding Smith was ordained an apostle on April 7, 1910, the *Salt Lake Tribune* published criticisms against him, his father, and the Smith family for nepotism. This vilification ignored his qualifications for the apostleship. In this difficult time, he took refuge in his family, which had special reason to have confidence in the call because of a revelation to his mother that her son would become an apostle (Bruce R. McConkie, pp. 24–31). In a patriarchal blessing he received at nineteen, Joseph Fielding Smith had also been told, "It shall be thy duty to sit in council with thy brethren, and to preside among the people" (John Smith, Patriarchal Blessing to Joseph Fielding Smith, Jan. 19, 1896; copy in LDS Church Historian's Library).

During his apostolic tenure, amid many responsibilities and duties, Joseph Fielding Smith was best known, and is best remembered, as a theologian and gospel scholar. President Heber J. GRANT called him "the best posted man on the scriptures of the General Authorities of the Church that we have" (Letter to Joseph Fielding Smith, Dec. 31, 1938, *HDC*). He published more books and articles than any other man who became President of the Church, though it was never his main intent to become an author. Many of his writings were discourses, answers to questions posed to him, instructions for Church leaders, and efforts to clarify common uncertainties.

One book, *The Signs of the Times* (1942), was published after requests mounted for copies of lectures he had given on the LAST DAYS. *The Restoration of All Things* (1945) was a compilation of radio talks; the two-volume *Church History and Modern Revelation* (1953) was a manual of instruction for the Melchizedek Priesthood quorums; and the five-volume *Answers to Gospel Questions* (1957–1966) was a compilation of answers to gospel questions printed in Church magazines over a period of years.

At a time when many were concerned with the issues of organic evolution, Elder Smith published *Man: His Origin and Destiny* (1954), in which he provided a scriptural and theological defense of the Church position that mankind is the offspring of and placed on earth by God, not a product of random evolutionary processes. His calm throughout this intellectual storm showed both his serenity and wisdom.

He always built his sermons on scriptural themes. "I never did learn to deliver a discourse," he said, "without referring to the scriptures" (Joseph F. McConkie, pp. 44–45). In his sixty-two-year ministry as an apostle and prophet, Joseph Fielding Smith preached on almost every facet of the gospel. Few Latter-day Saints have spoken so emphatically on the fact that God is a personal being, that he is the creator of all things, that he is literally the Father of Jesus Christ, and that the atonement of Christ grows out of the fact of his divine Sonship. His defense of the Prophet Joseph Smith, the Book of Mormon, and the doctrine of a latter-day restoration fulfilled a promise in a second patriarchal blessing that his teachings and writings would stand as a "wall of defense against those who are seeking and will seek to destroy the evidence of the divinity of the mission of the Prophet Joseph Smith" (Joseph D. Smith. Patriarchal Blessing to Joseph Fielding Smith, May 11, 1913; copies in family possession).

He explained the doctrine of the "divine law of witnesses" (*CR*, Apr. 1930) with a force and clarity not found elsewhere in the literature of the Latter-day Saints (*see* WITNESSES, LAW OF). *The Way to Perfection* (1931) and *Elijah the Prophet and His Mission* (1957) stand as classic expositions of the doctrines of salvation for the dead. His compilation *Teachings of the Prophet Joseph Smith* (1938) is one of the most widely used reference texts in LDS literature. *Essentials in Church History* (1922) and *The Life of Joseph F. Smith* (1938) are examples of interpreting history through scriptural and prophetic eyes.

Yet, while he is remembered as a gospel scholar, Joseph Fielding Smith's love of life and those he worked with was broader than his scholar-one-half-year tenure was marked by steady missionary growth; the dedication of the Ogden and Provo temples; some significant organizational restructuring, including reorganizations in the Church Sunday School system and the Church Department of Social Services; and a revamping of portions of the Church internal communication systems, which led to the consolidation of all general Church magazines into three.

After a long life of scholarship and influence, one of his most significant acts was his reaffirmation, as President of the Church, of the doctrines that he had taught throughout his apostolic ministry. "What I have taught and written in the past," he said in the October general conference of 1970, "I would teach and write again under the same circumstances" (*CR*, Oct. 1970, p. 5). He died July 2, 1972, in Salt Lake City.

BIBLIOGRAPHY

McConkie, Bruce R. "Joseph Fielding Smith, Apostle, Prophet, Father in Israel." *Ensign* 2 (Aug. 1972):23–31.

McConkie, Joseph F. *True and Faithful: The Life Story of Joseph Fielding Smith.* Salt Lake City, 1971.

Smith, Joseph Fielding, Jr., and John J. Stewart. *The Life of Joseph Fielding Smith.* Salt Lake City, 1972.

AMELIA S. MCCONKIE
MARK L. MCCONKIE

Shown here (c. 1970) with his third wife, Jessie Evans Smith. They were married in 1938, and she was famous as a singer. Joseph Fielding Smith was the tenth President of the Church, serving in that position from 1970 to 1972.

ship. When President Smith was ninety-three, Elder Gordon B. Hinckley said, "I have never heard him say a mean or evil or unkind thing. . . . He speaks generously of those he discusses." He repeatedly said, "I love my brethren," and with regard to the wayward, he urged giving "them the benefit of the doubt; there are two sides to the story." His counsel to bishops was similar: "If you make any mistakes in judgment, make them on the side of mercy." He frequently financed missions, paid the hospital bills of the sick, and sent groceries to the needy. He always disciplined his children with love, avoiding physical punishment, preferring to look them in the eyes and say, "I wish my children would be good." "No spanking or whipping," said one daughter, "could accomplish what this kindly father did with love" (Joseph F. McConkie, pp. 71–90).

Joseph Fielding Smith became President of the Church on January 23, 1970, following the death of President David O. McKay. His two-and-

SMITH, LUCY MACK

Lucy Mack Smith (1775–1856) was the mother of the Prophet Joseph SMITH and his main biographer for the crucial formative years of the restored Church. A marked tenderness existed between the Smith parents and children, and Lucy lived near or in the Prophet's household through hardships in New York, Ohio, Missouri, and Illinois. Mother and son maintained the strongest mutual respect throughout these years of change, sacrifice, and persecution.

Faith in God was central to Lucy Smith's personality. When a young mother, she became critically ill and spent a night very near death, but a voice promised her life after she pleaded for the power to "bring up my children, and comfort the heart of my husband," with a vow to serve God completely. More than forty years later, she publicly reviewed the result of her parental leadership with her husband, Joseph SMITH, Sr. Of eleven children, nine reached maturity, and with typical intensity, Lucy said, "We raised them in the fear of God. . . . I presume there never were a family that were so obedient as mine" (MS conference minutes, Oct. 8, 1845, HDC).

Her father, Solomon Mack, was a dynamic venturer who showed courage and self-reliance in close combat in the French and Indian Wars and afterward as merchant, land developer, contractor, miller, seafarer, and farmer. Unsatisfied with the seeming meaninglessness of his way of life, he finally found God after severe sickness. He then published his concise biography—the saga of how God protected him in his wanderings and at the end showered his soul with love and insight. Lucy Mack Smith identified deeply with her mother, Lydia Gates, who came from the home of a prosperous Congregational deacon. Lydia used her schoolteaching skills in the home, creating what Solomon called an atmosphere of "piety, gentleness, and reflection" (Anderson, 1971, p. 27). All of the Mack children possessed mixtures of the daring enterprise of their father and the assertive piety of their mother. Lucy was true to this heritage of seeking light and then sharing it.

Lucy was born in Gilsum, New Hampshire, where town records enter her birthday as July 8, 1775, the year the American Revolution began. Her education included attending school there and at Montague, Massachusetts, supplemented by private instruction by her mother. Lucy Smith's speeches and writing reveal an intelligent believer who used English capably. In her late teens Lucy was also greatly influenced by the courageous deaths of her older sisters; each died in her early thirties, after testifying to personal revelations of the hereafter and of Christ's love.

Lucy's entrepreneur brother, Stephen Mack, took her to Tunbridge, Vermont, where she met her future husband, Joseph Smith, Sr. She evaluated his family as "worthy, respectable, amiable, and intelligent." To their marriage on January 24, 1796, Lucy brought a dowry of a thousand dollars, a gift of her brother and his business partner; her husband owned a farm of almost equal value. A huge exporting investment failed because of the dishonesty of their agent, and the couple used their total assets to pay the debt rather than default on merchandise obtained for their Vermont store. Their first twenty years of marriage were spent in neighboring Vermont and New Hampshire towns. They climbed back to prosperity through the schoolteaching of Joseph Smith, Sr., assisted with farming and home industry. Yet setbacks came with agonizing sickness in the family in 1812–1813 and frozen crops in 1814–1816, which precipitated their move to Palmyra, New York.

Lucy and Joseph Smith, Sr., were active seekers. As a young, sensitive woman, Lucy sought the conversion that she heard preached in churches. As she "perused the Bible and prayed incessantly," Lucy concluded that the biblical church "was not like" any existing church. Thus, after a miraculous healing in early marriage, she asked a minister to baptize her without commitment to attend his denomination. Finding New England Presbyterianism wanting, she investigated Methodism, only to be opposed by her unaffiliated husband. In these years, he received periodic dreams promising future answers. And Lucy in turn dreamed of Joseph Smith, Sr., as a pliant tree; she concluded that he would yet receive the full truth from God.

Lucy Smith was a vigorous forty years of age when regional crop failure forced the family to the opening wheat land of western New York. Their move was evidently in 1816, and her husband preceded her, sending Lucy the means to bring a few goods and their eight children, ranging from eighteen-year old Alvin to the new baby, Don Carlos. Mother Smith showed independence in publicly dismissing her unprincipled teamster (who had been hired to help the family, but proved to be selfish and undependable). She also showed tender emotions in the reunion of "throwing myself and my children upon the care and affection of a tender husband and father" (Coray MS).

In the Palmyra area the family rebuilt financial security, only to have it slip away again amid the hostility of their neighbors to their son's revelations. Lucy first began to "replenish" her home furnishings by continuing "painting oil cloth coverings for tables, stands, etc." Like many new settlers, the Smiths signed a short-term contract to purchase about a hundred acres of uncleared land. Over several years the family cleared forty acres, built fences and outbuildings, kept up a coopering business, and ran farm operations for a large sugar maple harvest, orchard production, and the main wheat crop. These activities objectively contradict one of two charges in neighborhood affidavits that Lucy and her family were lazy and superstitious. The realities behind such accusations were poverty and a belief in the miraculous. Obvious attempts were made to discredit the new religion by denigrating its founders and their families.

Mother Smith's history admits that the family was accused of occult treasure searching, but it passes over the issue by stating the intense goal of their New York years: "Whilst we worked with our hands we endeavored to remember the service of [God] and the welfare of our souls" (Coray MS). In this context, she relates how the prayers of her son Joseph were answered. The Prophet does not suggest that he confided his FIRST VISION to his family, and his mother reports only that she had early knowledge that an angel later revealed the Book of Mormon. Lucy carefully describes that she handled the URIM AND THUMMIM and the ancient breastplate. Her conviction of the divinity of the Book of Mormon was total, as suggested by a letter to her brother in 1831: "I want you to think seriously of these things, for they are the truths of the living God" (Kirkham, p. 67).

For a time, Lucy affiliated with a Presbyterian church in Palmyra, though she was excommunicated for nonattendance the month before the LDS Church was organized. Her powerful faith in the young Church was expressed in her taking a large New York group to Ohio by canal boat to Buffalo and by steamer across a partially frozen Lake Erie in 1831. She braved cold weather and discouragement, leading in prayer, missionary work, and practical arrangements until again united with her husband and sons in upper Ohio. She then went to teach her Mack relatives in Detroit, converting Stephen Mack's widow, Temperance. Mother Smith endured two later migrations, one in the spring rains on the way to Missouri in 1838 and a move to Illinois in the wet snows of early 1839.

Joseph Smith, Sr., died in late 1840, a casualty of a decade of trauma and exposure. Shortly before he died, he blessed his children and expressed love for his "most singular" wife, promising her that her last days would be her best days. But other searing partings preceded the fulfillment of this promise of peace. Lucy early had lost two infant sons, and later came the sudden death of her oldest son, Alvin, during her New York days. She buried her husband in Illinois and, within the next four years, endured the deaths of four more sons—Samuel and Don Carlos in sickness and Joseph and Hyrum murdered by a mob.

"O God, why were my noble sons permitted to be martyred?" was her cry upon seeing their corpses (Anderson, 1977, p. 135). An inner voice assured her that divine purpose was accomplished in the tragedy. Lucy never lost her faith in God, in the revelations to her son, and in the destiny of her family. She was cared for by Joseph and Emma Smith until 1844, by her daughter Lucy Millikin some years thereafter, and by Emma once more in her final years in Nauvoo. Feeble and unable to write, she impressed visitors with her spiritual and social vitality. She passed from life May 14, 1856, at nearly eighty-one.

For a time after 1844, Lucy Smith depended emotionally on her only surviving son. Yet William seems to have overused her name in his cause. In 1845 he sought to expand his patriarch's office, and John TAYLOR's journal records visions briefly circulated from Lucy about William's supposed authority to lead the Church. Perhaps William helped her write them, since the apostles who met with Lucy found her questioning whether they had "a correct copy." Taylor described her "good feelings" toward the Twelve (pp. 63–68). She and most of her sons' widows were in the first companies receiving higher ordinances in the Nauvoo Temple. She received WASHINGS AND ANOINTINGS on December 11, 1845, and the ENDOWMENT the following day (HC 7:542–44).

Lucy Smith gave a spirited talk before the October 1845 conference, expressing her need to stay with her children in Nauvoo but giving her blessing to the Twelve and their plans for the exodus: "I feel that the Lord will let Brother Brigham take the people away." She also said that her memoirs were complete: "I have got all in a history, and I want this people to be so good as to get it printed" (MS conference minutes, Oct. 8, 1845, HDC). This was dictated to Martha Jane Knowlton Coray, whose first narrative survives. Lucy's history was not printed until Orson PRATT obtained a copy and published it in England in 1853.

The first edition of Lucy's memoirs was recalled by Brigham Young. However, his goal was accuracy, not suppression, since he initiated a second edition. According to Wilford WOODRUFF's journal, the President charged the careful Woodruff and two Smith family members to "correct the errors in the History of Joseph Smith as published by Mother Smith, and then let it be published to the world" (Apr. 22, 1866).

Lucy Smith's history gives more than two hundred names in its various drafts, and hundreds of details. Nearly all of these individuals and episodes are confirmed by independent contemporary records. Astute John Taylor evaluated her capacity after talking with her about her history: "Though now quite an aged woman, the power of her memory is surprising; she is able to relate circumstances connected with the family, with great distinctness and accuracy" (p. 52). Beyond facts, her history burns with the dedication that made the events of the Restoration possible. She achieved religious greatness—as a mother and as a dynamic contributor to the infant church. Furthermore, her history is irreplaceable, judged by her expressed goal to give "the particulars of Joseph's getting the plates, seeing the angels at first, and many other things which Joseph never wrote or published" (Lucy Smith to William Smith, Jan. 23, 1845, HDC).

BIBLIOGRAPHY

Anderson, Richard Lloyd. "The Reliability of the Early History of Lucy and Joseph Smith." *Dialogue* 4 (Summer 1969):13–28.

———. *Joseph Smith's New England Heritage.* Salt Lake City, 1971.

———. "Joseph Smith's Home Environment." *Ensign* 1 (July 1971):57–59.

———. "His Mother's Manuscript: An Intimate View of Joseph Smith." BYU Forum address, Jan. 27, 1976.

———. "The Emotional Dimensions of Lucy Smith and Her History." In *Dedication Colloquiums, Harold B. Lee Library,* pp. 129–37. Provo, Utah, 1977.

Kirkham, Francis W. *A New Witness for Christ in America,* 4th ed., Vol. 1. Salt Lake City, 1967.

Smith, Lucy. All unidentified quotations from Lucy Smith in this article are from Martha Jane Knowlton Coray's preliminary manuscript in the Historical Department of the Church. Most are also found in edited form in Lucy Mack Smith, *Biographical Sketches of Joseph Smith, the Prophet, and His Progenitors for Many Generations* (Liverpool, 1853). Among reprints, the most widely distributed is the early Utah edition, lightly modified by editor Preston Nibley, *History of Joseph Smith, by His Mother, Lucy Mack Smith* (Salt Lake City: n.d.).

Taylor, John. "The John Taylor Nauvoo Journal," ed. Dean C. Jessee. *BYU Studies* 23 (Summer 1983):63–68.

Youngreen, Buddy. "The Death Date of Lucy Mack Smith." *BYU Studies* 12 (Spring 1972):318.

RICHARD LLOYD ANDERSON

Mary Fielding (1801–1852) married Hyrum Smith, elder brother of the Prophet Joseph Smith, following the death of his first wife. She was mother of Joseph F. Smith and the grandmother of Joseph Fielding Smith, the sixth and tenth presidents of the Church. A nineteenth-century portrait. Artist unknown.

SMITH, MARY FIELDING

Mary Fielding Smith (1801–1852) has the unique distinction of being the mother of one President of The Church of Jesus Christ of Latter-day Saints (Joseph F. SMITH) and the grandmother of another (Joseph Fielding SMITH).

Born on July 21, 1801, at Honidon, Bedfordshire, England, Mary Fielding was the sixth child of John Fielding and Rachel Ibbotson, staunch Methodists. In 1834, Mary migrated to Toronto, Canada, where her brother and sister, Joseph and Mercy, had moved two years earlier. Nearby at Charleton, the three Fieldings were baptized into the Church in May 1836. The following year, Mary moved to KIRTLAND, OHIO.

Attractive and well educated, Mary became a live-in governess and teacher for various families in Kirtland. On December 24, 1837, Mary Fielding married the widower Hyrum SMITH, whose first wife had died while giving birth to their fifth child. Though reluctant to become a stepmother, Mary accepted this responsibility as the will of the Lord.

Mary and Hyrum were forced to flee Kirtland for Far West, MISSOURI, in early 1838. That November 13th, while Hyrum was incarcerated in LIBERTY JAIL in Clay County, Missouri, and the Missouri Saints were under siege, Mary gave birth to a son, whom she named Joseph Fielding Smith, and who would become the sixth President of the Church in 1901.

Ill for several months after the birth of her son, Mary was transported on a bed in a wagon to Quincy, Illinois, in February 1839. Freed from imprisonment in April, Hyrum joined her there. Soon they settled in nearby Commerce, which became NAUVOO. On May 14, 1841, Mary gave birth to a daughter, Martha Ann. Mary assisted Hyrum as he served as vice-mayor of Nauvoo, PATRIARCH to the Church, and Associate President of the Church. She and her sister Mercy helped organize the women of the Church to raise funds for the Nauvoo Temple. Tragedy befell the entire Church on June 27, 1844, with the MARTYRDOM OF JOSEPH AND HYRUM SMITH in Carthage Jail.

Mary and her children left Nauvoo in the fall of 1846. After living in WINTER QUARTERS eighteen months, they crossed the plains to the Salt Lake Valley in 1848. Her son Joseph F., only nine years of age, drove one of the wagons. When Peter Lott, captain of their company, complained that Mary was underequipped and would be a burden on the entire company, she replied that she would beat him to the valley—and without his help. A deeply spiritual person, Mary often relied on prayer. On one occasion while crossing the plains, two of her finest oxen disappeared. Several men looked for them at length but without success. Back in camp, Mary knelt in prayer and then walked straight to a ravine, where she found her oxen caught in a clump of willows. Her family arrived in Salt Lake City on September 22, 1848—ahead of Captain Lott.

Mary secured a lot in Salt Lake City and a farm in Mill Creek. Her two-room adobe farmhouse is preserved in the pioneer village near the "THIS IS THE PLACE" MONUMENT in Salt Lake City. Although a widow with few means, she directed her children to pick the best of their farm produce for the tithing office. When a clerk at the office suggested that the Widow Smith should not tithe when she had so little, she scolded him. It was a privilege to pay tithing, she insisted, and to recommend that she not pay her tithing was to deny her the blessings that she needed.

Mary Fielding Smith died September 21, 1852, probably from pneumonia, at the age of fifty-one. She was widely respected and admired during her lifetime. Later generations saw her through the eyes of her son, President Joseph F. Smith, who often spoke of her as a model of courage and faithfulness.

BIBLIOGRAPHY

Arrington, Leonard J., and Susan Arrington Madsen. *Mothers of the Prophets*, pp. 89–107. Salt Lake City, 1987.

Corbett, Don C. *Mary Fielding Smith: Daughter of Britain.* Salt Lake City, 1966.

Smith, Joseph Fielding. *Life of Joseph F. Smith.* Salt Lake City, 1938.

SUSAN ARRINGTON MADSEN

SMITH FAMILY

Joseph and Lucy Mack SMITH, parents of the Prophet Joseph Smith, were married in Tunbridge, Vermont, in 1796. Joseph, Sr., worked as a cooper, shopkeeper, schoolteacher, farmer, and laborer to provide for a growing family. Accounts of these years describe hard work, severe economic reversals, and strong family loyalty. Both parents were dissatisfied with the religions of their time, but family members believed in God, prayed, read the Bible, and were concerned about the salvation of their souls.

After the failure of a number of business and farming ventures, they moved to the village of Palmyra, New York, in 1816, near which Joseph Smith, Jr., experienced his early visions (*see* VISIONS OF JOSEPH SMITH). From the beginning, the Smith family supported young Joseph's claim to angelic visitations and prophetic power. Nine children grew to adulthood (a first son was stillborn; another, Ephraim, died shortly after birth in 1810), and all were loyal to their belief in their brother Joseph's divine mission.

Alvin (1798–1823), the oldest son, was a great strength to his family as he cleared land and worked to build a house for the family in Manchester. He died in November 1823 of an overdose of calomel prescribed for a stomach ailment. On his deathbed Alvin encouraged the seventeen-year-old Joseph to "be a good boy, and do everything that lies in your power to obtain the Record," referring to the Book of Mormon plates (Smith, p.

Smith family home south of Palmyra, New York (c. 1960). The family lived here, c. 1825–1829, leaving New York in 1831 for Kirtland, Ohio. In the grove to the west of this house, Joseph Smith received his First Vision (1820). Joseph brought the golden plates into this house from the Hill Cumorah to the southeast (1827).

87). In an 1836 vision, Joseph saw Alvin in the CELESTIAL KINGDOM (D&C 137).

The Smiths participated in the early events of the RESTORATION and followed young Joseph first to Ohio and then to Missouri and Illinois, suffering hardship and persecution, but continuing faithful. Don Carlos Smith (1816–1841), the youngest brother, was president of the HIGH PRIESTS at Kirtland and Nauvoo and an editor of the *Times and Seasons*. He died in August 1841 at the age of twenty-five.

The close relationship of Hyrum SMITH (1800–1844) and his younger brother Joseph is a prominent theme in the history of the Church. John TAYLOR declared of them, "In life they were not divided, and in death they were not separated!" (D&C 135:3). Hyrum became Second Counselor in the FIRST PRESIDENCY and was named PATRIARCH and assistant Church President in 1841. He married Jerusha Barden in 1826, and after her death in 1837 he married Mary Fielding (*see* SMITH, MARY FIELDING). He was the father of eight children and was assassinated with Joseph at CARTHAGE JAIL on June 27, 1844.

Samuel Harrison Smith (1808–1844) was the first missionary in the Church. Along with Hyrum and his father, Joseph, Sr., he was one of the eight witnesses of the Book of Mormon. He married Mary Bailey and, after her death, Levira Clark. Upon hearing of the danger to his brothers at Carthage, Samuel attempted to ride to their aid, but was fired upon and chased away by the mob. He eluded his pursuers with hard riding, but arrived too late to intervene. He died within the month, apparently of an injury sustained in that ride. Samuel's family went west with the Saints, as did the family of Hyrum Smith.

William Smith (1811–1893) was the only brother in the family to survive the Nauvoo period. He became a member of the QUORUM OF THE TWELVE APOSTLES in 1835 and Church Patriarch after the death of his brother Hyrum in 1844. Unwilling to accept the leadership of the Twelve over the Church after the death of Joseph, he was excommunicated in 1845. He may have been a pivotal influence in the decision of the Smith sisters and their mother to remain in Illinois after the main body of the Church moved west. He vigorously encouraged Mary Fielding Smith and Hyrum's children to remain in the area, but they chose to follow Brigham Young and the Twelve. William joined the REORGANIZED CHURCH OF JESUS CHRIST OF LATTER DAY SAINTS in 1878.

The three sisters in the Smith family were Sophronia, Catherine, and Lucy. Sophronia (1803–1876) married Calvin Stoddard in 1828 and bore him two daughters. After Calvin's death in 1836, she married William McCleary. Their temple ENDOWMENTS are recorded after Joseph and Hyrum's martyrdom, which indicates that they were in harmony with Church leadership at that time, but they did not go west with the Saints.

Catherine (1813–1900) fulfilled her father's blessing that she would live to a good old age. She married Wilkins Jenkins Salisbury in 1831, and they were the parents of eight children. After his death in 1856, she remained in Hancock County, Illinois, a prominent member of the community.

Lucy (1821–1882), the youngest, was especially beloved by all the family. She married Arthur Millikin when almost nineteen and became a welcome support to her mother, who lived with the couple for seven years after the death of Joseph, Sr. Lucy stayed in Illinois and with her sisters joined the RLDS Church in 1873. The sisters maintained cordial relationships with their Utah relatives throughout their lives.

BIBLIOGRAPHY

Anderson, Richard Lloyd. "What Were Joseph Smith's Sisters Like?" *Ensign* 9 (Mar. 1979):42–44.

———. "Joseph Smith's Brothers: Nauvoo and After." *Ensign* 9 (Sept. 1979):30–33.

Bushman, Richard L. *Joseph Smith and the Beginnings of Mormonism.* Chicago, 1984.

Smith, Lucy Mack. *History of Joseph Smith by His Mother, Lucy Mack Smith.* Salt Lake City, 1956.

SYDNEY SMITH REYNOLDS

SMITH FAMILY ANCESTORS

Five generations of the Prophet Joseph SMITH's ancestors lived in Topsfield, Massachusetts. The first was his great-grandfather's grandfather, Robert Smith, who came from England to Boston in 1638. He married Mary French in 1659 at Topsfield. They were the parents of ten children. When Robert died at Boxfield, Massachusetts, in 1693, he left an estate valued at the comparatively large amount of 189 pounds. Robert and Mary's son Samuel was born in 1666. He was listed on the town and county records as a "gentleman" and apparently held public office. He married Rebecca Curtis, and the third of their nine children, also named Samuel, was born in 1714.

Samuel Smith, Jr., was a distinguished community leader and supporter of the American War of Independence. He served six terms in the Massachusetts state legislature and twelve as a town selectman. He was chairman of the Tea Committee at Topsfield in 1773, which sustained the action of the Boston Tea Party, and he was elected to the First Provincial Congress in Massachusetts in 1774. Samuel married Priscilla Gould, a descendant of Zaccheus Gould, the founder of Topsfield.

Asael Smith, the Prophet Joseph Smith's grandfather, was born to this couple in 1744. His mother died just six months after he was born. Asael married Mary Duty at Topsfield in 1767. Their son Joseph SMITH, Sr., was born in Topsfield in 1771. They later moved to New Hampshire. Asael served in the Revolutionary War, following which he was town clerk of Derryfield, New Hampshire, from 1779 until 1786. When his father died, Asael returned to Topsfield at great personal sacrifice and worked for five years to liquidate his father's debts. In 1791 Asael left Topsfield to make a new life, first in Ipswich, Massachusetts, and then that same year in Vermont. He continued his trade as a cooper, settling in Tunbridge, Vermont, where he served as selectman, grand juror, and surveyor of highways. Over the years, he held nearly every public office in Tunbridge.

Although Asael believed in a personal God and Savior, he came to oppose the established churches. He served as moderator of a meeting that established one of the early Universalist societies in Vermont in 1797. He always subscribed to the Universalist doctrine that the atonement of Christ was sufficient to redeem all men. Despite this departure from traditional New England orthodoxy, his writings show him to have been a man of warm Christian faith. Asael said that he felt that God intended to raise a branch of his family to be of great benefit to mankind (R. L. Anderson, p. 112).

The maternal ancestors of the Prophet Joseph Smith were named Mack(e). John Macke was born in 1653 at Inverness, Scotland, a descendant of a line of clergymen. He emigrated to Salisbury, Massachusetts, in 1669, and then on to Lyme, Connecticut. His son Ebenezer inherited his father's large estate in Lyme and married Hannah Huntley. For a while Ebenezer was able to keep his family in good style, but their prosperity was short-lived. Their son Solomon, born in 1732, was apprenticed to a neighboring farmer in Lyme at the age of four. Solomon later reported that he was treated as a slave and never given instruction in religion or taught to read and write, which was a great hardship to him in later life.

In 1759 Solomon Mack married Lydia Gates, a young schoolteacher and a member of the Congregational church. She was well educated and from a well-to-do religious family. Although Solomon and Lydia came from contrasting backgrounds, theirs was an enduring marriage. Lydia took charge of both the secular and religious education of their eight children. They pioneered the upper Connecticut River Valley and settled Marlow, New Hampshire. They later moved to Gilsum, New Hampshire, where the Prophet Joseph's mother, Lucy Mack, was born in 1775 (*see* SMITH, LUCY MACK).

During the American Revolution, Solomon helped with the manufacture of gunpowder, served in an artillery company, and shipped aboard a privateer. Although he worked hard as a merchant, land developer, shipmaster, mill opera-

Genealogy of Joseph Smith, Jr.

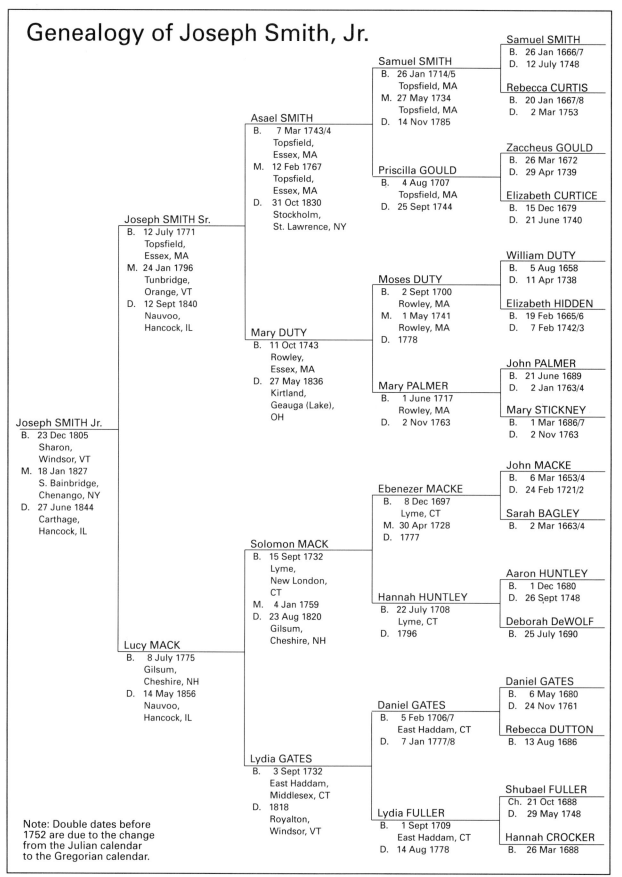

Joseph SMITH Jr.
B. 23 Dec 1805
Sharon,
Windsor, VT
M. 18 Jan 1827
S. Bainbridge,
Chenango, NY
D. 27 June 1844
Carthage,
Hancock, IL

Joseph SMITH Sr.
B. 12 July 1771
Topsfield,
Essex, MA
M. 24 Jan 1796
Tunbridge,
Orange, VT
D. 12 Sept 1840
Nauvoo,
Hancock, IL

Lucy MACK
B. 8 July 1775
Gilsum,
Cheshire, NH
D. 14 May 1856
Nauvoo,
Hancock, IL

Asael SMITH
B. 7 Mar 1743/4
Topsfield,
Essex, MA
M. 12 Feb 1767
Topsfield,
Essex, MA
D. 31 Oct 1830
Stockholm,
St. Lawrence, NY

Mary DUTY
B. 11 Oct 1743
Rowley,
Essex, MA
D. 27 May 1836
Kirtland,
Geauga (Lake),
OH

Solomon MACK
B. 15 Sept 1732
Lyme,
New London,
CT
M. 4 Jan 1759
D. 23 Aug 1820
Gilsum,
Cheshire, NH

Lydia GATES
B. 3 Sept 1732
East Haddam,
Middlesex, CT
D. 1818
Royalton,
Windsor, VT

Samuel SMITH
B. 26 Jan 1714/5
Topsfield, MA
M. 27 May 1734
Topsfield, MA
D. 14 Nov 1785

Priscilla GOULD
B. 4 Aug 1707
Topsfield, MA
D. 25 Sept 1744

Moses DUTY
B. 2 Sept 1700
Rowley, MA
M. 1 May 1741
Rowley, MA
D. 1778

Mary PALMER
B. 1 June 1717
Rowley, MA
D. 2 Nov 1763

Ebenezer MACKE
B. 8 Dec 1697
Lyme, CT
M. 30 Apr 1728
D. 1777

Hannah HUNTLEY
B. 22 July 1708
Lyme, CT
D. 1796

Daniel GATES
B. 5 Feb 1706/7
East Haddam, CT
D. 7 Jan 1777/8

Lydia FULLER
B. 1 Sept 1709
East Haddam, CT
D. 14 Aug 1778

Samuel SMITH
B. 26 Jan 1666/7
D. 12 July 1748

Rebecca CURTIS
B. 20 Jan 1667/8
D. 2 Mar 1753

Zaccheus GOULD
B. 26 Mar 1672
D. 29 Apr 1739

Elizabeth CURTICE
B. 15 Dec 1679
D. 21 June 1740

William DUTY
B. 5 Aug 1658
D. 11 Apr 1738

Elizabeth HIDDEN
B. 19 Feb 1665/6
D. 7 Feb 1742/3

John PALMER
B. 21 June 1689
D. 2 Jan 1763/4

Mary STICKNEY
B. 1 Mar 1686/7
D. 2 Nov 1763

John MACKE
B. 6 Mar 1653/4
D. 24 Feb 1721/2

Sarah BAGLEY
B. 2 Mar 1663/4

Aaron HUNTLEY
B. 1 Dec 1680
D. 26 Sept 1748

Deborah DeWOLF
B. 25 July 1690

Daniel GATES
B. 6 May 1680
D. 24 Nov 1761

Rebecca DUTTON
B. 13 Aug 1686

Shubael FULLER
Ch. 21 Oct 1688
D. 29 May 1748

Hannah CROCKER
B. 26 Mar 1688

Note: Double dates before 1752 are due to the change from the Julian calendar to the Gregorian calendar.

tor, and farmer, fortune did not favor him, and accidents, hardships, and financial reverses beset him most of his life.

Solomon Mack was not outwardly religious, though he was a God-fearing and good-hearted man. He showed little inclination toward scripture reading or churchgoing until 1810, when rheumatism forced him to reassess his values. "After this I determined to follow phantoms no longer, but devote the rest of my life to the service of God and my family" (quoted in Smith, pp. 7–8). That winter, he read the Bible and prayed earnestly, eventually finding peace of soul and mind. From then on until his death in 1820, Solomon spent much of his time telling others of his conversion and admonishing them to serve the Lord. He wrote an autobiography in the hope that others would not become enamored with the desire for material gain as he had. He enthusiastically shared his religious conviction with his grandchildren, among whom was young Joseph Smith, Jr. Solomon Mack died in 1820, three weeks before his eighty-eighth birthday and shortly after his grandson's remarkable FIRST VISION of the Father and the Son.

BIBLIOGRAPHY

Anderson, Mary Audentia Smith. *Ancestry and Posterity of Joseph Smith and Emma Hale.* Independence, Mo., 1929.

Anderson, Richard L. *Joseph Smith's New England Heritage.* Salt Lake City, 1971.

Bushman, Richard L. *Joseph Smith and the Beginnings of Mormonism.* Urbana, Ill., 1984.

Hill, Donna. *Joseph Smith, the First Mormon.* Garden City, N.Y., 1977.

Smith, Lucy Mack. *History of Joseph Smith.* Salt Lake City, 1958.

A. GARY ANDERSON

SMOOT HEARINGS

Before seating senator-elect Reed Smoot, a member of the Quorum of the Twelve Apostles, the U.S. Senate conducted lengthy hearings into his alleged involvement in PLURAL MARRIAGE and into the policy and government of the Church. Few events have had greater impact on the Church and its public image than the highly publicized Smoot Hearings of 1903–1907.

The 1890s had seen the Church pass through some of its most challenging times, including the tumultuous political fight for Utah statehood following the MANIFESTO OF 1890 (officially curtailing new plural marriages) and presidential amnesty for Church officers who had practiced POLYGAMY, initiating the process of accommodation and acculturation to mainstream America. Euphoria, however, was short-lived.

The election to the U.S. Senate of Reed Smoot, a highly visible Church leader, unleashed intense anti-Mormon sentiment, which had subsided after statehood. Within a year of his election, more than 3,100 petitions arrived in Washington, D.C., protesting his seating and creating a furor that forced the Senate to examine the case. The prosecution focused on two issues: Smoot's alleged polygamy and his expected allegiance to the Church and its ruling hierarchy, which, it was claimed, would make it impossible for him to execute his oath as a United States senator. Although the proceedings focused on senator-elect Smoot, it soon became apparent that it was the Church that was on trial.

The case opened with Church leaders subpoenaed to testify as to the power the Church exerted over its members in general and over General Authorities in particular. Investigators probed into past and present polygamous relationships of leaders and lay members alike. They raised questions on points of doctrine that affected how Church members and their leaders interacted with American society at large.

Some of the testimony revealed situations and circumstances that put the Church in an unfavorable light. President Joseph F. SMITH received especially harsh treatment in cross-examination. Some members of the Quorum of the Twelve refused to testify, which increased the hostility of senators already concerned about the Church's motives and conduct. Faced with intense pressure, Church leaders accepted the resignations of apostles Matthias Cowley and John W. Taylor, who were rumored to have performed plural marriages after the Manifesto. To further evidence good faith, in the annual April conference of 1904 President Smith issued a "Second Manifesto" that added ecclesiastical teeth to the Manifesto of 1890. Excommunication would now follow for those who refused to relinquish the practice of plural marriage.

Despite some damaging testimony, Senator Smoot gradually won support for three reasons. First, his character was found to be above reproach, and charges against him and the Church proved groundless. Second, U.S. President Theodore Roosevelt was sympathetic to Smoot's position; his motivation was partly personal but also political, as Senator Smoot and a Republican Utah were important to him. Third, the defense convinced a majority of senators that Smoot's apostleship would not impair his ability to put the oath of the senator first in executing his responsibilities.

The victory for Elder-Senator Smoot was a victory for the Church, providing the political legitimacy it had been seeking since 1850. It also launched a thirty-year career in the Senate that saw Senator Smoot reach the pinnacle of political success as one of the two or three most powerful senators in America during the 1920s. Perhaps more than any other individual, Reed Smoot molded and shaped the positive national image the Church was to enjoy throughout the twentieth century.

BIBLIOGRAPHY

Alexander, Thomas G. *Mormonism in Transition: A History of the Latter-Day Saints, 1890–1930.* Chicago, 1986.

Heath, Harvard. "Reed Smoot: The First Modern Mormon." Ph.D. diss., Brigham Young University, 1990.

Merrill, Milton R. *Reed Smoot: Apostle in Politics.* Logan, Utah, 1990.

United States Senate, Committee on Privileges and Elections. *In the Matter of the Protests Against the Right of Hon. Reed Smoot, A Senator from the State of Utah to Hold His Seat,* 4 vols. Washington, D.C., 1904–1906.

HARVARD S. HEATH

SNOW, ELIZA R.

Dubbed "Zion's poetess" by Joseph Smith, Eliza Roxcy Snow (1804–1887) is still noted widely for her hymn-texts, ten of which are included in the 1985 LDS Hymnal (*see* HYMNS AND HYMNODY). Of those, "O My Father," written in Nauvoo in 1845 and sung to various tunes since its first publication, is one of Mormondom's favorites. Her poems "How Great the Wisdom and the Love" and "Though Deepening Trials" are also sung frequently. Her most significant legacy, however, was not her poetry but her 1867 assignment to organize RELIEF SOCIETIES throughout the Church, and her involvement in the organization of the Young Ladies Mutual Improvement Association

Eliza Roxcy Snow (1804–1887), second general president of the Relief Society (1866–1887), was one of the most influential women in Utah in the nineteenth century. She was sealed to Joseph Smith and a wife to Brigham Young. Known as "Zion's poetess," she wrote many poems and hymns. She presided over ordinances for women in the Endowment House and served on the boards of the Deseret Hospital and civic organizations. Courtesy Rare Books and Manuscripts, Brigham Young University.

(later YOUNG WOMEN), the PRIMARY Association, and other economic and ecclesiastical movements. She was unchallenged in her position as "captain of Utah's woman-host."

She is described by her contemporaries as being of average height, and delicate in appearance. In her sixties she seemed to observers to be as young as forty, despite the fact that her dark brown hair was silvered with gray. She had dark eyes and a high forehead, and she habitually wore a cap over her center-parted hair and dangling earrings. Her manner was quiet and dignified. She was simple in her attire, calm, ladylike, and rather cold, observed several of her contemporaries. At age seventy, her now wrinkled face appeared to many to be stern. Most remarkable are the descriptions of her in her eighties, however, revealing a woman with mental faculty in full vigor, industrious beyond her physical strength, and tireless as a woman half her age. Throughout her life she was perceived as neat and orderly, with "old school" manners. Where her detractors saw her as outrageously bigoted, her friends admired her precision and enthusiasm in defense of her faith.

Born in Becket, Berkshire County, Massachusetts, on January 21, 1804, Eliza Roxcy (most often Eliza R. or misspelled Roxey) Snow was raised from her second year in Mantua, Portage County, Ohio. Her father, Oliver Snow, of Becket, and mother, Rosetta Pettibone, of Simsbury, Connecticut, along with daughters Leonora and Eliza, and family members on both sides, were 1806 pioneers to Connecticut's "Western Reserve" in northeastern Ohio. They cleared a good farm and in 1814 built one of Mantua's first permanent homes. Oliver was a town and county official, and Eliza, as she matured, served often as his secretary.

A precocious child, Eliza was gifted in language, reading, and writing beyond her years. Her earliest publications, odes in the neoclassical style of the century past, indicate wide knowledge of the literary masters, Shakespeare, Milton, and the ancients. "Trained to the kitchen," as she later wrote in her autobiography, she was skilled in domestic arts as well. She completed an education in the local grammar school; unlike her younger brother Lorenzo SNOW, however, she did not attend secondary schools.

Eliza claimed to have had suitors as a young woman, yet did not marry in Ohio. A member of the Reformed Baptist congregation of Sidney RIGDON, she was, with her family, introduced to Joseph Smith within a year of his arrival in Ohio. Not until 1835 did she follow her mother and older sister into the new faith, she having had first to "prove all things." Shortly after her baptism she moved to KIRTLAND, where she lived in the household of Joseph and Emma SMITH. There she taught a school for their children and others. She witnessed and recorded the dedication of the KIRTLAND TEMPLE, purchased land, and brought her family to Kirtland, but was, with them, compelled to move with the Saints to Missouri.

Settling in ADAM-ONDI-AHMAN, north of Far West, the Snows stayed only nine months before they were forced to leave with the migration to Illinois. There the family was split three ways: Lorenzo had gone on a mission through the southern states; the parents and younger boys moved to LaHarpe; and Eliza with Leonora and her two daughters stayed in Quincy. The local newspaper, the *Quincy Whig*, published several of Eliza's verses in defense of the Saints.

On invitation from Sidney Rigdon, Eliza moved to what would become NAUVOO, again to teach a school. Though Father Snow eventually came to Nauvoo, he soon became disaffected from the Church and took his remaining family to settle in Walnut Grove, Illinois, where he and Rosetta died.

Left alone in Nauvoo, Eliza continued to publish verses in the several Latter-day Saint newspapers. When in March 1842 the women's Relief Society was organized, she was invited first to draft its bylaws, and then to be its secretary. At the discontinuance of that organization in 1844, she was custodian of the minute book. That record would prove invaluable as a guide to the reorganization of the Relief Society in Utah in the 1860s, containing as it did reports of the Prophet Joseph Smith's instructions to the women.

Less than ten weeks after the founding of the Nauvoo Relief Society, on June 29, 1842, Eliza Snow was sealed as a plural wife to Joseph Smith, and lived for six months in the Smith home (*see* PLURAL MARRIAGE). Again she taught a school, which included the Smith children. Following the death of Joseph, by which time she was living in the attic room of the Stephen Markham home, she was married "for time" to President Brigham YOUNG. She never took President Young's name, however, and at his death claimed the name—and was buried as—Eliza Roxcy Snow Smith.

With the Markhams, and later with the Robert Peirce family, she made her way across the plains in the pioneer migration to the Great Basin. The winter that divided the two seasons of travel she spent at WINTER QUARTERS, Nebraska, much of it in ill health. Recovering, she found a place in the network of "leading sisters," those wives and daughters of the leaders of the Church who would, in years to come, direct the activities of LDS women in the Utah settlements. Traveling with the "big company," she arrived in the Salt Lake Valley on October 9, 1847.

Little is known of her activities in her first decade in Utah. Susa Young GATES, who knew her later, wrote that she was ill with tuberculosis, from which she recovered in the late 1850s; other indications suggest something less severe. During the first two decades in Utah she wrote and compiled poetry until she had enough for two volumes. The first, *Poems: Religious, Historical, and Political*, was published in Liverpool in 1856. Eliza Snow's reputation as poet and thinker made her the center of a female intelligentsia in Utah society. In 1854, she and her brother Lorenzo founded a Polysophical Society, where a select group of friends met regularly to perform for and address one another. Some of her most thoughtful writings were composed for those occasions. The assembly displeased some Church authorities, and so was discontinued in 1856.

The same year as the founding of the Polysophical Society, Relief Societies sprang up in various Salt Lake City wards, later to be encouraged by Brigham Young. Eliza Snow was herself only peripherally involved in the movement, and only in her own Eighteenth Ward. The reborn societies were interrupted by the Utah War (*see* UTAH EXPEDITION), however, and few survived.

In December 1866, following the Civil War, President Young once more saw need for the women to be organized, and called Eliza R. Snow to "head up" the movement, this time on an all-Church basis. Thus began the Relief Society as it has continued to the present: a central board setting directions to be followed by stake and ward officers wherever the Church has members. Loosely organized at first, the movement took advantage of existing networks of women until lines of responsibility were firmly established. Always at the center was "Sister Snow," or "Aunt Eliza," visiting or sending envoys to the various settlements to instruct, aid, and encourage. The Cooperative Junior and Senior Retrenchment Association, established in 1869 to promote frugality and HOME INDUSTRY, served as an early central meeting place for the sisters, meeting semimonthly in the Fourteenth Ward meetinghouse. It was replaced gradually by more directed organizations.

Included under her direction as "presidentess" of the women's organizations were, by 1884, the Relief Society, Young Ladies Mutual Improvement Association, and Primary Association, all of which she helped found. She also held responsibility for the women's work of the ENDOWMENT HOUSE, and sat on an advisory board of the WOMAN'S EXPONENT, the semimonthly newspaper edited for Mormon women by Lula Greene [Richards] and Emmeline B. Wells.

Various ad hoc projects came under Eliza Snow's direction: the encouragement of women to attend medical schools and then to offer classes in practical nursing and midwifery (*see* MATERNITY AND CHILD HEALTH CARE); the celebration of the United States Centennial by the preparation of handicrafts, later sold in the Ladies' Commission Store; the preparation, with Edward Tullidge, of a manuscript later published in New York as *Women of Mormondom*; and the establishment of the DESERET HOSPITAL, the first to be founded by the Latter-day Saints.

In addition to all of her public efforts, Eliza Snow carried on her private projects. She wrote, or edited, and published nine books, including her two poetry volumes, a biography of her brother Lorenzo, a collection of letters from her 1872–1873 tour of Europe and the Holy Land, and five instructional books for children.

Revered in her own time, she was honored during her many visits to the settlements of the Saints by feasts, celebrations of her birthday, odes in her praise, and invitations to address meetings of both men and women. Accounts of her healings, blessings, and prophesies are extant; her instructions to the women were accepted as binding. There was no intended exaggeration in the Kanab Relief Society's 1881 acknowledgment of her position as president "of all the feminine portion of the human race" and as "leading Priestess of this dispensation" (*Woman's Exponent* 9 [Apr. 1, 1881]:165), and Primary children two decades after her death in 1887 were encouraged in reverence for "the prophet, the priesthood, and Eliza R. Snow."

BIBLIOGRAPHY

Autobiographical writings:

Three holograph diaries and a brief autobiography are extant, two diaries at the Huntington Libraries, San Marino, Calif., one at the LDS Church Archives, and the autobiography at the Bancroft Library, Berkeley, Calif.; they have been published, in greater or lesser completeness, in the following places: Trail journals, 1846–1849, serially in the *Improvement Era*, in 1943–1944; "Sketch of My Life" in *Relief Society Magazine*, March to October 1944; also in part in Edward Tullidge, *Women of Mormondom* (New York, 1877). Parts of the trail journals are found, with other writings, in *Eliza R. Snow: An Immortal* (Salt Lake City, 1957). The Nauvoo diary and notebook, 1842–1844, are published as "Eliza R. Snow's Nauvoo Journal" in *BYU Studies* 15 (Summer 1975):391–416.

Publications by Eliza R. Snow:

Poems, Religious, Historical, and Political, 2 vols. Liverpool, 1856, and Salt Lake City, 1877.

Correspondence of Palestine Tourists . . ., edited. Salt Lake City, 1875.

Biography and Family Record of Lorenzo Snow. . . . Salt Lake City, 1884.

Publications about Eliza R. Snow:

Beecher, Maureen Ursenbach. "The Eliza Enigma." *Dialogue: A Journal of Mormon Thought* 11 (Spring 1978):30–43.

———. "'The Leading Sisters': A Female Hierarchy in Nineteenth Century Mormon Society." *Journal of Mormon History* 9 (1982):26–39.

———. "Leonora, Eliza, and Lorenzo: An Affectionate Portrait of the Snow Family." *Ensign* 10 (June 1980):64–69.

———; Linda King Newell; and Valeen Tippetts Avery. "Emma and Eliza and the Stairs." *BYU Studies* 22 (Winter 1982):87–96.

Madsen, Carol Cornwall, and Susan Staker Oman. *Sisters and Little Saints: One Hundred Years of Primary.* Salt Lake City, 1979.

Mulvay-Derr, Jill, and Susan Staker Oman. "The Nauvoo Generation: Our First Five Relief Society Presidents." *Ensign* 7 (Dec. 1977):36–43.

Terry, Keith, and Ann Terry. *Eliza.* Santa Barbara, Calif., 1981.

MAUREEN URSENBACH BEECHER

SNOW, LORENZO

Lorenzo Snow (1814–1901) was the fifth President of The Church of Jesus Christ of Latter-day Saints, from 1898 to 1901. A well-educated and refined man, he served many missions for the Church, traveling to England, Italy, and the Pacific, as well as in the southern and northwestern United States. Coming to the presidency when the Church suffered under a crushing weight of debt, President Snow reinvigorated tithe-paying among the Saints and put the Church on the road to financial solvency.

Born on April 3, 1814, the oldest son of Oliver and Rosetta Pettibone Snow, Lorenzo was the fifth of seven children. He grew to manhood in Mantua, Portage County, Ohio, where his parents had established themselves as leaders in the community. His father's public duties often took him from home, so the responsibility of the farm fell to Lorenzo and his younger brothers. Bookish by nature, Lorenzo pursued his education beyond the common schools in Mantua to the high school in nearby Ravenna, and completed one term at newly founded Oberlin College.

The family were Baptists with broad religious interests. While Lorenzo was in his teens, the Prophet Joseph SMITH took up residence in Hiram, four miles from the Snow farm. Although Lorenzo's sister Eliza, in her biography of him, claims to have whetted his interest in Mormonism while he was at Oberlin, his own account tells of hearing the Book of Mormon being read in his home in Mantua and of later meeting with the Prophet at Hiram in 1831. Contrary to the common accusations that Joseph Smith was a "false prophet," Lorenzo judged him to be "honest and sincere." He later said that at that time "a light arose in my understanding which has never been extinguished" (*IE* 40 [Feb. 1937]:82–83; Lorenzo Snow journal, Church Archives).

Lorenzo's mother, his two oldest sisters, and probably his father were soon baptized into the Church, but Lorenzo left for Oberlin uncommitted. A chance meeting with David W. PATTEN, an apostle, provided further information on the new Church, and as the young scholar began his work at Oberlin, he lost favor among the students and faculty by arguing in defense of Mormonism. Seeing an opportunity to continue his studies in Kirtland, he joined his two sisters there and on June 19, 1836, was baptized. He soon after received a manifestation that confirmed for him "a perfect knowledge that God lives, that Jesus Christ is the Son of God, and of the restoration of the holy Priesthood, and the fulness of the Gospel" (Smith, pp. 7–8). That conviction directed his actions for the remainder of his life.

Giving up his plans for further formal education, Lorenzo set out on a series of missions for the Church in early spring 1837, first to the Mantua area, where he baptized some of his friends and relatives, and then to other Ohio counties before returning to Kirtland. In 1838 the Snows joined the Saints in Missouri, and Lorenzo left for another mission, this time to Illinois and Kentucky. While the Saints settled Nauvoo and his parents moved farther on, to Walnut Grove, Illinois, Lorenzo went as a missionary to England.

Elder Snow taught in and around Birmingham for three months, during which time he baptized people in Greet's Green and organized a branch in Wolverhampton. In February 1841 the twenty-six-year-old missionary was called to preside over the ten established branches in London. He returned to Nauvoo in 1843 as leader of a shipload of 250 converts. En route, Elder Snow's quiet confidence, his healing of a dying steward, and the faith of his company of Saints led to the baptism of the ship's first mate and several of the crew. The party arrived in Nauvoo on April 12, 1843.

Lorenzo Snow (1814–1901) joined the Church in Kirtland, Ohio, in 1836. In 1840 he had a spiritual manifestation of the pathway of God and man, and he penned the famous couplet which expresses that revelation: "As man now is, God once was: As God now is, man may be." He was ordained an apostle in 1849. Courtesy Rare Books and Manuscripts, Brigham Young University.

In accordance with the revelation on plural marriage, Snow married Charlotte Squires, Mary Adaline Goddard, Sarah Ann Prichard, and Harriet Amelia Squires before leaving Nauvoo in the 1846 exodus. On the way west, the family had to stop at Mt. Pisgah, Iowa, because of his illness. Two of his three children born there survived. Called to preside over the temporary settlement, Snow actively raised money to assist the Saints in the move west. The family moved on to Salt Lake City in 1848.

On February 12, 1849, Lorenzo Snow was ordained a member of the Quorum of the Twelve Apostles. Assigned that summer to direct the first celebration of the Saints' entry into the Salt Lake Valley, Elder Snow established a reputation for pageantry as a way of building morale and group identity. For decades afterward, settlements throughout the Church followed his lead in celebrating significant events.

At the October 1849 conference, Elder Snow was assigned to fill a mission in Italy. Traveling with the first company of missionaries from Utah, he went first to England and there determined by study and by "a flood of light" that the work should begin among the Waldenses in the Piedmont area of northern Italy. He and his companions were successful in bringing several Waldensian converts to Utah, but the mission itself did not remain active. Snow extended the work to Switzerland, left missionaries there, and sent two more to India. Returning to Britain, he superintended the publication of an Italian translation of the Book of Mormon. Crossing France once more, he visited Switzerland and the Piedmont and concluded his mission in Malta.

After an absence of nearly three years, Elder Snow returned to Utah, arriving July 30, 1852, to discover that his wife Charlotte had died in his absence. He was immediately caught up in community activities. He organized the Polysophical Association to promote cultural refinement for the community. That fall, he was elected to the Utah legislature, where he served with distinction for twenty-nine years, ten of them as president of the Legislative Council.

In 1853, Elder Snow was called to lead a colonization group of fifty families and preside over the Saints in Box Elder County, Utah, headquartered in a struggling settlement of modest adobe huts later known as Brigham City. He established a dramatics society, a public school system, and the Brigham City Mercantile and Manufacturing Association, with forty departments. The association, a branch of the united order, became the most successful cooperative in the territory; its production for 1875 was valued at $260,000.

In 1864, Elder Snow accompanied four other missionaries on a short-term mission to the Sandwich (Hawaiian) Islands. He drowned when their small boat capsized in Lahaina Harbor but was restored to life when his friends were impressed to perform mouth-to-mouth resuscitation, a procedure unknown at that time. On Lanai the elders excommunicated the self-appointed Hawaiian mission president, Walter Murray Gibson, for organizing a new church, selling priesthood offices to men and women, and usurping Church property.

After all these missions abroad, still more were to come. Eight years later, Elder Snow accompanied George A. Smith, a member of the First Presidency, and others to Palestine, where, on the Mount of Olives, they blessed the land to be fruitful and dedicated the country for the return of the JEWS. In 1885 he served a short-term mission among the Native Americans in the Pacific Northwest.

Shortly after his return to Utah, Snow was tried and imprisoned for violation of the 1882 Edmunds Act, which prohibited the practice of polygamy. The territorial governor, Caleb W. West, promised amnesty if he would renounce plural marriage, but Elder Snow replied, "I thank you, Governor, but having adopted sacred and holy principles for which we have already sacrificed property, home and life on several occasions, . . . we do not propose, at this late hour, to abandon them because of threatened danger" (Romney, p. 381). He remained in prison for eleven months before being released under mandate of the U.S. Supreme Court.

Elder Snow radiated a purity and holiness that were extraordinary. He dedicated the Manti Temple in south-central Utah in 1888. Rhoda W. Smith, who was present, wrote, "When Apostle Lorenzo Snow arose, a beautiful heavenly light enveloped his head and shoulders; he looked angelic" (Spiritual Manifestations in the Manti Temple, *Millennial Star*, 50, Aug. 13, 1888, p. 522).

About the time of his conversion as a young man, Elder Snow had been promised an ancient apostolic power by Joseph Smith, Sr.: "If expedient the dead shall rise and come forth at thy bidding" (Romney, p. 406). In 1891, he restored life to a young woman, Ella Jensen, after she had been dead for two hours.

During the April 1889 general conference, Lorenzo Snow was sustained as President of the Quorum of the Twelve Apostles. He became the first president of the Salt Lake Temple in 1893, and on September 13, 1898, at age eighty-four, he was sustained as the fifth President of the Church. Worried about his advanced age, he pleaded for a manifestation of divine will. He testified that the Lord appeared to him in the Salt Lake Temple and affirmed that he should serve and that he should immediately reorganize the First Presidency (pp. 677–79). The reorganization took place without the

"**He that judgeth a Matter before he heareth it is not wise.**"*Solomon.*

THE

LATTER-DAY SAINTS

MEET FOR

Public Worship,

In the Room under that lately occupied by the Socialists,

Well Lane,

Allison-street, Birmingham,

Every Sabbath Morning at Half-past Ten, and in the Evening at Half-past Six o'Clock.

ALSO ON TUESDAY AND THURSDAY EVENINGS, at Half-past SEVEN o'Clock each Week.

LECTURES

WILL BE DELIVERED BY

ELDERS

A. CORDON & L. SNOW.

The Inhabitants of Birmingham are respectfully invited to attend.

The First Principles of the Everlasting Gospel in its Fulness, The Gathering of Israel, The Second Coming of

THE SAVIOUR.

And the Restitution of all things spoken of by all the Holy Prophets, will be among the Subjects Illustrated.

"THE LATTER-DAY SAINTS' MILLENNIAL STAR," Published Monthly, and other Publications, can be had at No. 24, PARK STREET.

Thomas Vale, Printer, Freeman-street, Birmingham.

A broadside announcing a lecture by Lorenzo Snow on the gospel, the gathering of Israel, and the second coming of the Savior. Birmingham, England, 1841.

lengthy interval that had followed the deaths of the first four Presidents of the Church and established a custom of immediate succession.

Another question firmly resolved by his succession was that seniority among the Twelve was determined not by chronological age but by date of ordination to the quorum.

Humble and self-effacing, President Snow told the Council of the Twelve, "I do not want this administration to be known as Lorenzo Snow's administration, but as God's in and through Lorenzo Snow" (*L.D.S. Biographical Encyclopedia*, Vol. 1, p. 30, Salt Lake City, 1901).

By 1898 the Church owed $2.3 million, an overwhelming burden of debt considering its resources. The major cause of debt was the U.S. government's escheat of Church properties under the provisions of the Edmunds-Tucker Act of 1887. Most of the Church's assets, including tithing funds, had been seized by federal agents. Many Saints reacted by curtailing financial donations; tithing receipts declined from more than $500,000 a year in the 1880s to about $350,000 in the 1890s.

The First Presidency consolidated debts, offered two $500,000 bond issues, and sold its controlling interest in many businesses. These measures, though helpful, were not sufficient. In 1899, President Snow, addressing the debt problem in a talk in the St. George (Utah) Tabernacle, received a spiritual manifestation: "This is the answer to our financial problems. Even though as a Church we are heavily in debt, I say unto you that, if this people will pay a full and honest tithing, the shackles of indebtedness will be removed from us" (*MFP* 3:322; see also Journal History entry for May 8, 1899). Carrying this message to the Saints throughout the territory, he stimulated a renewed commitment to tithing, and the Church's debt problems were resolved before he died.

As the new century dawned in 1901, President Snow stressed the worldwide mission of the General Authorities of the Church: "Here are the Apostles and the Seventies, their business is to warn the nations of the earth and prepare the world for the coming of the Savior" (*CHC* 6:377). He also encouraged the Saints in foreign lands to remain there and build up the Church rather than migrate to Salt Lake City.

President Snow spoke of introducing missionary work in Russia, Austria, and Latin America. He reopened the Mexican Mission and assigned Heber J. Grant of the Quorum of the Twelve Apostles to establish a proselytizing mission in Japan. Locally, young men were called to serve as stake missionaries of the Young Men's Mutual Improvement Association (YMMIA) to recommit youth to participation in the YMMIA (*see* YOUNG MEN).

Suffering from declining health, President Snow died of pneumonia in the Beehive House, the residence of the President, on October 10, 1901. At the time of his death, there were 50 stakes and 292,931 members in the Church, an increase of 10 stakes and 25,680 members during his three-year presidency.

Lorenzo Snow was small and slender in appearance. He stood five feet, six inches tall, weighed 140 pounds, and had tranquil gray eyes and a full beard. He was a scholar, schoolmaster,

Lorenzo Snow became the fifth President of the Church in 1898. He is remembered for his masterful leadership of the Brigham City United Order, his visionary prophetic gifts, and his reemphasis of the law of tithing following two difficult decades. Courtesy Rare Books and Manuscripts, Brigham Young University.

missionary, legislator, cooperative leader, financier, temple worker, and prophet. He had a profound effect upon Latter-day Saints and non-Mormons alike, with his heavenly countenance and sweet, gentle dignity. Meeting him for the first time, a Protestant minister said, "I was startled to see the holiest face I had ever been privileged to look upon. . . . The strangest feeling stole over me, that I stood on holy ground." Another minister said, "The tenor of his spirit is as gentle as a child. You are introduced to him. You are pleased with him. You converse with him, you like him. You visit with him long . . ., you love him" (Romney, pp. 14–16).

BIBLIOGRAPHY

Gibbons, Francis M. *Lorenzo Snow, Spiritual Giant, Prophet of God.* Salt Lake City, 1982.

Romney, Thomas C. *The Life of Lorenzo Snow, Fifth President of the Church of Jesus Christ of Latter-day Saints.* Salt Lake City, 1955.

Smith, Eliza R. Snow. *Biography and Family Record of Lorenzo Snow.* Salt Lake City, 1884.

Snow, Leroi C. "An Experience of My Father." *IE* 36 (Sept. 1933):677–79.

Swinton, Heidi S. "Lorenzo Snow." In *Presidents of the Church,* ed. Leonard J. Arrington. Salt Lake City, 1987.

Williams, Clyde J. *The Teachings of Lorenzo Snow, Fifth President of the Church of Jesus Christ of Latter-day Saints.* Salt Lake City, 1984.

MAUREEN URSENBACH BEECHER
PAUL THOMAS SMITH

SOCIAL CHARACTERISTICS

The major social characteristics and attitudes of Latter-day Saints in the United States, along with the challenges and problems they face, can be compared to those of other religious groups. Comparisons can be based on information that has been gathered about Latter-day Saints in the United States regarding their family characteristics, such as marriage, divorce, fertility, and sexual attitudes, as well as their social class, gender roles, substance use and health, political affiliation, attitudes toward social issues, religiosity, and migration.

SOURCES. Each year a random sampling of about 1,500 U.S. adults is interviewed in the National Opinion Research Center's Cumulative General Social Survey (NORC). From 1972 to 1988 this yielded a sample of 23,356, of whom 288 (1.2%) were LDS, a very small sample of the total Church population.

A supplemental source is the annual national survey of high school seniors conducted by Johnston, O'Malley, and Bachman (1988) for the National Institute on Drug Abuse (NIDA). They survey approximately 16,000 U.S. high school seniors each year regarding their lifestyles and substance use (62,570 students from 1984 to 1987). Beginning in 1984 they included "LDS" as one of the responses to the religion question (1.6% chose that response). These proportions of Latter-day Saints are similar to Stark's (1989) estimate that 1.6 percent of the population of the United States is LDS.

In addition, data on Church members have been published in various professional journals. Heaton and Goodman (1985) report information from a national, random sample of 1,500 Latter-day Saints and make comparisons with NORC data.

For comparisons in this article between Latter-day Saints and other religious groups, percentage differences larger than 5 percent are statistically significant.

MARRIAGE. Heaton and Goodman (1985) reported that 97 percent of Latter-day Saints over age thirty have married, which is higher than the marriage rate in the same category for Catholics, Protestants, or those with no religious affiliation. According to NORC data, a higher percentage of LDS Church members have been married than any other religious group. Eighty-nine percent of LDS adults have been married, compared to 87 percent of Protestants, 81 percent of Catholics, and 83 percent of Jews (Table 1).

AGE AT MARRIAGE. Latter-day Saints also tend to marry early. Forty-five percent of LDS women and 23 percent of LDS men have married by age nineteen. By age twenty-one 74 percent of LDS women and 49 percent of LDS men have married. This is considerably higher than for any other religious group (Table 1).

MARITAL HAPPINESS. Sixty-six percent of married Latter-day Saints say they are "very happy" in their marriages, compared with 65 percent of Protestants and Catholics and 57 percent of those with no religion. LDS women tend to report more marital happiness than other women, particularly Protestant and Catholic women. On the other hand, LDS men report lower levels of marital satisfaction than all other men except those with no religion (Table 1).

DIVORCE AND REMARRIAGE. The divorce rate is lower among Latter-day Saints than among Protestants, "other," and "none," but higher than among Catholics or Jews, as shown in Table 1. Eighteen percent of Mormons report that they have been separated or divorced, compared with only 11 percent of Catholics and 10 percent of Jews. In the survey of Latter-day Saints by Heaton and Goodman (1985), they reported that 17 percent had been divorced. NORC data for 1978, 1980, 1982, and 1983 showed considerably higher rates of divorce for the non-LDS or "other" religious groups than those shown in Table 1 (additional research is needed to resolve this discrepancy). After divorce, Latter-day Saints are more likely to remarry than persons from other religious groups (Heaton and Goodman, 1985).

TABLE 1. MARITAL CHARACTERISTICS BY RELIGIOUS AFFILIATION

				Religious Affiliation			
		Protestant	Catholic	Jew	Other	None	Mormon
Percent ever married		87	81	83	74	66	89
Percent married by 19	Female	49	37	24	34	40	45
	Male	18	12	3	13	18	23
Percent married by 21	Female	70	61	50	56	65	74
	Male	42	33	17	32	40	49
Percent "very happy" in marriage	Female	63	62	69	70	60	72
	Male	67	68	65	63	55	62
Percent ever divorced or separated		18	11	10	20	23	18
SAMPLE SIZE		14,678	5,809	515	368	1,626	288

Source: NORC pooled surveys for 1972–1988.

FERTILITY. Thornton (1979) found that Latter-day Saints in the United States and Canada have a high fertility rate. Although LDS fertility has decreased substantially during the twentieth century, it remains considerably higher than that of other religious groups. Heaton and Goodman (1985) found that LDS women average about one child more than women in other religious groups.

NORC data illustrate the relatively high rate of childbearing among Church members. More than 50 percent of Latter-day Saints have three or more children, compared with 36 percent of Catholics and 37 percent of Protestants. About one in five Church members has five or more children, compared with only one in ten among Protestants and Catholics. Only about 2 percent of Jews have five or more children.

Among all religious groups except Latter-day Saints, the ideal number of children is two. Forty-three percent of Catholics said that two is the ideal number of children, compared with only 23 percent of Latter-day Saints. More than 50 percent of

TABLE 2. RELIGION AND FERTILITY

				Religious Affiliation			
		Protestant	Catholic	Jew	Other	None	Mormon
Children ever born							
Percent with 3 or more children		37	36	21	25	20	52
Percent with 5 or more children		11	11	2	5	5	22
Ideal number of children							
Percent who say ideal number of children is . . .							
	2	50	43	49	54	56	23
	3	22	26	29	20	16	18
	4	14	15	7	8	12	26
	4 or more	22	26	16	19	17	54
SAMPLE SIZE		14,678	5,809	515	368	1,626	288

Source: NORC pooled surveys for 1972–1988.

TABLE 3. SEXUAL ATTITUDES AND RELIGION

| | Religious Affiliation | | | | | |
	Protestant	Catholic	Jew	Other	None	Mormon
Percent who said that . . .						
Premarital sex is always wrong	34	25	13	22	7	58
Extramarital sex is always wrong	76	71	46	43	58	90
Homosexuality is always wrong	77	67	33	55	40	90
SAMPLE SIZE	14,678	5,809	515	368	1,626	288

Source: NORC pooled surveys for 1972–1988.

Latter-day Saints said that the ideal number of children is four or more, compared with 26 percent of Catholics and 22 percent of Protestants (Table 2).

SEXUAL ATTITUDES. A greater percentage of Latter-day Saints disapprove of premarital sex, extramarital sex, and homosexuality than any other religious group. As shown in Table 3, 58 percent of the Latter-day Saints said that premarital sex is always wrong, compared with 34 percent of Protestants and 25 percent of Catholics. About three-fourths of Protestants and more than two-thirds of Catholics said that extramarital sex and homosexuality are always wrong, compared to 90 percent of Latter-day Saints.

SOCIAL CLASS. LDS Church members tend to be middle class in terms of education, occupation, and income. They tend to have somewhat fewer people in high-status occupations than Jews or those with no religion, but somewhat more than Protestants and Catholics.

EDUCATION. Eighteen percent of LDS women and 22 percent of LDS men in the NORC survey have graduated from college. This is significantly higher than the comparable percentages among Protestants and Catholics, but lower than among Jews and those with no religious affiliation. Fourteen percent of LDS men and 8 percent of LDS women have received graduate education. Jews and those with no religion have higher percentages, while Catholics and Protestants have lower percentages (Table 4).

OCCUPATION. The data on occupations are similar to the data on education. Among both men and women, Latter-day Saints have more professionals and managers than Catholics or Protestants but fewer than Jews or "others." They have fewer operative workers than any other religious group except Jews. LDS women are overrepresented among service occupations, with 25 percent in service occupations, compared with only 19 percent of Catholic women, the religion with the next highest percentage (Table 5).

INCOME. Table 6 gives a distribution of family income by religious affiliation. About one in five LDS families has an income less than $10,000 per

TABLE 4. EDUCATION BY RELIGION (IN PERCENT)

| | Religious Affiliation | | | | | |
	Protestant	Catholic	Jew	Other	None	Mormon
Women						
College graduate	12	11	35	17	25	18
Postgraduate	4	4	14	11	9	8
Men						
College graduate	17	19	52	37	27	22
Postgraduate	8	8	31	13	17	14

Source: NORC pooled surveys for 1972–1988.

TABLE 5. PERCENT IN SELECTED OCCUPATIONS BY RELIGION

			Religious Affiliation			
	Protestant	Catholic	Jew	Other	None	Mormon
Women						
Professional	15	15	25	19	23	23
Manager	7	7	16	8	12	8
Clerical	29	37	37	27	30	30
Operative	14	13	6	21	9	6
Service	19	16	5	15	15	25
Men						
Professional	14	16	35	26	21	17
Manager	14	14	26	19	11	16
Clerical	5	8	10	5	7	8
Operative	18	15	3	10	16	10
Service	8	8	3	10	8	7
SAMPLE SIZE	14,678	5,809	515	368	1,626	288

Source: NORC pooled surveys for 1972–1988.

year, while 15 percent earn more than $50,000 per year. The only religious group dramatically different from Latter-day Saints in income distribution is the Jewish: Almost half of Jewish families earn $50,000 or more, while less than 10 percent have incomes below $10,000. Although the differences are not large, Latter-day Saints have a few more middle-income families than the other religions. Thirty-nine percent of LDS families have incomes between $25,000 and $50,000, which is higher than for any of the other religious groups.

GENDER ROLES. Brinkerhoff and Mackie (1985) studied how religion is related to gender role attitudes among college students. They found that the more religious students tend to have more traditional attitudes. Those with no religion were the most egalitarian, followed by Catholics, Protestants, and Latter-day Saints.

As shown earlier in Table 4, LDS women are more likely to graduate from college than Catholic or Protestant women, but less likely than Jewish or nonaffiliated women. For graduate education the pattern was similar—a higher percentage of LDS than Catholic or Protestant women have received graduate education.

As shown in Table 5, LDS women are more likely to be employed in professional occupations than Catholic or Protestant women. Twenty-three percent of LDS women are employed in professional occupations, which is similar to Jewish women and women with no religious affiliation.

Respondents to the NORC survey were asked if they agreed or disagreed with the following statement: "A preschool child is likely to suffer if his or her mother works." Agreement with this statement is higher among Latter-day Saints than among any other religious group. As shown in

TABLE 6. FAMILY INCOME BY RELIGION (IN PERCENT)

			Religious Affiliation			
	Protestant	Catholic	Jew	Other	None	Mormon
Income level						
$0–9,999	26	15	10	29	18	22
10,000–24,999	33	34	17	23	33	24
25,000–49,999	30	36	24	34	34	39
50,000 or more	12	15	49	14	15	15
TOTAL	101	100	100	100	100	100
SAMPLE SIZE	14,678	5,809	515	368	1,626	288

Source: NORC pooled surveys for 1972–1988.

TABLE 7. PERCENT WHO STRONGLY AGREE THAT A PRESCHOOL CHILD IS LIKELY TO SUFFER IF HIS/HER MOTHER WORKS

			Religious Affiliation			
	Protestant	Catholic	Jew	Other	None	Mormon
Percent who strongly agree	13	16	14	8	15	22
SAMPLE SIZE	14,678	5,809	515	368	1,626	288

Source: NORC pooled surveys for 1972–1988.

Table 7, 22 percent of LDS strongly agree with the statement, compared with only 16 percent of Catholics and 13 percent of Protestants.

SUBSTANCE USE. LDS doctrine prohibits the use of alcohol, tobacco, and other addictive drugs. Among adults and adolescents, usage rates are considerably lower among Latter-day Saints than among other religious groups (Table 8). Only 28 percent of adult Latter-day Saints say they drink alcohol, compared with 65 percent of Protestants, 85 percent of Catholics, and 86 percent of Jews. Fourteen percent say they smoke tobacco, compared with 36 percent of Protestants, 38 percent of Catholics, and 28 percent of Jews.

The NIDA survey of substance use among high school seniors reveals substantial differences between Latter-day Saints and other religious groups (Table 8). About 33 percent of LDS high school seniors said they had used alcohol within the previous thirty days, compared to 62 percent of Protestants and 75 percent of Catholics. The percentage of LDS seniors who smoke is half as large as among the other religious groups—14 percent among LDS, 28 percent among Protestants, and 32 percent among Catholics. The differences for mari-

juana are not as large, but are still lower for LDS students. For example, 14 percent of LDS seniors had used marijuana during the past month, compared to 22 percent among Protestants and 25 percent among Catholics. LDS students also have low rates of cocaine use. Five percent had used cocaine during the past month, compared to 5 percent among Protestants, 7 percent among Catholics, and 8 percent among Jews.

HEALTH. Jarvis and Northcott (1986) observed that Latter-day Saints have longer life expectancy than non-LDS because of lower than average rates of cancer, heart disease, and infant deaths. Self-reported health of NORC respondents (Table 9) shows 85 percent of Latter-day Saints report that their health is good or excellent, which is higher than any other religious group. Only 3 percent of LDS rate their health as poor.

POLITICAL AFFILIATION. Stark (1989) reported that Utah is the most Republican state in the nation, judging from the fact that a higher percentage of people voted for Reagan there in 1984 than in any other state. Data on religion and political party affiliation confirm that Latter-day Saints strongly

TABLE 8. SUBSTANCE USE BY RELIGIOUS AFFILIATION

			Religious Affiliation			
	Protestant	Catholic	Jew	Other	None	Mormon
Adults						
Percent who drink alcohol	65	85	86	66	87	28
Percent who smoke	36	38	28	34	49	14
SAMPLE SIZE	14,678	5,809	515	368	1,626	288
High school seniors*						
Percent who drink alcohol	62	75	79	51	70	33
Percent who smoke	28	32	30	25	32	14
Percent who use marijuana	22	25	28	18	32	14
Percent who use cocaine	5	7	8	5	9	5
SAMPLE SIZE	29,949	18,704	914	3,642	7,046	972

*Percent who used during the past 30 days.
Source: Adults: NORC pooled surveys for 1972–1988.
Seniors: NIDA pooled surveys for 1984–1987.

TABLE 9. PERCEIVED HEALTH BY RELIGIOUS AFFILIATION (IN PERCENT)

| | Religious Affiliation | | | | | |
	Protestant	Catholic	Jew	Other	None	Mormon
Health						
Good or excellent	72	77	78	81	79	85
Fair	21	18	17	16	17	12
Poor	7	5	6	4	3	3
	100	100	101	101	99	100
SAMPLE SIZE	14,678	5,809	515	368	1,626	288

Source: NORC pooled surveys for 1972–1988.

favor Republicans. Almost half of Church members are Republicans, compared with only 27 percent of Protestants, 18 percent of Catholics, and 11 percent of Jews. Nineteen percent of Latter-day Saints say they are "strongly Republican" compared to only 10 percent of Protestants and 6 percent of Catholics. The percentage of people who are Democrats is smaller among LDS members than among any other religious group (Table 10). In 1984, 85 percent of Mormons voted for Reagan compared to 57 percent of Protestants, 57 percent of Catholics, and 41 percent of Jews.

ABORTION. Jews are the most accepting of abortion, while Latter-day Saints are the least accepting. Less than one-fourth of Latter-day Saints favor abortion if the reasons are lack of money, being unmarried, or not desiring the child. The next-closest group is the Catholics, and more than one-third of them favor abortion in the above-stated circumstances. Sixty-seven percent of Latter-day Saints favor abortion if the fetus is deformed, compared with 74 percent of Catholics and 96 percent of Jews. Almost 90 percent of Latter-day Saints favor abortion if the health of the mother is endangered by the pregnancy. This percentage is similar to most other religious groups, although Jews and

those with no religion have percentages of 97 and 95, respectively (Table 11).

DEATH PENALTY. A majority of Americans approve of the death penalty for murderers. Of the six religious groups shown in Table 11, Latter-day Saints show the greatest support for the death penalty while "others" give the least support. Eighty-nine percent of Latter-day Saints favor the death penalty compared to 67 percent of Protestants, 71 percent of Catholics, and 60 percent of "others."

LEGALIZATION OF MARIJUANA. Only one in ten Latter-day Saints supports the legalization of marijuana, compared with about two in ten among Protestants and Catholics. Forty-one percent of Jews and half of those with no religion favor legalization of marijuana.

RESIDENCE AND MIGRATION. Latter-day Saints are less likely than individuals from other religious groups to have grown up in a large city and somewhat more likely to have lived in "open country but not on a farm." Only 9 percent of Mormons were living in a large city at the age of sixteen, compared to 11 percent of Protestants, 22 percent of Catholics and 51 percent of Jews. Twenty percent of Mormons were living on a farm at sixteen,

TABLE 10. POLITICAL PARTY BY RELIGION (IN PERCENT)

| | Religious Affiliation | | | | | |
	Protestant	Catholic	Jew	Other	None	Mormon
Democrat	41	46	55	34	30	26
Independent	30	35	32	48	54	26
Republican	27	18	11	14	13	46
Other	2	1	2	4	3	1
Strongly Democrat	18	18	20	10	16	6
Strongly Republican	10	6	2	4	7	19
SAMPLE SIZE	14,678	5,809	515	368	1,626	288

Source: NORC pooled surveys for 1971–1988.

TABLE 11. PERCENT FAVORING ABORTION, DEATH PENALTY, AND LEGALIZATION OF MARIJUANA BY RELIGION

| | Religious Affiliation | | | | | |
	Protestant	Catholic	Jew	Other	None	Mormon
Abortion if . . .						
Endangered health	88	83	97	88	95	88
Rape	79	75	96	81	91	71
Defective fetus	79	74	96	80	91	67
Poor	45	40	85	61	74	24
Unmarried	41	37	85	53	71	24
Do not desire child	40	36	81	71	53	22
Death penalty	67	71	68	60	62	89
Legalization of marijuana	18	22	41	28	50	10
SAMPLE SIZE	14,678	5,809	515	368	1,626	288

Source: NORC pooled surveys for 1972–1988.

compared to 27 percent of Protestants, 10 percent of Catholics, and 11 percent of Jews.

Do certain religious groups tend to grow up and live in the same city or state? When Latter-day Saints become adults, do they tend to stay in the area where they were raised, or migrate elsewhere? NORC respondents were asked if they lived in the same city, same state, or a different state than they lived in at age sixteen (Table 12). Forty-one percent of Latter-day Saints lived in a state different from the one where they lived at age sixteen, while 31 percent lived in the same city as they did at age sixteen. In this, Latter-day Saints are not dramatically different from members of other religious groups. They appear somewhat more mobile than Catholics and Protestants in that a higher percentage live in a different state than they did at age sixteen.

When one compares various selected social characteristics of Latter-day Saints with other religious groups in the United States, one finds both similarities and differences. Latter-day Saints as a whole have higher rates than other religious groups with respect to marriage rates, rates of marital satisfaction, fertility, and life expectancy, as well as higher disapproval rates on sexual relations outside of marriage, abortion, and the legalization of marijuana. Latter-day Saints have fewer divorces than most Protestant groups, but more than Catholics and Jews; they tend to have higher rates of education, income, and occupational status than Protestants and Catholics, but typically lower rates in these respects than Jews.

BIBLIOGRAPHY

Brinkerhoff, Merlin B., and Marlene MacKie. "Religion and Gender: A Comparison of Canadian and American Student Attitudes." *Journal of Marriage and the Family* 47 (1985):415–29.

Heaton, Tim B., and Kristen L. Goodman. "Religion and Family Formation." *Review of Religious Research* 26 (1985):343–59.

Jarvis, George K., and Herbert C. Northcott. "Religion and Differences in Mortality." Mimeographed, Department of Sociology, University of Alberta, Edmonton, Alta., 1986.

Johnston, Lloyd D.; Patrick M. O'Malley; and Herald G. Bachman. *Illicit Drug Use, Smoking, and Drinking by America's*

TABLE 12. MIGRATION SINCE AGE 16 BY RELIGION

| | Religious Affiliation | | | | | |
	Protestant	Catholic	Jew	Other	None	Mormon
Current residence compared to residence at age 16						
Same city	43	46	38	30	41	31
Same state	26	25	20	21	23	28
Different state	32	29	42	50	36	41
TOTAL	14,678	5,809	515	368	1,626	288

Source: NORC pooled surveys for 1972–1988.

High School Students, College Students, and Young Adults: 1975–1987. Rockville, Md., 1988.

Stark, Rodney. *Sociology*, 3rd ed. Belmont, Calif., 1989.

Thornton, Arland. "Religion and Fertility: The Case of Mormonism." *Journal of Marriage and the Family* 41 (1979):131–42.

STEPHEN J. BAHR

SOCIAL AND CULTURAL HISTORY

[*For nineteenth-century beliefs and customs related more directly to worship, see* Pioneer Life and Worship.]
As a people, members of The Church of Jesus Christ of Latter-day Saints have over time taken on distinctive qualities as their beliefs and historical experience have given shape and force to their society. Indeed, geographers speak frequently of a "Mormon Culture Region" covering all of Utah and extending into neighboring states, with identifiable traits that set it apart. Observers have long seen LDS social organization as more coherent and tightly knit than most societies in the United States.

Several forces have shaped LDS cultural and social life. Belief in the GATHERING motivated most early converts to migrate to areas where they could live with other Saints. Joseph Smith urged

Saltair (c. 1920). This resort on the Great Salt Lake, west of Salt Lake City, was built by the Church in 1893 as a contribution to the greater community in the area. It burned in 1925 and was rebuilt a number of times thereafter, but is no longer standing. Photographer: Albert Wilkes. Courtesy Utah State Historical Society.

them, once gathered, to build homes in towns rather than on their farms, thus minimizing the physical distance between households and enhancing opportunities for social interaction (*see* CITY PLANNING). Joseph Smith founded programs to help build a more cohesive society and taught that cooperation was superior to individual enterprise. PRIESTHOOD power was extended to all the faithful, thus breaking down traditional class-based social hierarchies. The LDS belief that God inspired those acting in Church CALLINGS invested both local and general leaders with legitimacy at a time when authority in general was questioned widely among Americans. Priesthood office and Church position became a fluid alternative hierarchy, providing an effective mechanism for directing social and cultural change.

Other elements have combined with these to shape the distinctive aspects of LDS society. The Church did not, as did many rapidly growing Christian movements of the early nineteenth century, reject popular public entertainments. Indeed, excelling in fine arts, music, dance, drama, and other forms of cultural expression could be seen as a sacred obligation. Individual creative works were recognized and appreciated, but the more robust Mormon cultural expressions were those requiring unified action and cooperation. Moreover, the influx of immigrants—beginning in the 1840s from Great Britain and in the 1850s from Scandinavia—brought directly to Utah pioneer settlements institutions not as readily accessible to many other agrarian societies in the western United States.

Distinctive elements of social and cultural life in the first LDS areas—KIRTLAND, OHIO, and the various MISSOURI settlements—were related principally to religious activities. They included the designing and constructing of the KIRTLAND TEMPLE (1836), with Aaronic and Melchizedek pulpits that corresponded to priesthood organization; the writing of HYMNS expressing distinctive beliefs; the forming of a choir to sing LDS hymns at the dedication of the Kirtland Temple; and the founding of the SCHOOL OF THE PROPHETS to encourage both secular and religious learning. Popular amusements, vernacular architecture, and crafts were similar to those in other rural American districts, with the exception that horseracing and cardplaying were avoided. In the mid-1830s, the movement was as yet too young and the number of Latter-day Saints too few for either new doctrines or historical experience to have made them markedly different culturally from other Americans.

By the mid-1840s, however, some distinctive elements were becoming evident. Because earlier persecutions had reinforced a natural group solidarity, members looked inward and limited association with those not of their faith, whom they came to call GENTILES. Resulting isolation focused the process of selecting and adapting cultural and social forms from the greater society, making them more distinctive. NAUVOO, ILLINOIS, a temporary respite from persecution, saw the largest group "gathered" yet, further favoring the development of distinctive social and cultural institutions. The division of Nauvoo into political "wards" led eventually to a practice of dividing Church membership into geographically defined congregations called WARDS. The ward was to become a social institution of first importance—perhaps the most powerful single instrument of LDS social organization.

Nauvoo also saw the introduction of temple-related teachings and practices that had important implications for social and cultural life. BAPTISM FOR THE DEAD permitted Church members to be baptized as proxies for deceased ancestors; SEALINGS united husbands and wives through eternity; and the ENDOWMENT, another ordinance with eternal implications, also strengthened group commitment to building together the KINGDOM OF GOD. Celestial and PLURAL MARRIAGE, popularly called polygamy, was taught privately (publicly in 1852); with the LAW OF ADOPTION, plural marriage extended the concept of family to incorporate all of society.

Some left the Church over Nauvoo innovations. Those who embraced the restoration of these additional doctrines and ordinances found themselves farther from a Protestant Christianity that came to seem increasingly hostile. The result was even stronger identity and solidarity among those who accepted the teachings and endured the opprobrium they engendered.

Folk amusements in Nauvoo were those commonly found elsewhere in the United States. The city had bowling alleys and billiard halls. Men engaged in horsemanship and in personal contests, such as foot races and wrestling matches. Swimming, an early version of baseball called "Old Cat," and fencing were popular recreations.

Intellectual life was encouraged by lyceums, a debating society, a lending library, and art exhibits. The NAUVOO CHARTERS provided for a university, which administered the public school system and kept salient the hope of developing an LDS-controlled intellectual center for the Saints—a hope not realized until the founding in Utah of the UNIVERSITY OF DESERET (1850), BRIGHAM YOUNG UNIVERSITY (1875), and numerous ACADEMIES. The TIMES AND SEASONS (1839–1846) continued a tradition of LDS journalism that had begun in 1832 with the publication of the EVENING AND THE MORNING STAR in Missouri (1832) and in Ohio (1832–1834), and would culminate in founding the DESERET NEWS in 1850, which remains a Church-owned Salt Lake City daily newspaper.

Recent convert Gustavus Hills organized the Nauvoo Musical Lyceum in 1841. Partly through his efforts, choral music became so popular that in 1842 the women's RELIEF SOCIETY organized its own choir, as did several outlying settlements. These choirs continued throughout the Nauvoo period to sing a varied repertoire of religious, popular and even comedic songs, at both religious services and civic events. The first band to become an enduring institution was a twenty-piece ensemble, mostly percussion instruments and fifes. The band or other musicians provided music for the most popular entertainment in the city, dancing. Dances were held on every possible occasion and became an enduring feature of LDS social life. So important was music to the city's cultural life that in 1845 the Saints completed a Music Hall that would seat more than seven hundred persons.

In 1846 the Saints left Nauvoo for the West. That winter as many as 16,000 (by some estimates) gathered into settlements across Iowa and, especially, on both banks of the Missouri River (see WINTER QUARTERS). Band and choral music, and dancing, continued even in these severe circumstances. Though advance parties reached Utah the next year, the settlements on the river's east bank, centered in Kanesville (see COUNCIL BLUFFS), remained heavily LDS until 1852. This Iowa interlude (1846–1852) was of great importance in shaping LDS social and cultural institutions. Wards clearly became, for the first time, ecclesiastical jurisdictions with their own leaders and meeting schedules. Dancing, singing societies, and schools proliferated. The women, meeting frequently and informally, blessed and comforted one another and ministered to those needing assistance. Efforts were made to work the law of adoption and plural marriage into viable institutions that would enhance the cohesiveness of the larger COMMUNITY.

Perhaps most important, the FIRST PRESIDENCY was reorganized in December 1847, with Brigham YOUNG, just returned from the SALT LAKE VALLEY, being sustained in place of the martyred prophet. In Utah Brigham Young would take the lead in elaborating developments already begun in Nauvoo.

The earliest years of pioneering in Utah left little time for cultural and social activities beyond the perennial dancing, singing, and band music. But by 1852 the population was again sufficiently concentrated, this time in SALT LAKE CITY, to recommence the ambitious agenda begun in Nauvoo. That winter Church leader Lorenzo SNOW and his sister Eliza R. Snow organized the Polysophical Society, an informal discussion and debating society for men and women; comparable societies founded in many wards continued their activities throughout the decade. In 1853 a public lending library opened in the city. In 1852 Sicilian-born convert Domenico Ballo came to Salt Lake City with a band he had organized in St. Louis. The Ballo and the older William Pitt bands played, in addition to favorite hymns, such popular songs as "Auld Lang Syne," an occasional patriotic rendering of "Yankee Doodle" or "La Marseillaise," and selections from Mozart, Meyerbeer, and Rossini.

Choral music remained widespread and popular. In 1852 members revived the old Nauvoo choir. Because they performed first in the just-completed old adobe tabernacle and, after 1867, in a new TABERNACLE (which still graces TEMPLE SQUARE), it became known as the TABERNACLE CHOIR. Eventually the "Mormon Tabernacle Choir" became one of the two or three most widely recognized symbols of the Latter-day Saints. Its several hundred members from different backgrounds express themselves as a unified, harmonious whole—the epitome of LDS cultural expression. In 1929 the choir began regular weekly network radio broadcasts, which continue.

Cultural life in early Salt Lake City was not limited to music. The Deseret Dramatic Association, organized in 1852, first performed in the old Social Hall. The Social Hall housed musical performances, balls, and receptions as well as theatrical productions. It was superseded in 1862 by the SALT LAKE THEATRE, a lavish building seating 1,500 and constructed at some sacrifice, one of the important cultural institutions of the early west. The Deseret Dramatic Association maintained an

Actress Maude Adams was born in Salt Lake Valley in 1872. Her mother was a regular performer in the Social Hall and Salt Lake Theatre, for which her father furnished timber. Her career on stage in New York earned her a reputation for charm and naturalness. *Young Woman's Journal* 14 (June 1903):244–49. Photographer: Charles Ellis Johnson. Courtesy Rare Books and Manuscripts, Brigham Young University.

ambitious repertory schedule, in some seasons performing three times a week. A typical program began with prayer, featured a long, serious play, and ended with a short comedy or farce.

Dancing was popular throughout the territory, and every community prized its fiddlers. Most holidays ended with a grand ball that might last until two or three in the morning. "Square dances," ordered in prescribed patterns like the Virginia Reel, were the usual fare. An occasional risqué round dance such as the waltz was permitted as the century wore on. In Salt Lake City the Social Hall routinely hosted dances; larger affairs could be held at the Salt Lake Theatre, whose orchestra seats could be covered by a spring floor.

Architecture in Salt Lake City was for the most part spare, practical, and derivative. Greek Revival style, ordered and simple, was as popular in Utah as elsewhere in the United States. The Gothic Revival style can be seen in the SALT LAKE TEMPLE, and in other buildings, notably, Brigham Young's residence, the Lion House. The Federal-style architecture of public buildings the Saints had used in the Midwest was replicated in the city hall and other early civic structures. Homes were generally simple adobe or brick, built in traditional or pattern-book styles and sometimes reflecting the ethnic background of the owner. Such homes were commonly symmetrical, ornamented according to the combined tastes of owner and builder, and designed to look complete while awaiting the addition of a second story or wing as family needs and means permitted.

The considerable variety seen in houses was contained by a rigid city plan, an adaptation of principles Joseph Smith recommended in his 1833 "plat of the city of Zion" (see CITY PLANNING). The plan called for homes of adobe, rock, or brick on large city lots uniformly set back from the broad, square-surveyed streets. A central square was set aside for the TEMPLE, and streets were named for their direction and distance from it. In outlying towns the central square contained churches, schools, and other civic structures. Farm land was outside the town proper. Early visitors were invariably impressed with the neatness and order of Mormon towns, always noting, in addition to the street pattern, the gardens, and the clear, mountain water that ran in small ditches along the streets.

This general pattern was followed in remote villages as well as in Salt Lake City. The compactness of the village system made it possible to sustain, even in towns with as few as two hundred or three hundred citizens, a full complement of bands and choirs, theater groups, and the ubiquitous community dances. Church leaders were acutely conscious of the social consequences of such a settlement pattern, pointing out in an 1882 letter the "many advantages of a social and civic character which might be lost . . . by spreading out so thinly that intercommunication is difficult, dangerous, inconvenient and expensive."

Despite the stress on group activities, there were several fine ARTISTS in early Utah. These included William W. Major, an accomplished painter, and C. C. A. Christensen, trained at the Royal Academy in Denmark, who painted faith-promoting scenes from LDS history. Norwegian convert Danquart A. Weggeland also did excellent work, mainly in painting sets for the Salt Lake Theatre and scenes in LDS temples and MEETINGHOUSES. George M. Ottinger worked extensively with historical representations, portraits, and landscapes.

Landscape painting played a lesser role in Utah ART until, in the 1890s, John Hafen, Lorus Pratt, Edwin Evans, and John Fairbanks studied in Paris under Church sponsorship. They returned to devote their considerable talents to painting Church scenes adorning interiors of LDS temples. Alfred Lambourne and H. L. A. Culmer, also prominent landscape artists of this later period, emphasized the romantic qualities of Utah landscapes in a style worthy of the famous Rocky Mountain painters Albert Bierstadt and Thomas Moran. Since Latter-day Saints did not commonly use statuary in adorning church interiors, there was relatively little public demand for sculpture. Two early pieces are well known: the lion that dominated the entryway to Brigham Young's Lion House, and the eagle carved in 1859 by Ralph Ramsey for the entrance to Brigham Young's estate.

Early photographers Marsena Cannon, Charles W. Carter, Charles Savage, George Anderson, and Elfie Huntington did excellent work, often recording important events as well as everyday scenes in Utah folk life. The notable writers included Parley P. PRATT, Eliza R. SNOW, Hannah Tapfield King, and Sarah Elizabeth Carmichael. Most of their work was devotional poetry, often set to music to become part of the rich repertoire of LDS hymnody. Newspapers and magazines were published wherever opportunity permitted, including manuscript newspapers laboriously copied by hand and circulated from house to house in smaller towns. For a time the *Peep O'Day* (1864) served the literary set in the capital. Thousands of diaries and journals kept by individuals, recording the routine of their lives and their interpretation of the world about them, provide an often eloquent literary legacy.

There have been several distinct periods in LDS social and cultural life, each influenced by a different relationship between the Saints and the society around them. From 1847 to 1857 the LDS community was relatively small and undisturbed. Ward organizations played a secondary role to the

Salt Lake City Main Street, looking north from Fourth South Street (c. 1925). Photographer: Shiplers.

central community, and since almost all in Mormon communities were Church members, community endeavor was LDS endeavor. This began to change in 1857–1858 when the UTAH EXPEDITION brought a large non-Mormon military and freighting population to UTAH TERRITORY. During the 1860s, the Civil War and gold and silver strikes in Utah and the surrounding territories brought a continuous stream of new settlers. That decade culminated in the completion of the transcontinental railroad, forever ending earlier autonomy and isolation.

As a more secular Utah sprang up, the Latter-day Saints, also growing in numbers, found themselves for the first time unable to dominate all the central public institutions. They responded by changing the center of community life from the Salt Lake downtown area to the dozens of individual wards. Each ward began to foster a full range of religious, educational, social, economic, recreational, and cultural activities designed to keep the growing numbers of young within the fold. Ward grammar schools, for example, avoided the secu-

larization of public education, as did the later academies for secondary education.

Many wards founded cooperative stores as local outlets for the central Zion's Cooperative Mercantile Institution (ZCMI). In 1874 President Young took a dramatic step in founding the UNITED ORDER of Enoch, a regionwide economic plan aimed at placing production and distribution under community-owned cooperatives. Though almost every ward organized an order, the plan had an important economic effect in only a few localities. Nonetheless the effort indelibly impressed upon Latter-day Saints the understanding that they would one day live and work under a celestial economic order based on cooperation and sharing.

Beginning in 1849, individual wards founded SUNDAY SCHOOLS for children, their activities first coordinated on a Churchwide basis in 1872. The RETRENCHMENT ASSOCIATION for young women was begun in 1869—its name changing in 1875 to the Young Women's Mutual Improvement Association (YWMIA), a complement to the Young Men's Mutual Improvement Association (YMMIA), also founded that year. Both societies aimed to provide a full complement of cultural and recreational activities for LDS youth, thus shielding them from the influences of the outside world. Even younger children were brought into this net of concern with the founding of the PRIMARY organization in 1878, which held weekly recreational and instructional programs for children between the ages of three and eight (later raised to eleven). Beginning in 1867, Relief Societies were reinstituted throughout the Church. They provided women an organization for mutual assistance that was concerned with maternal and child health matters, administering to the needs of the poor, socializing, and adult education. Their leaders also published the WOMAN'S EXPONENT, which was discontinued in 1914 and replaced by the RELIEF SOCIETY MAGAZINE (1915–1970).

As these organizations proliferated, the Latter-day Saints were moving toward their ultimate confrontation with the federal government over plural marriage. By the end of the 1880s, the U.S. Congress had passed laws disincorporating the Church, taking over most of its properties, and disfranchising its women (see ANTIPOLYGAMY LEGISLATION). Faced with the destruction of the Church as an institution, in 1890 Church President Wilford WOODRUFF issued the MANIFESTO and began the process of better integrating the Saints into American society. Whereas in the 1860s Latter-day Saints had responded to the broader society by creating complete ward-centered societies, they now involved themselves in secular workplaces and civil governance, and sent their children to public schools. Ward schools fell into disuse, between 1913 and 1924 many Church-sponsored academies were closed, and ward stores were sold to private entrepreneurs.

Still, the Church remained committed to institutional responses that helped meet the needs of members in a changing world. Though they could not duplicate tax-supported public schools, they began in 1912 to build SEMINARY buildings near high schools, where Church-supported religious instruction (and social and recreational activities) could be offered to LDS youth. In the 1920s, they extended the same concept to higher education with the institute program (see CHURCH EDUCATIONAL SYSTEM). Leaders stressed as never before the importance of attending Church services regularly. They gave new emphasis to observance of the WORD OF WISDOM, a health code revealed in

1833, as a principal index of faithfulness and group identity. Determined to co-opt entertainments popular in the outside world, they sponsored parallel activities—they were always opened with prayer, were alcohol and tobacco free, and were carefully chaperoned. If in the secular world competition in SPORTS became popular, the Latter-day Saints would found their own leagues. If public dances were tempting youth, they would have more and better dances.

Through Mutual Improvement Associations (MIA), Relief Societies, Primary, and the various priesthood QUORUMS, ward BISHOPS administered a remarkable array of social and cultural activities, involving youth and adults in choirs, dancing, speech, drama, and sports. In 1895 the MIAs founded the "Mutual Improvement League," opening gymnasiums that sponsored athletic and fitness programs for men and women. After this league's demise, the YMMIA and the University of Utah built Deseret Gymnasium in 1910 to foster physical fitness in a wholesome environment.

As team sports became more popular in the broader society, the Church began to sponsor these activities within the wards as well. Beginning in 1901, Church leaders held a special "June conference" annually for the Mutual Improvement Associations. Leaders sponsored an athletic field day in connection with the 1904 conference, an event that continued for some years. By 1906 baseball, basketball, and track and field competitions were being held among the various wards, and in 1910 the General Board of the MIA set up a standing "Committee on Athletics and Field Sports."

One consequence of this Church sponsorship of athletics was the development of Churchwide tournaments and competitions. Young men of 17–24 years ("M-Men") held their first Churchwide basketball tournament in 1922 and added a softball tournament in 1934. Boys were at first not deemed physically capable of the strenuous sport of basketball, so a new sport, "Vanball," was invented, combining elements of basketball and volleyball; it was played in competition until the end of World War II. From World War II until the 1960s the Church held competitions at both senior and junior levels in basketball, softball, volleyball, and golf, with more than a thousand teams from the United States, Canada, and Mexico competing for the chance to play in all-Church tournaments. Tennis tournaments also were held in the 1950s, but were dropped partly because, as an individual sport, tennis was not the kind of "mass participation" activity the Church had generally favored.

Beginning with the exercise and fitness movement at the turn of the century, sports activities for young women somewhat paralleled those for young men but lagged behind a little. Young women participated fully in annual sports field days. Later came camping programs that, by 1950, saw as many as 20,000 girls certifying annually. Because wards and stakes had flexibility to meet local needs and interests, compared with young men's athletics, the girls' team program varied widely. A swimming achievement program and all-Church golf and tennis tournaments accommodated individual young women who wished to participate. Eventually young women competed in volleyball, softball, and basketball, and by the 1970s sports opportunities for young men and women were generally comparable.

In addition to social dances in ward meetinghouses, dance festivals with colorful pageantry became a common feature of June Conference. Beginning in the 1930s, "Road Show" competitions were held at STAKE and higher levels, the youth of each ward (with leaders) preparing an original fifteen-minute musical that could quickly be moved from meetinghouse to meetinghouse, so that members of each congregation could enjoy an evening of theatricals in their own neighborhood. Youth also competed for local, stake, and general awards in speech.

The primary site for all of these activities was the local ward MEETINGHOUSE. In one sense the home became a place from which the Saints commuted to their main center of socializing and worship—the ward meetinghouse. Ward activities occupied at least some family members part of virtually every day of the week, much of Saturday, and most of Sunday. Because Latter-day Saints learned to see the meetinghouse as the primary place for socializing, it was difficult for those not part of the ward to become part of their world.

Though the ward still remains the center of social and cultural life for committed Latter-day Saints, since the 1960s Church leaders have initiated changes that have diminished its role as the focal point of LDS neighborhoods and communities. A consolidated meeting schedule greatly reduced the amount of time spent at the meetinghouse. A more restricted definition of Church purposes, "to spread the gospel, perfect the Saints, and redeem the dead," called into question the relevance of Church-sponsored cultural and social activities not contributing to these aims. Reallocating TITHING funds to pay ward expenses reduced the need to cooperate in fundraising events to pay for socials and other activities. With both construction and maintenance of buildings managed by centrally funded contract, meetinghouses were no longer a product of community labor and sacrifice. At the same time, Churchwide competitions in speech, drama, and athletics were discontinued, leaving strong regional competition in some areas and perhaps less incentive for good local programs in others.

Church leaders saw gains in these new initiatives that would outweigh the losses. The great sacrifices members had made to sustain the many ward and Church programs would be reduced. There would also be a better distribution of Church resources, with more equality across geographical and class lines. Though the Saints in heavily LDS Utah might have a leaner program, members in developing areas could have more.

Latter-day Saints have proudly borne the stamp of being "a PECULIAR PEOPLE," an identity that helped maintain the energy and commitment that characterized the classic, close-knit ward community. Some observers feel that this cohesive sense of community is the genius of LDS society. Latter-day Saints face the challenge of maintaining that cohesiveness and their sense of special identity and mission in a complex, changing world. Bereft of many occasions when the Saints traditionally were brought together to worship, work, and play, LDS society must continue to adjust or it could lose its focus. Drawn out of the broader society by faith in the Restoration, early Latter-day Saints learned to select and adapt cultural and social forms upon which they put a distinctive and compelling stamp. As the Church expands internationally, that process must continue. The challenge facing the Church in the twenty-first century is to find ways to maintain that energy and develop that sense of identity among peoples of diverse cultures throughout the world.

BIBLIOGRAPHY

No comprehensive study exists of the social and cultural history of the Latter-day Saints. Much useful material can be gleaned from studies of particular periods of LDS history; see bibliographies accompanying HISTORY OF THE CHURCH entries. See also bibliographies for articles on Education, Music, Dance, Sports, Art, Artists, Sculpture, and Drama. Also helpful is

Davis Bitton, "Early Mormon Lifestyles; or the Saints as Human Beings," in *The Restoration Movement: Essays in Mormon History*, ed. F. Mark McKiernan et al. Lawrence, Kans., 1973.

DEAN L. MAY

SOCIALIZATION

In general, socialization refers to the processes used to internalize the ways of a particular group in order to function therein (Elkin and Handel, p. 4). In this light, LDS socialization faces a number of challenges in the contemporary world, notably in aiding its members to observe a health code (*see* WORD OF WISDOM); to oppose all forms of premarital and extramarital sexual behavior (*see* CHASTITY); to spend two years at their own expense in MISSIONARY work; and in the face of social pressures to the contrary, to have large families—generally two more children than the national average (Heaton; Thomas, 1983).

Many processes that lead to effective socialization within the LDS culture are similar to those found in American culture generally. Mormon parents are similar in many respects to other American parents, including the love and support they express to their children and the nurturing and disciplinary controls they exercise within the family (Kunz; Thomas, 1983). Nevertheless, some researchers contend that Latter-day Saints are more effective than some other groups in socializing their members to accept specific group values and behavior (Christensen; Smith). Some hints at possible reasons may be found in the degree to which LDS families participate in home religious observance (family prayer, SCRIPTURE STUDY, and FAMILY HOME EVENING).

The influence of home religious observance is perhaps best understood through research conducted by the Church on young men between the ages of twelve and eighteen. It found that home religious observance is a reliable predictor of what an adolescent's private religious observance (individual prayer, study of the scriptures, etc.) will be. Home religious observance also somewhat predicts public religious observance, but only half as accurately as does private religious observance. In turn, private religious observance is the single best predictor of a young man's internalizing religious goals and values specific to the LDS lifestyle, such

as serving a mission for the Church, temple marriage, premarital chastity, and Church activity (Thomas, Olsen, and Weed). Having these as part of one's future plans is the best predictor of both private and public religious behaviors during the young adult years, ages twenty to twenty-eight (Roghaar).

This research also indicates that LDS male adolescents decide at a relatively young age on a general lifestyle that either includes or excludes plans to serve a mission or marry in the temple. In interviews, many said they could not remember when they made their mission decision but that it was a long time ago. Some said it was made before baptism (eight years of age). Thus, many adolescents at an early time form a general view of themselves that either includes or does not include a mission, and then they construct a lifestyle consonant with that orientation.

Research shows that other dimensions of the young person's religious world are important to understanding LDS socialization. While Church programs such as participation or nonparticipation in AARONIC PRIESTHOOD activity, SCOUTING, and daily religious education (*see* SEMINARY) during the school year has limited direct effect on socialization outcome, independent of family influences, research shows that these programs can reinforce basic orientations and internalization of values begun in the family. Cornwall shows that religiously committed LDS families usually channel their children into seminary, which in turn influences their peer associations, who then reinforce the religious values held by the parents. Roghaar further shows the positive influence of seminary education by pointing out that children from Latter-day Saint families who do not participate extensively in Church-sponsored activities will more likely remain active as young adults if they do complete four years of religious education during their adolescent years.

During the expanding social world of the late adolescent years, the family influences tend to weaken, whereas the influence of an adult adviser who represents the religious organization increases. Indeed, the influence of these adult representatives of the Church often exceeds that of the family for late adolescents between the ages of sixteen and eighteen. The crucial dimension of this relationship between the adolescent and the adult seems to center on the degree to which the adolescent has association with an adult whom he or she respects, admires, wishes to emulate, and finds easy to talk to.

[*See also* Individuality; Values, Transmission of.]

BIBLIOGRAPHY

Christensen, Harold T. "Mormon Sexuality in Cross-Cultural Perspective." *Dialogue* 10 (Autumn 1976):62–75.

Cornwall, Marie. "The Influence of Three Agents of Religious Socialization: Family, Church, and Peers." In *The Religion and Family Connection: Social Science Perspectives*, ed. D. Thomas, pp. 207–31. Provo, Utah, 1988.

Elkin, F., and G. Handel. *The Child and Society: The Process of Socialization*, 3rd ed. New York, 1978.

Heaton, Tim B. "Four C's of the Mormon Family: Chastity, Conjugality, Children, and Chauvinism." In *The Religion and Family Connection: Social Science Perspectives*, ed. D. Thomas, pp. 107–24. Provo, Utah, 1988.

Kunz, Phillip R. "Religious Influences on Parental Discipline and Achievement Demands." *Marriage and Family Living* 25 (1963):224–25.

Roghaar, Bruce. "Young Men of Sound Understanding." Paper presented at Church Education System Symposium, Brigham Young University, Provo, Utah, Aug. 15, 1990.

Smith, Wilford E. "Mormon Sex Standards on College Campuses, or Deal Us Out of the Sexual Revolution!" *Dialogue* 10 (Autumn 1976):76–81.

Thomas, Darwin L., ed. "Family in the Mormon Experience." In *Families and Religions: Conflict and Change in Modern Society*, ed. William V. D'Antonio and Joan Aldous, pp. 267–88. Beverly Hills, Calif., 1983.

———, and Joseph Olsen. "Young Men Study Revisited: A Five-Year Follow-up of Priest Age Young Men's Mission Decisions." Unpublished report, Research and Evaluation Division, The Church of Jesus Christ of Latter-day Saints, Nov. 1986.

———. *The Religion and Family Connection: Social Science Perspectives*. Provo, Utah, 1988.

———; Joseph Olsen; and Stan E. Weed. "Missionary Service of L.D.S. Young Men: A Longitudinal Analysis." Paper presented at the Society for the Scientific Study of Religion, Salt Lake City, Oct. 1989.

Weed, Stan E., and Joseph Olsen. "Policy and Program Considerations for Teenage Pregnancy Prevention: A Summary for Policymakers." *Family Perspective* 22 (1988):235–52.

DARWIN L. THOMAS

SOCIAL SERVICES

The Church of Jesus Christ of Latter-day Saints calls upon LDS Social Services, a separate corporation, to help meet the social and emotional needs of Church members and others. Services include:

1. Placement of children for adoption with couples who meet legal requirements and the Church's personal worthiness standards.
2. Counseling and support for unwed parents, to help them with issues and decisions pertaining to MARRIAGE, ADOPTION, and single parenthood.
3. Placement of children in foster homes that will promote healthy individual development and positive family relationships.
4. Therapy and referrals for members having personal or family problems, to allow them to receive help from resources that are respectful of LDS values.

Members are generally referred for assistance to LDS Social Services by their BISHOPS. The agency staff strives to work in harmony with ecclesiastical leaders and, at moderate fees, to provide services consistent with LDS values, such as individual responsibility, the sanctity of the FAMILY and human life, the eternal worth of souls, and the importance of experiences in mortality.

Charitable work among Latter-day Saints dates back to the organization of the Church in 1830. In the nineteenth century, most charitable work was done through the women's RELIEF SOCIETY, whose representatives began regularly calling upon members in their homes to obtain contributions for the poor, assess the needs of families, distribute food or clothing, or perform other compassionate services. Care of the needy is still viewed as a local responsibility, best addressed at the WARD level and provided through local ecclesiastical leaders, mainly the bishop. The bishop regularly involves the RELIEF SOCIETY and, when needed, the local Social Services agency.

To help with the relief effort in World War I, the Church sent Amy Brown LYMAN, General Relief Society President, together with another Relief Society delegate, to the National Conference of Charities and Correction in 1917. There these two women learned of charity and relief methods used by the Red Cross and became convinced that adopting these could strengthen their own charity program. Encouraged by Presidents Joseph F. SMITH and Heber J. GRANT, Sister Lyman founded the Relief Society Social Service Department in 1919. The department provided casework services for LDS families, served as a liaison between the Church and public and private charities, operated an employment bureau for women, and provided social work training for volunteers from local Relief Societies. It also provided adoptive placements and family services, including foster care and counseling for unwed mothers. During the Great Depression of the early 1930s, this department expanded its cooperation with Salt Lake County, providing commodity relief to the poor.

In the 1930s many federally funded public assistance and Social Security programs were established in the United States. Consequently, the Relief Society Social Service Department, like many other private agencies, changed its focus from providing financial relief to offering direct services, or counseling, mostly on child welfare matters.

During the next three decades (1937–1969), the department began hiring trained professionals, mostly social workers. Adoptive placements increased and services to unwed mothers expanded. More children were placed and supervised in foster care. An extensive youth guidance program was developed. The INDIAN STUDENT PLACEMENT SERVICES, a special foster care program for NATIVE AMERICANS, officially began in 1954. It provided Native American children with educational, religious, and cultural experiences in LDS homes. Belle S. SPAFFORD, General Relief Society President, provided direction during those years. In 1962, geographical expansion began, and, by 1969, Social Service agencies had been established in Arizona, Nevada, Idaho, and California.

In October 1969, Church leaders consolidated the Relief Society adoption services, the Indian Student Placement Services, and the Youth Guidance Program under a single department known as Unified Social Services. The change was part of the CORRELATION of all Church programs. Counseling and adoption services continued to increase. Professional employees were encouraged to obtain at least a master's degree in the behavioral sciences, preferably in social work. They began responding to requests from local Church leaders for assistance in counseling members with a variety of social-emotional needs and problems.

In September 1973, Unified Social Services became a separate corporation, renamed LDS Social Services. The new corporation began charging moderate fees for clinical, adoption, and foster care services. Services were expanded with Church growth and with the demand for licensed and clinical services. Agencies were established in the United States, Canada, Australia, New Zealand,

and Great Britain. In 1974, there were 16 agencies and 9 suboffices; in 1979, 35 agencies and 13 suboffices; in 1991, 41 agencies with 24 suboffices. Staff size increased to a peak of 280 in 1980, then began decreasing slightly due to reductions in the Indian Student Placement Services and a trend toward emphasizing referral services for personal and family problems.

Shortly before 1990, LDS Social Services began placing greater emphasis on services for adoptive and unwed parents. Outreach efforts were instigated to assist greater numbers of unwed parents. The First Presidency issued letters to local leaders encouraging unwed parents to ensure their children are raised in stable homes with two parents, placing them for adoption through LDS Social Services when marriage is not feasible. At the same time, LDS Social Services changed the focus of its foster care program with a greater emphasis on placing troubled children in the homes of relatives, and on working closer with community agencies to provide services.

Currently, LDS Social Services continues to respond to the requests of Church members for adoption services, counseling for unwed parents, foster care, and referral or therapy for personal or family problems.

BIBLIOGRAPHY

Benson, Ezra T.; Gordon B. Hinckley; and Thomas S. Monson. "Unwed Parents." A letter from the First Presidency to local leaders. Salt Lake City, May 25, 1989.

Derr, Jill M. "A History of Social Services in The Church of Jesus Christ of Latter-day Saints." Unpublished manuscript at Director's office, LDS Social Services, 1988.

C. ROSS CLEMENT

SOCIETIES AND ORGANIZATIONS

The vitality and relevance of The Church of Jesus Christ of Latter-day Saints have spawned the formation of a wide assortment of unofficial organizations serving various Church-related interests and needs. Because the Church encompasses a comprehensive belief system about deity and the purpose of life, some members feel an intense need for outlets that allow them to share their personal insights, question ideas, and apply religious beliefs to daily living.

Unofficial organizations have existed since the early years of the Church (for a discussion of many nineteenth-century organizations, see Heinerman; Jenson). Some eventually became official Church programs, such as the Deseret Sunday School Union in 1849, the Mutual Improvement Association in 1875, and the Primary organization in 1878. Publications by these organizations similarly evolved from unofficial to official Church publications: *Juvenile Instructor* (Sunday School), *The Contributor* and later the *Improvement Era* (Mutual Improvement Association), and *Children's Friend* (Primary).

In recent years, hundreds of unofficial societies and organizations have been created primarily to provide four kinds of activities: They (1) hold regular study groups, usually monthly; (2) meet as professional associations; (3) publish journals and newsletters; or (4) hold annual symposiums or conferences.

The least formal organizations are study groups of neighbors or friends sharing common interests who meet periodically to discuss preselected topics. Although most of these groups have a temporary and unstable life, some have met regularly for many years and have invited scholars or Church leaders to address them. Several professional associations have been formed by members who originally met as special interest groups at professional conferences.

The Society for Early Historic Archaeology (SEHA) was originally chartered with the state of Utah in 1949 as the University Archaeological Society, a nonprofit organization for the purposes of collecting and disseminating information about archaeological research on the scriptures. SEHA distributes a quarterly newsletter, plus papers presented at its annual symposium.

The Mormon History Association was formed in 1965 by both Mormon and non-Mormon historians who wanted an opportunity to share ideas in an atmosphere of openness. The Mormon History Association publishes the *MHA Newsletter* (quarterly) and the *Journal of Mormon History* (annually). The journal contains scholarly articles related to Mormon history that have passed an editorial review board. The association holds a three-day conference annually, usually in historically significant locations, such as Nauvoo, Kirtland, Lamoni, Palmyra, Omaha, England, and Salt Lake City. An annual awards banquet honors distinguished scholars who have written about LDS history from the perspective of their discipline. These conferences have attracted many who are not professional historians plus many non-Mormons. The Mormon History Association has facilitated extensive contacts between Latter-day Saint and Reorganized Latter Day Saint scholars that have contributed to the exchange of historically significant original documents.

Among the organizations that restrict their activities to publishing, one of the best known is *Dialogue: A Journal of Mormon Thought*. The title page of this journal states that it is "an independent national quarterly established to express Mormon culture and examine the relevance of religion to secular life." Started in 1966, it is edited by Latter-day Saints whose intent is to bring their faith into dialogue with human experience as a whole and to foster artistic and scholarly achievement based on their cultural heritage.

Exponent II is a quarterly newspaper founded in 1974 to discuss Mormonism and feminism to help LDS women develop their talents.

The Sunstone Foundation was started in 1975 by a group of graduate students at Berkeley, California, who initially issued a quarterly magazine that was later published bimonthly. The purpose of the magazine is to provide a forum for young scholars to express themselves without being restricted by the professional, literary, and academic standards of established journals or Church publications. In 1979 the first annual Sunstone Symposium was held. Selected presentations from the annual symposium have been published in *Sunstone* and other journals. In addition to full-length articles, *Sunstone* features poetry, fiction, interviews, opinion columns, book reviews, and discussions of contemporary issues, theology, history, art, and drama.

The Association of Mormon Counselors and Psychotherapists (AMCAP) was organized in 1975 to promote fellowship and to enhance personal and professional development of LDS counselors and psychotherapists. AMCAP meets twice annually and publishes a quarterly newsletter and a semiannual journal containing articles on psychotherapy with an LDS emphasis.

The Association of Mormon Letters (AML) was organized in 1976 to promote the writing and study of LDS literature. AML gives awards for outstanding literature and publishes an annual volume of essays on Mormon literature plus a quarterly newsletter.

In 1977, a group of LDS media artists formed an association called ALMA (Associated Latter-day Media Artists), which publishes a bimonthly newsletter and meets monthly to "promote quality media." In 1978, the Society for the Sociological Study of Mormon Life was formed to encourage sociological research on Mormon life.

The Foundation for Ancient Research and Mormon Studies (F.A.R.M.S.), headquartered in Provo, Utah, was organized as a California nonprofit corporation in 1979 to promote, coordinate, finance, and popularly disseminate research on ancient scriptures, particularly the Book of Mormon. F.A.R.M.S. publishes books, an annual review of publications on the Book of Mormon, a bimonthly newsletter, reprints, research reports, tapes, videos, and the writings of Hugh W. Nibley and other Mormon and non-Mormon scholars.

The B. H. Roberts Society was established in 1980 as an association "dedicated to the study of timely issues in Mormonism" and sponsors quarterly meetings in Salt Lake City. Similar societies have been formed in Denver, Los Angeles, and San Francisco.

A group called Affirmation was founded in 1980 to provide a forum and newsletter for discussing homosexuality.

In 1982, a group of medical practitioners formed Collegium Aesculapium for physicians, medical students, and those in the paramedical professions. This professional association publishes the *Journal of Collegium Aesculapium* and holds a semiannual conference. The main purpose of the association is to promote service to society and help to the underprivileged.

The Mormon Women's Forum was founded in 1988 to publish a newsletter and discuss women's issues in monthly meetings in various cities.

Several organizations have been formed by people associated with programs and activities of BRIGHAM YOUNG UNIVERSITY. For example, in 1975 the BYU Management Society was organized under the auspices of the School of Management, and in 1988 the J. Reuben Clark Law Society was formed at the Law School to enhance the professional careers of their members through educational and professional opportunities. An International Society was organized in 1989, coordinated by the David M. Kennedy Center for International Studies at BYU. Many other centers and organizations are funded and operated by the university itself.

Unofficial organizations and their publications may serve at least six important functions for Church members and/or the Church.

First, a few serve ecumenical functions, bringing people of different faiths together in an exchange of ideas and understanding. Increased understanding has reduced ignorance, hostility, and intolerance and has led to greater sharing of ideas, historical documents, and research, especially in relationships fostered by the Mormon History Association.

Second, some unofficial organizations provide increased affiliation and social support for members by allowing them to associate with others whose religious beliefs provide a feeling of kinship. Having a common religious heritage provides a social bond that facilitates friendship and the formation of a social support system. Many monthly study groups are attended primarily for the purpose of association.

Third, unofficial publications provide an opportunity to learn and distribute new insights regarding theology, the scriptures, ancient cultures, historical events, and current practices. Dedicated members wanting to combine their religious beliefs with their professional training have made significant scholarly contributions, and unofficial journals provide outlets for publishing them.

Fourth, the creative efforts of those who contribute to these publications add to the collection of Mormon literature by allowing members to write about life and events from a unique LDS perspective. Some literary articles represent personal expressions of faith and testimony in artistic or scholarly ways that most authors would not choose to use in a monthly testimony meeting.

Fifth, certain publications serve as an outlet where individuals with unorthodox beliefs can share their questions, concerns, and doubts in an open forum where they feel adequate acceptance.

And sixth, for members who feel a need to promote change, publications of such organizations provide a forum where they can take an advocacy position. The targets of change have included the elimination of racism and sexism, the acceptance of altered social practices (such as birth control, dress, and grooming standards), and interpretation of the scriptures or historical events.

BIBLIOGRAPHY

Anderson, Edward H. "The Past of Mutual Improvement." *IE* 1 (Nov. 1897):1–10.

Arrington, Leonard J. "Reflections on the Founding and Purpose of the Mormon History Association, 1965–1983." *Journal of Mormon History* 10 (1983):91–103.

Bradford, Mary L., ed. *Personal Voices: A Celebration of Dialogue.* Salt Lake City, 1987.

Heinerman, Joseph. "Early Utah Pioneer Cultural Societies." *Utah Historical Quarterly* 47 (Winter 1979):70–89, discusses the Universal Scientific Society, the Polysophical Society, the Deseret Theological Institution, the Deseret Dramatic Association, and others.

Jenson, Andrew. *Encyclopedic History of the Church of Jesus Christ of Latter-day Saints,* e.g., "Daughters of the Utah Pioneers," "Deseret Agricultural and Manufacturing Society," p. 183, "Deseret Pottery Society," p. 188, and "Utah Silk Association," p. 795. Salt Lake City, 1941.

Warner, Cecelia. "A Guide to the Mormon Network." *Sunstone* 10 (June 1985):42–47.

DAVID J. CHERRINGTON

SOCIETY

[*Mormon life is inseparably involved with people. See, generally,* Children; Community; Family; Lifestyle; Marriage; Men, Roles of; Social and Cultural History; Social Characteristics; Socialization; Values, Transmission of; Vital Statistics; Women, Roles of; *and* Youth.

Belonging to the Church is the basis of many aspects of Latter-day Saint societal values and concepts. See Activity in the Church; Brotherhood; The Church of Jesus Christ of Latter-day Saints; Lay Participation and Leadership; Membership; Orthodoxy, Heterodoxy, and Heresy; Senior Citizens; Sisterhood; Volunteerism; *and* Ward.

On the single individual in LDS society, see Dating and Courtship; Divorce; Individuality; *and* Single Adults.

For discussions of specific social topics, see various entries under Business; City Planning; Education; Family; Fine Arts; Folk Art; Folklore; Holidays; Humor; Language and Culture; Literature; Material Culture; Mental Health; Minorities; Music; Politics; Science; Societies and Organizations; Sports; Symbolism; *and* Welfare.

Social relations with members of other religious groups are treated under Interfaith Relationships; Non-Mormons, Social Relations with; *and* Tolerance.]

SOLEMN ASSEMBLIES

In the Old Testament, ISRAEL met in solemn assembly on the seventh day of the Feast of the Passover (Ex. 23:14–17; Deut. 16:8, 16) and the eighth day of the Feast of Tabernacles (Lev. 23:33–36;

The Assembly Hall upstairs in the Salt Lake Temple (1991) where solemn assemblies are held.

Neh. 8:18). The dedication of Solomon's Temple occurred during the latter feast (2 Chr. 5:2–3; 7:9–11).

By commandment, the Prophet Joseph SMITH convened a solemn assembly on March 27, 1836, in the KIRTLAND TEMPLE and in a nearby schoolhouse. During the meeting, the SAINTS sustained Joseph and other Church leaders in their CALLINGS, Joseph offered the dedicatory prayer for the new temple, and Church leaders instructed each other and bore TESTIMONY, which led to a rich outpouring of the Spirit of God (D&C 88:70; 108:4; *HC* 2:410–28).

Church leaders have called solemn assemblies for many purposes since then. The foremost is to sustain general Church leaders. Following the death of a PRESIDENT OF THE CHURCH, the Church holds a solemn assembly in the Salt Lake TABERNACLE to approve and sustain its new FIRST PRESIDENCY. Church members participate at the Tabernacle and in other places where the proceedings are broadcast (see, e.g., *CR* [Apr. 1986]:93–95).

A second purpose is to dedicate new or refurbished temples. Worthy Church members attend dedicatory services, which are held in the temples themselves and in other nearby facilities (*see* DEDICATIONS).

A third purpose is to instruct and encourage Church members in their responsibilities. Such solemn assemblies generally take place in temples or STAKE centers. Church members invited to these assemblies are usually PRIESTHOOD leaders. Sometimes in such assemblies the sacrament is served, but traditionally the main function is for those assembled to receive counsel from the presiding Church authorities.

BIBLIOGRAPHY

Norman, Robert J. "I Have a Question." *Ensign* 18 (Dec. 1988):53–54.

Peterson, H. Burke. "A Glimpse of Glory." *Speeches of the Year* [1975], pp. 424–25. Provo, Utah.

Widtsoe, John A. "The Sacred Assembly." *IE* 48 (Nov. 1945):672.

RICHARD E. TURLEY, JR.

SON OF GOD

See: Jesus Christ: Names and Titles of

SONS OF PERDITION

In LDS scripture Lucifer and CAIN are called Perdition, meaning "destruction" (D&C 76:26; Moses 5:24). The unembodied SPIRITS who supported Lucifer in the WAR IN HEAVEN and were cast out (Moses 4:1–4) and mortals who commit the UNPARDONABLE SIN against the HOLY GHOST will inherit the same condition as Lucifer and Cain, and thus are called "sons of perdition."

Perdition is both a place and a spiritual condition. As a place, it is synonymous with that HELL to which both unembodied and resurrected sons of perdition will be consigned following the last JUDGMENT (2 Ne. 28:23; D&C 29:38; *TPJS*, p. 361). This future kingdom of the DEVIL will be devoid of any of the Spirit and glory of GOD. (D&C 88:24).

The spiritual condition of those in this realm is described metaphorically as a lake of unquenchable fire and brimstone and as "a worm [that] dieth not" (Jacob 6:10; D&C 76:44). They will be "vessels of wrath, doomed to suffer the wrath of God" (D&C 76:33). God's wrath will originate within them when they contrast his holiness and majesty with their own filthiness and ignominy (2 Ne. 9:14; Alma 12:14–17; Morm. 9:4–5; *TPJS*, p. 361). The Prophet Joseph SMITH explained, "A man is his own tormentor and his own condemner. . . . The

torment of disappointment in the mind of man is as exquisite as a lake burning with fire and brimstone" (*TPJS*, p. 357). Fire and brimstone characterize the person, not the place.

The awful realization that they are truly damned, have lost all favor with God, have rejected all that he represents, and have lost the opportunity for repentance will be compounded by their subjection to Lucifer and Cain, who are consumed with like misery and frustration (2 Ne. 2:27; Moses 1:22). Such is the ultimate "damnation of hell" (*TPJS*, p. 198; *see* DAMNATION).

Perdition is the second death: total banishment not only from God's literal presence but also from the influence of his Spirit (2 Ne. 9:15–16; Hel. 14:18; D&C 88:32). Those who sin against the Holy Ghost commit the unpardonable sin and will suffer the fulness of the second death (Alma 39:6; Hel. 14:16–19). All others will be saved eventually in one of the DEGREES OF GLORY (D&C 76:40–43; *JD* 8:154).

Sons of perdition are not merely wicked; they are incorrigibly evil. In sinning against the revelations of the Holy Ghost, they have sinned against the greater light and knowledge of God. They willfully and utterly pervert principles of RIGHTEOUSNESS and truth with which they were once endowed, and transform them into principles of evil and deception. Joseph Smith declared, "You cannot save such persons; you cannot bring them to repentance" (*TPJS*, p. 358). No divine principle can cleanse the sons of perdition; following the last judgment, they will remain "filthy still" (D&C 29:44; 88:35). It is revealed that "it had been better for them never to have been born" (D&C 76:32).

Those who become sons of perdition while in mortality will be resurrected with unglorified physical bodies and "rise to the damnation of their own filthiness" (*TPJS*, p. 361). Cain, thus resurrected, will then rule over the unembodied Lucifer (Moses 5:23; *MD*, p. 109).

It has been suggested that in the absence of the life-sustaining powers of God's Spirit, sons of perdition will eventually become disorganized and return to "native element" (*JD* 1:349–52; 5:271; 7:358–59). However, scripture declares that "the soul can never die" (Alma 12:20) and that in the Resurrection the spirit and the body are united "never to be divided" (Alma 11:45; cf. 12:18; D&C 93:33). The ultimate fate of sons of perdition will be made known only to those who are partakers thereof and will not be definitely revealed until the last judgment (D&C 29:27–30; 43:33; 76:43–48; *TPJS*, p. 24).

Few individuals have been identified as sons of perdition. Although Judas is often so regarded, there is a question whether he had received the Holy Ghost sufficiently to sin against it at the time of his betrayal of Christ (John 17:12; Smith, pp. 433–34).

BIBLIOGRAPHY

Smith, Joseph F. *Gospel Doctrine.* Salt Lake City, 1946.

RODNEY TURNER

SOUL

In Latter-day Saint terminology "soul" is used in various ways, with diverse connotations found throughout the scriptures and in other Church writings. However, the word also has a precise definition given in latter-day REVELATION: the soul is the united entity of the SPIRIT with the PHYSICAL BODY (D&C 88:15–16). This concept is enhanced by an understanding of (1) the creation of humankind as a uniting of the SPIRIT BODY and the physical body (Gen. 2:7; Moses 3:7; Abr. 5:7); (2) the knowledge that God himself is embodied (D&C 130:22); and (3) the doctrine that all mortals will ultimately undergo a literal resurrection of the physical body (Alma 40:17–23; 41:2; 2 Ne. 9:13). Only in this resurrected and permanently united form can a soul receive a fulness of joy (D&C 93:33–34; cf. D&C 138:17). The glory with which the soul arises in the resurrection is related to the glory, form, and qualities of the resurrected body (1 Cor. 15:40–45; D&C 88:28).

"Soul" in a generic sense, however, means a person. This was common usage in the nineteenth century and earlier (i.e., Gen. 17:14 and Mosiah 18:28) as it is today. "Soul" is sometimes synonymous with "the whole self," or what might be described as one's "being" or "essence." Scriptural passages speak of "enlarging" the soul (Alma 32:28; D&C 121:42) and of imploring others with all the "energy" of one's soul (Alma 5:43). The word occasionally also appears as a metaphor implying "strength" (D&C 30:11; 31:5) or "heart" (2 Ne. 26:7, 10–11). "Soul" often is likewise used to refer to a person's intimate feelings or desires, as when one pours out one's "whole soul" (Enos 1:9; Mosiah 26:14) or when one is commanded to love God with "all thy soul" (Matt. 22:37; Mark 12:30–33; Luke 10:27). Other connotations are suggested by the word when it describes an entire community (Num. 21:4; 1 Sam. 30:6; Acts 4:32).

"Soul" is often used where the term "spirit" might also apply (1 Ne. 19:7; 2 Ne. 1:22; D&C 101:37). Here the soul is essentially that aspect of all human beings which persists independent of the physical body (Matt. 10:28; 1 Ne. 15:31; Mosiah 2:38; Alma 40:11). In LDS doctrine the soul, in this sense, exists both before and after mortal life, and is truly eternal (Abr. 3:22–23; *see also* INTELLIGENCES).

Consistent with the idea that all spirits (or souls) existed prior to their mortal life, LDS doctrine holds that all vegetable and animal life was created spiritually before the physical creation (Moses 3:5; cf. Gen. 2:5). In this sense, every living thing (plant, animal, human) is spoken of as having a soul (Moses 3:9, 19).

The human soul is innately endowed with an AGENCY that should be honored and guarded as sacred and eternal (D&C 134:4). The soul (spirit), being eternal, cannot be fully destroyed but can suffer a type of destruction or SPIRITUAL DEATH through sins that result in total and ultimate estrangement from God (1 Ne. 14:3; Alma 12:16–18, 36; 30:47; 42:9, 16). Scripture teaches that all human souls are children of God and are of infinite worth (Matt. 16:26; Alma 39:17; D&C 18:10–16). God has great joy in a repentant soul, and there is no more important work than the saving of souls and bringing them to God (D&C 18:10–16; 15:6; 16:6).

RICHARD N. WILLIAMS

SOUTH AMERICA, THE CHURCH IN

[*This entry consists of three articles:*

Brazil

South America, North

South America, South

The first article discusses the establishment, growth, and development of the Church in Brazil. The second article covers the same points in Bolivia, Colombia, Ecuador, Peru, and Venezuela; and the third article covers Argentina, Chile, Paraguay, and Uruguay.

After Parley P. Pratt, an apostle, his wife Phoebe Soper Pratt, and Elder Rufus C. Allen were unsuccessful in establishing a foothold in Valparaiso, Chile, in 1851–1852, it was not until 1925 that The Church of Jesus Christ of Latter-day Saints sent Melvin J. Ballard, another apostle; and Elders Rulon S. Wells, who spoke German, and Rey L. Pratt, who spoke Spanish, both of the Seventy, to open the South America Mission. Under assignment from President Heber J. Grant, these men dedicated the vast area of South America for the preaching of the gospel in Buenos Aires on December 25, 1925. The establishment of the Church in South America began in Argentina when some German LDS families emigrated there in the 1920s, and requested that missionaries and Church supplies be sent to Buenos Aires to help them build the Church among their families and friends. The Church moved into Brazil in 1928, also in answer to requests of LDS German emigrants living there. The first Latter-day Saints in Chile apparently were North American miners who worked in the mining district in northern Chile. The first missionaries were sent there from Argentina in 1956, and the Chilean Mission was established in 1961. The Church moved into Uruguay from Argentina in 1944, and into Paraguay from Uruguay in 1948. The first missionaries were sent to Peru from Uruguay in 1956.

Speaking at a sacrament meeting in Buenos Aires in 1926, Elder Ballard likened the Church's potential in South America to a strong, mighty oak growing from a tiny acorn. He said there would be thousands of members and many missions growing from the tiny begin-nings of the Church there, and South America would become one of the strongest areas of the Church. True to that prophecy, although the work went slowly for a number of years, with the location of a General Authority, Elder A. Theodore and Sister Marné Whittaker Tuttle, in South America in the 1960s to supervise missionary work, a dramatic surge of conversions began. The Church moved into the northern countries with the creation of the Andes Mission in Peru and Chile in 1959. The first units were established in Bolivia in 1964; in Ecuador in 1965; and in Colombia and Venezuela in 1966. Many of the LDS missionaries in South America are local members who have been strengthened and prepared for service and leadership by attending seminary and institute programs of the Church Educational System. Where the Church originally had only one mission in all of South America, in January 1991 it had 43 missions, 381 stakes and districts, and 3,791 wards and branches serving over 1.35 million members.]

BRAZIL

The LDS Church first came to Brazil in 1928, when several German converts emigrated to the German colonies in the southern states of Brazil and asked the Church for materials to teach their children. The Church grew slowly in Brazil until the 1960s and 1970s, when great numbers of Brazilians began joining. The first mission was divided to make new missions, STAKES were organized and then divided, and in 1985 Brazil became an AREA

A sacrament meeting in the Curitiba South Stake, Brazil, c. 1981.

Caracas
1977

VENEZUELA
(53,000)

GUYANA *

SURINAME *

FRENCH GUIANA *

Bogota
1977

COLOMBIA
(83,000)

Quito

ECUADOR
(81,000)

Guayaquil
1978

PERU
(178,000)

Lima 1970
1986

BOLIVIA
(64,000)

Santa Cruz
1979

BRAZIL
(366,000)

PARAGUAY
(12,000)

Asuncion
1979

1966
1978

São Paulo

CHILE
(298,000)

ARGENTINA
(171,000)

Santiago
1972
1983

Buenos Aires
1966
1986

URUGUAY
(52,000)

Montevideo
1967

0   500   1000

Scale in Miles

SOUTH AMERICAN AREAS

▢ North (459,000 members)

▢ South (533,000 members)

▨ Brazil (366,000 members)

✪ Area Headquarters

◆ First Stake in Country

⛪ Temple

✳ Membership less than 100

BYU Geography Department

1394

Joseph Receives the Plates, by Max Rezler (1973, Brazil, inlaid wood, 24″ × 21″). This work by LDS Brazilian artist Max Rezler portrays the occasion when the Angel Moroni, on September 22, 1827, delivered to Joseph Smith the plates containing the Book of Mormon record. Church Museum of History and Art.

with a resident area presidency of General Authorities. In January 1991 Brazil had an LDS temple, an area presidency, 12 missions, more than 2,100 LDS missionaries (over half local Brazilians), 87 stakes and districts, and over 800 wards and branches serving 366,000 members of the Church.

When President Reinhold Stoof visited the German members in Brazil in 1928 as president of the South American Mission, he was impressed with the potential he saw for missionary work there. The first LDS missionaries assigned to Brazil spoke German rather than Portuguese and began their missionary labors in the German colonies at Joinville, Santa Catarina State, on September 12, 1928. The first converts were baptized on April 14, 1929. Although the work progressed slowly at first, by October 1931 Joinville had the first LDS meetinghouse chapel in South America. The first Relief Society was organized there in 1933 with twenty-four members.

⟵ The Church of Jesus Christ of Latter-day Saints in South America as of January 1, 1991.

In 1935 the Brazil Mission was divided from the South American Mission with only 143 members of the Church in the entire mission. President Rulon S. Howells began preparing Church materials in Portuguese and then assigned some of the missionaries to learn Portuguese so that they could work with the Brazilians and not just with the German immigrants. In 1938 the Brazilian government prohibited the use of the German language in public meetings and schools, which made Church activities very difficult for the German-speaking members. With the advent of World War II and the North American missionaries being called home, many of the local branches of the Church were closed. However, some units, such as the Campinas Branch, had developed sufficient local leadership to be able to keep the branch functioning throughout the war and to bring in new members.

With the return of the North American missionaries in 1945 and the calling of local Brazilians to serve missions, the Church began to grow more rapidly in Brazil. That growth was aided by the visit of Stephen L Richards, an apostle, who toured the mission in 1948, and of President David O. MCKAY in 1955. Lifting the members spiritually, and recognizing their strength, President McKay authorized the building of meetinghouses (chapels) in which the Saints could worship. With this manifestation of confidence by the President of the Church, the local members reached out to share the gospel with their friends and neighbors. They especially shared the Church youth auxiliary program, which attracted many converts and became the center of proselytizing for the mission. They also developed pageants and theatrical presentations that showed the Brazilians what blessings being a member of the Church brings.

Another important event in the history of the Church in Brazil was the organization of its first stake, the São Paulo Brazil Stake, on May 1, 1966, with Walter Spät as president. By mid-1990 that first stake had grown to fifty-six stakes and almost six hundred wards and branches, all presided over by local Brazilian priesthood bearers.

The most significant event in the history of the Church in Brazil was the construction of the São Paulo Temple in 1978. That brought all the blessings of the Church to the Brazilian and other South American Saints. Former Mission President Finn B. Paulsen was called as temple president, and his wife, Sara Broadbent Paulsen, as the temple matron. With a temple in Brazil, the Church organized the first missionary training center in South America at São Paulo in 1979.

One of the most effective missionary tools the members used to present the message of the Church was a theatrical presentation, "The Gate," written by Ana Gláucia Ceciliato and presented to more than 20,000 people at the open house for the São Paulo Temple before it was dedicated. To make the presentation required some sixty talented Church children, youth, and adults to travel many miles from several cities to São Paulo for rehearsals. The introduction of the Church seminary and institute programs also greatly strengthened the youth of the Church in Brazil.

The first translation of the Book of Mormon into Portuguese was printed in 1940. Some of the missionary tracts were translated and published a year earlier. The Portuguese translation of the Doctrine and Covenants was published in 1950, and the Pearl of Great Price in 1952, making all the latter-day scriptures available in the language of the people. The Church magazine for Portuguese-speaking members, A Gaivota (now A Liahona), began publication in 1948. Other Church materials are translated into Portuguese in Brazil for all Portuguese-speaking countries. The work of Elder William Grant and Sister Geri Hamblin Bangerter and of Elder James E. and Sister Ruth Wright Faust greatly expanded the Church in Brazil.

Two native Brazilians have been called as General Authorities of the Church. Hélio da Rocha Camargo, born in Rezende, Rio de Janeiro, on February 1, 1926, became a Seventy on April 7, 1985. A former Protestant minister, he was baptized a member of the Church on June 1, 1957. He was released from the Seventy in October 1990 and called as the president of the São Paulo Temple. Helvécio Martins, born in Rio de Janeiro on June 27, 1930, and baptized on July 2, 1972, was called to the Seventy on March 31, 1990. He is the first General Authority of African lineage.

BIBLIOGRAPHY

Grover, Mark L. "Mormonism in Brazil: Religion and Dependency in Latin America." Ph.D. diss., Indiana University, 1985.

Labarca, Ana Rosa. "Dias inesquecíveis de 1978—Uma nova era para a Igreja no Brasil." A Liahona 41 (Oct. 1988):4–5.

Williams, Frederick S., and Frederick G. Williams. From Acorn to Oak Tree: A Personal History of the Establishment and First Quarter Century Development of the South American Missions. Fullerton, Calif., 1987.

FLAVIA GARCIA ERBOLATO

SOUTH AMERICA, NORTH

BOLIVIA.   The Church became legally established in Bolivia in 1963 through the work of North American LDS families living in La Paz and in Cochabamba. The first Bolivian was baptized and the first branch organized in 1964. The Bolivian Mission was organized in 1968, with headquarters in La Paz. Some of the first families who joined the Church are still active in leadership roles.

The first Bolivian stake was organized in January 1979 in Santa Cruz de la Sierra, with Noriharu Ishigaki Haraguichi as president. In March of the same year, the La Paz Stake was established, with Jorge Leano as president. In January 1991, he was serving as president of the Colombia Cali Mission.

Church materials going to Bolivia are printed in the three principal languages of the country: Spanish, Quechua, and Aymara. The LDS Bolivian youth, strengthened by the seminary and institute programs, have responded enthusiastically to the call to share the restored gospel; they currently make up 70 percent of the missionaries serving in the country. As a result of the dedicated missionary effort, approximately 64,000 members of the Church lived in Bolivia in January 1991. The Church enjoys the respect and admiration of the citizens and of government authorities because of the members' stability, spiritual contribution, and exemplary lifestyle. The construction of one hundred meetinghouses between 1987 and 1990, has given the members places in which to worship, as well as work opportunities to many Bolivians. The meetinghouses are also used as classrooms wherein the Bolivians are given the advantage of religious education and literacy training.

COLOMBIA.   On March 20, 1966, the first branch of the Church was organized in Bogotá, Colombia, with Harold M. Rex as president. When the government officials signed the record of the proceedings, The Church of Jesus Christ of Latter-day Saints was established in Colombia. Elder Spencer W. Kimball rededicated the country to the preaching of the gospel in Bogotá on May 11, 1966. Colombia was part of the Andes Mission until 1968, when it became part of the Colombia-Venezuela

Mission. The Colombia Bogotá Mission began operations on July 1, 1971. That mission was divided in 1975, creating the Colombia Cali Mission. On July 1, 1988, a third mission, the Colombia Barranquilla Mission, was established.

The first chapel built in Colombia was built at Cali in 1975, in a section of the city where the Versalles Ward is located. The First Presidency has announced plans for the construction of a temple in Bogotá.

The first stake in Colombia was organized at Bogotá on January 23, 1977, by Elder Bruce R. McConkie, of the Quorum of the Twelve Apostles, with Julio E. Dávila as president. On April 6, 1991, President Dávila became the first native Colombian called to be a General Authority. In January 1991 there were nine stakes in the country: Bogotá, Kennedy, Ciudad Jardín, El Dorado, Cali, Américas, Medellín, Bucaramanga, and Barranquilla. The progress of the Church in Colombia is noteworthy. More than 83,000 members are enjoying the benefits of the spiritual and temporal programs offered by the quorums of the priesthood, the auxiliary organizations, and the religious educational courses, as well as literacy classes in seminaries and institutes.

The feeling of unity has grown strong among Church members in Colombia, as was shown during the 1983 earthquake in the city of Popayán, in the southern part of the country. The Colombian Saints united to help provide the necessities of life as well as housing for the thousands injured and made homeless by the quake.

The March 1977 area conference with President Spencer W. Kimball was of great significance to the people of Colombia, as were the regional conferences of 1987 and 1989 with Elder Russell M. Ballard, of the Quorum of the Twelve Apostles, presiding.

ECUADOR. On April 27, 1964, Sterling Nicolaysen, president of the Andes Mission, was instructed by Elder A. Theodore Tuttle to register the "Corporation of the Church" in Ecuador. On Saturday, October 9, 1965, Elder Spencer W. Kimball, then of the Council of the Twelve Apostles, dedicated the land of Ecuador to the preaching of the restored gospel, offering the dedicatory prayer from the top of Panecillo Hill in Quito. In June 1969, the Ecuador Quito Mission was organized, with Louis Latimer as president. In January 1991 there were two missions in Ecuador, headquartered in Quito and Guayaquil.

The first nine members in Quito were baptized on October 31, 1965. Missionary work began in Guayaquil on January 20, 1966. Napoleón Trujillo, the first local missionary called from Ecuador, served in Uruguay. His father, José G. Trujillo, was serving as the patriarch of the Quito Stake in 1991.

Church materials for Ecuador are prepared in Spanish and Quechua, its two official languages. In 1978 Amado Ruíz, a member from Otavalo, translated some the materials needed by the Otavalo Indians, who received their own stake on December 6, 1981, with Luis Alfonzo Morales C. as president. Having Church materials in their native language has been a great help to the indigenous peoples who inhabit the diverse regions of the country.

Elder Mark E. Petersen, of the Quorum of the Twelve Apostles, organized the first stake in Guayaquil on June 11, 1978, and called Lorenzo Garaycoa as president. The first stake in Quito was organized on August 22, 1979, by Elder Gordon B. Hinckley, then of the Quorum of the Twelve, with Ernesto Franco as president.

The Church Educational System has performed an important role in the religious education of the Ecuadorian youth in seminaries and institutes and has made great strides in the area of literacy, especially among the indigenous Indian peoples. The many youths of Ecuador who serve as missionaries among their countrymen have brought the missionary work of the Church to all corners of their country. As of January 1991, the Church had 81,000 members served by two missions, 18 stakes and districts, and 121 wards and branches in Ecuador.

The First Presidency of the Church has announced plans to construct a temple in Guayaquil, Ecuador.

PERU. The first LDS contact with the people of Peru was in 1926, when Elder Melvin J. Ballard, returning to the United States after dedicating South America to the preaching of the gospel, visited Peru and was impressed that it would be a good place to send missionaries. Although several members lived in Peru in the 1940s and possibly even earlier, it was not until July 8, 1956, that Elder Henry D. Moyle, of the Quorum of the

Twelve, and Frank K. Parry, president of the Uruguayan Mission, organized the first branch in Lima. Frederick S. Williams, former president of the South American and Uruguay missions, was called to be president of the branch, which began in his home. On November 1, 1959, Elder Harold B. Lee, then of the Quorum of the Twelve Apostles, organized the Andes Mission, which included Peru and Chile, and later Bolivia, Ecuador, Colombia, and Venezuela. Headquarters were in Lima. Two years later Peru had twelve branches of the Church and more than a thousand members.

Selected passages of the Book of Mormon and other Church materials have been translated into the Quechua and Aymara languages to help the new indigenous members gain a better understanding of the gospel.

The Lima Peru Stake was organized on February 22, 1970, with Roberto Vidal as president. It had six wards, three branches, and approximately 5,000 members. In January 1991 there were 5 missions, 57 stakes and districts, and over 500 wards and branches serving the 178,000 members of the Church in Peru. At the April 1989 multiregional conference held in Lima, more than 10,000 Latter-day Saints from nine of Lima's eighteen stakes attended. The Lima Peru Temple was dedicated by President Gordon B. Hinckley, First Counselor in the First Presidency, on January 10, 1986, with Samuel and Clara Lorenzi Boren as the first president and matron. In 1990 the Lima Temple operated with an average of nine endowment sessions a day.

The Church is received with respect and enthusiasm throughout the country, where an ever-increasing number of local missionaries carry the message of the restored gospel to their people. Much credit for this success among the youth has been given to the significant role played by the Church members' religious education. More than 12,500 young Peruvians between the ages of fourteen and thirty have benefited from the courses available in the Church Educational System's seminaries and institutes. Sixty percent of the members of the Church in Peru are under thirty years of age.

VENEZUELA. On November 2, 1966, on special assignment from President David O. McKay, Elder Marion G. Romney, of the Quorum of the Twelve, dedicated the land of Venezuela for the preaching of the restored gospel. Present at that dedication was Elder F. Burton Howard, who was responsible for the legal registration of the Church in Venezuela, and Ted E. Brewerton, president of the Central American Mission (to which Venezuela belonged). Both men were later called to the Seventy.

From 1966 to 1968 there were only a few LDS missionaries in Venezuela, and progress was slow. From July 1968 to 1971, Venezuela formed a part of the Colombia-Venezuela Mission, but in 1971 the Venezuela Caracas Mission was organized, and the Church began a new era of growth. In 1978 the Venezuela Maracaibo Mission was divided from the Venezuela Caracas Mission, and President Alejandro Portal Campos, who had been the president of the Caracas Mission and the first Venezuelan to preside over a mission, was assigned the new mission.

The Caracas Stake, the first in Venezuela, was organized on May 15, 1977, under the direction of Elder Bruce R. McConkie; Adolfo Mayer was the president. In January 1991 there were seven stakes in Venezuela: two in Caracas, two in Maracaibo, and one each in Valencia, Oriente, and Guayana. There were also nine districts in the two missions. More than fifty thousand members of the Church in Venezuela have benefited from Church influence and have contributed significantly to the quality of life in their country. Because of the leadership training and skills that Church members receive and develop, many businesses and industries prefer to hire members of the Church. The Church seminary and institute programs have made significant contributions to the Venezuelan LDS youth. The influence that daily scripture study has had in their lives has made them want to participate in missionary work.

BIBLIOGRAPHY

Cowan, Richard O. "The Church in Latin America." In *The International Church*, ed. James R. Moss et al., pp. 157–91. Provo, Utah, 1982.

Williams, Frederick S., and Frederick G. Williams. *From Acorn to Oak Tree: A Personal History of the Establishment and First Quarter Century Development of the South American Missions*. Fullerton, Calif., 1987.

JULIO E. DÁVILA
(Translated from Spanish by Lyman Sidney Shreeve and Afton Kartchner Shreeve.)

SOUTH AMERICA, SOUTH

ARGENTINA. The Church was brought into Argentina by a few German immigrant families who had joined it in their homeland before they emigrated. They felt they needed to await the visit of Elder Melvin J. Ballard before they could baptize even their family members who wished to join. The first non-German convert was baptized in 1926. For several years the missionaries spoke only English and German, but emphasis was later placed on teaching also in Spanish, and that brought limited success to the Church's missionary work. The Church grew slowly in Argentina until the 1960s, when the emphasis was placed on training local member leadership. Mission President C. Laird Snelgrove organized a mission council in which he trained most of the men who would become the leaders during the next twenty-five years. A member of that council, Juan Carlos Avila, became the first native Argentine to be called as a mission president (1974–1977). The first Argentine stake was organized on November 20, 1966, presided over by a local priesthood bearer, Angel Abrea, who in 1976 would become the first Latin American General Authority. The mission was first divided in 1962, and by January 1991 the Church had nine missions, 64 stakes and districts, and over 500 wards and branches serving Argentina's 171,000 Latter-day Saints. The Buenos Aires Temple was dedicated on January 17, 1986, by Thomas

Santiago Chile Temple, dedicated 1983.

S. Monson, Second Counselor in the First Presidency. Angel and Maria Victoria Chiapparino Abrea were the president and the matron. Argentina received a missionary training center in Buenos Aires, established in 1986 under President Lyman Sidney and Sister Afton Kartchner Shreeve, who had served missions in Argentina and presided over the Uruguay Mission.

CHILE. After Parley P. Pratt's unsuccessful attempt to establish a Church foothold in Chile in 1851–1852, the Church did not officially come to Chile until Brother William Fotheringham moved to Santiago, Chile, in 1952, and requested that the Church send missionaries there. The first regular missionaries arrived in Santiago just two weeks before Elder Henry D. Moyle, then of the Quorum of the Twelve Apostles, called Brother Fotheringham as the president of the first Chilean branch on July 5, 1956. It was made up primarily of expatriate members, the first local Chilean convert being baptized that same year.

The first mission in Chile was organized on October 8, 1961, with A. Delbert Palmer presiding. That single mission has grown to become six missions, with more than 50 percent of the missionaries called from the local members, many of whom have been prepared in large measure by their seminary and institute training. They are generally called to attend the Missionary Training Center in Santiago, the second such center in South America. The Church has grown rapidly in Chile, with almost 298,000 members on March 31, 1990. On January 1991, Carlos Cifuentes, one of

Liniers chapel in Liniers, Argentina, the first constructed in South America by the Church, at the time of its dedication on April 9, 1939. Courtesy Frederick G. Williams, III.

those local converts, became the first native Chilean branch president and stake president. On September 15, 1983, the Santiago Chile Temple was dedicated. Eugene F. and Rae Stephens Jones Olsen were the president and matron. On March 31, 1990, Elder Eduardo Ayala, a former mission president in Uruguay, became the first native Chilean called to be a Seventy.

PARAGUAY. Even though in 1939 President Frederick S. Williams of the Argentine Mission traveled to the upper Pilcomayo River and visited Indian tribes there, as well as the people in Asunción, it was not until 1948 that the Church baptized its first Paraguayan convert. The Church was officially established when missionaries were sent to Paraguay from the Uruguay Mission in October 1949. Since the first baptism, Church growth has been steady. The Paraguay Mission was created in 1977, and the first stake was organized in Asunción on February 25, 1979, with Carlos R. Espinola as president. In 1980, the Church established an active branch made up of Indian converts from the Churupi-Nivacle tribe, in Mistolar village, about 800 kilometers northwest of Asunción.

URUGUAY. The first member of the Church to gain attention in Uruguay was Elder Rolf L. Larson, a missionary in the Argentina Mission who was named the most valuable basketball player in South America during the championship games held at Montevideo in January 1940. The first branch in Uruguay was organized with twelve members on June 25, 1944; the mission was organized on August 30, 1947, with the first converts being baptized on November 1, 1948. In the 1960s President and A. Sister Theodore Tuttle moved the headquarters of the South American Mission to Montevideo, which then became the center for the development of the Church throughout South America. The headquarters were later moved to Buenos Aries. The Montevideo Uruguay Stake was organized on November 12, 1967, with Vicente C. Rubio as president. Although the first plans for a temple in South America called for it to be built in Uruguay, it was eventually built in São Paulo, Brazil, in 1978. On January 1991, the Church had one mission, 18 stakes and districts, and 111 wards and branches serving over 50,000 Uruguayan Latter-day Saints.

BIBLIOGRAPHY

Cowan, Richard O. "The Church in Latin America." In *The International Church*, ed. James R. Moss et al., pp. 157–91. Provo, Utah, 1982.

Tullis, F. LaMond, ed. *Mormonism: A Faith for All Cultures.* Provo, Utah, 1978.

Williams, Frederick S., and Frederick G. Williams. *From Acorn to Oak Tree: A Personal History of the Establishment and First Quarter Century Development of the South American Missions.* Fullerton, Calif., 1987.

TOMÁS F. LINDHEIMER

SOUTH BAINBRIDGE (AFTON), NEW YORK

In October 1825, Josiah Stowell (sometimes spelled Stoal) of Bainbridge Township (now Afton), Chenango County, New York, hired Joseph SMITH and his father to assist in digging for Spanish treasure near the Susquehanna River in Harmony Township (now Oakland), Pennsylvania. The men lodged with Isaac Hale, where Joseph Smith met his future wife, Emma Hale, and began their courtship. The treasure hunters gave up excavating in mid-November 1825, but Joseph continued his employment at the Stowell farm.

Josiah Stowell's home was situated on the west side of the Susquehanna River about two miles southwest of the village of South Bainbridge (Afton since 1857), on the road to Nineveh, twenty-six miles northeast of the Hale home in Harmony. Joseph Smith worked as a farmhand, a laborer in the Stowell sawmill, and as a "wool carder." Josiah Stowell, Jr., remembered that Joseph "went to school with him one winter" and that "he was a fine likely young man" (letter of Josiah Stowell, Jr., to John S. Fullmer, Feb. 17, 1843, HDC).

Joseph Smith encountered difficulty when Peter G. Bridgman (Bridgeman), who was Stowell's nephew, swore out a complaint against him for being a "disorderly person." He appeared before Justice of the Peace Albert Neeley in South Bainbridge during March 1826 and was acquitted (Madsen, pp. 106–107; *see* SMITH, JOSEPH: TRIALS OF JOSEPH SMITH). That same year Joseph Smith found employment with Joseph Knight, Sr., in Colesville township, Broome County, a few miles south of the Stowells. He continued to call on Emma Hale in Harmony, and requested her hand in marriage. Isaac Hale strenuously objected and Joseph Smith found himself "under the necessity of taking her elsewhere" (*HC* 1:17). The couple were married in South Bainbridge on January 18, 1827, by Justice of the Peace Zachariah Tarbell. Joseph Smith was twenty-one and Emma Hale was twenty-two.

On June 28, 1830, while proselytizing at the home of Joseph Knight, Sr., in Colesville, Joseph Smith was arrested on a warrant from Chenango County, taken to South Bainbridge for trial before Justice of the Peace Joseph Chamberlain, and was again acquitted (Firmage, pp. 50–51). Despite strong sectarian opposition, Joseph and other LDS missionaries were successful in converting a number of individuals in the South Bainbridge area, including Josiah Stowell.

BIBLIOGRAPHY

Firmage, Edwin B., and Richard C. Mangrum. *Zion in the Courts*. Urbana, Ill., 1988.

Hill, Marvin S. "Joseph Smith and the 1826 Trial: New Evidence and New Difficulties." *BYU Studies* 12 (Winter 1972):223–33.

Madsen, Gordon A. "Joseph Smith's 1826 Trial: The Legal Setting." *BYU Studies* 30 (Spring 1990):91–108.

Porter, Larry C. "A Study of the Origins of The Church of Jesus Christ of Latter-day Saints in the States of New York and Pennsylvania, 1816–1831." Ph.D. diss., Brigham Young University, 1971.

GORDON A. MADSEN

SPAFFORD, BELLE SMITH

Marion Isabelle (Belle) Sims Smith Spafford (1895-1982) was a gifted administrator and an able assistant and adviser to six Presidents of the Church during her twenty-nine years as General President of the RELIEF SOCIETY (1945–1974).

President Spafford served through the late 1940s, when the Church rallied to rebuild war-weary Saints both physically and emotionally; the 1950s, when the Church endeavored to bridge its tremendous national and international growth; and the 1960s, when the Church correlated its programs and reemphasized the family and selfless service. Commanding in stature, she displayed invaluable energy, stamina, wisdom, and forthrightness during those turbulent decades.

Belle Smith Spafford (1895–1982), ninth general president of the Relief Society, served from 1945 to 1974. She is shown here with her counselors Marianne Clark Sharp (left, daughter of J. Reuben Clark, Jr.) and Louise W. Madsen (right). Courtesy Utah State Historical Society.

Belle Smith was born October 8, 1895, in Salt Lake City, to Hester Sims and John Gibson Smith. Following her graduation from LDS High School, she completed a two-year degree at the University of Utah. After her marriage to widower Earl Spafford on March 23, 1921, she studied at the BYU Training School, and later, while her children, Mary and Earl, were growing up, she took courses at the University of Utah. A lifelong student, she designated daily study hours during which she was not to be called or disturbed; as a grandmother, she established "scholar night" on which she would study with each of her grandchildren, on a one-to-one basis.

Called early to leadership, Belle Spafford served as president of her ward YWMIA at age seventeen, and she also taught religion classes. She later served as a counselor in her ward Relief Society presidency and on the Relief Society stake board of Salt Lake Belvedere Stake. In 1935 she was called to the Relief Society General Board, and in 1942 she became a counselor to General Relief Society President Amy Brown LYMAN. She edited the history of Relief Society, *A Centenary of Relief Society* (1942), and also the RELIEF SOCIETY MAGAZINE from 1937 until her call as general president in 1945.

Named as general president of the Relief Society near the end of World War II, Spafford felt an urgent need to aid the members of the Church in Europe who had suffered from the conflict. Within weeks, Relief Society members had gathered and shipped thousands of items of food, clothing, and bedding to the members abroad. In addition to providing for physical needs, President Spafford placed special emphasis in the *Relief Society Magazine*, as well as in the lesson manuals, on social and spiritual issues of love and tolerance, in an attempt to lessen some of the anger and bitterness that existed as a result of the war. The leadership of the Relief Society organization was restructured to meet local needs worldwide. With increased emphasis on training, members of the Relief Society General Board visited every stake to develop leadership skills in local officers and to establish or reestablish local units.

Amid all the aid and effort aimed at repairing war damage, the Relief Society gained permission and raised money to construct a new Relief Society Building in Salt Lake City. Having their own headquarters building, dedicated on October 3, 1956, gave the Relief Society new cohesion and support. The early 1960s brought new emphasis on music and choirs at the local level and almost every stake in the Church formed a women's chorus called "The Singing Mothers." These groups appeared both nationally and internationally over the next twenty years.

In an effort to solidify the family, the FIRST PRESIDENCY and the QUORUM OF THE TWELVE APOSTLES assigned the Relief Society the responsibility of reemphasizing the Family Home Hour. These efforts grew into the regular Monday night FAMILY HOME EVENING program in 1964.

In the 1960s, the Relief Society also placed special emphasis on strengthening the community by encouraging women to do volunteer service at the Red Cross, Traveler's Aid, March of Dimes, child-care clinics, and hospitals. A health missionary program was instituted in 1971, using specially trained nurses and others to teach health principles and welfare concepts to the disadvantaged. Under President Spafford's direction the Social Service and Child Welfare departments provided specialized services, including programs for abused children, unwed mothers, and youth guidance, and established licensed agencies for adoption, foster care, and Indian student placements in Utah, Nevada, Arizona, and Idaho. For her pioneering efforts in social work, the Utah State Conference of Social Work awarded her an honorary life membership, and the University of Utah established the Belle S. Spafford Endowed Chair in Social Work.

President Spafford traveled the world widely and was affiliated with a number of national and international organizations. She served two terms as president of the National Council of Women (1968–1970). Recognized as one of the leading women in the world, she was presented with the National Council of Women's highest honor (1978). She died on February 2, 1982.

BIBLIOGRAPHY

History of the Relief Society, 1842–1966. Salt Lake City, 1966.

Peterson, Janet, and LaRene Gaunt. *Elect Ladies.* Salt Lake City, 1990.

Spafford, Belle S. *A Woman's Reach.* Salt Lake City, 1974.

MAREN M. MOURITSEN

SPAULDING MANUSCRIPT

The Spaulding Manuscript is a fictional story about a group of Romans who, while sailing to England early in the fourth century A.D., were blown off course and landed in eastern North America. One of them kept a record of their experiences among eastern and midwestern American Indian tribes. The 175-page manuscript was first published as a 115-page monograph in 1885, some seventy years after the death of its author, Solomon Spaulding (sometimes spelled Spalding). The only known manuscript was lost from 1839 until its discovery in Honolulu, Hawaii, in 1884. It was promptly published by both the Latter-day Saints and Reorganized Latter Day Saint churches to refute the theory of some critics that it had served as an original source document for the Book of Mormon, supposedly supplied to Joseph Smith by Sidney Rigdon.

Spaulding was born in Ashford, Connecticut, on February 21, 1761. He served in the American Revolution, later graduated from Dartmouth College, and became a clergyman. He subsequently lost his faith in the Bible, left the ministry, and worked unsuccessfully at a variety of occupations in New York, Ohio, and Pennsylvania until his death near Pittsburgh in 1816. About 1812 he wrote *Manuscript Found*, which he attempted to publish to relieve pressing debts.

There are similarities in the explanation for the origins of both *Manuscript Found* and the Book of Mormon. The introduction to the Spaulding work claims that its author was walking near Conneaut, Ohio (about 150 miles west of the place in New York where Joseph Smith obtained the gold plates), when he discovered an inscribed, flat stone. This he raised with a lever, uncovering a cave in which lay a stone box containing twenty-eight rolls of parchment. The writing was in Latin. The story is primarily a secular one, having virtually no religious content. A character in the novel possessed a seerstone, similar to objects used by Joseph Smith. However, none of the many names found in either volume matches any of those in the other, nor is there the remotest similarity in literary styles.

The first to assert that a direct connection existed between the Book of Mormon and *Manuscript Found* was Doctor Philastus Hurlbut, who was excommunicated from the Church in June 1833. Desiring to discredit his former coreligionists, Hurlbut set out in the ensuing months to refute Joseph Smith's claims for the origins of the Book of Mormon. He interviewed members of Spaulding's family, who swore that there were precise similarities between Spaulding's work and the Book of Mormon. He also located the neglected manuscript, but must have been disappointed to discover that it had no demonstrable connection with the Book of Mormon.

In 1834, Hurlbut was involved with Eber D. Howe in preparing a significant anti-Mormon publication, *Mormonism Unvailed*. Its final chapter dealt with the Spaulding theory of the origin of the Book of Mormon. Howe admitted in the book that the only document known to have been authored by Spaulding had been found, but he asserted that this was not *Manuscript Found*. The title penciled on the brown paper cover was *Manuscript Story— Conneaut Creek*. Howe speculated that Spaulding must have composed another manuscript that served as the source of the Book of Mormon, but no additional writings of Spaulding have ever surfaced. By the 1840s, the so-called Spaulding theory had become the main anti-Mormon explanation for the Book of Mormon.

Spaulding's manuscript, lost for forty-five years, was among items shipped from the office of the Ohio *Painesville Telegraph*, owned by Eber D. Howe, when that office was purchased in 1839 by L. L. Rice, who subsequently moved to Honolulu. Rice discovered the manuscript in 1884 while searching his collection for abolitionist materials for his friend James H. Fairchild, president of Oberlin College. Believers in the Book of Mormon felt vindicated by this discovery, and they published Spaulding's work to show the world it was not the source for the Book of Mormon.

Since 1946, no serious student of Mormonism has given the Spaulding Manuscript theory much credibility. In that year, Fawn Brodie published *No Man Knows My History*. This biography of Joseph Smith, hostile to his prophetic claims, dismissed the idea of any connection between Spaulding and Smith or their writings. Rigdon first met Joseph Smith in December 1830 after the Book of Mormon was published.

Nevertheless, some have continued to promote the Spaulding theory (e.g., see Holley). In 1977, graphologists claimed to have detected similarities between the handwriting of Spaulding and of one of the scribes who transcribed some of the Book of Mormon from Joseph Smith's dictation. After considerable media attention and further scrutiny, anti-Mormon spokespersons acknowledged that they had been too hasty. The handwriting evidence did not support a connection between Solomon Spaulding and Joseph Smith.

BIBLIOGRAPHY

Bush, Lester E., Jr. "The Spaulding Theory Then and Now." *Dialogue* 4 (Autumn 1977):40–69.

Bushman, Richard L. *Joseph Smith and the Beginnings of Mormonism*. Urbana, Ill., 1985.

Fairchild, James H. "Manuscript of Solomon Spaulding and the Book of Mormon." *Bibliotheca Sacra*, pp. 173–74. Cleveland, Ohio, 1885.

Holley, Vernal. "Book of Mormon Authorship: A Closer Look." Ogden, Utah, 1983; this booklet is reviewed by A. Norwood, *Review of Books on the Book of Mormon* 1 (1989):80–88.

LANCE D. CHASE

SPIRIT

The existence of both good and evil spirit beings is a prominent doctrine in LDS theology. Spirits are intelligent, self-existent, organized matter and are governed by eternal laws. Moreover, all living things had a pre-earthly spirit existence. LDS understanding on this subject is formulated by biblical and latter-day scripture and the teachings of latter-day prophets.

Latter-day revelation declares that "all spirit is matter, but it is more fine or pure" than the physical materials of earth life (D&C 131:7–8). The Prophet Joseph SMITH explained:

> A very material difference [exists] between the body and the spirit; the body is supposed to be organized matter, and the spirit, by many, is thought to be immaterial, without substance. With this latter statement we should beg leave to differ, and state the spirit is a substance; that it is material, but that it is more pure, elastic and refined matter than the body; that it existed before the body, can exist in the body; and will exist separate from the body, when the body will be mouldering in the dust; and will in the resurrection, be again united with it [*TPJS*, p. 207].

Although the Lord has revealed much in ancient and latter-day scripture about spirit matter and spirit beings, many unknowns remain, especially the full meaning of such terms as "INTELLIGENCE," "light," and "truth," which are used in the revelations in association with the word "spirit." Spirit matter is identified with intelligence or the light of truth (D&C 93:29). Joseph Smith taught that elements were not created or made, but can be organized into a spirit being. This spirit, intelligence, or light has always existed, being coeternal with God. It can act and be acted upon; it can be organized, but it cannot be destroyed. Spirits exist upon a self-existent principle, and "all . . . spirits that God ever sent into the world are susceptible of enlargement" (*TPJS*, pp. 351–54), meaning that they are capable of intellectual growth and maturation and that "there is never a time when the spirit is too old to approach God" (*TPJS*, p. 191).

It is LDS doctrine that human spirits are the literal offspring of perfected, exalted parents, a Father and a MOTHER IN HEAVEN (cf. Num. 16:22; Heb. 12:9). God instituted a PLAN OF SALVATION whereby his spirit children could advance and become like him (*see* COUNCIL IN HEAVEN). Paul said that the human family is God's offspring (Acts 17:29). All men and women lived as personal, individual spirit children with God in a PREMORTAL LIFE before they were born into physical bodies. Likewise, one's personal, individual spirit existence extends beyond the death of the mortal body.

Jesus Christ was the firstborn of all God's spirit children and is thus the elder brother of the rest of mankind (*see* JESUS CHRIST: FIRSTBORN IN THE SPIRIT). Because of the faith of the BROTHER OF JARED (c. 2200 B.C.), he was permitted to see the Lord's premortal spirit body. The Lord explained to him, "Seest thou that ye are created after mine own image? Yea, even all men were created in the beginning after mine own image. Behold, this body, which ye now behold, is the body of my spirit; . . . and even as I appear unto thee to be in the spirit will I appear unto my people in the flesh" (Ether 3:15–16). Since spirits are the offspring of Heavenly Parents, they are in that image and likeness, both male and female (Gen. 1:26–27; Moses 3:4–7; Abr. 3:18–23).

Enoch was shown a vision of the spirits of all men and women who had lived or who would yet live on the earth and who were first created as spirits in heaven (Moses 6:28; 7:38–40, 57). Abraham also saw the premortal spirits of mankind and noted that they varied in intelligence and obedience (Abr. 3:18–19). Among these were many noble and great ones whom God said he would make rulers and leaders in his kingdom. Abraham was told that he was one of these and was chosen before he was born (Abr. 3:22–23). Many were foreordained to perform certain tasks when upon the earth (*see* FOREORDINATION). In the premortal state, spirits received their first lessons in the gospel and the work of God that they would do on the earth (D&C 138:55–56; cf. Jer. 1:5; Eph. 1:3–4; Titus 1:2). Many of these spirit beings were called and prepared from the foundation of the world because of their faith and good works, to bear the priesthood and teach the gospel and the commandments of God in mortality (Alma 13:1–6).

Inherent in the makeup of their intelligent nature, spirits have AGENCY and are able to make choices. The scriptures teach that spirits are capable of all the emotions, passions, and intellectual experiences exhibited by mortals, including love, anger, hate, envy, knowledge, obedience, rebellion, jealousy, repentance, loyalty, activity, thought, and comprehension. Using their agency, some of God's children rebelled in the premortal life, and WAR IN HEAVEN ensued. The rebellious spirits followed Lucifer and with him were cast down to the earth and became devils or evil spirits, never to receive physical bodies on earth (Moses

4:1–4; D&C 76:25–27; cf. Rev. 12:4, 7–9; D&C 29:36). Satan and his followers remain spirit beings made in the image of God but are still rebellious and evil. They are desirous of having a mortal body. The Prophet Joseph Smith explained, "The great principle of happiness consists in having a body. The devil has no body, and herein is his punishment. He is pleased when he can obtain the tabernacle of man, and when cast out by the Savior he asked to go into the herd of swine, showing that he would prefer a swine's body to having none" (*TPJS*, p. 181; cf. pp. 297–98).

Latter-day revelation has not identified or clarified the nature of seraphim or cherubim mentioned in the Bible (Gen. 3:24; Isa. 6:2) and whether these are spirit beings or merely symbolic representations. Some spirits are messengers of the Lord and minister to mortals (Heb. 1:14; D&C 129), but spirit ministrants cannot perform all the functions of those angels who have resurrected bodies (*TPJS*, pp. 191, 325).

A spirit being who has never entered mortality is in an "unembodied" state. A spirit with a mortal body is in an "embodied" state and the body and spirit constitute the SOUL (D&C 88:15). Death is the separation of the mortal, physical body from the spirit (James 2:26), after which the spirit lives in a "disembodied" state in the postmortal SPIRIT WORLD, while the mortal, physical body, without life, decays in the grave. In the postmortal world, the spirit awaits being "reembodied" in the RESURRECTION, which is the reuniting of the spirit and the body, never to be separated (Alma 11:44–45). Every person in the mortal world has come from the spirit world, and all will eventually die and then be resurrected.

Latter-day revelation teaches that God the Father and Jesus Christ are resurrected, exalted beings, meaning that they have glorified bodies of flesh and bones (D&C 130:22). Man exists that he "might have joy" (2 Ne. 2:25), and the revelations teach that a fulness of joy can be experienced only in the resurrected state—with the spirit and the body inseparably united (D&C 93:33–34). Therefore, existence as a spirit alone in either the premortal or postmortal spirit world has its limitations. Departed spirits who know the plan of God and the value of a physical body are anxious to be resurrected (D&C 45:17; 138:50). Because they rejected God's plan of salvation, Lucifer and his followers have been denied forever the privilege of having a physical body and thus are limited or cur-tailed in their progress. The Lord declared, "Where I am they cannot come, for they have no power" (D&C 29:29).

The spirit creation pertains not to the human family alone but to all living things. Latter-day scriptures teach that the human spirit is in the likeness of that which is physical, as was demonstrated in the case of the spirit of Jesus Christ, who appeared to the brother of Jared, noted above. Thus, "the spirit of man [is] in the likeness of his person, as also the spirit of the beast, and every other creature which God has created" (D&C 77:2; *see also* ANIMALS). Moses wrote that every plant of the field, every herb, indeed every thing, was created "in heaven" before it was naturally upon the face of the earth (Moses 3:5–7).

[*See also* First Estate; Hell; Spirit Body; Spirit Prison.]

BIBLIOGRAPHY

"The Father and the Son: A Doctrinal Exposition by the First Presidency and the Twelve." *AF*, pp. 465–73. Salt Lake City, 1963.

Millet, Robert L., and Joseph F. McConkie. *The Life Beyond*. Salt Lake City, 1986.

"The Origin of Man," An official declaration in *MFP* 4:200–206.

Packer, Boyd K. "The Law and the Light." In *The Book of Mormon: Jacob Through the Words of Mormon, To Learn with Joy*, ed. M. Nyman and C. Tate, pp. 1–31. Provo, Utah, 1990.

Smith, Joseph. *Teachings of the Prophet Joseph Smith*, ed. Joseph Fielding Smith, pp. 202–215. Salt Lake City, 1938.

Top, Brent, L. *The Life Before*. Salt Lake City, 1988.

JAY E. JENSEN

SPIRIT BODY

Latter-day Saints believe that each person was born in PREMORTAL LIFE as a spirit son or daughter of God. The spirit joins with a physical body in the process of birth on the earth. At death the spirit and the body separate until they reunite in the RESURRECTION. SPIRITS are capable of intellectual advancement, love, hate, happiness, sorrow, obedience, disobedience, memory, and other personal characteristics. Latter-day Saints believe that "all spirit is matter," but this matter is so fine that it cannot be discerned by mortal eyes (D&C 131: 7–8).

The DOCTRINE AND COVENANTS explains that "the spirit of man [is] in the likeness of his person, as also the spirit of the beast; and every other creature which God has created" (D&C 77:2). That spirit bodies resemble physical bodies is demonstrated in the account of the premortal Jesus visiting the BROTHER OF JARED many centuries before Jesus' birth (Ether 3:9–16). On this occasion, the Lord revealed his spirit body and said, "this body, which ye now behold, is the body of my spirit; . . . and even as I appear unto thee to be in the spirit will I appear unto my people in the flesh" (3:16).

According to Latter-day Saint doctrine, the spirit (sometimes called the SOUL) does not die (Alma 42:9; cf. James 2:26). However, a spirit, though immortal, cannot have a fulness of joy without being inseparably connected to a resurrected physical body (D&C 93:33–34; 138:50). For additional references see Job 32:8; Hebrews 12:9; 1 Nephi 11:11; Abraham 3:18–23.

WILSON K. ANDERSEN

SPIRIT OF GOD

See: Light of Christ

SPIRIT PRISON

In Latter-day Saint doctrine the "spirit prison" is both a condition and a place within the postearthly SPIRIT WORLD. One "imprisons" himself or herself through unbelief or through willful disobedience of God. In such circumstances, one's opportunities in the AFTERLIFE will be limited. Those who willfully rebel against the light and truth of the gospel and do not repent remain in this condition of imprisonment and suffer SPIRITUAL DEATH, which is a condition of hell (Alma 12:16–18; D&C 76:36–37). Furthermore, since a fulness of joy is not possible without the resurrected body, the waiting in the spirit world for the RESURRECTION is a type of imprisonment (D&C 45:17; 93:33–34; 138:16, 17, 50). However, through the ATONEMENT of Jesus Christ all have a promise of resurrection, and thus of eventual release from this type of spirit prison, although the unrepentant will still be imprisoned by their unbelief (see DAMNATION).

Another more far-reaching definition of "spirit prison" is HELL. In this sense, spirit prison is a temporary abode in the spirit world of those who either were untaught and unrighteous, or were disobedient to the gospel while in mortal life (cf. Alma 40:11–14; D&C 138:32).

As part of his redemptive mission, Jesus Christ visited the spirit world during the interlude between his own death and resurrection, and "from among the righteous, he organized his forces and appointed messengers, clothed with power and authority, and commissioned them to go forth and carry the light of the gospel to them that were in darkness"—in other words, to the spirits in prison (D&C 138:30; cf. 1 Pet. 3:18–20; 4:6). Thus, the gulf between paradise and hell that is spoken of in Jesus' parable of the rich man and Lazarus (Luke 16:19–31) was bridged by the Savior's ministry in the spirit world. This bridging allows interaction among the righteous and wicked spirits to the extent that the faithful present the gospel to "those who had died in their sins, without a knowledge of the truth, or in transgression, having rejected the prophets" (D&C 138:32). Latter-day Saints believe that preaching the gospel in the spirit world continues today and will continue until every soul who wishes to do so and repents properly will be released from such imprisonment.

Repentance of imprisoned spirits opens the doors of the prison, enabling them to loose themselves from the spiritual darkness of unbelief, ignorance, and sin. As they accept the gospel of Jesus Christ and cast off their sins, the repentant are able to break the chains of hell and dwell with the righteous in paradise.

[See also Salvation of the Dead.]

BIBLIOGRAPHY

Pratt, Orson. "Deity; The Holy Priesthood." In *Masterful Discourses and Writings of Orson Pratt*, N. B. Lundwall, comp., pp. 260–68. Salt Lake City, 1946.

ROBERT J. PARSONS

SPIRIT OF PROPHECY

Spirit of prophecy is equated in Revelation 19:10 with "the testimony of Jesus." For members of The Church of Jesus Christ of Latter-day Saints, having a TESTIMONY OF JESUS CHRIST means receiving personal spiritual assurance through REVELATION by the HOLY GHOST that Jesus is the literal Son of God, the creator of the world, and that through his

ATONEMENT all people will be resurrected and live forever.

According to the Prophet Joseph SMITH, the spirit of prophecy is vital to the principles of salvation, revelation, and the teaching and ministering of the gospel. Each person must receive a testimony of Christ in order to attain salvation and ETERNAL LIFE with him (*TPJS*, p. 160). Since the gospel is to be taught to everyone, it follows that all people of every race and gender can experience the spirit of prophecy. Moreover, in the words of Joseph Smith, "God in his superior wisdom, has always given his Saints, wherever he had any on the earth, the same spirit, and that spirit, as John says, is the true spirit of prophecy, which is the testimony of Jesus" (*TPJS*, p. 300).

It is through the spirit of prophecy that God's continuing revelations are brought to the people of the earth, not only through his ordained prophets but also through all those who have received a testimony of Christ. The gospel cannot be taught on the earth without the spirit of prophecy or a testimony of Christ, because it is only through testimony received by revelation that Christ's teachings are validated in the heart and mind of the person taught. One who preaches the gospel and denies the spirit of prophecy is, according to Joseph Smith, an "imposter" (*TPJS*, p. 269).

While only one person (the PRESIDENT OF THE CHURCH) may exercise all the keys of the priesthood of God at one time on the earth and receive revelation for the whole Church, the underlying principle of the spirit of prophecy is that all SAINTS who receive a testimony of Christ are PROPHETS in the limited sense that they may receive revelation and INSPIRATION for themselves (*TPJS*, p. 119). This same idea is implicit in Moses' response to Joshua: "Would God that all the Lord's people were prophets, and that the Lord would put his spirit upon them!" (Num. 11:29).

LOUISE PLUMMER

SPIRITUAL DEATH

Spiritual death is the condition of one who is spiritually cut off, temporarily or permanently, from the presence of God. LDS SCRIPTURES speak of two spiritual deaths, and the concept manifests itself in many ways.

The first type of spiritual death is the actual separation from God that automatically comes upon all born into MORTALITY as a consequence of the FALL OF ADAM. All mortals will be redeemed from this death, as well as from physical death, through Christ's atonement and RESURRECTION (1 Cor. 15:21–23; 2 Ne. 9:10–15; Hel. 14:15–19; D&C 29:41), to be brought back into God's presence to stand before him.

The second spiritual death will be finalized on the day of JUDGMENT for those who have not repented (Rev. 2:11; 20:6–15; Alma 12:16–36). It is the result of a lifetime of choices. For those who ultimately lose the inclination or ability to repent, or commit unpardonable sin, it becomes perdition (2 Pet. 3:7; Alma 34:35; 40:25–26) or "banishment from the presence of God and from his light and truth forever" (*DS* 2:216–30). This does not extinguish the spirit of man, however, for it is eternal (see Alma 12:18; 42:9). The Savior's atonement gives all mankind the opportunity to avoid the second spiritual death and gain IMMORTALITY and ETERNAL LIFE.

The spiritually "dead" may be grouped into several types and categories. For example, Satan and the spirits who joined him during the WAR IN HEAVEN are eternally spiritually dead (D&C 29:36–39; 76:25–29). They are SONS OF PERDITION (see 2 Ne. 9:8–9). Mortals who sin "unto death" (D&C 64:7) by denying the Son after the Father has revealed him will join "the only ones on whom the second death shall have any power" (D&C 76:30–38). In yet another sense, all people on earth over the age of ACCOUNTABILITY are to a certain extent spiritually dead, depending on their present state of REPENTANCE and their degree of sensitivity to the LIGHT OF CHRIST and to the HOLY GHOST.

Buddhism, Islam, Christianity, Judaism, and most other religions believe in some form of life after death, judgment, and ultimate punishment for the unrepentant. For example, the ancient Egyptians believed that the hard-hearted would die a second death by being devoured by the Chaos monster (Keel, pp. 72–73). Major differences between the Mormon concept of spiritual death and those of others center on the ATONEMENT OF JESUS CHRIST. The only permanent spiritual death is that which individuals bring upon themselves by refusing to repent of their sins, having denied the Holy Spirit after having received it, and having denied the Only Begotten Son of the Father, having crucified him unto themselves (D&C 76:35).

BIBLIOGRAPHY

Keel, O. *The Symbolism of the Biblical World*, pp. 72–73. London, 1978.

Lund, Gerald N. "The Fall of Man and His Redemption." In *The Book of Mormon: Second Nephi, The Doctrinal Structure*, ed. M. Nyman, pp. 83–106. Provo, Utah, 1989.

Matthews, Robert J. "The Fall of Man." In *The Man Adam*, ed. J. McConkie, pp. 37–64. Salt Lake City, 1990.

Romney, Marion G. "The Resurrection of Jesus." *Ensign* 12 (May 1982):6–9.

RICHARD M. ROMNEY

SPIRIT WORLD

The spirit world is the habitation of spirits. The earth itself and the living things on the earth have spirit counterparts that existed before the physical creation, and a living SOUL consists of a spirit body united with a physical body. This spirit existence, where living things are composed of organized, refined spirit matter, extends beyond the human family and includes animals and plants. Little is revealed about plant spirits beyond the fact that all living things, including plants, were created as spirits before they were created with physical bodies (Moses 3:5, 9). However, latter-day revelation indicates that human and animal spirits are living, active, intelligent beings and that spirits do not need physical bodies for existence (*see* SPIRIT). Since spirits exist before mortality, as well as afterward, there is both a premortal and a postmortal spirit world.

The premortal spirit existence, for mankind at least, was "in heaven," in the kingdom where God lives. Explaining this phase of the Creation, the Lord said, "I, the Lord God, created all things, of which I have spoken, spiritually, before they were naturally upon the face of the earth, . . . for in heaven created I them" (Moses 3:5).

More detail is known about the place and conditions of departed spirits—the postmortal spirit world—than about the premortal. Concerning the postmortal place of human spirits, ALMA₂ sought an answer to the question "What becometh of the souls of men from this time of death to the time appointed for the resurrection?" (Alma 40:7). It was revealed to him by an angel that at the death of the body "the spirits of all men, whether they be good or evil, are taken home to that God who gave them life" (Alma 40:11). They are then assigned to a place of PARADISE or a place of HELL and "outer darkness," depending on the manner of their mortal life (Alma 40:12–14).

President Joseph F. SMITH discussed this subject further:

The spirits of all men, as soon as they depart from this mortal body, whether they are good or evil, . . . are taken home to that God who gave them life, where there is a separation, a partial judgment, and the spirits of those who are righteous are received into a state of happiness which is called paradise, a state of rest, a state of peace, where they expand in wisdom, where they have respite from all their troubles, and where care and sorrow do not annoy. The wicked, on the contrary, have no part nor portion in the Spirit of the Lord, and they are cast into outer darkness, being led captive, because of their own iniquity, by the evil one. And in this space between death and the resurrection of the body, the two classes of souls remain, in happiness or in misery, until the time which is appointed of God that the dead shall come forth and be reunited both spirit and body, and be brought to stand before God, and be judged according to their works. This is the final judgment [p. 448].

President Brigham YOUNG declared:

When you lay down this tabernacle, where are you going? Into the spiritual world . . . Where is the spirit world? It is right here. Do the good and evil spirits go together? Yes they do. . . . Do they go beyond the boundaries of the organized earth? No, they do not. . . . Can you see it with your natural eyes? No. Can you see spirits in this room? No. Suppose the Lord should touch your eyes that you might see, could you then see the spirits? Yes, as plainly as you now see bodies [Widtsoe, pp. 376–77].

The postmortal spirit world is an actual place where spirits reside and "where they converse together the same as we do on the earth" (*TPJS*, p. 353). "Life and work and activity all continue in the spirit world. Men have the same talents and intelligence there which they had in this life. They possess the same attitudes, inclinations, and feelings there which they had in this life" (*MD*, p. 762).

The postmortal spirit world is a place of continued preparation and learning. In this sense, it is an extension of mortality. Those who have died without an opportunity to hear the gospel of Jesus Christ will have opportunity to hear and accept it in the spirit world. "The great work in the world of spirits is the preaching of the gospel to those who are imprisoned by sin and false traditions" (*MD*, p.

762). The faithful elders and sisters who depart this life "continue their labors in the preaching of the gospel of repentance and redemption . . . Among those who are in darkness" (D&C 138:57; Smith, p. 461; *see also* SALVATION OF THE DEAD).

Bruce R. McConkie explained, "Until the death of Christ these two spirit abodes [paradise and hell] were separated by a great gulf, with the intermingling of their respective inhabitants strictly forbidden (Luke 16:19–31). After our Lord bridged the gulf between the two (1 Pet. 3:18–21; Moses 7:37–39), the affairs of his kingdom in the spirit world were so arranged that righteous spirits began teaching the gospel to wicked ones" (*MD*, p. 762).

An important LDS doctrine states that Jesus Christ inaugurated the preaching of the gospel and organized a mission in the spirit world during his ministry there between his death and resurrection. This is the substance of a revelation recorded as Doctrine and Covenants section 138. Since Jesus' visit there, the gospel has been taught vigorously in the spirit world (*see* SPIRIT PRISON).

The relative conditions and state of mind in the two spheres of the postmortal spirit world are described by the Prophet Joseph Smith: "The spirits of the just are exalted to a greater and more glorious work; hence they are blessed in their departure to the world of spirits. Enveloped in flaming fire, they are not far from us, and know and understand our thoughts, feelings, and motions, and are often pained therewith" (*TPJS*, p. 326). On the other hand, "The great misery of departed spirits in the world of spirits, where they go after death, is to know that they come short of the glory that others enjoy and that they might have enjoyed themselves, and they are their own accusers" (*TPJS*, pp. 310–11).

A statement regarding conditions in the spirit world among the righteous was given in 1856 by Jedediah M. Grant, a member of the First Presidency. He had related to President Heber C. KIMBALL a vision he had had of the spirit world, which President Kimball subsequently discussed at Grant's funeral a few days later on December 4, 1856. Although an unofficial statement, it represents concepts generally held by Latter-day Saints. A summary follows: Jedediah Grant saw the righteous gathered together in the spirit world; there were no wicked spirits among them. There were order, government, and organization. Among the righteous there was no disorder, darkness, or con-

fusion. They were organized into families, and there was "perfect harmony." He saw his wife, with whom he conversed, and many other persons whom he knew. There was "a deficiency in some" families, because some individuals "had not honored their calling" on earth and therefore were not "permitted to . . . dwell together." The buildings were exceptionally attractive, far exceeding in beauty his opinion of Solomon's temple. Gardens were more beautiful than any he had seen on earth, with "flowers of numerous kinds." After experiencing "the beauty and glory of the spirit world" among the righteous spirits, he regretted having to return to his body in mortality (*JD* 4:135–36).

Since all who have possessed a body in mortality will be resurrected, a time will ultimately come when the postmortal spirit world pertaining to this earth will cease to exist as the earth will become the celestial home for resurrected beings (*MD*, p. 762).

BIBLIOGRAPHY

Smith, Joseph F. *GD*, pp. 428–77.

Smith, Joseph Fielding. *DS* 2:132–61.

Young, Brigham. *Discourses of Brigham Young*, ed. John A. Widtsoe, pp. 376–81. Salt Lake City, 1946.

WALTER D. BOWEN

SPORTS

The LDS Church was a pioneer among religious faiths in promoting physical activity, sports, and recreation for members (Parkin, p. 67). Joseph SMITH, the first Prophet of the Church, enjoyed and excelled in running, wrestling, jumping, and playing ball. Brigham YOUNG, his successor, taught that recreation (including sports) is a spiritual activity that develops not only the body but also the mind and the spirit. He encouraged the building of recreation halls in conjunction with chapels for worship (Parkin, p. 15). These halls, later called cultural halls, are still part of a meetinghouse and are used extensively for sports, recreational, and cultural activities.

During the early years of the Church, participation in sports was informal. But gradually programs became well structured. In 1904 in Salt Lake City, one of the earliest leagues for "outdoor activities and friendly competition" was organized

Basketball at Brigham Young Academy was originally a women's sport. This team in 1900 won the championship. The Church encourages members to live a well-rounded life, including the development of physical skills and a healthy body. From the Brigham Young University Centennial Collection.

(Strong, p. 101–102). In 1904 and for a few years thereafter, an annual field day that included a variety of athletic activities was held in the Salt Lake Valley. The first formal basketball league for boys was started in Salt Lake City in 1908. During the decade 1910–1920, competition in baseball and basketball spread from the Salt Lake Valley to many other LDS settlements.

The completion of the Deseret Gymnasium in 1910, near the Salt Lake Temple, made it apparent that Church leaders continued to encourage physical activity and sports. The facility included a gymnasium, a swimming pool, bowling lanes, tennis courts, and dressing rooms. It accommodated sports and exercise activities for both men and women (*Deseret Evening News*, Sept. 20, 1910, p. 5). By 1922, gym membership exceeded four thousand.

The 1911 June CONFERENCE sessions for activity leaders of individual WARDS (congregations) focused on volleyball, wrestling, fencing, swimming, gymnastics, running, jumping, vaulting, and baseball (*IE* 14 [June 1911]:751–52). In 1922 Church leaders issued formal guidelines for recreation and sports. "The recreation program under the direction of the MIA [a Church program that served youth and young adults] must do more than provide amusement. Through it we must emphasize the fundamental ideals and standards of the Church. Ours is the opportunity to enrich leisure, to spiritualize recreation" (*M.I.A. Activity Manual*, p. 5).

By 1926 team sports such as baseball, basketball, and soccer, and lifelong activities such as walking, hiking, camping, tennis, swimming, skating, and dancing, were being encouraged. At this time the need for emphasis on sportsmanship came into focus. Quoting Walter Camp, one leader counseled, "Play fair, but play hard, win if you can, lose if you must, but take a whipping without whimpering" (*Recreation Organization and Leadership*, pp. 50–51). Leaders taught that the desire to win should not be so intense that participants could not enjoy the game.

For two decades following World War II, "all-Church" tournaments flourished in sports such as basketball, softball, and volleyball, and to a lesser degree in tennis, golf, and horseshoes. By 1962 more than 3,500 basketball teams and 50,000 players were involved. Teams came to Salt Lake City not only from neighboring states but also from as far away as Washington, D.C., Canada, and Mexico (*Church News*, Feb. 24, 1962, p. 9).

In 1963 Elder Ezra Taft BENSON, later to become the thirteenth President of the Church, spoke to more than 1,400 participants attending the all-Church softball tournament banquet. "This is the greatest softball tournament in the world. Its purpose is to build men, men of character, men of strength, and faith, to build testimonies, to build men who love the Lord" (*Church News*, Aug. 31, 1963, p. 4). So popular was all-Church tournament competition in the major sports involved that it grew to include three divisions of play: juniors (ages 16–17), seniors (ages 18–29), and college students. Televised finals, devotional meetings, banquets, and other features of highly organized competitive sports became the custom for all-Church tournaments. Sportsmanship trophies, superior in importance and appearance to championship trophies, became a highlight of the tournaments.

Worldwide Church growth in the 1960s made it impractical to continue these popular tournaments. In 1971 Church leaders announced that sports would henceforth be emphasized on a local basis and teams would no longer travel to Salt Lake City. Where practical, tournaments were to be held in various REGIONS of the Church (*New Era* 1 [Sept. 1971]:44–45). This change accommodated larger numbers of new members with differing interests in sports appropriate to their cultures.

Today LDS meetinghouses continue to have large cultural halls that accommodate sports and recreation. With more than 15,000 wards in the Church in 1990, combined male and female sports participation in three selected team sports is estimated to be as follows: basketball, 552,000; softball, 690,000; volleyball, 207,000.

Since the first printed guidelines in 1922, Church authorities have continued to provide local leaders with instructions that give purpose and direction to Church sports: "Sports programs should provide year-round opportunity for involvement and should include a wide variety of individual and team sports. All who have a desire to participate should have the opportunity" (*Physical Fitness, Sports, and Recreation Manual*, p. 17). President David O. MCKAY aptly summarized the position of the Church on sports and play when he taught that practicing Mormons work, worship, pray, and play (*Family Home Evening Manual*, p. iii).

Since 1977 the coordination and leadership of Church sports have been the responsibility of activities committees at the ward and STAKE levels. These committees give local leadership to cultural arts, socials, service projects, and sports. Regional (three to six stakes), multiregional (fifteen to thirty stakes), and area sports directors are called as needed to organize and supervise tournaments in the eighteen designated geographical AREAS of the worldwide Church.

The Church also supports a full intercollegiate athletic program at Brigham Young University and BYU—Hawaii. But beyond intercollegiate athlet-

"Club Benson," a basketball team in Peru composed of Church members (1988). The Church sponsors and conducts athletic activities among local Church members in many team sports, including basketball, softball, and volleyball. Photographer: Jed Clark.

ics, both schools have large intramural programs that serve thousands of students.

The Church promotes both physical and spiritual fitness for all members. Sports for females have somewhat paralleled sports for males through the years, except that all-Church tournaments for women in team sports have never been held. Characteristic of the Church sports program from the beginning is that there is no practice or play on Sunday.

[*See also* PHYSICAL FITNESS; RECREATION.]

BIBLIOGRAPHY

Family Home Evening Manual. Salt Lake City, 1968.

M.I.A. Activity Manual. Salt Lake City, 1933.

Parkin, Darrell Lloyd. "The Athletic Program of the Mormon Church: Its Growth and Development." Master's thesis, University of Illinois, 1964.

Physical Fitness, Sports, and Recreation Manual. Salt Lake City, 1984.

Recreation Organization and Leadership. Salt Lake City, 1926.

Strong, Leon M. "A History of the Young Men's Mutual Improvement Association, 1875–1938." Master's thesis, Brigham Young University, 1939.

CLAYNE R. JENSEN

STAKE

Stakes are an intermediate unit of organization between Church headquarters and the local WARDS. A stake ordinarily comprises between five and twelve wards, totaling at least 3,000 members. Depending on LDS population density, a stake may cover only a small part of one city or include many towns or cities spread over hundreds of miles. Where there are not sufficient Latter-day Saints to organize functioning wards, members belong to BRANCHES, which are supervised by MISSIONS or stakes. The stake is "a miniature Church to the Saints in a specific geographic area" (Benson, p. 4); the STAKE PRESIDENCY is fully charged and authorized to implement all the programs of the Church within the stake boundaries and directly supervises the BISHOPS of wards. Stake presidents are supervised by AREA presidencies, who report directly to the presiding quorums of the Church. For the sake of administrative convenience, training and support are provided to geographically proximate stakes by REGIONAL REPRESENTATIVES.

The Box Elder Tabernacle in Brigham City, Utah (built 1865–1890, burned in 1896, and rebuilt in 1897 with additional spires added). In pioneer Utah, the tabernacle and other stake buildings were the religious and social center of LDS community life. These outlying stakes were viewed symbolically as the "stakes" holding in place the tent of God's covering over the Church. Courtesy Utah State Historical Society.

THE SCRIPTURAL CONCEPT OF STAKES. When the resurrected Jesus visited the Nephites in the Western Hemisphere, he taught them the words of Isaiah: "Enlarge the place of thy tent, and let them stretch forth the curtains of thy habitations; spare not, lengthen thy cords and strengthen thy stakes . . . and make the desolate cities to be inhabited" (3 Ne. 22:2–5; cf. Isa. 54:2–3). He promised to reveal to them his new covenant of priestly sacrifices and ordinances, including those of the temple (3 Ne. 9:19–20; 10:6–7; WJS, pp. 212–13). The rich imagery of Isaiah chapter 54 associates the concept of "stake" with the tent pegs that firmly held the curtains around the tabernacle that Moses built, the central Israelite sanctuary and seat of the Lord. In Doctrine and Covenants 101:43–62, this imagery is expanded: the stakes of Zion are represented as twelve thriving olive trees nurtured in peace (WJS, p. 415); in the redemption of Zion, they will never "be removed" (Isa. 33:20).

Stakes are gathering places for the Saints, "the curtains or the strength of Zion" (D&C 101:21).

They are established as protected enclaves of spiritual strength and righteousness around the globe, symbolically holding the curtains around God's presence in the Church and among his people, in preparation for the establishment of the NEW JERUSALEM (D&C 115:6; Isa. 4:6) and the rebuilding of the "old" Jerusalem in the Holy Land.

The portable tabernacle of Moses with its sustaining cords and stakes eventually came to rest in Shiloh, and was replaced centuries later with the construction of the temple of Solomon in Jerusalem. In all ages, "the main object" of the gathering of people is to construct a temple, "to build unto the Lord an house whereby he [can] reveal unto his people the ordinances of his house and glories of his kingdom and teach the people the ways of salvation" (WJS, p. 212; cf. Benson, p. 4). In the modern Church, stake presidents hold the keys to issue TEMPLE RECOMMENDS, and stake high priests quorums coordinate temple participation to strengthen Zion: "Put on thy beautiful garments, O daughter of Zion; and strengthen thy stakes and enlarge thy borders forever, that thou mayest no more be confounded, that the covenants of the Eternal Father which he hath made unto thee, O house of Israel, may be fulfilled" (Moro. 10:31; cf. Isa. 52:1).

President Ezra Taft Benson listed four purposes that stakes serve in the Church: (1) "to unify and perfect the members . . . by extending to them the Church programs, the ordinances, and gospel instruction"; (2) to be models or standards of righteousness to the world; (3) to provide a defense from error, evil, or calamity; and (4) to be "a refuge from the storm" prophesied to come upon the earth in the LAST DAYS (pp. 4–5).

THE ORGANIZATIONAL HISTORY OF STAKES. For the first several months following its organization, the Church had no need for a complex organizational structure. In response to increasing membership, the first stake was organized in Kirtland, Ohio, in 1832. The Kirtland Stake was presided over by Joseph Smith and his counselors in the FIRST PRESIDENCY. Most affairs of this original stake that did not fall under their direct purview were handled by a council of high priests who operated under the direction of the bishop (Allen and Leonard, p. 79).

In 1834 the Kirtland HIGH COUNCIL was organized and became the official judicial body for the stake. The First Presidency continued to function as the presidency of the stake until Kirtland was abandoned, but as new stakes were organized, these roles changed. In July 1834, a stake was organized in Clay County, Missouri, with its own presidency and high council (Allen and Leonard, p. 79). From that time forward, stakes were presided over by a president with two counselors, who were assisted by a high council comprised of twelve high priests residing within the stake's boundaries.

For several decades, stake organization tended to be less emphasized and often quite haphazard in comparison with the ward. While there was a functioning stake in Salt Lake City following the migration westward, most other areas of the Church had none. Where stakes existed, they filled two major functions: they held conferences designed to bring together members of several wards for instruction and spiritual guidance, and they had responsibility for many disciplinary actions that were brought before the stake high councils. However, much direction from the top proceeded directly between general Church authorities and the local ward bishops (Arrington and Bitton, p. 212).

When President Brigham YOUNG began a major restructuring of Church organization in 1877, changes were made that significantly affected the role of the stake (Hartley, p. 3). Earlier, President Young had declared that the Salt Lake Stake held no authority over other stakes of the Church, all stakes being equal and autonomous relative to each other (Hartley, p. 5). He also released members of the QUORUM OF THE TWELVE from their callings as stake presidents so that they could assume more fully their general Church leadership assignments. New stake presidencies were called for most of the stakes, and several new stakes were organized by dividing those that had become too large.

As part of the organizational change instituted by Brigham Young, stake presidencies were given responsibility for all Church matters within their stake boundaries. Stake presidencies were instructed to hold quarterly CONFERENCES, which would be visited and presided over by General Authorities. Stake presidencies were also instructed to visit the wards in their stake on a regular basis and to call local priesthood leaders as home missionaries to help them preach in the wards.

Other changes in stake organization were designed to improve administrative efficiency. Stakes were made into more manageable units to give stake presidents more time for their private commitments and to create smaller and more cohesive units with which members could more readily identify (Alexander, pp. 95, 107). During this same period, financial accounting procedures were regularized and Church membership records systematized, and the newly streamlined stakes were given greater oversight responsibility in both areas.

Following these important organizational changes, the stake assumed its role as the major governing unit between the wards and Church headquarters. Stakes were now expected to have responsibility for every person and every program within their boundaries. Decentralization by the transference of more priesthood responsibility to the stakes has continued as Church membership has expanded. Stake presidents and bishops have been clearly identified as the links in the organizational chain between the General Authorities and local Church members.

The historical importance of stakes in the Church is exemplified by the stake-level innovations that have been adopted throughout the Church. FAMILY HOME EVENINGS and the WELFARE program began as programs of the Granite Stake in Salt Lake City in the early 1900s. The "Home Evening" program was designed to help parents develop closer relationships with their children. The suggested format for these weekly family meetings included prayer, music, scripture reading and gospel instruction, discussion of family concerns, recreational and cultural activities, and refreshments. The Granite Stake welfare plan was designed to promote temporal well-being by stressing home industry and cooperation. Stake committees were appointed to promote gardening, the development of canneries, livestock raising, and the establishment of new industries. This program foreshadowed the work of President Harold B. Lee as president of the Pioneer Stake during the Great Depression, which led to the establishment of a Churchwide welfare program. Other Church programs that originated in stakes include the seminary program for high school students, stake missionary work, systematic stake supervision of temple and genealogical work, and a variety of youth programs.

THE CONTEMPORARY STAKE. The continuing centrality of stakes in the Church's organizational structure is emphasized by additional recent expansions of the responsibilities assigned to stakes. Stake conferences are held semiannually, with stake presidents responsible for presiding when Regional Representatives or General Authorities are not present. Other functions formerly performed by General Authorities but now assigned to stake presidents include issuing temple recommends, setting apart counselors in the stake presidency and missionaries, ordaining bishops and stake patriarchs, and giving special temple recommend clearances.

Stake officers have primary responsibility for training ward priesthood and auxiliary officers. Stake presidencies recommend new bishops to the General Authorities and, with their high councils, train ward bishoprics and quorum leaders. Under the direction of the stake presidency and the high council, stake auxiliary leaders hold regular leadership meetings to train their counterparts at the ward level (see LEADERSHIP TRAINING). Stake presidencies and high councils continue to serve as the major judicial organization of the Church and conduct DISCIPLINARY COUNCILS for members who have committed serious sins.

New stakes are created when the membership of an existing stake becomes too large or when Church numbers and leadership strength in a mission district where a stake has not previously existed reach a level that justifies its organization

(Kimball, p. 11). This process has accelerated greatly since the mid-twentieth century, with stakes being organized in many nations. Before 1840, 11 stakes had been established in Ohio, Missouri, and Illinois. In 1870 there were 12, all located in Utah. By 1882 the number had grown to 27, and by 1940, to 177. The 321 stakes in 1960 included one in Mexico and 19 in English-speaking countries outside the United States. In 1991 there were over 1,800 stakes worldwide, with almost weekly additions.

Stake presidents are called by revelation and set apart by a General Authority under the direction of the Quorum of the Twelve Apostles. They are sustained by the membership of the stake in the stake conference following their call. After a period of service (often about ten years), they are released from their assignment and a replacement is selected in the same manner.

[See also Area, Area Presidency; Bishop, History of the Office; Organization: Contemporary; Region, Regional Representative; Ward; Stake President, Stake Presidency.]

BIBLIOGRAPHY

Alexander, Thomas G. *Mormonism in Transition*, pp. 93–115. Urbana, Ill., 1986.

Allen, James, and Glen Leonard. *Story of the Latter-day Saints*. Salt Lake City, 1976.

Arrington, Leonard, and Davis Bitton. *The Mormon Experience*. New York, 1979.

Benson, Ezra Taft. "Strengthen Thy Stakes." *Ensign* 21 (Jan. 1991):2–5.

Coleman, Neil K. "A Study of The Church of Jesus Christ of Latter-day Saints as an Administrative System, Its Structure and Maintenance." Ph.D. diss., New York University, 1967.

Hartley, William G. "The Priesthood Reorganization of 1877: Brigham Young's Last Achievement." *BYU Studies* 20 (Fall 1979):3–36.

Kimball, Spencer W. "The Image of a Stake." Unpublished speech to regional representatives, Salt Lake City, Oct. 4, 1973.

Soltau, Henry W. *The Tabernacle, the Priesthood, and the Offerings*, pp. 135–41. Grand Rapids, Mich., 1972.

STAN L. ALBRECHT

STAKE PRESIDENT, STAKE PRESIDENCY

The Church officer who presides over several WARDS (congregations) that comprise a STAKE is the stake president. A stake president is selected

Interior of the St. George Tabernacle in St. George, Utah, built 1863–1875 and regular site of local stake conferences, concerts, and community events. Courtesy Utah State Historical Society.

by the General Authority assigned by the Quorum of Twelve Apostles to preside at that stake's conference. He typically interviews many MELCHIZEDEK PRIESTHOOD leaders in the stake and then seeks inspiration from God to determine whom to call. The General Authority calls the stake president and instructs him to nominate two counselors who are interviewed and called. These three men constitute the stake presidency. They serve voluntarily, receiving no financial remuneration from the Church. Counselors to the stake president advise and assist him in his responsibilities and counsel with him in decision making. As with all officers in the Church, members of the stake presidency must be sustained by the vote of the members over whom they preside (D&C 20:65; see COMMON CONSENT). Each stake president supervises and is responsible for the progress of the Church in his stake, including all Church activities, callings, ORDINANCES performed, and programs.

Members of the stake presidency hold the office of HIGH PRIEST, and they serve as the presidency of the high priest quorum and supervise all Melchizedek Priesthood quorums. This means they hold the proper priesthood authority to act as the Lord's agent in behalf of the members (see KEYS OF THE PRIESTHOOD).

What the stake president performs and authorizes within the scope of his calling is recognized as official and binding by the Church. For example, the stake president authorizes ordinations of worthy men to offices in the Melchizedek Priesthood, such as ELDER and high priest. He submits to the FIRST PRESIDENCY for their approval the names of men to be called as BISHOPS. When the approval is granted, the stake president issues the call and ordains the man a bishop, after he has been sustained by his ward. The stake president calls the presidents of the women's organizations of the stake. He sets them apart after they have been sustained by vote of the stake. Both stake and full-time MISSIONARIES are SET APART and later released by stake presidents. With a few exceptions, stake presidents may delegate to their counselors, or to high councilors, the authority to perform ordinances, issue calls to serve, ordain others to priesthood offices, and give spiritual blessings. Stake presidencies are to draw upon the scriptures and are to seek inspiration through prayer. The stake president is the one ultimately responsible for decisions made, but the stake presidency is to act as a unified quorum when decisions are made and actions taken. The stake presidency is accountable to members of the General Authorities of the Church for the administration of their stake.

During semi-annual stake conferences, members of the stake gather to hear instruction and inspirational messages from the stake presidency and other leaders. Stake presidents provide additional spiritual direction through counseling individuals and families and by visiting members' homes.

The stake president also presides over certain council meetings in which the spiritual welfare of Church members is the focus, such as meetings to address the needs of the poor or to prepare for emergencies, or councils that conduct DISCIPLINARY PROCEDURES for Church members who have transgressed fundamental standards of the gospel. Through personal interviews, stake presidencies certify the worthiness of members to enter TEMPLES and to be ordained to Melchizedek Priesthood offices, after they have been recommended to the stake president by their bishop. Bishops are to report their stewardship and the welfare of their congregations to their stake president.

Stake presidents are charged with fiscal responsibility for the stake. CLERKS are called to help with RECORD KEEPING and payments, but the expenditures of all wards, priesthood quorums, and AUXILIARY ORGANIZATIONS within the stake are the responsibility of the stake president. Financial assistance provided to needy individuals is administered by ward bishops, supervised by the stake president. In addition, since most wards meet in Church-owned buildings, the maintenance and operation of all physical facilities in the stake fall under the auspices of the stake president.

The stake president serves until he is released. As is the case with all callings in the Church, he neither campaigns for the position nor chooses the time of his release.

BIBLIOGRAPHY

McConkie, Bruce R. MD, p. 763.

Richards, LeGrand. A Marvelous Work and a Wonder, chap. 12. Salt Lake City, 1968.

KIM S. CAMERON

STANDARD WORKS

Standard works are the books accepted by Latter-day Saints as SCRIPTURE: the BIBLE, BOOK OF

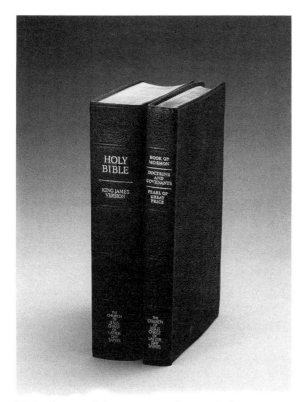

LDS editions of the scriptures from 1979 (King James Version of the Bible) and 1981 (Book of Mormon; Doctrine and Covenants; Pearl of Great Price). Latter-day Saints accept these four books as "standard works" containing the word of God.

MORMON, DOCTRINE AND COVENANTS, and PEARL OF GREAT PRICE. In early Latter-day Saint usage, the term apparently included more writings than the scriptures. In 1874 George A. Smith described "standard works" as the scriptures and other works published by the Church that illustrate "the principles of life and salvation made known in the gospel of Jesus Christ" (JD 17:161; cf. 11:364). By 1900, however, the phrase "standard works" came to refer only to the scriptures (Smith, pp. 363–65; AF, p. 7).

Anciently, the Lord declared to the prophet NEPHI₁ that the words of his seed, joined with the Lord's words, would be declared "unto the ends of the earth, for a standard unto my people" (2 Ne. 29:2). In this sense, a standard is a rule for measuring or a model to be followed. The scriptures contain the DOCTRINE and principles that serve as the rules and models by which Latter-day Saints are to live. Hence, they become the standard by which spiritual and other matters are to be judged or measured.

The standard works are different from other writings in the Church, for they have been formally accepted by the Church as revelation and are viewed as containing the word of God. It is his voice that has given them through his PROPHETS (see D&C 18:34–36). Latter-day Saints accept the Bible as the word of God, but recognize that some errors and omissions have occurred in the processes of transmission and translation (A of F 8). The Book of Mormon, Doctrine and Covenants, and Pearl of Great Price, brought forth in modern times by the Prophet Joseph SMITH, are likewise accepted as the word of God (see MD, p. 364).

Although The Church of Jesus Christ of Latter-day Saints accepts the present scriptures as "standard works," the canon of scripture is not closed. "We believe all that God has revealed, all that He does now reveal, and we believe that He will yet reveal many great and important things pertaining to the Kingdom of God" (A of F 9). Latter-day Saints also esteem the words of the living prophets of God as scripture, for when they "speak as they are moved upon by the Holy Ghost," they speak the will, mind, and word of the Lord (D&C 68:3–4). Latter-day Saints are encouraged to study and ponder all these in connection with the standard works and to apply them to their own lives, that all "might be for our profit and learning" (1 Ne. 19:23).

BIBLIOGRAPHY

Smith, Joseph F. GD.

CLYDE J. WILLIAMS

STEREOTYPING OF LATTER-DAY SAINTS

From the time Joseph SMITH's visions became public knowledge, many stereotypes—pejorative and nonpejorative generalized impressions—have shaped the public image of the Church and its members. In general, stereotypes travel by word of mouth or through the media of popular culture and tend to exaggerate or to distort selected characteristics.

The Church's first century produced media stereotypes that were largely pejorative and relatively uniform. In the early years, Joseph Smith and the fundamental claims of the Church were the principal targets. The dominant images questioned prophetic credibility and impugned the validity of the Book of Mormon. Although some sympathy was evoked by the persecutions in Missouri, the martyrdom of Joseph and Hyrum Smith, and the expulsion of Mormons from Illinois, negative stereotypes predominated.

When the practice of plural marriage was publicly announced in 1852, the stereotypes changed. From then on the dominant images in Europe as well as in the United States were of treacherous, cruel, lustful males; degraded and gullible females; and neglected, unmanageable children. Brigham YOUNG became the major target of denunciation. He was depicted as wily and unscrupulous, and his followers as credulous and victimized.

Pejorative stereotypes peaked in conjunction with the antipolygamy legislation of the 1880s. They declined for a few years after the Church discontinued plural marriage in 1890, but reappeared in the early twentieth century. While occasional nonpejorative images were generated by travelers' accounts or other sympathetic sources, images of Latter-day Saints in the media between 1830 and 1930 were, for the most part, derogatory.

By the 1930s, however, the prevailing stereotype of Latter-day Saints had become positive. The next few decades consolidated that image, portraying the Saints as loyal citizens with a circumspect lifestyle and a communal ethic that "took care of their own." Factors supporting this stereotype included more exposure to Latter-day Saints and their lifestyle, more favorable media coverage, increasing stature as a worldwide Church, and gradual, if sometimes reluctant, acceptance into the sociopolitical, economic, and religious establishment of America. Still, pejorative images continued to compete with the more favorable versions, and most people outside the intermountain region knew little about the Church beyond the abandoned practice of polygamy, the exodus west to Utah under Brigham Young, and the weekly broadcasts of the MORMON TABERNACLE CHOIR.

Since 1960, the substantial growth of the Church in Latin America and other parts of the world has supported the overall view that international impressions were improving. Yet Church growth was sometimes a mixed blessing, for LDS missionaries and members became stereotyped targets for those who mistakenly associated the Church with the politics of the United States. In the United States, both positive and negative views provided the public with information, true and false, about the Church and piqued their curi-osities. Church positions on social issues such as abortion and the Equal Rights Amendment evoked both favor and opposition. The Church's own PUBLIC RELATIONS efforts, intended to educate the public about Church doctrines and the importance of the family, have offered alternative stereotypes of the Mormons as wholesome people and good citizens.

As others become more acquainted with Latter-day Saints, they realize that Church members include the normal variety of human beings with differing personalities and interests (see INDIVIDUALITY). Given the vagaries of public opinion and private belief, however, stereotypes of Latter-day Saints will continue to exist, although they are becoming more positive.

BIBLIOGRAPHY

Bunker, Gary L., and Davis Bitton. *The Mormon Graphic Image, 1834–1914*. Salt Lake City, 1983.

"Imagemakers: Mormons and the Media." *Dialogue* 10 (Spring 1977):12–113.

GARY L. BUNKER

STERILIZATION

Sterilization, including voluntary vasectomies, tied fallopian tubes, or premature hysterectomies, are serious matters with moral, spiritual, and physiological ramifications. God's primordial instruction to mankind is to "be fruitful, and multiply and replenish the earth" (Gen. 1:28). The privilege and power to procreate may be God's greatest gift to mankind and, within the sacred marriage covenant, is an obligation for which God will hold men and women fully accountable. Latter-day Saints affirm that life's most lofty and ennobling values are found in marriage, procreation, parenthood, and family life. Any impediment or interference with this sacred opportunity may warrant God's judgment:

> Surgical sterilization should only be considered (1) where medical conditions seriously jeopardize life or health, or (2) where birth defects or serious trauma have rendered a person mentally incompetent and not responsible for his or her actions. Such conditions must be determined by competent medical judgment and in accordance with law. Even then, the person or persons responsible for this decision should consult with each other and with their bishop . . . and receive divine confirmation through prayer [*General Handbook of Instructions*, 11-15].

Consistent with Church policies concerning BIRTH CONTROL and ABORTION, leaders have advised its married members not to resort to any practices that destroy the power of having children. The FIRST PRESIDENCY has declared, "We seriously deplore the fact that members of the Church would voluntarily take measures to render themselves incapable of further procreation" (p. 11-5).

BIBLIOGRAPHY
General Handbook of Instructions. Salt Lake City, 1989.

LORRY E. RYTTING

STEWARDSHIP

"Stewardship" in LDS vocabulary is responsibility given through the Lord to act in behalf of others. It is based on the understanding that all things ultimately belong to the Lord, whether property, time, talents, families, or capacity for service within the Church organization. An individual acts in a Church CALLING as a trustee for the Lord, not out of personal ownership or privilege. Every position in the Church is received as a calling, a stewardship, from the Lord made through others who are responsible for the supervision of the position. Such stewardships are temporary responsibilities.

Because the stewardship of a lay leader is not a permanent calling, a member of the Church may hold a position of extensive responsibility at one time in life and one of lesser responsibility at another time. Each member given a stewardship is expected to sacrifice time and talent in the service of others, but at the completion of such callings, most report that they have personally grown and benefited. Every calling is important. As members bear one another's burdens, they build a sense of community. When all serve, all may partake of the blessings of service. The ideal attitude toward stewardship suggests that it is not the position held but how well the work is done that counts (see MAGNIFYING ONE'S CALLING).

Faithful stewards seek a thorough understanding of their responsibilities and a knowledge of the Lord's will concerning them and their callings. A person with a stewardship reports to an immediate superior in the Church. For example, a ward RELIEF SOCIETY president reports to the BISHOP of her ward. A bishop reports to his STAKE PRESIDENT.

Stewards are accountable to and will be judged by the Lord (Luke 16:2; 19:17). To whom much is given, much is required (cf. Luke 12:48; D&C 82:3). The primary accounting is with the Lord. He knows a person's heart, intentions, and talents. The faithful and wise steward is rewarded; the unjust or slothful steward gains but little, and may even lose what he has (cf. Matt. 25:14–30; D&C 82:3, 11; 78:22).

BIBLIOGRAPHY
Cuthbert, Derek A. "The Spirituality of Service." Ensign 20 (May 1990):12–13.
Larsen, Dean L. "Self-Accountability and Human Progress." Ensign 10 (May 1980):76–78.
Malan, Jayne B. "The Summer of the Lambs." Ensign 19 (Nov. 1989):78–79.
Nelson, Russell M. "The Five A's of Stewardship." Ensign 2 (Apr. 1972):24–25.
Pace, Glenn L. "A Thousand Times." Ensign 20 (Nov. 1990):8–9.

J. LYNN ENGLAND

STICK OF JOSEPH

[For Latter-day Saints, the "Stick of Joseph" and the "Stick of Ephraim" refer to the Book of Mormon. Both phrases appear in the book of the prophet Ezekiel (37:16, 19). The view that the Stick of Joseph consists of a scriptural record receives support from the Book of Mormon and the Doctrine and Covenants (1 Ne. 13:35–40; 2 Ne. 3:11–12, 18–21; D&C 27:5). Articles that deal with this subject are Book of Mormon, Biblical Prophecies about; Ezekiel, Prophecies of; Joseph of Egypt: Writings of Joseph; and "Voice from the Dust."]

STICK OF JUDAH

[In LDS terminology, the "Stick of Judah" refers to the Bible. The phrase appears in the book of the prophet Ezekiel (37:19). The belief that the Stick of Judah consists of a scriptural record is stated in the Book of Mormon (1 Ne. 3:9–12; 5:5–6, 10–13; 13:20–29; 2 Ne. 3:11–12; cf. D&C 27:5). Articles that discuss this subject are Book of Mormon, Biblical Prophecies about; and Ezekiel, Prophecies of.]

STILLBORN CHILDREN

Medically, a stillborn child is a dead fetus developed to a point at which it normally would have been viable. Religiously, one major question is whether a stillborn child ever was "a living soul" (Moses 3:7) that can be resurrected and be part of its parents' eternal family. Because "there is no information given by revelation" (*DS* 2:280), the Church has made no official statement on the matter. President Brigham YOUNG once stated as his opinion that "when the mother feels life come to her infant it is the spirit entering the body" (*JD* 17:143). Others have speculated that the spirit might not enter the fetus until just before birth, and still others have suggested that three elements constitute a living soul—body, SPIRIT, and "breath of life" (Moses 3:7).

Because Church policy permits temple sealings to be performed for children who die after birth, but not for those who die before birth, some have concluded that stillborn children will not be resurrected. However, the current *General Handbook of Instructions* (1989) states that the policy of not sealing stillborn children to their parents implies "no loss of eternal blessings or family unity" (6-8). Latter-day Saints trust God's loving kindness to accord to each of his spirit children the eternal state which is proper, through judgment which is both just and merciful.

BIBLIOGRAPHY

Greenwood, Val D. "I Have a Question." *Ensign* 17 (Sept. 1987):27–28.

JEANNE B. INOUYE

STRAIT AND NARROW

Latter-day Saints speak of following the "strait and narrow" path to ETERNAL LIFE. These words are found in both ancient and modern scripture. For them as for other Christians, probably the best-known passage in which these words are conjoined is Matthew 7:13–14: "Enter ye in at the strait gate: . . . because strait is the gate, and narrow is the way, which leadeth unto life, and few there be that find it."

"Strait" and "narrow" mean approximately the same: constricted, tight. The juxtaposition of synonyms is a typical Hebrew literary parallelism. The terms thus translated reveal diverse nuances, enhancing the implications of the metaphors. The Greek word *stene(s)*, translated "strait" in the King James Bible, is defined as "narrow." The word for "narrow" is the perfect passive participle of *thlibo*, meaning "pressed together, made narrow, oppressed." Several Hebrew words exhibit similar meanings. Jesus Christ and a number of prophets utilized such terms in constructing an image with diverse applications, but with the ultimate end of portraying the strict path to God's presence.

In the Book of Mormon, LEHI uses especially vivid imagery in recounting his vision of the TREE OF LIFE: "And I beheld a rod of iron, and it extended along the bank of the river. . . . And I also beheld a strait and narrow path, which came along by the rod of iron" (1 Ne. 8:19–20). Near the end of his record, NEPHI₁, son of Lehi, offers the clearest explanation of the images in this vision, pointing out that the gate to the strait and narrow path consists of repentance, baptism, and remission of sins. The gospel, then, is the good news that there exists such a path, which men and women can follow to eternal life by "press[ing] forward, feasting upon the word of Christ, and endur[ing] to the end" (2 Ne. 31:17–20). This emphasis on Christ is in harmony with the observation that the strait and narrow path is the "way." One may compare Jesus' response to Thomas in John 14:6: "I am the way, the truth, and the life: no man cometh unto the Father, but by me."

The connotations of the Hebrew and Greek words for "strait" and "narrow" suggest that the path is not easy. One's journey on the path is to be a challenge, but not so strenuous a one that it is hopeless. Jesus affirmed, "My yoke is easy, and my burden is light" (Matt. 11:30). A related concept is found in a homophone of "strait," with different etymological roots. It is expressed in a poignant psalm wherein Nephi prayed to the Lord, "Wilt thou make my path straight before me! Wilt thou not place a stumbling block in my way—but that thou wouldst clear my way before me, and hedge not up my way" (2 Ne. 4:33).

BIBLIOGRAPHY

Stapley, Delbert L. "The Straight Gate—Repentance and Baptism." *IE* 58 (June 1955):416–18.

Wirthlin, Joseph B. "The Straight and Narrow Way." *Ensign* 20 (Nov. 1990):64–66.

DANIEL B. MCKINLAY

SUCCESSION IN THE PRESIDENCY

Upon the death of the President of The Church of Jesus Christ of Latter-day Saints, the senior APOSTLE in the Church's governing quorums (*see* FIRST PRESIDENCY; QUORUM OF THE TWELVE APOSTLES) becomes presiding officer of the Church (*see* PRESIDENT OF THE CHURCH).

The principles underlying the succession process were established at the death of the Prophet Joseph Smith in 1844. Since there was at the time no precedent and no clear procedure providing for succession to the office of president, competing views arose. Brigham YOUNG, then President of the Quorum of the Twelve Apostles, presented the proposition that the Twelve, ordained apostles who held all the KEYS necessary to govern the Church, should be sustained as the authorized leaders in the absence of Joseph Smith. In his favor was the fact that the Twelve in Nauvoo had been carefully tutored by the Prophet in all aspects of Church leadership and had served as his right hand. The Church also understood that this position was in harmony with the 1835 revelation on priesthood (D&C 107). After describing the FIRST PRESIDENCY ("three Presiding High Priests, chosen by the body, appointed and ordained to that office, and upheld by the confidence, faith, and prayer of the church"), that revelation affirmed that the Twelve Apostles "form a quorum, equal in authority and power to the three presidents previously mentioned" (D&C 107:22–24).

Inherent in the Twelve's proposal was the assumption that, although the Quorum of the Twelve Apostles had equal authority and power with the Quorum of the First Presidency, as long as the First Presidency was intact and functioning, they, and not the Twelve, possess the necessary jurisdiction to govern the Church. But the death of the president, thereby disorganizing the presidency and automatically releasing the president's counselors, bestows on the Quorum of the Twelve the required authorization to exercise the keys they already possess and assume full responsibility for governing the Church—including the reorganization of the First Presidency. Representing the Twelve, Brigham Young also reminded the Saints in 1844 of Joseph Smith's "last charge to the Twelve," stipulating that in the event something happened to him, the Twelve were responsible for carrying on the work he had begun (Esplin, pp. 319–20).

Sidney RIGDON, who had been a counselor to Joseph Smith, presented an alternative view. He argued that Joseph Smith's death did not disorganize the presidency or the Church and that, therefore, as first counselor to Joseph Smith, he should be sustained as "guardian" over the Church. This ran directly counter to the Twelve's position that the death of the president automatically dissolves the First Presidency, leaving the counselors without authority over the Church.

Though there were theoretically other possibilities for succession besides these two, the competing claims of Sidney Rigdon and of Brigham Young, representing the Twelve, were the only two practical alternatives at that time. After several private meetings during which leaders reviewed the options, on August 8, 1844, thousands of Church members gathered in the grove near the Nauvoo Temple to decide by a public sustaining vote (*see* COMMON CONSENT) whether Sidney Rigdon or the Twelve would lead the Church. Rigdon, an eloquent speaker, took the stand first and spoke at length of his right and position. Then Brigham Young, with less polish but confident that the Twelve held authority and that they were prepared to "direct all things aright," presented the other view. The result was overwhelming support recognizing the Quorum of the Twelve Apostles as the authorized leaders of the Church, specifically with the keys to act as the First Presidency and with the power to reorganize the First Presidency. Although that decision was clearly sanctioned by the 1835 revelation and was in harmony with the position of the Twelve in Nauvoo, many Latter-day Saints claimed a further deciding factor: when Brigham Young spoke on August 8, his voice and appearance bore a striking resemblance to those of Joseph Smith. Wilford WOODRUFF, one who was present, later said that if "I had not seen him with my own eyes, there is no one that could have convinced me that it was not Joseph Smith" (*Deseret News*, Mar. 15, 1892; cf. *JD* 15:81).

For the next three years the Church was governed by the Quorum of the Twelve Apostles with Brigham Young as president of the quorum. In December 1847, following the pioneer journey to the Rocky Mountains, the First Presidency was reorganized and Brigham Young was named President of the Church.

Though the right of the Quorum of the Twelve to reconstitute the First Presidency was firmly established, there have been other short periods when the Quorum of the Twelve Apostles governed the Church before a new First Presidency was organized. John TAYLOR, president of the quorum when Brigham Young died in 1877, did not have the Quorum of the Twelve Apostles formally reorganize the First Presidency until 1880. A similar interim existed after his death in 1887. Wilford Woodruff as President of the Quorum of the Twelve Apostles directed the affairs of the Church on the basis of that position until 1889. Several years later, he instructed Lorenzo SNOW, then President of the Twelve Apostles, that it was the will of the Lord that the First Presidency should be organized without delay upon the death of the president (Lorenzo Snow Notes, Dec 3, 1892, Church Archives). Lorenzo Snow, therefore, was named President of the Church in a new First Presidency eleven days after President Woodruff's death, a precedent of reorganizing the presidency without delay that has since been followed.

Since a fundamental doctrine of the Church is the reality of continuing REVELATION, and since the Twelve Apostles are sustained as PROPHETS, SEERS, AND REVELATORS, there is no apparent reason that the Quorum of the Twelve could not depart from this precedent and select someone other than the senior apostle to lead the Church, if so directed by revelation. Established principles, however, require (1) that a revelation directing any other course of action must come through the senior apostle in the presiding quorum and approved by unanimous vote of the members of the quorum and (2) that the senior apostle in the presiding quorum by virtue of that position immediately presides over the Church following the death of the president.

The fundamental organizing principle of the Church rests on the reality that it was established by direct commandment from God to Joseph Smith and that those who lead it are specifically called of God to those positions. The existing succession process does not violate that principle, which it would do if succession were decided by a contested election either within the Quorum of the Twelve or by the body of the Church. In keeping with the principle of common consent, the name of each new president is submitted to the body of the Church for its sustaining approval. But this procedure is in no wise an election nor does it affect the legitimacy of the president's divine commission. Rather than empowering the new leader, the vote is an expression by members that they recognize the legitimacy of the calling and that it is binding upon them. To sustain the president is a commitment that no assistance that can aid his success will be withheld and that no barriers that might hinder his efforts will be erected.

BIBLIOGRAPHY

Arrington, Leonard J. *Brigham Young: American Moses*, pp. 113–16. New York, 1985.

Durham, Reed C., Jr., and Steven H. Heath. *Succession in the Church*. Salt Lake City, 1970.

Esplin, Ronald K. "Joseph, Brigham and the Twelve: A Succession of Continuity." *BYU Studies* 21 (Summer 1981):301–341.

MARTIN B. HICKMAN

SUFFERING IN THE WORLD

Suffering is inherent in mortality. Physical bodies are subject to pain and discomfort from hunger, disease, trauma, violence, and exposure. As a social being, man is vulnerable to emotional suffering that often rivals physical pain—anxiety, rejection, loneliness, despair. Among the sensitive there are also other levels of profound suffering. They may relate, for example, to the awareness of the effects of sin or the anguish of the abuse or indifference of one's loved ones. And there is vicarious suffering in response to the pain around one and the sense of the withdrawal of the Spirit. For Latter-day Saints, Jesus' words on the cross "My God, my God, why hast thou forsaken me?" is a measure of the depth of his suffering (Matt. 27:46).

Mankind's attempts to explain the necessity of suffering are varied: (1) it is an essential element in testing and building moral character; (2) it is the unavoidable side effect of agency; (3) it is illusory or utterly mysterious. Whatever partial consolations these attempts provide, suffering remains.

LDS doctrine provides two explanations that are uncommon in the Judeo-Christian tradition. First, all mankind chose to enter mortality with full knowledge of the great price that would be required of the Christ and of discipleship in his name. Second, one's suffering is to be in the image of that of the Lord, whose suffering was requisite "that his bowels [might] be filled with mercy . . . that he [might] know according to the flesh how to succor his people according to their infirmities" (Alma 7:12). In no other way could the redemption of the universe and the unleashing of authentic love and compassion be achieved. Jesus described his own mission almost entirely in terms of healing: "to bind up the brokenhearted, to proclaim liberty to the captives, and the opening of the prison to them that are bound; . . . to comfort all that mourn; to appoint unto them that mourn in Zion, to give unto them beauty for ashes, the oil of joy for mourning, the garment of praise for the spirit of heaviness" (Isa. 61:1–3; Luke 4:18–19).

Only in the life to come amid the glories of the NEW JERUSALEM will the full effect of Christ's mission "wipe away all tears from their eyes; and there shall be no more death, neither sorrow, nor crying, neither shall there be any more pain" (Rev. 21:4). Even so, for Latter-day Saints the embrace of his messiahship and the proclamation of his gospel were intended to relieve needless pain and suffering. They do so in many ways. First, they provide a foundation for hope that through the ATONEMENT OF JESUS CHRIST one may find reunion with God. Second, they offer continuous access to the HOLY GHOST, the Comforter, and, through this, to an inner peace that "passeth all understanding" (Philip. 4:7). Third, they teach the law of the harvest, that many blessings follow naturally from obedience to the laws that govern them and that much unhappiness can be avoided, including sin and its accompanying pain, shame, and spiritual bruising. And finally, they establish a community built on kinship, a society of mutually supportive and protective fellow believers whose charge is to "bear one another's burdens, that they may be light; yea, and are willing to mourn with those that mourn; yea, and comfort those that stand in need of comfort" (Mosiah 18:8–9).

Latter-day Saints do not believe that pain is intrinsically good. In their teaching there is little of asceticism, mortification, or negative spirituality. But when suffering is unavoidable in the fulfillment of life's missions, one's challenge is to draw upon all the resources of one's soul and endure faithfully and well. If benefit comes from pain, it is not because there is anything inherently cleansing in pain itself. Suffering can wound and embitter and darken a soul as surely as it can purify and refine and illumine. Everything depends on how one responds. At a time of terrible desolation and imprisonment, the Prophet Joseph SMITH was told, "My son, peace be unto thy soul; thine adversity and thine afflictions shall be but a small moment; and then, if thou endure it well, God shall

exalt thee on high. . . . Know thou, my son, that all these things shall give thee experience, and shall be for thy good. The Son of Man hath descended below them all. Art thou greater than he? Therefore, hold on thy way, . . . fear not what man can do, for God shall be with you forever and ever" (D&C 121:7–8; 122:7–9).

BIBLIOGRAPHY

Kimball, Spencer W. "Thy Son Liveth." *IE* 48 (May 1945):253, 294.

———. "Tragedy or Destiny." *IE* 69 (Mar. 1966):178–80, 210–12, 214, 216–17.

Madsen, Truman G. "Evil and Suffering." *Instructor* 99 (Nov. 1964):450–53.

CARLFRED BRODERICK

SUICIDE

From an LDS perspective, suicide is a moral issue and is to be handled with particular sensitivity and human caring. The *General Handbook of Instructions* (1989) says, "A person who takes his own life may not be responsible for his acts. Only God can judge such a matter. A person who has considered suicide seriously or has attempted suicide should be counseled by his bishop and may be encouraged to seek professional help" (11-5). Such contacts need to be personalized and enduring. The inclination to commit suicide represents a crisis in a person's life and should not be taken lightly. Underlying causes should be identified and treated.

The body of a person who has committed suicide is not dishonored. If the person has been endowed and otherwise is in good standing with the Church, the body may be buried in temple clothes. Normal funeral procedures are followed (*see* BURIAL).

Suicide and attempted suicide are painful and dramatic aspects of human behavior, but this does not mean that they should not be dealt with in terms of the same basic principles as those applicable in understanding and managing any other aspect of human behavior. Thus, principles associated with concepts of agency, accountability, atonement, eternal life, immortality, resurrection, and family establish the frame of reference Latter-day Saints use to guide their responses to such behaviors as they occur.

Despite traditions and beliefs that recognize and honor the ways in which value decisions led to the death and martyrdom of Jesus Christ and of Joseph Smith, there is no support in LDS doctrine for anyone intentionally seeking death.

The ancient commandment "Thou shalt not kill" is interpreted in most traditions to include a prohibition against killing oneself. In LDS doctrine, "Thou shalt not kill" has been extended to "nor do anything like unto it" (D&C 59:6). This extension is relevant in considering a variety of life-threatening behaviors that suicidologists identify as suicide equivalents (e.g., death as a result of deliberate reckless driving) or "slow suicide" (e.g., drug and alcohol abuse).

Suicide prevention sometimes is criticized by people who claim that individuals have an innate right to do whatever they want with their lives, including a right to kill themselves if they want to. Suicide, however, is never fully an individual matter. Even when difficult physical and biological factors are present, suicide is a social act, with interpersonal, family, and social systems ramifications.

A social milieu organized to help people find adequate housing and life goals of learning, loving, and working provides genuine choices between life and death. It is the position of the Church that when there are such choices, the majority of people, including those who are suicidal, will choose life. This is not to deny inequity, unfairness, conflict, instability, evil, aging, and illness of loved ones, but to provide a basis for behavior so that when crises occur, they will be seen as resolvable.

BIBLIOGRAPHY

Ballard, M. Russell. "Suicide: Some Things We Know, and Some We Do Not." *Ensign* 17 (Oct. 1987):6–9.

General Handbook of Instructions. Salt Lake City, 1989.

CLYDE E. SULLIVAN

SUNDAY

Whereas the seventh or SABBATH DAY was established as a day of rest and worship and a commemoration of the Creation (Ex. 20:10–11), the "first day of the week" Sunday, or the Lord's Day, was consecrated to remember the atonement and resurrection of Jesus Christ (Acts 20:7; 1 Cor. 16:2; Rev. 1:10). Moreover, a new ORDINANCE, the SACRAMENT, was introduced so that Christian wor-

shipers on that day might venerate Jesus' atoning sacrifice. For Latter-day Saints, modern revelation fixes the day of weekly worship and holy rest as "the Lord's day," which is Sunday, the first day of the week (see D&C 59:9–12).

Jesus' fulfillment of the LAW OF MOSES brought several changes, including the practice of meeting on the first day of the week to commemorate Jesus' resurrection. That the Lord intended a change in the day of worship is suggested by certain events of his postmortal ministry. For instance, it was on the first day of the week (Sunday) that he initially appeared to the apostles (John 20:19). It was also on the first day of the week that he reappeared to these same apostles, then in company with Thomas (John 20:26). After Jesus' resurrection, it was on the day of Pentecost, a festival on the first day of the week observed by ancient Israel fifty days after Passover (cf. Lev. 23:15–16), that the assembled Saints and others received their most essential guide to eternal life, the HOLY GHOST (Acts 2:1–12). On that day of Pentecost the apostolic ministry began with the CONVERSION of three thousand souls through the preaching of PETER (Acts 2:37–41).

The early Christians understood the significance of this change in the day of their worship, as can be seen by their continued practice of congregating on the first day of the week: "And upon the first day of the week, when the disciples came together to break bread, Paul preached unto them" (Acts 20:7; 1 Cor. 16:2; cf. Col. 2:16). Early Christian writers confirm the continued use of the first day of the week as the accepted new day of worship, only noting exceptions (e.g., Eusebius, *Ecclesiastical History* 3.27.5). By A.D. 321, Constantine had officially designated the first day of the week as a day of rest. The word "Sunday" for the first day came from the weekly pagan worship of the sun god in Rome.

In a revelation received on August 7, 1831, a Sunday, the Lord confirmed his prescribed design in changing the day of public worship: "But remember that on this, the Lord's day [Sunday], thou shalt offer thine oblations and thy sacraments unto the Most High" (D&C 59:12).

For members of The Church of Jesus Christ of Latter-day Saints, the day of the week on which they gather to pay devotion to God and his Son matters less than receiving the edification and enlightenment that may be gained from worship. This observation is confirmed, for example, by the

Church's custom of worshiping weekly in countries in the Middle East on a day other than Sunday.

As President Joseph F. SMITH explained, Latter-day Saints are to gather on a day to "mingle with the saints that their moral and spiritual influence may help to correct our false impressions and restore us to that life which the duties and obligations of our conscience and true religion impose upon us" (Smith, p. 243; see D&C 59:9–19).

BIBLIOGRAPHY

Kittel, Gerhard, ed. *Theological Dictionary of the New Testament*, Vol. 8, pp. 1–34. Grand Rapids, Mich., 1964–1974.

Smith, Joseph F. *GD*, pp. 241–47. Salt Lake City, 1939.

GLEN E. BARKSDALE

SUNDAY SCHOOL

Sunday School in The Church of Jesus Christ of Latter-day Saints is held weekly in each local WARD or BRANCH. It lasts about an hour. Each Sunday, ward members assemble at the meetinghouse chapel for prayer and hymn singing, following which those twelve years and older attend age-group classes for religious instruction while younger children attend PRIMARY. The Sunday School courses provide a forum for discussions, socialization, and the integration of gospel principles into everyday life. The adult curriculum includes a gospel doctrine course based on the STANDARD WORKS, a gospel essentials class, and elective alternative classes on family history, teacher development, and family relations. The courses of study between twelve and eighteen are coeducational and focus on gospel principles, teachings of the Savior, Church history, scripture study, and the lives and teachings of the modern prophets. Under the direction of a three-person Sunday School presidency in each ward or branch, members are called to serve as the course teachers, usually for a term of several years.

EARLIEST SUNDAY SCHOOLS. Following the organization of the Church in 1830, most Sunday gatherings were general meetings for all members and visitors. In good weather, large meetings were usually held outdoors. The Prophet Joseph SMITH notes, for example, on July 3, 1842, at Nauvoo,

Illinois, "This morning I preached at the grove to about 8,000 people" (*HC* 5:56). Smaller groups met in homes or other buildings. Those meetings typically included praying, singing, partaking of the SACRAMENT of the Lord's Supper, and preaching.

Before the exodus from Nauvoo that followed the MARTYRDOM OF JOSEPH AND HYRUM SMITH in 1844, a few small Sunday School groups met regularly in scattered communities, notably in Nauvoo, Kirtland, and various cities in England. Only after the Saints arrived in the Salt Lake Valley in 1847, however, did Sunday School begin to take on its present form.

In May 1849, Richard BALLANTYNE began plans to start a Sunday School to educate the young people in the principles of the gospel and the scriptures. Some years before, in his native Scotland, he had organized a Sunday School in the Relief Presbyterian Church of which he was then a member. Having no suitable place in his Salt Lake City neighborhood for such a gathering, Ballantyne built a structure to serve both as his home and a place to hold Sunday School. Today, a monument on the northeast corner of 100 West and 300 South streets in Salt Lake City commemorates the location of this first Sunday School. The original building was eighteen feet wide and twenty feet long, furnished with wooden benches, and warmed by a stone fireplace.

On Sunday, December 9, 1849, Ballantyne gathered a group of fifty children into his newly completed home for instruction from the scriptures. Of his purpose Ballantyne wrote, "There is growth in the young. The seed sown in their hearts is more likely to bring forth fruit than when sown in the hearts of those who are more advanced in years" (Sonne, p. 51). Disturbed by observing children at play on the Sabbath day and sensing that their spiritual growth was being neglected, he added, "I wanted to gather them into the school where they could learn not to read and write, but the goodness of God, and the true Gospel of salvation given by Jesus Christ" (Sonne, p. 51).

The following year the Fourteenth Ward, in which Richard Ballantyne was serving as second counselor to Bishop John Murdock, completed its meeting house, and the rapidly growing Sunday School was moved from the Ballantyne home to the new building. The expanding Sunday School class was also divided into a number of smaller classes with additional teachers being called into

Deseret Sunday School general board (between 1918 and 1934). David O. McKay, general superintendent of the Sunday School (center second row). Courtesy Rare Books and Manuscripts, Brigham Young University.

service. Others in the valley soon followed the Ballantyne pattern. Each Sunday School functioned somewhat autonomously, but generally under the direction of a ward bishop.

In 1858 the Sunday School movement was suspended when Johnston's Army (*see* UTAH EXPEDITION) entered Salt Lake Valley and many of the Saints moved south to other settlements. When the military climate stabilized in the early 1860s, Sunday Schools and other Sabbath meetings resumed. By 1870, more than 200 Sunday Schools were regularly attended by 15,000 youths and adults.

DESERET SUNDAY SCHOOL UNION. The first Sunday Schools functioned independently, devising their own curricula and administrative guidelines. Seeing the value of a central organization, however, Church leaders interested in the work being done organized a Sunday School Union on November 11, 1867. President Brigham YOUNG and Daniel H. Wells, a counselor in the FIRST PRESIDENCY, attended along with Elders George A. SMITH, Wilford WOODRUFF, George Q. Can-

non, of the QUORUM OF THE TWELVE APOSTLES, and Brigham Young, Jr., who became a member of the Quorum in 1868.

At this meeting, first steps were taken toward a permanent organization. Elder Cannon became general superintendent of the Deseret Sunday School Union. A committee of three was appointed to decide on books suitable for Sunday School use. A general secretary and two corresponding secretaries were also appointed. Commencing in June 1872, monthly meetings of the teachers and superintendents were held in Salt Lake City. In 1877, a three-man general board was added, and expanded to six members in 1879.

The organization addressed lesson topics and source materials, punctuality, grading, prizes and rewards, use of hymns and songs composed by members of the Church, recording and increasing the attendance, developing an elementary catechism, and libraries. It also sponsored the publication of administrative guidelines and materials for classroom use, resulting in increased uniformity in Sunday School administration and lesson content.

The Deseret Sunday School Union also sponsored efforts beyond the scope possible for individual schools. The Deseret Sunday School Musical Union was formed and its brass band organized, with Charles J. Thomas serving as director. The Musical Union, though of short duration, was artistically and financially successful. Contributing to its success were many whose compositions left a lasting imprint upon music in the Church, including Evan Stephens, George Careless, and Joseph J. Daynes. Commencing in 1874, annual musical festivals were presented in the TABERNACLE at Salt Lake City, with similar festivals being sponsored in many of the larger settlements. A Union Music Book was published, containing hundreds of pieces of original music.

In 1866, before the Deseret Sunday School Union was formed, publication of the JUVENILE INSTRUCTOR commenced privately, with Elder Cannon as editor. Early editions included catechisms on the Bible, Book of Mormon, and Doctrine and Covenants. Its pages also presented a variety of musical compositions, editorial teachings, and other aids to gospel instruction. As the Deseret Sunday School Union grew in stature, the *Juvenile Instructor* became its official voice. In January 1901, the Deseret Sunday School Union purchased the *Juvenile Instructor* from the Cannon family but continued publishing under that name until 1929, when the name was changed to INSTRUCTOR.

As stakes increased in size and number, it became customary to designate a stake Sunday School superintendency to supervise local Sunday Schools operating within the stake boundaries.

SACRAMENT IN SUNDAY SCHOOL. Following the organization of the Church in 1830, partaking of the sacrament of the Lord's Supper became a customary part of Sabbath meetings held on a community or stake basis and attended principally by adults. Gradually these meetings were replaced by ward sacrament meetings. In early 1877, President Young asked bishops and their counselors to attend Sunday School and administer the sacrament to all children under eight years of age as well as to those over that age who had been baptized and confirmed members of the Church. The practice of administering the sacrament in Sunday School was discontinued in 1980, when the three Sunday meetings were consolidated in a three-hour block.

GROWTH OF SUNDAY SCHOOLS. Upon the death of Superintendent Cannon on April 12, 1901, he was succeeded by Lorenzo SNOW, President of the Church. But President Snow died within a few months and was succeeded in both callings by President Joseph F. SMITH.

In 1884 stake Sunday School superintendencies began holding monthly meetings of Sunday School officers and teachers for instruction and coordination. General meetings of the Deseret Sunday School Union convened twice a year in connection with general conferences of the Church.

In the early 1900s the Sunday School added five new classes for the older children and youth. In 1904, the Sunday Schools in the Weber Stake introduced an adult class. Shortly thereafter, adult classes became an integral part of the Sunday School program.

When President Joseph F. Smith died in 1918, Elder David O. MCKAY became general superintendent of the Sunday Schools. He was succeeded by George D. Pyper, who served until early 1943. Others serving included Milton Bennion (1943–1949), George R. Hill (1949–1966), and David Lawrence McKay (1966–1971).

SUNDAY SCHOOL CORRELATION. As the Church expanded throughout the world, the Sunday School general board was enlarged and its members traveled extensively to provide support and training for local leaders in diverse lands, languages, and cultures. Growth in the number of Sunday School units and in attendance have matched the growth of the Church.

Over the years, there emerged an effort to draw all Church functions and programs into harmonious coordination under priesthood leadership. The Deseret Sunday School Union, designated an AUXILIARY, had functioned with considerable autonomy under separate organizational leadership, sending correspondence and instructions directly to local leaders. However, in April 1971 Church leadership created an all-Church coordinating council composed of three age-group committees (child, youth, and adult) assigned to correlate the curricula within the priesthood and auxiliary organizations of the Church.

In June 1971, Russell M. Nelson was called as general superintendent, with Joseph B. Wirthlin and Richard L. Warner as assistants. Spurred by the correlation movement, they brought dynamic changes to the Sunday School organization between 1971 and 1979. Reflecting the Sunday School's transition to an integrated part of the worldwide, unified Church organization under priesthood direction, the name was changed from Deseret Sunday School Union to simply Sunday School. The title of superintendent was changed to president to comport with traditional terminology commonly used in the priesthood and other auxiliary organizations.

Curriculum planning and writing became coordinated and centralized. Separate Sunday School general conferences were discontinued, and communication to Sunday School leaders was directed principally through priesthood channels. The frequency of regional visits by general board members was significantly reduced. Materials and programs were simplified and consolidated. Stake boards and ward Sunday School faculties were reduced in size, and reporting relationships were simplified as accountability of ward Sunday School officers to their ward priesthood leaders, rather than to stake auxiliary leaders, was strengthened.

An eight-year cycle of scripture instruction for the adult gospel doctrine course was instituted. Later reduced to four years, it focused one year of study each on (1) the Old Testament and the Pearl of Great Price, (2) the New Testament, (3) the Book of Mormon, and (4) the Doctrine and Covenants and Church history.

In October 1979, Russell M. Nelson was succeeded as general president by Elder Hugh W. Pinnock, of the Seventy, initiating a pattern of having GENERAL AUTHORITIES serve as the general presidency of the Sunday School, thus completing the organization's full integration as a correlated arm of the priesthood-directed Sunday School efforts throughout the world.

Attendance at Sunday School has continued to increase each year. By 1990 there were 17,676 Sunday Schools in the Church throughout the world, with more than 4.7 million members age eleven and older.

BIBLIOGRAPHY

"Brief Review of the Sunday School Movement." *Juvenile Instructor* 34 (Nov. 1, 1899):666–74.

Hartley, William G. "Mormon Sundays." *Ensign* 8 (Jan. 1978):19–25.

Jubilee History of the Latter-day Saint Sunday Schools, pp. 9–28. Salt Lake City, 1900.

McKay, David O. "Sunday Schools of the Church." *IE* 33 (May 1930):480–81.

Nelson, Russell M. *From Heart to Heart*, pp. 125–140. Salt Lake City, 1979.

Sonne, Conway B. *Knight of the Kingdom: The Story of Richard Ballantyne*. Salt Lake City, 1949.

Sunday School Handbook. Salt Lake City, 1990.

B. LLOYD POELMAN

SWORD OF LABAN

Laban, a Book of Mormon contemporary of NEPHI₁ in JERUSALEM (c. 600 B.C.), possessed a unique sword. "The hilt thereof was of pure gold, and the workmanship thereof was exceedingly fine, and the blade thereof was of the most precious steel" (1 Ne. 4:9). Nephi was "constrained by the Spirit" to kill Laban (1 Ne. 4:10). Among other things he had opposed the Lord's imperative to relinquish the plates and had "sought to take away" Nephi's life (1 Ne. 4:11). Using Laban's "own sword," Nephi slew him (1 Ne. 4:18), retained the sword, and brought it to the Western Hemisphere.

Nephi made many swords "after the manner" of the sword of Laban (2 Ne. 5:14) and used the sword in "defence" of his people (Jacob 1:10), as did King BENJAMIN (W of M 1:13). Benjamin later delivered the sword to his son MOSIAH₂ (Mosiah 1:16). The sword of Laban seems to have been preserved as a sacred object among the Nephites, as was Goliath's sword in ancient Israel (1 Sam. 21:9).

In June 1829 the three WITNESSES to the Book of Mormon plates were promised a view of the sword (D&C 17:1). According to David WHITMER's report, that promise was fulfilled "in the latter part of the month" (Andrew Jenson, *Historical Record*, nos. 3-5, May 1882, Vol. VI, Salt Lake City, p. 208).

President Brigham YOUNG also reported that the Prophet Joseph SMITH and Oliver COWDERY saw the sword of Laban when they entered a cave in the hill CUMORAH with a large room containing many PLATES. "The first time they went there the sword of Laban hung upon the wall; but when they went again it had been taken down and laid upon the table across the gold plates; it was unsheathed, and on it was written these words: 'This sword will

The gold-hilted dagger (left) with a blade of rare nonmeteoric iron, from the tomb of Tutankhamun (d. 1325 B.C.), is reminiscent of another treasure, the sword of Laban (c. 600 B.C.), described in the Book of Mormon: "the hilt thereof was of pure gold, and the workmanship thereof was exceedingly fine, and I saw that the blade thereof was of the most precious steel" (1 Ne. 4:9). Courtesy the Egyptian Government.

never be sheathed again until The Kingdoms of this world become the Kingdom of our God and his Christ'" (*JD* 19:38).

BIBLIOGRAPHY

Alan R. Millard. "King Og's Bed." *Bible Review*, VI, no. 2 (Apr. 1990):19. Contains a description of a sword or dagger discovered in Pharaoh Tutankhamen's tomb in 1922 that is remarkably similar to the sword of Laban.

REED A. BENSON

SYMBOLISM

The word "symbol" derives from the Greek word *súmbolon*, which means literally "something thrown together"; this word can be translated "token." Contracting parties would break a *súmbolon*, a bone or tally stick, into two pieces, then fit them together again later. Each piece would represent its owner; the halves "thrown together" represent two separated identities merging into one. Thus this concept of "symbol" (unity; separation; restoration) provides a model for love, the Atonement, separation and reunification, our original unity with God, our earthly separation, our eventual return to the divine presence and renewed perfect unity with God (*see* DEIFICATION). Furthermore, this meaning of symbol shows that understanding any symbol requires the "throwing together" of an earthly, concrete dimension and a transcendent, spiritual dimension. Plato's idea that knowledge is remembrance (of a premortal existence) (*Meno* 81c–d) has relevance here.

Symbolism plays a significant role in LDS life. The overriding theme is that all things bear record of Christ, "both things which are temporal, and things which are spiritual; things which are in the heavens above, and things which are on the earth, and things which are in the earth, and things which are under the earth, both above and beneath: all things bear record of me" (Moses 6:63). The use of symbols among the Latter-day Saints expresses religious roots, cultural connections, and modes of life. More connected to Hebrew traditions than most Christian churches and at the same time eschewing many traditional Christian symbols, LDS symbolism is unique among modern religions.

Since LDS worship services are nonliturgical and, except for Christmas, Easter, and the Sunday Sabbath, do not adhere to the usual Christian calendar, many Christian symbols are absent from LDS religious practices. Thus, although the atonement and crucifixion of Jesus Christ are at the heart of their scriptures and theology, traditional symbols such as the cross and the chalice are not prominent. Nor are the rich iconographic materials associated with the traditional churches, especially the emblems, signs, colors, patterns, and symbols that developed during the Middle Ages and during the Renaissance.

The Church embraces biblical symbolic rituals such as BAPTISM (with its attendant associations

The Book of Life, by Alfred Raymond Wright (1949, carved pine, 40″ high). Among the symbols included in this wood carving are twelve oxen, representing the Twelve Tribes of Israel, with a temple baptismal font resting on their backs; the four standard works of LDS scripture; a beehive, symbol of industry; spheres representing the telestial (stars), terrestrial (moon) and celestial (sun) kingdoms of glory; and a replica of the Salt Lake Temple, representing the attainment of the highest degree in the celestial kingdom. Church Museum of History and Art.

with death, burial, and rebirth), the sacrament of the Lord's Supper (with its connection to the blood and body of Christ), and marriage (which signifies both human and divine unity).

Some LDS symbols derive from the Book of Mormon. For example, the iron rod (1 Ne. 8:19) symbolizes the word of God as man approaches the tree of life (1 Ne. 11:25); the Liahona, the compass or pointer used by the Nephites in their travels (1 Ne. 16:10; Alma 37:38–39), symbolizes guidance

through sensitivity to the Spirit; the large and spacious building stands for the corruption of worldly values (1 Ne. 8:31); though the cosmic tree is a universal symbol, the Book of Mormon describes it uniquely as the love of God (1 Ne. 11:21–23).

The Church's history, especially the period of the exodus from the Midwest and the settlement of the Intermountain West, has been a fountainhead of symbols. The covered wagon and the handcart symbolize the faith, courage, and sacrifice of the pioneers; the seagull, the miraculous delivery from a natural disaster; the tabernacle, the quest for sanctuary; and the beehive, the industry and ingenuity required of true disciples.

The architecture of most LDS MEETING-HOUSES is plain and uniform. There are spires, but no crosses; few buildings have cruciform design; and very few have stained-glass windows. Again, reflecting plain, New England-style origins, the interiors of LDS churches contain no crosses or other religious symbols. The sacrament or communion table is plain and adorned only with white tablecloths. It usually rests at the same level with, and is generally adjacent to, the pews, reflecting emphasis on a lay ministry and congregational principles.

LDS temples, both in their structure and ordinances, reflect the glory of God. Their entrances are inscribed, "The House of the Lord/Holiness to the Lord," symbolizing both a sanctuary from the world and heaven itself. The Nauvoo Temple had a frieze consisting of sun stones, moon stones, and star stones, symbolizing DEGREES OF GLORY. Temples built in pioneer Utah had elaborate spires and pinnacles, bas relief, and stained-glass windows, most of which contained symbolic materials. Often temples are built on a hill and near water to suggest not only their elevation from the world, but also their separateness from it and the beauty of the living water of Christ's redemption and exaltation.

The interiors of the temples, too, are highly symbolic, suggestive of the progressive stages of the plan of salvation. By the use of films and murals, symbolic presentations are given of the creation of the world, the Garden of Eden, the telestial or present world, the postmortal terrestrial world, and the celestial kingdom where God dwells. Also associated with the temples are the symbols of the all-seeing eye and the handclasp. Like many Mormon symbols, these have Masonic parallels, though they are by no means original to Masonry, and have different meanings in an LDS context.

Temples contain baptismal fonts that rest on the backs of twelve oxen symbolizing the twelve tribes of Israel. The rooms where marriages and family sealings are solemnized contain altars and mirrored walls in which participants can see their reflections multiplied to infinity, symbolizing the eternal nature of marital love and the family unit. At the conclusion of the temple service, those participating in the endowment ceremony pass from the terrestrial room to the celestial room through a veil, which symbolizes the transition from time into eternity.

The temple ceremony is richly symbolic, with sacred symbolism in the signs, tokens, clothing, covenants, dramatic enactment, and prayer circle. The unifying connection of this symbolic material is the idea of centering. Everything in the temple is suggestive of centering oneself on Christ. The enactment of this privilege precedes the symbolic entrance into the celestial world and the presence of God.

Because it has some unique scriptures and theology and because it has both correspondence with, and independence from, its Judeo-Christian roots, The Church of Jesus Christ of Latter-day Saints will continue to have its own unique symbolic system.

BIBLIOGRAPHY

Andrew, Laurel B. *The Early Temples of the Mormons.* New York, 1977.

Eliade, Mircea. *Patterns in Comparative Religion.* Cleveland and New York, 1958.

——. *The Sacred and the Profane.* New York, 1959.

Hamilton, C. Mark. *The Salt Lake Temple: A Monument to a People.* Salt Lake City, 1983.

Lundquist, John, and Stephen Ricks, eds. *By Study and Also By Faith*, Vol. 1. Salt Lake City, 1990. See esp. Hamblin, pp. 202–21; Parry, pp. 482–500; Porter and Ricks, pp. 501–22; Compton, pp. 611–42.

Madsen, Truman G., ed. *The Temple in Antiquity.* Provo, Utah, 1984.

Nibley, Hugh. *The Message of the Joseph Smith Papyri.* Salt Lake City, 1976.

——. "Treasures in the Heavens." *Nibley on the Timely and the Timeless*, pp. 49–84. Provo, Utah, 1978.

Paulsen, Richard. *The Pure Experience of Order*, pp. 45–55. Albuquerque, N.M., 1982.

TODD COMPTON

SYMBOLS, CULTURAL AND ARTISTIC

LDS cultural and artistic symbols express a distinctive view of the universe and the purpose of life, and tie the present to the historical past. These symbols derive principally from four basic sources: religious ordinances, scriptures, historical experience, and adaptations of other traditions. In the Church today, symbols can be seen in a variety of contexts, including in the continuation of ordinances; in presentations of music, poetry, literature, and drama; in visual arts, sermons, and architecture; and even in settlement patterns of pioneer towns.

The scriptures revealed through the Prophet Joseph SMITH give perspective to the symbolism of the ordinances of the gospel (*see* BAPTISM) and to the creation of the earth. A key passage contains the word of God to Adam, which revealed that everything in the universe has an important and unique role in the PLAN OF SALVATION:

> And behold, all things have their likeness, and all things are created and made to bear record of me, both things which are temporal, and things which are spiritual; things which are in the heavens above, and things which are on the earth, and things which are in the earth, and things which are under the earth, both above and beneath: all things bear record of me [Moses 6:63].

The focal point of "all things" and of symbolism relating thereto is Jesus Christ (*see* JESUS CHRIST, TYPES AND SHADOWS OF). Baptism by immersion is symbolic of the death, burial, and resurrection of Christ (Rom. 6:3–5; D&C 76:51–52). Adam was given instruction regarding the symbolism of baptism: "Inasmuch as ye were born into the world by water, and blood, and the spirit, which I have made, . . . even so ye must be born again into the kingdom of heaven, of water, and of the Spirit, and be cleansed by blood, even the blood of mine Only Begotten" (Moses 6:59). This ordinance also symbolizes the atonement of Christ, which makes the cleansing of mankind possible and makes of the repentant new creatures.

Symbols are associated extensively with sacred gospel ordinances performed in the TEMPLE. The temple is a house of order. The orderliness is symbolized in the ENDOWMENT ceremony, which portrays the journey of individuals from the premortal existence through mortal life and death to life after death. The temple, or House of the Lord, is also symbolic of the Lord's dwelling place, where one can go to learn godliness. For some, the temple symbolizes the conjunction of heaven and earth, where those who seek heaven come out of the world for instruction and receive symbolic reminders of God's plan for his children. Symbols in the temple are linked to the biblical events of the Creation and the fall of Adam, and to the need for redemption. Dramatic presentations, special clothing, and symbolic instruction during the temple ceremonies represent various stages in an individual's eternal progression. The temple clothing is white, suggesting purity and the equality of all mankind before God.

Various levels or ways of living are reflected in the architecture of the temple, including the sun, moon, and stars as representative of kingdoms in the hereafter, and the "all-seeing eye" as suggesting the total knowledge, love, and concern that God has for his children (*see* SALT LAKE TEMPLE). Entry into God's kingdom requires prescribed ordinances, including baptism. Baptismal work is conducted in some temples on a level below ground, to symbolize the eventual burial and resurrection of all from the grave (D&C 128:12–13). The baptismal font rests on the backs of twelve oxen, representing the twelve tribes of Israel.

Latter-day scriptures also contain striking symbols that depict the passage through mortal life. In the dream of Lehi in the Book of Mormon (1 Ne. 8:5–34), a desolate waste represents an individual's position in this world, where one is blinded by "mists of darkness" (the temptations of the devil). Many are in a "great and spacious building," which stands for the pride and vanities of the world that must be abandoned. An iron rod represents the word of God, leading one to the TREE OF LIFE. The universal symbolism of the cosmic tree is described by an angel as a representation of the love of God (cf. 1 Ne. 11:8–25, 35–36).

Latter-day scriptures are thus teleological in tone and theme, reflecting that all things and happenings in the universe have a purpose and are under God's ultimate direction. The motion of earth and the planets "denote there is a God" (Alma 30:44), as do other orbs of light, which "roll upon their wings in their glory, in the midst of the power of God, . . . and any man who hath seen any or the least of these hath seen God moving in his majesty and power" (D&C 88:45, 47).

Church history has been a fountainhead of symbols that reflect similar patterns of the spiritual quest for a better world. The SACRED GROVE in which Joseph Smith in his first vision beheld the Father and the Son may symbolize for some the human potential for contact with God and the enlightenment that comes through personal revelation; CARTHAGE JAIL (where Joseph and Hyrum Smith were murdered), the cost of discipleship; the expulsion from Missouri and exodus from NAUVOO, the adversity that the Church must overcome; and the establishment of the Church in the West, the fulfillment of God's promises.

The BEEHIVE has become the symbol of the industry and cooperative behavior necessary to achieve an ideal society. The symbolism of pilgrimage and pioneering also depicts the path of personal commitment and perseverance that a person must pursue through mortality in order to partake of the fruit of the tree of life and inherit the kingdom whose glory is that of the sun. The sacrifices required to participate in both temporal and spiritual journeys convey that the events of one's life are imbued with eternal significance, and that God is working in and through history.

LDS theology and symbolism have both correspondence with and independence from Judeo-Christian roots. Indeed, the fresh combinations of rich religious symbols are to Latter-day Saints a part of God's continuous revelations to man.

[*See also* Angel Moroni Statue; Architecture; Ceremonies; City Planning; Dove, Sign of; Folk Art; Historical Sites; Kirtland Temple; Nauvoo Temple; Sculptors; Symbolism.]

BIBLIOGRAPHY

Andrews, Laurel B. *The Early Temples of the Mormons*. Albany, N.Y., 1978.

Cooper, Rex E. *Promises Made to the Fathers*. Salt Lake City, 1990.

Eliade, Mircea. *The Sacred and the Profane*. New York, 1959.

Hamilton, C. Mark. "The Salt Lake Temple: A Symbolic Statement of Mormon Doctrine." In *The Mormon People: Their Character and Traditions*, ed. Thomas G. Alexander, pp. 103–127. Provo, Utah, 1980.

Heiss, Matthew K. *The Salt Lake Temple and the Metaphors of Transformation*. Master's thesis, University of Virginia, 1986.

Olsen, Steven L. *The Mormon Ideology of Place: Cosmic Symbolism of the City of Zion, 1830–1846*. Ph.D. diss., University of Chicago, 1985.

REX E. COOPER